Mastering
Autodesk® Revit®
Architecture 2011

Mastering

Autodesk® Revit®
Architecture 2011

Autodesk®
Official Training Guide

Eddy Krygiel

Phil Read

James Vandezande

WILEY

Wiley Publishing, Inc.

Senior Acquisitions Editor: Willem Knibbe
Development Editor: Kim Wimpsett
Technical Editor: Dave Willard
Production Editor: Rachel McConlogue
Copy Editor: Liz Welch
Editorial Manager: Pete Gaughan
Production Manager: Tim Tate
Vice President and Executive Group Publisher: Richard Swadley
Vice President and Publisher: Neil Edde
Book Designers: Maureen Forys and Judy Fung
Compositor: Craig Johnson, Happenstance Type-O-Rama
Proofreader: Publication Services, Inc.
Indexer: Ted Laux
Project Coordinator, Cover: Lynsey Stanford
Cover Designer: Ryan Sneed
Cover Image: Hassell

ISBN: 978-0-470-62696-2
ISBN: 978-0-470-90819-8 (ebk)
ISBN: 978-0-470-90822-8 (ebk)
ISBN: 978-0-470-90821-1 (ebk)

Library of Congress Cataloging-in-Publication Data:

Krygiel, Eddy, 1972-
 Mastering Autodesk Revit architecture 2011 / Eddy Krygiel, Phil Read, James Vandezande. 1st ed.
  p. cm.
 ISBN 978-0-470-62696-2 (pbk.)
 1. Architectural drawing—Computer-aided design. 2. Architectural design—Data processing. I. Read, Phil, 1965– II. Vandezande, James, 1972– III. Title.
 NA2728.K795 2010
 720.28'40285536—dc22
                    2010021345

10 9 8 7 6 5 4 3 2 1

Dear Reader,

Thank you for choosing *Mastering Autodesk Revit Architecture 2011*. This book is part of a family of premium-quality Sybex books, all of which are written by outstanding authors who combine practical experience with a gift for teaching.

Sybex was founded in 1976. More than 30 years later, we're still committed to producing consistently exceptional books. With each of our titles, we're working hard to set a new standard for the industry. From the paper we print on, to the authors we work with, our goal is to bring you the best books available.

I hope you see all that reflected in these pages. I'd be very interested to hear your comments and get your feedback on how we're doing. Feel free to let me know what you think about this or any other Sybex book by sending me an email at nedde@wiley.com. If you think you've found a technical error in this book, please visit http://sybex.custhelp.com. Customer feedback is critical to our efforts at Sybex.

Best regards,

Neil Edde
Vice President and Publisher
Sybex, an Imprint of Wiley

Writing a book is definitely a team effort. None of this would be possible without the support of my family—Angiela, Zoë, and Maya—who not only put up with my around-the-clock writing but help me take the breaks that keep me mostly sane. Thank you.
—Eddy

Dearest Jasper, Millicent, Harrison, and Justine—thanks so much for being particularly patient with me over these past months. Please address all your "Where's my Spring Break 2010?" questions to Eddy Krygiel. And if he puts up a fight, you can take him, as he doesn't have good depth perception. I'd also like to express my deepest gratitude to the many wonderful people who I've worked with while implementing Revit. The vast majority were gracious beyond expectation, many of you remain close personal friends, and only a few of you were complete ******. The bottom line is all of you taught me about myself and life. Thanks!
—Phil

I couldn't have even thought about authoring a book without the patience and understanding of my wife Tara and our beautiful kids, Stephen, Christopher, Arianna, and Joseph. My parents, brother, and extended family have gone a long way in bringing me to where I am today, and I am grateful to each and every one of you. Along my professional journey, I've been inspired by a great number of wonderfully talented people, all of whom I couldn't list in this space; however, I would like to thank those who have had a profound impact on my direction: Carl Galioto, Paul Seletsky, Felicia Davis, Charles D'Alessio, Joe Randazzo, Frank Messano, Chuck Mies, Matthew Jezyk, Angelo Arzano, Kevin Peters, and the crew of the Pioneers Lunch. Thank you.
—James

Acknowledgments

First, we, the authoring team, would like to extend our sincere thanks to the fine folks at Autodesk Revit. Thanks to the hard work of Anthony Hauck and the rest of his team; they have continued to build a fine product and make it better. While it's not possible to name them all, the work of the developers, product designers, quality assurance team, and all the others doesn't go unrecognized or unappreciated. Thank you, gals and guys, for taking a tough job and doing it with a great attitude.

Second, we were fortunate enough to have the help of some of the leading industry experts for a portion of this book. Part 6, "Construction and Beyond," features chapters about cutting-edge technologies and workflows that you can perform using Revit. We cover topics such as dealing with a BIM model during construction, using Revit in direct-to-fabrication, creating Revit models for film and stage, creating BIM clouds, and even teaching fellow architectural students to approach Revit and design with an open mind. To that end, we'd like to thank contributors David Light, Josh Lowe, Mike Whaley, Laura Handler, Adam Thomas, Jereme Smith, Don Rudder, Jeffery McGrew, Peter Streibig, Chris France, and Bryan Sutton for pushing the boundaries and taking the time to put their thoughts into words. It's material we couldn't have created without your help and knowledge.

And finally, thanks are due to our friend and technical editor, Dave Willard, and our excellent support team at Sybex, who helped us develop and focus the content. Thanks to Kim Wimpsett for helping us form complete sentences and finally bring justification to our fifth-grade grammar class; to Liz Welch and Rachel McConlogue for not letting us spell *allright* as one word; and a special thanks to Willem Knibbe, for convincing us that this would be a fun thing to do in the first place.

We would like to express our sincerest gratitude to our friends, the architects who generously shared their work, allowing us to inspire you with it: Bohlin Cywinski Jackson, Davison Architects, Elerbe/AECOM, HNTB, HOK, Lake Flato, RTKL, Hassell, and SOM.

About the Authors

Eddy Krygiel is a senior project architect, a LEED Accredited Professional, and an Autodesk Authorized Author at HNTB Architects headquartered in Kansas City, Missouri. He has been using Revit since version 5.1 to complete projects ranging from single-family residences and historic remodels to 1.12-million-square-foot office buildings. Eddy is responsible for implementing BIM at his firm and also consults for other architecture and contracting firms around the country looking to implement BIM. For the last four years, he has been teaching Revit to practicing architects and architectural students in the Kansas City area and has lectured around the nation on the use of BIM in the construction industry. Eddy also coauthored *Green BIM: Successful Sustainable Design with Building Information Modeling* with Bradley Nies (Sybex, 2008).

Phil Read is a vice president and director of practice integration at HNTB Holdings, where he helps lead research and development on visualization, BIM, and cloud-based collaboration. After working in both civil engineering and architecture, he downloaded Revit version 1.0 (at the suggestion of an ArchiCAD reseller) and was hooked. Less than a year later, he began working for Revit Technology and then Autodesk as a project implementation specialist, where he had the honor and pleasure of working with some of the most remarkable people and design firms around the world. He's a regular speaker, blogger, and Twitterer and relishes the role of "change agent" as long as it makes sound business sense. Phil holds degrees in communications and architecture, as well as a master's degree in architecture.

James Vandezande is a registered architect and a senior associate at HOK in New York City, where he is a member of the firm-wide BIM leadership and is managing their buildingSMART initiatives. After graduating from the New York Institute of Technology in 1995, he worked in residential and small commercial architecture firms performing services ranging from estimating to computer modeling to construction administration. In 1999, he landed at SOM and transformed his technology skills into a 10-year span as a digital design manager. In this capacity, he pioneered the implementation of BIM on such projects as One World Trade Center, a.k.a. Freedom Tower. James has been using Revit since version 3.1 and has lectured at many industry events, including Autodesk University, VisMasters Conference, CMAA BIM Conference, McGraw-Hill Construction, and the AIANYS Convention. He is a co-founder and president of the NYC Revit Users Group and is an adjunct lecturing professor at the NYU School for Continuing and Professional Studies, as well as the Polytechnic Institute of NYU.

Contents at a Glance

Contents

Foreword

If you have come this far, the concept of building information modeling (BIM) is on your mind, and I commend you for that! I can also assure you that you are in the right place. My name is Lynn Allen, Autodesk Technical Evangelist, and after 25 years in the CAD and design industry, the writing couldn't be clearer on the wall. BIM is here to stay, and Revit is the software product that will take you there.

If I were to take a Revit course right now, the writers of this book—Eddy Krygiel, Phil Read, and James Vandezande—would be the ultimate teachers. Each of them is a BIM star in their own right—top-rated Autodesk University speakers, highly respected industry leaders, the true Revit and BIM evangelists. Having their combined mindshare in one book is the perfect combination. These are the writers who will get you to where you need to go in BIM!

In my profession, I speak to about 30,000 customers a year, and each day I see more and more architects making the move to Revit Architecture. I also see the enthusiasm from those who have made the move, which solidifies to me that Revit and BIM are clearly the correct route to take. As more and more architectural firms are making the move to BIM every day, it is clear the BIM is now the current standard for architectural design, and not just the future standard. I am mostly known for my AutoCAD expertise and hate to lose all these great customers to another product, but even I can see the light here!

Technology is changing, the world is changing, and in order to stay current you'll need to embrace the world of BIM. Here you can model, render, analyze, test for sustainability, prototype, and validate. These 3D intelligent models can be passed down through all the phases of the building cycle with the building owner as the final recipient. Which would you rather have someone hand you, a huge roll of paper drawings or an intelligent 3D model? The answer seems pretty clear to me.

So, here is your chance to get started with the pros! I know many of you are currently AutoCAD users, so let me assure you that if you can learn AutoCAD, you can certainly learn Revit. Revit Architecture was designed specifically for architects, to think the way they think and to work the way they work. AutoCAD has had to be all things to all people over the years and is not the easiest product to learn.

So what are you waiting for? Don't let BIM pass you by; jump on the Revit bandwagon, and be ready for an exciting future of smart buildings you can really be proud of!

—*Lynn Allen*
Autodesk Evangelist
www.autodesk.com/lynnallen

Introduction

Welcome to the second edition of *Mastering Autodesk Revit Architecture 2011*, based on the Revit Architecture 2011 release.

When we sat down to plan this book, we realized that in the past three years, so many have made such great advances in their use of Revit that we felt we needed to start this book from scratch and work to fill it with really solid content. We looked to serve the needs of individuals who had used Revit in the past, but wanted to take it up a notch all the way to teams that were looking for advanced content. We hope you will find that our efforts to that extent were successful.

Writing a book looks easier than it truly is. It is an effort that we each have taken on beyond our day jobs in the hopes of sharing our experience and knowledge about Revit and BIM with the greater design community. We want to help make better designs and stronger document sets, and continue pushing the envelopes of what you can build. We hope you find the techniques, workflows, and processes, as well as the tips on software, useful and inspiring.

We also wanted to write a book that is as much about architectural design and practice as it is about software. Architecture is a way of looking at the world and the methods that inspire creatively solving the problems of the built world. We hope you'll agree that we've succeeded because the book follows real-life workflows and scenarios and is full of practical examples that show how to use Revit both inside and outside the box.

The book is based on a project that is already in motion—a theoretical project for the Jenkins Music building in Kansas City. The Jenkins Music building was built at the turn of the century as a terracotta block façade building that housed the Jenkins Music store. This was one of many stores nationwide where musical instruments were made, and you could come to purchase them or take classes. The company went out of business in Kansas City, and the property was eventually sold to a developer. In the 1980s, the building was going to be torn down for a parking garage. The historic façade was saved as well as the first bay of the building. This has left Kansas City with 100' of beautiful, historic terracotta on an 18' deep building. The model shown in this book is a representation of the remaining building taken and made into living units. How great would it be to have an 18' × 100' apartment overlooking the downtown skyline?

All the tutorial files necessary to complete the book's exercises plus sample families are hosted online at www.sybex.com/go/masteringrevit2011. To download the trial version of Revit Architecture, go to www.autodesk.com/revitarchitecture, where you'll also find complete system requirements for running Revit.

Who Should Read This Book

This book is written for architects and designers who have had some exposure to Revit and are eager to learn more. It's for architects of any generation—you don't need to be a computer wizard to understand or appreciate the content within. We've designed the book to follow real project workflows and processes to help make the tools easier to follow, and the chapters are full of handy tips to make Revit easier to leverage.

This book is also for the entire range of architects, from those who are fresh out of school to the seasoned project managers. We have endeavored to include content for all walks of the profession so that regardless of your role on the project you can learn how BIM changes both workflow and culture within a project team. With that, a basic understanding of Revit will make it easier to work through the book. Revit is a very robust tool requiring more than one project iteration to master.

For BIM managers, the book offers insights into the best practices for creating good project or office templates; these managers should also take a sneak peek into the powerful world of building content and Revit families. We've added many time-saving and inspiring concepts to the book, supported by examples from our own projects and the rest of the real world, to help motivate and inspire you on your journey through building information modeling.

What You Will Learn

This book will help you take the basics of Revit and BIM that you already know and expand on them using real-world examples. We will show you how to take a preliminary model and add layers of intelligence to help analyze and augment your designs. We'll show you how to create robust and accurate documentation, and then help you through the construction process.

We go beyond introductory topics. To that end, we won't be starting a project from scratch or teaching you how to build a simple BIM model. If you are interested in learning at that level, we strongly recommend you pick up *Introducing Autodesk Revit Architecture 2011* (Wiley, 2010), before plunging headlong into this book. Instead, our book begins with a brief overview of the BIM approach. As you are already aware, BIM is more than just a change in software; it's a change in architectural workflow and culture. To leverage the full advantages of both BIM and Revit in your office structure, you will need to make some changes to your practice. We've designed the book around an ideal, integrated workflow to help you make this transition.

Starting with the project team, standards, and culture, we'll discuss how BIM changes your project approach and how to best build your team around a newer workflow. From there, we will delve into conceptual design and sustainability studies, continuing through best practices for design iteration and refinement. You'll learn about powerful modeling techniques, design documentation best practices, how to make compelling presentation graphics, parametric design with the Family Editor, workflow topics like tracking changes and worksharing, and some strategies moving beyond traditional concepts of BIM. The book concludes with an appendix on troubleshooting and best practices so you can avoid common pitfalls. Throughout the book we've tried to share our practical experience with you, particularly in the form of real-world scenario sidebars.

Whether you're studying Revit on your own or in a class or training program, you can use the "Master It" questions in the "Bottom Line" section at the end of each chapter to test your mastery of the skills you've learned.

Also featured is a color project gallery containing inspirational Revit projects from friends and colleagues who were generous enough to share their good work with the rest of the world.

The Mastering Series

The Mastering series from Sybex provides outstanding instruction for readers with intermediate and advanced skills, in the form of top-notch training and development for those already working in their field and clear, serious education for those aspiring to become pros. Every Mastering book includes the following:

◆ Real-world scenarios, ranging from case studies to interviews, that show how the tool, technique, or knowledge presented is applied in actual practice

◆ Skill-based instruction, with chapters organized around real tasks rather than abstract concepts or subjects

◆ Self-review test questions, so you can be certain you're equipped to do the job right

Contacting the Authors

In all, we welcome your feedback and comments. You can find the three of us on our blog, www.architecture-tech.com, or email us at MasteringRevit@architecture-tech.com. We hope you enjoy the book.

Part 1

Fundamentals

Although this is a Mastering book, we recognize that not everyone will know how to find every tool or have a mastering of the Revit workflow. The chapters in Part 1 are devoted to rounding out that knowledge and helping to fill in any of those gaps in your knowledge of the toolbox, the UI, or the Revit workflow.

Chapter 1

Beyond Basic Documentation

In this chapter, we'll cover some of the principles of a successful building information modeling (BIM) approach within your office environment and summarize some of the many tactics possible using BIM in today's design workflow. We'll explain the fundamental characteristics of maximizing your investment in BIM and moving beyond documentation with the BIM model.

In this chapter, you'll learn to

♦ Leverage the BIM model

♦ Know how BIM affects firm culture

♦ Focus your investment in BIM

Leveraging the BIM Model

Building Information Modeling or BIM is a parametric, 3D model that is used to generate plans, section, elevations, perspectives, details, schedules—all of the necessary components to document the design of a building. Drawings created using BIM are not a collection of 2D lines and shapes that represent a building, but a series of parametric, interactive elements that allow a model to become infinitely more data-rich. These elements can be changed by manipulation of their parametric data. This means creating one door or window can quickly be made into several simply by changing specific parameters associated with that object. Additionally, all of the elements within the model share a level of bidirectional associativity—if the elements are changed in one place within the model, those changes will be visible in all the other views. So, move a door in plan and that door will be moved in all of the elevations, sections, perspectives, and so on in which it is visible.

We have all seen the growth in the use of BIM in the past few years within the design and construction industries. Firms have been moving from a two-dimensional (2D) documentation process to take advantage of the benefits of BIM and a model-based document set. According to a recent survey by McGraw-Hill (`http://construction.ecnext.com/coms2/summary_0249-296182_ITM_analytics`), the adoption of building information modeling has taken quite a hold within the architecture, engineering, and construction (AEC) industry. By 2009, almost 50 percent of the industry had fully adopted BIM as a workflow, and many of those firms use BIM for their sustainable design and analysis. Figure 1.1 shows the impact of current BIM adoption and the levels of involvement in sustainable projects.

FIGURE 1.1
Impact of BIM
and use in green
projects

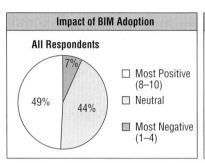
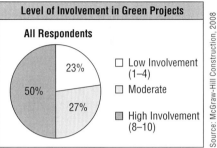

If you look at this growth in a bit more detail (see Figure 1.2), you'll note an increase across the board of BIM use. Heavy users—firms that have been invested in BIM and are building on that investment—increased 10 percent in 2009 alone. Light users—typically those firms that are making their initial foray into BIM—have jumped 20 percent over the same time frame.

FIGURE 1.2
Growth in BIM
use on projects

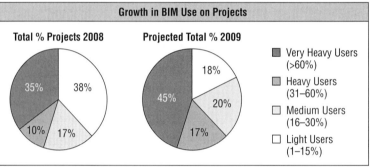

Source: McGraw-Hill Construction, 2008

Even in economically challenging times, it seems that the industry is looking for ways to get projects done better, faster, and greener. The same survey goes on to state that at the 2005 National American Institute of Architects (AIA) convention, out of a room of 4,000 people, there were only about 15 percent of the attendees who could identify with BIM as a workflow and documentation methodology. Four years later, in 2009, more than half the firms are using BIM on a regular basis to document their designs.

Planning for BIM

As architects or designers, we have accepted the challenge of changing our methodology to adapt to the nuances of documentation through modeling rather than drafting. We are now confronted with identifying the next step. Some firms look to create better and better documents, whereas others are leveraging BIM in building analysis. As we continue to be successful in visualization and documentation, industry leaders are looking to move BIM to the next plateau. Many of these new possibilities are, like BIM was a decade ago, new workflows and potential changes in our culture or habits, which require you to ask yourself a very critical question:

What kind of firm do you want to be, and how do you plan to use BIM?

As the technology behind BIM continues to grow, so does the potential. There are a host of things now possible using a BIM model; in fact, that list continues to expand year after year. Figure 1.3 shows some of the potential opportunities.

When moving to the next step with BIM—be that better documentation, sustainable analysis, or facility management—it's important to identify where you land in three primary goals for your use of BIM. Understanding these areas, and specifically how they overlap within your firm, will help you define how cutting edge your firm is willing to be regarding BIM. These three areas are as follows:

◆ Visualization

◆ Analysis

◆ Strategy

FIGURE 1.3
The integrated
BIM model

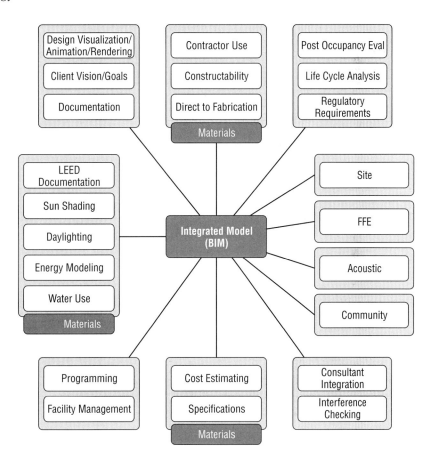

We'll first define each of these areas individually and then discuss what it means to begin combining them in practice.

VISUALIZATION

Creating documentation using BIM has the added advantage of being able to graphically visualize the project in 3D. Although this was initially conceived as one of the "low-hanging fruits" of using BIM as a workflow, this has led to an explosion of graphics—3D perspectives, wireframes, renderings, and gaming engines—within the industry as a means to communicate design between stakeholders on a project.

This digital creation of the project has given us a variety of tools to communicate aspects of the project. It becomes "architecture in miniature," and we can take the model and create a seemingly unlimited number of interior and exterior visualizations. The same model can be imported directly into a gaming engine like an Xbox and be used to create realistic walk-throughs. Clients no longer need to rely on the designer's preestablished paths in a fly-through—they can virtually "walk" through the building at their own pace, exploring an endless variety of directions. The same model again can then be turned into a physical manifestation either in part or in whole by the use of digital printers creating small, monochromatic vignettes of space. A variety of types of visualization are currently accessible through a BIM model; we'll cover some of the different types and their relationships with BIM.

The still image might be one of the easiest creations from the BIM model. Once the first shapes are established, you have created a still image, be it in plan, elevation, or perspective. The still images, however, have taken on a variety of uses beyond simple communication of design intent. These images are used to not only describe design intent but also to illustrate ideas about proportion, form, space, and functional relationships. The ease to which these kinds of views can be mass-produced makes the perspective more of a commodity. In some instances, as shown in Figure 1.4, materiality is intentionally removed to focus on the building form and element adjacencies.

By adding materiality to the BIM elements, you can then begin to explore the space in color and light, creating photorealistic renderings of portions of the building design. These highly literal images, as shown in Figure 1.5, begin to convey information about both intent and content of the design. Iterations at this level are limited only by processing power. These images can also become analytical tools for the project stakeholders by demonstrating spatial and functional adjacencies and interactions. The photorealism allows for an almost lifelike exploration of color and light qualities within a built space even to the extent of allowing analytic footcandle calculations to reveal the exact levels of light within a space.

Finally, the next logical step is taking these elements and adding movement. In Figure 1.6, you can see a still image taken from a photorealistic rendering of a project. These renderings not only can convey time and movement through space but also have the ability to be highly physically accurate in demonstrating how the building will react or perform under real lighting and atmospheric conditions. All of this creates a better idea of building predictability and performance before the built form is realized.

FIGURE 1.4
Sectional
rendering

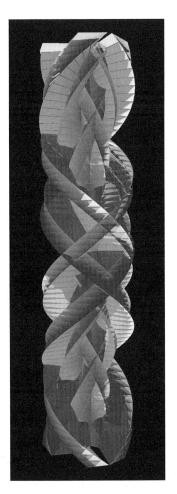

FIGURE 1.5
An analytic
rendering

FIGURE 1.6
A still from an animation showing accurate physical conditions for the project

ANALYZE

As with visualization, the authoring environment of a BIM platform isn't necessarily the most efficient one to perform analysis. Although you can create some rendering and animations within Revit, a host of other applications are specifically designed to capitalize on a computer's RAM and processing power to minimize the time it takes to create a rendering or animation. Analysis is much the same way—although some basic analysis is possible using Revit, other applications are much more robust and can create more accurate results. The real value in BIM is the interoperability of model geometry and metadata between applications. Consider energy modeling as an example. In Figure 1.7, we're comparing three energy modeling applications: A, B, and C. In the figure, the darkest bar reflects the time it takes to either import model geometry into the analysis package or redraw the design with the analysis package. The middle shaded color reflects the amount of time needed to add data not within Revit, such as loads, zoning, and so on. The lightest bar represents the time it takes to perform the analysis once all the information is in place.

FIGURE 1.7
BIM environmental analysis time comparison

BIM Environmental Analysis Time Comparison

◼ Geometry Manipulation ◻ Adding Load Data ◻ Simulation

A

B

C

In A and B, we modeled the project in Revit but were unable to use the model geometry in the analysis package. This caused the re-creation of the design within the analysis tool and also required time to coordinate and upkeep the design and its iterations between the two models. In application C, you can see we were able to import Revit model geometry directly into the analysis package, saving almost 50 percent of the time needed to create and run the full analysis. Using this workflow, it is possible to bring analysis to more projects, perform more iterations, or do the analysis in half the time.

This same workflow is true for daylighting (Figure 1.8) and several other types of building performance and design analysis. By being able to repurpose the Revit model geometry, we are able to lose many of the "rules of thumb" we have created as designers along the way and begin to rely on calculated results. The Revit model also ensures consistency and accuracy of design through analysis by using the model as the sole point source for design geometry.

FIGURE 1.8
Daylighting overlay from 3ds Max Design

Building analysis can reach beyond just the design phase and into facility management. Once the building has been constructed, that doesn't mean the use of the BIM model needs to end. More advanced facilities management systems allow us to track—and thereby trend—building use over time. Building use historically changes over a building's life span. By trending building use, you can begin to then predict future use patterns and help anticipate future use. This can help you become more proactive with maintenance and equipment replacement because you will be able to "see" how equipment performance begins to degrade over time. Trending will also aid you in providing a more comfortable environment for the building occupants by understanding historic use patterns and allow you to keep the building tuned for optimized energy performance.

STRATEGIZE

To maximize your investment in a BIM-based workflow, it's necessary to apply a bit of planning. As in design, a well-planned and flexible implementation is paramount to a project's success. By identifying goals on a project early on in the process, it allows the BIM model to be created to efficiently reach those ideals. A good BIM strategy answers three key questions about a project:

◆ What processes do we need to employ to achieve our project goals?

◆ Which people and team members are key to those processes?

◆ What technology or applications do we need in place to support the people and process?

Ask these questions to your firm as a whole so you can collectively work toward an expertise in a given area, be that sustainable design or construction, or something else. Ask the same questions of an individual project as well so you can begin building the model in the early stages for the proper downstream use. In both cases (firm-wide or project-based), the processes will need to change in order to meet the goals you've established. Modeling techniques and workflows will need to be established. Analysis-based BIM requires different constraints and requirements than a model used for clash detection. If you're taking the model into facilities management, you'll need to add a lot of metadata about equipment but might need the level of detail significantly lower than if you are looking to perform daylighting. Having to apply a new level of model integrity after the fact (like halfway through documentation) can be a frustrating and time-consuming endeavor. Regardless of the goal, setting and understanding those goals early on in the project process is almost mandatory for success.

Setting Firm Goals for BIM

Combining visualization, analysis, and strategy will help you define your adoption curve and help you locate your future direction. It's important to note that no matter where you fall or how these elements are combined, there is no wrong answer. Identifying a direction is the critical piece so you can better plan for the success of your projects. BIM ultimately is a communication tool. It can aid in analysis and documentation, but the primary goal is to communicate design ideas and concepts to the team in all the various states of the project's life cycle.

The adoption curve isn't really much of a curve. We'll discuss the process of moving beyond basic documentation with the use of three concentric circles. Each circle represents one of the primary elements we discussed in the previous sections. Figure 1.9 shows two of the iterations possible with the curve. The combination on the left shows a late adopter and one where each of the elements—visualization (V), strategy (S), and analysis (A)—are fairly separate of each other. The other iteration shows almost a complete integration of these tools.

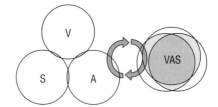

Although the graphic shows a fairly balanced use of each of these tools, any of them can be used in any combination depending on your goals and uses for BIM. To better understand where you fall into any of the possible iterations, we'll discuss three examples and what those possible workflows will look like to your projects: late adopters (the image on the left), intermediate adopters, and early adopters.

LATE ADOPTERS

Late adopters, shown with the configuration in Figure 1.10, see each of these tools as very distinctive efforts. There is little overlap between each of the systems, and any of them can be taken and removed from a process without negatively impacting any of the others. Late adopters typically come to new technologies as a strong second. This means you're not picking up the latest and newest tools or workflows that come to the industry, but instead you're waiting for others to test these new ideas a bit before adoption. In late adoption, the *I* in BIM is not critical. Information within the model will be used for documentation (i.e., door schedules), but analysis will probably be done using different model sources.

FIGURE 1.10
Late adoption

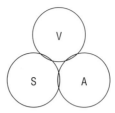

INTERMEDIATE ADOPTION

Intermediate adopters, as shown in Figure 1.11, tend to assume a much stronger relationship between visualization, analysis, and strategy. These elements are seen in a more concurrent workflow and are more dependent on each other for their individual successes. For intermediate adopters, the *I* in BIM is very important, and a more robust level of data is pulled from various model resources. Intermediate adopters see the changes in technology as a means to help improve current processes and make them more efficient and effective. These changes in technology are used to explore new markets and help create new opportunities for growth.

FIGURE 1.11
Intermediate
adoption

EARLY ADOPTION

Early adoption, shown in Figure 1.12, focuses on a combination of all these elements in a dependent relationship. Early adopters are creating new tools, technologies, and workflows to implement new processes and opportunities that did not previously exist in the marketplace. In each of these cases, there is a significant development investment and a perception where higher risk can equal higher reward. It is not nearly enough to have the best or most advanced applications available on the marketplace, but there is a need to create the "next best thing." The *I* in BIM to early adopters becomes a core part of their strategy for project success. They do not wait to follow markets but instead work to create new ones, which they can then lead.

FIGURE 1.12
Early adoption

How BIM Affects Firm Culture

In understanding where you are and where you want to be in this adoption curve, it's also important to understand that moving between any of the iterations of this curve requires a shift in your internal firm culture. As anyone who's adopted BIM can tell you, the difficulties you might experience do not come from learning a new application but understanding how that application affects your workflow—and managing that change. That ability to adapt and accept that change within an organization will in some way determine where you fall on the adoption curve.

Predictability vs. Innovation

To understand the process of any change, think about it as a product of happiness over time, as shown in Figure 1.13. The process of any change, be it adoption of a new workflow or tool within your office to a more personal one, such as acquiring a new cell phone, can be described by this curve.

FIGURE 1.13
Happiness vs. time in technological adoption

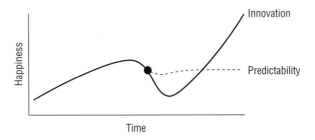

Let's use the simple example of a new cell phone. When you first get the new cell, there is an increase in your happiness. The new device might have a color screen, allow you to send or receive emails, play games, or find the nearest Starbucks. As you gain familiarity with these features, your happiness goes up. At some point in your adoption or process, there is an initial pinnacle to your happiness. You briefly plateau. This occurs when you are now asked to do something within a limited time frame or utilize a new feature that is outside your comfort zone—and things don't proceed as planned.

In our cell phone example, this could occur the first time you try to synchronize your phone with the office email server, and instead of performing correctly, it duplicates or shuffles your contacts. Now the names are no longer associated with the proper phone numbers or email addresses, and the system you've come to rely on is now unpredictable. In a BIM-based example, this could mean you have a schematic design deadline, or you need to create a wall section or model a set of ornate stairs in a limited amount of time. You might know that the task is techni-cally possible, but you have yet to ever perform that task personally.

There comes a point as your stress level goes up that your happiness begins to decline and you hit a point (shown as a dot on the graph in Figure 1.13). At this point, you perceive a crossroads: do you go back to the previous technology (the old phone) and choose a path of predictability, or do you muscle forward and push for mastering the change for the hopes of innovation? Any system, no matter how inefficient, if it is predictable, there is a certain amount of comfort associated with the existing system. As you try to find your way along the adoption curve, understand that part of what you are trying to manage—either personally or for your project team—is this predictability versus innovation while trying to maintain a level of happiness and morale.

Evolution vs. Revolution

While you're in the process of trying to manage the amount of change you're willing to endure, you also need to consider the rate that change will affect your project teams. Progress and innovation are iterative and can take several cycles to perfect a technique or workflow. That can become a real challenge if you're working on a very large-scale design. The process of change and creating new methodologies using BIM is an evolution, not a revolution.

Figure 1.14 shows two bicycles. The image on the left is the penny-farthing bicycle taken from *Appleton's Cyclopaedia of Applied Mechanics* of 1892. Although not the first bicycle (which was invented in 1817 in Paris), it does demonstrate many of the rudimentary and defining features of what we think of a bicycle today: two wheels, a handlebar, and pedals to supply power. The image on the right is the 2006 thesis design of Australian University student Gavin Smith. The bike was designed to assist people with disabilities or those with impaired motor skills in riding a bike unaided. The basic concept is that the bike would supply its own balance at low speeds, and the wheels would remain canted. As the bike moves faster and wheel speed increases, the wheels become vertical and the rider is able to ride at faster speeds while balancing mostly on his or her own. As the bike slows, the wheels cant back in again, giving the rider the necessary balance needed at lower speeds. The bike on the right, still possessing all of the distinguishing characteristics of what we define as a bicycle, is an evolution of the bike over many, many iterations. A similar evolution will occur with your use of BIM—the more often you iterate the change, the better and more comfortable it will become.

FIGURE 1.14
Understanding replication vs. innovation

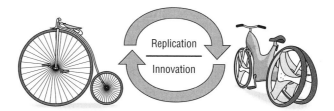

Focusing Your Investment in BIM

One of the common assumptions is that larger firms have a bigger investment than smaller firms in their capacity to become early adopters, take on new technologies, or innovate. Although larger firms might have a broader pool of resources, much of the investment is proportionally the same. We have been fortunate enough to help a number of firms implement Revit over the years, and each has looked to focus on different capabilities of the software that best express their individual direction. Although all of these firms have varied in size and individual desire to take on risk, their investments have all largely been relatively equal. From big firms to small, with very little variation, the investment ratio consistently equals about 1 percent the size of the firm. If you consider a 1,000-person firm, that equals about 10 full-time people; however, scale that down to even a 10-person firm, and if you apply the same one percent, that becomes one person's time for three full weeks.

The key to optimizing this 1 percent investment is focusing the firm's energy and resources. As the technologies behind BIM continue to expand, so do the opportunities for specialization, so you will need to pick and choose strategically to focus the efforts and direction of your firm. The following list highlights many of the expanded uses possible today based on a BIM model. Some of these things are core precepts of what BIM is and does, such as 3D visualization; some, like energy modeling, are more emerging technologies; and others, such as facility management, are truly cutting edge.

- Construction documentation
  - Coordinated documentation
  - Automated keynoting
  - Consultant coordination (integrating multiple models)
  - Design visualization
  - Scheduling systems/materials/quantities
  - Specifications
  - Furniture, Finishes, and Equipment (FF&E): tracking/logging/procurement
- Spatial program validation
- Construction
  - Constructability analysis
  - Clash detection
  - Quantity take-offs
  - Cost analysis/estimating
  - Direct to fabrication
- Traffic studies
- Building performance analysis
  - Rainwater reclamation
  - PV access
  - Energy analysis
  - Daylighting
  - Solar studies
  - Computational fluid dynamics analysis
  - LEED documentation

- Programming
- Facilities management
  - Asset tracking
  - Trending

If the investment (regardless of scale) is focused and planned, it can still leverage strong potential. Identifying the importance of visualization, analysis, and strategy to your firm and process will help guide you in selecting areas of focus within your own practice. When choosing the specialization or how much focus to give to visualization, analysis, or strategy within BIM, there are no wrong answers. Just choose a path that reflects the comfort level of your firm to take risks while focusing on selected areas of specialization.

Throughout this book, we will elaborate on many of these elements and demonstrate, using real-world examples, how to use these techniques to visualize, analyze, and strategize with your use of Revit.

The Bottom Line

Leverage the BIM model.   Understanding the level of risk your firm is willing to take in new technologies will help you establish goals for your future use of BIM.

Master It   Using the three areas of firm integration (visualization, analysis, and strategy), define how those areas overlap for your firm or project.

Know how BIM affects firm culture.   Not only is the transition to BIM from 2D CAD a change in applications, but it's also a shift in workflow and firm culture. Understanding some of the key differences helps to ensure project and team success during the transition.

Master It   What are some of the ways that BIM differs from CAD, and how does this change the culture of an office or project team?

Focus your investment in BIM.   One of the key elements to understanding BIM beyond documentation is simply to have an awareness of the possibilities. This allows you to make an educated decision as to what direction your firm or project would like to go.

Master It   List some of the potential uses of a BIM model beyond documentation.

Chapter 2

Principles of Revit

After one decade in the AEC space, Revit continues to be unique in its holistic "whole-building BIM" approach to design integration. Sure, there are other BIM-ish tools that allow you to design in 3D. And 10 years ago, 3D might have been a differentiator, but today 3D is a commodity!

Whole-building BIM is the ability to design, manage, and document your project information from within a single file, something that no other BIM tool will allow you to do. In a non-Revit workflow, you'd have to design your project across multiple files—not just across disciplines but within the same discipline! Imagine the dysfunctional workflow of having separate files for the building shell, roof, and each interior level for a modest 50-story building. That means you'll be managing at least 50 files just for the architecture. Count on another 50 files for the MEP and structural design, and now your team has to juggle more than 150 separate files that have to be manually linked together. Then you would have to export your files to separate sheets and views for documentation.

So, now your building has been smashed up into 2D information. And when you have changes, expect to go back to the model and repeat the process, because you can't risk making changes in 2D when they're not bidirectionally associative. No thanks!

How would you complete the same project in Revit? Well, worst case is that you're probably looking at *three* files for the same building (architecture, structure, and MEP), because design is a team sport, and you're not all in the same office or geography. So, everyone does their work and links each other's projects. Three files!

And as for documentation, it's all in the same file as the respective project. No exporting required. It's a completely bidirectional, multiuser working environment, so if you're trying to compare Revit to what you're used to in other 2D CAD or 3D BIM tools, stop now.

As for the UI, well, there have been some much needed changes in Revit Architecture 2011. Last year's introduction of the Ribbon introduced us all to what one well-respected Revit expert succinctly referred to as "drunken leprechaun mode" because the tools were not only highly contextual, but they kept moving around in subjective ways. We're glad to tell you the Ribbon UI has evolved into what we like to call "sober leprechaun mode"! Yes, the UI is still contextual because the now-sober leprechaun keeps contextually hiding commands and panels the moment you put them down. But at least he's learned to put the commands and panels in the same place the moment you start to do something else. And we think this is a terrific improvement.

In this chapter, you'll learn to:

◆ Understand Revit project organization

◆ Understand Revit interface organization

Project Organization

If you are coming from 2D CAD background, you are already familiar with a lot of terms and concepts that don't have exact corollaries in Revit. You're probably used to thinking in terms of what needs to be drawn and coordinated: plans, sections, elevations, details, schedules, and so on. You're also used to keeping that information in a lot of separate files that have to be linked together in order to reference other parts of the building. And you're used to being allowed to have only one person in one file at a time (which can be particularly frustrating from a workflow standpoint). And finally, maintaining all your project settings and management is a struggle across so many disconnected files.

Revit contains all of these kinds of things. But at a high level Revit is about the four key components of a holistic and successful design process: relationships, repetition, representations, and restrictions. These concepts are respectively managed in Revit by data, content, views, and project management. And they are managed from within a single, bidirectional database.

Figure 2.1 shows what we like to think of as a Revit organization chart, which should give you a visual description of these four top-level categories and the kinds of things these categories contain. In the following sections, we'll discuss each of these categories and describe their particular role in your Revit project environment.

Datum

Datum consists of references, grids, and levels (Figure 2.2). The reason that datum is all about the relationships of your Revit project is because they establish and control your content (the building, stuff that goes in a building, and the stuff you need to document your building).

Reference planes can be created in any 2D view from the Home tab, but once created they may be visible in 3D. After you add reference planes to your project, they can be set and seen from the Work Plane panel. This will allow you to work with respect to the desired work plane.

Like reference planes, grid lines can also be added to any 2D view. Keep in mind that grids may only be perpendicular to levels. Furthermore, grids are only visible in views that are aligned with the grid. So if the grid is in a North/South orientation, you'll only be able to see it in plan and from the North/South–oriented views.

Levels may be seen and created only in views that are parallel to the analytic ground plane in Revit. So you can't create levels in plan and they can't be diagonal to the ground plane. To create any datum in Revit, simply select the desired type and then pick two points to define the start and end location.

FIGURE 2.1
Revit organization
chart

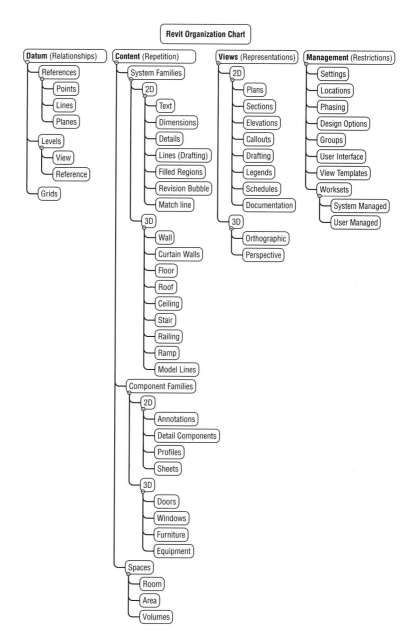

FIGURE 2.2
Datum in Revit

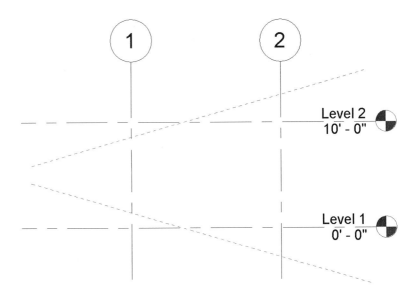

CREATING AND DUPLICATING LEVELS

Creating a new level may or may not create a corresponding plan view (controlled by the Make Plan View option). Sketching a level defaults to creating a plan view. But copying an existing level will default to not creating a plan view, which is useful for creating relationships to content where no plan view is needed (for example, if you want to control multiple window elevations). The graphic indication of a level, which doesn't have a corresponding view, will be that the head of the level is black rather than blue.

CERT OBJECTIVE

If you want to convert a datum level that doesn't have a view to one that does, simply select the Plan View option in the Create panel on the View tab. This will open the dialog box shown in Figure 2.3. You'll be able to select among all the non-view levels in your project and convert them to view corresponding levels.

FIGURE 2.3
Converting datum
level to view level

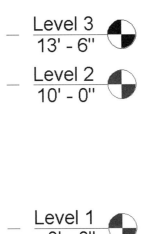

You can also use this option to create duplicate views of existing levels. Simply uncheck the option at the bottom of the dialog box (Figure 2.4) and you'll see all the levels in your project.

FIGURE 2.4
All project-level datum

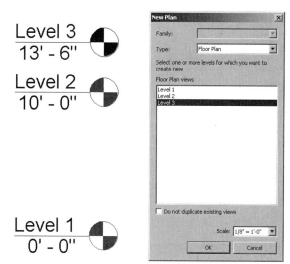

ANALYTIC AND GRAPHIC DATUM EXTENTS

We need to mention two important notes about the control and visibility of levels and grids. First, you can control both the graphic and analytic ends of levels and grids. If you control the analytic end of the grid, you're controlling the extents of the datum across the entire project and all views, and the 3D option will be visible as you pull the datum, as shown in Figure 2.5 (seen above Level 2).

FIGURE 2.5
Controlling the analytic extents of datum

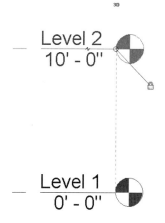

If you only want to move the graphic extents of your datum, first click the 3D icon. Now you can graphically modify the datum but not the analytic extents (Figure 2.6).

FIGURE 2.6
Controlling the
extents of datum

Second, datum can only be visible in a view that is being crossed by its analytical extents. Here's the difference. The elevation in Figure 2.6 shows lowering the ends of the grid above Level 2. This might be done to make an elevation graphically "cleaner" at a large scale.

In Figure 2.7, the analytic (3D) extents of the grid don't cross the levels. As a result, the grids would not be visible in those views.

FIGURE 2.7
Analytic (3D)
datum extents

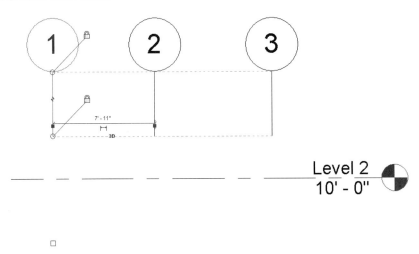

But in Figure 2.8, the analytic extents cross both Level 1 and Level 2 datum. But the graphic (2D) extents are above Level 2. This means that the grid datum would still be visible in both levels.

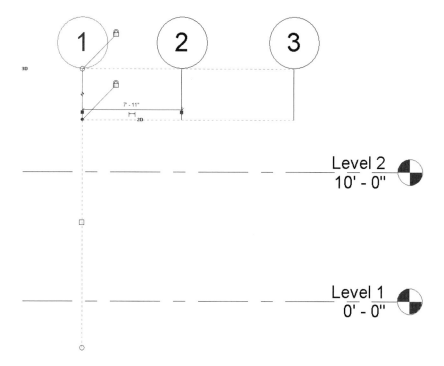

When you move datum in Revit, one way or another content is going to respond. If you move a level, walls and furniture are going to move accordingly. If you move a grid, structural elements are going to relocate. And if you move references, the elements associated with them update. As a matter of fact, you'll often pin datum or lock dimensions in order to restrict movement of datum after your project is starting to develop.

In turn, content can have a relationship to other content. For example, content can be hosted or associated with other content. Walls host doors and windows. A wall can be "attached" to a roof above it (or a floor or even another wall below it). Tops and bottoms of walls can even be attached to the top or bottom of other walls. But did you know that walls can maintain relationships inside other walls?

Here's a simple exercise to understand these relationships between content:

1. First, create a simple wall. Now let's edit the profile of the middle segment. Select the wall and click Edit Profile. Now you can't edit the middle wall's profile as shown in Figure 2.9 until you select the Edit Profile option. Once you're in Edit Profile mode, simply delete all the boundary lines and then redraw them as shown.

FIGURE 2.9
Editing the
wall's profile

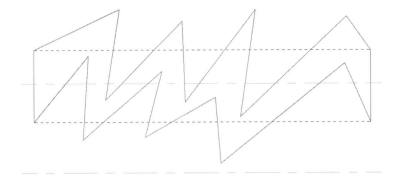

2. Now finish Edit Profile mode. Then in a plan view, draw another wall directly on top of the one that you just created. Go ahead and use a different type that's wider than the first wall you used. Initially the walls will overlap and you'll get a warning, which is fine and can be ignored (Figure 2.10). In this case, the view is also set to Wireframe so you can see the edited wall's profile that's being enveloped by the second wall.

FIGURE 2.10
Overlapping walls

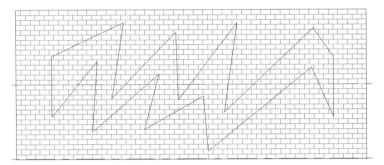

3. Now here comes the fun part. Using your Cut Geometry tool, cut the enveloped wall from the enveloping wall. Figure 2.11 shows the result.

FIGURE 2.11
Cutting geometry

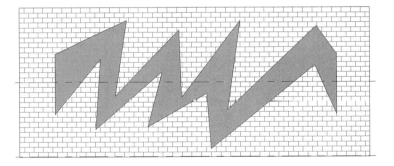

4. This builds a relationship between the wall that's being cut and the wall that's cutting. This relationship will be maintained even if you change the inner wall's profile or type. Go ahead and change the wall to a Storefront Wall type. Now edit the elevation profile and finish the sketch. The relationships are immediately updated (Figure 2.12).

FIGURE 2.12
Finished wall

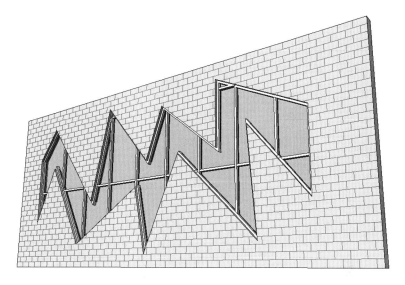

So, objects in Revit are able to maintain relationships between other objects. But here's the thing—you may not always have associate geometry (like walls, floors, and roofs) to relate to other geometry. This is why datum is so important.

If you've been using Revit for a reasonable amount of time, it seems obvious that levels and grids would control content, but reference planes aren't often appreciated. Here's a simple exercise to demonstrate this special kind of relationship between reference planes and walls:

1. Go to a plan view and create a series of concentric walls, as shown in Figure 2.13.

FIGURE 2.13
Concentric walls

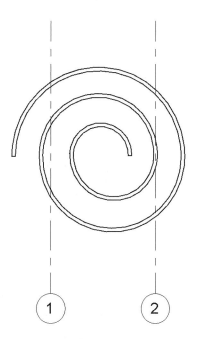

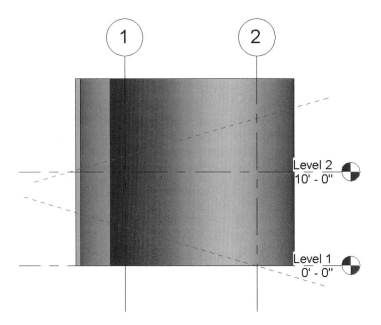

FIGURE 2.14
Datum and walls
in context

2. Now go to the front elevation view, as shown in Figure 2.14. If you move Level 1, you'll notice that the walls all move with it. You don't have ti select the walls; it's in the properties of the walls to maintain a relationship to the Level 1 datum. You could make the top of the walls maintain this same kind of relationship to Level 2.

3. You can also create a relationship to the Revit planes. To do this, simply select all the walls (just hover your mouse over one wall and then click and release the tab button to select the chain of walls) and then click the Attach Top/Base button. By default, Attach Wall ➤ Top is the default selection, so make sure that Attach Wall ➤ Base is selected when attaching the base of walls to the lower reference plane.

Figure 2.15 shows the results in the elevation view, once you've attached the top and bottom of the walls to the upper and lower reference planes.

The incredible thing is that moving and rotating the attached reference planes can modify the attached relationships. This is shown in a perspective view of the walls in Figure 2.16.

There are situations where you need a particular relationship to be maintained without attached relationships to geometry but the top or bottom condition isn't a straight line. What to do? Well, here's another solution:

1. First, copy all the walls from the previous exercise over to the side, as shown in Figure 2.17.

FIGURE 2.15
Finished wall

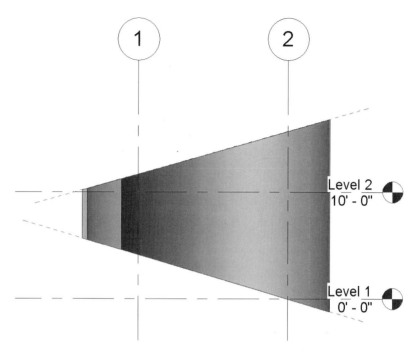

FIGURE 2.16
Perspective view

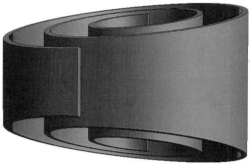

FIGURE 2.17
Copied walls

2. Now select all the walls and attach their Top Constrain to Level 2, as shown in Figure 2.18.

FIGURE 2.18
Finished wall

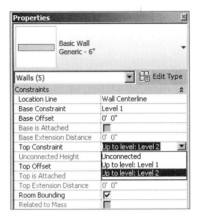

What do you do you do when you want a curved or nonlinear attachment and there's no geometry to attach to? You model an in-place void of the same category:

1. First, select Component ➤ Model In Place, select the category of Walls, and name the family **Top of Wall Void**. Now return to your Level 1 view and create a reference plan, as shown in Figure 2.19. Go ahead and name the reference plan **Top of Wall Void**.

FIGURE 2.19
Wall and reference
plane

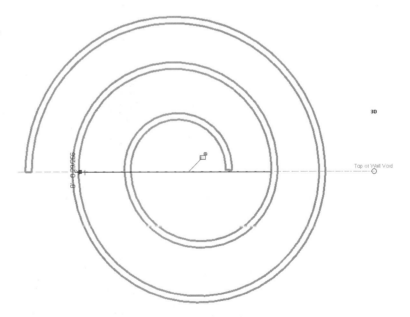

2. Return to your South elevation and you'll start to model the void that carves the top of the walls.

3. When you start to create the revolve, you'll need to set the reference plane as shown in Figure 2.20. This will control the work plane with respect to the center of the series of tangent walls.

FIGURE 2.20
Setting the reference plan

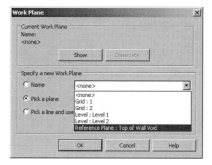

4. Now create the void revolve, as shown in Figure 2.21. To maintain relationships to Level 2, align and lock the top line to Level 2, and then dimension either side of the revolve sketch and lock those dimensions as well. This will force the void to move up with Level 2. Since the walls are also constrained to Level 2, they will move up as well.

FIGURE 2.21
Revolving the sketch

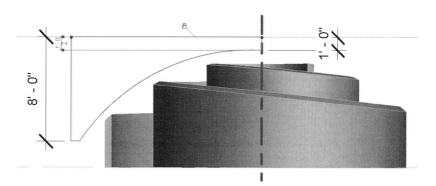

5. Go ahead and finish the sketch. Now you can use your Cut tool to remove the top of the walls from the in-place void (Figure 2.22).

FIGURE 2.22
Cutting with void

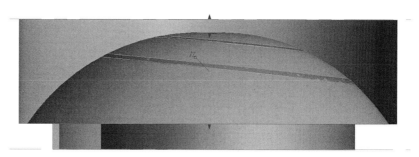

When you finish the in-place family, the walls will look similar to Figure 2.23. If you move Level 2 up or down, the void and walls will maintain relationships to their datum.

FIGURE 2.23
Finished walls

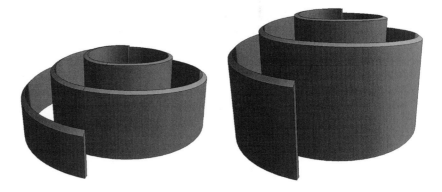

Overall, it's the role of datum, levels, grids, and reference planes to create your project's key relationships.

Content

Content is all about repetition that you put in your Revit project to design, develop, and document your project. Content can often maintain relationships with other content, but more importantly, content maintains relationships to your project datum. As you can see from the Revit organization chart shown earlier in Figure 2.1, content includes system families, component families, and spaces.

System families (also called *host families*) are project content that is part of the Revit project environment. These families are not created in the Family Editor—they're already in your project environment. If you need another type, you'll duplicate an existing type from within the project. Content can be 2D or 3D. Walls, Floors, Roofs, Ceilings, Stairs, and Railings are common 3D system families. Text, Dimensions, Revision Bubbles, and Insulation are commonly used 2D system families.

Component families are created in the Family Editor and are also 2D or 3D content. This means that you'll have to create and load these kinds of families or files outside the Revit project environment. When you start to create a component family, you'll initially be given the dialog box in Figure 2.24. This is Revit prompting you to select the right family template. And by selecting the right family template, you'll be certain that the component that you're creating is going to behave, view, schedule, and (if necessary) export properly.

The next category of content is *spaces*, such as rooms, areas, and volumes. Obviously this isn't the same thing as geometry. But they're also an important part of your project and maintain relationships to datum (as well as some system families). Like some system families, they're also phase, design option, and workset aware and can be scheduled.

FIGURE 2.24
Selecting a family
template

TYPE AND INSTANCE PARAMETERS

Everything in Revit has *parameters*, which are simply the information or data about something.
The kind of information that you can assign to something is extensive (Figure 2.25).

FIGURE 2.25
Types of
parameters

There are two kinds of parameters: type and instance. It's important that you understand the
difference between the two kinds of parameters. Type parameters control information about every
element of the same type. So for example, if you change the Material type of a piece of furniture,
the material for all the furniture of that type will change. Instance parameters control only the
instances that you have selected. So if the material of the piece of furniture that you've selected is
an *instance* parameter, you'll only be editing the selected elements.

Both instance and type parameters can be constantly exposed and docked in the Properties
dialog box. Simply selecting something will initially display the instance parameters. Figure 2.26
shows the instance parameters of a wall that control the relative height, constraints, and structural usage.

FIGURE 2.26
Instance parameters of a wall

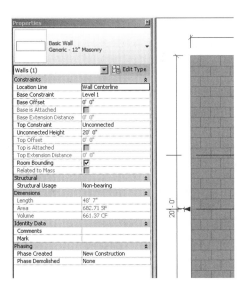

By clicking the Edit Type button, you expose the type parameters (Figure 2.27). These parameters control values such as the structure, graphics, and assembly code.

FIGURE 2.27
Type parameters of a wall

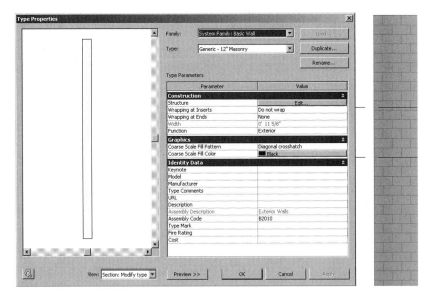

Views

Views are used to see the project. As you can see in the Revit organization chart shown earlier in Figure 2.1, there are both 2D and 3D views. Two-dimensional views are analytically oriented to specific coordinates, like plan, elevation, section, and so on. We've also grouped schedules under 2D areas of views. Views also have type and instance parameters (relative to each kind of view). Three-dimensional views are either orthographic or perspective in nature.

Understanding how to create and modify the properties of a view is important. First of all, every view has some kind of visibility parameters specific to that view (even schedules) that control what you want to be seen. Figure 2.28 shows the visibility parameters for an elevation. We'll discuss the other View Properties when we describe the UI later in this chapter.

FIGURE 2.28
Visibility graphics

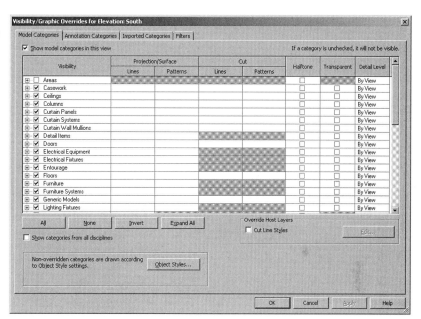

CREATING AND DUPLICATING VIEWS

It's important that you understand how to create different view types and how to control their extents after they're created.

Plans

When you create a corresponding level in elevation, you typically create plan views for your project. Figure 2.29 shows all of the level instance properties.

FIGURE 2.29
Plan view instance
parameters

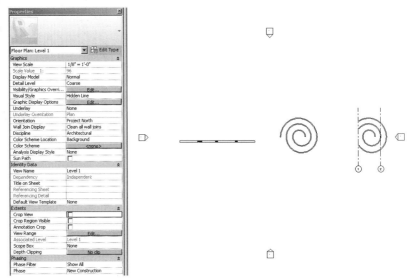

If you have a level without a corresponding view, you can also use the Plan Views function, as shown in Figure 2.30, to create a plan view.

FIGURE 2.30
Creating plan
views

Next to the Plan Views option is the Duplicate View option, which allows you to duplicate the active view (Figure 2.31).

FIGURE 2.31
Duplicating exist-
ing views

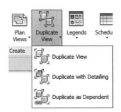

**CERT
OBJECTIVE**

You can also right-click a view name in the Project Brower and access the same option to duplicate the view (Figure 2.32).

FIGURE 2.32
Duplicating views
from the Project
Browser

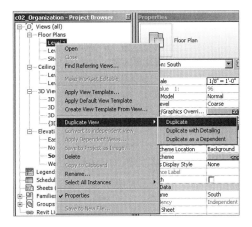

The vertical (in plan) and horizontal (in elevation) extents can also be controlled from View Properties. The View Range settings, as shown in Figure 2.33, define the vertical range of the view.

FIGURE 2.33
View Range
dialog box

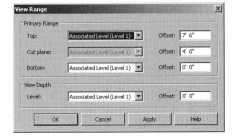

Checking the Crop Region Visible option can turn on the horizontal extents of a view. The shape may only be rectilinear (Figure 2.34).

FIGURE 2.34
Crop region

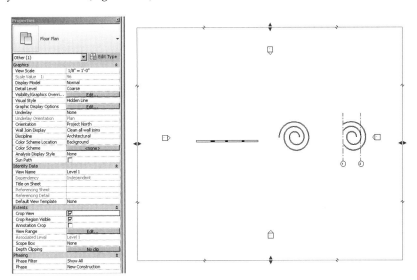

Although you can control the visibility of the crop region from this same dialog box, we recommend that you keep it turned on since you can control the visibility when you print (Figure 2.35).

FIGURE 2.35
Hiding the crop
when printing

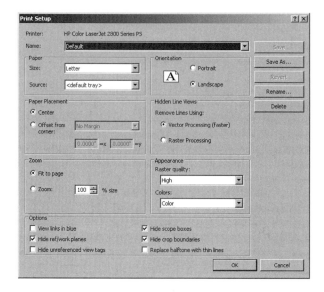

Elevations

Selecting the Elevation function on the View tab creates elevations. You'll also notice that as you place an elevation tag, they automatically orient to walls (Figure 2.36). If there's no host element nearby to reference, they'll automatically orient to the west.

FIGURE 2.36
Elevation tag
orientation

Selecting the center of the tag will allow you to create additional elevation (more typically done for interior elevations) by selecting the unchecked boxes that surround the elevation tag (Figure 2.37).

FIGURE 2.37
Creating additional elevations

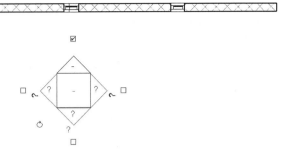

If you select the nose of the elevation tag, you'll see a blue line that defines the beginning of the cut plane for the elevation as well as a dashed line that defines the side and rear extents (Figure 2.38). This allows you to control the analytic extents of the elevation without moving the graphic tag, which is useful if you want the tag in a particular location but you want the actual elevation to start apart from the tag's location.

FIGURE 2.38
Elevation extents

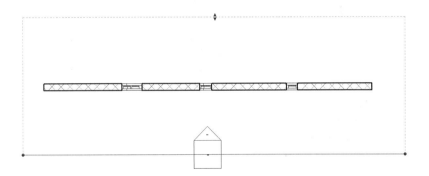

Finally, there are three types of elevations in Revit: exterior, interior, and framing. Their differences are more than graphic. *Exterior elevations* by default don't have an active crop boundary, only a starting cut plane. *Interior elevations* have their crop boundary on by default and attempt to find boundaries of host elements, like walls, floors, and ceilings. *Framing elevations* become active in the presence of grids, and their cut plane corresponds to their grid.

Sections

Selecting the Section function on the View tab creates sections. By default, there are three types of sections: Building, Wall, and Callout (Figure 2.39). This allows them to be grouped with better clarity in the Project Browser, but there are also other important properties.

FIGURE 2.39
Section types

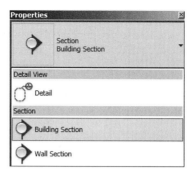

Unlike elevations, the cut plane of a section must correspond with the line of the section. Figure 2.40 shows the Instance Properties of a Building section. The far and side cut planes of a section can also be controlled. This goes for both Building and Wall sections.

FIGURE 2.40
Section properties
and extents

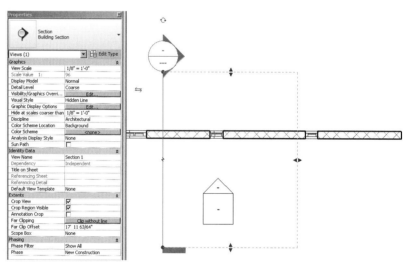

Neither Building nor Wall sections may be created in a nonperpendicular orientation with regard to project levels. But after you create them, they can be rotated in elevation. But this would lead to confusion in your project because once rotated, the section wouldn't be available in plan.

This is where the Detail section is such a great help. A Detail section that's created in plan can not only be seen in corresponding views, but it will also presume different graphic conventions.

CERT OBJECTIVE

For example, take a look at the two Detail sections in Figure 2.41 that are to the right of the Building section. When you create a Detail section, it will look like Detail Section 1. But when you view it in referring views, it will look like Detail Section 2.

The other thing that you should note is the color of callout and selection heads in Figure 2.41. These "blue" icons act as hyperlinks to the other views in your project. The great thing about them is they are automatically coordinated numerically when you place the views on your document set.

FIGURE 2.41
Detail sections in plan view

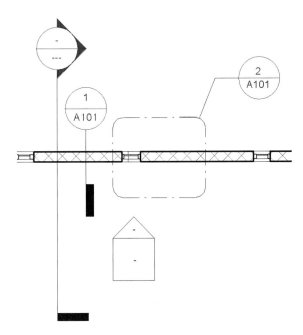

If we go to the view of the Building section, we see that the Detail sections are graphically the opposite of what you've seen in plan view (Figure 2.42).

FIGURE 2.42
Detail sections in section view

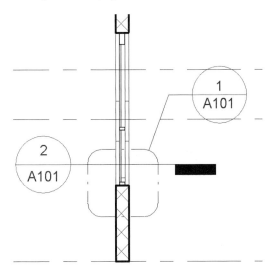

Callouts

There are two types of callouts: Detail and Floor Plan (Figure 2.43). Although Detail callouts may look like Detail sections graphically, they're not visible inside other perpendicular views. So a callout created in plan view will not be visible in elevations or sections like a Detail section.

FIGURE 2.43
Callout types

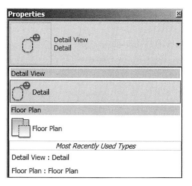

It's probably best to think of a Detail callout as an enlarged view. Its Far Clip settings are by default the same as the parent view (Figure 2.44).

FIGURE 2.44
Detail callout

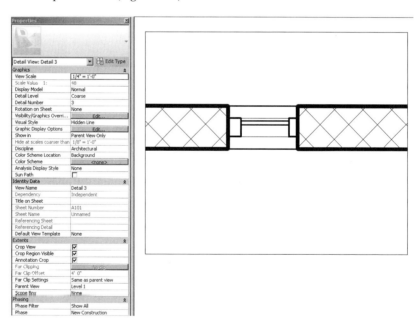

CERT OBJECTIVE

You can think of a Floor Plan callout as another plan view but with associated callout graphics. Floor Plan callouts also have all the same view controls as a regular plan view, such as Depth Clipping and View Range (Figure 2.45). Take a moment to note the line and control arrows around the border of the view. By modifying the location of these arrows, you're modifying the extents of the view. Of course, more than plan views can have their extents modified; elevations, sections, and callouts can all have their view extents modified in the same way.

FIGURE 2.45
Floor Plan callout

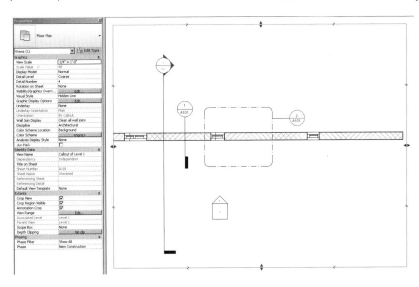

Drafting Views

Drafting views give you the ability to draw without first creating a reference to something in your project. They may contain Detail and Repeating Detail components, as well as all the annotation and documentation tools that Revit has to offer. Drafting views are great for drafting standard or analytic conditions that don't require an actual geometric underlay.

And once you've created a drafting view, you may refer to this view when creating an elevation, section, detail, and so on that would normally rely on an actual view of the model. As you start to create a standard project view (Figure 2.46), simply select the Reference Other View option and then you'll be allowed to select a reference view from all the other like views in your project, as well as any drafting views.

FIGURE 2.46
Drafting view
reference

Legends

There are two types of legends: legends and keynote legends. Regular legends are used to assemble analytic views of content in your project, graphics, geometry, tags, and so on—anything that lives in your project. Legends may contain Detail, Repeating Detail, and Legend components (Figure 2.47).

FIGURE 2.47
Types of legends

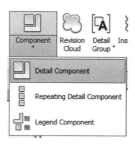

A Legend component (Figure 2.48) is a special bidirectionally associative representation of 3D system and component families that may only appear in legend views (not drafting views). If the actual thing in your project changes, the representation of that thing in your legend will change as well.

FIGURE 2.48
Legend
components

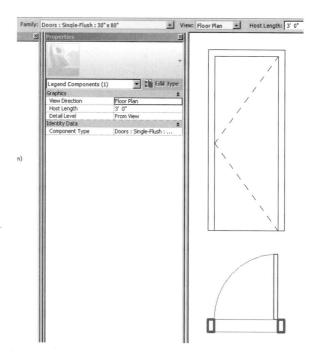

Keynote legends are special schedules. When creating a keynote legend, you'll be prompted much the same way as you are when creating a schedule (Figure 2.49).

FIGURE 2.49
Creating keynote
legends

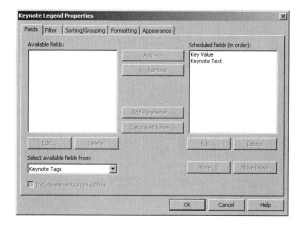

Schedules

There are five types of schedules in Revit: Schedule/Quantities, Material Takeoff, Sheet List, Note Block, and View List (Figure 2.50).

FIGURE 2.50
Schedule types

Schedules/Quantities in Revit are used to quantify the actual building elements that are being *used* in the project, not the elements that are loaded in the project (Figure 2.51).

FIGURE 2.51
Creating a
schedule

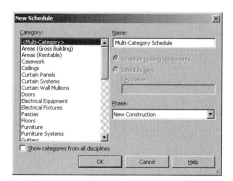

Three categories of elements may be scheduled via Schedules/Quantities:

◆ Masses: Mass and Mass Floors

◆ Spaces: Rooms and Areas

◆ Content: System and component families

There is also a special schedule called a Multi-Category schedule. It is used to create and *master* schedule component families (and may only contain component families) across many categories.

We think that being able to create a Multi-Category schedule that could contain everything in one place would be great, as it would allow you to see your entire project in one schedule. We hope this is being planned for the future.

Documentation

Sheets in Revit ultimately contain all the documentation for your project and will come in a variety of standard as well as custom sizes. The important thing to remember is that you're not going to select a "scale" when you print a sheet; it's really more like printing than "plotting." If you need your sheet to be smaller or fit on the desired page, these options are available and little different than printing from a word processing application.

3D Views

There are two kinds of 3D views in Revit: orthographic and perspective. 3D views are orthographic, and Camera and Walkthrough views are in perspective. You can't change one to another after the fact, so select carefully (Figure 2.52). We'll also cover 3D views in more detail in Chapter 12 when we discuss visualization.

FIGURE 2.52
3D view types

Orthographic views will always show parallel edges along Cartesian X-, Y-, and Z-axes. Orthographic views are best if you need to show model information to scale. A lot of people don't realize that it's possible to dimension and detail in Revit from a 3D orthographic view.

After isolating the part of the model that you want to dimension, the trick is to set the appropriate work plane (Figure 2.53) before dimensioning.

As long as you're careful about setting the work plane as you work, you can add dimensions and text to your views, as shown in Figure 2.54.

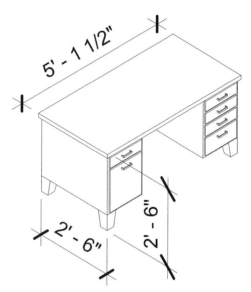

Create perspective views by placing the start and end points of a camera (typically from a plan view). It should be noted that the first point you select in plan is where the view will be taken from, but the second point is also the rotation origin for the view (Figure 2.55). This is important because if you select a second point that is far beyond your view, when you open the view and attempt to modify it, it will rotate around a target that doesn't seem to make sense. That's because the target location of the view is off in the distance.

A perspective view will not be to scale, but it can be made relatively larger or smaller by selecting the view's boundary and then selecting the size crop from the Modify | Camera tab (Figure 2.56). Once you do this, you'll have the option to change the view size and field of view (proportionally or nonproportionally). You can also simply drag the nodes of the bounding box.

FIGURE 2.55
Setting eye and
target origin

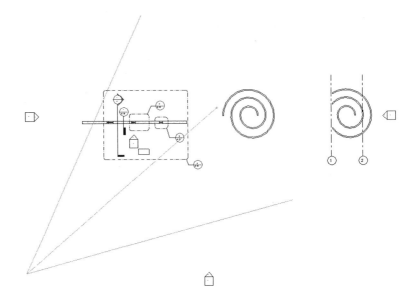

FIGURE 2.56
Modifying the
view size and field
of view

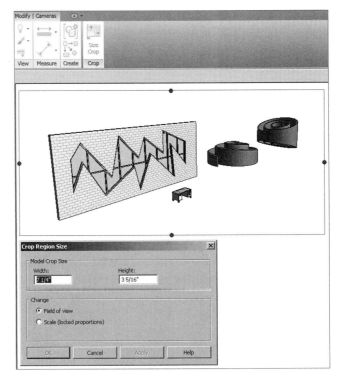

Camera extents are defined by the Far Clip Offset option, accessed in the View Properties' View Extents settings (Figure 2.57).

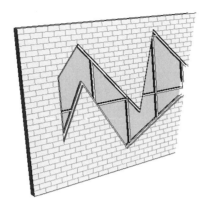

If the Far Clip Offset is too shallow, the view will look something that Figure 2.58. Geometry that you'd expect to see will be "clipped" in the view.

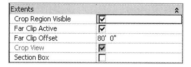

Simply increase the Far Clip Offset value to show more of the model. You may also do this graphically by returning to a plan view, right-clicking the view, and selecting Show Camera (Figure 2.59).

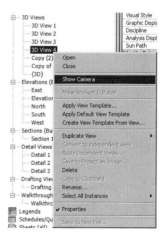

Once the camera is shown in your plan view, you may select the node at the far end of your clipping plane and manually drag the node to extend the Far Clip Offset of your view (Figure 2.60).

FIGURE 2.60
Extending the Far
Clip Offset

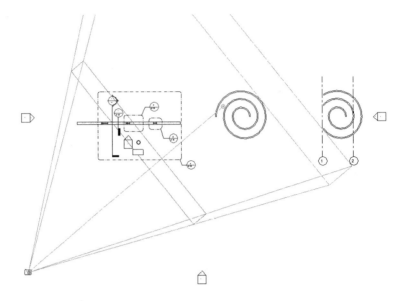

Finally, 3D views (even walkthroughs) contain section boxes, which become active when selecting the Section Box option (Figure 2.61). This will allow you to control how much of the project is shown and is helpful for creating cutaway visualizations in real time or in renderings.

FIGURE 2.61
Section box

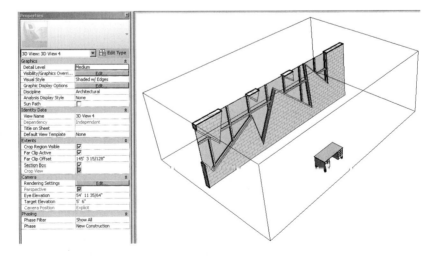

Management

Project management has to do with all the project settings that control (and therefore restrict) any number of project variables. Looking at the Revit organizational chart shown in Figure 2.1, we'll discuss each of the management options in the rest of the chapter as we discuss the UI. At the moment, the most important part of project organization to discuss is worksets, because this has to do with workflow and how the team comes together to work on the project simultaneously. Worksharing is covered in more detail in Chapter 6, but we'll cover this topic here at a high level as it relates to overall workflow of Revit.

There are two kinds of worksets: system managed and user managed. The user cannot create, manage, or assign system-managed worksets. Users can only create, manage, and assign worksets and elements that are assigned to user-created worksets (Figure 2.62).

FIGURE 2.62

Only user-created worksets are visible by default.

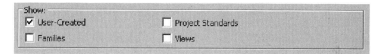

When worksharing is enabled, Revit creates worksets for everything in the project: datum, content, views, and settings. Revit manages the worksets related to families, views, and project standards.

But as for the actual content that is being used in your project (not just loaded, but actually in use) such as datum, 3D host and system families, and spaces, Revit allows you to create, manage, and assign worksets to those elements. The elements that are assigned to user-defined worksets are illustrated in Figure 2.63.

FIGURE 2.63

Elements assigned to user-defined worksets

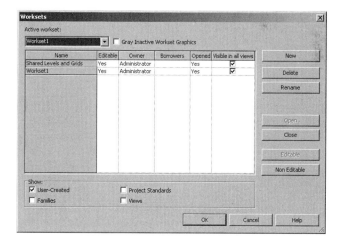

Levels and grids are assigned to the Shared Levels And Grids workset. All other 3D project geometry (system or components) is assigned to Workset1.

The great thing is that you only need to create and assign workset to a limited number of things that you're using in your project. Revit is managing the worksets assigned to everything else.

If you want to review any of the content from this portion of the chapter, you can download file c02_Organization.rvt from the Chapter 2 folder. This will allow you to investigate the complex 3D forms that were created using reference planes, hosted relationships, edited elevation profiles, and more.

Interface Organization

As mentioned, the interface has evolved for Revit Architecture 2011 and has improved in a lot of areas. Persistence of command location is the key. So even though functions remain contextually exposed and hidden depending on what you're working on, the majority of those contextual commands are in the same place.

Figure 2.64 shows the Revit 2011 UI. To illustrate some different project views, we've tiled four different view windows: Plan, Elevation, 3D, and Sheet.

FIGURE 2.64

Revit 2011 user interface

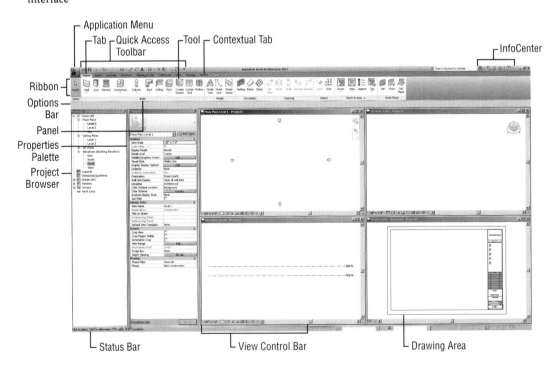

Application Button

The Application button (Figure 2.65), also called the *application menu*, allows you to access commonly used commands: New, Open, Save, Print, and so on. You can also export your project to a number of 2D and 3D formats from this menu. This is also where you would manage licensing information. The Publish option will allow you to publish RFA files to Autodesk Seek.

FIGURE 2.65
Application button

Quick Access Toolbar

The Quick Access toolbar (QAT) allows you to create a group of frequently used tools into one selection area (Figure 2.66).

FIGURE 2.66
Quick Access
toolbar

Right-clicking a command in one of the tabs will allow you to add elements to the QAT (Figure 2.67).

FIGURE 2.67
Adding commands
to the QAT

By clicking the small, down-facing arrow to the far right of the QAT, you'll find that commands may be further customized, grouped, and removed from the toolbar (Figure 2.68). You also have the option to show the QAT below the Ribbon.

FIGURE 2.68
Customizing
the QAT

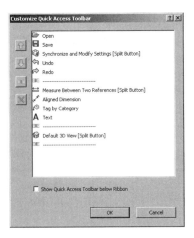

InfoCenter

To the far right of the QAT is the InfoCenter (Figure 2.69).

FIGURE 2.69
InfoCenter

From left to right, you have the ability to search, access the Subscription Center, access the Communication Center, save favorites, and get help.

Properties

The Properties tab contains the instance parameters of whatever you're currently working on. From this palette you can access the Type Selector, filter properties, and edit type parameters (Figure 2.70).

FIGURE 2.70
Properties Palette

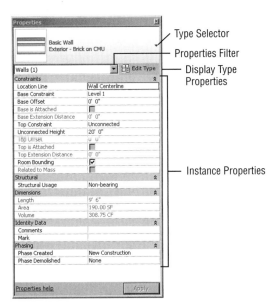

Project Browser

The Project Browser (Figure 2.71) is a project tree of all the views, legends, schedules, sheets, families, groups, and links in your Revit project. You can collapse and expand the project tree by selecting the + or – icons.

FIGURE 2.71
Project Browser

The Project Browser can also be filtered and grouped into folders based on a number of user-defined parameters. To access the type properties of the Project Browser, simply right-click the Views portion at the top of the palette (see Figure 2.72).

FIGURE 2.72
Project Browser's
Type Properties

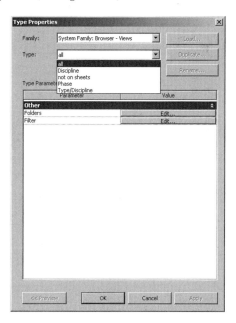

Status Bar

The status bar provides useful project information on files that are opening or already open (Figure 2.73). Project information such as worksets, design options, and filters is immediately accessible from the status bar.

FIGURE 2.73
Status bar

Drawing Area

The drawing area is the window into your design space. In this example, we've tiled four different view types: plan, elevation, 3D, and sheet view (Figure 2.74). Rather than jump between expanded drawing areas that obscure each other, it's sometimes helpful to tile many views in the same area.

FIGURE 2.74
Drawing area

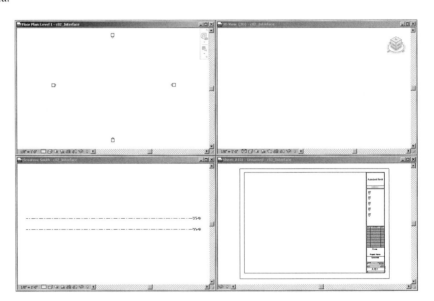

When you do this, you'll only be able to zoom into the extents that are defined by the drawing area. If you want to get around this limitation, here's a helpful tip.

Create a new sheet, but then delete the sheet (keeping the view). This is your "working" space for any view of the project. Now you can create duplicate views of any of your project views and assemble them in this working space (Figure 2.75). Zooming in and out is much more fluid, and you're not limited to the extents of one drawing area. You can create a keyboard shortcut to activate and deactivate views, which is helpful as well.

FIGURE 2.75
Working
sheet view

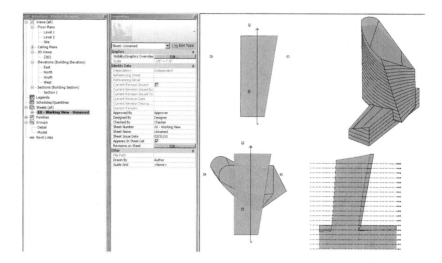

View Control Bar

The View Control bar is at the bottom of every view and is contextual based on the type of view that you're working in (Figure 2.76). Some views (like sheet views) won't have them. Perspective views won't show a scale.

FIGURE 2.76
View Control bar

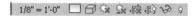

From left to right you have Scale, Detail Level, Visual Style, Sun Path (on/off), Shadows (on/off), Rendering Show/Hide (only in 3D views), Crop (on/off), Show Crop (show/hide), Temporary Hide/Isolate, and Reveal Hidden Elements.

One of the nice features in Revit Architecture 2011 is the ability to see realistic colors from the visual style (Figure 2.77).

FIGURE 2.77
Realistic option

The difference is subtle, but when combined with other graphic features, it will likely lead to users not rendering project views that are part of the document set. Rather, they'll opt for having real-time views.

ViewCube

You'll find the ViewCube in 3D views (Figure 2.78).

FIGURE 2.78
ViewCube

Hovering over the ViewCube will reveal the Home option (the little "house" above the ViewCube), which will bring you back to your home view. Right-clicking the ViewCube will open a menu that allows you to set, recall, and orient your view (see Figure 2.79).

FIGURE 2.79
ViewCube options

Selecting the Options menu will take you directly to the ViewCube options in the Options Bar (see Figure 2.80).

FIGURE 2.80
ViewCube
Options Bar

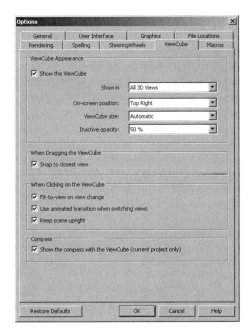

Navigation Bar

The Navigation bar contains the Navigation Wheel, View Zoom, and Pan controls (Figure 2.81).

FIGURE 2.81
Navigation bar

Ribbon

The Ribbon contains all of the Revit functionality for designing and documenting your Revit project (Figure 2.82). There are specific portions of the Ribbon that you should be familiar.

FIGURE 2.82
Ribbon

TABS

Tabs are used to select from among the various groups of functionality in Revit. There are nine tabs in the Revit Ribbon (Figure 2.83).

FIGURE 2.83
There are nine tabs
in the Ribbon.

We'll take a moment to briefly describe these tabs.

Home   The Home tab is used to create or place content (both system and component families) as well as datum (Figure 2.84).

FIGURE 2.84
Home tab

Insert   The Insert tab is used to link external files (2D, 3D, image, and Revit file types) as well as search for external content via Autodesk Seek (Figure 2.85).

FIGURE 2.85
Insert tab

Annotate   The Annotate tab contains many of the tools necessary to annotate, tag, dimension, or otherwise graphically document your project (Figure 2.86).

FIGURE 2.86
Annotate tab

Structure The Structure tab contains the tools necessary to add elements, which can be structurally analyzed in Revit Structure (Figure 2.87). You can also add datum from this tab.

FIGURE 2.87
Structure tab

Massing & Site The Massing & Site tab contains the tools necessary to add massing- and site-related elements (Figure 2.88).

FIGURE 2.88
Massing & Site tab

Other than infrequency of use, Massing and Site elements are so conceptually dissimilar that we believe they should occupy separate tabs.

Collaborate The Collaborate tab refers to the tools that you'll use to coordinate and manage the project within your own team as well as across other teams and their linked files (Figure 2.89).

FIGURE 2.89
Collaborate tab

View The View tab refers to the tools that you'll use to create all your project views, 2D and 3D, as well as schedules, legends, and sheets. You can also modify your user interface from this tab, including your keyboard shortcuts (Figure 2.90).

FIGURE 2.90
View tab

Manage The Manage tab contains all your project standards and other settings (Figure 2.91). This tab also contains your design option and phase tools. We believe it would make more conceptual sense to locate design option and phase tools in the Home tab.

FIGURE 2.91
Manage tab

CERT
OBJECTIVE

One of the most important settings that you'll use during your project is Object Styles on the Manage tab. Selecting this option will allow you to manage the global visibility settings for just about everything in your project: how it projects, how it cuts, and its associated color and pen weight.

Modify   The Modify tab contains the tools you'll use to manipulate all the content that you're creating in your Revit project (Figure 2.92).

FIGURE 2.92
Modify tab

Contextual Modify   Contextual Modify tabs are contextually revealed as part of an addition to the Modify tab when specific elements are selected (Figure 2.93). Contextual tabs are located to the far right of all the other panels in your Ribbon.

FIGURE 2.93
Contextual tabs

PANELS

Panels identify areas of grouped functionality in the Ribbon. They can also be pulled out of tabs and arranged so that functionality is persistently exposed. To relocate a panel, simply click and drag the panel portion out of the Ribbon (Figure 2.94).

FIGURE 2.94
Panels

The panels will snap together if you hover over a previously placed panel. To return a panel to the Ribbon, simply click the small down arrow that is in the upper portion of the right grey bar in the panel set.

OPTIONS BAR

CERT
OBJECTIVE

The Options Bar is a contextually sensitive area that gives you feedback as you create and modify content (Figure 2.95).

FIGURE 2.95
Options Bar

 **Real World Scenario**

UI Limitations and Evolution

Although there's been a lot of improvement in the Revit Architecture 2010 UI compared to the Revit Architecture 2011 UI, we believe there's room for improvement. Here's where we'd like to see the UI to develop for Revit Architecture 2012. These improvements can happen in two specific areas:

◆ Although the user is able to undock panels, it would be more helpful if the user had the option to undock entire tabs (as the functionality is so related). As it is, undocking and organizing panels is tedious and time-consuming.

◆ Undocked panels may not exist within the Ribbon or Options Bar area. This is really unfortunate. Having undocked panels in the drawing area leaves the overall view feeling cluttered and inconsistent. And as much as the implementation of the Ribbon was about "saving" space on your monitor, it's pretty clear to see every View tab has a considerable amount of unused space from the right of each tab and all the way to the right side of the monitor.

To resolve both conditions, we recommend that tabs have the ability to be undocked from the Ribbon and exposed persistently below the default Ribbon.

In this scenario, the user wants to be able to quickly and easily create, annotate, view, and modify their project. Since this is such a considerable portion of their workflow, the corresponding tabs are undocked from the default Ribbon and persistently exposed below it. This is far more sensible than having frequently used items placed in the hard-to-reach (and see) Quick Access toolbar.

Here's a mockup:

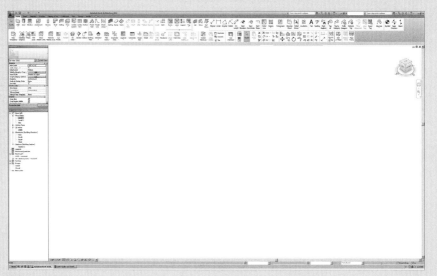

As you can see, the Home tab remains in its default location. But the Annotate, View, and Modify tabs are now to the side of and below the default Ribbon. And there is enough space to the right of the Modify tab for contextual panels. The Properties Palette and Project Browser are vertically stacked. Overall, this arrangement maximizes the drawing area while minimizing contextual selection between commonly used tabs.

The Bottom Line

Understand Revit project organization.   Revit has been available for about 10 years, and yet, after a decade, it remains unique in its approach to "whole-building BIM." The compelling advantage of being able to design, document, and manage your project across multiple disciplines—the architect, structural, and mechanical disciplines—is something that you can only do in Revit, and understanding project workflow in Revit is key to getting off on the right foot.

Master It   Thinking back to the Revit organization chart shown in Figure 2.1, what are the main components of a Revit project, and how can you use them apply to your design process? How do these categories directly affect your design workflow?

Understand Revit interface organization.   In addition to understanding how your project is organized, to use Revit well you must understand how the user interface is organized. Once you grasp both these concepts, you'll be ready to move ahead.

Master It   The "big" areas of the Revit UI are the Ribbon, properties, the Project Browser, and the drawing area. How do these areas work together, and what tabs correspond to an iterative design process?

Chapter 3

The Basics of the Revit Toolbox

The road to mastery will always include reinforcement of fundamental skills. Just as an accomplished musician will always practice her scales, we will review the fundamental selection and editing tools throughout the Revit Architecture program. There are many tools in Revit that can assist you in refining your models and project designs. Some are simple geometry editing functions whereas others possess more powerful capabilities. In this chapter, we'll review these tools and provide some exercises for you to remain productive.

In this chapter, you'll learn to:

◆ Select, modify, and replace elements

◆ Edit elements interactively

◆ Use other editing tools

Selecting, Modifying, and Replacing Elements

Knowing how to efficiently select, modify, and replace elements is fundamental to working productively in Revit. These interface operations are the foundation upon which you will build skills in creating and editing your project models. In this section, we will review methods for selection, filtering, and modifying properties.

Selecting Elements

Revit was one of the first programs that had the ability to highlight elements as you hovered the mouse pointer over them before you actually selected them. Not only does this give you a clear idea of what you are about to select, it displays information about that object in the status bar and in a banner near the mouse pointer. When you hover over an element, it highlights (turns purple); click the highlighted element and it turns blue, indicating that it is selected.

Once an element is selected, the ribbon changes to Modify mode where consistent editing tools are located in the left side and context-sensitive tools will appear to the right. Notice the subtle differences in the ribbon, as shown in Figure 3.1 when a roof, stacked wall, and floor are selected.

FIGURE 3.1
The right end of
the Modify tab
changes based on
the element that is
selected.

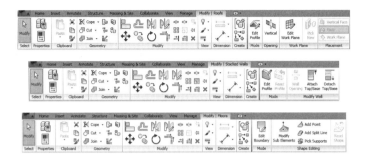

CHANGING SELECTION COLORS

Note that you can change Revit's default colors for selection, highlighting, and alerts to your liking. Click the Application button and select Options. In the Options dialog box that opens, switch to the Graphics tab to edit the settings for colors.

You can select elements in many different ways:

Add or Subtract   You can build a selection of individual elements by using the Ctrl and Shift keys on your keyboard. Hold down the Ctrl key while picking to *add* elements, and hold down the Shift key while picking to *remove* elements. Notice the mouse pointer will indicate a plus (+) when you hold the Ctrl key and a minus (-) when you hold the Shift key.

Window   To select large amounts of elements in a view window, you can click and drag the mouse to form two different types of selection windows. Click and drag from left to right, and only the elements completely within the window will be selected—this implied window is displayed as a solid line. Click and drag from right to left, and any element within or crossing the window will be selected—this implied window is displayed as a dashed line.

Chain   Although there are no polylines in Revit as there are in AutoCAD, chain-select is an intelligent method for selecting connected elements. To activate this mode, hover your mouse over (but don't click yet) one wall that is connected to several other walls. While the element is pre-highlighted, press the Tab key once, and the connected elements should be selected. When selecting objects, note that the Tab key is used to cycle through all available objects near your mouse pointer. If a floor edge happens to be near the edge of a wall you are trying to chain-select, you can skip the chain of walls and select the floor. Be sure to look at the status bar; it will indicate "Chain of walls or lines" when you have selected correctly.

Selection Count   Whenever you select any number of objects, the count of selected objects is displayed at the right end of the status bar. Clicking the Filter icon next to the selection count will open the Filter dialog box, allowing you to further refine the elements you want to modify.

Select Previous   A little-known feature allows you to select elements you had previously selected. Either right-click and choose Select Previous from the context menu or press Ctrl and the left arrow key on your keyboard.

Filtering Your Selection

Once you have elements selected, you can filter the selection by object categories using the Filter tool. This tool allows you to select large amounts of elements and then focus your selection by removing categories you don't need, as shown in Figure 3.2. For example, if you box-select an entire floor plan, you will have a selection set of many different categories. Using the Filter tool, you can limit the selection to just the Doors category—or perhaps Doors and Door Tags.

FIGURE 3.2
Use the Filter dialog box to fine-tune your selections.

Note that the Filter tool in the ribbon appears only if you have elements from multiple categories selected. If you have elements of only one category selected, you can still open the Filter tool by clicking the Filter icon in the status bar. You can use the Properties Palette as a filter as well; see "Using the Properties Palette" for more information.

Selecting All Instances

Another fast and powerful method for selecting objects is the Select All Instances function. When you right-click a single object in the drawing area or right-click a family in the Project Browser, the Select All Instances tool gives you two options: Visible In View or In Entire Project. Selecting the Visible In View option will select only those items you can see in the current view. This will *not* select elements that have been either temporarily or permanently hidden in the view.

Use the In Entire Project option carefully because you can modify elements in many places that you did not intend to change. Always remember to look at the selection count in the status bar when you use Select All Instances. Here are some common situations where you might use this tool:

◆ View titles—when updating graphics

◆ Walls—when switching from generic to specific types

◆ Title blocks—moving from design to detail documents

◆ Viewports—useful when trying to purge unused viewports

Note that Select All Instances does not work on model lines or symbolic lines. This limitation exists because lines are not only drawn in project views; they are integral parts of other objects such as filled regions and shaft openings.

Using the Properties Palette

The Properties Palette is similar to the Instance Properties dialog box in previous versions of Revit. In the latest version, it is a floating palette that can remain open while you work within the model. The palette can be docked on either side of your screen, or it can be moved to a second monitor. Open the Properties Palette by:

◆ Clicking the Properties icon in the Properties panel of the Modify tab in the ribbon

◆ Selecting Properties from the right-click context menu

◆ Pressing Ctrl+1 on your keyboard (like in AutoCAD)

As shown in Figure 3.3, the Properties Palette now contains the Type Selector at the top of the palette. When placing elements or swapping types of elements you've already placed in the model, the palette must be open to access the Type Selector.

FIGURE 3.3
The new Properties
Palette contains
the Type Selector
and is used to set
View Properties.

When no elements are selected, the Properties Palette displays the properties of the active view. This supersedes the View Properties command in older versions of Revit. If you need to change settings for the current view, simply make the changes in the Properties Palette, and the view will be updated. For views, you may not even need to use the Apply button to submit the changes.

Finally, you can also use the Properties Palette as a filtering method for selected elements. When you select a large number of disparate objects, the drop-down list below the Type Selector will display the total number of selected elements. Open the list and you will see the elements listed per category, as shown in Figure 3.4. Select one of the categories to modify the parameters for the respective elements. This is different from the Filter tool in that the entire selection set is maintained, allowing you to perform multiple modifying actions without reselecting elements.

FIGURE 3.4
Use the Properties
Palette to filter
selection sets.

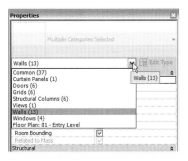

Matching Properties

Located on the Modify tab of the ribbon under the Clipboard panel, the Match Type Properties tool allows you to select one element and apply its Type and Instance Properties to other elements of the same category. Once you select one element, the brush icon near the mouse pointer appears filled. Each subsequent pick on elements of the same category will replace the selected element with the properties of the first element picked. Clicking in an open space will clear the brush icon and allow you to pick a new source object without restarting the command.

Be careful when using this tool with walls, because not only does it change the wall type, but it also changes the top and bottom constraints of the walls being matched. Thus, the best practice for changing wall types without affecting height constraints is to simply use the Type Selector.

Using the Context Menu

The context menu that appears when you right-click in the drawing area contains several new options in Revit Architecture 2011. You can activate the last command or select from a list of recent commands, as shown in Figure 3.5.

FIGURE 3.5
Run recent com-
mands from the
context menu.

In addition to the other right-click commands listed throughout this chapter (such as Create Similar), zoom commands including Previous View are on the context menu. There are also useful commands when you right-click views in the Project Browser. For example, activate a plan view and then try right-clicking a 3D view in the browser. Select Show Section Box, and you can edit the extent of the 3D view's section box while in a floor plan.

Editing Elements Interactively

Revit provides a range of options to interactively edit elements in the model. The most obvious is to select elements to drag on the screen or use the blue control grips to extend walls, lines, shape faces, and region boundaries; however, you often need more precise ways of moving and copying objects. Let's look at some ways to do this.

Moving Elements

You can move elements in several ways, ranging from traditional tools to using intelligent dimensions that appear on the fly when you select elements. Become familiar with each method and determine what is best for your workflow.

USING TEMPORARY DIMENSIONS

You have likely noticed by now that dimensions appear when elements are selected or newly modeled in Revit. These dimensions are called *temporary* dimensions and are there to inform you of the location of the elements relative to other elements in the model as well as to help you reposition them. Clicking the blue dimension value makes it an active and editable value. Type in a new value, and the selected element will move accordingly. Remember that when you are editing the position of an element via the dimensions, it will always be the selected element that moves. You can't change a dimension value if nothing is selected.

If a temporary dimension isn't referencing a meaningful element, you can choose a different reference by dragging the small blue square on the dimension's witness line to a new parallel reference, which will highlight when the mouse moves over them (Figure 3.6). For example, if you want to position a door opening at a specific dimension from a nearby wall, you will need to drag the grip of the temporary dimension that references the center of the door to the side of the opening. Then you can edit the value of the dimension as required. When you are dragging the grip of a temporary dimension, you can also use the Tab key on the keyboard to cycle through available snapping references near the mouse pointer.

FIGURE 3.6

Drag or click the blue grip to change the reference of the temporary dimension.

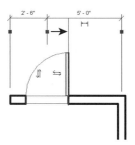

If you click a blue grip, it cycles to the next possible reference in the element. For example, clicking the grip of a dimension to a door or window cycles between the left and right openings and the center reference. The same applies to walls: try clicking the grip on the temporary dimension extending from a wall and see how the dimension cycles through the various references in the wall (interior face, centerline, exterior face). Note that when you drag a temporary dimension reference to a different position, the new reference is remembered when you return to the element for future editing.

You can also change the default behavior of temporary dimensions using the Temporary Dimension Properties dialog box shown in Figure 3.7 (on the Manage tab, click Additional Settings and then select Temporary Dimensions). Here you can specify how temporary dimensions will reference walls, doors, and windows independently.

FIGURE 3.7
The Temporary Dimension Properties dialog box lets you define default behaviors based on your modeling needs.

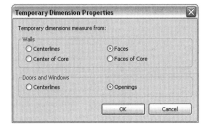

You can now modify the font size and transparency of temporary dimensions in the program options. To customize these values, click the Application button and select Options. In the Options dialog box that opens, switch to the Graphics tab and locate the Temporary Dimension Text Appearance settings. Adjust the text size and transparency according to your needs.

If you have many elements selected at the same time or select an element within the proximity of a large number of other elements, temporary dimensions sometimes don't appear. Check the Options Bar for the Activate Dimensions button; clicking it will make the temporary dimensions appear in the view.

NEW BEHAVIORS FOR MODIFY TOOLS

In Revit Architecture 2011, the Modify tools behave differently than in previous versions. Now you have the option to activate the tools without any elements selected. If you choose this method, you must press the Enter key when the objects you intend to modify are selected.

You can also switch between any of the Modify panel tools while you have elements selected. For example, if you initially chose Mirror – Pick Axis and selected an element during the command, you can simply activate the Mirror – Draw Axis command without reselecting the elements.

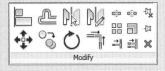

USING THE MOVE TOOL

Use the Move tool to relocate elements with more precision than by simply dragging them. The tool allows you to type in values or use temporary dimensions as helpers.

Moving elements is a two-click process: first you define a start point, and then you click to define a destination. If you know you need to move something a specific distance, it doesn't matter where your two picks take place. All that matters is the distance between the two clicks is the specified distance. Alternatively, you can simply type the desired value after picking the first point and guiding the mouse pointer in the desired direction of the move. This behavior is similar to the move command in AutoCAD.

There are a few options on the Options Bar to be aware of when the Move command is active:

Constrain   When this option is selected, it constrains movements to horizontal and vertical directions. Deselecting it allows you to move the elements freely as long as the element is not hosted. Hosted elements such as windows or doors always move in a constrained manner parallel to their host's axis.

Disjoin   Hosted elements can't change hosts and move to another host without being explicitly disjoined from their original host. This option lets you disconnect inserts from their hosts and move them to new hosts. For example, if you need to move a door from one wall to another, select the door and activate the Move tool. Select the Disjoin option and move the door to another host. Similarly, you can use the Disjoin option to move one wall away from another without maintaining the join between the two elements.

Multiple   The Multiple option is not active for the Move tool. This option is only available when you switch to the Copy tool.

Nudging Elements

Nudging is a simple way to push things around quickly, as you would in software programs such as Microsoft Office. When elements are selected, you can use the arrow keys on the keyboard to move the elements horizontally or vertically in small increments. Each press of an arrow key nudges the element a specific distance based on your current zoom factor. The closer you zoom, the finer the nudge is. Note that your snap settings do not affect the nudging distances set by the zoom level.

Moving with Nearby Elements

A simpler way to constrain freestanding elements is to use the Moves With Nearby Elements option. This setting is designed to capture logical relationships between elements without establishing an explicit constraint. When furnishing a space, for example, you probably want to align the bed or dresser with an adjacent wall. If you change the design of the space, you want the furniture to follow the wall to the new location. For this purpose, select the furniture and then select Moves With Nearby Elements in the Options Bar, as shown in Figure 3.8.

By setting this option, you create an invisible relationship between the bed and the wall so that each time you move the wall, the bed moves with it. To clarify the difference between this approach and other constraint relationships, you could create a wall-hosted family, but that would limit your placement options and would subject instances to deletion if the host is deleted. You could align and constrain the family to its host, but too many explicit constraints will adversely affect model performance.

FIGURE 3.8

Once an object is selected, it can be set to move with nearby elements.

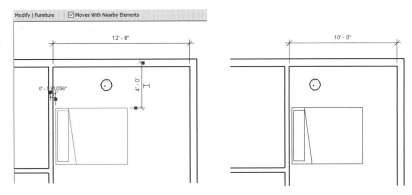

Copying Elements

CERT
OBJECTIVE

The Copy tool is another modifying tool that is nearly identical to the Move tool but makes a copy of the selected element at the location of the second pick. This tool doesn't copy anything to the clipboard; it copies an instance of an element or selection of elements in the same view. If you change views while using this tool, your selection is lost.

To activate this tool, either choose elements you want to copy and then select the Copy tool in the Modify tab in the ribbon, or activate the Copy tool first, select elements you want to copy, and then press the Enter key to start the copy process. Using the Options Bar, you can choose to make multiple copies in one transaction by selecting the Multiple option.

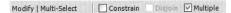

An alternative to the Copy tool is to use standard Windows accelerator keys to copy elements. To quickly copy a single element without the precision of the Copy tool, click and drag on an element while pressing the Ctrl key on your keyboard. This technique is useful for quickly populating a quantity of elements in a design without the required precision of the multiple picks of the Copy tool.

COPYING USING WORKSETS

If you are working in a model in which worksharing is enabled, be careful when performing any type of copying method. These methods include pasting from the clipboard, mirroring, and arraying, as well as using the Copy tool. Copied elements will always be placed on the *active workset*, not the workset of the original object. For example, if you are copying chairs that have been placed on the workset named Furniture but your active workset is Structure, the copied chairs will be assigned to the Structure workset.

Rotating and Mirroring Elements

CERT
OBJECTIVE

When refining or expanding your building design, you will likely find a frequent need to rotate or mirror one or more objects. Just as with moving or copying, Revit provides a few methods for these types of interactive operations. The quickest way to rotate elements in 90-degree increments is by pressing the spacebar on your keyboard. For more precision, you can use the Rotate tool to rotate elements to any specific angle you require.

USING THE SPACEBAR

You can use the spacebar to rotate elements both at the time of placement and after an element has been placed. In addition to rotating an object through 90-degree increments, pressing the spacebar will locate any nearby diagonal references (walls, grids, or reference planes) as rotation candidates. This is a great timesaving command to become familiar with because you can forgo the necessity of using an additional tool such as Rotate and Mirror after placing an object. Here are a few examples:

Doors and Windows   If you have a door with its swing in the wrong direction, select it and press the spacebar. You can cycle through all four possible orientations of the door using the spacebar. The same holds true for windows; however, many window families are built to only let you flip the window from inside to outside because many windows are symmetrical in elevation. If you are creating an asymmetrical window family, be sure to add flip controls to the window family during its creation. These controls allow the spacebar to work on hosted elements.

Walls   If you select a wall, pressing the spacebar flips the element as if it were being mirrored about its length. Walls flip based on the wall's Location Line, which often isn't the centerline of the assembly. If you aren't sure which direction your wall is facing, select it and look for the flip-control arrows. These are always located on the exterior side of walls (Figure 3.9).

FIGURE 3.9
The flip arrow is another way to reorient an element. For walls, it is always found on the exterior side.

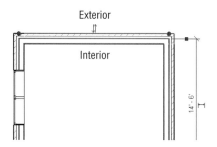

Freestanding Elements   If you select a freestanding element, the spacebar rotates the element about the center reference planes defined in the family. Depending on how the family was built, the rotation origin may not make the most sense. If you decide to edit a family to change the location of the geometry relative to the center reference planes, be careful: when the family is loaded back into a project, all instances of the family will jump to a new location based on the change you made relative to the reference planes.

USING THE ROTATE TOOL

To rotate an element, select it and click the Rotate tool. Remember, you can also activate the Rotate tool first, select one or more elements, and then press Enter to begin the operation. This is a two-click operation similar to the Move and Copy tools. Alternatively, you can enter numeric values for the desired rotation angle. Revit locates the geometric center of the selected elements and uses that as the default center of rotation; however, you will most likely want to designate a more meaningful center.

To choose a new center of rotation, select and drag the center icon to a new location before clicking to set the starting reference angle. Note that you might have to zoom out in order to find the center icon. Once the center is established, begin rotating the element using the temporary dimensions as a reference or by typing in the angle of rotation explicitly.

You'll notice that while moving the center of rotation, you lose the ability to pan and zoom the view. To overcome this, drag the center into the Project Browser and release the mouse button; then, move the mouse pointer back into the view. The mouse pointer changes to a rotation icon, and you can freely zoom and pan to the desired location. The next click you make places the origin and you can continue with the rotation operation. Note that you can also use keyboard snap shortcuts to refine the location of the center of rotation while dragging it. For example, type **SE** to snap to an explicit endpoint while dragging.

USING THE MIRROR TOOL

The Mirror tool allows you to mirror elements across an axis in order to create a mirror image of an element or multiple elements. You can either pick an existing reference in the model with the Mirror – Pick Axis tool or draw the axis interactively using the Mirror – Draw Axis tool. In Figure 3.10, the centerline of the plumbing chase wall was picked as the axis for mirroring the plumbing fixtures.

FIGURE 3.10
The sink, toilet, and bath fixtures are mirrored about the centerline of the chase wall.

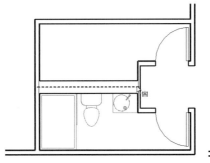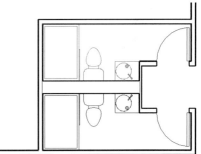

As with the other modify tools you have seen so far, the Mirror tools have the option to create a copy of the selected elements or to simply mirror the selected elements to a new position. You can find the Copy option in the Options Bar after you activate either of the mirror tools.

BE CAREFUL WHEN MIRRORING

The mirror tools should be used carefully on any type of freestanding elements that may be asymmetrical in design. Revit does not restrict you from using the mirror tools on any object; however, performing this operation to suit a design may distort a product component. For example, if an asymmetrical chair family was loaded into your model and you decide to mirror it to fit a space layout, the mirrored version of that chair may not be a viable product offered by the manufacturer. Remember that although an object can be scheduled, the schedule cannot determine if the object has been mirrored.

Arraying Elements

An array allows you to copy instances of an element with equal spacing between the instances. Revit provides the option to create intelligent arrays that can be grouped and associated for further refinement as well as one-off, unassociated arrays. Like the other tools we've reviewed in the Modify tab of the ribbon, the array options are presented on the Options Bar.

You can create two types of arrays: linear and radial. *Linear* arrays are set as the default because they're the most common. As you would expect, a linear array creates a series of elements in a line. Each element in the array can be given a defined distance from the previous element (Move To 2nd option) or can be spaced equally based on a defined overall array length (Move To Last option). Figure 3.11 shows a linear array where the Move To 2nd option was selected in order to define a fixed distance between each instance in the array. Think of this type of array as additive and subtractive: if you change the number, the length of the array increases or decreases.

FIGURE 3.11
The Move To 2nd option is used in the Array tool to set a fixed distance between instances.

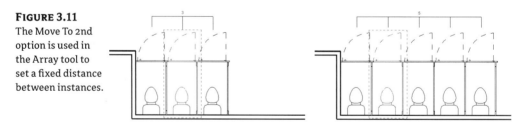

If you want to arrange elements in a fixed space and the exact spacing between elements is less important, use the Move To Last option. Figure 3.12 shows an array where the location of the last element in the array was picked and the elements were placed equally between the first and last elements in the array. With this option, the length is fixed and the array squeezes elements within that constraint as the number changes.

FIGURE 3.12

This array uses the Move To Last option and fills instances between the first and last instances.

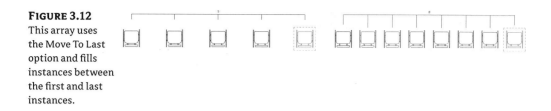

A *radial* array uses the same options as a linear array, but it revolves around a center point. The Move To 2nd and Move To Last options function as angles instead of distances in a radial array. You can specify the instance angle or overall array angle with two picks or you can enter a specific value. With this type of array, elements autorotate so that each element faces the center of the array, as shown in Figure 3.13.

FIGURE 3.13

Elements will autorotate in a radial array.

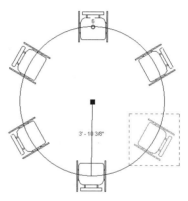

The radial array is a little trickier than a linear array. Here is how to achieve the example shown in Figure 3.13:

1. Before starting the radial array, draw a detail line to help locate the intended center of the array.

2. Select the element and activate the Array tool from the Modify tab in the ribbon. Select the Radial option button, change the Number to **6**, and choose the Move To Last option.

3. Drag the center of rotation off the element and to the endpoint of the detail line you drew in step 1.

4. Click the mouse to define any starting point. An exact starting point is not important because you will be defining a complete circle in the next step.

5. Do not click a second time; instead, go to the Options Bar, type **360** in the Angle option, and press Enter on the keyboard.

Enabling the Group And Associate option allows you to treat an array as a group that can be modified later to adjust the number and spacing of the array. If this option is unchecked, then the array is a one-off operation and you have no means of adjusting the array after it is created.

As shown in Figures 3.11 and 3.12, when an element in a grouped array is selected, a control appears indicating the number of elements in the array. Editing that number changes the number of elements in the array. This tool comes in handy when you're creating certain families because the array number can be associated with a parameter or driven by a mathematical formula. See Chapter 15 for a detailed exercise.

GROUPING ARRAYS OF DATUM ELEMENTS

When developing a project for a multistory building, you may find the Array tool a quick and easy way to generate many levels and grid lines. We recommend not using the Group And Associate option when arraying datum elements. Maintaining grids and levels inside groups can cause problems with elements that refer to those data.

Scaling Elements

The Scale tool lets you scale certain lines and graphic elements in 2D that are appropriate to be scaled, such as imported raster images and 2D line shapes. While not an obvious option, the Scale tool can be used in Sketch mode for any type of sketch-based element in a project or for solid and void geometry sketches in the Family Editor.

Keep in mind that you are working with a model made out of real-world objects, not abstract primitive forms. You cannot scale most elements in Revit because it's not practical or meaningful and may cause dangerous errors in scheduling and dimensions. For example, you can't scale the size of a door, wall, or sink because they represent real assemblies and scaling them would mean resizing all their components. This would lead to impractical results, such as a sink being displayed as a fraction of its actual manufactured size.

Aligning Elements

If you've been using Revit for any amount of time, you have likely discovered the power of the Align tool. It has the ability to supplant the need to use many of the tools we've already discussed. The Align tool lets you line elements up in an efficient way that works on almost all types of objects.

With this tool, you explicitly align references from one element to another regardless of the type of either object. For example, you can align windows in a façade so their centers or openings are all in alignment. To use the Align tool, activate it from the Modify tab in the ribbon and first select the target reference—a reference to which you want to align another element. Next, select what you want to align to that reference—the part or side of the element whose position needs to be modified. The second element picked is the one that always moves into alignment. This selection sequence is the opposite of the other editing tools we've discussed so far, so remember: *destination first*, then the element to be aligned.

As soon as you make your second pick and the aligned element is moved, a lock icon appears allowing you to constrain the alignment. If you click the icon, thereby constraining the alignment, the alignment is preserved if either element moves. Figure 3.14 illustrates the use of the Align tool to align multiple windows in an elevation view using the Multiple Alignment option on the Options Bar.

The Align tool also works within model patterns such as brick or stone on surfaces of model objects. Select a line on an object such as the edge of a wall then select a line in the surface pattern. Use the Tab key if you cannot get surface patterns selected with the first mouse click. Note that the Align tool will also rotate elements in the process of aligning them to objects which are not parallel. This is a real time-saver compared to moving and rotating.

FIGURE 3.14
You can use the Align tool for lining up edges of windows in a façade.

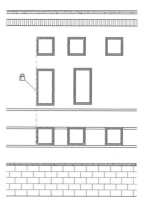

Trimming or Extending Lines and Walls

CERT
OBJECTIVE

You can trim and extend lines and walls to one another using the Trim/Extend tools on the Modify tab of the ribbon. In older versions of Revit, this function was assigned to a single button with three options in the Options Bar. In the latest version, there are three separate tools in the ribbon: Trim/Extend To Corner, Trim/Extend Single Element, and Trim/Extend Multiple Elements. With the Trim/Extend tools, you first activate the tool and then operate on elements in the model, selecting two lines or walls that need to meet in a corner or as a T intersection.

The Trim/Extend tools are used frequently for editing sketches of floors and roofs because it's easy to end up with overlapping lines that need to be trimmed to form a closed loop. Keep in mind that with the Trim/Extend tools, you are selecting pairs of elements to *remain*, not to be removed. While the Single Element and Multiple Elements tools are similar to the Extend command in AutoCAD, the behavior of the Trim/Extend To Corner tool in Revit is more like that of the Chamfer or Fillet commands, rather than its Trim command.

The Trim/Extend tools for extending a single element or multiple elements function in a slightly different way than Trim/Extend To Corner. To extend a wall or line, first select a target reference; then select the element you want to extend to that target (Figure 3.15). Using the Multiple Elements tool, you first select the target reference; then each subsequent pick extends the selected element to the target reference.

FIGURE 3.15
Extend walls to references by picking the target (1), then the wall to extend (2).

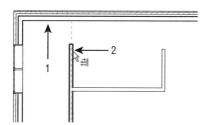
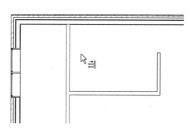

USE TRIM/EXTEND ON LINE-BASED COMPONENTS

You can use the Trim/Extend tools on line-based families that are either model or detail components. Try this using a line-based detail component for batt insulation or gypsum wallboard. The Trim/Extend tools will help make your detailing process much more efficient and fun!

Splitting Lines and Walls

The Split tool operates on walls and lines and lets you divide an element into two pieces. To cut an element, activate the Split tool from the Modify tab in the ribbon and place the mouse pointer over the edge of a wall or line. Before you click, you'll see a preview of the split line. The split line will automatically snap to any adjoining geometry.

The Options Bar displays a nice feature called Delete Inner Segment that removes the need to use the Trim tool after a splitting operation. In Figure 3.16, you need to remove the middle section of a wall and end up with a clean set of wall joins. Using the Split tool with the Delete Inner Segment option checked, you can accomplish this with two clicks and get a clean condition without having to return with the Trim command.

FIGURE 3.16
Using the Split tool with the Delete Inner Segment option checked

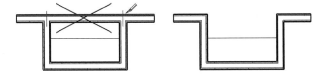

SPLIT WITH GAP

A new feature has been added to Revit 2011 that extends the functionality of the Split tool. The Split With Gap tool allows you to specify a gap distance and pick a single point on a wall. Although the wall is divided into two separate segments, the gap distance is maintained with an automatic constraint. To use Split With Gap, follow these steps:

1. Go to the Modify tab and from the Modify panel, select Split With Gap.

2. Specify the Joint Gap distance in the Options Bar. Note that this distance can only be set between 1/16" [1.6 mm] and 1'-0" [304.8 mm].

3. Move the mouse pointer over a wall and click to place the gap.

Once you have successfully split a wall with a gap, select the wall and notice the constraints (locks) on the gap and between the two parallel wall segments. Try to drag either of the wall ends separated by the gap and you will see the gap distance is maintained. Try to move the wall in a direction perpendicular to the wall segments and you will notice the two wall segments remain aligned.

If you'd like to rejoin walls that have been split with a gap, follow these steps:

1. Select a wall split with a defined gap.

2. Click the constraint icon in the gap to unlock the dimension constraint.

3. Right-click the end grip of one wall segment and select Allow Join.

4. Select the other wall and repeat step 3.

5. Drag the wall end grip of one wall segment to the end of the other segment. The walls should join.

Note that on walls with smaller gaps, the segments may automatically join as soon as you select Allow Join; however, rejoined segments may not form a single segment. If you have trouble joining two parallel wall segments into one, try to drag one of the wall ends away from the other and release the mouse button; then drag the segment back to the other end.

Offsetting Lines and Walls

Offset is similar to the Move and Copy tools in that it moves and makes a copy of an element by offsetting it parallel to an edge you select. You can find the Offset tool in the Modify tab of the ribbon. You can also specify an offset distance as an option in the Options Bar when you are sketching lines or walls.

This tool is especially useful in the Family Editor when you're making shapes that have a consistent thickness in profile, such as extruded steel shapes. The Offset tool has a Copy option available in the Options Bar that determines whether the offsetting operation generates a copy of the selected elements or simply moves them.

Remember that you can Tab-select a chain of elements and offset them in one click, as shown in Figure 3.17.

FIGURE 3.17
Use Offset with
Tab-select to copy
a chain of elements

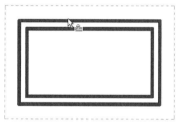

Keeping Elements from Moving

In some cases, you may want to make sure some elements in the model never move. An example of this is when you work on a renovation to an existing building. For obvious reasons, you would not like to move walls in the model that are already built in reality. Other examples include imported drawings, grids, levels, and exterior walls. Revit provides two ways to deal with this and lock certain elements, thus preventing them from moving.

PINNING ELEMENTS

You can restrict an element's ability to move by pinning it with the Pin tool. Use this tool to lock down critical elements that need to remain fixed for long periods of time. This is an important tool to use on imported CAD files, because it's easy to accidentally select an import and drag it or move it. This kind of accidental modification can lead to coordination problems, even in a BIM environment. Use pins to lock down gridlines as well, because you certainly don't want those to move accidentally either.

This tool is located in the Modify panel of the Modify tab in the ribbon. Select one or more elements for which you want to prevent movement and click the Pin tool. If you try to move the element, nothing will happen—you won't even get a preview of a potential move. To unpin an element, select it and click the Unpin icon, which is also located in the Modify panel. You can also unpin an element by clicking the pin icon that appears near a pinned element when it is selected.

DELETING PINNED ELEMENTS

Pinned elements can be deleted. This unfortunately is misunderstood by users who believe that a pinned element is safe from deletion. Revit will give you a warning after a pinned element is deleted, so pay close attention to these types of alerts.

> **Warning**
> Pinned objects deleted.

CONSTRAINTS

Constraints aren't as rigid as the Pin tool, but they do allow you to create dimensional rules in the model so that elements remain fixed relative to other elements. You can create a constraint using dimensions or alignments and then click the lock icon that appears upon creation of a dimension or completion of an alignment operation.

A simple example of using constraints is maintaining a fixed distance between a door and a side wall. If the wall moves, the door will also move. If you try to move the door, Revit will not let you move it. Look at Figure 3.18: the door has been constrained to remain 4″ from the wall face.

FIGURE 3.18
A door constrained to a wall can't be moved independently of the wall.

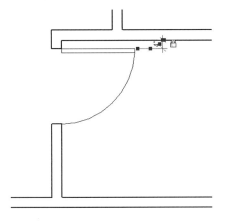

This type of constraint is accomplished by placing a dimension string between the side of the door and the face of the wall and then clicking the lock icon on the dimension. Note that the dimension can be deleted while preserving the constraint. If you delete a constrained dimension, an alert will appear giving you the option to unconstrain the elements or simply delete the dimension while maintaining the constraint (Figure 3.19). Note that you can determine where constraints were by creating new dimensions; constrained relationships will still display with the lock icon. You can also view these relationships when a constrained element is selected. Simply hover the mouse pointer near the constraint icon and you will see the dimension constraint represented as a dashed dimension string.

FIGURE 3.19
Deleting a constrained dimension generates an alert.

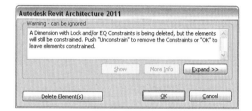

Exploring Other Editing Tools

A range of other editing tools are available in Revit, and we'll cover them in subsequent chapters when they're used in specific operations; however, there are a few tools you should know about now because they are generic tools you can put to immediate use on any project.

Using the Join Geometry Tool

Joining walls to floors and roofs creates cleaner-looking drawings, and Revit will attempt to create these joins automatically; however, in some cases, elements don't look right until they are explicitly joined. This is where the Join Geometry tool comes into play. This tool creates joins between floors, walls, ceilings, roofs, and slabs. A common use for this tool is in building sections, where floors and walls may appear overlapped and not joined. Figure 3.20 shows a floor intersecting with some walls that aren't joined. Using the Join Geometry tool, these conditions can be cleaned up nicely.

FIGURE 3.20
Intersections at Level 2 have been joined.

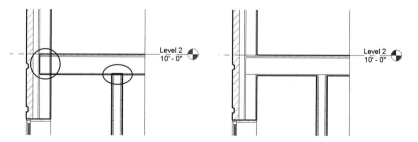

You might notice that some joins—especially in a view set to coarse detail level—contain a thin dividing line between two elements. This is usually because the two elements you joined consist of differing materials. Ensuring consistent material application will give you increased graphic quality in your project views.

You should also be aware that joining large host elements to many other elements may cause degraded model performance. One way to avoid this is to apply a black solid fill to elements in the cut plane of your coarse sections and avoid overall manual joining; then selectively join for medium and fine views.

Using the Split Face and Paint Tools

Occasionally you may need to apply a thin material to the face of an object without making a new type of element. You may also need to divide an overall surface into smaller regions to receive different materials. Revit provides the Paint tool to apply materials and the Split Face tool to divide object surfaces. With the Paint tool, you can apply alternative materials to the exterior faces of walls, floors, roofs, and ceilings. This material has no thickness, but you can schedule it with a material takeoff schedule and annotate it with a material tag. A typical use case for these two tools is the application of a carpet or thin tile to a floor. See Chapter 14, "Floors, Ceilings, and Roofs," for a detailed exercise on this topic.

Copying and Pasting

Copying and pasting is a familiar technique used in almost all software applications, and Revit provides the basic features you'd expect (Ctrl+C and Ctrl+V). It also has some additional time-saving options that are specific to working on a 3D model.

To copy any element or group of elements to the clipboard, select them and press Ctrl+C. To paste, press Ctrl+V. In the majority of cases, Revit pastes the elements with a dashed bounding box around them. You then determine where to place the elements by clicking a point to define its final position. In the Options Bar you will find a Constrain option that when clicked will only let you define the location of the pasted content orthogonally to the original elements.

Edit Pasted

Immediately after you select a point for the location of the pasted content, you will find a new panel in the ribbon called Edit Pasted (Figure 3.21). You can click Finish to complete the pasting action or simply start another command. If you are unsatisfied with the pasting action, select Cancel.

FIGURE 3.21
Additional actions
are available when
pasting elements.

If you select Edit Pasted Elements, a special mode will be started with the Edit Pasted tools appearing at the top left of the active window (Figure 3.22). In this mode, only the pasted elements are editable. You can use the Select All or Filter button to refine those elements within the pasted selection. When your edits are completed, click the Finish button.

FIGURE 3.22
Edit Pasted mode allows additional modification of pasted elements.

PASTE ALIGNED

If you need to paste elements with greater location control, Paste Aligned offers options to make the process simple and efficient. These options allow you to quickly duplicate elements from one view or one level to another while maintaining a consistent location in the X-Y coordinate plane. After selecting elements and copying them to the clipboard, find the Paste button in the Clipboard panel, as shown in Figure 3.23.

FIGURE 3.23
Paste Aligned options

Five options are available when you click the Paste drop-down button, in addition to the Paste From Clipboard option. Depending on the view from which you copy and what kinds of elements you copy, the availability of these options will change. For example, if you select a model element in a plan view, you won't have the Aligned To Selected Views option. These options are as follows:

Aligned To Selected Levels   This is a mode you can use to quickly paste copied elements to many different levels simultaneously. When you select this option, you choose levels from a list in a dialog box. This is useful when you have a multistory building design and you want to copy a furniture layout that repeats on many floors and selecting level graphics in a section or elevation would be too tedious.

Aligned To Selected Views   If you want to copy view-specific elements such as drafting lines, text, or dimensions, this option allows you to paste them by selecting views from a list of views in a dialog box. In the list available for selection, you don't see levels listed but rather a list of parallel views. For example, if elements are copied from a plan view, all other plan views are listed. Likewise, if you copy from an elevation view, only elevation views are listed.

Aligned To Current View   This option pastes the elements from the clipboard into the active view, in the same spatial location. For example, if you copy a series of walls in one view, switch to another view in the Project Browser, and choose to paste with the Aligned To Current View option, Revit pastes the walls to the same X-Y location in the view you switched to.

Aligned To Same Place   This option places elements from the clipboard in the exact same place from which it was copied or cut. One use for this tool is copying elements into a design option; see Chapter 11, "Designing with Design Options and Groups," for an explanation of design options.

Aligned To Picked Level   This is a mode you can use to copy and paste elements between different floors by picking a level in a section or elevation. Although you can cut or copy elements from a plan view, you must be in an elevation or section to paste using this option. You might use this paste option to copy balconies on a façade from one floor to another.

Using the Create Similar Tool

Rather than hunting through a list of families or making copies you'd have to edit later, try using the Create Similar tool to add new instances of a selected element to your model.

This tool is available in the Create panel of the Modify tab of the ribbon when an object is selected or from the right-click context menu. To use this tool, simply select an existing instance of the same type of element you'd like to create and click the Create Similar tool, and you will immediately be in a placement or creation mode according to the type of element. For example, if you use Create Similar with a floor selected, you're taken directly into Sketch mode, where you can start sketching the boundary for a new floor.

Using Keyboard Shortcuts (Accelerators)

To increase your productivity even further, you may like to use keyboard shortcuts to speed up common commands and minimize interruptions to your workflow. When you hover your mouse pointer over any tool in the ribbon, the keyboard shortcut is indicated to the right of the tool name, as shown here.

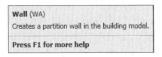

You can customize the keyboard shortcuts assigned to all commands in Revit through a new interface. To access this tool, go to the View tab in the ribbon, find the Windows panel, and select User Interface ➤ Keyboard Shortcuts. When the Keyboard Shortcuts dialog box appears (Figure 3.24), you can search for commands in the Search box. Once you find a command to which you'd like to assign a shortcut, select it and type the shortcut in the Press New Keys box. Click the Assign button, and you will see the new shortcut added to the selected command. Click OK to close the dialog box, and the keyboard shortcuts will be ready for immediate use.

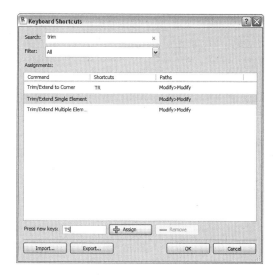

Modeling Site Context

In the previous sections of this chapter, you learned about the fundamental tools for editing and modifying model elements. Another set of tools you should become familiar with are the site tools. These allow you to create a context within which your building models can be situated. For example, a toposurface will create a hatched area when you view your building in a section, and it will function as a hosting surface for site components such as trees, shrubs, parking spaces, accessories, and vehicles (Figure 3.25).

FIGURE 3.25
A toposurface can host components such as trees, entourage, and vehicles.

The site tools in Revit are only intended to be used for the creation of basic elements, including topography, property lines, and building pads. Although editing utilities are available to manipulate the site elements, these tools are not meant to be used for civil engineering like the functionality found in Autodesk Civil 3D.

In the following sections you'll learn about the different ways to create and modify a toposurface, how to generate property lines with tags, and how to model a building pad within a toposurface.

Using a Toposurface

As its name suggests, a toposurface is a surface-based representation of the topography context supporting a project. It is not modeled as a solid in Revit; however, a toposurface will appear as if it were solid in a 3D view with a section box enabled (Figure 3.26).

FIGURE 3.26
Toposurfaces will appear as a solid in a 3D view only if a section box is used.

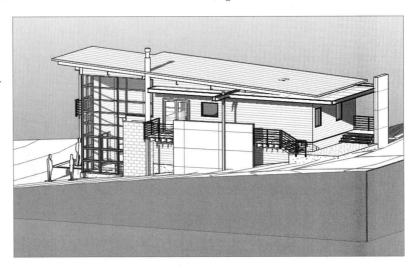

You can create a toposurface in three different ways: by placing points at specific elevations, by using a linked CAD file with lines or points at varying elevations, or by using a points file generated by a civil engineering application. We'll examine these techniques in the following exercises.

CREATING A TOPOSURFACE BY PLACING POINTS

CERT
OBJECTIVE

The simplest way to create a toposurface is by placing points in your Revit project at specific elevations. To create a clean outer edge for your toposurface, we suggest drawing a large rectangle using detail lines in your site plan. When you are creating a toposurface by placing points, there are no line-based geometry tools; however, points can be snapped to the detail lines. The following exercise will show you how to create a toposurface by placing points.

1. Begin by opening the file c03-Site-Tools.rvt, which can be downloaded from this book's companion website at www.sybex.com/go/masteringrevit2011.

2. Activate the floor plan named Site and you will see a rectangle created from detail lines.

3. Go to the Massing & Site tab and from the Model Site panel, click Toposurface. Notice in the contextual tab in the ribbon that the default tool is Place Point.

4. Notice the Elevation value in the Options Bar. Set the value of the points you are about to place.

Also note that the elevation values are always related to the Revit project base point. They do not relate to the elevation of any shared coordinates.

5. With the Elevation value set to 0'-0" (0mm), place a point at each of the left corners of the rectangle.

6. Change the Elevation value to 20'-0" (6000mm) and then place a point at each of the right corners of the rectangle. You will notice the contour lines of the surface begin to appear after the third point of the surface is placed.

7. In the contextual tab of the ribbon, click Finish Surface (green check) to complete the toposurface. Activate the default 3D view and you will see the sloping surface, as shown in Figure 3.27. Notice that the 3D view in this project already has the Section Box property enabled. To adjust the section box, activate the Reveal Hidden Elements tool in the View Control bar.

8. Save the project file for use in subsequent exercises.

FIGURE 3.27
A simple topo-
surface created by
placing points

CREATING A TOPOSURFACE FROM IMPORTED DATA

A common workflow you may encounter involves the use of CAD data generated by a civil engineer. In this case, the engineer must create a file with 3D data. Blocks, circles, or contour polylines must exist in the CAD file at the appropriate elevation to be used in the process of generating a toposurface in Revit.

In the following exercise, you will download a sample DWG file with contour polylines. You must link the file into your Revit project before creating the toposurface.

1. Create a new Revit project using the `default.rte` or `DefaultMetric.rte` template.

2. Download the file `c03-Site-Link.dwg` from this book's companion website at `www.sybex.com/go/masteringrevit2011`.

3. Activate the Site plan in the Project Browser.

4. Go to the Insert tab in the ribbon and click the Link CAD button. Select the `c03-Site-Link` `.dwg` file and set the following options:

- ◆ Current View Only: Unchecked

- ◆ Import Units: Auto-Detect

- ◆ Positioning: Auto - Center To Center

- ◆ Place At: Level 1

5. Click Open to close the dialog box and complete the insertion of the CAD link. Open a default 3D view to examine the results (Figure 3.28).

FIGURE 3.28
Linked CAD file as seen in a 3D view

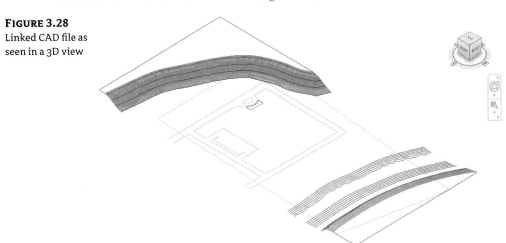

6. From the Massing & Site tab in the ribbon, click the Toposurface button. In the Tools panel of the Modify | Edit Surface ribbon, select Create From Import and then Select Import Instance.

7. Pick the linked CAD file and the Add Points From Selected Layers dialog box will appear (Figure 3.29). Click the Check None button and then select the layers C-TOPO-MAJR and C-TOPO-MINR.

FIGURE 3.29
Select only the layers containing 3D contour information.

8. Click OK to close the dialog box. It may take a few seconds to generate the points based on the contour polylines in the linked file, but they will appear as black squares when they have all been placed.

9. If you would like to use fewer points to define the toposurface, click the Simplify Surface button in the contextual ribbon and enter a larger value such as 1'-0" (250mm).

10. Click the Finish Surface button in the contextual ribbon to complete the toposurface. Change the visual style of the view to Consistent Colors to examine your results.

CREATING A TOPOSURFACE FROM A POINTS FILE

A less common method for creating a toposurface, although equally effective when using linked CAD data, is using a points file. A points file is a text file that is usually generated from a civil engineering program. It must be a comma-delimited file (TXT or CSV format) in which the x, y, and z coordinates of the points are the first numeric values in the file. In the following exercise, we have provided a sample points file that was exported from Autodesk Civil 3D using the XYZ_LIDAR Classification (comma-delimited) format setting.

1. Open the file c03-Site-Points.rvt, which can be downloaded from this book's companion website at www.sybex.com/go/masteringrevit2011.

2. Download the file c03-Points.csv from this book's website to your local computer.

3. Activate the Site plan in the Project Browser.

4. From the Massing & Site tab in the ribbon, click the Toposurface button. In the Tools panel of the Modify | Edit Surface ribbon, select Create From Import and then choose Specify Points File.

5. Navigate to the c03-Points.csv file and click Open. Note that if you were using a TXT format file, you'd change the Files Of Type option to Comma Delimited Text.

6. In the Format dialog box, select Decimal Feet. It is important to understand the units of the values in the points file to ensure the toposurface will be created at the correct scale. Click OK to close the dialog box.

7. Click the Finish Surface button in the contextual ribbon to complete the toposurface. Open the default 3D view to examine your results. You may have to use the Zoom All command to see the extents of the new toposurface.

8. Save the project file for use in subsequent exercises.

In the following sections, you will continue to use this file to explore the tools available for modifying a toposurface.

MODIFYING THE SURFACE WITH SUBREGION

The points file example we provided in the previous exercise represents a section of terrain across Lake Mead, Nevada. If you wanted to define an area of the toposurface with a different material but not change the geometry of the overall surface, you would use the Subregion tool. In the following exercise, you will use this tool to create a region that will represent the water of the lake.

1. Using the c03-Site-Points.rvt file, activate the Site plan from the Project Browser. In this view, there are dashed detail lines that represent the edge of the water.

2. Go to the Massing & Site tab in the ribbon and click the Subregion tool.

3. Switch to Pick Lines mode in the Draw panel of the contextual ribbon.

4. Hover your mouse pointer over one of the dashed detail lines at the left side of the surface, Tab-select the chain of lines, and then click to select them. You will see a purple sketch line appear.

5. Repeat step 4 for the dashed detail lines at the right side of the surface.

6. Switch to Line mode in the Draw panel of the contextual ribbon and draw a line connecting each open end of the water edge lines, as shown in Figure 3.30.

FIGURE 3.30
The sketch boundary for a subregion must be a closed loop but can overlap the edge of the toposurface.

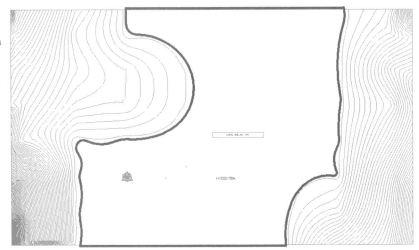

7. Click Finish Surface in the contextual ribbon to complete the subregion.

8. Activate the default 3D view and select the subregion you created in the previous steps.

9. In the Properties Palette, locate the Material parameter and click the ellipsis button to open the Materials dialog box. Locate and select the material named Site - Water. Note that you can easily find this material by typing **Water** in the search field at the top of the dialog box.

10. Click OK to close the Materials dialog box, you will see the results in the 3D view, as shown in Figure 3.31.

When you use the Subregion tool, the geometry of the original surface remains unchanged. If you no longer need the subregion, you can simply select it and delete it. Be aware that topographic surfaces cannot display surface patterns assigned to materials.

FIGURE 3.31
The subregion is assigned a different material for visualization purposes.

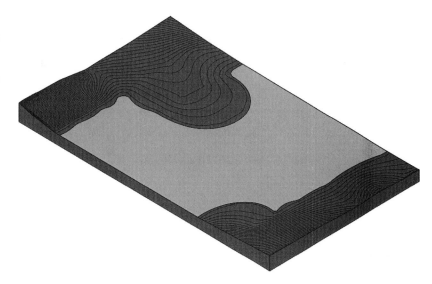

USING THE SPLIT SURFACE TOOL

If you need to divide a topographic surface into separate parts for the purpose of editing the geometry, you would use the Split Surface tool. With this tool, you can sketch a single line along which the surface will be divided into two editable entities. These separate entities can be recombined later using the Merge Surfaces tool. In the following exercise, you will split a topographic surface and edit some of the points. Remember that you can also use Split Surface to delete a portion of a topographic surface.

1. Open the file c03-Site-Tools.rvt you saved after the earlier lesson in this section.

2. Activate the Site plan in the Project Browser.

3. Go to the Massing & Site tab in the ribbon and click the Split Surface tool. Remember that you should use the Subregion tool if you only plan to assign a different material to the split region of the original surface.

4. Select the topographic surface and you will enter Sketch mode. Using the Line mode in the Draw panel of the contextual ribbon, draw two lines that overlap the edges of the surface, as shown in Figure 3.32.

FIGURE 3.32
Sketch lines that overlap the edge of the topographic surface

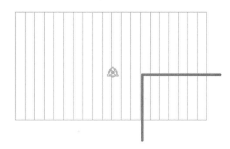

5. Click Finish Edit Mode in the ribbon and you will see the split surface highlighted in blue.

6. Activate the default 3D view and turn off the Section Box option in the Properties Palette.

7. Select the split surface and click the Edit Surface tool in the Modify | Topography tab of the ribbon.

8. Select the point at the outer corner of the topographic surface and change the elevation value in the Options Bar from 20′-0″ (6000mm) to 10′-0″ (3000mm).

9. Click Finish Surface in the contextual ribbon and you will see the result as shown in Figure 3.33.

FIGURE 3.33
A split region after editing the elevation of a corner point

10. To illustrate the difference between a split surface and other topographic surface edits, select the main surface and click Edit Surface in the contextual ribbon. Select the point at the upper corner opposite from the split region and change the elevation value to 10′-0″ (3000mm). Notice the difference in how the surface slope is interpolated between the other points on the surface (Figure 3.34).

FIGURE 3.34
Compare the difference between an edited split region (left) and an edited point directly on the surface (right).

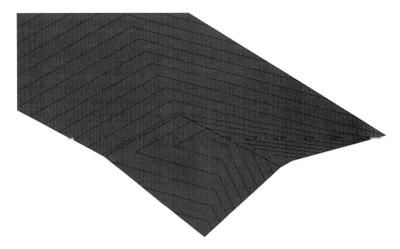

Creating a Building Pad

A building pad in Revit is a unique model element that resembles a floor. It can have a thickness and compound structure, it is associated with a level, and it can be sloped using slope arrows while you're sketching its boundary. The building pad is different from a floor because it will automatically cut through a toposurface, defining the outline for your building's cellar or basement.

The process to create a building pad is virtually identical to that of creating a floor. Let's run through a quick exercise to create a building pad in a sample project.

1. Open the file c03-Site-Pad.rvt, which can be downloaded from this book's website at www.sybex.com/go/masteringrevit2011.

2. Activate the floor plan named Site in the Project Browser. You will see an existing topographic surface and property line. Notice that reference planes were created to demarcate the required zoning setbacks from the property line. Foundation walls have been created within these reference planes.

   Note that you don't have to create a property line and walls before creating a building pad. You might create a building pad before any other building elements. Just realize that you can utilize the Pick Walls mode to associate the boundary of the building pad with the foundation walls.

3. Activate the Cellar floor plan from the Project Browser.

4. Go to the Massing & Site tab in the ribbon and click the Building Pad button. In the Properties Palette, change the Height Offset From Level value to 0.

5. Switch to Pick Walls mode in the Draw panel of the contextual ribbon and then pick the inside edges of the four foundation walls. You can use the Tab-select method to place all four lines at once.

6. Click the Finish Edit Mode button in the contextual ribbon to complete the sketch and then double-click the section head in the plan view to examine your results. Notice the top of the building pad is at the Cellar level and the poche of the topographic surface has been removed in the space of the cellar (Figure 3.35).

FIGURE 3.35
This section view illustrates how the building pad adjusts the extents of the topographic surface.

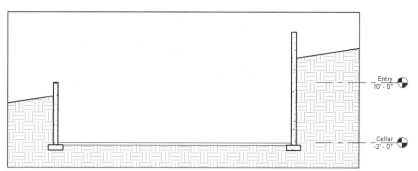

Entry
10'- 0"

Cellar
-2'- 0"

ADJUSTING THE SECTION POCHE FOR TOPOGRAPHIC SURFACES

If you would like to customize the settings for the fill pattern and depth of poche, locate the small arrow at the bottom of the Model Site panel in the Massing & Site tab of the ribbon. Clicking on it will open the Site Settings dialog box as shown here:

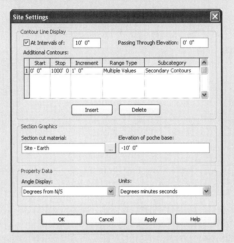

As you can see in this dialog box, you can change the Section Cut Material and the Elevation Of Poche Base settings. Note that the elevation value is in relation to the Revit project base point. You can also adjust the display format of contour lines shown on topographic surfaces as well as the units displayed by property lines.

Generating Property Lines

Property lines are used to delineate the boundary of the lot within which your building will be constructed. These special types of lines are different from simple model lines or detail lines because they can be tagged with standard property line labels that will display segment lengths along with bearings. The property line object can also report its area in a special tag.

You can create a property line in one of two ways: by sketching lines or by entering distances and bearings in a table. In the following exercise, you will create a simple property line by sketching, and then convert the sketched property line into a table of distances and bearings for comparison.

1. Start a new project using either the Default.rte or MetricDefault.rte template file and activate the Site plan in the Project Browser.

2. Go to the Massing & Site tab and click the Property Line button. When prompted with the Create Property Line dialog box, choose Create By Sketching.

3. Switch to the Rectangle tool in the Draw panel of the contextual ribbon and draw a rectangle measuring $120' \times 70'$ (36m × 21m).

4. Click the Finish Edit Mode button in the contextual ribbon to complete the sketch.

5. With the property line still selected, click the Edit Table button in the Modify | Property Lines tab of the ribbon. You will be prompted with a warning that you cannot return to Sketch mode once the property line has been converted to a table of distances and bearings. Click Yes to continue.

6. You will now see each vertex of the property line expressed as a distance and a NE bearing, as shown in Figure 3.36.

FIGURE 3.36
A property line can be defined in a table of distances and bearings.

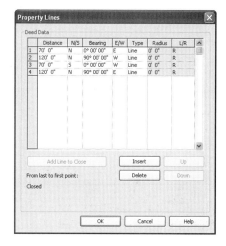

TAGGING PROPERTY LINES WITH AREA

In standard construction documentation, it is customary to annotate each vertex of a property line with its distance and bearing. There are two different types of tags you can use to annotate property lines. In the following exercise you will load these two types from Revit's default library and tag each segment of the property line as well as display the area contained within it.

1. Go to the Insert tab of the ribbon and click the Load Family button. Navigate to Revit's default library; double-click the Annotations folder and then the Civil folder.

2. Locate the following files and select them both by pressing the Ctrl key (the equivalent Metric library families are shown in parentheses):

   ◆ Property Line Tag.rfa (M_Property Line Tag.rfa)

   ◆ Property Tag - SF.rfa (M_Property Tag.rfa)

3. Click Open to load both families.

4. Go to the Annotate tab of the ribbon and click Tag By Category and uncheck the Leader option in the Options Bar.

5. Click on each segment of the property line to place the tags indicating the distance and bearing, as shown in Figure 3.37.

FIGURE 3.37
Tags are applied to display the distance and bearing of each segment of the property line.

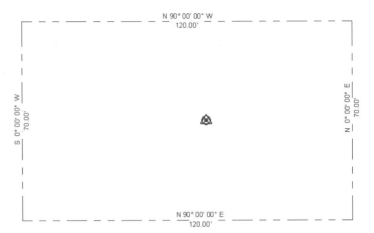

Now that you have tagged the individual vertices of the property line, it is time to display the area within the property line. This process is not the same as applying an area tag because an area object doesn't exist for the property line. Instead, the annotation family `Property Tag - SF.rfa` (`M_Property Tag.rfa`) is designed to be applied to the property lines when all its segments are selected.

You can try this with the property line you created earlier. Go back to the Annotate tab in the ribbon and click Tag By Category. Instead of picking a single vertex of the property line, hover your mouse pointer over one segment and use Tab-select to highlight the entire chain of property line segments. Click to place the property area tag. Click the question mark above the area to change the name of the property line, as shown in Figure 3.38.

FIGURE 3.38
Use Tab-select to place a property area tag for all segments.

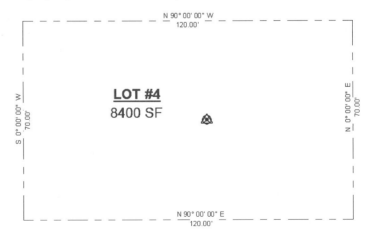

Cut and Fill Schedules

As we mentioned earlier in this section, Revit's site tools are not meant to replace civil engineering software programs. We have shown you how to create a topographical surface in a variety of ways as well as some methods of modifying these objects. There is also a way to quickly quantify how much earth is displaced by proposed changes to existing topography. This is commonly referred to as a cut/fill schedule.

One easy way to demonstrate the use of a cut/fill schedule is through the creation of a building pad which automatically modifies the topographic surface. Let's go through a quick exercise to examine this process.

1. Open the file c03-Site-Cut-Fill.rvt, which can be downloaded from this book's website at www.sybex.com/go/masteringrevit2011.

   In this file, notice that the topographic surface has been assigned to the Existing phase.

2. From the View tab in the ribbon, click Schedules and then select Schedules/Quantities to open the Edit Schedule dialog box.

3. From the Category list, choose Topography and then click OK.

4. In the Fields tab of the Schedule Properties dialog box, choose Name, Projected Area, and Net Cut/Fill, clicking Add after each one.

5. Activate the Cellar plan from the Project Browser and create a building pad in the same way you created one earlier in this section.

   After you complete the creation of the building pad and the topographic surface is modified, notice that the Net Cut/Fill values in the topography schedule still have a value of 0. This is because the Graded Region tool must be used on a surface to generate the differences required to calculate what volume must be cut versus filled in the proposed design.

6. Tile the open Revit windows so you can see both the default 3D view and the topography schedule.

7. From the Massing & Site tab, click the Graded Region tool and then select the topographic surface. When the Edit Graded Region dialog box appears, choose the option Create A New Toposurface Exactly Like The Existing One. This effectively creates overlapping existing and proposed surfaces, which will allow Revit to schedule the differences between the two.

8. When you select the surface, you will see the volume values in the topography schedule update to reflect how the excavation for the building pad affected the overall soil. Note that this type of calculation does not account for various construction methods such as backfilling.

   Try selecting the building pad and changing the Height Offset From Level value. Observe how the Net Cut/Fill values change as the pad helps define the scope of excavation on the site.

   You can also make the topography schedule easier to read by assigning descriptive information to each topographic surface. Simply select the surface and enter a value in the Name field in the Properties Palette. Change the name of the main surface to **Existing Grade** and then locate the surface where the building pad is. Change its name to **Pad Area** and observe the topography schedule once again.

The Bottom Line

Select, modify, and replace elements. There are many fundamental interactions supported by Revit to select just what you need and to modify elements efficiently.

Master It How can you quickly select only the door tags in a plan view and switch them to another type?

Edit elements interactively. The editing tools in Revit are similar to those found in other CAD and BIM software programs. Tools such as Move, Copy, and Trim are available on the Modify tab of the ribbon.

Master It How do you create a parametric repetition of an element?

Use other editing tools. Beyond the basic editing tools are more advanced commands to help you consistently and intelligently populate a building model with content.

Master It How do you copy model elements in the same location for a multistory building?

Creating site context for your Revit project The site tools in Revit allow you to create context for your building models including topographic surfaces, graded regions and property lines.

Master It Describe the different methods used to create a topographic surface.

Part 2

The Revit Workflow

In Part 1, you became more familiar with Revit's user interface and editing tools. Now we'll take a look at what makes a Revit project tick. Part 2 sets you on the path toward using Revit on a team or throughout your firm.

Chapter 4

Configuring Templates and Standards

In this chapter we discuss how to configure and manage graphic standards through the development and use of a project template. Such templates can be rich with information that goes beyond the out-of-the-box content provided by Autodesk. We will present proven methods for establishing template settings and content as well as explain how the reuse of work will increase productivity with each successive project.

In this chapter, you will learn to:

♦ Define settings for graphic quality and consistency

♦ Organize views for maximum efficiency

♦ Create custom annotation families

♦ Start a project with a custom template

♦ Develop a template management strategy

Introducing Project Templates

Like many other programs, Revit allows you to start with a basic template and then evolve your own custom templates to suit specific needs. As your knowledge of the software progresses, you'll begin to create new and reusable content such as wall types, roof types, ceilings, stairs, tags, and other families in order to meet your design and documentation needs. This is also the case with regard to the graphical language that you or your firm has established and needs to implement within Revit. How you graphically present elements such as text, dimensions, annotations, keynotes, and hatch patterns defines your graphic style of design documentation. In reality, the architectural profession tends to develop stylized graphics to convey design intent, and Revit respects this by enabling the customization of almost all aspects of the project template.

With Revit, project templates are configured by one or more of the following tasks:

♦ Defining all project settings to meet graphic requirements

♦ Preloading model and annotation families

♦ Defining standard system families

We'll explain these tasks in greater detail throughout this chapter. For now, know that you can save the completed settings as a new project template (.rte) and use them whenever you start a new project. You can create templates either by using a completely blank project, by saving an existing project as a template, or by using one of the default templates provided with the Revit installation. To start from scratch, click the Application button and choose New ➤ Project. In the New Project dialog box, as shown in Figure 4.1, choose None for the Template File option, and choose Project Template for the Create New option. Note that this dialog box does *not* appear when you press Ctrl+N or click New in the Recent Files window.

FIGURE 4.1
Starting a new
project template
from scratch

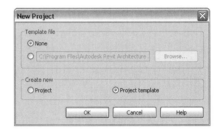

Starting a new project template without a base template requires you to develop *all* common content such as levels, grids, sections, callouts, tags, and model elements. If you have completely custom graphics and system families, this approach would be appropriate; however, if much of your graphic style is similar to the defaults, we suggest you start with one of Revit's default templates and edit it as necessary. You can find these templates by clicking Browse in the Template File area of the New Project dialog box. The files are usually installed in the root folder of the templates directory such as C:\Documents and Settings\All Users\Application Data\ Autodesk\RAC 2011\Imperial Templates.

In the older versions of Revit, when the program was launched, a new project was created using the specified default template. This behavior was similar to AutoCAD opening Drawing1.dwg when launched or Microsoft Word with Document1. If a heavier custom template was the default, Revit would take much longer to open. This forced users to think about providing lighter templates or to use an empty template as the default and train fellow users to create new projects by manually specifying the appropriate template. In recent years, Revit has eliminated the use of a new project at startup in lieu of a Recent Files page. This allows greater flexibility when developing a strategy for managing custom project templates.

Customizing Project Settings for Graphic Quality

One of the most common complaints from teams implementing Revit on their first projects is poor graphic quality of printed documents. When you first install the software, only some default settings are defined to approximate a standard graphic appearance of architectural drawings. For example, walls cut in sections are thicker than those shown in projected views and callout boundaries are dashed; however, all annotation categories are set to a line weight of 1. Fortunately, you can easily overcome these problems with some basic configuration.

Object Styles

The primary means of controlling graphic consistency throughout a project is through *object styles*. To access these settings, switch to the Manage tab and choose Object Styles. As shown in Figure 4.2, the dialog box is divided into three tabs: Model Objects, Annotation Objects, and Imported Objects. Settings for line weight, line color, line pattern, and material are established for each category.

FIGURE 4.2
The Object Styles dialog box gives you graphic control of all Revit categories and their subcategories.

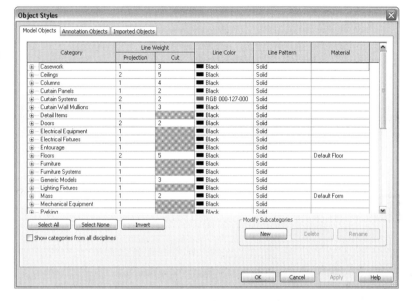

Model Objects   The Category column on the Model Objects tab lists all available categories and subcategories of model elements. It is important to note that the subcategories for model and annotation objects are created in families, which are loaded into the project or template. This will be discussed in greater detail in Chapter 15, "Family Editor."

The next two columns, under Line Weight, define the line weight used when the elements are displayed in *projection* or *cut* modes. In some categories, the Cut setting is unavailable; these element categories will never be cut in plan or section views, regardless of the location of the view's cut plane. For other categories that enable Cut display, element geometry in the Family Editor can be set to follow that rule or not, as shown in Figure 4.3.

FIGURE 4.3
Customizing the cut display of geometry in a family

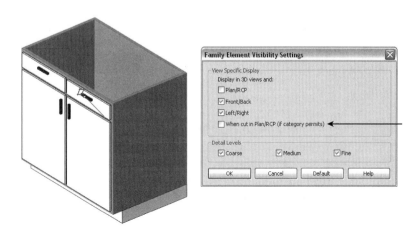

Line Color and Line Pattern allow customization of the display properties of each category and subcategory, but remember that printing a Revit view is WYSWYG (what you see is what you get)—colors will print as colors unless you override them to print as grayscale or black in Print Setup. The last column, Material, allows the definition of a default material to be associated with the category or subcategory in case family components in that category don't have materials explicitly defined. If a family has materials set to By Category, it references the material set in Object Styles.

Annotation Objects   The Annotation Objects tab is similar to the Model Objects tab except there are no material definitions. There is also only one column for line weight (Projection) because lines do not have three-dimensional properties like model objects and cannot be "cut."

Imported Objects   You can control the graphic appearance of layers (DWG) and levels (DGN) within linked or imported CAD files throughout the project on the Imported Objects tab of the Object Styles dialog box; however, we will cover this in greater detail in Chapter 8, "Interoperability: Working Multiplatform."

ASSIGNING LINE WEIGHT 1

You may want to avoid assigning line weight 1 to objects, because this is the weight used by most fill patterns. Reserving its use will help object profiles stand out compared to their patterns.

Line Settings

You can use lines in a variety of ways in Revit. Some lines relate to obvious tools such as Detail Lines and Model Lines, while you can place others with Filled Regions and the Linework tool. Lines also relate to the graphic representation of model and annotation elements as previously discussed. Achieving the desired graphic quality requires a review of Revit's line weights, patterns, and styles.

SETTING LINE WEIGHTS

The dialog box shown in Figure 4.4 manages the printed line weights relative to a numbered assignment from 1 to 16. For model objects, heavier line weights vary between view scales. If you require more granular control between scales, click the Add button to insert another scale value column and edit the line weights as required.

We recommend that you first customize the graphic appearance of model and annotation elements with object styles. You should only attempt to refine the line weight settings with a rigorous investigation of printed views in multiple scales.

FIGURE 4.4
Model line weights
vary depending on
the view scale.

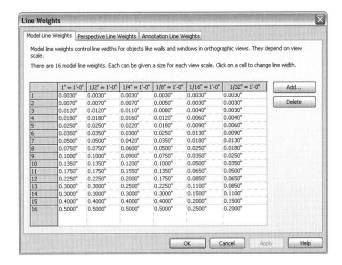

SETTING LINE PATTERNS

Repetitive series of line segments, spaces, and points comprise line patterns in Revit. To edit or create line patterns, switch to the Manage tab and choose Additional Settings ➤ Line Patterns. The Line Patterns dialog box, as shown in Figure 4.5, displays a list of existing line patterns in the project.

FIGURE 4.5
Displays all line
patterns in the
project

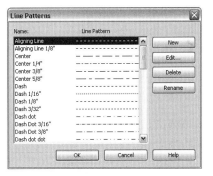

To edit an existing pattern, click the Edit button, or click New to create your own. You create patterns by specifying dash and space lengths, which will form a repeating sequence as shown in Figure 4.6. For dots, a length value isn't required.

USE CAUTION WHEN DELETING LINE PATTERNS

Before deleting a line pattern, you must verify that it hasn't been used anywhere in your project. This can only be done manually by checking Object Styles, Line Styles, and Visibility/Graphic Overrides. If you fail to do so, all line styles using the deleted pattern will be assigned as Solid.

FIGURE 4.6
Line patterns
consist of dashes,
spaces, and dots.

Frequently, a line pattern is required to include a symbol or text for elements such as fence lines, piping, or underground utilities. In AutoCAD, shape definitions could be used within linetype definitions to achieve the desired results. In Revit, these special lines can be created as line-based detail components. A sample of this type of custom line can be found by downloading the file c04-Lines.rvt from this book's companion website at www.sybex.com/go/masteringrevit2011.

CREATING A NEW LINE PATTERN

Follow these steps to create a new simple line pattern:

1. Switch to the Manage tab and choose Additional Settings ➤ Line Patterns.

2. In the Line Pattern dialog box, click New.

3. Give the new line pattern a name.

4. Define the sequence, as follows:

   ◆ Name: Dash - Dot - Double Dash - Dot

   ◆ Dash: $\frac{7}{16}$″ (10 mm)

   ◆ Space: $\frac{3}{16}$″ (5 mm)

   ◆ Dot

   ◆ Space: $\frac{1}{16}$″ (2 mm)

   ◆ Dash: $\frac{1}{8}$″ (3 mm)

   ◆ Space: $\frac{1}{16}$″ (2 mm)

   ◆ Dash: $\frac{1}{8}$″ (3 mm)

   ◆ Space: $\frac{1}{16}$″ (2 mm)

   ◆ Dot

   ◆ Space: $\frac{3}{16}$″ (5 mm)

5. Confirm by clicking OK.

The resulting line pattern looks like this:

SETTING LINE STYLES

Now that we have discussed the basic components of lines—color, weight, and pattern—the three are combined to create *line styles* for use in Detail Lines, Model Lines, Filled Regions, and Masking Regions. They are also available when the Linework tool is used to override a part of a model element. Access the Line Styles dialog box on the Manage tab under Additional Settings (Figure 4.7).

FIGURE 4.7

Line styles consist of weight, color, and pattern.

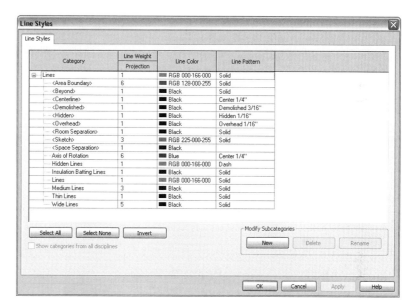

In the Line Styles dialog box, notice that some of the style names are bracketed—for example, <Hidden>. These are internal, "system" types of lines that cannot be renamed or deleted; however, their weight, color, and pattern can be modified.

USE CAUTION WHEN DELETING LINE STYLES

If you delete a line style used in a project, any elements utilizing the deleted style will be unable to reference that style anymore. The lines assigned to the deleted style will be reassigned to a common style such as Thin Lines—possibly producing undesirable results.

Establishing the best styles for your templates will be completely up to you, but we will offer some proven examples for inspiration. First, realize that Revit already uses common line styles such as Thin Lines, Medium Lines, and Wide Lines. If you are creating a complete array of customized line styles for your colleagues to use, rename the common styles to fit into your standard.

One common approach is to create line styles organized by their weight number along with any variable to its appearance, such as (3) Gray Dashed. Note the parentheses keep your custom line styles sorted to the top of the list in the Line Styles dialog box as well as the Type Selector when using a line-based tool. This approach has proven to be effective and efficient when creating details in drafting views or generating fill or masking regions.

Another approach reserves certain line styles for special circumstances where lines represent aspects of a building in a plan, elevation or section and must be assigned to a specific layer when views are exported in CAD format. For example, the crossing lines typically used to indicate an area in plan that is "open to below" may need to be assigned to a CAD layer "A-FLOR-BELW." This is difficult if you used a line style based solely on weight and pattern alone such as (2) Dashed. You cannot separately assign that line style to "A-FLOR-BELW" for the floor plan export and "A-DETL-THIN" for all other exports. Here are some examples of line styles you could create:

- Open to Below
- ADA Circles
- Curbs
- Fire Rating

In summary, take care to understand the different settings when you are beginning to customize graphic settings for lines in the Revit template. To change the displayed weight of an element in a project, changes should *not* be made in Line Weights, but rather through the Object Styles dialog box. For example, if you wanted to increase the cut line weight of a wall already set to (5), do not increase the value of (5) in the Line Weights dialog box. You would change this value by selecting (6) or (7) as the cut weight of a wall in the Object Styles dialog box.

Materials

Defining materials in your project template is another important task that can help maintain graphic consistency in many other areas of Revit. Materials drive the graphic representation of elements—not just in a rendered view—but in hidden line views, 2D or 3D. They are also responsible for cleanups because materials can merge with one another when elements of the same material are joined. A material also defines how an element's surface looks in shaded views, when cut in plan or section, and when seen in 3D views. In Figure 4.8, the surface patterns are all derived from the material used in the element.

To access the Materials Editor (Figure 4.9), switch to the Manage tab and choose Materials on the Settings panel. At the lower left of the dialog box (a) are icons for basic editing commands—duplicate, rename, and delete. At the upper left (b) is a search bar for quickly locating specific materials in the project and all material properties are found at the right side (c) of the dialog box.

FIGURE 4.8
Materials define
the surface and
cut patterns,
color, and render
material of the
elements.

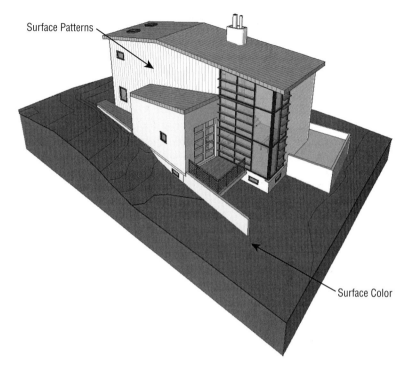

FIGURE 4.9
Manage material
properties using
the Materials
Editor.

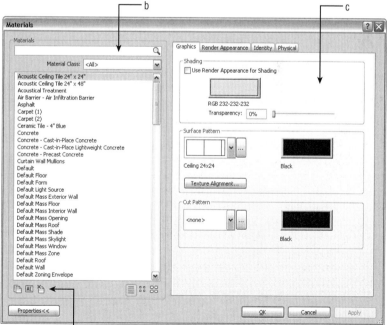

MATERIAL PROPERTIES

The material properties are divided into four tabs: Graphics, Render Appearance, Physical, and Identity.

Graphics   Defines shading color, surface patterns, and cut patterns.

> **Shading**   Defines the color and transparency of a material when the view is set to Shaded, Shaded with Edges, or Consistent Colors display mode. Note that the color can be dependent on the material's render appearance. If the Shading option is selected, the color and transparency are adopted from the Render Appearance settings and the shading controls will be disabled.
>
> **Surface Pattern**   Allows the selection of a *model pattern* to be displayed on the faces of elements in elevation, plan, and 3D views. Note that a material's surface pattern does not appear in rendered views; a pattern can be defined in the Render Appearance tab.
>
> **Cut Pattern**   Allows the selection of a drafting pattern to be displayed when an element is cut in a model view. Some elements can't be cut as discussed earlier in this chapter; in these cases, this setting has no effect on the graphic display and the pattern will not be displayed.

Render Appearance   Defines rendering attributes. Click the Render Appearance tab to view render properties. These properties will only become visible when you render a view and will not affect construction documentation graphics.

Physical   Defines structural properties of a material for analysis.

Identity   Defines schedule values and keynotes for materials. Specifying correct identity data for your standard or typical materials will increase efficiency when using annotation such as material tags as well as facilitate quality management by aligning model data such as manufacturer, model, and mark with your project specifications. In Figure 4.10, some sample identity data has been entered. Notice how the Material Class field can be customized to group project materials. Keywords can be entered for use with the Search bar and cost data has been entered for use in a Material Takeoff schedule. The use of material identity data in project annotation and detailing is discussed in greater detail in Chapter 19, "Annotating Your Design."

FIGURE 4.10
Use identity data to classify, find, tag, and schedule materials.

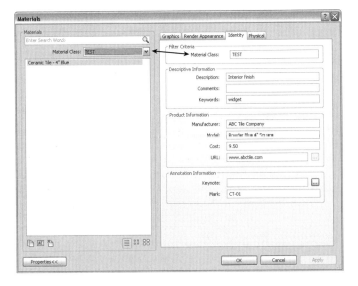

MATERIAL STRATEGIES

It may seem impossible to imagine all the materials you'll need in a project, making building a template seem daunting. Think of the basic materials you're likely to use—wood, brick, concrete, glass, and so on—and build from those. Remember, a template is just a starting point, and you can always expand it. If you end up making a lot of nice materials over the course of a project, use the Transfer Project Standards function to move materials back into your templates.

When you start to organize materials in Revit by name, there are many prevailing theories too numerous to list here, but here are a few suggestions:

By Type   Each material is prefixed with a descriptor such as Metal, Paint, Carpet, Wood, and so on.

By Use   Each material is prefixed with a description of its application such as Cladding, Interior, Exterior, Site, and so on.

Alphabetical   Materials have no prefixes.

By CSI Division   Each material is prefixed with a MasterFormat numerical descriptor corresponding to its specification section.

By Mark   Each material is prefixed with the designation of its Mark annotation parameter (for example, WD01-Wood-Cherry).

CREATING A SIMPLE EXTERIOR GLAZING MATERIAL

In the early phases of design, you may want to keep the level of detail to a minimum. In fact, guidelines for modeling levels of development may be established as part of a BIM execution plan (see AIA E202 BIM Protocol Exhibit at www.aiacontractdocuments.org/bim or the model progression specification at www.ipd-ca.net). To simplify the creation of exterior enclosures such as a curtain wall, try creating a glass material with a surface pattern approximating the layout dimensions of a curtain wall system (such as 5″ × 12″). Then create a generic wall type using this material, and you will have a much lighter wall type to explore design options with great ease.

Fill Patterns

Materials are often represented with simple hatch patterns. For any material used in Revit, you can define a *surface pattern* and a *cut pattern*. For simple parallel hatches and crosshatches, you can use the patterns already supplied in Revit or you can make your own patterns.

For more complex patterns, you need to import an external pattern file (.pat). Such pattern definitions can be imported from pattern files used by AutoCAD—a process we explain later in this chapter. To create, modify, or view an available fill pattern, switch to the Manage tab and choose Additional Settings ➢ Fill Patterns (see Figure 4.11). On the left side of the Fill Patterns dialog box, you can view the names and small graphic previews of the patterns. Below those are the Pattern Type options, where you choose what type of patterns to create and specify what type of pattern you wish to edit (Drafting or Model).

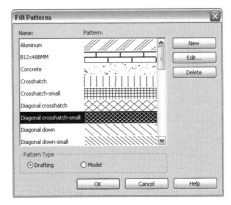

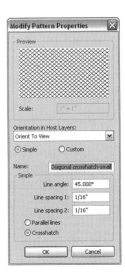

Model patterns are used to convey real-world dimensional patterns to represent a material, whereas *drafting patterns* are intended for symbolic representations. For example, a model pattern is used to show a brick pattern in 3D and elevation views, whereas a brick drafting pattern is used to represent the material in plan and section. Figure 4.12 shows how concrete masonry units (CMUs) are represented with a running bond pattern (model) as well as a crosshatch (drafting).

FIGURE 4.12
The CMU wall has
both a drafting
pattern (cut) and
a model pattern
(surface) defined.

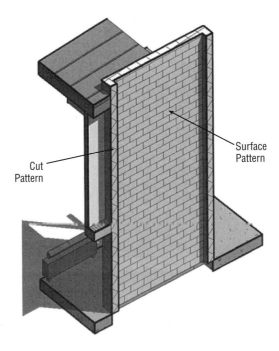

Surface Pattern

Cut Pattern

Model and drafting patterns have specific behaviors. In this example, you have a CMU wall with blocks that measure 16″ × 8″ (40mm × 20mm), regardless of the view scale. With a drafting pattern, the opposite is true: the pattern adjusts with the view scale, so the pattern looks identical in all scales.

CREATING A NEW DRAFTING PATTERN

To create a new pattern, first choose either Model or Drafting, and then click the New button. A generic pattern appears in the New Pattern dialog box. You can then design your pattern and assign some behaviors.

The option Orient In Host Layers is particularly useful when you're making drafting patterns. This allows you to specify how a pattern orients itself relative to host elements such as walls, floors, roofs, and ceilings when they're represented as cut. Note that the option isn't available for model pattern types. As shown in Figure 4.13, the orientation options are Orient To View, Keep Readable, and Align With Element.

FIGURE 4.13
From left to right: Orient To View, Keep Readable, and Align With Element

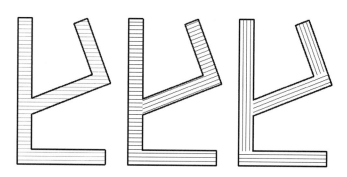

Orient To View   When this orientation is applied, the patterns used in the project all have the same orientation and the same origin. They're always perfectly aligned with the origin of the view.

Keep Readable   This orientation will maintain alignment with the view (i.e., horizontal lines will remain horizontal), but will be adjusted relative to angled host elements.

Align With Element   This orientation ensures that the pattern orientation depends on the orientation of the host element. Patterns essentially run parallel with the element.

You can choose to make either simple or custom patterns with this dialog box, using the radio button options. Figure 4.14 illustrates some examples of each option:

FIGURE 4.14
From left to right: simple fill pattern, simple fill pattern with the crosshatch option selected, and a custom fill pattern

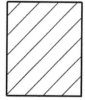

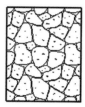

Simple   These patterns are generated with parallel or crosshatch lines that can have different angles and spacing. With both the crosshatch and parallel options, you can specify only one angle for the entire pattern. Using crosshatch, you can set two spacing values.

Custom   To create a more complex custom pattern, you have to import a pattern (.pat) file from an external source. This is often necessary because of Revit's current limitation in creating natively complex patterns. Your office may have a set of established patterns they've been using for years, and the Custom option allows you to import and reuse them without having to make them again from scratch. Custom patterns let you import a PAT file from anywhere on your hard drive or on a network and use it as a base pattern for a new fill pattern in Revit. The next section shows some best practices for importing a PAT file.

CREATING A CUSTOM COMPLEX PATTERN

Custom patterns require an external file that contains the definition of the pattern. The file extension of that pattern should be .pat, which is what you'll make in this section by editing an existing AutoCAD PAT file. An advantage of specifying patterns in the template file is that the PAT file won't need to be installed on each computer where Revit is installed; Revit stores each pattern internally in each template or project.

Before modifying PAT files, always make a copy of the original PAT file you intend to use as a base; you don't want to risk messing up other files that might already be using that original PAT file. PAT files can be edited with Notepad, but any text-editing application will also do. For this exercise, you'll choose the AutoCAD pattern called Grass, which you can find in acadiso.PAT (in metric units) or acad.pat (Imperial units) located on this book's companion web page: www .sybex.com/go/masteringrevit2011.

IMPORTING A CUSTOM PATTERN

Follow these steps to make a custom fill pattern by importing an existing pattern definition:

1. Using Notepad, open the file acadiso.PAT or acad.PAT.

2. Highlight the lines that define the pattern, and select them:

   ```
   45, 6.35, 0, 4.49013, 4.49013, 1.5875, -5.80526, 1.5875, -8.98026
   *GRASS, turfed surface
   90, 0, 0, 17.9605, 17.9605, 4.7625, -31.1585
   45, 0, 0, 0, 25.4, 4.7625, -20.6375
   135, 0, 0, 0, 25.4, 4.7625, -20.6375
   *GRATE, grid
   0, 0, 0, 0, 0.79375
   ```

3. Choose Edit ➢ Copy.

4. Open a new text file, and paste the selection. (You can also open the PAT file located in C:\Program Files\Autodesk\Revit Architecture 2011\Data, in which all Revit patterns are already saved. In that case, you can paste the selected text in that file.)

5. This is the important part: in the new text file where you pasted the selected text, add the two lines shown highlighted here:

```
;%UNITS=MM
*GRASS, turfed surface
;%TYPE=DRAFTING
90, 0, 0, 17.9605, 17.9605, 4.7625, -31.1585
45, 0, 0, 0, 25.4, 4.7625, -20.6375
135, 0, 0, 0, 25.4, 4.7625, -20.6375
```

The first line that you write before the pattern text, ;%UNITS=MM, can appear only once in the text file. It defines the value for the units used in the pattern. In the example, the units are millimeters (MM); if you wanted to work in imperial units, it would be ;%UNITS=INCH. (If you use the option in step 4 to collect all patterns the master PAT file, then this line already exists and you don't need to add it.)

The second statement, ;%TYPE=DRAFTING, helps define whether you're creating a drafting or model pattern. In this example, the pattern is the Drafting type.

6. Save your text file with a .pat file extension.

7. In Revit, on the Manage tab, choose Additional Settings ➢ Fill Patterns.

8. In the Fill Patterns dialog box, verify that the Drafting option is selected, and click New.

9. In the New Pattern dialog box, select the Custom option. The lower part of the dialog box offers new options.

10. Click Import.

IMPORTING PAT FILES

It's important to know that when you import a new pattern, the type of pattern needs to be the same as the new type of pattern you're making. In other words, if you're making a new model pattern, you can't import a drafting pattern. If you try to do so, you'll see a warning message like the one shown here:

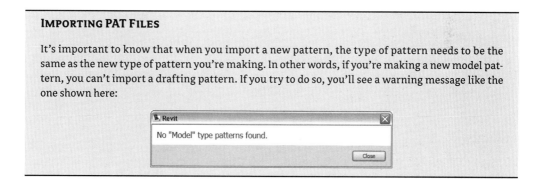

---

11. Navigate to the place on your hard drive or network where you saved the PAT file, and click Open.

12. In the list that appears to the right of this button, you can see the name of the pattern you created: GRASS, as shown in Figure 4.15. (If you have a PAT file with many patterns defined, you see all the other drafting patterns available in that list.) The name of the pattern automatically becomes the name of your fill pattern, but you can change that if you like.

FIGURE 4.15
The New Pattern
dialog box displays
the imported PAT
file in the Custom
group.

13. If necessary, you can adjust the scales of the imported pattern. The Preview window displays the graphic of the pattern, always in 1:1 scale. This informs you if you need to scale the pattern up or down. You'll know that you need to scale the pattern if the preview appears as a solid black box—that means the pattern is too dense.

14. If you're happy with the result, confirm by clicking OK.

Color Schemes

The use of color schemes in project documentation will be covered in greater detail in Chapter 20, "Presenting Your Design"; however, for now, just know that you can preconfigure them in project templates for a variety of scenarios. As an example, an architect may perform many projects for a single client who utilizes the same department names in all of their program design requirements. The architect would like to ensure that the colored plans in all projects for this client use the identical color scheme. In the following steps, you will create a new color fill legend with some predefined department values and associated colors to be saved in a custom project template.

1. On the Home tab, go to the Room & Area panel and select the Legend tool.

2. Place a legend in any available floor plan view, and you will see the Choose Space Type And Color Scheme dialog box, as shown in Figure 4.16. Choose Space Types: Rooms And Color Scheme: Department. (These choices can be modified later.)

FIGURE 4.16
Select criteria for
assigning a color
scheme to a view.

Edit
Scheme

3. Select the color fill legend you placed in the previous step and find the Edit Scheme icon at the right end of the ribbon. The Edit Color Scheme dialog box will appear, as shown in Figure 4.17.

FIGURE 4.17
Edit color schemes to add predefined values, colors, and fill patterns.

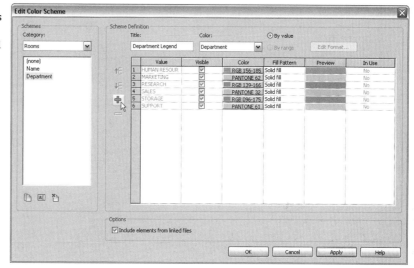

4. As shown in Figure 4.17, click the Add Value icon to populate the list of departments in the Scheme Definition area. Choose colors and fill patterns according to your graphic requirements.

5. Click OK to close the dialog box.

6. When rooms are placed, you can either type values for departments that match the predefined values in the color scheme or select the values in the Element Properties of the room, as shown in Figure 4.18.

FIGURE 4.18
Select from predefined values in the Element Properties of a room.

As shown in Figure 4.19, the department values utilized in every project started with your project template will have the same colors and fill patterns according to those specified in the original color scheme. You also have a predefined list of your client's department names.

FIGURE 4.19
Color-filled plans can utilize pre-defined values in templates.

Department Legend

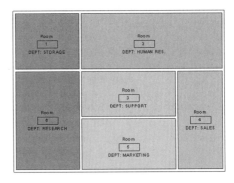

Efficient View Management

Once you've customized the settings for graphic quality, you can use several other tools and techniques to increase efficiency and ensure your visual standards are applied consistently throughout your projects. The properties of all views within Revit can be used to your advantage in creating a browser organization that meets the needs of your teams. You can apply filters to views for generating graphic overrides based on model element parameters. You can manage and deploy these settings and more in view templates that can be applied to many views simultaneously.

Organizing Views

Maintaining a clear and consistent organization of views within a Revit project can generate measurable increases in project productivity. Especially in larger projects, a Revit file can have more than 1,000 views, which can easily cause confusion and wasted time if the right view cannot be found in the Project Browser when needed. The default project template contains a few simple browser organization types that can be copied and/or customized—except for the type named All. To access these settings, switch to the View ribbon, find the Windows panel, click the User Interface drop-down button, and select Browser Organization, as shown in Figure 4.20.

FIGURE 4.20
Accessing browser organization settings in the ribbon

Select any one of the listed types in the Browser Organization dialog box and click the Edit button. Remember, you can't edit or delete the type named All.

In the Browser Organization Properties dialog box (Figure 4.21), there are two tabs called Folders and Filter. Folders allow you to group views together based on selected view parameters, whereas the Filter tab will give you the opportunity to display only views that pass selected criteria.

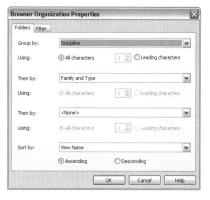

FIGURE 4.21
Use view parameters to create folders in the Project Browser.

Choose the Folders tab to specify up to three levels of "folders" to be shown in the Project Browser. Some examples are:

◆ Family and Type, Discipline, Scale

◆ Phase, Discipline, Family and Type

◆ Detail Level, Family and Type

To further organize the views in your project, you can create additional parameters and assign them to views and sheets. The following is one example of adding custom text parameters to views for more refined organization:

1. On the Manage tab, find the Settings panel and click Project Parameters.

2. In the Project Parameters dialog box, click Add.

3. In the Parameter Properties dialog box, create a parameter named `Custom View Type`; for Type Of Parameter, specify Text. Select the Instance option; then find and check the Views category, as shown in Figure 4.22.

FIGURE 4.22
Create custom project parameters for additional view organization options.

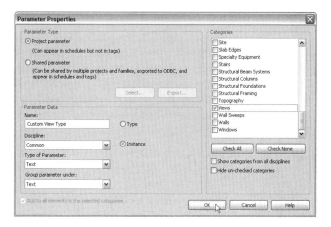

4. Repeat steps 2 and 3 and create another text parameter named **Custom View Sub-Type** assigned to the Views category. Remember to set the Type Of Parameter option to Text.

5. Click OK to close the window.

6. Return to the Browser Organization dialog box and click New. Name the new type **Custom Type/Sub-Type**, and click OK.

7. Set the following values on the Folders tab:

   ◆ Group By: Custom View Type

   ◆ Then By: Custom View Sub-Type

8. Click OK to close the open dialog box. The Project Browser is now ready to support the use of the custom view parameters you created earlier.

It is now up to you to assign values to the custom view parameters created in the previous exercise. These values can be assigned directly to the view properties in the Properties Palette or by adding them to View Templates. Views that do not have values for these parameters will be found under the folders listed as "???" (three question marks). Figure 4.23 illustrates this scenario in which plans and elevations have been assigned to the Custom View Type and Custom View Sub-Type parameters but the 3D view was not.

FIGURE 4.23
Customized browser organizations can make larger projects easier to navigate.

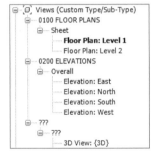

Creating and Assigning Filters

Filters are another view configuration and customization tool that can be developed and deployed in Revit project templates. They are similar to the filters available in schedules in that they can either display or hide elements matching user-specified criteria. But view filters can also override the graphic appearance of such elements affected by them. The possible combination and application of view filters is virtually limitless, so let's take a look at a few real-world examples.

First, we'll review the steps to create and assign a view filter. The fundamental steps are as follows:

1. Create a named filter.

2. Assign it to object categories.

3. Assign data criteria.

4. Add to the Visibility/Graphics settings of a view.

5. Define graphic overrides.

In the following example, you will create view filters to identify fire-rated walls with different colors. You can download the sample file c04-JenkinsMusicBldg.rvt from this book's companion web page at www.sybex.com/go/masteringrevit2011.

1. Open the file c04-JenkinsMusicBldg.rvt. Switch to the View tab, find the Graphics panel, and click Filters.

2. Add a new named filter by clicking the New icon at the bottom of the Filters zone at the left side of the dialog box. Name the first new filter **Walls-Fire-1** and click OK.

3. Find Walls in the center zone and check the category.

4. In the Filter Rules zone at the right side, define the following criterion:

- ◆ Filter by: Fire Rating equals **1 HR**

5. Click Apply. With the Walls-Fire 1 filter still selected, click the Duplicate icon twice and Walls-Fire 2 and Walls-Fire 3 should be created.

6. Select Walls-Fire 2 and change the value in Filter Rules to **2 HR**.

7. Select Walls-Fire 3 and change the value in Filter Rules to **3 HR**, as shown in Figure 4.24.

FIGURE 4.24
Filter rules applied to walls for fire ratings

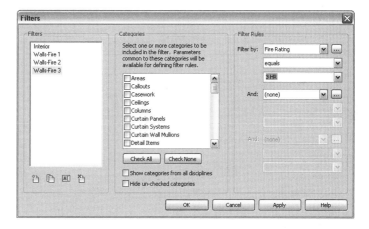

8. Click OK to close the window.

9. Activate the Level 2 floor plan, open the Visibility/Graphics settings, and select the Filters tab.

10. Click the Add button, select all three Walls-Fire filters, and click OK.

11. Click the Override button in each filter row under Cut-Lines and change the line color as follows:

◆ Walls-Fire 1 = Green

◆ Walls-Fire 2 = Yellow

◆ Walls-Fire 3 = Red

12. Click OK to close the Visibility/Graphic Overrides dialog box.

With the filters now applied to the floor plan, walls that have been assigned a fire rating value will appear with the color overrides you had assigned to the respective filters. You can create more filters to define graphic styles for specific model elements such as furniture by owner, interior walls, secure doors, or equipment not in contract.

Applying View Templates

After you have defined your desired settings in as many view types as possible, you can use view templates to manage these settings and apply them to other views of the same type. They will be described in greater detail in Chapter 18, "Documenting Your Design," but we will discuss their importance to the project template in this section. Let's begin by opening the View Templates tool:

1. On the View tab, find the Graphics panel and select View Templates ➢ View Template Settings.

2. In the View Templates dialog box (Figure 4.25), you will find icons to duplicate, rename, or delete view templates below the list on the left. On the right are the View Properties that can be applied when the view template is applied to a view.

FIGURE 4.25
View Templates
dialog box

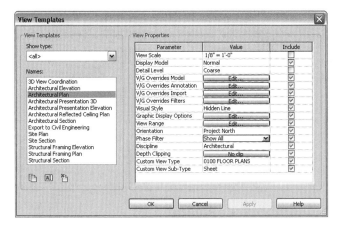

3. Notice the column named Include. This allows you to include or exclude various View Properties when applying the View Template. In Figure 4.25, notice that View Scale and Detail Level are not included. This would allow you to apply this template to plans of multiple scales and detail levels, while applying settings such as visibility of object styles, phase filter, and view range.

4. Also notice in Figure 4.25 the two custom view parameters: Custom View Type and Custom View Sub-Type, which we described earlier in this chapter. These values can be applied with the View Template, which will have the effect of cataloging the views in your standardized folders within the Project Browser.

5. Click OK to close the window.

Changes to view templates are not automatically reflected in the views to which they have been applied; however, Revit has a method for making these updates easy to maintain. When a View Template is applied to a view for the first time, it becomes the default View Template for that view. Subsequent View Template applications will not change a view's default View Template; rather it can only be changed in the View Properties.

When you apply a template as the Default View Template, it is easy to update all views prior to publishing sheets. Simply select the sheets you are about to print or publish from the Project Browser, right-click, and select Apply Default View Template To All Views, as shown in Figure 4.26.

FIGURE 4.26
Reapplying default templates to views on sheets

Including view templates in your project template will give your teams the ability to quickly apply your standard view settings. It will also support continued consistency as each building project grows in scope and size. Remember that view templates are easily shared between projects using the Transfer Project Standards tool, which we will discuss later in this chapter in the section "Strategies for Managing Templates."

Creating Custom Annotations

The authors of this book are avid supporters of global graphic standards for architecture and engineering such as the US National CAD Standard (`www.nationalcadstandard.org`), but each architect or designer will likely have their own set of standards that will need to be implemented in their Revit projects. Placing customized annotation families in your project template will save time when starting new projects and ensure maximum compliance with your firm's standards. You can load tag families into the template using several methods:

◆ Switch to the Insert tab, and in the Load Library panel, select Load Family.

◆ Using Windows Explorer, select `.rfa` tag families and drag them into the Revit project environment with the template open. If you try to drag more than one family at once, Revit prompts you to either open each of those files in an independent window (so you can modify them) or load them all in the current project. Choose the second option.

◆ Use the Loaded Tags tool available in the Annotate tab when you expand the Tag panel (Figure 4.27). This allows you to preview all loaded and preset tags that will be used for respective element categories.

FIGURE 4.27
The Tags dialog box shows loaded annotation families assigned to selected categories.

In this section, we'll walk you through creating some common element tags and customizing system annotation.

ARCHIVING AND MANAGING CUSTOM CONTENT

Many new users of Revit are unsure where to store custom created families. It isn't advisable to save them in the system folders created during the installation of Revit, because you may lose track of them or inadvertently delete them when you reinstall the software. Reinstalling Revit erases just about any folder and the entire contents of it. It is thus advisable to keep your personally created content somewhere else, under a separate independent folder; if you are not a single user, store that folder on a shared network drive.

You should also keep your templates up to date as you add more content; that way, you only need to maintain a few template files rather than dozens of separate family files. It's even better if you can establish a template manager as a role within the office so everyone isn't making graphical changes to your templates.

Tag Family Fundamentals

Before you begin to customize annotation families or create your own, it is important to review the fundamental difference between text and labels.

Text   In the Family Editor, placing text in an annotation or title block means you're defining text that will always be the same and is unchangeable when that annotation is placed in the project environment. Figure 4.28 shows the words AREA and VOLUME as text. Regardless of where this room tag is placed, the text will always say AREA and VOLUME. Section tags work the same way: if you add static text, that text appears exactly the same for all section marks. This isn't typically used for sections, because each section is a reference to a unique view, and you want that information to be dynamic and parametric. That's where label functionality comes into play.

FIGURE 4.28
A custom room tag showing room name, number, area, and volume

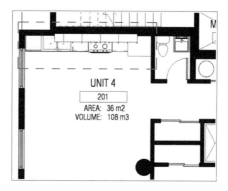

Labels Like static text, a label offers textual information; however, it's a live reference to a parameter value of an element in the project. For example, if you add an Area label, it will pull the value of the area of the room; if you add a Sheet Number label in a Section Head family in the Family Editor environment and then use that section head in a project, the label will automatically display the actual sheet number on which the section is placed in the project. If you move the section from one sheet to another, the label will automatically report the new sheet number.

In Figure 4.28, Unit 4 is a label of the room name; the number 201 is a label of the room number. The label behaves as dynamic text and is always fully coordinated with the value of the parameter it represents.

Creating a Custom Door Tag

As an example of creating custom tags for a basic model element, use the following steps to create the custom door tag shown in Figure 4.29.

FIGURE 4.29
Custom door tag with parametric label

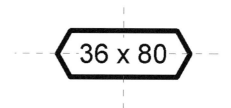

1. Click the Application button, and select New ➢ Annotation Family.

2. In the Select Template File dialog box, select the family template called `Door Tag.rft` or `M_Door Tag.rft` and click Open.

   The Family Editor opens in a view with two crossing reference planes, the intersection of which represents the origin of the tag. To avoid problems later, don't move these planes.

3. On the Home tab, find the Text panel and select Label. Click the intersection of the two planes to position the label.

4. In the Edit Label dialog box that opens, select Width and click the Add Parameter To Label icon between the Category Parameters and Label Parameters fields. Then do the same for Height, as shown in Figure 4.30.

FIGURE 4.30
Adding more than one parameter to a single label

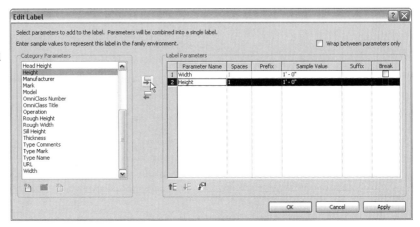

The Width and Height parameters will be concatenated in a single label, which will display the actual size of the door in the tag. In the subsequent steps, you will customize the display of the label.

5. Add a space and the letter *x* in the Suffix column of the Width parameter and change the Sample Value to 36 [in] or 1000 [mm]. Change the Sample Value of the Height parameter to 80 [in] or 2000 [mm].

6. With the Width row selected, click the Edit Parameter's Units Format icon. In the Format dialog box, uncheck the Use Project Settings option and set the following:

◆ Units: Decimal Inches or Millimeters.

◆ Rounding: 0 decimal places

◆ Unit symbol: None

7. Repeat the previous step for the Height parameter.

8. Click OK in all open dialog boxes.

9. On the Home tab, activate the Masking Region tool and sketch a six-sided polygon, as shown in Figure 4.29.

Remember to finish the sketch by clicking the green check in the Mode panel.

10. Save your tag and load it into your project template. Make sure that it is specified as the default tag for doors in the Tags dialog box and use the Tag By Category or Tag All Not Tagged tools or place new doors with the Tag On Placement option. Using concatenated parameters in tag labels allows a great deal of flexibility while utilizing actual parametric values. In this example (Figure 4.31), the actual width and height parameters driving the door size become the text displayed in the tag.

FIGURE 4.31
Actual door sizes comprise the custom tags applied to doors.

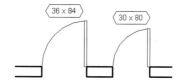

SET SOME DEFAULTS

To aid the users of your custom templates, take some time to establish default values for common elements, such as doors, windows, rooms, grids, sheets, and levels. Create one of each element and change the Mark value to a number just below the value at which you'd like your users to begin. Unfortunately, this approach does not work for letters, because nothing comes before A.

View Tags

Section, callout, and elevation tags are graphic indicators that reference (link to) other views in your project. The graphics for these elements can be customized to meet most scenarios. To create a custom section tag, for example, you have to first create a custom section tag family and load it into a template or project. You must then associate it with a section tag system family type, which is then assigned to a section type. Switch to the Manage tab, and choose Additional Settings ➤ Section Tags; you will see the application of separate section head and tail families in a section tag system family type in Figure 4.32.

FIGURE 4.32
Section tag system family properties

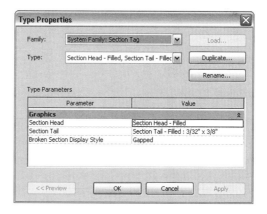

In simple terms, view tags in Revit are organized in the following hierarchy:

◆ System Family: Section

  ◆ System Family: Section Tag

    ◆ Annotation Family: Section Tag/Tail

By default, there is a predefined view tag for each view type. The graphics can vary depending on the language version of Revit you have installed on your machine. The tags shown in Figure 4.33 are displayed and available by default in the US English version.

FIGURE 4.33
Samples of graphic content as supplied by Autodesk

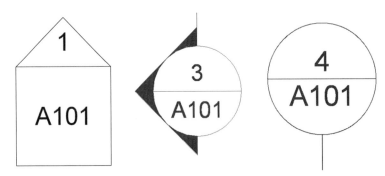

CREATING A CUSTOM SECTION TAG

In the next exercise, you will create a section tag that looks like the one shown in Figure 4.34. You'll first need to create a section tag family using the Family Editor before loading it into the template.

FIGURE 4.34
Custom section tag

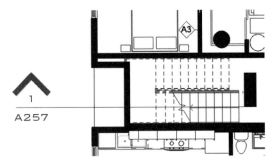

To begin, follow these steps:

1. Click the Application button, and select New ➤ Annotation Symbol.

2. In the Open dialog box, select the family template called `Section Head.rft` or `M_Section Head.rft`, and click Open.

3. The Family Editor environment automatically opens, and the drawing area shows a view in which three green reference planes (two vertical and one horizontal) have already been drawn. Do *not* change the position of either the horizontal reference plane or the vertical reference on the right. In some templates, this is indicated with help text in red (which you can later remove).

   The intersection of horizontal and right reference planes defines the connection location with the section line. This means your annotation will be located in between the two intersections points.

A proposed geometric shape is drawn for the annotation: a circle (two arcs) and a horizontal line. You're free to delete this default geometry and create your own tag shape. The default shape is there to help you visually understand where to begin drawing your new tag geometry.

4. Select the arcs that create the circle (use the Ctrl key for faster selection), and delete them.

Label

5. On the Home tab of the Text panel, click the Label button. Position your cursor between the two vertical reference planes and below the horizontal plane, and click to position the start of the label.

6. In the Edit Label dialog box, select Sheet Number. Click the Add Parameter(s) To Label button. In the Sample Value column, you can enter a value; the default is A101.

The label is placed and displays blue grips when selected. These let you change the length of the label text field. The length is important, because any value that is added (in a project) that is longer than the length of this box will begin to wrap and could cause undesirable results.

7. Following the same principle, place the label Detail Number above the horizontal reference but still between the vertical references, as shown in Figure 4.35.

FIGURE 4.35
Place labels for
Detail Number and
Sheet Number.

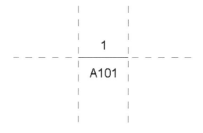

8. You can reposition a label by selecting it and using the Move button to move it around. For more precise positioning, use the arrow keys on your keyboard to nudge elements in small increments. You can also help yourself by zooming in for a better view. (Note that zooming in refines the increment for the nudge tools.)

9. On the Detail panel of the Home tab, click the Filled Region button. You'll be put into Sketch mode. Using the Line tool, draw the shape shown in Figure 4.36. In the Region Properties, check that Color is set to Black and Cut Fill Pattern to Solid Fill. Make sure the lines form a closed loop (no gaps or overlapping lines).

FIGURE 4.36
Draw the outline
of the filled region
to form the section
arrow.

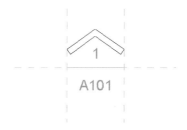

10. Click Finish on the Mode panel of the Modify | Create Filled Region Boundary tab.

11. Save the tag you just created as `Custom Arrow.rfa` somewhere on your hard drive or network, and you're ready to use it in the template or a project. To load it into your project, click the Load Into Projects button located in the Family Editor panel. Choose the project you want to use the symbol in, and click OK.

Next, you'll assign this tag to a section mark system family type in the context of a project or template.

CREATING A SECTION TYPE WITH A CUSTOM HEAD/TAIL GRAPHIC

To create a section type that utilizes the section head family you created previously, you need to load the created section head in the template file (if you've already loaded the custom arrow family in the previous exercise, skip to step 3):

1. If the family isn't already loaded, switch to the Insert tab, and on the Load From Library panel, choose Load Family.

2. In the Load Family dialog box, find the `Custom Arrow.rfa` section head you created previously, select it, and click Open.

3. Switch to the Manage tab and select Additional Settings ➤ Section Tags.

4. In the Type Properties dialog box, click Duplicate.

5. In the Name dialog box, name the new type **Custom Filled Arrow** and click OK.

6. In the section head's Type Properties dialog box, click the drop-down menu for Section Head and select Custom Arrow. For Section Tail, click <none>. This means the other end of the section line will not use a symbol. Click OK.

The final step is to create a customized section type, which will utilize the new section tag type created in the previous step.

7. Switch to the View tab, and on the Create panel, select Section.

8. On the Properties tab, select the Type Properties button.

9. In the Type Properties dialog box, select Duplicate.

10. Name the new type **Custom Arrow - No Tail**, and click OK.

You can now place a section in your drawing area and see the results shown in Figure 4.37.

FIGURE 4.37
Custom section
mark after section
is placed on a sheet

The custom section tag exercise can also be applied to the creation of custom callouts, as shown in Figure 4.38.

FIGURE 4.38
Custom callout annotation (left); custom callout annotation associated with callout boundary (right)

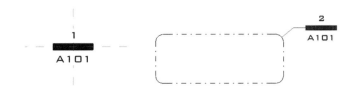

CREATING A CUSTOM ELEVATION TAG

We can't help but get excited over this long-awaited new feature for Revit Architecture 2011—the ability to create custom elevation tags! You are no longer limited to either a circle or square tag. Here's how it works:

1. Click the Application button, and select New ➢ Annotation Symbol.

2. In the Open dialog box, select the family template called Elevation Mark Body.rft or M_Elevation Mark Body.rft, and click Open.

3. Using similar steps from the section tag exercise, place the Sheet Number label and draw lines as shown in Figure 4.39.

FIGURE 4.39
Define the custom linework and sheet number for the elevation mark body.

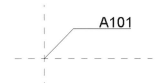

4. Make sure the label has the properties Keep Readable and Fixed Rotation checked.

5. Save the family as **Custom Elev Head.rfa**.

6. Click the Application button, and select New ➢ Annotation Symbol.

7. In the Open dialog box, select the family template called Elevation Mark Pointer.rft or M_Elevation Mark Pointer.rft, and click Open.

8. Using similar methods in previous steps, place labels for the Detail Number and Reference Label parameters. Draw a diamond with lines and a small triangular filled region, as shown in Figure 4.40.

FIGURE 4.40
Custom elevation pointer composed of lines, filled region, and labels

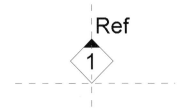

9. Again remember to make sure the labels have the properties Keep Readable and Fixed Rotation checked.

10. Save the family as **Custom Elev Pointer.rfa** and load it into the `Custom Elev Head.rfa` family.

11. Place four instances of the Custom Elev Pointer family around the intersection of the visible reference planes, as shown in Figure 4.41.

FIGURE 4.41
The nested pointer family is placed four times in the head family.

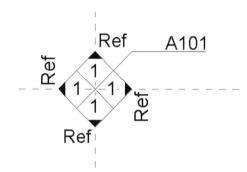

When this custom elevation tag family is loaded into a project and associated with an elevation type, it will function much like standard elevation symbols.

After the views are placed on a sheet, you get a preview of the completed elevation symbol, as shown in Figure 4.42.

FIGURE 4.42
A customized elevation tag for interior elevations

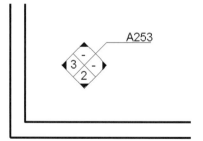

Starting a Project with a Custom Template

Now that we have covered many areas of customization within project templates, you can configure Revit to use your new template. To do so, follow these steps:

1. Click the Application button, and at the bottom of the menu click Options.

2. In the Options dialog box, select the File Locations tab. The first option in the dialog box lists the default template location.

3. Click the Browse button to choose a new path to your default template file (see Figure 4.43).

Change the path to your default template.

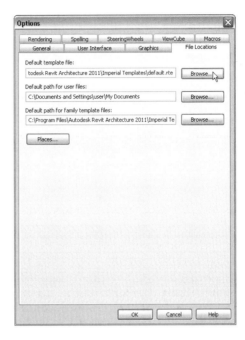

Strategies for Managing Templates

During the implementation of Revit, you can take one of two approaches when managing project templates: additive or subtractive. An *additive* approach, as shown in Figure 4.44, assumes that more than one project template will be developed to manage standards and content for a single project. Typically, a "base" template is used to start a project with a minimum amount of settings, whereas content and settings from "supplemental" templates are appended based on region, project type, or project style. In this scenario, each template file is lighter, but managing the templates becomes more difficult because changes in common settings or families must be applied to all templates.

FIGURE 4.44
Additive template approach

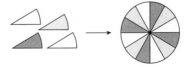

In contrast, the *subtractive* approach, shown in Figure 4.45, uses a single master template that contains all standard settings and content and relies on the project teams to remove and purge unused content. Although these templates tend to be heavier, graphic settings are easier to manage within a single file.

FIGURE 4.45
Subtractive template approach

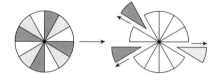

 Real World Scenario

USING PROJECT TEMPLATES TO REDUCE REDUNDANT WORK

Based on a survey conducted by Robert Manna for an Autodesk University class, the majority of responders indicated they develop two to five project templates primarily to differentiate between project types and/or market sectors. For example, if you're an architectural firm that is usually contracted to perform work on large transportation sector projects, you might need to create a Revit file just to manage the site data for every project.

In that case, you would use a specific template as a "site" project template. Within such a template, you could use the following settings to reduce the amount of redundant work every time different teams attempt to establish a site model into which other building models are linked:

◆ Levels named Sea Level and First Floor Reference

◆ Setting default view scales to larger sizes

◆ Changing default project units to reflect civil engineering

◆ Adding a Cut/Fill schedule

◆ Creating dimension types useful for large drawings

◆ Pad types including "gravel"

More information on template management, including results of the survey, can be found on Robert Manna's website at http://revit.krarchdesign.net. His Autodesk University content can be found at au.autodesk.com.

Aggregating Template Data

Whether you are managing the settings between templates or developing a project with multiple templates in an additive approach, Revit has some useful tools to help share data between projects, such as Transfer Project Standards, Insert Views From File, and Insert 2D Elements From File.

Transferring Project Standards

You can easily share Revit families between project files by loading their RFA files; however, most other types of content can be transferred with the Transfer Project Standards command. Some types of elements commonly transferred with this command include, but are not limited to, the following:

◆ Materials

◆ System family types (Walls, Floors, Roofs, and so on)

◆ Text and dimension styles

◆ Grid and level types

◆ Line styles and patterns

◆ Object style settings

◆ Viewport types

To use this command, you must first have both the source and target Revit files open; then make the target file the active project. Switch to the Manage tab, and select Transfer Project Standards on the Settings panel. In the Select Items To Copy dialog box (Figure 4.46), choose as many item categories as you'd like to transfer, and then click OK.

FIGURE 4.46
Select categories to be transferred between projects.

If you choose an element category containing some of the same types that already exist in your current project, you will be prompted with the option to overwrite the existing types or import the new types only (New Only), as shown in Figure 4.47.

FIGURE 4.47
Transferring project standards with duplicate types

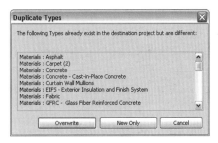

INSERTING VIEWS FROM A FILE

The Insert Views From File command is useful for sharing Drafting Views of standard or typical details with other Revit project files. It can also insert entire sheets with all attached Drafting Views and associated properties. You can use the Insert Views From File command with the following view types:

- ◆ Drafting views

- ◆ Sheets

- ◆ Schedules

Switch to the Insert tab, and choose Insert From File ➢ Insert Views From File in the Import panel. Browse to a Revit project (.rvt) file, and you will see the Insert Views dialog box (Figure 4.48). In the left pane, all eligible drafting views, sheets, and schedules will be listed. If necessary, use the drop-down list above to filter the choices.

FIGURE 4.48
Insert Views can be used to transfer an entire sheet of drafting views into your project.

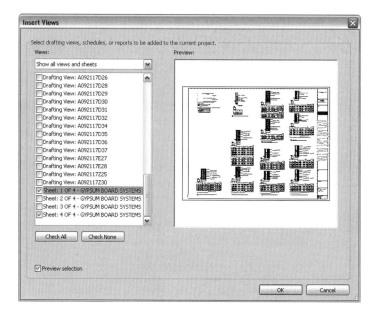

If one or more sheets are selected in the Insert Views dialog box, all eligible drafting views placed on those sheets will be inserted into the current project as well. Note that repeating this process will not update the drafting views in the project, but instead will create new renamed drafting views and sheets. Also note that any custom view parameters are maintained during the transfer and can fit right into your customized Project Browser organizations, as we discussed earlier in this chapter.

INSERTING 2D ELEMENTS FROM A FILE

Similar to Insert Views From File, the Insert 2D Elements From File command imports the 2D elements of the selected view as a detail group into the active view in the current project instead of the entire view. For best results, make sure you have a drafting view active before using this command. On the Insert tab, find the Import panel, choose Insert From File ➤ Insert 2D Elements From File, and then navigate to a project file. Choose one of the available drafting views in the Insert 2D Elements dialog box (Figure 4.49).

For consistency, be sure to select the Transfer View Scale option to convert the scale of the active drafting view to that of the view you are inserting. You can move the elements into position using the Move command and, after placing the 2D elements, be sure to click Finish in the Edit Pasted panel or double-click anywhere outside the elements to complete the command.

FIGURE 4.49

Insert 2D Elements dialog box

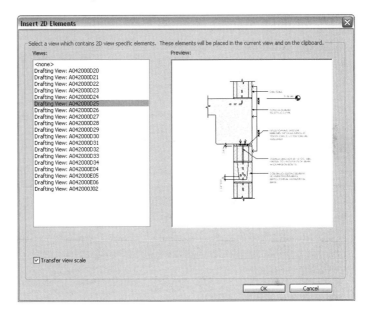

DUPLICATE TYPES WHEN INSERTING

When using Insert Views From File or Insert 2D Elements From File, be sure to watch for warnings about duplicate types being renamed, as shown here. You may be able to use the Purge Unused tool to remove any renamed styles; however, some types may need to be manually modified.

If duplicated types cannot be removed with Purge Unused, you will need to swap the duplicated types with the originals. Find the duplicated family types in the Project Browser, right-click on it, and choose Select All Instances. This selects all instances of that type throughout the entire project. Open the Properties Palette and select a different type. You will then be able to remove the duplicated type with Purge Unused or by right-clicking on it in the Project Browser and choosing Delete. Note that the Select All Instances method does not work on line styles.

The Bottom Line

Define settings for graphic quality and consistency. The fundamental building blocks for any template are the customized settings to object styles, line styles, fill patterns, materials, and more.

Master It How can a complex custom fill pattern be imported into Revit?

Organize views for maximum efficiency. The project template can be used to capture a framework supporting your visual and organizational standards.

Master It How can you customize the Project Browser to support your business needs?

Create custom annotation families. Developing a graphic style to match your standards will usually require some annotation families to be edited or created from scratch.

Master It Can a single label display more than one parameter? How are custom view tags loaded into a project?

Start a project with a custom template. Making your custom template available for new projects ensures all future projects will maintain the same level of graphic quality and efficiency you expect.

Master It How do you set your own custom project template to be the default for new projects?

Develop a template management strategy. Organizing your standards, content, and settings while using Revit's tools to transfer content will make your effort more efficient.

Master It How do you insert your standard details from one Revit project to another? How do you transfer settings such as materials?

Chapter 5

Managing a Revit Project

Understanding Revit and how to use the software is not a difficult challenge. The real challenge in understanding Revit and BIM is determining how it changes your organization's culture and your project's workflow. Revit can be more than just a different way to draw a line. In this chapter, we'll focus on what those changes are and provide some tools, tips, and tricks on how to manage the changes.

In this chapter, you'll learn to:

- ◆ Understand a BIM workflow
- ◆ Staff a BIM project
- ◆ Work in a large team
- ◆ Create details in Revit
- ◆ Perform quality control on your Revit model

Understanding a BIM Workflow

Regardless of the workflow you have established, moving to BIM is going to be a change. In Chapter 1, "Beyond Basic Documentation," we discussed some of those changes and tried to help define your place in the process of managing that change. Regardless of where you fall on our adoption curve, you'll still need some tools to help transition from your current workflow to one using Revit. To begin, we'll cover some of the core differences between a CAD-based system and a BIM-based one.

Moving to BIM is a shift in how designers and contractors look at the design and documentation process throughout the entire life cycle of the project, from concept to occupancy. In a traditional CAD-based workflow, represented in Figure 5.1, each view is drawn separately with no inherent relationship between drawings. In this type of production environment, the team creates plans, sections, elevations, schedules, and perspectives and must coordinate any changes between files manually.

FIGURE 5.1
A CAD-based
workflow

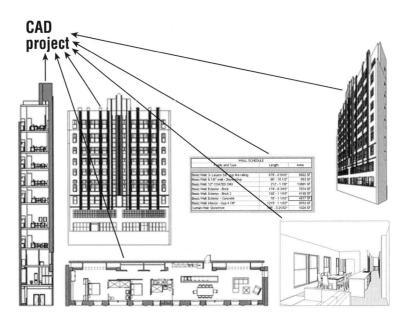

In a BIM-based workflow, the team creates a 3D, parametric model and uses this model to automatically generate the drawings necessary for documentation. Plans, sections, elevations, schedules, and perspectives are all by-products of creating an embellished a BIM model, as shown in Figure 5.2. This enhanced documentation methodology not only allows for a highly coordinated drawing set, but also provides the basic model geometry necessary for analysis such as daylighting studies, energy, material takeoffs, and so on.

FIGURE 5.2
A BIM workflow

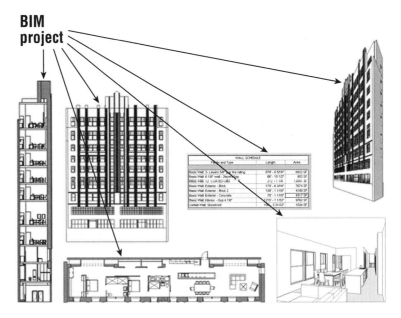

Using Revit becomes more than a change in software; it becomes a change in workflow and methodology. To better address the impacts and nuances of this change in process, let's look at the existing paradigm. A traditional or standard design and documentation workflow looks like Figure 5.3.

FIGURE 5.3
The traditional method of design review

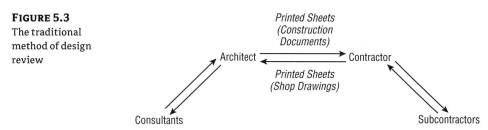

To describe this better, you need to understand that design is a cyclical process and one of continual refinement. As you share ideas and coordinate information with the entire project team, you can make adjustments to your own portion of the project. A standard architectural project might go something like this:

1. The architect draws a building design and shares this information with consultants.

2. Various consultants, working separately, will reuse parts of the architect's drawings to create a new series of their own drawings specific to their specialization.

3. The consultant's drawings will be shared with the architect who will need to use them to further coordinate their own work. Portions that affect the architectural drawings such as building structure or mechanical ductwork are in a large portion redrawn within the architectural set.

4. At a certain point in the project process, all of the drawings (typically in printed form only) are shared with a contractor or builder. The contractor disseminates the drawings to various subcontractors who will need to utilize their specialties to embellish the information in the original drawings.

5. The contractor will create new sets of drawings with added detail, but all based on the original set of documents.

With all of these separate teams making their own sets of drawings, a system of checks and balances is needed to ensure the information is communicated accurately and effectively. In our traditional model shown earlier, the subcontractors will send their drawings back to the contractor to verify the work. The contractor will create multiple copies of the drawings (based on the number of parties needed to review) and pass them to the architect. The architect will review their own set while giving the other copies to various consultants to do the same. All of these changes will be manually transcribed to one set before being sent back to the contractor to be passed back to subcontractors for further revisions and clarifications.

This entire chain of information sharing has many opportunities for a miscommunication error in manual transcription. Much of the information is redundantly reproduced as a way of error checking, which can just as easily create its own errors. If you can utilize the advantages inherent in a BIM-based method (Figure 5.4), you can eliminate many of the redundant efforts, improve communication, and focus more time on improving the design and expediting construction.

FIGURE 5.4

An integrated approach to design review

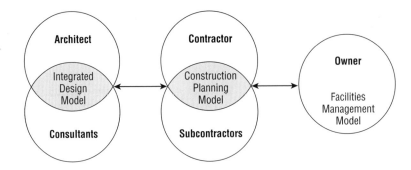

In an ideal BIM-based system, the following occurs:

1. The architect and consultants would work together on a single building model. This might be one model or a model consisting of interconnected parts.

2. After this model reaches a stage of refinement, it is passed on to the contractor and building team to further embellish with information specific to their trades and expertise.

3. As they construct the physical building, the BIM model can be adjusted to reflect the changes that happen in the field.

4. The revised model can then be shared with the owner and facilities operator. The model can contain the necessary product information about the systems installed to aid the owner's facility operator in maintaining the building. The model can also be used for future personnel moves or even building additions.

As various design specializations interact and create the building model (Figure 5.5), you can see how structure, mechanical, energy, daylight, and other factors inform design direction. You can also draw relationships between some of these elements that might not have been as obvious in a more traditionally based approach. Although some of these specialties (such as structure and mechanical) are historically separate systems, by integrating them into a single design model, you can see how they interact in relation to other systems with a building. Analysis such as daylighting can inform your building orientation and structure. Depending on your glazing, it can also affect your mechanical requirements (as solar gain). You can see some of these effects through a computational fluid dynamics (CFD) model (used to calculate airflow). Geographic information system (GIS) data will give you your relative location globally and allow you to see how much sunlight you will be receiving or what the local temperature swings will be during the course of a day. As you can see, all of these variables can easily affect building design.

As with any methodological change, you'll have success if you address all the factors. Project success happens on more than a financial or chronological level. It is also determined by a team's ability to replicate successful results. A difficult aspect of transitioning to BIM is predictability. Any system or method, even if it is inherently inefficient, is at some level successful if the system is predictable. If you can say that x effort + y time will yield z result, there is an established comfort level with that system even if it is an inefficient system. When you move to BIM, the system automatically becomes unpredictable because team members need to experience the new system to establish a comfort level with the given results. No longer does x effort + y time yield z; instead, the result is unknown.

FIGURE 5.5
The integrated
design model

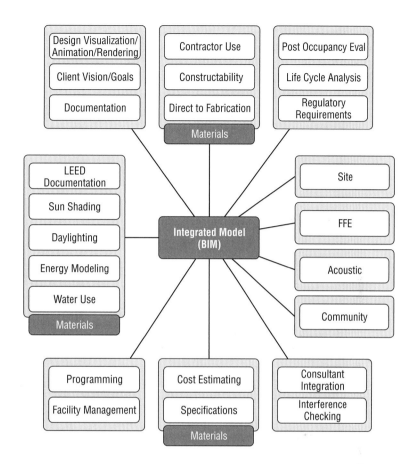

Eventually, you reach a point of temporary diminishing returns. The amount of effort you need to put into understanding the new process feels like it has begun to exceed the value you derive from the change, and happiness plateaus or slightly declines. At a point during this plateau, you're put in a position where you need to perform a task in a given amount of time using the new technology. It might be represented by needing to get a schematic-level design sent out to a contractor or create something as simple as a stair. Regardless, the process is a foreign one and by its nature is unpredictable in time. You'll be faced with a decision to forge ahead using an unpredictable method or revert to a more familiar yet inefficient process.

Here your path can split. By regressing to your previous process, you'll enjoy an immediate increase in happiness with the familiarity and predictability of the former method, but this will only level out and never reach any greater heights than it did before you contemplated the initial change. If you stay the course with the new process, happiness will decrease (and frustration increase) as you struggle with the change. However, eventually as the new method becomes more predictable and comfortable, your happiness can achieve greater value.

Although this might be an oversimplification of a process change, the core meaning is critical. Change can be challenging. However, to realize greater goals and adapt to an ever-changing environment both professionally and globally, you will need to rethink our process in order to achieve success. Moving to BIM is acknowledging a change in workflow and process—from abstraction to virtualization (Figure 5.6). As you transition from a traditional workflow to a BIM-based one, keep in mind the change in culture. It will help you to manage expectations, time, and team members' stress levels.

FIGURE 5.6
From abstraction
to virtualization

Staffing for BIM

As you rethink the process of design and documentation, one of the semantic changes you will need to address is staffing. A common misconception of project management when teams are first moving from CAD to BIM is that staffing the project will be the same in both workflows. This couldn't be further from the truth. When the workflow changes, staffing allocations, time to complete tasks, and percentage of work by phase are all affected as a by-product of the change of method.

To better understand how to staff your new workflow, we'll compare the two methodologies, CAD and BIM. In Figure 5.7, we have superimposed CAD and BIM workflows. The chart in the x-direction represents project phases from conceptual design through occupancy. The chart in the y-direction represents the amount of effort in each phase. This effort can also be translated into the amount of staff or person-hours put into the project by phase.

FIGURE 5.7
Staffing in BIM

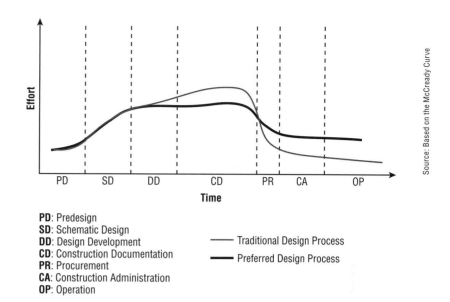

PD: Predesign
SD: Schematic Design
DD: Design Development
CD: Construction Documentation
PR: Procurement
CA: Construction Administration
OP: Operation

—— Traditional Design Process
—— Preferred Design Process

In a CAD-based project, the level of effort during each of the phases is fairly well known. The industry has been using some metrics over the past several years that should be fairly familiar. Typically in a CAD-based project process, effort by phase breaks down similar to what you see in Figure 5.7. The darker gray line represents a traditional or CAD-based project process. There is modest effort and staffing in conceptual design and schematic design phases, and this effort builds until it crescendoes during construction documentation. At this phase, a CAD project can greatly increase the amount of staff in an effort to expedite the completion of the drawing set. This can be effective because the CAD drawings are typically separate files and moving lines in one drawing won't dynamically change another.

The lighter gray line in Figure 5.7 represents an idealized BIM workflow. In this framework, there is still a gradual increase of staffing and effort through conceptual design and into the schematic phase, but the effort during schematic design is greater using BIM than in CAD. During SD and DD, the project team is still performing all the same tasks that occur in any design process; testing design concepts, visualizations, or design iteration. The increase in effort during the early design phases allows the team to use the parametric nature of the model to significantly reduce the effort later during construction documents, allowing for a decrease in the overall effort over the project cycle.

Project Roles Using Revit

With such a significant change in the effort behind a BIM-based project flow, it's also important to understand how this can change the various roles and responsibilities for the project team. The changes in traditional roles can become a burden to many projects successfully adopting BIM. Project managers need to be able to predict staffing and time to complete tasks throughout the project phases and have relied on past precedent of staff and project types to do this. Since a BIM-based project can significantly alter the project workflow, many of the historic timetables for task completion are no longer valid. However, a BIM-based project can be broken down into a few primary roles that will allow you some level of predictability through the various project phases. Although the specific effort and staffing will vary between offices (and even projects), there are some general roles that will need to be accounted for on every project.

There are three primary roles on every BIM project:

Architect   Deals with design issues, code compliances, clear widths, wall types, and so on

Modeler   Creates content in 2D or in 3D

Drafter   Deals with annotations, sheet layout, view creation, and detail creation

These roles represent efforts and general tasks that you need to take into account on any Revit project. On a large project, these roles could also represent individual people, whereas on a smaller project they might be all the same person or one person might carry multiple roles. We'll now cover each of these in a bit more detail and discuss how these roles interact with the project cycle.

ARCHITECT

The role of the architect is to deal with the architectural issues revolving around the project. As the model is being created, you will naturally have to solve issues like constructability and wall types; set corridor widths; deal with department areas; and deal with other issues involving either codes or the overall architectural design. This role will be the one applying standards to the project (as in wall types, keynotes, and so on) and organizing the document set. This role will need to be present on the project from the beginning to ensure consistency of the virtual building creation and isn't necessarily limited to only one person. This role also might or might not be a "designer." Although it is possible to do early design in Revit, many project teams prefer to utilize other tools such as Google SketchUp or even pencil and trace paper. The job of the architect is steering the creation of the building within Revit. Tasks for this role include the following:

- Leading the creation of architectural elements and building from within the model

- Designing around code requirements and other building logistics

- Constructability and detailing aspects of the design

MODELER

The role of the modeler is to create all the 2D and especially the 3D content needed in the project. This would include all the parametric families for things such as windows, doors, casework, wall types, stairs, railings, furnishings, and so on. Typically, this role is the responsibility of less experienced staff, who might not be able to fulfill the role or architect. These less experienced positions tend to have longer periods of undisturbed time, making them better suited to deal with some of the longer, more involved tasks in modeling content. Finally, they also tend to have some 3D experience coming out of school. They might not have worked with Revit directly, but possibly Autodesk 3ds Max or Google SketchUp, and are thereby familiar with working in a 3D environment. Tasks for this role include the following:

- Creating model content and families

DRAFTER

The role of the drafter is to create sheets and views and embellish those views with annotations or other 2D content. This role will be doing the bulk of the work needed to document the project. In earlier stages of the project, this role is typically assumed by either the architect or the modeler, but as documentation gets moving into high gear, this can quickly become the role of multiple people on a larger project. Tasks for this role include the following:

- Keynoting
- Dimensioning
- Setting up sheets and views
- Creating schedules

Now let's apply these same roles to the project timeline. It's important to understand how these various roles can be best integrated into the typical project workflow. If you look at a typical project process, outlined in Figure 5.8, you see Time on the x-axis and Effort on the y-axis. Superimposed on this chart is the light gray line shown in Figure 5.7 that represents the effort in a BIM workflow to help demonstrate staffing intensity at various times of the project cycle. We have also taken the roles of architect, modeler, and drafter and shown them in the graph represented by the numbers 1, 2, and 3, respectively.

From a staffing planning purpose, we are demonstrating the ideal times to bring in some of these various roles. At the inception of a project design, a modeling role will be of the best use. This person can help create building form, add conceptual content, and get the massing for the building established. If you're using the conceptual modeling tools (covered in Chapter 11, "Working with Consultants"), the modeler can even do some early sustainable design calculations.

FIGURE 5.8
Roles over the project cycle

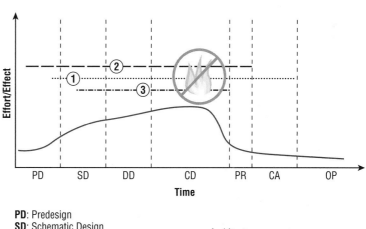

PD: Predesign
SD: Schematic Design
DD: Design Development
CD: Construction Documentation
PR: Procurement
CA: Construction Administration
OP: Operation

········ Architect
— — Modeler
··—··· Drafter
Fire Fighters

Once the project begins to take a more established form and you complete conceptual design, you'll need an architect role to step in the project. As in a typical project, you'll have to mold the form into building by applying materials, applying wall types, and validating spatial requirements and the owner's program.

During schematic design, you'll need to include the role of the drafter to begin laying out sheets and creating views. These sheets and views don't have to be for a construction document set as of yet, but you'll need to establish views for any schematic design submittals. If these views are set up properly, they can be reused later for design development and construction document submittals as the model continues to gain a greater level of detail.

What you'd like to avoid for your project staffing, if possible, is adding staff during the construction document phase. In a BIM/Revit workflow, this can sometimes cause more problems than it solves and slow down the team rather than get work done faster.

 Real World Scenario

TAKING PERMISSIONS OF ELEMENTS

Teams in Revit will invariably structure the model in different ways to optimize individual tasks and roles on a project. Regardless, if you have one workset or several, there are a few simple tips to making sure your workflow stays fluid. In a team structure, typically you will find that certain sheets or views will inevitably become the responsibility of particular team members. Checking out an entire workset can usually cause some angst on a project team because you'll take permission over more than you need, so team members typically borrow elements from the central file. The downside of borrowing is that depending on your network environment, it can take a second or two per element to get the permissions established. This can be a real drain when you have a few hundred elements in the view you are working on. What you need is a simple way to take permission over a group of elements quickly and easily. Fortunately, Revit has a tool for that.

If you are working within a particular view, you take permission of all the elements within that view in just two clicks. By choosing the view name in the Project Browser, right-clicking on the view name, and choosing Make Workset Editable from the context menu, you'll be able to take permission over all the elements with that view. The workset discussed here isn't the workset the elements reside on but the workset of the view.

You can also take permission of all the views and their contents for an entire sheet. By right-clicking the sheet name in the Project Browser, you'll be able to take permission over all the elements in all the views on a particular sheet. Either of these methods is a quick, handy way to only take permission of the elements you can use and leave the rest available to other team members.

This shortcut was especially handy when we were recently working on a large project and had several people pulled into documentation to help meet a deadline. By allowing everyone to focus their work on specific sheets in the set, we were able to quickly take permission over just the elements and views on those sheets and get the project out the door without fear of people stepping on each other in the file.

Adding Team Members to Fight Fires

In many projects, there is might come a time when the schedule gets tight and the project management wants to add more staff to a project to meet a specific deadline. When in a 2D CAD environment, new team members would be added to help meet a deadline and would have the burden of trying to learn the architecture of the building, the thoughts behind its design, and how its various systems interact. In a Revit project, they have that same obligation, but they have the additional task of learning how the *model* goes together. The model will have constraints set against various elements (such as locking a corridor width), and various digital construction issues (such as how floors and walls might be tied together or what the various family names are, or workset organization). This can take some additional time to ramp up to being viable on a project.

Regardless of planning, deadlines still escape the best of architects and project managers. It's a good idea to know when and how you can "staff up" to make sure to meet those deadlines. Keeping in mind that your team member new to the project has to learn about both the design and the model they have been thrown into, here are some easy things to have them do to both help production and make sure they don't accidentally break anything:

Create Content, Content, Content   You will find that you will be making model families or detail components until the end of the project. This will help get the newbie engaged in a specific part of the project and also isolate them enough until they learn a bit more about how the model has gone together.

Put Them into a Drafting Role   Even if this isn't their ultimate role, having them help create views and lay out sheets will get them familiar with the architecture while still allowing the team to keep progressing on the document set.

Working on Detailing   Every project can always use someone who knows how to put a building together. If you have someone new to the project and possibly even new to Revit, let them embellish some of the views already created and laid out on sheets. These can be layered with 2D components, linework, and annotations.

Detailing in Revit

Today, in the industry's current design workflow, we still submit 2D printed construction document sets in the majority of our work. These sets, while created from a 3D Revit model, still contain a good portion of 2D linework and embellishment (and sometimes straight-up 2D details) to get the building documented and the drawing set out the door.

When detailing within Revit, you can create and lay out three primary types of details on sheets. Knowing how and when to use each will help get your document set done, keep your model running and responsive, and minimize the amount of frustration as you adapt to a new workflow.

3D Details

This type of detail is taken directly from the 3D model and used to show conditions that are otherwise difficult to visualize in a flat, 2D view. A good example of a common use for this detail type is flashing details in a brick building exterior on the interior corner of an exterior wall. Figure 5.9 shows a 3D detail in another condition at a corner balcony condition.

FIGURE 5.9
Detailing building components in 3D

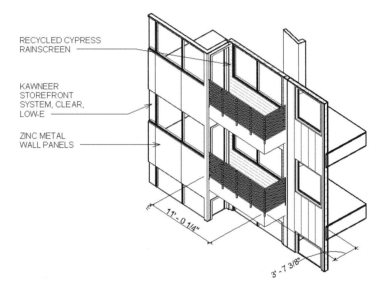

RECYCLED CYPRESS
RAINSCREEN

KAWNEER
STOREFRONT
SYSTEM, CLEAR,
LOW-E

ZINC METAL
WALL PANELS

11'- 0 1/4"

3' - 7 3/8"

Note that in these types of details, it is only possible to add dimension strings that are with the same plane as the working plane. That plane can be redefined with the particular view, but the dimensions will only be able to be placed parallel to that plane. The annotations, however, will sit "flat" against the view as they would any other view.

2D Details from 3D Views

Probably one of the most commonly created views in Revit are 2D views created directly from the model. These types of views consist of the floor plans, elevations, sections, plan details, and sectional details within the project. Figure 5.10 shows some examples.

These view types are created by taking plans, sections, or elevations from within the model and then embellishing them with two-dimensional detail components, linework, and annotations. In this way, you can add the necessary elements to the view to communicate the design and construction intent to the contractor while ensuring that when the model is updated, all the elements within the view are updated as well.

FIGURE 5.10
A building section cut from the model (left) and a parapet and roof detail take from a separate model. Both have been embellished using 2D linework but originated from a 3D section.

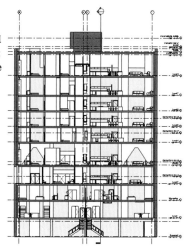
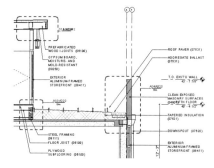

2D Details

Sometimes within the drawing set it becomes necessary to draft a 2D detail. These kinds of details are drafted in a similar manner to how you'd draft the same detail using a 2D CAD system. Revit has the ability to create 2D views, and using a series of drafting commands, you can create the types of details needed for any drawing set. These detail types are typically used when you large-scale details (1½″ = 1′-0″ for example) as at this scale, these are elements you typically won't model. This can be used for details like doorjambs, as seen in Figure 5.11, flashing details, or similar conditions.

FIGURE 5.11
A drafted doorjamb

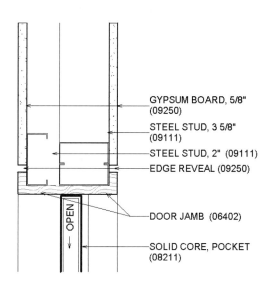

THREE SIMPLE GUIDELINES FOR DETAILING IN REVIT

Since you can create the same details and sheet views using a few different methods, it becomes important to understand when to use each of these detail methodologies. Knowing when to use each will depend on how your model was constructed, the scale of your view, and ultimately your comfort level and experience with Revit. To help you choose the right type of workflow to use, there are three simple questions you should ask yourself when you are detailing in Revit:

How many times will you see the detail in the model? There are many detail conditions within the model environment that you will see a variety of times. Knowing how often you will see that condition will help you gauge whether it is worth taking the time to model in 3D or whether it will be better as a simple, 2D detail. As a general rule of thumb, if you are going to see the condition more than once, it will probably be worth your time to model it. If you will only see the condition once, it will probably be a good idea to simply draft it as a 2D detail. Take a doorjamb condition, as shown in Figure 5.11 earlier, as an example. You will have many doorjamb conditions within the model, but you'll need to see the detail condition only once. In this case, it's probably better to simply draft that detail in 2D because you'll never see the exposed conditions within the doorjamb beyond this detail. As another example, if you were working on a window detail (the whole window, not head or sill or jamb), you will see this window cut in several plan locations and several sectional locations—so many times with the document set. Because of all these cuts, it makes more sense to model the window once and set the parametric conditions to reflect the level of detail needed for the scale of the drawing.

What scale are you drawing your detail in? The scale you are drawing in will have a large impact on whether to model the elements or draft them. A good rule of thumb I have used for teams new to Revit is to draft all of your details 1-1/2″ = 1′-0″ and larger. Obviously, the smaller the scale, the more likely you are to see the building elements within the context of the rest of the model and of other components. So, a wall section at 3/8″ = 1′-0″ scale would include a lot of the modeled building context, while our doorjamb condition (Figure 5.11) would show very little of the building context.

How good are you at using Revit? This is a critical question for modeling and detailing. As we have discussed, using Revit is an iterative process. You cannot expect to master the entire application the first time you model a building. So, it's important to be honest with your skill level so you don't bite off more than you can chew in any phase of the project. If it is your first use of Revit and the deadline is short and modeling the detail is complicated, draft it. You'll still be able to take advantage of many other key elements of the application, like its ability to organize your sheet set, automatic section cuts, and detail flags, among other things. You can take on modeling the complex detail in the next project when you have a bit more experience with the application.

Working in a Large Team

Revit is a single-file environment. This single file can be used individually by one person, or it can be tapped by multiple people using a feature built into Revit called *worksharing*. Worksharing allows more than one user to access Revit at a time, which lets a team of designers work on the same model simultaneously. The concepts and use of worksharing are covered in depth in

Chapter 6, "Understanding Worksharing," so in this chapter, we'll just touch on how you would manage and plan a large project in Revit. In a large-project environment—when you have half a dozen or more people actively in the Revit file—it takes some additional coordination and planning for a successful BIM implementation.

Breaking Up a Model

Revit's worksharing environment can allow for multiple people within a model at the same time. Although this multiuser workflow is supported within Revit, because of the nature and workflow inherent to design, it is possible to get too many people with a model at the same time. How many is too many will vary based on the size of the model and what people are working on, but it will become obvious when the model is overburdened with team members. Save times will be slow, there will be frequent occurrences of team members asking others to Synchronize With Central (SWC) so they can acquire permission over elements, and saving work to get everyone an updated model will become a time-consuming process. As a general rule of thumb, this number seems to be about six or eight users. About this point, you'll notice a significant decrease in speed and model performance.

When this happens, it's a good idea to discuss with your project team and consultants breaking up the model into separate models that can be linked back to each other. Breaking up the model involves taking sections of the model and splitting them into distinctive parts. As an example, you might have a project that will put out a Shell and Core package followed later by an Interiors package. If the project is a large one or you're planning on more than a half dozen people working on each set, it would be wise to divide those sets into distinctive Revit files. One file would contain the Shell and Core aspects of the project. The second file would contain all the elements of the Interiors. Because the second package is going to need to show elements of the first, it's a simple matter of linking the Shell and Core Revit file into the Interiors file.

As another example, let's say you are working on a campus project so your project has multiple buildings on a site. In this case, each building can easily become a separate Revit file.

A note of caution: you can split your model apart at any time in the project process, but once it is split, it is difficult to recombine it. Trying to recombine a model will also mean that you will only be able to merge model elements. Two-dimensional information and content from one model cannot be readily combined into another.

Within this workflow, there are some things that you'll want to make sure are consistent across all the files. Here are some of these potential pitfalls and their solutions:

You need your drawing sheets consistent between Revit files.   This can easily be addressed by either using the same template file for both projects or by exporting the Revit sheet family from one model and importing it into the other.

Your building plans and elevations need to show the context of the other file.   This can easily be fixed by linking one file into another. This same issue can be used to solve showing the building site as well. Create the site in a third Revit file and link it in on its own workset.

You are planning to do some renderings in Revit and need consistent materials or both models shown.   When you are working across multiple files, don't think that your building model necessarily has to be the source for all of your content. If you are creating walkthroughs or renderings, typically you are populating the view you are rendering with all kinds of entourage. You are adding people, trees, automobiles. You might also be constantly tweaking materials and lighting to get the view to render or look just right. In your production set, you don't want to see these elements popping up all over your drawings or your entourage accidentally getting printed as part of your building sections. Create a separate Revit file for this sort of production work and link your model geometry from the buildings into it. In this file, you can perform all of your renderings, add entourage, and adjust materials without the worry of interfering with the production workflow. You'll also get updates dynamically to the design every time you SWC.

You have details that need to be consistent in multiple packages. Any details you create within Revit can be moved from one file to another. By right-clicking the view in the Project Browser, you can use Save As to save the view and it will be saved to a separate file. This file can then be imported as a group into your other file or files and used again.

Using Worksets

Worksets, which are part of the worksharing process, allow you to divide up portions of the model along logical building divisions. Don't think of these as layers; think of them more as building assemblies and components. Where in 2D CAD you might have doors and walls as separate layers, in Revit you might have Building Skin, Building Core, and Interior Walls as separate worksets.

Worksets on a large project give team members a way to manage what goes into the active RAM on their individual workstations. Each workset can be selected to load or not load when you open a project. In Figure 5.12, you can see how we have chosen to open only selected worksets. To open this dialog box and change this, click the Workset button on the Manage tab.

FIGURE 5.12
Turning worksets on and off

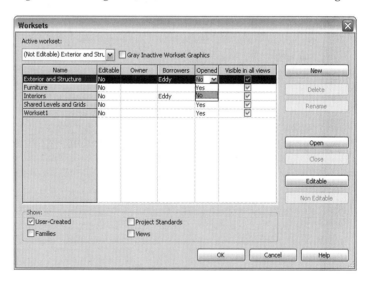

Choosing to leave a workset off means that you won't load that information into the active memory of the computer, making the model easier to manipulate and manage. It will be "lighter" and more responsive. Views will open quicker. And when you need to see your work in context with the other worksets, simply turn them back on. Figure 5.13 shows the same view with the Shell workset turned off and then turned back on. Just don't forget to turn them back on before you print your set; otherwise, you might be wondering where some of the walls have gone.

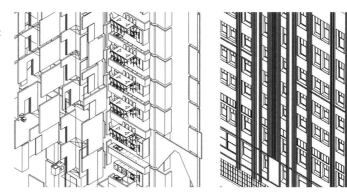

FIGURE 5.13
The Shell workset turned off (left) and turned on (right)

 Real World Scenario

SETTING NAMING STANDARDS

When working on a large team, one of the problems you eventually run into is trying to find families in the Project Browser or the Type Selector. As the project grows in size and more people are added, everyone seems to self-stylize their own family naming conventions. When inserting casework, you don't know if you're looking for Base-Cabinet-2 door or Cabinet-Base or Casework. Since both the family list and Type Selector sort alphabetically, it can be quite a challenge to find the family you want to insert when the list grows long.

On a recent, very large project we worked on where the architectural model alone consisted of five separate files, we needed a family-naming convention that would allow people to move back and forth between models and still be able to insert families easily. We settled on a naming convention that would utilize the first four digits of a material's MasterSpec number as the prefix to the family name. Instead of having Cast In Place Concrete in one location and Precast Concrete further down the list, the families were renamed to 0330 Cast in Place Concrete and 0345 Precast Concrete. This sorted them numerically before sorting alphabetically and allowed all the families to be located quickly. The short prefix was also useful so the description wouldn't be too truncated in the Type Selector.

Quality Control and BIM

In any project process, you should always maintain a level of quality control to ensure a solid workflow. When working in a BIM environment, good model maintenance is an imperative part of the process. A well-maintained model will open quickly and be responsive when changing views or manipulating content. A model that is not well maintained can have a very large file size, take a long time to open or save, or even become corrupted. Letting the quality control of your model suffer can negatively impact the team's overall production and lead to frustration because they cannot be as efficient as they'd like to be. The model size will grow, it will take a long time to save locally or SWC, and the file can suffer corruption or crashes.

Maintaining a good, healthy model is not a hard thing to accomplish. It takes about as much effort as regularly changing the oil in your car. The important thing, as with your car, is actually doing the regular maintenance so you don't have to fix a big problem that could have been avoided. In the following sections, we'll cover some simple things you can do and watch using some of the tools already built into Revit that will help flag whether there is a problem.

Keeping an Eye on File Size

Watch the size of your file. The size of your file is a good metric for general file stability. A typical Revit file size for a project in construction documents will be between 100MB and 250MB—250MB is really on the high side of file sizes. Beyond that, you will find that the model will be slow to open and hard to rotate in 3D views, and other views, such as building elevations and overall plans, will also be slow to open.

Should your file become large or unwieldy, you have several ways you can trim your file down and get your model lean and responsive again.

PURGING UNUSED FAMILIES AND GROUPS

On the Manage tab is a command called Purge Unused. This command removes all the unused families and groups from your model by deleting them. There are many times within a design process where you will change window types or wall types or swap one set of families for another. Even if those elements are not being used in the project, they are being stored within the file, and therefore when the file is opened, they are being loaded into memory. Depending on the stage of your project, you should periodically delete these elements from the model to keep your file size down. Don't worry—if you find you need a family you've removed, you can always reload it.

Select the Manage tab and choose Purge Unused from the Settings panel (Figure 5.14). Depending on the size of your model and how many families you have loaded, it might take Revit a few minutes to complete this command.

FIGURE 5.14
Selecting Purge
Unused

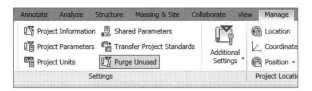

After Revit is done thinking, it will provide you with a list of all the families and groups in the file that are not actively within a view (Figure 5.15). At this point, you have the option to select the elements you want to delete or to keep and remove the rest.

Figure 5.15
The Purge Unused
dialog box

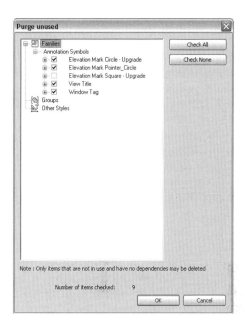

We don't recommend that you use this command in the early stages of design. This is largely because your file size won't be that large early on, and purging at this stage would eliminate any preloaded families that you might have included in your template. During schematic design and design development, you are typically going through design iteration and will likely be adding and removing content regularly. It can become a hassle to have to constantly load or reload families into the model. If your model is not suffering from performance issues or the file size isn't unruly, it's not necessary to perform a Purge Unused.

Cutting Down on the Number of Views

The ability to quickly create views within a model is one of the fast and easy benefits of using Revit. This ability can also be a detriment, though, if it is not managed. Beyond the simple hassle of having to sort through many views to find the one you need, having too many views in Revit can also impact your performance and file size.

Obviously, a number of views are needed within the model to create the construction documentation. Beyond those views, you will find yourself creating additional views to study the design, deal with model creation, or simply view the building or project from a new angle. These types of "working views" will never make it to the sheet set, and some will be used for only brief periods.

HOW MANY WORKING VIEWS IS TOO MANY?

How many working views is too many to have in your model? The obvious answer is when performance begins to suffer, you need to start looking at ways to make the model lean and speed up response times. We had a project team new to Revit, and they were complaining about the file being slow to open and manipulate. When reviewing their model, we saw their file size was around 800MB! We were surprised they were even able to do any work at all.

One of the first things we did to get the file size down to something more reasonable was look at all the views that were not on sheets. We found they had more than 1,200 views not being used. Deleting those views paired with a File ➤ Save (with the Compress box checked) brought the file size down to 500MB. Although still very high, it demonstrates the impact too many views can have on your file size.

Now, before you go through the effort of counting all your unused views to see how many you have, let's remember that Revit is a database. You can use this feature to let Revit perform the counting for you using schedules. To create a schedule that will track unused views, with the Jenkins model open, select the Schedules flyout from the View tab and choose View List (Figure 5.16).

This will pull up the View List Properties dialog box (Figure 5.17) and allow you to select the fields you want to have in your schedule. For your View List schedule, select the following fields:

◆ Sheet Number

◆ View Name

◆ Title on Sheet

FIGURE 5.16
Choosing the View
List schedule

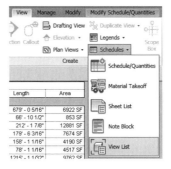

Use the Add button to move those fields from the left column to the right one and sort them in the order listed and shown in the figure.

Figure 5.17
Selecting fields
for the View List
schedule

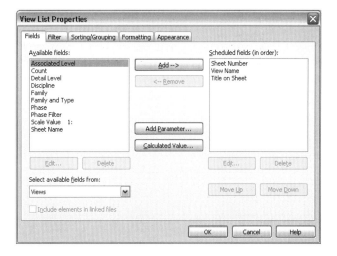

If you were to click OK right now, this would create a schedule of all the views you have within the model. Since you want to see only the views that are not on sheets, you have a bit more formatting to do. By selecting the next tab, Filter, you can choose to only see the views not on sheets. In the Jenkins model, there are two sheet types: those that begin with an *A* and ones that begin with a *K*.

1. On the Filter tab, choose to filter the sheets by Sheet Number.

2. Now from the drop-down menu, choose Does Not Begin With as a filter type.

3. Finally, in the text field, enter a capital **A** (see Figure 5.18).

Remember that since these are database functions, they are also case sensitive. Before moving on to the next tab, choose to add another filter selection. Copy the one you just created to filter A sheets, but now filter out all the K sheets.

Figure 5.18
Filtering out views
on sheets

As a last bit of formatting, select the Sorting/Grouping tab. On this tab, from the drop-down menu, select Sheet Number. Should you have missed a sheet number type (for instance, if we have "G" sheets in our list), it would appear at the top. Be sure to have the Grand Totals checkbox selected and the Itemize Every Instance box selected (Figure 5.19). Click OK when you're done.

FIGURE 5.19
Sorting the schedule by sheet name

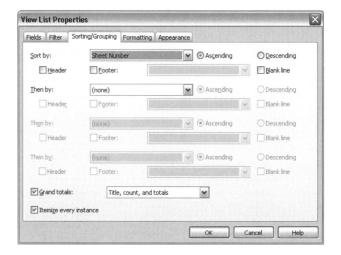

This will give you a schedule that will look similar to Figure 5.20; it shows a list and the total of all the views not on sheets in your model. You can see that in our model we have 36 views not currently on sheets. You can add this schedule to your office template where it will keep a running list of views not on sheets that you can refer to at any time in the project process.

FIGURE 5.20
The finished schedule

View List		
Sheet Number	View Name	Title on Sheet
	Basement	
	Basement	
	Level 1	
	PARAPET	
	ROOF	
	Level 5	
	Level 1	
	Level 3	
	Level 2	
	Level 4	
	Level 6	
	Level 7	
	Level 8	
	Mezzanine	
	ROOF	
	PENTHOUSE ROOF	
	PENTHOUSE	
	PENTHOUSE ROOF	
	Level 2	
	Mezzanine	
	Level 3	
	Level 4	
	Level 5	
	Level 6	
	Level 7	
	Level 8	
	Section 1	
	Solar Array	
	3D View 1	
	3D View 2	
	West Elevation	
	3D View 3	
	Section 2	
	3D View 4	
	exterior worm-eye	
	(3D)	
Grand total: 36		

Using Schedules

Using schedules, as you just saw in the previous example, is a great way to use tools already in Revit to perform quality control on your model or drawings. Don't think that all schedules need to be placed on sheets. There are several uses for schedules as a quality assurance measure. In the previous example of the views, we were using schedules to help troubleshoot poor model performance; however, you can use schedules to help you QA/QC all kinds of things. In effect, schedules are used to track elements within the model, so using that logic, there are many things that would be worth tracking from a quality assurance standpoint. On larger projects, we have sometimes made a separate sheet in the drawing set and placed some of these schedules onto this sheet, allowing the project manager to have a sheet to refer to for the stewardship of the drawing set. What other kinds of quality control can you use schedules for? The following sections highlight two more examples.

WALL SCHEDULES

Every project we've ever worked on has needed a series of wall partition types. Although Revit still lacks the ability to directly link wall partition types to both tags and schedules, the project still needs to track all the wall types used on the project.

Using the schedules, create a simply wall schedule and add Wall Type, Length, and Area to the schedule. Creating a schedule like this will give you a result something like Figure 5.21.

FIGURE 5.21

Creating a wall schedule

WALL SCHEDULE		
Family and Type	Length	Area
Basic Wall: 3- Layers 5/8" gyp fire rating	679' - 0 5/16"	6922 SF
Basic Wall: 6 1/8" wall - 2layersGyp	66' - 10 1/2"	853 SF
Basic Wall: 12" COATED CMU	212' - 1 7/8"	12881 SF
Basic Wall: Exterior - Brick	179' - 6 3/16"	7674 SF
Basic Wall: Exterior - Brick 2	158' - 1 1/16"	4190 SF
Basic Wall: Exterior - Concrete	78' - 1 1/16"	4517 SF
Basic Wall: Interior - Gyp 4 7/8"	1215' - 1 1/32"	9762 SF
Curtain Wall: Storefront	106' - 3 21/32"	1024 SF

Creating a schedule like this can tell you several things. First, it will give you an up-to-date list of all the walls used in a project. If you find a wall type listed in this schedule that doesn't appear in your wall types, then you know the two have to be coordinated. Possibly you have a new wall type condition or possibly someone has used a different wall type in error.

A second use for this schedule is in pricing. This can be used to double-check contractor takeoffs for wall lengths and areas. Now remember, Revit will report actual wall areas. If you have a 10′ × 10′ wall, that's 100 sq. ft. of wall area. If you add a 3′ × 7′ door to that wall, you now will only see 79 sq. ft. of wall area in the schedule even though the length and height of the wall hasn't changed. Although this schedule won't reflect the actual amounts of materials a contractor will need to purchase to build a wall, it will reflect actual lengths and areas that can be used to cross check takeoffs.

A final use for this wall schedule is BIM-deliverable standardization. More and more clients are asking for BIM models as a deliverable in lieu of CAD files. Although standardization and naming conventions are not as robust yet as they are for 2D CAD submittals, you'll want your family-naming conventions to be easy to understand and relatively similar in style. Regularly reviewing this schedule will ensure that you are not submitting a BIM model to the client with wall names like "Susan's Wall" or "1/2″ Gyp Wall"—a wall type that we recently found in one of my projects that was truly only a ½″ wide wall.

KEYNOTES

As a final example for using schedules to manage the consistency of a project, we'll discuss how to use keynotes and textnotes in the construction document process. Regardless of whether you use keynotes (the numerical notes) or textnotes (the text-based notes), you will invariably need to use one of them to add annotations to your project. Although Revit can easily produce both types of annotation, for the sake of ease and consistency we will refer to them as *keynotes* for the remainder of this section because that is the name of the command within Revit.

If you are keynoting a project, you are adding annotations that call out specific materials or conditions within your details. Those notes need to not only be consistent across multiple details, but they will also link directly back to the specification—a whole separate document published outside of Revit. Historically on a project, to maintain any sort of consistency between notes in different views, you needed to manually coordinate all the notes and manually check them. When you are talking about hundreds of sheets in a drawing set and thousands of notes, there is plenty of room here for error. In a manual process, you can have notes on one sheet that read "Cast-in-Place Concrete" while on another sheet they read "CIP Concrete" and on a third sheet "Cst in Place Conncrete" (note the typos).

The Keynote tool in Revit has some built-in checks and balances to ensure a level of consistency when it is being used, and we'll go into using the keynoting tool in Chapter 19, "Annotating Your Design." However, it should be pointed out that schedules are another good way for the project manager to maintain a level of oversight across the project. A keynoting schedule will give you a running list of what notes are being used and how often a note has been inserted into a project. This list can be used to verify that all the notes read as desired (proper abbreviations are being used and the notes are free of typos) and how many times a note is being used with the project. Knowing the frequency of note use can tell you whether someone used an incorrect note; perhaps there was only one instance of a note. This overall list can also be cross-checked against the specifications so you can ensure that everything you've added to the drawings has a corresponding spec section.

To create a keynote schedule, follow these steps:

1. On the View ribbon, select the Schedule drop-down, and choose Note Block (Figure 5.22).

FIGURE 5.22
Creating a Keynote schedule

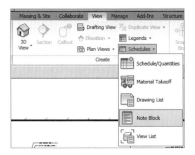

2. The fields for a Note Block schedule are fairly limited. From the fields list on the left, choose the following:

- ◆ CSI Number
- ◆ Description
- ◆ Count

Then sort them in that order, as shown in Figure 5.23.

FIGURE 5.23
Adding fields to the Note Block schedule

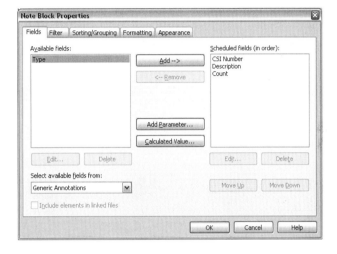

3. Select the Sorting/Grouping tab. From the first drop-down menu, choose CSI Number for the sort order. Make sure that both checkboxes, Grand Totals and Itemize Every Instance, are unchecked (see Figure 5.24).

FIGURE 5.24
Sorting the Note Block schedule

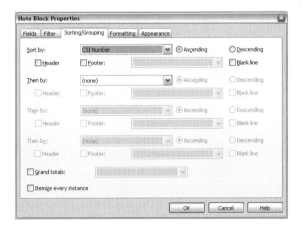

4. Select the Format tab and then highlight Count in the list on the left. For ease of reading the finished schedule, change the alignment of the Count field from Left to Right (Figure 5.25).

FIGURE 5.25
Setting Count to
align right

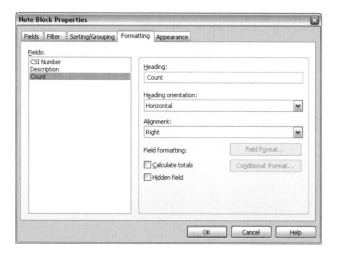

The finished schedule will look like Figure 5.26. If you look at the elements displayed in the schedule, you'll notice that it is organized by CSI division and every note will be listed so you can verify the spelling and accuracy of each item. You'll also see each time that note is used within the drawing set—GYPSUM BOARD, TYPE X 5/8″ (09250)—being our most used note.

FIGURE 5.26
The Note Block
schedule

CSI Number	Description	Count
05400.AF	STEEL FRAMING (05400)	13
05400.BC	STEEL STUD (05400)	10
09111.AF	STEEL FRAMING (09111)	24
09111.BA		13
09111.BD	HAT CHANNEL (09111)	1
09111.BH	STEEL RUNNER (09111)	5
09111.BZ	HANGER (09111)	1
09250.AD	GYPSUM BOARD, TYPE X 5/8″ (09250)	28
09250.AE		2
09250.AH	GYPSUM BOARD, CEILING 1/2″ (09250)	11
09250.AM	GYPSUM BOARD, 5/8″ (09250)	32
09250.AN	GYPSUM BOARD, MOISTURE- AND MOLD-RESI	15
09250.AO	TRIM BEAD (09250)	3
09250.AU	SOUND-ATTENUATION BLANKET (09250)	7
09250.ZZ	EDGE REVEAL (09250)	12
09310.AD	GLASS WALL TILE (09310)	5
09385.AF	STONE TILE BASE (09385)	2
09385.AX		4
09385.AY	1/4″ CEMENTITIOUS BACKER UNIT (09385)	5
09385.AZ	4″ x 4″ TRAVERTINE TILE (09385)	5
09640.AA	WOOD FLOORING (09640)	6
09640.AB	WOOD BASE (06402)	6
09640.ZZ	BAMBOO WOOD FLOORING (09640)	7

Notice that three lines are blank. These are 09111.BA, 09250.AE, and 09385.AX. In each of these conditions, we have a CSI number that has two different notes assigned to it. Since Revit cannot have multiple values in the same field within a schedule, it will show the condition as a blank. This should tell you, in this schedule, that someone has used the same number to refer to two different notes. To see which notes these are, simply highlight the line item you want to view and choose Highlight In Model in the Element panel (Figure 5.27).

FIGURE 5.27
Showing selected
elements from a
schedule

Finding Errors and Warnings

A seemingly obvious place to troubleshoot your model is the Errors And Warnings tool. Although this will do very little to affect your overall file size, the Errors And Warnings box will alert you to problems within the model that should regularly be addressed to ensure file stability. To locate this dialog box, on the Inquiry panel of the Manage tab, click the Errors And Warnings button (Figure 5.28).

FIGURE 5.28
The Errors And
Warnings button

Selecting this tool will give you the dialog box shown in Figure 5.29, which will list all of the errors and warnings still active in your project file.

FIGURE 5.29
The Errors
And Warnings
dialog box

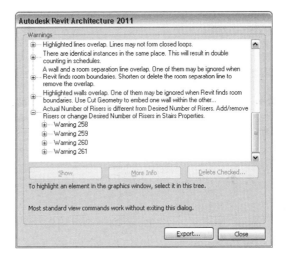

Errors and warnings are essentially all types of issues Revit has resolving geometry, conflicts, or formulas that do not equate. Things that will appear in this dialog box are instances where you have multiple elements sitting directly on top of each other, thereby creating inaccurate schedule counts; wall joints that do not properly clean themselves up; wall and room separation lines overlapping; stairs that have the wrong number of risers between floors; and so on. This dialog box basically shows you all the times the yellow warning box showed up at the bottom-right corner of the screen and you ignored it. Errors that go unchecked not only can compound to create other errors but can lead to inaccurate reporting in schedules or even file corruption. You'll want to check the Errors And Warnings dialog box regularly as part of your periodic file maintenance and try to keep the number of instances to a minimum. You might also notice that the Errors And Warnings dialog box has an Export feature. This will export your error list to an HTML file, allowing you to read it at your leisure outside the model environment (Figure 5.30). Pulling this list into a Microsoft Word or Excel document can allow you to also distribute the errors across the team for them to be resolved.

FIGURE 5.30
Exporting
the errors and
warnings

JenkinsMusicBldg-Cntrl-Eddy Error Report (1/3/2010 11:51:07 AM)

Error message	Elements
Highlighted walls are attached to, but miss, the highlighted targets.	Exterior and Structure : Floors : Floor : CIP Concrete : id 263090 Exterior and Structure : Walls : Basic Wall : 12" COATED CMU : id 613698
Highlighted walls are attached to, but miss, the highlighted targets.	Exterior and Structure : Floors : Floor : CIP Concrete : id 263090 Exterior and Structure : Walls : Basic Wall : Exterior - Brick 2 : id 693453
Highlighted walls are attached to, but miss, the highlighted targets.	Exterior and Structure : Floors : Floor : CIP Concrete : id 269226 Interiors : Walls : Basic Wall : Interior - Gyp 4 7/8" : id 605102
Highlighted walls are attached to, but miss, the highlighted targets.	Exterior and Structure : Walls : Basic Wall : Exterior - Brick 2 : id 325781 Exterior and Structure : Floors : Floor : CIP Concrete : id 334468
Highlighted walls are attached to, but miss, the highlighted targets.	Exterior and Structure : Walls : Basic Wall : Exterior - Brick 2 : id 325861 Exterior and Structure : Floors : Floor : CIP Concrete : id 334468

In the example shown in Figure 5.30 using the Jenkins model, we have 261 errors and warnings in the file. How many errors in a file are too many? A lot of that depends on your model, computer capabilities, what the error types are, and your deliverable. For instance, if you are delivering a BIM model to your client or to the contractor, you might have a zero error requirement. In that case, no errors are acceptable. If you still actively in the design phase of the project, however, you will always have some errors—it is an inescapable part of the process of iteration. As you refine the drawings, errors will be resolved, and as you add new content to the model that is in need of resolution, new errors will be created. If you are not worried about a model deliverable, you can get away with having fewer than 1,000 errors in the project without too much trouble. That said, the cleaner the model, the smoother it will run.

Activating Design Options

Design options are a great way to work through possible design iterations while keeping all the content within the same model. We'll discuss how to use them specifically later in this book, but also understand they are not meant to become a permanent part of the model. Having design options within your model will eventually increase your file size the longer they stay in there. Over time, you will have difficulty in removing them as elements and views will be created and associated to the various elements within a particular design option. As a general rule of thumb, you'll want to leave the design options active in your model long enough for you to make a decision on the design direction. Then, once that decision is reached, it is in your best interests to remove them.

To tell if you have design options active within your model, choose the Manage tab. There is a Design Options button located on this tab (Figure 5.31).

FIGURE 5.31
The Design
Options button on
the Manage tab

You can also look at the status bar at the bottom of the screen for the same information (Figure 5.32).

FIGURE 5.32
The Design
Options button in
the status bar

Clicking the Design Options button will pull up the Design Options dialog box shown in Figure 5.33. This dialog box will list all design options you have actively within the file. You can also delete the options here and merge the geometry back into the main model. Make sure you coordinate removing options with the rest of the project team so no work is lost.

FIGURE 5.33
The Design
Options dialog box

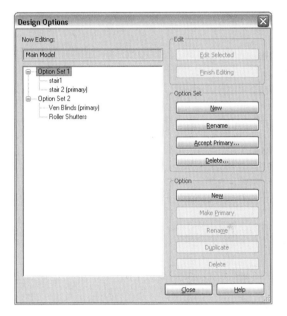

The Bottom Line

Understand a BIM workflow.   Understand how projects are completed in BIM and how the use of Revit on a project can change how information within a project is created.

Master It   Explain one of the primary differences between a more traditional 2D CAD-based workflow and producing documents using Revit.

Staff a BIM project.   Since Revit is a change in workflow, it is also important to understand the change in staffing and who is needed to perform what roles on a project.

Master It   What are the three primary roles in a Revit project and what are the responsibilities of those roles?

Work in a large team. Many projects require multiple team members. Some require having a very large team assembled on a project. Working with a large team in Revit is a matter of collectively managing a series of smaller models. Know how to manage these smaller models.

> **Master It** How many people is too many to have working in a single Revit file? What do you do when you reach that limit?

Create details in Revit. Revit is a combination of model content in 3D and annotations and embellishment in 2D to create any document set. It is important to understand when to use 3D within a model environment and what elements are best done in 2D to maintain model integrity and keep the model responsive.

> **Master It** What are the three questions you should ask yourself before modeling or drafting any views in Revit?

Perform quality control on your Revit model. Since you have several people using one file to create possibly hundreds of drawing sheets, it's important to keep a model clean of errors and functioning well. Performing regular maintenance on your model is essential to maintaining a file stability and functionality. Should a file happen to become corrupted, you stand to lose the work of the entire team. Understand how to maintain a model and how to regularly check under the hood.

> **Master It** There are several ways to keep an eye on the model so it stays responsive and free of corruption. List some of these ways.

Chapter 6

Understanding Worksharing

Most projects involve more than one person working together at any given time. It's common in design for many people to work collaboratively to meet deadlines and create a set of construction documents. Revit has tools that allow for a collaborative design and documentation process while allowing multiple people simultaneous access to its single-file building model. Keeping with the theme of an integrated single-file building model, Revit allows for this workflow without breaking apart the model. A complex model can be edited by many people at once using a feature called worksharing. In this chapter, we'll focus on enabling the worksharing feature of Revit.

In this chapter, you learn how to:

◆ Understand key worksharing concepts

◆ Use worksharing in your project

◆ Manage workflow with worksets

◆ Understand element ownership in worksets

Understanding Worksharing Basics

CERT OBJECTIVE

Worksharing in Revit refers to the use of *worksets* to divide a model for the purpose of sharing the workload among multiple people. A workset is a collection of building elements and components (building skin; core; interior walls; furniture, fixtures, and equipment [FF&E]; and so on) that can be used to manage project responsibilities. By separating these various building components into sets (worksets) that allow control over visibility and element ownership, multiple people can collaborate and work within the same file. By default, worksharing is not enabled when you start a project in Revit because Revit assumes you are in a single-user environment at project startup.

Work is shared by creating and saving to a *central file* located on a network drive. This central file becomes the repository where all the individual work is stored. Access to elements is managed through permissions as in a database. By taking permission of a workset or element—checking out elements or worksets—the central file can manage all the components within a model and make sure that none of the team members are working on the same things.

You share your work by saving the central file to a shared network location. This central file becomes the repository where all the individual work on the project is collected and permissions are managed.

Once the central file has been established, each team member then makes a "local copy" by copying the central file to the desktop or C: drive. All the project work is then done solely in this local copy, which keeps an active association with the central file. All work is done directly in these copied local files. This enables all users to open their local files simultaneously and work concurrently on the project (see Figure 6.1).

FIGURE 6.1
The worksharing concept

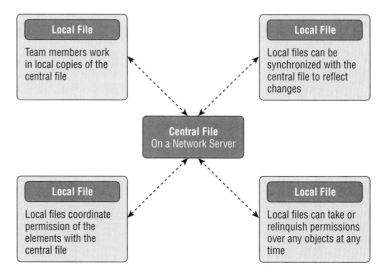

The elements in each local file are tied to permissions linking them back to the central file. This makes it impossible to edit an element in one local file if that same element is owned or has been edited by someone else on the same team in another local file.

Remember, Revit is built on top of a database. In effect, when you are working on elements within the model, you're obtaining permission to edit one or more of them from the central database. Once permission to modify an element is granted, no one else can make changes to that element until the changes are reconciled with the central file. This occurs when you use the Synchronize With Central (SWC) command on the Collaborate tab to copy changes you've made back to the central file and simultaneously update your local file with any other changes that have been published to the central file by other team members. If one team member has ownership over an element, no other team members can edit that element until its permissions or changes have been reconciled with the central file.

Worksets allow you to group building elements into collections of objects for the purpose of managing visibility, file performance, or work activity. The actual use of worksets can vary greatly from project to project. Simply enabling worksharing facilitates a multi–team member file and using the worksets beyond the defaults is technically not necessary. However, using the worksets allows you to take advantage of other benefits such as the following:

◆ You can control the visibility of groupings of building components such as building skin, core, interior walls, and so on, without having to use temporary view settings or control visibility manually.

◆ Closing worksets or turning them on or off as needed removes those elements from active memory and thus improves performance.

◆ You can quickly take permission of the entire workset and all the elements contained within at one time.

Using Worksharing in Your Project

The worksharing feature is designed to accommodate a variety of ways to group elements within your model. There are no inherent restrictions in how you use worksharing. For example, you can use worksharing to divide a model into one workset for the shell and core and another workset for interior partitions. You can turn worksharing on during any stage of the project, create and remove worksets, or move elements between worksets.

WORKSHARING IN THE PROJECT PROCESS

Once worksharing is enabled in a project, it cannot be turned off, and it will remain on for the future life of the file. When you choose to enable the worksharing feature, make sure that the team is aware of the change to the file and that it is planned within the project process.

Revit's worksharing feature is designed to accommodate any division of labor you see fit. There are no inherent restrictions in how you use worksharing to divide up a model. For example, you can break up a model and have one group work on the shell and another work on the interior core of a building. You can turn worksharing on at any stage of the project, and you can create or remove individual worksets during the project cycle.

You can find the worksharing feature on the Worksets panel of the Collaborate tab, as shown in Figure 6.2.

FIGURE 6.2
The
Collaborate tab

You can initiate worksharing by clicking the Worksets button, as shown in Figure 6.3. It will initially be the only active button on the panel.

FIGURE 6.3
The Worksets
button

Selecting this button opens the Worksharing dialog box alerting you that you are about to enable worksharing for your project (Figure 6.4). Remember, once activated, worksharing cannot be turned off. Click OK to confirm you want to enable worksets. Depending on the size of your model and your processor speed, this process can take a few minutes for Revit to complete.

FIGURE 6.4
Activating work-
sharing

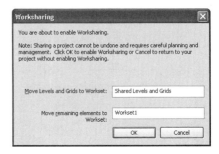

Once that is done, Revit will open the Worksets dialog box and automatically create two worksets within your project: Shared Levels and Grids, which contains only the levels and grids within the model, and Workset1, which will contain everything else (Figure 6.5). New levels and grids created in the project will automatically be placed on the Shared Levels and Grids workset.

FIGURE 6.5
The Worksets dia-
log box

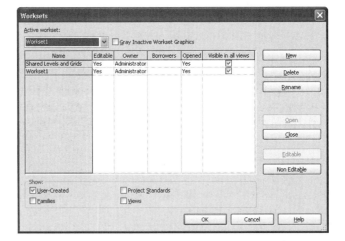

Types of Worksets

There are four types of worksets in any project: User-Created, Families, Project Standards, and Views. User-Created worksets such as Shared Levels and Grids and Workset1 are shown by default, and you have the option to make the others visible by selecting the check boxes at the bottom of the Worksets dialog box.

User-Created Worksets   Besides the Shared Levels and Grids and the Workset1 worksets that Revit created for you, all of the worksets created in the Worksets dialog box will fall under this category. The User-Created worksets are the only ones by default that will appear in the Worksets dialog box when it is first opened. Only elements on User-Created worksets can be moved between other User-Created worksets.

Families Worksets   For each family type created or loaded in the project, a workset is automatically created. When editing the properties of a family, you will automatically take ownership over that family. You cannot make changes to a family or family type without first having permission over the family itself.

Project Standards Worksets   The Project Standards workset type is dedicated to all the project settings such as materials, dimension styles, annotations, tags, line styles, and so on. Any time you need to edit a project standard, such as modifying the graphics of a dimension string, you will be taking ownership of the element's workset.

Views Worksets   Every view created in a project has its own view workset type. The Views workset type controls ownership of the View Properties and any view-specific elements such as annotations, dimensions, tags, detail lines, and so on. You can take ownership of a particular view workset by selecting it from the workset list and clicking the Editable button. Alternatively, you can also take permission of a view by right-clicking the view in the Project Browser and choosing Make Workset Editable from the context menu. This can be a helpful shortcut in construction documents when much of the effort on the project is more view specific. Regardless of ownership, any team member always has the ability to add elements, components, annotations, or whatever to any view.

The Worksets dialog box lets you add and remove User-Created worksets and take and relinquish permissions over existing worksets. By default, when a new workset is created, it does not contain any model elements or components.

MANAGING WORKSET STRUCTURE

Worksets are groupings of elements logical to a three-dimensional, virtual building. One of the biggest challenges facing teams new to Revit is conceptualizing the difference between layers in 2D CAD and worksets in Revit. These teams typically want to try to manage worksets in Revit as they managed layers in 2D CAD, which can result in worksets named Doors, Windows, Walls, and so on. Although this is effective management in a 2D CAD environment, it poses certain problems for a Revit workflow. For instance, if you choose to take possession of the Doors workset and a teammate takes ownership of the Walls workset, neither of you can edit the elements in your workset if it is hosted in (or has hosts from) the other workset. How do you move a wall that has noneditable doors? Or add a door to a wall when you cannot edit the wall? You need to own both elements for the door to be placed.

However, much like layers, the workset is a standard that the team will need to understand and follow to use it successfully. Worksets should be structured by a team's BIM manager or project manager familiar with a BIM workflow. Ultimately, though, it is up to the team members to place elements on the proper worksets and ensure project standards are being followed.

Organizing Worksets

When dividing your project into worksets, it's important to think about the holistic building rather than trying to isolate its individual components. A good way to think about dividing up worksets is to consider the building elements and the number of people working on each of these elements. A basic breakdown of a project's elements might include the following:

- Exterior skin
- Core
- Interior partitions (in a larger building, by floor)
- Site
- FF&E

This breakdown mirrors some of the roles and responsibilities on the project as well. There might be a small group working on exterior skin design and detailing, another group working on interior partitions, and a third working on FF&E.

HOW MANY WORKSETS DO YOU NEED?

As a good rule of thumb, you should have one or two worksets for every person working on the project (besides Shared Levels and Grids). On a small project with two or three people, you might only have three or four worksets. On larger projects, you could have a dozen or so.

Also keep in mind that once you have six to eight people working in a project, Revit's performance will begin to degrade, not to mention that you will spend a good deal of time each day getting everyone's local files synchronized; each person will need to save two times (once to save changes to central and another to download everyone else's changes). If your project is large enough to warrant more than six to eight people concurrently in the model, consider dividing the model into multiple files, as we discussed in Chapter 5, "Managing a Revit Project."

For the Jenkins Building, we have divided the model into four worksets, as shown in Figure 6.6.

FIGURE 6.6
Workset organization for the Jenkins Building

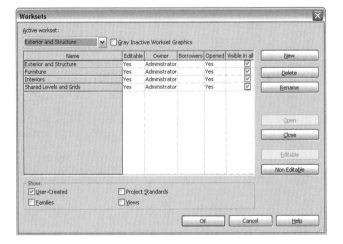

Exterior and Structure   This workset contains all the exterior skin of the building as well as the elevator, stair, slabs, and columns.

Furniture   This workset contains all the furniture, fixtures, casework, and appliances.

Interiors   This workset contains all the interior walls, furniture, and other items are managed with this workset.

Shared Levels and Grids   This workset contains the level and grid information from the model, as was originally established when worksharing was enabled.

Notice that Workset1 has been renamed, in our case, to Exterior and Structure. The title Workset1 is not descriptive enough to be of much use, so it can be modified once all the model elements have been moved to relevant worksets. The worksets we've set up demonstrate how a typical breakdown might occur in a project of this size, but it's by no means limited to this scheme. Depending on how you structure work in your office, the worksets might be quite different.

Managing Workflow with Worksets

Once worksharing is enabled, there is always a single central file that is used to manage element permissions and create local files. This is the file that will collect all the work done by your team members and allow the team to see regular updates of changes being made to the model or documents. After initializing worksharing, there are a few more steps to complete before all the team members can begin working in a multiuser environment.

THE GOOD THINGS ABOUT LOCAL FILES

Using Revit in a worksharing environment requires you to do everything your IT department typically asks you *not* to do: work directly off your C: drive. Although working off a network file is typically a good idea, in Revit there are several reasons why a local copy offers some additional benefits:

◆ It allows more than one user to make changes to the central file by editing local files and synchronizing those changes with the central file.

◆ Your local copy will be more responsive than a networked local file because your access speed to your hard drive is much faster than it is across most networks.

◆ If anything bad happens to your network or your central file, such as file corruption, each local file is basically a backup that can be used to create a new local file by performing a Save As operation.

Creating a Central File

Now that you've activated worksharing, you need to set up the new central file to initiate the multiuser environment. To do this, you'll first create the central file on your network; then you'll create the local files that the team will be using.

To create the central file, click the Application button and choose Save As ➤ Project. You'll be presented with the typical Save As dialog box, as shown in Figure 6.7.

FIGURE 6.7

Save As dialog box

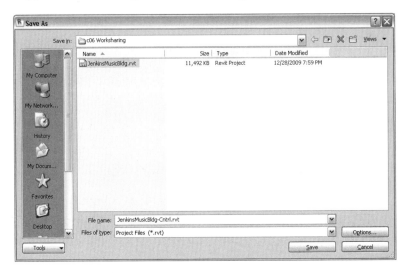

Before renaming the new file, click the Options button at the lower right of this dialog box. A File Save Options dialog box opens that will look like Figure 6.8.

FIGURE 6.8

File Save Options dialog box

This dialog box contains some important settings. At the top, you can set the number of backups the file will keep in the folder history after saves. The default value is 20. Depending on the storage availability on your network, how often your network is backed up, and the number of people working in the model (remember, local files are also backups), you might want to reduce this number. Because of our space limitations, we've reduced this number to 3.

Also note here that the Make This A Central File After Save check box is selected and grayed out. This is because we've activated worksharing in this file and Revit assumes that we will be making a central file on the next save. Click OK to exit the dialog box.

Back in the Save As dialog box, choose a network location for your central file that everyone on the team has access to. Be sure that when you are naming your new central file, you choose a new name. Do not save over the existing Revit file. There are two reasons for this. First, it automatically gives you a backup of your pre-workshared file in case you need to revert to a non-multiuser file for some reason. Second, saving over an open Revit file can sometimes cause corruption, even if it is the same model.

Once you've entered a new name for the file, click OK to save the file. Now that your file is saved to the network, close all the open windows. Make sure that you *never work directly within the central file*. Doing so will change the file attributes on the server and prohibit anyone with a local file from being able to synchronize with the central file. The possibility of losing a lot of work and effort from team members exists, so it is safer to err on the side of simply never opening the file.

As one final step, make sure that as the person who has created the central file, you don't accidentally retain any rights over the objects and elements within the central file, thereby prohibiting anyone from editing those elements.

To do this, select the Collaborate tab and click the Worksharing button again to open the Worksets dialog box. In the Editable column, change all the Yes entries to No, as shown in Figure 6.9. This will ensure that you have relinquished all the permissions over elements before creating any local files.

FIGURE 6.9
Relinquishing permissions

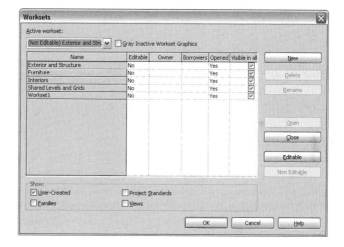

Creating the Local File

Now that you've made a central file, you'll need to create a local file to work from. To do this, simply open the network location of the central file and drag a copy from the network to your desktop or anywhere on your C: drive. Be careful not to *move* the file—only copy it.

Now, open the new local file. The first time any local file is opened, you'll see a warning message alerting you that you are opening a local file (Figure 6.10). All this means is that you've made a local file and you'll be the owner of the local file. Click Close to dismiss the warning and continue the file-opening process.

FIGURE 6.10

Opening a local file
for the first time

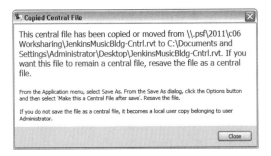

FIGURE 6.10

Opening a local file
for the first time

Each local file is "owned" by the local machine, and once it's opened, Revit will pair the local machine with that local file. By default, Revit assigns a username to the local file that matches the login name on the active workstation. So, a typical Windows login might be first initial and the last name, such as ekrygiel. That user would then become the owner of the local file. In this case, the local login is Administrator, which you can see in the Owner column of Worksets dialog box (Figure 6.11).

FIGURE 6.11

Workset and ele-
ment ownership

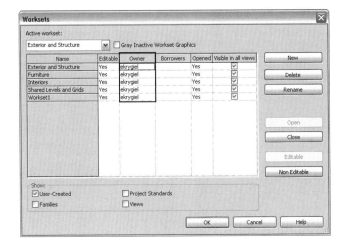

It can be a good idea to adjust this naming convention to help team communication and identification of who owns what on a project. In a smaller office, it might not be as necessary, but in a larger office or if you're working across multiple offices, clarification of ownership is vital. A good workflow is to change this name to a first name, last name, and phone extension. This way, team members can quickly identify and contact you if they need you to relinquish permission over a given element. To make this modification, follow these steps:

1. Navigate to the Application button, and choose Options at the bottom.

2. In the Options dialog box, select the General tab.

3. In the Username field, enter a new value (Figure 6.12). Click OK to exit. You'll need to close and reopen Revit for the change to take effect.

FIGURE 6.12

Changing the
default username

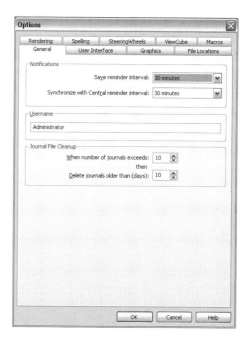

Once in a worksharing environment, every element in the file and added to the file belongs to a workset. To make sure that you are placing elements in the proper workset while working, there are a couple places to ensure the right workset is selected.

One such location is on the Collaborate tab, where we originated worksharing to begin with. In Figure 6.13, our active workset is Exterior and Structure. Note that this also tells us that the Exterior and Structure workset is not editable. What this means is that as a user, we have not taken ownership of this workset. However, as we mentioned earlier, you don't need to own a workset to add elements to the workset. It just needs to be visible in this window.

FIGURE 6.13

Changing the
active workset

The second location is new to Revit 2011 and is located in the status bar at the bottom of the application (Figure 6.14). This drop-down menu serves the same function as the Collaborate tab, but it allows you to visually verify the proper workset is active without having to bounce between tabs and interrupt your workflow. From this location you can also change the active workset and even open the Worksets dialog box using the small button to the left of the drop-down menu.

FIGURE 6.14

Changing the
active workset
from the status bar

A helpful tool located on the Collaborate tab is the Gray Inactive Worksets button. This disables all the elements that aren't active, helping you identify what elements are in your current, active workset. This is a temporary view state and will not affect any printing or other output.

Once in a workset environment, you can see or change an object's workset by accessing its Element Properties. At the bottom of the Element Properties dialog box, you can view which workset an object or group of objects belongs to, and you can modify that workset. Note that you can move elements to other worksets only if you own the elements. You do not need to own the entire workset to do this—just the individual elements.

Additionally, you can always tell what workset an object belongs to by hovering your mouse pointer over the object and viewing its workset in the status bar. This location will also display an object's family and category. In the example shown here, the chair is in the Interiors workset, in the Furniture category, and its type is an Armless Chair.

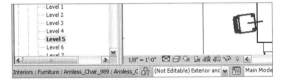

Saving Work

Once you begin working in a worksharing environment, it will eventually become necessary to save your work and share your progress with others in the model. There are three ways for you to both save work and view others' efforts:

Save   The Save button saves the work you've done to your local copy only; the work isn't shared or published back to the central file. This can be a useful step if you're in the middle of a process, want to make sure your work is saved, but aren't ready to share the changes with the rest of the team. You can find the Save tool either by clicking the Application button and selecting Save or by clicking the save icon on the Quick Access toolbar (QAT).

Synchronize With Central   You can use the Synchronize With Central (SWC) command when you are ready to publish your work to the central file for the rest of your team to see. Using SWC also acquires all the changes that other team members have made and loads those into your local file. You can access this command in a couple of ways. The first is on the Collaborate tab in the Synchronize panel, as shown in Figure 6.15. The Synchronize With Central button is located on the left of this panel.

FIGURE 6.15
Synchronize With
Central command
on the ribbon

Alternatively, you can use the Synchronize With Central button located on the QAT. Both buttons perform the same action and will open the Synchronize With Central dialog box (Figure 6.16). This dialog box gives you some additional tools to assist your workflow:

◆ The Compact Central File check box allows you to compact the model to save on disk space. It will take some additional save time, but it can temporarily decrease your file size significantly. This should not be seen as a permanent solution to managing a large file, however. Compaction will decrease the file size, but use of the file will expand the compacted elements. Reducing file size is discussed in Chapter 5.

◆ There are five additional check boxes that will be available (depending on what work you've done to the file) to allow you to relinquish or keep permission over the elements you've previously edited. Unchecking these boxes means that you will retain ownership over all the elements you currently own with the model. This can be useful if you are planning to continue working on the same elements and only want to publish recent changes of the model.

◆ A final check box, Save Local File Before And After Synchronizing With Central, allows you to save your changes locally, get any new changes from the central file, and then save locally again, ensuring your local copy is up-to-date. This is the longest of save options, and you might choose to uncheck this periodically if you're pressed for time or have a large file that typically takes longer to save.

FIGURE 6.16
Synchronize With
Central dialog box

Synchronize With Central ➤ Synchronize Now   By selecting the fly-out from the Synchronize With Central button on the QAT, you'll see another save option, shown in Figure 6.17. Choosing this option allows you to bypass the Synchronize With Central dialog box and simply sync your file immediately. Keep in mind that when choosing this option, you'll be saving your changes to the central file and relinquishing all your permissions over any elements you happen to own.

FIGURE 6.17
Using the
Synchronize
Now option

Saving at Intervals

Revit will remind you to save your work at regular intervals. Once worksharing is enabled, you will receive an additional reminder to synchronize with the central file as well as to save your work (Figure 6.18). You can always dismiss these dialog boxes by clicking Cancel at the lower right, but remember, it's always a good idea to save regularly so you don't lose any work.

FIGURE 6.18
Changes Not Syn-
chronized With
Central dialog box

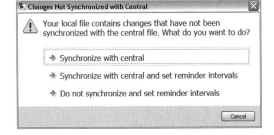

When the Save To Central dialog box appears, you'll have three options to choose from:

◆ Synchronize With Central, which will save identically to the Synchronize Now command

◆ Synchronize With Central And Set Reminder Intervals, which will synchronize your file, then pull up the Options dialog box, allowing you to set the intervals in which you receive this message

◆ Do Not Synchronize And Set Reminder Intervals, which will cancel all future reminders for the remainder of your Revit session

The reminder time shown in the dialog box can be modified at any time by clicking the Application button and selecting Options and then choosing the General tab.

Loading Work from Other Team Members

It is possible to update your model and review or load work from other team members without publishing your own work back to the central file. This process, called Reload Latest, basically updates your model and refreshes the content so you can continue working with current information. Since you are only downloading content from the central file, this process only takes a portion of the time a full SWC does. To do this, click the Collaborate tab on the ribbon, and choose Reload Latest from the Synchronize panel (Figure 6.19).

FIGURE 6.19
Using Reload
Latest

Moving Elements Between Worksets

Once your worksets have been established, you'll need to separate your existing model elements between those worksets. The easiest way to move elements between worksets is by subtracting them from a 3D view. The following exercise will walk you through moving elements from Workset1 to the worksets we have established using a subtractive method to locate and move the model geometry. Note this should be done by a single person who owns all the elements. This is will ensure there are no permissions issues when elements are being moved between worksets.

1. Open the default 3D view, {3D}, so you can see all of the model. Open the Visibility/ Graphics Overrides dialog box, and choose the Worksets tab. Choose to hide all the worksets except for Workset1, and click OK. This will turn off any elements that are visible on those worksets and allow you to "subtract" elements from this view as you move them to the nonvisible worksets.

2. Now, depending on your model size, you have a few options:

   ◆ For a smaller model, in your 3D view, select a comfortable number of elements and click the Element Properties button (if it is not active in your Project Browser). What constitutes a "comfortable" number of elements depends on your computer capabilities. Then use the Filter tool located on the Modify Elements tab to filter out all the elements that are in opposing worksets. As an example, if we select a series of elements in our Jenkins model, we can choose to keep the furniture and casework active and uncheck the remaining items. Click OK. Finally, in the Element Properties dialog box, choose a new workset (Figure 6.20).

FIGURE 6.20
Moving objects
between worksets

◆ For a larger model, it might first be necessary to select some individual components and move those separately. Although the process remains the same (select elements, change the workset using the Element Properties), the selection system can vary. Another example of moving elements by selection would be to highlight an exterior wall and use the Tab key to select a chain of exterior walls. Those can be moved to the Exterior and Structure workset.

3. Using the same technique, you can move the remainder of the site elements to their respective worksets. When the default 3D view is empty, you'll know that all the elements have been reassigned to new worksets.

At any point in this process, you can check your work by opening the Workset tab in the Visibility/Graphic Overrides dialog box and clearing all the boxes but one to see what is in each workset. Figure 6.21 shows the Furniture workset with all its elements.

FIGURE 6.21
The Interiors workset

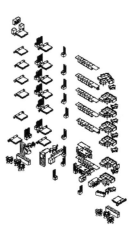

MOVING EVERY INSTANCE OF AN ELEMENT

A quick way to move every instance of an element type to a new workset is to use the Select All Instances option from the context menu. For example, select a chair in the model and right-click it. From the context menu, choose Select All Instances ➢ In Entire Project. This will select all the family elements in the entire model, allowing you to quickly move them all to the same workset with the Element Properties dialog box.

Another way to select all instances of an element is to right-click the family name in the Project Browser tree under the Family node. Simply navigate to your family in its proper category.

Understanding Element Ownership in Worksets

One of the fundamental processes in working in a workshared model is taking ownership of an element. You can do this to directly edit the element, or take ownership to keep other team members from editing an element key to your area of responsibility or your design process.

Determining whether you own an element is fairly easy. Simply select it. It will highlight in blue. If you do not own it, you will see three blocks, as shown in Figure 6.22. To take permission of an unowned element, simply click the stack of blocks. If you already own an element, you won't see any blocks, but the element will still highlight in blue.

FIGURE 6.22
Making an element
editable

There are a few other ways you can obtain ownership of an element or group of elements:

◆ Using the Workset dialog box, you can obtain permission of any workset and all the elements contained therein.

◆ Using the technique we just discussed, you can highlight any element or series of elements and take permission of them by clicking the blue stack of boxes.

◆ If you edit, move, or modify any element in Revit, Revit will automatically grant you permission over the element.

◆ You can right-click any element and choose Make Elements Editable from the context menu (see Figure 6.23). Note that you also have the ability to make editable the entire workset this object is on.

◆ You can right-click any element in the Project Browser under the Family node. In the context menu that appears, you can take ownership of a group or name of elements.

FIGURE 6.23
Making an element
editable using the
context menu

Using any of these options, if it is already owned by another team member, Revit will alert you and you will not be able to modify the element or take permission of it.

 **Real World Scenario**

ACCIDENTS HAPPEN

It's human nature: eventually an accident will occur on a project, and elements will get modified or deleted unexpectedly. It's important to know how to recover when these accidents occur.

On one project we worked on, someone new to Revit and new to the team was working on detailing windows in a three-sided building. In the detailing process, he somehow deleted one of the walls in the project. By deleting the wall, he also deleted the elevation as well as all the wall sections associated with that wall, along with any of the details in plan and section. When the new team member deleted the element, he wasn't aware of the mistake and then performed Synchronize With Central, publishing all the deletions to other team members. Fortunately, we caught the mistake before everyone performed a Synchronize With Central, and we did not have to resort to restoring the model from the previous night's backup. We were able to use another team member's local file to create a new central file, thereby minimizing the loss of work. Once everyone on the team made a new local copy, we were back in business.

Had the deleted elements been more isolated (like a conference room layout), recovery would have been much less invasive. In such a case, you simply group all the elements you would like to save, then right-click the group in the Project Browser. You'll have the option to save the group out of the file, which can then be inserted into a different file and ungrouped again.

Borrowing Elements

When working in a worksharing project, it is not always necessary to take ownership of an entire workset in order to begin editing elements. As we discussed earlier in this chapter, it is possible to take permission of singular elements (one by one or in groups). This process is referred to as *borrowing*.

By borrowing elements, team members can take ownership of only portions of a workset, leaving the remainder of the workset to be edited by someone else. Taking permission of elements in this style creates a more "take what you need" approach to editing and usually results in less overlap between team members.

If you need to work on an element that already belongs to someone else, Revit will alert you that the element(s) have already been checked out, and you'll be given the option to request permission.

Borrowing is a critical concept in Revit for multiuser teams; it allows users to transfer permission of objects without having to constantly save all their work to the central file and relinquish all worksets. Let's look at this interchange of permissions in more detail.

Requesting Permission

Imagine you are happily working away on your model in a workshared environment and you realize that someone else is an owner of an element that you need to modify. What do you do? When that situation occurs, you will be presented with a dialog box that allows you to request permission of that element from the other user (Figure 6.24). This will happen every time you are working in a model with worksharing enabled and you attempt to modify (even if it's indirectly) an element owned by another team member.

FIGURE 6.24
Placing a request
for permission

Looking at the dialog box, you have two options:

◆ You can click Cancel and not take permission of the element and then focus your efforts on another part of the design.

◆ You can click Place Request to ask your team member to relinquish permission over the element in question. When you click Place Request, the dialog box shown in Figure 6.25 opens.

FIGURE 6.25
Check Editability
Grants dialog box

Once you have placed your request, you're in a bit of a holding pattern. You cannot continue to edit this element until the other user has granted permission over it, and you cannot continue working on other portions of the project. It is also important to note that the other team member will not receive any notification through Revit that you have placed a request. You will need to contact the team member so your permission can be granted, and you can get back to work.

Once you've made your request known to your team member, you can click Check Now and see whether the request has been granted or whether there are additional steps you'll need to take to gain permission over that element. While this is happening, you always have the option to click Continue. This will undo your most recent edit to the element you are attempting to borrow and let you get back to working on another portion of the project.

Once the other user has granted your editing request and you click Check Now, you'll see the dialog box shown in Figure 6.26, alerting you that your permission has been granted and you can resume your workflow with your edits intact.

FIGURE 6.26
Permission
granted

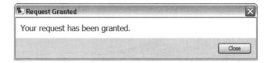

ALERTING THE TEAM TO PERMISSION REQUESTS

Since Revit doesn't currently have a tool to alert team members that you are requesting permission of elements within the model, it is necessary for you to contact them yourself. Depending on the project phase and the number of people in the model, these requests can happen several times a day. You'll want to find a way that is the least disruptive to your workflow so you can remain focused on the project. A great way to get attention of your other team members for permission is through an intraoffice IM or chat service. It is invasive enough to alert another team member to the fact that you are requesting permission of an element and can get their attention even if they are on a call or talking with someone else.

Another way to get a hold of team members is by calling them on the phone. If your office doesn't support IM services, this might be your best recourse. A good way to make this process quicker is to click the Application button, click Options, and choose the General tab. Append your phone extension to your username so team members can reach you quickly.

Granting Permission

Now suppose you are on the other end of this scenario, where you have been working away and you receive a call or IM or visit from someone looking to acquire permission for an element you own in the model. How do you grant permission?

On the Worksets panel of the Collaborate tab, there is a button called Editing Requests. Clicking this button will open a dialog box allowing you to see all the outstanding requests you have for elements in the model.

To deal with the request for permission, you have a few options, as shown in Figure 6.27:

Grant Gives permission for the requested element to your team member

Deny/Retract Denies permission to your team member

Show Shows you which element or elements have been requested to help you make an informed decision

Once you are ready to grant permission of the element, one of two things will happen. If there have been no edits to the element, you can simply click Grant and the permission for the element will be transferred to your team member.

If you have made edits to this element or one that is dependent or hosted to the element in question, you will be alerted that you'll need to SWC before the permission can be switched. Your team member on the other end will also need to SWC to receive the recent changes, and then they can begin editing the most recent version of that element. Permission requests that require an SWC are flagged in this dialog box by an asterisk next to the permission request.

FIGURE 6.27
Editing Requests
dialog box

Relinquishing Permission

It is not always necessary to wait for a request from another team member to relinquish permission over your elements. Fortunately in Revit, there is a tool to do just that. On the Worksets panel of the Collaborate tab is a button called Relinquish All Mine (Figure 6.28). This feature returns the permissions for any elements you have not edited back to the central file so they are freely available to the rest of your team.

FIGURE 6.28
Relinquish
All Mine

Closing Revit

Eventually, you will need to close your project and Revit and leave for lunch or go home for the day. Don't worry—the project will still be there tomorrow. But in the meantime, it's important to understand how to close the project correctly so you don't accidentally leave the office and maintain permission over any elements. This situation—where a team member has accidentally left the office and not closed Revit or relinquished permissions—leaves the other team members without a way to edit those elements or even request permission. So that you are not the unfortunate victim of their wrath upon your return, make sure you close Revit properly.

The most thorough way to close the file is to simply quit the application completely. You can do this by clicking the red X at the upper right or clicking the Application button and selecting Close. Both will provide the same results. You'll be presented with a dialog box asking you to save your file locally. After that, you'll see a second dialog box asking you to Synchronize With Central (Figure 6.29). As we noted, if you do not SWC, your changes will not appear on the network for other users to see and you'll maintain permission over some of your elements.

FIGURE 6.29
Saving to the central file

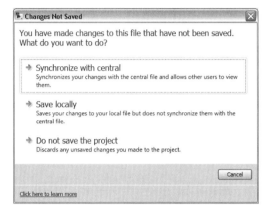

GETTING PERMISSION OF SOMEONE ELSE'S OBJECTS

Inevitably it happens on a project. Someone leaves their desk for a meeting or goes home without relinquishing permission over all their elements and worksets, leaving the rest of the team in a lurch. The best solution is to contact the person and gain their network password and just synchronize their file with central. This will ensure that all their changes as well as permissions are synchronized and no work is lost. If that is not possible, there is a workaround for this problem. We should note that the workaround will result in the loss of the work by the missing team member, but will clear up all the permissions issues.

If the immediate team needs outweigh the potential loss of the missing person's work, follow these steps:

1. Open a new session of Revit.

2. Click the Application button, select Options, and choose the General tab.

3. Change the name listed in the Username field from your username to the person's whose permissions you are looking to release.

4. Create a new local file of the project and open it. Now simply SWC, and all their elements will be available to the team to edit.

5. Before closing Revit, be sure to go back to the Application button, select Options, and select the General tab so you can change the username back to your own.

Sometimes you've opened a file to do something simple such as review a detail or print a set. You might have inadvertently taken permission over an element or group of elements but not performed any edits. On closing the file, you'll get a dialog box like Figure 6.30, alerting you that you have permissions that need to be reconciled. Again, the proper workflow is to choose to relinquish elements and worksets.

FIGURE 6.30
Editable Elements
dialog box

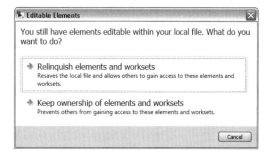

The Bottom Line

Understand key worksharing concepts.   Once the team has created local files, it is necessary to understand how to keep both the local file and central file up-to-date as changes occur on the project. This ensures that everyone is working from an updated and recent copy of the model at all times.

Master It   Once you've begun working out of your local file, how do you publish your changes to the central file? How do you download changes from the central file to your local file?

Use worksharing in your project.   Knowing how to activate and utilize worksharing is indispensible to working in a team environment using Revit.

Master It   How do you transition a single-user Revit file to a multiuser environment using worksharing?

Manage workflow with worksets.   Once the central file has been created, you'll need to organize and structure the model into logical worksets to maintain workflow with Revit.

Master It   How do worksets differ from layers in 2D CAD? What are some logical ways to create worksets within a model?

Understand element ownership in worksets.   Editing elements in a central file means you have sole ownership over further changes to those elements. Understanding the permissions will be critical to working in a team.

Master It   How do you edit an element in the model if someone has already taken permission of it in a worksharing environment?

Chapter 7

Working with Consultants

Whether you work on large or small projects—on residential, commercial, or industrial building types—collaboration is an almost certain aspect of the workflow you will encounter when implementing BIM. This chapter will discuss important considerations for interdisciplinary coordination as well as the tools within Revit to help manage the process. While this chapter will cover aspects of collaboration solely utilizing the Revit platform, Chapter 8, "Interoperability: Working Multiplatform," will focus on collaborating with other software programs.

In this chapter, you'll learn to:

- ◆ Prepare for interdisciplinary collaboration
- ◆ Collaborate using linked Revit models
- ◆ Use Copy/Monitor between linked models
- ◆ Run interference checks

Preparing for Collaboration

Working alone in Revit will deliver measureable increases in productivity, quality, and consistency; however, the true benefit of BIM is the ability to effectively collaborate between design disciplines with contractors and deliver useful data to facility operators.

Social BIM

The difference between these working paradigms has been described as *lonely BIM* vs. *social BIM* by John Tocci of Tocci Building Corporation (`www.tocci.com`), which is a forward-thinking construction company with headquarters in Woburn, Massachusetts. Lonely BIM can also be referred to as the use of "isolated BIM techniques for targeted tasks," whereas social BIM is the underpinning for the goals set forth by organizations such as the National Institute for Building Sciences' (NIBS) buildingSMART Alliance (according to Penn State's BIM wiki at `http://bim .wikispaces.com/BIM+Project+Execution+Planning+Project`). The ability to support information exchanges, such as the facility life cycle helix concept shown in Figure 7.1, necessitates the proper use of 3D models and nongraphic data in a highly collaborative environment. Furthermore, the buildingSMART Alliance and the National BIM Standard (NBIMS) stress the need for platform-neutral, open interoperability *between* applications, not just within a program such as Revit.

FIGURE 7.1
BIM data
exchanges accord-
ing to NBIMS

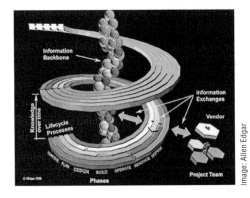

Image: Allen Edgar

BIM EXECUTION PLAN

Once a project team decides to participate in social BIM—either through desire or the requirements of a client—they must decide how to deliver this information in a useful way to all constituents throughout the project life cycle. Whether your client requires it or not, you should
develop a BIM *execution plan* to define the goals, exchanges, and results related to the use of BIM.

The buildingSMART Alliance (www.buildingsmartalliance.org)—in an effort sponsored
by the Charles Pankow Foundation, The Construction Industry Institute, Penn State Office of
Physical Plant, and the Partnership for Achieving Construction Excellence (PACE)—has created a BIM Execution Planning Guide and template BIM Execution Guide. You can find the two
guides at the Penn State Computer Integrated Construction (CIC) website: www.engr.psu.edu/
ae/cic/bimex.

One of the most critical parts of a BIM execution plan is the definition of the goals and uses
of BIM. If you are just beginning your implementation of Revit, perhaps you are using it because
it is the latest parametric program to enter the AEC industry, or perhaps you are attempting to
increase your drafting productivity. Defining clear and concise reasons for implementing BIM
on each project will help you define where to concentrate your modeling efforts. According to
the buildingSMART Alliance, "a current challenge and opportunity faced by the early project
planning team is to identify the most appropriate uses for Building Information Modeling on a
project given the project characteristics, participants' goals and capabilities, and the desired risk
allocations." A listing of the common uses of BIM along with potential value opportunities and
required resources is also available on the Penn State CIC website.

According to the American Institute of Architects' (AIA) "Integrated Project Delivery: A Guide,"
a BIM execution plan "should define the scope of BIM implementation on the project, identify
the process flow for BIM tasks, define the information exchanges between parties, and describe
the required project and company infrastructure needed to support the implementation." To be
clear, the development of such a plan does not imply the application of integrated project delivery
(IPD). IPD is "a project delivery approach that integrates people, systems, business structures and
practices into a process that collaboratively harnesses the talents and insights of all participants
to optimize project results, increase value to the owner, reduce waste, and maximize efficiency
through all phases of design, fabrication, and construction." For the purpose of this chapter,
we will consider only the collaboration and coordination between members of a project design
team, not the interactions with a client or contractor.

For additional reading on IPD, refer to these sources:

◆ IPD and BIM white papers by Ted Sive: `www.tedsive.com`

◆ Integrated Practice/Integrated Project Delivery: `www.aia.org/ipd`

◆ buildingSMART Alliance: `www.buildingsmartalliance.org`

◆ McGraw-Hill Construction, BIM Special Section: `bim.construction.com`

Coordination in Revit

The coordination process within Revit will begin by linking multiple files together to form a composite view of your building project. A project can be divided in many different ways to meet a variety of workflow requirements. Most often each discipline will develop at least one separate Revit project file, many of which will be linked into each other for reference. Because there are several workflow possibilities, this chapter will focus on the coordination among a traditional design team consisting of the following:

◆ Architect

◆ Structural engineer

◆ Mechanical, electrical, and plumbing engineers

The workflow within a traditional design team is more complex than you might assume. If you were to graph the dependencies and coordination between these parties (Figure 7.2), you would see a web of primary relationships (architect to/from structure, architect to MEP) and secondary relationships (structure to/from mechanical and piping).

FIGURE 7.2
The relationships of interdisciplinary coordination

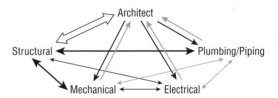

In addition, these relationships can be further parsed into physical and logical relationships. If we use mechanical and electrical as an example, you can see that making sure that a light fixture is not hitting the bottom of a duct is a physical relationship, while making sure that the electrical design properly accounts for the load of the heating coil in a variable air volume (VAV) box (being designed by the mechanical engineer) is a logical relationship.

It is the complexity of these possible workflow scenarios that makes this process prone to errors and a major source of coordination between the traditional design team. So, what are the tools that can be used for collaboration between Revit products? There are three distinct tools that typically are used in a collaboration scenario:

Linked Models   Linking models together using the Revit link tool provides full visual fidelity of the referenced content, showing the complete context of the other discipline's data, fostering a complete understanding of their geometry. The data can also be controlled and shown in any manner appropriate to the use. You can turn it on or off, half-tone the data, or enhance it with color or line pattern overrides. Linking also provides support for the Interference Check and Coordination Monitor tools.

Copy/Monitor   Copy/Monitor is a powerful tool available in all products built on the Revit platform and is considered the most intelligent of the coordination tools offering these benefits:

> **Intelligent Bond**   Using Copy/Monitor, you can choose items from another model that you want to monitor for change and the degree to which you want to monitor them.

> **Multiple Modes**   Many people do not realize that there are two distinct modes of this tool: Copy and Monitor. Using the correct mode can provide additional functionality flexibility.

> **Geometry Creation**   When this tool is used in Copy mode, you can create geometry in the source file based on objects in the linked file. In this mode, you will also be establishing a monitor relationship.

Interference Check   In many cases, the only workflow requirement is to verify that items from another discipline are not interfering with your items. The Interference Check tool can be used to check between categories within a single model or between linked models.

 Real World Scenario

INDIANA UNIVERSITY BIM REQUIREMENTS

In 2009, the Indiana University (www.iu.edu) Architect's Office announced that it would require the use of BIM on all projects with a capital value of over $5 million. Accompanying the announcement was the release of the IU BIM Standards and Project Delivery Requirements, which included a BIM execution plan template and IPD template—developed under the guidance of Autodesk and SHP Leading Design (www.shp.com/leadingdesign). Although the university's BIM requirements may seem new, the desire to ensure the maximum reuse of information has been evolving at IU for several years, beginning with its implementation of integrated GIS tools for campus and facility management in 1996.

One important excerpt from these requirements focuses on the organization of the interference checking (aka *clash detection*) process. Within the IU BIM Standards & Guidelines for Architects, Engineers, & Contractors, rules have been established for classifying clashes between modeled elements. Level One clashes are considered critical and include ductwork and piping clashing with ceilings, rated walls, or structure; and equipment clearances interfering with structure. Level Two clashes are less critical but include casework clashing with electrical fixtures and structure versus specialty equipment. Finally, Level Three clashes are still important but are a lower priority. These include casework clashing with walls and plumbing interfering with mechanical equipment.

These requirements may be defined differently by other clients, but it's important to understand the importance of using interference checking tools for logical groups of model elements. Checking for clashes throughout an entire model will yield a plethora of unusable data and will limit the effectiveness of model-based coordination.

For more information, visit the IU BIM site at www.indiana.edu/~uao/iubim.html or read a review of these standards at the Arch | Tech blog at www.architecture-tech.com/2009/11/indiana-university-requires-bim.html.

Given the range of available tools for collaboration in Revit, they are not necessarily applicable to all interdisciplinary relationships. As shown in Figure 7.3, only the most appropriate tools should be applied to each collaborative situation. Note that these situations are merely suggestions based on the experience of the authors. Your needs for collaborative workflows may vary.

FIGURE 7.3
Suggestions for collaboration tools to be used between disciplines

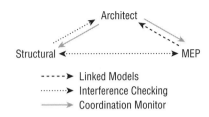

Architect – Structural Engineer   The relationship between the architect and structural engineer is becoming closer as we strive for lighter structures and more innovative design. In many respects, structural engineers may be affecting the building aesthetic as much as the architects. As such, this workflow may be considered the most crucial and should be bi-directional.

Architect – Structural Engineer: Coordination Monitor   By using Copy/Monitor, the structural engineer is able to create a strong, intelligent link between the structural and architectural models. In doing so, he can easily track the changes in the architect's model that will affect the structural design. He is also able to create geometry in his model using these tools, which can be directly or indirectly related to architectural elements such as walls and floors.

Remember that coordination of relationships for datum (grids and/or levels) should be established at the beginning of a project. For example, does the architect "own" the levels and the grids—or will the structural engineer? Conflicts due to a lack of proper planning will negatively impact the effective use of the Copy/Monitor tools on your projects.

Structural Engineer – Architect: Interference Check   The architect's primary requirement for the structural model is to include the structure in context, and to know if the structure is interfering with any architectural elements. For this workflow, it is recommended that the architect link in the structural model and use interference checking. The rules governing what clashes are considered critical may be established by a client's BIM standards and protocols.

Architect – MEP Engineer   The relationship between architecture and MEP is not quite as dynamic as that between architecture and structure, but represents specific opportunities to benefit from collaboration.

Architect – MEP Engineer: Coordination Monitor   The MEP engineer needs to link in the architect's model to have the architectural model for context and positional relationships for ceiling based items, and the avoidance of clashes. Copy/Monitor is used to copy and monitor the architects levels and rooms. These room objects take on the additional properties, such as light levels and airflow. Note that levels are required to copy or monitor the rooms.

MEP Engineer – Architects: Linked Models The architect's primary benefit from linking in the MEP model(s) is the ability to reference this geometry within the context of the architectural model and drawings. Although there is not usually a strong need to use the Coordination Monitor from MEP back to architecture, interference checking may be required under certain circumstances.

Structural to MEP engineer(s) This relationship is almost always best served by cross-linked models using interference checking. The most important aspect of collaboration between these disciplines is the early detection and correction of clashes.

Linked Models

The first rule governing all Revit-to-Revit coordination situations is that all linked project files must be generated with the same platform version of Revit. For example, the architecture model must be generated with Revit Architecture 2011, the structure model must be generated with Revit Structure 2011, and the MEP model must be generated with Revit MEP 2011. In a worksharing environment, it is also important to ensure that the computers of all team members working on a project have the same build of the agreed-to Revit version installed (Figure 7.4). As discussed earlier in this chapter, a BIM execution plan should include an agreement on all modeling and coordination software to be used on a project, including the versions of each listed program.

FIGURE 7.4
Linked files must use the same platform version, while all worksharing team members should use the same build.

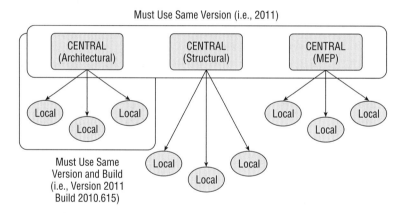

You can find the build information for your Revit product by clicking the Help drop-down button and selecting About. As shown in Figure 7.5, the build appears at the upper right of the About Autodesk Revit Architecture 2011 dialog box.

FIGURE 7.5
Click the Help button flyout and select About to find the build of your Revit software.

SHARED POSITIONING

In the collaborative process of sharing information via linked models, the coordinated positioning of each model is of paramount importance. Agreement on a common coordinate system and origin must be included in every project's BIM execution plan to ensure accuracy. This section will help you develop a fundamental understanding of the coordinate systems within Revit so you can configure and manage them in your projects. For a more complete history of coordinate systems and various examples of using them within Revit, we recommend the following class material from Autodesk University 2009, available at www.au.autodesk.com:

◆ AB118-3 Finding Your Way Around Shared Coordinates, By Teresa Martin, Ideate Inc.

◆ AB9114-1 Autodesk Revit Collaboration: Shared Coordinates for Projects Big and Small, By Steve Stafford, AEC Advantage, Inc.

There are two coordinate systems in a Revit project: *project internal* and *shared*. Each system has essential features and limitations.

Project Internal   Every Revit project has an internal coordinate system referred to in several places as Project. You can find this reference in the type properties of datum measuring objects such as levels and spot coordinates as well as in the settings for exporting CAD files. The project coordinate system cannot be changed and your model should be constructed within a *one mile radius* of the project origin. The true origin in Revit is referred to as the Project Start Up Point and the Project Base Point can be reset to this point by setting it to unclipped, right-clicking on the icon and selecting Move To Start Up Location.

A complementary component of the project internal coordinate system is the view orientation of Project North. This setting is the default and can be found in the View Properties of any plan. We strongly recommend that your model is created in an orthogonal relationship to project north or as you expect the plans to be oriented on a typical sheet. Your project's actual relation to True North will be established via shared coordinates.

Shared Coordinates   According to Ideate's Teresa Martin, "shared coordinates are simply a way for the project team to utilize the same definitive work point." In other words, the shared coordinate system consists of a single origin and true north orientation which can be synchronized between models and even AutoCAD drawings. In the diagram shown in Figure 7.6, you will see an architectural model and structural model linked together. Each model was created using a different project base point (not the recommended method), but their shared coordinates were synchronized.

LIMITATIONS ON USING SHARED COORDINATES FOR EXPORTING

Although you can use either Project Internal or Shared as the setting for Coordinate System Basis when exporting CAD formats, there are some limitations. If you are exporting sheet views, the plan data will always use the Project Internal coordinate system. Using the XRef Views On Sheets option during export does not change this limitation. We recommend using views—not sheets—for issuing 2D CAD backgrounds to project participants not using Revit.

The shared coordinates are also not supported if you export your project to IFC format. Only the project internal coordinates are used. If you are planning to utilize IFC exported data in tools such as Solibri Model Checker, BIMServer, TOKMO or Horizontal Glue; you will have to either manually transform the coordinates between linked models after export or make sure that each linked model in your project has the same relation to the project internal origin before beginning the project.

FIGURE 7.6
Diagram of the relationship between project base points and shared coordinates in linked models.

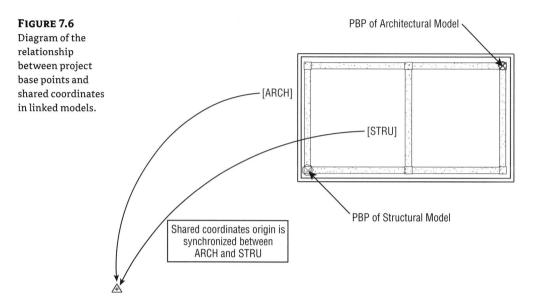

You can export views from Revit using the Shared setting for Coordinate System Basis; however, there are limitations when using shared coordinates for exporting. Refer to Chapter 8 for more detailed information on exporting.

ACQUIRING OR PUBLISHING COORDINATES

When you attempt to synchronize shared coordinates between linked projects, there are two tools to achieve this: Acquire Coordinates and Publish Coordinates. A simple way to understand the difference between these tools is to think of them in terms of pulling versus pushing:

♦ Acquire = Pull

♦ Publish = Push

It is important to understand the situations where you would pull or push coordinates between linked files. A typical workflow for establishing a synchronized shared coordinate system on a single building project would be as follows:

1. A site model is generated in which the survey point in Revit is coordinated with geodetic survey markers or station lines. The site model is linked into the architectural Revit model. This file can be placed manually, then moved and rotated into a position relative to the building. *Do not move or rotate your building to the linked site model!*

2. From the Manage tab, select Coordinates, then Acquire Coordinates. Pick the linked file and the origin of the shared coordinate system and angle of true north in your Revit model will be synchronized with those in the linked file.

3. For all engineers or consultants using Revit, they should obtain a copy of the site model and repeat steps 1 and 2. When linking other project models that have already been synchronized with the site model, they can be placed using the Auto - By Shared Coordinates option.

ACQUIRING COORDINATES FROM A CAD FILE

A common scenario in a project workflow begins with the architect commencing a design model and receiving a 2D survey file in DWG format from a civil engineer. The survey is drawn in coordinates that are geospatially correct but may not be orthogonal to true north. The architect should create the model close to the internal project origin; however, the architect will need to ensure the building and survey coordinates are synchronized for properly oriented CAD exports and for coordination with additional linked Revit models from engineers in later phases of the project.

The architect will link the 2D CAD file into the Revit model but will first manually place it—moving and rotating the CAD file to be in proper alignment with the building model. Once the link is in place and constrained (or locked), the architect will acquire the coordinates from the DWG survey by switching to the Manage tab and from the Project Location panel, selecting Coordinates ➢ Acquire Coordinates, and then clicking the DWG link. This will not affect any views that are oriented to Project North—only those set to true north will display the orientation established by the coordinates acquired from the survey file.

For a campus-style project in which you might be creating multiple instances of a linked building model, you would most likely use Publish Coordinates to push information from a site model into the linked building model. Here's how that would work in a hypothetical scenario:

1. Assuming a site model and building model were created in Revit, you would begin by opening the site model and linking the building model into the site.

2. Adjust the position of the first instance of the linked building model to location A.

3. From the Manage tab in the ribbon, select Coordinates then Publish Coordinates and pick the linked model.

4. The Location Weather and Site dialog box will open and you will create a duplicate location named **Location A** as shown in Figure 7.7.

FIGURE 7.7
Creating multiple locations for a single linked model.

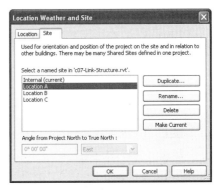

5. Copy the linked building model as required for each subsequent location. Repeat steps 2–4 for each copy.

6. When you close the site model and open the building model, you can link the site model to the building using any of the named location references you *pushed* into the building model.

USING PROJECT BASE POINT AND SURVEY POINT

In prior versions of Revit, locating the project origin or shared coordinate point was only accomplished by using an imported AutoCAD file or by using spot coordinates and moving elements as required. Revit now provides two objects to identify these points: the *project base point* and the *survey point*. In the default templates, these points are visible in the floor plan named Site; however, they can also be displayed in any other plan view by opening the Visibility/Graphics Overrides dialog box, selecting the Model Categories tab and expanding the Site category as shown in Figure 7.8.

FIGURE 7.8

Project base point and survey point are found under Site in Visibility/ Graphics Overrides.

Project Base Point   The Project Base Point (PBP) defines the 0,0,0 point of the project. Notice that we are not calling it the *origin*. Using that term, you might confuse the PBP with Revit's internal project origin. The unclipped PBP *can* be moved in relation to the internal origin, thus creating a secondary reference point for spot coordinates, spot elevations and levels—as long as the measuring control is set to Project in the respective type properties. Moving the clipped PBP icon is the equivalent of using the Relocate Project tool, moving the project relative to the shared coordinates system.

Unless your project requires the use of a secondary point of reference other than the survey point, we recommend you **do not** adjust the PBP and make sure your building model lies within a close reference of this point such as the corner of a property line or intersection of column grids A and 1.

Survey Point   The survey point is the equivalent of a station pin or geodetic survey marker in a civil engineering drawing (Figure 7.9). This is the point that will be coordinated to real geospatial coordinates. For coordination with Autodesk Civil 3D, the survey point is used when a Revit project is exported to the ADSK file format.

FIGURE 7.9

Survey point can be considered similar to a real world geodetic survey marker.

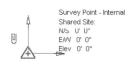

Note that specifying a particular location for the survey point based on civil engineering data is not a requirement. For smaller projects, the survey point and shared coordinates may never be used at all; however, these are critical in the use of analytical tools for daylighting and solar analysis.

To further expand your understanding of these points and what happens when they are modified, we have created a sample file for your reference. Open the file c07-Shared-Points.rvt from this book's companion web page (www.sybex.com/go/masteringrevit2011). In this file you will find three copies of the floor plan Level 1. Each is configured to display the project coordinates, the shared coordinates and a combination of the two. There are also two types of spot coordinates—one indicating project coordinates in which the values are prefixed with the letter p; the other indicates shared coordinates with the prefix of s. You can open these three floor plans and tile the windows (View tab, Window panel, Tile or type the keyboard shortcut WT) to get a better sense of how these points affect each other (Figure 7.10).

FIGURE 7.10
Tiled windows to examine the affect of project and shared coordinates.

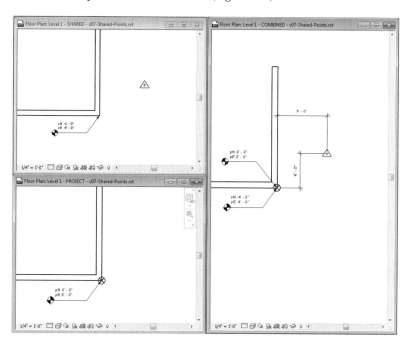

Within this sample file, you can explore the effects of moving the project base point and survey point on your model's coordinates. When selected, the project base point and survey point have paperclip icons that determine the behavior of the points when you move them. Clicking the paperclip icon changes the state from clipped to unclipped and back to clipped.

Following is a list of the possible point modifications and explanations of how they affect the project. Note that in most cases you shouldn't have to move the survey point or project base point if you are using a linked civil file (2D or 3D) and acquiring the coordinates from the linked file.

Project Base Point (PBP): Clipped

◆ Move the PBP

◆ PBP values change

◆ Project-based spot coordinates don't change

◆ Model elements 'move' relative to shared coordinates

Moving a clipped PBP is the same as using Relocate Project. That is, the model elements maintain their relationship to the PBP, but the relationship of the PBP to the survey point is changed.

Project Base Point: Unclipped

◆ Move the PBP

◆ PBP values change

◆ Project-based spot coordinates change

◆ Model doesn't move

Unclipping the PBP essentially *detaches* it from the internal project origin. Moving the unclipped PBP is really only used to affect the values reported in spot coordinates set to the Project origin base. It does not have any effect on exported files.

Survey Point (SP): Clipped

◆ Move the SP

◆ SP values don't change

◆ Shared spot coordinates change

◆ Model doesn't move

The clipped survey point represents the origin of the shared coordinate system. Moving it is the equivalent of setting a new origin point. Use caution if you must move the shared coordinates origin if linked models already exist in which the shared coordinates have already been synchronized. In such a case, each linked model must be opened and manually reconciled with the model in which the origin has changed.

Survey Point: Unclipped

◆ Move the SP

◆ SP values change

◆ Shared spot coordinates don't change

◆ Model doesn't move

Moving an unclipped survey point essentially doesn't do anything. It doesn't affect spot coordinates and it doesn't affect the origin of exported files.

USE PINNING TO PROTECT COORDINATE ORIGINS

An excellent way to prevent accidental modification of your project's coordinate systems is to pin them. To do this, you must first make sure the survey point and project base point are visible in a view (as we discussed earlier in this section). Next, select each point and click the Pin button from the Modify panel when the Modify | Project Base Point or Modify | Survey Point ribbons appear.

ATTACHMENT VS. OVERLAY

Linked Revit models utilize what we will call a *portability setting* that is similar to the way XREFs are handled in AutoCAD. Although this setting is not exposed when you initially link a Revit model, you can modify the setting by switching to the Insert tab and selecting Manage Links. Change the setting in the Reference Type column as desired (Figure 7.11).

FIGURE 7.11
Determining the Reference Type of linked Revit models

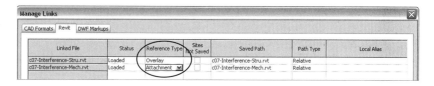

Attachment   The Attachment option ensures that the linked model will be included if the host model is subsequently linked into other hosts. For example, if Project A is linked into Project B as an *attachment*, when Project B is linked into Project C, Project A will automatically be included as well.

Overlay   The Overlay option prevents linked models from being included if the host model is subsequently linked into other hosts. For example, if Project A is linked into Project B as an *overlay*, when Project B is linked into Project C, Project A will not be included.

LINKS WITH WORKSHARING

If you are utilizing linked Revit models where one or more of the project files have worksharing enabled, there are a few guidelines to follow as well as tangible benefits to be reaped. Be sure to read more about worksharing in Chapter 6, "Understanding Worksharing."

The first guideline is to ensure that the files received from consultants are set up as central files within your own domain. Even though you may not have direct access to your consultants' servers, Revit will attempt to reconcile the location of each project model's central file location. We recommend opening each received Revit file and using the following steps to set up a copy as a central file:

1. From the Application button, select Open ➢ Project.

2. In the Open dialog box, make sure you have the worksharing-enabled project selected and check the Detach From Central option (Figure 7.12).

FIGURE 7.12
Open a worksharing project detached from its central file.

3. After the file opens, return to the Application button, and select Save or click the save icon on the Quick Access toolbar (QAT). Note that the Detach From Central option has created an unnamed project.

4. Save the project to a new location. When a worksharing project is detached from its central file, the first save will automatically consider the project a new central file. If you did not use the Detach From Central option when opening, you must click the Options button in the Save dialog box and choose the option Make This A Central File After Save (Figure 7.13).

FIGURE 7.13
Save option to establish a new central file

5. Finally, click the Synchronize And Modify Settings button in the QAT and be sure to check the option to relinquish all user-created worksets before clicking OK to complete the process (Figure 7.14).

FIGURE 7.14
Relinquish all user-created worksets when saving a file that has been detached from central.

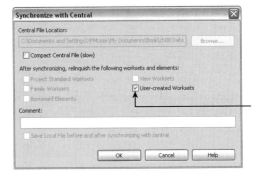

When the host model is enabled for worksharing, we recommend you create and reserve a workset for each linked Revit model, such as Link-RVT-Structure or Link-RVT-HVAC. This simple step will allow your team members to choose whether they would like any, all, or none of the linked models to be loaded when working on a host model. To enable this functionality, use the Specify setting in the drop-down options next to the Open button.

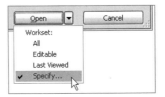

When the Worksets dialog box appears, select the worksets reserved for the linked models and set their Open/Closed status as you desire. The benefit of using worksets to manage linked Revit models is the flexibility it offers a project team. When a workset containing a linked model is closed, the linked model is unloaded only for that person—it does not unload for the entire team.

Additional flexibility can be leveraged through the use of the Workset parameter in both Instance and Type Properties of a linked model. In a large and complex project that consists of multiple wings where some of the wings are identical, each wing may consist of multiple linked models: architecture, structure, and MEP. Figure 7.15 shows a simplified representation of such a design where Wings A, D, and E are identical as are Wings B, C, and F.

FIGURE 7.15
Schematic representation of a complex project assembled with multiple linked models

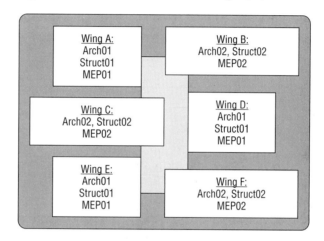

In Figure 7.15, there are two Revit models for each discipline that represent wing design 01 and 02 (Arch01, Arch02, and so on). Note there are three instances of each linked model. For each instance of a linked model, the Workset parameter can be specified where the workset instance property represents the wing and the type property reflects either the entire discipline or one of the discipline models. For example:

♦ Instance workset: Wing A

♦ Type workset: Link-Architecture01 or simply, Link-Architecture

Using this example, you can choose to open the Wing A workset, which would load all the discipline models, but only for Wing A. Or, you could choose to open the Link-Architecture workset, which would load only the architectural models, but for all the wings. Note that the workset Type Properties can be modified only after a linked model has been placed in your project. Access this setting by selecting an instance of a linked model and opening the Properties Palette, and then click Edit Type. Although this functionality can offer a variety of benefits to your project team, it should be used with care and proper planning as it can adversely affect model visibility if you are using worksets for visibility manipulation.

Worksharing-enabled linked models also afford you the flexibility to adjust the visibility of project elements for the entire project, without relying on individual settings per view or maintenance of view templates. For example, grids and levels are not usually displayed from linked models because their extents are not editable in the host model and the graphics may not match those in the host model. Without worksets, the owner of the host model would have to establish visibility settings for the linked model within all views and hopefully manage those settings in view templates. Assuming the owner of the linked model maintains the levels and grids on an agreed workset such as Shared Levels and Grids, you will be able to close that workset in one place, thus affecting the entire host project. To modify the workset options for linked Revit models, follow these steps:

1. Open the Manage Links dialog box and switch to the Revit tab.

2. Select one of the linked files and click the Manage Worksets button.

3. In the Linking Worksets dialog box, select the worksets you would like to unload, click the Close button, and then click Reload.

4. Click OK to close the Manage Links dialog box.

RELATIVE PATHS OF LINKED MODELS

If your team is working in a situation where your project file(s) is regularly transferred between multiple locations throughout the design process, you may find it difficult to maintain linked files (they are unloaded when the file is returned), even if you are using relative paths. To alleviate this problem, try keeping the linked models and CAD files within subdirectories of the central file. For example, if your central file is saved in W:\Architecture\BIM, try keeping linked CAD files in W:\Architecture\BIM\Links-CAD and linked Revit models from consultants in W:\Architecture\BIM\Links-RVT.

BENEFITS AND LIMITATIONS

To summarize using linked Revit models, let's review some of the benefits and limitations. You should carefully consider these aspects not only when preparing for interdisciplinary coordination, but also when managing large complex projects with linked files.

The following list highlights some of the benefits:

Tagging Elements in Linked Files   A new feature in the Revit 2011 platform of products, most model elements (not rooms) from a linked model can be tagged in a host model. Linked views can also be utilized if the annotation exists in the linked model and needs to be displayed in the host.

Scheduling Elements in Linked Files   In the Fields tab of the Schedule Properties dialog box, check the option Include Elements In Linked Files.

Copying/Pasting Elements from Linked Files   In a host model, use the Tab key to select any individual element within a linked file and you can use standard copy and paste techniques to create a copy of the element in the host model.

Hiding Elements in Linked Files   In addition to having full control of a linked model's visual fidelity through object styles, you can use the Tab key to select an individual element in a linked file and use the Hide In View commands as you would on any element within the host model.

The following list highlights some of the limitations:

Joining Walls   Walls cannot be joined between linked Revit models. Consider alternative graphic techniques such as using coarse scale black solid fill to mask unjoined walls.

Opening Linked Models   You cannot have a host model with loaded linked models open in the same Revit session as the linked model files. Either separate sessions of Revit must be launched or the host file must be closed before opening a linked model.

EXERCISE: USING LINKED MODELS

CERT OBJECTIVE

Before beginning the exercises in this chapter, download the related files from this book's companion website: www.sybex.com/go/masteringrevit2011. The project files in each section's exercise should be saved because the lessons will build upon the data. In this exercise, you will do the following:

◆ Link the architectural model to a blank project

◆ Establish shared coordinates

Note that the structural model is essentially a blank project with a few element types specifically built for this chapter's lessons.

1. Open the sample project file c07-1-Structure.rvt.

2. Switch to the Insert tab and select Link Revit.

3. Navigate to the file c07-2-Architecture.rvt.

4. Set the Positioning option to Auto – Center To Center and click Open.

5. Activate the South elevation view and use the Align tool to bring the linked model's Level 1 down to align with Level 1 in the host model if necessary.

   Remember, linked files should be adjusted to keep the geometry in the host model as close to the host's internal project origin as possible.

6. Switch to the Manage tab and from the Project Location panel, select Coordinates ➢ Acquire Coordinates. Pick the linked model.

   Notice that the elevation value displayed in the level within the current file has changed to match the shared elevation in the linked file. This is because the Elevation Base parameter of the level's Type Properties has been set to Shared.

7. Save the project file for subsequent exercises in this chapter.

MODIFYING ELEMENT VISIBILITY IN LINKED FILES

Once you have linked one or more Revit files into your source project file, you may want to adjust the visibility of elements within the linked files. By default, the display settings in the Visibility/Graphics dialog box are set to By Host View for linked files, which means model objects in the linked files will adopt the same appearance as the host file. In the following exercise, we'll show you how to customize these settings to turn the furniture off in the linked file and then display the room tags.

1. Continue this exercise with the file c07-1-Structure.rvt which you saved with the linked architectural model.

2. Activate the Level 1 floor plan from the Project Browser.

3. Go to the View tab in the ribbon, locate the Graphics panel, and select Visibility/Graphics. In the Visibility/Graphics dialog box, select the Revit Links tab.

   You will see the linked architectural model listed as an expandable tree. Click the plus sign next to the linked file name and you will see a numbered instance of the link. This allows you to customize the visibility for each instance of a linked file if you have multiple copies of the link in the host file.

4. In the row displaying the linked file name, click the button in the Display Settings column which is labeled By Host View. This opens the RVT Link Display Settings dialog box.

5. To begin customizing the display of elements in the linked file, you must first choose the Custom option in the Basics tab as shown in Figure 7.16. This will enable all of the options in each tab of the RVT Link Display Settings dialog box.

FIGURE 7.16
Enable all custom display settings for a linked RVT file.

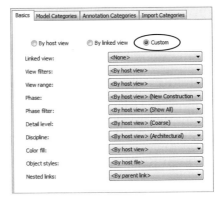

6. Select the Model Categories tab and choose <Custom> in the drop-down list at the top of the dialog box as shown in Figure 7.17.

FIGURE 7.17
Enable custom display settings for model categories of a linked RVT file.

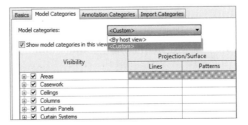

7. Clear the checks from the following categories: Casework, Furniture and Furniture Systems.

8. Click OK to close all open dialog boxes.

You should observe that all the furniture and casework from the linked architecture file are no longer visible in the Level 1 floor plan. It is important to mention that in a typical architecture to structure collaboration scenario, the Structural Engineer is likely to have a view template in which typical architectural elements are already hidden. In such a case, the default By Host View settings would be sufficient. The previous exercise illustrates a scenario where additional visual control is required.

While the previous exercise focused on the display of model elements, a slightly different approach is required to utilize annotation elements from a linked file. In the following exercise, we will show you how to display the room tags from the linked architectural model. Note that many other tags can be applied to linked model elements in Revit 2011 products.

1. Continue with the c07-1-Structure.rvt file saved from the previous exercise and make sure you have activated the Level 1 floor plan.

2. Open the Visibility/Graphics dialog box and select the Revit Links tab.

3. The button in the Display Settings column should be labeled as *Custom* based on the previous exercise. Click the Custom button to open the RVT Link Display Settings dialog box.

4. Select the Basics tab and click the Linked View drop-down box. You will see the floor plans available for reference in the linked file. Only view types similar to the current view in the host file will be available for use as a linked view.

5. Select the linked view named Level 1-A-Anno.

6. Click OK to close all open dialog boxes.

After completing these steps, you should see the room tags from the linked architectural file in the host file. Remember that you can tag other model elements in linked files. Try using the Tag By Category tool to place some door tags on the linked architectural model.

Coordination Tools

Once you have established the configuration of linked Revit models for your project, the next step is to create intelligently bound references between specific elements within the models. In the past, CAD users might have referenced files containing grid lines or level lines to establish some level of coordination between one user's data and another. Note that these elements in CAD are merely *lines*—not datum objects as they are in Revit. If these referenced elements were modified in a CAD setting, the graphic appearance of the referenced lines would update, but there would be no additional automated response to the geometry. It would be the responsibility of the recipient to update any referring geometry in their host files.

Revit's coordination tools—Copy/Monitor and Coordination Review—allow a project team to ensure a high degree of quality control while achieving it at an increased level of productivity. These tools can function on datum (levels and grids) as well as model elements such as columns, walls, and floors. The Copy/Monitor command is used first to establish the intelligent bonds between linked elements and host elements, whereas the Coordination Review command automatically monitors differences between host and linked elements which were previously bound with the Copy/Monitor command.

Although these tools are indeed powerful and have no similar discernable similarities to CAD workflows of the past, it is important to employ proper planning and coordination with your design team constituents. The familiar adage of "quality over quantity" holds true for the implementation of coordination tools in Revit. It may not be necessary to create monitored copies of all structural elements within the architectural model. How would this affect project-wide quantity takeoffs for the sake of minor improvements in graphic quality?

Again, we reiterate the necessity of developing a BIM execution plan to determine important aspects of the collaboration process. When using specific coordination tools such as those in Revit, teams might plan on issues such as these:

- "Owner" of grids and levels

- "Owner" of floor slabs

- Are structural walls copied, monitored, or just linked?

- How often are models exchanged?

- How are coordination conflicts resolved?

A seemingly powerful BIM tool will not replace the need for professional supervision and the standard of care implicit to respective disciplines in the building industry. As such, there is no substitution for the most important part of effective collaboration: *communication*. Without open and honest communication, the coordination tools will discover conflicts, but the results may be ignored, dismissed, or overwritten to the detriment of the team's progress.

COPY/MONITOR

CERT OBJECTIVE

The Copy/Monitor command allows you to create local copies of linked elements for better graphic control of the elements, while maintaining an intelligent bond to the linked elements. If the linked element changes in a subsequent iteration of the project file, the changes are detected in the Coordination Review tool, which will be discussed later in this chapter.

With the project file saved from the previous exercise, switch to the Collaborate tab and select Copy/Monitor ➢ Select Link. Pick the linked architectural model and the ribbon will change to Copy/Monitor mode. Click the Options icon (Figure 7.18); note that the options seen in the Copy/Monitor tool in Revit Architecture are slightly different from those in the Structure and MEP products. For the purpose of this book, we will focus only on the options available in Revit Architecture.

FIGURE 7.18

Element tabs available for Copy/Monitor in Revit Architecture

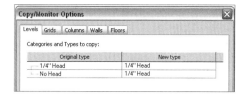

As shown in Figure 7.18, the Copy/Monitor Options dialog box in Revit Architecture is divided into five tabs representing the elements available to be copied and/or monitored. For each element tab, there is a list called Categories And Types To Copy. As shown in Figure 7.19, the Floors tab lists the available floor types in the linked model in the left column and host model floor types in the right column. Notice that any of the linked types can be specified with the option Don't Copy This Type. This can be used for quality control if your project's BIM execution plan states that certain elements are not to be copied. For example, if walls are not to be copied, switch to the Walls tab and set all linked wall types to Don't Copy This Type.

FIGURE 7.19

The Copy/Monitor Options dialog box allows customization for intelligent collaboration.

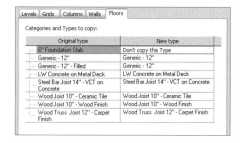

At the bottom of the Copy/Monitor Options dialog box, you will find a section called Additional Copy Parameters for each element tab (Figure 7.20). Note that the additional parameters are different for each element category. For example, when levels are copied and monitored, an offset and naming prefix can be applied to accommodate the difference between the finish floor level in a linked architectural model and the top of steel level in the host structural model.

FIGURE 7.20

Additional copy parameters can be applied to each element category.

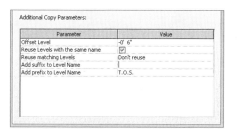

Let's take a closer look at each of the element category options available for the Copy/Monitor tool:

Levels In most cases, the difference between the location of a structural level and an architectural level may lead to the presumption that you would not want to copy levels between files; however, this is a good case where you can apply additional copy parameters to build in an offset distance. Keep in mind the offset will apply to all copy/monitor selections. Thus, if a structural level needs to be offset by a different value, simply create the level in the host model and use the Monitor command to create the intelligent bond to the linked model's level. The difference will be maintained through any modifications in the linked model.

Grids Copying in the grids is usually a strong workflow. You can use the options on these tabs to convert the grid bubbles used by the architect into those used by the structural engineer. It is also possible to add a prefix to the grid names. For instance, you could add the value "S-" in the prefix field and then grid "A" from the architectural model will come into the structural model as "S-A."

Columns The structural engineer can chose to replace any column—architectural or structural—in the architectural model with an appropriate structural column; however, this implies that the architect will maintain an understanding of where differentiating column types would exist. Realistically, the structural elements should only exist in the structural engineer's model and then linked into the architectural model. The architect may then choose to either copy/monitor the linked structural columns with architectural columns (which act as finish wrappers) or to simply place architectural columns along the monitored grid lines. In the latter option, architectural columns will move along with changes in grid line locations, but would not update if structural columns are removed in the linked model.

Walls and Floors Similar to columns, structural walls that are important to the coordination process may be better managed in the structural model and linked into the architectural model. If you decide to use a copy/monitor relationship for these types of elements, it is best to create uniquely named wall types for structural coordination. Name such wall types in a manner that makes them display at the top of the list in the Copy/Monitor Options dialog box. You can do this by adding a hyphen (-) or underscore (_) at the beginning of the wall type name.

Finally, make sure that you select the check box Copy Windows/Doors/Openings for walls or Copy Openings/Inserts for floors so that you also get the appropriate openings for those components in the monitored elements.

EXERCISE: USING COPY/MONITOR

Continue with the project file saved in the previous exercise in this chapter. In this exercise, you will do the following:

◆ Use Copy/Monitor to establish new levels and grids

◆ Use Copy/Monitor to create floors

◆ Link the new structural model back to the architectural model

◆ Use the Monitor option for grids in the architectural model

These steps will establish the intelligent bonds between elements in the host file with the related elements in the linked model. With the file c07-1-Structure.rvt open (saved from the previous exercise), activate the South elevation view.

1. Switch to the Collaborate tab and select Copy/Monitor ➤ Select Link. Choose the linked model.

2. On the Copy/Monitor tab, click the Options button.

3. Select the Levels tab and enter the following options under Categories And Types To Copy:

- ¼" Head = TOS Head

In the Additional Copy Parameters section, set the following options:

- Offset Level: -0' 6"
- Add prefix to Level Name: T.O.S.

4. Select the Grids tab and enter the following options under Categories And Types To Copy:

- ¼" Bubble = ¼" Square

5. Select the Floors tab and enter the following options under Categories And Types To Copy:

- Arch Slab 6" = LW Concrete on Metal Deck
- Set all other Original Types to Do Not Copy This Type

In the Additional Copy Parameters section, set the following option:

- Copy Openings/Inserts: Yes (checked)

6. Click OK to close the Options dialog box.

7. From the Copy/Monitor ribbon, choose the Copy button.

8. Select the Level 2 and Roof levels in the linked model. Levels in the host model should be created 6" below the linked levels with the prefix T.O.S. (Top Of Structure).

Note that there is already a Level 1 in the host model. You will need to use the Monitor tool to establish a relation to the Level 1 in the linked model.

9. From the Copy/Monitor ribbon, choose the Monitor button and select the Level 1 in the host model. Note that Revit will only allow you to select levels in the host model for the first pick.

10. Select Level 1 in the linked model to complete the monitored relationship.

11. Activate Section 1 and return to copy mode by clicking the Copy button in the Copy/Monitor ribbon.

12. Select the floor in the linked model at Level 2.

13. Activate the Level 1 floor plan and make sure the Copy tool is still active. Check the Multiple option in the Options Bar.

14. Select all the visible grids using any selection method you prefer.

15. Click the Finish button in the Options Bar to complete the copy process for the grids. Do not click the Finish icon in the Copy/Monitor ribbon without finishing the multiple selection mode first.

16. Click the Finish icon in the Copy/Monitor ribbon to exit Copy/Monitor mode.

If you now select any of the grids or levels in the host file, you will see a monitor icon near the center of the element. This indicates that the intelligent bond has been created between the host and the linked element and will evaluate any modifications in the linked file whenever the file is reloaded.

Save and close the file c07-1-Structure.rvt and then open the file c07-2-Architecture.rvt. Using the procedures you have learned earlier in this chapter, link the structural file into the architectural model. Placement should be done in the Level 1 floor plan using Auto – By Shared Coordinates positioning.

Use the Copy/Monitor tools in Monitor mode to establish the relationships of the grids between host and linked models. This will ensure that changes to grids in either model will be coordinated.

COORDINATION REVIEW

After intelligent bonds have been established between elements in linked models, it is the purpose of the Coordination Review tool to support the workflow when datum or model elements are modified. This tool was designed to allow the recipient of linked data to control how and when elements in host models are modified based on changes in the linked models.

When a linked model is reloaded, which will happen automatically when the host model is opened or by manually reloading the linked model in the Manage Links dialog box, monitored elements will check for any inconsistencies. If any are found, you will see a warning message that a linked instance needs coordination review.

The coordination review warning is triggered when any of the following scenarios occur:

◆ A monitored element in the linked model is changed, moved, or deleted.

◆ A monitored element in the host model is changed, moved, or deleted.

◆ Both the original monitored element and the copied element are changed, moved, or deleted.

◆ A hosted element (door, window, opening) is added, moved, changed, or deleted in a monitored wall or floor.

◆ The copied element in the host file is deleted.

To perform a coordination review, switch to the Collaborate tab and select Coordination Review ➢ Select Link. After picking one of the linked models, you will see the Coordination Review dialog box, which will list any inconsistencies in monitored elements (Figure 7.21).

FIGURE 7.21
The Coordination
Review dialog box
lists inconsisten-
cies in monitored
elements.

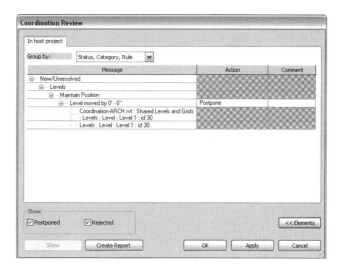

For each of the changes detected in Coordination Review, one of the following actions can be applied. Note that actions resulting in changes to elements will only be applied to the host model; they do not modify elements in a linked model. Also note that not all options are available for all monitored elements.

Postpone   Takes no action on the monitored element and changes the message status so that it can be filtered out or considered later.

Reject   Select this action if you believe the change made to the element in the linked file is incorrect. A change must then be made to the element in the linked file.

Accept Difference   Accepts the change made to the element and updates the relationship. For example, if a pair of grids was 200 mm apart, and one was moved to 300 mm away, the change would be accepted, and the relationship would now be set to 300 mm.

Modify, Rename, Move   The command name changes based on the action. If the name of the monitored element has changed, the command reads Rename. If a column or level is moved, the command is Move. If a grid is changed or moved, the command is Modify.

Ignore New Elements   A new hosted element has been added to a monitored wall or floor. Select this action to ignore the new element in the host. It will not be monitored for changes.

Copy New Elements   A new hosted element has been added to a monitored wall or floor. Select this action to add the new element to the host, and monitor it for changes.

Delete Element   A monitored element has been deleted. Select this action to delete the corresponding element in the current project.

Copy Sketch   The sketch or boundary of a monitored opening has changed. Select this action to change the corresponding opening in the current project.

Update Extents   The extents of a monitored element have changed. Select this action to change the corresponding element in the current project.

As you can see, Coordination Review can be a powerful tool to support the collaboration process. Remember that such a tool may not be appropriate for all elements at all times. For example, instead of copying and monitoring columns and grids, it may be sufficient to copy and monitor only grids, as the columns placed in your host model will move with the grids anyway.

EXERCISE: USING COORDINATION REVIEW

In this exercise, you will utilize two files that have already been linked together with monitored elements between both files. You can download the files c07-Review-Arch.rvt (architectural model) and c07-Review-Stru.rvt (structural model) from this book's companion website: www.sybex.com/go/masteringrevit2011. In this exercise, you will do the following:

◆ Modify elements in the architectural model

◆ Use Coordination Review to address these changes in the structural model

Remember that you can't have a host model and a linked model open in the same session of Revit. To make this lesson easier, you can launch a second session of Revit. Open c07-Review -Arch.rvt in one session and c07-Review-Stru.rvt in the other.

1. In the architectural model, activate the Level 1 floor plan and make the following modifications:

   ◆ Move grid line F to the north by 2'-0"

   ◆ Rename grid 6 to 8

2. Save the architectural model and switch to the structural model. Open the Manage Links window, select the linked structural model, and click Reload. Click OK to close the dialog box.

3. In the structural project, switch to the Collaborate tab and choose Coordination Review ➢ Select Link. Select the linked structural model.

4. When the Coordination Review dialog box opens, you will see changes to monitored elements detected in the reloaded architectural model (Figure 7.22). Note you may need to expand some of the statuses and categories to reveal the detected change and the drop-down list under the Action column.

FIGURE 7.22
Coordination Review detects changes to monitored elements.

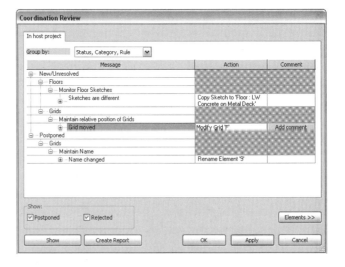

5. Apply the appropriate modifying action to each of the detected changes. (Copy the sketch of the changed floor, modify the moved grid, and rename the numbered grid.)

6. Click Apply and OK to close the dialog box.

In the previous exercise, you might have noticed the appearance of a monitored floor sketch. Why did a floor sketch change if you only moved a grid and renamed another? The answer lies in constraints and relationships. The exterior wall in the architectural model was constrained to be 2'-0" offset from grid line F. When it was moved, the exterior wall was moved to maintain the offset. The sketches of the model's floor slabs were created using the Pick Walls tools, creating an intelligent relationship to the wall. The modified grid affected the wall, which modified the floor, and the Coordination Monitor tools ensured that all changes were detected and presented to you for action.

Interference Checking

In addition to uses such as asset management, digital fabrication, and cost estimation, 3D coordination is one of the most important uses of building information modeling. It has an enormous potential to reduce costs of construction through the computerized resolution of clashing building elements as well as exposing opportunities for alternate trade scheduling or prefabrication. The key component to achieving 3D coordination is interference checking, also known as *clash detection*.

 **Real World Scenario**

INDIANA UNIVERSITY DEFINES CLASHES

As we mentioned earlier in this chapter, not only are some building and facility owners requiring BIM processes and deliverables for new projects, they are defining how these processes are to be utilized. When you focus on interference checking, the myriad of potential clashes can be distilled into a prioritized grouping of building elements. Borrowing from Indiana University's BIM Standards & Guidelines for Architects, Engineers, & Contractors, the following is an intelligent approach to the organization of potential interferences. (Always remember that the priorities listed here are based on the requirements of one organization. The needs of your firm and those of your clients may vary.)

LEVEL ONE CLASHES

Clashes in these categories are considered the most critical to the coordination process. They usually relate to more costly systems or construction techniques that are more costly to delay or reschedule.

◆ Mechanical Ductwork and Piping vs. Ceilings

◆ Mechanical Ductwork and Piping vs. Rated Walls (for coordination of dampers and other mechanical equipment needs)

◆ Mechanical Ductwork and Piping vs. Structure (columns, beams, framing, etc.)

◆ All Equipment and Their Applicable Clearances vs. Walls

◆ All Equipment and Their Applicable Clearances vs. Structure

◆ Mechanical Equipment and Fixtures vs. Electrical Equipment and Fixtures

◆ Mechanical Ductwork and Piping vs. Plumbing Piping

LEVEL TWO CLASHES

These categories of clashes are considered important to the design and construction process, but are less critical than those designated as Level One.

◆ Casework vs. Electrical Fixtures and Devices

◆ Furnishings vs. Electrical Fixtures and Devices

◆ Structure vs. Specialty Equipment

◆ Structure vs. Electrical Equipment, Fixtures, and Devices

◆ Ductwork and Piping vs. Electrical Equipment, Fixtures, and Devices

◆ Ductwork vs. Floors

LEVEL THREE CLASHES

These clashes are considered important to the correctness of the model; however, they will usually change on a regular basis throughout the design and construction process.

◆ Casework vs. Walls

◆ Plumbing Piping vs. Electrical Equipment, Fixtures, and Devices

◆ Plumbing Piping vs. Mechanical Equipment, Fixtures, and Devices

◆ ADA Clear Space Requirements vs. Doors, Fixtures, Walls, Structure

TOOLS FOR INTERFERENCE CHECKING

The Interference Check tool in Revit is a basic tool supporting 3D coordination. You can use it within a single Revit project model or between linked models. You can also select elements prior to running the tool in order to detect clashes within a limited set of geometry instead of the entire project.

For more powerful clash detection capabilities, Autodesk offers Navisworks Manage (www .autodesk.com/navisworks), which is a multiformat model reviewing tool with various modules supporting phasing simulation, visualization, and clash detection. Figure 7.23 shows an example of a model in Navisworks Manage comprised of Revit, Tekla Structures, and AutoCAD MEP. Some of the benefits of using Navisworks for interference checking over Revit include automated views of each clash, grouping of related clashes, enhanced reporting, clash resolution tracking, and markup capabilities. Although many other 3D model formats can be opened directly in Navisworks, Revit models can be exported directly to Navisworks format with an exporter add-in.

FIGURE 7.23

3D coordination model in Navisworks Manage

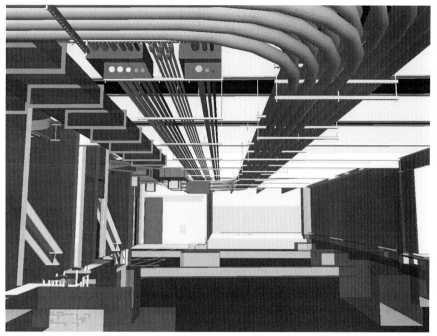

EXERCISE: RUNNING AN INTERFERENCE CHECK

CERT
OBJECTIVE

Let's take a look at the interference checking process within Revit. For this exercise, you will need to download three sample files to your computer or network: c07-Interference-Arch.rvt, c07-Interference-Mech.rvt, and c07-Interference-Stru.rvt. You can download these files from this book's companion web page: www.sybex.com/go/masteringrevit2011. The sample files are already linked into each other using relative paths, so be sure to place all three files into the same folder.

1. Open the file c07-Interference-Mech.rvt and activate the 3D view named Coord-STR -MEP. You should see some ductwork in the host model and the linked structural model. The architectural model has been turned off in this view.

2. Switch to the Collaborate tab, find the Coordinate panel, and choose Interference Check ➤ Run Interference Check.

3. When the Interference Check dialog box appears, choose c07-Interference-Stru.rvt from the Categories From drop-down list in the left column. Select Structural Framing in the left column and Ducts in the right column (Figure 7.24).

4. Click OK to close the dialog box.

FIGURE 7.24
Select categories
to be included in
an Interference
Report.

5. The Interference Report window will appear, listing all clashes detected between the categories you selected. The list can be sorted by either Category 1 or Category 2, representing the left and right columns in the Interference Check dialog box, respectively. In Figure 7.25, one interference condition has been selected and the corresponding element is highlighted in the 3D view.

FIGURE 7.25
Results of an
interference check
are displayed in
the Interference
Report window.

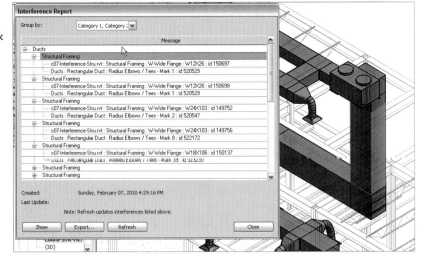

Note that you can navigate in the 3D view using any method (mouse, ViewCube, or Steering Wheel) while keeping the Interference Report open. This facilitates resolution of the clashing items. The results of the interference check can also be exported to an HTML format report. Simply click the Export button and specify a location for the report. You can now share this report with other members of your design team for remedial actions on linked models.

The Bottom Line

Prepare for interdisciplinary collaboration.   Proper planning and communication are the foundation of effective collaboration. Although only some client organizations may require a BIM planning document, it is a recommended strategy for all design teams.

Master It   What are the key elements of a BIM execution plan?

Collaborate using linked Revit models.   The most basic tool for collaboration is the ability to view consultants' data directly within the context of your own model. Project files from other disciplines can be linked and displayed with predictable visual fidelity without complex conversion processes.

Master It   How can worksharing complement the use of linked Revit models?

Use Copy/Monitor between linked models.   The Coordination Monitor tools establish intelligent bonds between elements in a host file and correlating elements in a linked model. They also support a workflow that respects the needs of discrete teams developing their own data, perhaps on a different schedule than that of other team members.

Master It   How can grids in two different Revit projects be related?

Run interference checks.   Interference checking—also known as *clash detection*—is one of the most important uses of building information modeling. It is the essence of virtual construction and has the greatest potential for cost savings during the physical construction process.

Master It   How do you find interfering objects between two linked Revit models?

Chapter 8

Interoperability: Working Multiplatform

In the previous chapter, we discussed working with others in a Revit-to-Revit environment; however, often you'll need to work with data from other software platforms. For example, you may need to coordinate data from other disciplines, reuse legacy data, or integrate disparate design platforms. Fortunately, there are several ways to use external data within your Revit model in both 2D and 3D. We will discuss not only the methods of importing and exporting data but also when to use each method and the reasons for using specific settings. In this chapter, you'll learn to:

◆ Use imported 2D CAD data

◆ Export 2D CAD data

◆ Use imported 3D model data

◆ Export 3D model data

◆ Work with IFC imports and exports

The BIM Curve

Based on a 2004 study, the National Institute of Standards and Technology (NIST) reported annual losses of $15.8 billion in the building industry due to insufficient interoperability. This underscores a problem that building information modeling as a whole is designed to address. Adequate interoperability will help rectify the problem illustrated in Figure 8.1, sometimes known as the *BIM curve*.

In Figure 8.1, the downward spikes in the lower line at the end of each project phase represent a loss of knowledge and acquired data. This usually occurs when a project is exported from BIM to a 2D CAD format or is printed to paper. Project data is then gradually reconstructed in another software platform. The upper line represents a more ideal paradigm where data and knowledge are gradually increased throughout the life of the project—a paradigm supported by BIM and full interoperability.

While full interoperability between BIM platforms is the ideal scenario, we realize that you are likely to be working with constituents who are using 2D CAD software or non-BIM 3D modelers. This chapter will show you not only how to export data and to use imported data in a variety of ways but also when and why to apply different settings to ensure the best results.

FIGURE 8.1
The BIM curve shows loss of data without interoperability at project milestones.

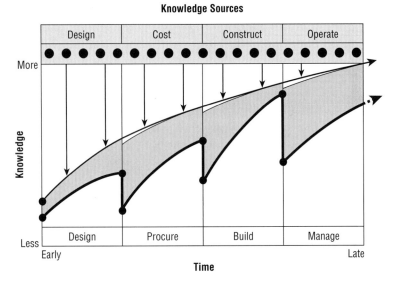

Overview of Importing

Although Revit provides ample means to generate 2D documentation based on a rich multi-dimensional (3D, 4D, 5D, and so on) model, there are a few real-world scenarios in which CAD data must be integrated with the building information model. Such scenarios might include the following:

- Using CAD details developed within your firm
- Coordinating with other firms using CAD software
- Converting projects from CAD to Revit
- Using external modeling tools for conceptual massing
- Using complex component models from other software

Import Settings

When you are importing data from a DWG or DXF file, layers within the file are assigned a Revit line weight based on the weight assigned to each layer. If the layer line weights are set to Default in the CAD file, they will follow a translation template you can configure in Revit that maps the layer colors to Revit line weights. To access these settings in Revit, select the Insert tab and click the shortcut arrow at the bottom right of the Import panel. This will open the Import Line Weights dialog box, shown in Figure 8.2.

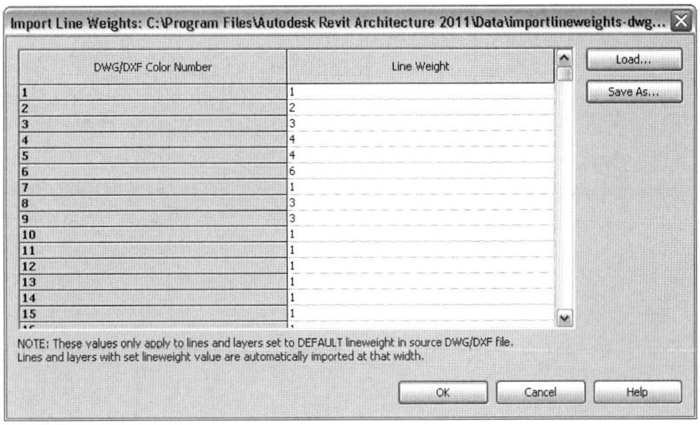

FIGURE 8.2

Defining settings
for imported
DWG/DXF line
weights

As you can see in the title bar of this dialog box, these settings are stored in a text file (TXT) in C:\Program Files\Autodesk Revit Architecture 2011\Data. There are several predefined text files based on international CAD standards for layer color:

◆ AIA (American Institute of Architects)

◆ BS1192 (British Standard)

◆ CP83 (Singapore Standard)

◆ ISO13567 (International Standards Organization)

Click the Load button to import one of these predefined line weight import templates or your own. Based on the unique needs of some projects, you might also consider creating customized import settings files and storing them along with the rest of your project data.

IMPORTING THE LINE WEIGHTS SETTING IN *Revit.ini* FILES

The file location for the imported line weights map is stored in the Revit.ini file under the following category:

```
[Directories]
ImportLineweightsNameDWG=< Full path to TXT file >
```

If you are using any kind of automation scripts to set up standards, your import line weights template file location can be written into the Revit.ini file for all your users. This will ensure consistency if several team members are linking CAD data into your Revit project.

FONT MAPPING

Another important aspect for imports and links is Revit's ability to map shape-based fonts to TrueType fonts. Usually a remnant of older CAD standards based on graphic performance, CAD files may contain fonts such as Simplex, RomanS, or Monotxt that do not have matches in standard Windows fonts. The `shxfontmap.txt` file tells Revit which TrueType font to substitute for each specified SHX font. You can find this text file at `C:\Program Files\Autodesk Revit Architecture 2011\Data`.

If your firm frequently uses imported CAD data as an integrated part of your final documentation, the `shxfontmap.txt` file should be configured to map your standard CAD fonts to your standard Revit fonts. This file should then be copied to the workstations of all team members using Revit. Failure to do so may result in undesirable results when utilizing linked CAD files in a worksharing environment.

Importing vs. Linking

You can bring CAD data into Revit in two ways: importing and linking. Each method has advantages and disadvantages.

Importing   Similar to the Insert command in AutoCAD, importing data integrates the CAD data into the Revit project but does not allow the imported data to be updated if the original CAD file is modified. In such a case, the imported data would have to be deleted and reimported. It also does not give you an easy way to purge the layers, linetypes, and hatch patterns of the imported file after it has been deleted.

Importing is the only method supported for accurate representation of 3D model geometry. The method for integrating external model data will be discussed later in this chapter in *Importing 3D Data*.

Linking   A linked CAD file in Revit is analogous to an external reference (XRef) in AutoCAD. When the original CAD file is modified, its reference is automatically updated in Revit. Linking also allows you to easily unload or remove a file when it is no longer needed, which will leave no trace of the file's contents after removal.

Linked data cannot be modified in Revit unless it is converted to an import in the Manage Links dialog box (Insert ➤ Manage Links) and then exploded.

Linking is the preferred method for external data integration; however, too many linked files will make it slower to open a Revit project. Although ceiling plan fixture layouts may change with every design iteration (where linking is preferred), static standard details that all share a minimal amount of standardized layers, linetypes, hatch patterns, text, and dimension styles might be better suited as imports.

COLLECT CAD LINKS IN A LINKED REVIT FILE

Another option to manage many CAD references in larger projects is to create a separate Revit project containing only the linked data. If the CAD data is placed with the Current View Only option, you must use linked views between Revit models. If the linked data does not use this option, it will be visible as any other modeled element in a linked Revit model.

Options During Importing/Linking

After you have configured the necessary settings for inserted CAD data and decided on whether to import or link, you will need to understand certain options during the import/link process. We'll discuss the preferred settings for each of the options based on real-world situations in sections *Importing 2D Data* and *Importing 3D Data*. To place your first CAD file into a Revit project, switch to the Insert tab and select either Link CAD or Import CAD. No matter which tool you use, there will be several important options at the bottom of the command dialog box, as shown in Figure 8.3.

FIGURE 8.3
Options available for import/link

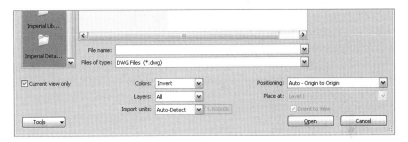

Let's examine the meaning of the settings in this situation:

Current View Only When this option is selected, the linked or imported file can be seen only in the view in which it was inserted and is thus considered a view-specific element. In a worksharing-enabled project, this data will be assigned to the view's workset. More often than not, you will want to choose this option to limit the number of views in which the referenced data will appear. If you need this data in other views, you can copy and paste it from one view to another.

If the option is not selected, the linked file can be seen in all views, including 3D, elevations, and sections. In a worksharing-enabled project, this data will be assigned to the active workset. A benefit to using links in a worksharing environment is the ability to create a workset specifically for linked data and uncheck its Visible In All Views option. The CAD file(s) placed in this manner will not appear in every view but are available when you need them by adjusting the workset visibility in the Visibility/Graphics Overrides dialog box.

Colors As stated earlier in the chapter, colors don't really matter for linked CAD files being used for model conversion; however, using Invert or Preserve may help distinguish the CAD data from the modeled elements during the conversion process.

Layers These options allow you to import or link all the layers, only the layers visible when the CAD file was last saved, or a selected group of layers you choose from the linked file in a separate dialog box. (Layers are a DWG-based terminology. Revit supports the same functionality with Levels from DGN files.)

Import Units For CAD files generated in an original program (that is, DWG from AutoCAD or DGN from MicroStation), the Auto-Detect option works well. If you are linking CAD data that has been exported from a different program, such as DWG exported from Rhino, you should specify the units to the respective CAD file.

Positioning To maintain consistency in a multilevel project during a CAD-to-Revit coordination or conversion process, you should use Auto – Origin To Origin or Auto – By Shared

Coordinates. Origin To Origin will align the world coordinates origin of the CAD file with the project internal origin. Although Autodesk claims Auto – By Shared Coordinates is only for use with linked Revit files, it can be used with CAD files if rotation of true north becomes inconsistent using the Origin To Origin option.

Place At   This option is available only if Current View Only is not selected; it specifies the level at which the inserted data will be placed.

Manipulating Linked Data

Once you have data imported or linked into a Revit project, you have several ways of manipulating the data to suit your needs:

Foreground/Background   This setting only applies to linked or imported CAD files placed with the Current View Only option. With the inserted file selected, a drop-down menu will appear in the Options Bar to adjust whether the data appears above or below your modeled Revit content.

Pay close attention to this option when integrating 2D CAD data with an existing Revit model—sometimes linked or imported CAD data may not appear at all until you set the option to Foreground because of floors or ceilings obscuring the 2D data.

Visibility of Layers/Levels   The layers or levels within a linked or imported CAD file can be accessed in two ways, the easiest of which is the Query tool. First, select a linked or imported CAD file, and you will see a special Modify panel appear at the right end of the ribbon. Select the Query tool and then pick an object in the CAD file.

You will see the Import Instance Query dialog box (Figure 8.4). Using this tool, you can hide the layer or level by clicking the Hide In View button. Note that the Query tool will remain active even after you click any of the command buttons in the Import Instance Query dialog box, and you must press the Esc key or select the Modify button.

FIGURE 8.4
Querying objects within a linked CAD file

The second way to make layers or levels in imported or linked CAD files invisible is to use the Visibility/Graphic Overrides dialog box by switching to the View tab and selecting Visibility/Graphics from the Graphics panel. Once the dialog box opens, select the Imported Categories tab, as shown in Figure 8.5. Every imported or linked CAD file in the project will be listed. Expand any listed file to expose the list of layers/levels within that file and use the checkboxes to customize visibility of the link within the current view. Note that this method is the only way to restore visibility of layers/levels that were hidden with the Query tool.

FIGURE 8.5

Controlling visibility of layers within imported objects

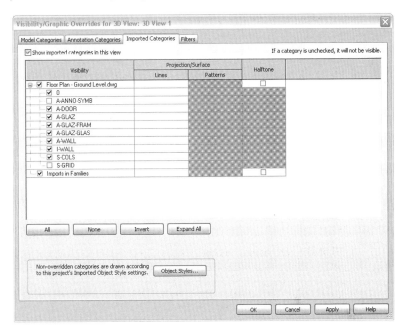

IMPORTED DATA IN FAMILIES

Remember that 2D and 3D data imported into Revit families will be listed under the Imports In Families category in both the Visibility/Graphic Overrides and Object Styles dialog boxes. They will not appear as separately listed files.

Graphic Overrides   If you need to change the appearance of the content within a linked or imported CAD file, you can accomplish that at the project level or within an individual view. To change a CAD file's appearance throughout the project, select the Manage tab on the ribbon, and click Object Styles in the Settings panel (Figure 8.6). Select the Imported Objects tab and expand any of the imported or linked CAD files to change the color, line weight, line pattern, or material of the layers/levels within the referenced file. Note that changing these properties in the row of the filename does not affect the contents of that file. You can also apply these settings in a specific view using the Visibility/Graphic Overrides dialog box.

FIGURE 8.6
Changing the
graphic appear-
ance of imported
layers via object
styles

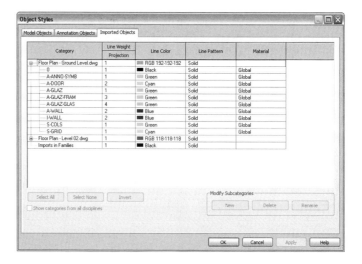

Exploding   Although we do not recommend the exploding of CAD data within a Revit project, you can do it to facilitate the modification of such data. Linked content must first be converted to an import in order to be exploded. You do this by selecting the Insert tab on the ribbon, choosing Manage Links from the Link panel, choosing a listed link, and clicking the Import button. To explode the imported file, select it, and choose Explode ➢ Full Explode or Partial Explode from the special Modify tab in the ribbon. The lines, text, and hatch patterns will become new line styles, text types, and fill regions in your Revit project. Remember that these types of objects cannot be removed from your project via the Purge Unused command; you must remove them manually.

TIPS ON IMPORTING CAD FILES

To minimize the adverse impact of unnecessary styles and types carried into the Revit environment via exploding imported CAD data, we recommend removing extraneous data in the CAD file *before* importing it. Here are some general tips for this workflow:

◆   If your import contains hatches or annotations not intended for use in Revit, delete them before importing.

◆   Consider consolidating data within the CAD file to a minimum number of layers or levels. This will ease the process of converting to standard Revit line styles if the file is exploded as well as facilitating graphic overrides.

◆   Revit doesn't allow line segments shorter than 1/32". Take care when exploding CAD details with very small line segments because these will be removed upon exploding.

Importing 2D Data

In this section, we will discuss how to import 2D CAD data from platforms such as AutoCAD (DWG) and MicroStation (DGN) or in the generic Drawing Exchange Format (DXF). You can also use files from other software platforms, but only if they are DWG, DGN, or DXF format. Most commercially available CAD programs are able to export in DWG or DXF format.

There are two fundamental ways 2D CAD data can be used with respect to a building project's floor plans, ceiling plans, or site plans:

◆ Using 2D data as backgrounds for BIM conversion

◆ Integrating 2D data with the model

Backgrounds for BIM Conversion

In this situation, we will assume that 2D CAD data will be linked into the Revit model to be converted into building elements. Although the positioning of the files is important, the color and line weights of the imported data are not.

To begin the next exercise, you will need the files c08-Plan01.dwg and c08-Start.rvt. You can download these files from this book's companion website: www.sybex.com/go/masteringrevit2011. After downloading, open the c08-Start.rvt file, and activate the Level 1 floor plan.

1. Switch to the Insert tab and select Link CAD from the Link panel. Browse to the file c08-Plan01.dwg.

2. In the Link CAD Formats dialog box, set the following options:

◆ Current View Only: Selected

◆ Colors: Invert

◆ Layers: All

◆ Import Units: Auto-Detect

◆ Positioning: Auto – Origin To Origin

LINKING VERY LARGE CAD DATA

Use caution when attempting to link or import CAD files with vector data very far from the origin. Revit has distance limitations on imported vector data that—if exceeded—may result in a warning, as shown here:

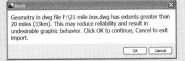 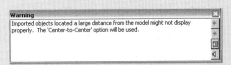

Notice in the warning message above that Revit will automatically use Center To Center positioning if the distance limitations are exceeded. This will preclude you from using the origin of the linked file for Origin To Origin placement. If you must link data that is physically larger than a twenty-mile cube—which may occur in projects such as airports or master plans—you should separate the data into smaller portions before linking. If the data is smaller than the twenty-mile cube but is located farther than twenty miles from its origin, an alternate origin should be coordinated with your project team, and the data should be moved closer to the origin.

Coordination

If you need to use 2D CAD data as an integrated component of your team coordination, different settings become important. Examples of these types of scenarios might include the following:

- Showing light fixture layouts from a lighting designer
- Integrating landscape design into a site plan
- Reusing existing CAD data for a renovation project

Most of the settings and procedures for conversion apply to the coordination process; however, color and the placement visibility will be different. Because this data will be included in the output from Revit, you will always want the color option to be set to Black and White in the options during linking. It is also likely that some sort of background plans will be exported from the Revit model for use in coordination by one or more consultants using a CAD-based program. The data returned in this process may still contain the background information originally exported from Revit; thus, we recommend agreement to a standard that establishes unique layers for the consultants' content. This will help you select layers to be loaded when linking your consultants' files into the Revit project.

Use these options when linking CAD files into Revit for plan-based coordination:

- Current View Only: Selected if data is needed in one view; unselected if data is needed in many views
- Colors: Black and White
- Layers: Specify (choose only designated layers to isolate consultant's content)
- Positioning: Auto – By Shared Coordinates

If the Current View Only is not selected, the 2D CAD data will be visible in all other views. This could be a nuisance in views such as sections and elevations; however, you might find it useful to visualize the data alongside the Revit model, as shown in Figure 8.7.

FIGURE 8.7
Existing CAD data integrated with the Revit model

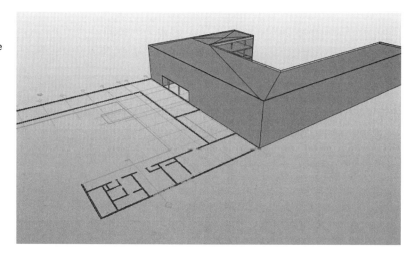

Details

Your company's CAD detail library does not need to go to waste when you implement Revit. External CAD data can be linked into drafting views, allowing you to leverage the powerful view coordination tools within Revit. Entire sheets of CAD details can be inserted to reduce the number of linked files Revit has to reconcile; however, we recommend linking one detail into each drafting view and utilizing Revit's ability to automatically manage the view references with callouts, sections, and detail views. You may also want to name these drafting views with a unique prefix to help keep track of where any linked CAD data might reside. For example, a drafting view might be named CAD-Roof Detail 04. Also refer to Chapter 4, "Configuring Templates and Standards," for additional information on view organization.

In this exercise, you will create a drafting view into which a single CAD detail will be linked. This view can be referenced throughout your Revit model using a section, callout, or elevation view with the Reference Other View option selected in the Options Bar, as shown in Figure 8.8.

FIGURE 8.8

Creating a view as a reference to a drafting view

To begin this exercise, open the c08-Jenkins.rvt file. You can download this file and the associated CAD file (c08-Detail.dwg) from the book's companion website: www.sybex.com/go/masteringrevit2011.

1. Switch to the View tab and select Drafting View from the Create panel.

2. Name the new drafting view **CAD Wall Detail 1**, and set the scale to 1-1/2″=1′-0″.

3. Switch to the Insert tab and select Link CAD.

4. In the Link CAD Formats dialog box, navigate to the c08-Detail.dwg file and set the following options:

   ◆ Colors: Black and White

   ◆ Layers: All

   ◆ Units: Auto-Detect

   ◆ Positioning: Auto – Center To Center

5. Click Open to complete the command. If you don't see the linked detail in the drafting view, use Zoom To Fit in order to reset the extents of the view.

6. Open the Section 2 view from the Project Browser, and zoom to a portion of the view where a floor meets an exterior wall.

7. From the View tab, select Callout from the Create panel, and select Reference Other View in the Options Bar. Choose Drafting View: CAD Wall Detail 1 from the drop-down list. You'll see the result shown in Figure 8.9.

FIGURE 8.9
Callout created to reference a drafting view containing a linked CAD detail

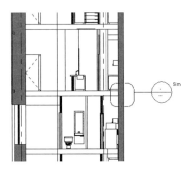

8. Double-click the callout head, and you will be taken to the drafting view with the CAD detail linked in the previous steps.

Importing 3D Data

Now that we have discussed using 2D reference data, we will cover how to use 3D model data within your Revit project. There are many valid reasons for modeling outside of Revit, including software expertise, availability of content or generation, and optimization of complex geometry. The following sections will explore some situations in which model data can be shared between programs, including:

◆ Imported data as a mass

◆ Imported data as a face

◆ Imported data as an object

Imported Data as a Mass

In Chapter 9, "Advanced Modeling and Massing," you will learn more about harnessing the impressive modeling tool set in Revit's conceptual massing environment; however, the fast and flexible process of design may lead architects toward a tool in which they have more expertise or comfort. This type of massing design workflow is supported in Revit under the following conditions:

◆ Masses require volumetric geometry to calculate volume, surface area, and floor area faces.

- Finely detailed complex geometry should be avoided as the Host By Face tools may not be able to generate meaningful objects.

- Refer to Revit Architecture's help system for even more details on using imported geometry in a Mass family.

This example demonstrates the process of creating an in-place mass by linking an external model—in this case, a SketchUp model. You can download the file `c08-Mass.skp` from the book's companion website: `www.sybex.com/go/masteringrevit2011`.

1. From the Massing & Site tab, select In-Place Mass from the Conceptual Mass panel.

2. Name the new mass family **SKP Mass** and click OK.

3. Switch to the Insert tab and select Link CAD from the Link panel. Note that this is a new option for the Revit 2011 platform.

4. Navigate to the SKP file downloaded from the book's companion web page and set the following options:

   - Colors: Invert

   - Layers: All

   - Import Units: Auto-Detect

   - Positioning: Auto – Center To Center

   - Place At: Level 1

5. Click Open to complete the link process.

6. Click Finish Mass in the In-Place Editor panel.

Now that a new mass has been created, you can assign mass floors and begin to see calculated results in schedules of masses and mass floors. (Refer to Chapter 9 for more information on these processes.) Calculation of volumes, perimeters, and mass floor areas will work well in this workflow, but be careful when using imported model geometry with the By Face tools because face updates will likely be more difficult for Revit to maintain than with native Revit massing.

Using linking instead of importing enables continued iteration of the form in the original software. In the case of this example, you may edit the original file in Google SketchUp, which is available as a free download from `http://sketchup.google.com`, or you can download the file `c08-Mass-2.skp` from the book's companion web page.

If you modify and save the original SKP file yourself, save, close, and reopen the Revit project. Alternatively, open the Manage Links dialog box, select the SKP file, and click Reload. If you want to use the alternate file downloaded from the book's companion web page, use the following steps:

1. Open the Manage Links dialog box from the Insert tab.

2. Select the SKP file and click Reload From.

3. Navigate to the file `c08-Mass-2.skp` and click Open.

4. Click OK to close the Manage Links dialog box.

With the modified mass loaded, notice the changes in the Mass Schedule and Mass Floor Schedule.

Imported Data as a Face

Similar to the data as mass workflow, externally modeled data can be used as a driver for more complex forms. An example might be the need to generate a complex curved roof surface. We will demonstrate this workflow using Rhinoceros by McNeel (www.rhino3d.com) to generate a shape, link the shape into Revit, and create a roof by face on the shape.

As shown in Figure 8.10, a complex surface is generated in Rhino from drawing two curves and using the Extrude Curve Along Curve tool. Note that some reference geometry was exported from a Revit model to DWG and linked into this study in Rhino.

FIGURE 8.10
Curves for a complex surface in Rhino

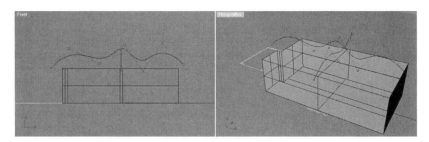

A flat surface model is enough to generate a roof by face in Revit; however, it may be difficult to see the imported surface, so use the Extrude Surface tool to give it a thickness. Once the surface is complete (Figure 8.11), select only the double-curved geometry, choose File ➤ Export Selected Objects, and choose the SAT file extension. SAT will generate the cleanest geometry for curved solids and surfaces.

FIGURE 8.11
Completed complex surface in Rhino

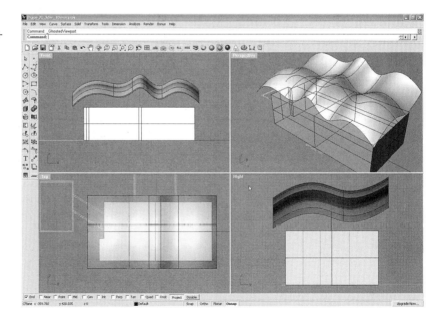

You can download the Rhino file (c08-Roof-Face.3dm) and SAT export (c08-Roof-Face.sat) from this book's companion web page. You can also download the sample Revit project and continue the process as follows:

1. Open the file c08-Roof-by-Face.rvt and make sure you are in the 3D view named 00-Start.

2. On the Massing & Site tab, choose In-Place Mass and name it **Rhino Roof**.

3. Switch to the Insert tab and select Link CAD. Navigate to the c08-Roof-Face.sat file downloaded from the book's companion web page.

4. Set the placement options as follows:

   ◆ Positioning: Auto – Origin to Origin

   ◆ Place At: Level 1

   ◆ Import Units: Inch

5. Click Open to complete the link and close the dialog box and then click the Finish Mass button in the ribbon. The mass should be seen above the tops of the walls in the Revit model, as shown in Figure 8.12.

FIGURE 8.12
Complex surface linked as an in-place mass

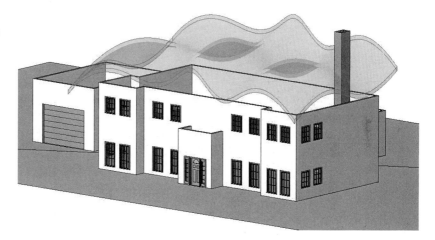

6. Return to the Massing & Site tab and select the Roof tool from the Model By Face panel. Choose the Basic Roof: Generic 12″ from the Type Selector, and click the top face of the mass created in the previous steps. Click the Create Roof button in the ribbon to complete the command and the roof will be generated along the mass surface as shown in Figure 8.13.

FIGURE 8.13
Roof By Face
applied to the mass
with linked SAT
geometry

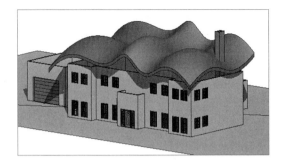

7. Select all the perimeter walls—either using the Tab key or using Ctrl to add individually to the selection.

8. Select the Attach Top/Base tool from the Modify | Walls tab, set the Top option in the Options Bar, and pick the roof by face created in step 6. The walls will connect to the underside of the complex roof shape, as shown in Figure 8.14.

The original shape can be edited in the originating software and will update in Revit via the link if the original exported SAT file is overwritten. To update the roof based on the newly modified massing geometry, select the roof and click the Update To Face button in the Modify | Roofs tab.

FIGURE 8.14
Completed roof
with tops of walls
attached

Imported Data as an Object

Yet another derivation of the reference data workflow supports the use of linked model geometry for specific instances of building components. Examples of this scenario might include a complex canopy structure being designed in SolidWorks or a building's structural framing being modeled in Bentley Structural Modeler. The workflow is again similar to that of using imported data as a mass or face; however, the file format will help you control the component's visualization in Revit. In the previous exercise, we used an SAT format to transfer complex curved geometry from Rhino to Revit; however, a limitation of an SAT file is that the geometry only contains one layer, making it impossible to vary material assignments for different components of the design. We recommend using a solids-based DWG, DGN, or DXF file format, which will maintain a layer structure in most cases.

In the following example, you will create an in-place structural framing component that will act as a placeholder for a consultant's structural model created in Bentley Structural Modeler. You will be using the file c08-Framing.dgn, which you can download from the book's companion web page: www.sybex.com/go/masteringrevit2011.

1. Launch Revit and start a new project using the default.rte template.

2. Switch to the Home tab and choose Component ➢ Model In-Place. Set the category to Structural Framing. For other scenarios, remember that some categories cannot be cut in Revit.

3. Name the new in-place model **DGN Structure**.

4. From the Insert tab, select Link CAD.

5. Change the Files Of Type option to DGN Files (*.dgn) and navigate to the downloaded file.

6. Set the following options and click Open:

   ◆ Current view only: Unselected

   ◆ Colors: Black and White

   ◆ Layers: All

   ◆ Positioning: Auto – Origin To Origin

   ◆ Place At: Level 1

7. Click Finish Model in the In-Place Editor panel to complete the process.

Switch to a 3D view, and you should see the entire contents of the DGN model (Figure 8.15). Because the linked content was created as a structural framing model, the linked data will be displayed similarly to any other structural framing element in Revit. Examine the linked model in different plans and sections to observe this behavior.

FIGURE 8.15
DGN structural
model linked into
Revit

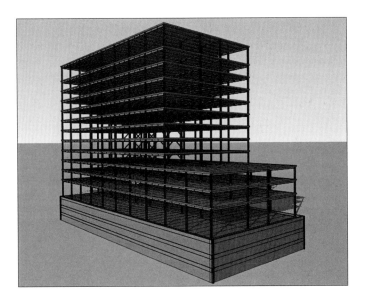

Utilizing linked models in DWG, DGN, or DXF format also allows you to modify the graphic representation of the elements within Revit. To adjust these settings, do the following:

1. Select the Manage tab, click Object Styles, and switch to the Imported Objects tab.

2. Find your linked file, expand it to expose the layers or levels included in that file, and modify the graphic settings as desired.

When you are using linked model data for custom components, the consistency of the data you bring into Revit from other programs depends on the ability of that software to generate organized information. Some programs utilize layers, and some don't. Recognizing this difference will give you the best opportunity for success in coordination through interoperability.

Overview of Exporting

Of equal importance to importing external data is the ability to export Revit data for use by others. This section will examine various processes for exporting data from your Revit project to other formats. To achieve your desired results when exporting, remember that exporting from Revit is essentially a WYSIWYG (what you see is what you get) process. For example, exporting a 3D view will result in a 3D model, exporting a floor plan will result in a 2D CAD file, and exporting a schedule will result in a delimited file that can be used in a program such as Microsoft Excel.

We will first review the process for preparing a set of files to be exported. This method is similar for almost all exports and will be referred to in subsequent sections.

Preparing for Exports

The first step to any export is to establish the set of files to be exported. The following steps will walk you through the process:

1. You can find all exporting commands by clicking the Application button and clicking the Export fly-out. As shown in Figure 8.16, check the bottom of the fly-out menu for additional commands available for use.

FIGURE 8.16
Export commands accessed by clicking the Application button

2. Beginning an exporting command such as DWF/DWFx, you will first see the typical Export Settings dialog box, as shown in Figure 8.17. Notice in the View/Sheet Set tab the Export value is usually set to <Current View/Sheet Only>.

FIGURE 8.17
First view of Export Settings dialog box

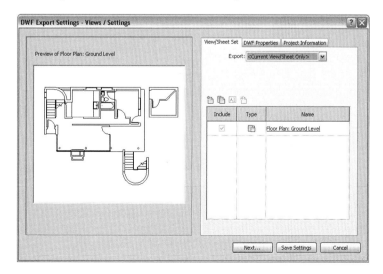

3. Begin to create your own list of views and/or sheets to export by picking <In session view/sheet set> from the Export drop-down list, as shown in Figure 8.18. Note the listings "Export Set 1" and "Export Set 2" are predefined lists I created for the purposes of this tutorial.

FIGURE 8.18
Viewing available export sets in the model

4. From this point, you can either use a temporary in-session set or create your own named set. We will continue these steps by creating a new set. Click the New icon above the view list, as shown in Figure 8.19, and name the set **Export Set 3**. Click OK to close the dialog box.

FIGURE 8.19
Create a new export list.

USING IN-SESSION LISTS WITH WORKSHARING

Be careful when using an in-session list for printing or exporting on a worksharing-enabled project. If two or more team members working on the same Revit project attempt to use the In-Session set, you may receive errors about the workset not being editable. Instead, always try to use predefined lists for exporting and printing on worksharing projects.

5. To begin adding views and/or sheets to your new export set, make sure the Show In list drop-down is set to Views In The Model, Sheets In The Model, or All Views And Sheets In The Model (see Figure 8.20).

FIGURE 8.20
Showing all views
and sheets in the
model

6. Select the views and/or sheets you need to export by checking the boxes next to the listed views in the Include column. Remember, you can sort the list by clicking any of the list headers (Figure 8.21).

FIGURE 8.21
Adding views/
sheets to the
export list

7. If you are done creating your list of views to export and don't want to continue exporting, click the Save Settings button; otherwise, click Next.

The subsequent steps in the exporting process are slightly different based on each export format. You will usually see a Save To Target dialog box that allows you to specify automatic or manual naming conventions for multiple exported files. Exporting FBX files or images simply requires a file location and name.

Export Layer Settings

In addition to creating and maintaining lists of views for various exporting tasks, we recommend that you create at least one standardized layer mapping file for CAD format exports. Revit stores these settings in a text file (*.txt) that can be loaded from any location on your computer or network. To access the Export Layers settings, click the Application button and select Export ➤ Options ➤ Export Layers DWG/DXF or Export Layers DGN. You can also access these settings by clicking the ellipsis button in the DWG Properties tab of the Export CAD Formats dialog box (Figure 8.22).

FIGURE 8.22
Accessing export layer settings on the DWG Properties tab

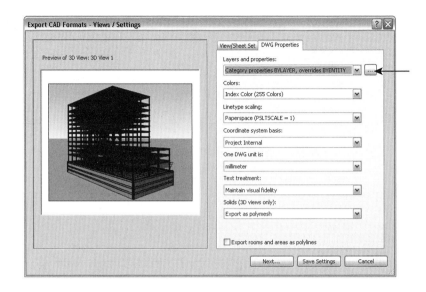

Several exporting templates based on the industry standard layering guidelines are included (Figure 8.23) with Revit Architecture and can be applied by clicking the Standard button in the Export Layers dialog box. Similarly to import settings, you may want to create customized layer export templates and save them with your project data for future reference. Note that export templates will inherit all layer names of linked CAD files in your active project. Because of this, we recommend saving a copy of your export templates in a zip archive in case you need to return to the original template.

FIGURE 8.23
Industry standard layering conventions can be applied to export settings.

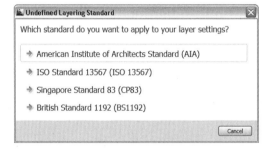

Layer names and colors can be customized by directly editing the values within the Export Layers dialog box (Figure 8.24). Notice when a layer's color is modified, the color of all other layers of the same name will update automatically. Layers listed in bracketed italics—for example, {A-WALL-FULL}—are automatically referencing the layer assigned to a parent category. For example, in Figure 8.24, the Cut layer for the subcategory Wall Sweeps will adopt the same layer (A-WALL) as the parent category of Walls.

FIGURE 8.24
Exported layer
names and colors
can be customized
for any standard.

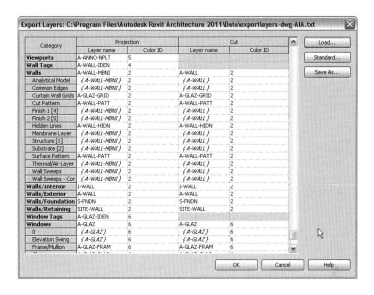

Category	Projection		Cut	
	Layer name	Color ID	Layer name	Color ID
Viewports	A-ANNO-NPLT	5		
Wall Tags	A-WALL-IDEN	4		
Walls	A-WALL-MBNI	2	A-WALL	2
Analytical Model	{ A-WALL-MBNI }	2	{ A-WALL }	2
Common Edges	{ A-WALL-MBNI }	2	{ A-WALL }	2
Curtain Wall Grids	A-GLAZ-GRID	2	A-GLAZ-GRID	2
Cut Pattern	A-WALL-PATT	2	A-WALL-PATT	2
Finish 1 [4]	{ A-WALL-MBNI }	2	{ A-WALL }	2
Finish 2 [5]	{ A-WALL-MBNI }	2	{ A-WALL }	2
Hidden Lines	A-WALL-HIDN	2	A-WALL-HIDN	2
Membrane Layer	{ A-WALL-MBNI }	2	{ A-WALL }	2
Structure [1]	{ A-WALL-MBNI }	2	{ A-WALL }	2
Substrate [2]	{ A-WALL-MBNI }	2	{ A-WALL }	2
Surface Pattern	A-WALL-PATT	2	A-WALL-PATT	2
Thermal/Air Layer	{ A-WALL-MBNI }	2	{ A-WALL }	2
Wall Sweeps	{ A-WALL-MBNI }	2	{ A-WALL }	2
Wall Sweeps - Cor	{ A-WALL-MBNI }	2	{ A-WALL }	2
Walls/Interior	I-WALL	2	I-WALL	2
Walls/Exterior	A-WALL	2	A-WALL	2
Walls/Foundation	S-FNDN	2	S-FNDN	2
Walls/Retaining	SITE-WALL	2	SITE-WALL	2
Window Tags	A-GLAZ-IDEN	6		
Windows	A-GLAZ	6	A-GLAZ	6
0	{ A-GLAZ }	6	{ A-GLAZ }	6
Elevation Swing	{ A-GLAZ }	6	{ A-GLAZ }	6
Frame/Mullion	A-GLAZ-FRAM	6	A-GLAZ-FRAM	6

Export Layers: C:\Program Files\Autodesk Revit Architecture 2011\Data\exportlayers-dwg-AIA.txt

Load... Standard... Save As...

OK   Cancel   Help

Special layer suffixes can be assigned to Revit model objects that are subject to graphic over-rides from phasing. The standard phasing overrides (Existing, Demolished, and Temporary) are listed as object styles in the Export Layers dialog box and can be customized as required. These settings are applied to the end of the specified layer for a given Revit object. For example, if a new wall was set to export to A-WALL, a wall displayed as demolished in a Revit view would be exported to the A-WALL-DEMO layer.

Exporting 2D CAD Data

When collaborating with others who require 2D CAD, planning a strategic workflow will allow you to share your Revit data more efficiently and consistently. We highly recommend that you determine and document the scope of data to be shared, the schedule by which it will be shared, and the software platforms to be used on a project. These aspects should be compiled in a BIM execution plan as explained in Chapter 7, "Working with Consultants."

To facilitate the setup and ultimate export of plan data, you can create copies of floor plans and ceiling plans with a standardized naming convention in your Revit project. These should be easy to recognize yet help in building the export list. In Figure 8.25, a series of duplicated plans have been created and named with the EXP- prefix. The rest of the view name conforms to the naming convention specified by the National CAD Standard (www.nationalcadstandard.org).

FIGURE 8.25
View organiza-
tion for plans to be
exported

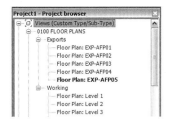

Project1 - Project browser
Views (Custom Type/Sub-Type)
0100 FLOOR PLANS
Exports
Floor Plan: EXP-AFP01
Floor Plan: EXP-AFP02
Floor Plan: EXP-AFP03
Floor Plan: EXP-AFP04
Floor Plan: EXP-AFP05
Working
Floor Plan: Level 1
Floor Plan: Level 2
Floor Plan: Level 3

When it is time to export floor plans or ceiling plans, make sure you are using the most appropriate settings according to the conventions your team has established in the BIM execution plan. You can find these settings in the DWG Properties tab of the Export CAD Formats dialog box, as shown in Figure 8.26.

FIGURE 8.26
DWG properties
for exporting

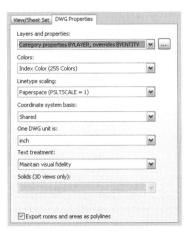

DWG Settings for Export

The following are the DWG settings for exporting:

Layers And Properties   Usually the best option is Category Properties BYLAYER, Overrides BYENTITY because of its fidelity to the original graphic appearance in Revit views; however, if the recipients of your exported data have scripts or macros to convert your data to their own graphic standards, the setting All Properties BYLAYER, No Overrides might be a better choice. This avoids necessary manual editing of object properties to be modified.

Coordinate System Basis   Any BIM execution plan or project CAD standard will contain specifications for a common origin and coordinate system. When you are exporting 2D CAD data from Revit, the Coordinate System Basis option should be set to Shared. This requires the establishment of a shared coordinate system, discussed in Chapter 7. The Project Internal option might lead to inconsistent results if data from others is being coordinated.

Export Rooms And Areas As Polylines   This check box is useful if the recipients of your data will need to extract area information from the exported CAD files. Closed polylines are the best vehicle for transferring this data efficiently.

Exporting 3D Model Data

You can also export your Revit model as a 3D model in several formats for use in other modeling software. A frequent destination for such data is Autodesk 3ds Max for its enhanced rendering and daylighting analysis capabilities. This workflow is supported by the FBX export format, which not only includes model geometry but materials, cameras, and lights as well. More generic exports in DWG, DGN, DXF, or SAT formats can provide numerous opportunities for you to become more creative with the presentation of your designs.

Studies in Google SketchUp

Earlier in this chapter we discussed using Google SketchUp for conceptual building massing studies. These studies were imported directly into the Revit environment for further development of a true building information model. Revit model data can also be exported via 3D DWG to Google SketchUp, where visualization studies can be conducted on an entire project or even a simple wall section. In the following exercise, we will create a wall section study from Revit to Google SketchUp using files you can download from the book's companion website: `www.sybex.com/go/masteringrevit2011`.

1. Open the file `c08-Sketchup-Wall-Study.rvt`.

2. Activate the default 3D view and enable the Section Box option in the Properties Palette for the view.

3. Set the detail level of the view to Medium.

4. Select the section box in the 3D view and shape handles will appear on each face. Grab the shape handle of one side of the section box parallel to the vertical edge of the wall sample and drag toward the wall until the section box intersects the wall, as shown in Figure 8.27. You should see the layers of the wall structure exposed.

FIGURE 8.27
Using the section box to expose the layers of the wall

5. With the section box still selected, right-click and choose Hide In View ➢ Elements, as shown in Figure 8.28. This will prevent the section box from being exported.

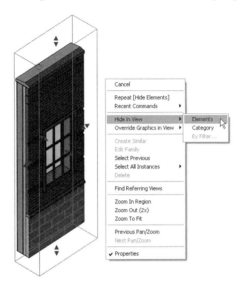

6. Click the Application button and select Export ➢ CAD Formats ➢ DWG Files.

7. In the Export CAD Formats dialog box, switch to the DWG Properties tab and set the Solids option to Export As Polymesh.

8. Click Next and save the DWG file to a location on your computer or network.

9. Launch Google SketchUp, and choose File ➢ Import.

10. Switch the Files Of Type option to AutoCAD Files, navigate to the file saved in step 8, and click Open.

11. Switch to the Select tool, select the entire DWG import, right-click and choose Explode. This will allow you to directly edit the elements in the SketchUp environment. Note that other components within the exploded model may need to be exploded again.

Once the DWG model is loaded in Google SketchUp, you can use the Paint Bucket tool to apply materials to individual components, use the Push/Pull tool to hide or expose layers of the wall construction, and use the line tools to customize the profile of the revealed layers, as shown in Figure 8.29.

FIGURE 8.29
Completed wall
study in Google
SketchUp

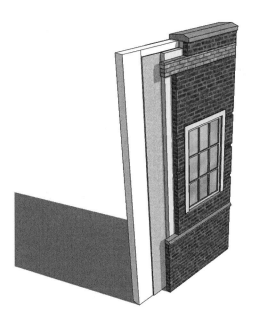

IFC Interoperability

According to Wikipedia, "Industry Foundation Classes (IFC) is a data model based on a neutral and open specification that is not controlled by a single software vendor or group of vendors. It is an object-oriented file format with a data model developed by the buildingSMART Alliance (International Alliance for Interoperability, IAI) to facilitate interoperability in the building industry." The IFC model specification is registered by the International Standards Organization (ISO) as ISO/PAS 16739 and is currently in the process of becoming the official International Standard ISO/IS 16739. Because of its focus on ease of interoperability between BIM software platforms, some government agencies are requiring IFC format deliverables for publicly funded building projects.

The use of IFC format in a Revit workflow can be useful if you understand its limitations. Some scenarios where IFC exchange may apply and facilitate data exchange include, but are not limited to, the following:

- Linking AutoCAD MEP into Revit

- Using Solibri Model Checker

- Coordination between Revit and Nemetschek Allplan, VectorWorks, or ArchiCAD

You can export the Revit model quite effectively to the IFC 2x2, 2x3 or BCA ePlan Check formats by clicking the Application button and selecting the Export menu. The resulting IFC file

(Figure 8.30) can be viewed in a number of programs that can be downloaded at no cost from any of the following websites:

◆ DDS CAD Viewer from Data Design System (www.dds-cad.net)

◆ Nemetschek IFC Viewer (www.nemetschek.com/ifc)

◆ IFC Engine Viewer (www.ifcbrowser.com)

FIGURE 8.30
Revit model exported to IFC format

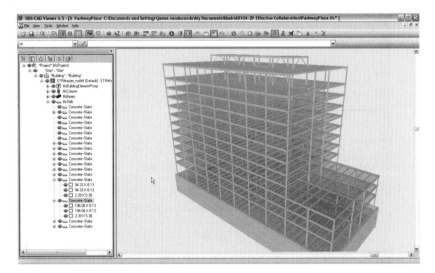

Importing IFC data into Revit is similar to the process for importing 3D CAD geometry; however, the data generated is intended to be more intelligent and editable. Although this method has great potential, the accuracy of Revit's IFC import is highly dependent on the software used to generate the IFC output. We recommend the use of one of the free IFC viewers listed previously to inspect IFC data prior to importing into a Revit project. (Note that only some tools, such as DDS CAD Viewer, have the ability to measure objects in an IFC format file.)

VIEWING THE CONTENTS OF AN IFC FORMAT FILE

Did you know that an IFC file can be viewed in a text editor such as Notepad? Download a sample file from the book's companion website and check it out! Right-click an IFC file, select Open With, and choose Notepad.

Once you've reviewed the contents of the IFC file, you can open it in Revit and integrate it into your coordination process as follows:

1. Click the Application button, and select Open ➤ IFC.

2. Navigate to the c08-Structure.ifc file and click Open.

3. Save the file as a Revit project file (*.rvt).

4. Start a new Revit project using the default template. You will link the saved RVT file into a blank project to simulate the process for a host project model.

5. On the Insert tab, select Link Revit from the Link panel.

6. Navigate to the file saved in step 3, and click Open.

If an updated IFC file is received, repeat steps 1–3, and overwrite the RVT file created in step 3. When the host project file is reopened, the linked RVT file containing the imported IFC content will be updated.

 Real World Scenario

3D EXPORTS BY LEVEL

Effective coordination between Revit Architecture and AutoCAD MEP frequently relies on the exchange of 3D DWG files of limited scope with respect to the overall project. MEP engineers using AutoCAD MEP will usually manage their BIM with one model file per level. Even though the entire architectural model can be exported to a single DWG model, they may not be able to reference such a large model efficiently. The good news? Your Revit project can be set up to achieve this by creating 3D views with section boxes for each level.

Begin by creating a series of floor plans designed for exporting (discussed earlier in this chapter). In the View Range settings for these plans, set the Top value to Level Above, Offset: 0 and the Bottom value to Associated Level, Offset: 0. Create a 3D view for each level required in the project and rename the views according to your standards. In each duplicated 3D view, right-click the ViewCube and select Orient To View ➢ Floor Plans and choose the corresponding floor plan with the adjusted view range. This series of 3D views can be saved in an export list and batch exported to 3D DWG when needed for collaboration, as shown here:

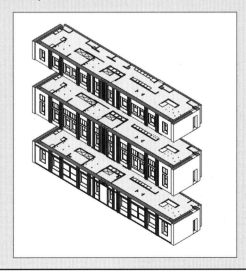

The Bottom Line

Use imported 2D CAD data. CAD data can be integrated into your Revit project in a number of ways: as plans of existing conditions, as fixture layouts from consultants, or as standard details from your company's library.

Master It How can CAD details be used within Revit?

Export 2D CAD data. The ability to deliver quality 2D information to other constituents involved in your project is as important as importing it into Revit. Appropriately formatted views, standardized layer templates, and proper coordinate settings will result in happy team members and a smooth coordination process.

Master It Does Revit comply with the National CAD Standard?

Use imported 3D model data. Model data generated outside of Revit can be integrated into your projects as whole building systems, massing studies, or unique components.

Master It How can a building's structural model created with Bentley Structure be integrated into Revit?

Export 3D model data. Your modeled elements don't have to remain in the Revit environment forever. Data can be exported to 3ds Max, Google SketchUp, AutoCAD MEP, and more.

Master It How can I coordinate my architectural Revit model with an engineer using AutoCAD MEP?

Work with IFC imports and exports. Industry Foundation Classes is a vendor-neutral model format designed to support interoperability in the AEC industry. It is widely used by some major BIM platforms available around the world.

Master It How is an IFC model integrated into Revit for coordination?

Part 3

Modeling and Massing for Design

In Part 2, we covered the topics that help define important project standards when using Revit—both within your team as well as across external Revit teams and other consultants. In this section—we'll begin to delve into the actual use of Revit from the earliest design stages, through analysis and iteration and finally with visualization.

- ◆ **Chapter 9: Advanced Modeling and Massing**
- ◆ **Chapter 10: Conceptual Design and Sustainability**
- ◆ **Chapter 11: Phasing, Groups, and Design Options**
- ◆ **Chapter 12: Visualization**

Chapter 9

Advanced Modeling and Massing

Nothing is more frustrating than getting into a design program by building the project in Revit only to find out the building is too big and somehow the program still doesn't fit. You think that you've done everything right—walls, floors, rooms, schedules—but somewhere, something is wrong. And you have no idea where to begin to change your design.

Massing is great for avoiding this kind of scenario. By creating the "big" design idea at a macro level, as a mass, you're able to quickly and easily quantify and analyze the results. This allows you to confidently work from general to specific as your design progresses, without starting with actual building elements (which would be too specific too soon anyway).

In addition, massing allows you to create forms and containers to control more granular components. Complex walls, curtain walls, curtain panels, and other elements would be incredibly difficult to make (much less update) without some underlying form to establish and drive their design. Massing is essential for this kind of design and design iteration.

Even though your overall design might not be represented by a complex massing form, it's very likely that somewhere in a more conventional design massing is essential to the success of your project.

In this chapter, you'll learn to:

◆ Create and schedule massing studies

◆ Know when to use solid and surface masses

◆ Use mathematical formulas for massing

Massing UI and Functionality

You might not think that you need to use massing tools when you first begin using Revit if you tend to design conventional or rectilinear buildings. But you'll quickly find that just because you don't create complex buildings, a lot of buildings contain complex features or parts that require a firm understanding of the massing tool.

Massing is certainly used to create *masses*, that is, forms with geometric substance (solids and voids). But the massing tool is also used to create complex surfaces that can be used to create relationships to other host elements. Without these mass- or surface-based relationships, it'd be really hard to create and reiterate system families such as walls and curtain walls. You'd essentially have to start over when the design changed. Massing allows you to create a lightweight design idea, evaluate it, and then associate some real-world building elements with the massing element. To change the real-world building element, you change the lightweight design idea first.

Another important thing to know about massing is that masses can be created in both the project environment as well as the Family Editor. There's a lot of overlap of functionality in each case, but there's also a lot of important functionality missing. So, what's the difference?

The main difference as to whether you create massing in-place or in the Family Editor doesn't depend on the kind of shape or surface you want to create. Solid and surface forms can be created in both the project and Family Editor environments. Rather, it depends on *how* you want to create the massing and how want to *change* the mass once it's been created.

Intuitive and Formula Mass Creation

Generally speaking, there are two ways to create form. The first approach tends to create masses more *intuitively*; the second approach tends to create masses more *formulaically*. Intuitively created masses could probably be created right in the project environment as an in-place mass, but if the shape that you're trying to create needs to be driven by formulas, you're probably better off opening the Family Editor and creating the shape there.

When using the intuitive method, you can model just about anything in the project environment, both host and component families. We strongly recommend that you don't model component families in-place unless the condition is quite unique and exceptional, because the moment you need to create another just like it, you will have created a copy. If you have to change both of them, you'll have to change them both manually. It's best to model component families in the Family Editor.

But once in a while you'll have to create a complex host element that can't be created with the standard tools, and you'll have to use the formulaic method. As you've noticed by now, there are no templates in the Family Editor for host (or system) families such as walls, roofs, and floors. If you need to create these, they'll have to be created in the project environment. This can be done in one of two ways: create a mass or surface (using massing) or simply model it in place. If the structure of the wall varies significantly, you'll probably just want to model the wall in place. But if the structure is more consistent, it'll be easier to create a mass or surface form, and then associate the wall with this form.

In-Place Masses

CERT OBJECTIVE

Figure 9.1 illustrates the intuitive method. It was created all the way back in 2001 when a lot of people thought Revit couldn't be used to create complex shapes. This was kind of true for a while, but once blends were introduced, these kinds of complex shapes were immediately possible.

This wall wasn't created by starting with a mass; it was created by creating the blend in-place in the Wall category. Notice how the top and base of the wall are not consistently thick. It's narrower in some places and wider in others as it moves from bottom to top.

But if the wall was meant to be consistently wide, it would be more appropriate to make the mass or surface first, and then assign the wall to the form (Figure 9.2). Notice how the top and bottom of the wall are the same width overall.

FIGURE 9.1
Complex
in-place wall

FIGURE 9.2
Wall created from
in-place mass
surface

At the end of the day, the previous two figures were created in the project environment through intuitive decision making. There were no formulas or parameters or rules; we just created the shape directly—in the moment, so to speak.

Family Component Masses

The other way to create a form is to first start to think about the rules that you want to create (and later reiterate) for the form you're trying to accomplish. Figure 9.3 illustrates this kind of form.

FIGURE 9.3
Massing created in the Family Editor

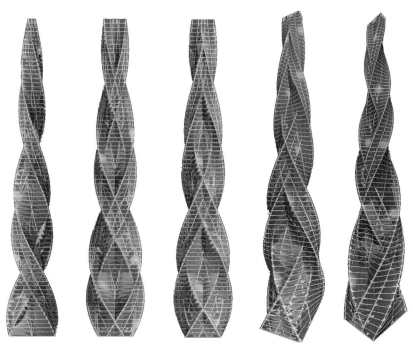

The rules that were created resulted in a form that would programmatically rotate and narrow depending on its relative elevation. Later, geometry was assigned to this form along the edges. Creating this kind of form as an in-place object would be tedious, and modifying it would be extremely time-consuming.

Now we'll talk about creating massing as both in-place and in the Family Editor.

Floor Area Faces and Scheduling Masses

Whether you create masses in-place or in the Family Editor, you're able to generate floor faces (not the actual floors) and schedule important metadata before you've even begun to assign actual geometry to the masses. This is important to do because the masses will be light in your project. You should use them to establish your design idea before committing a lot of complex geometry.

In-place mass forms can be both solid- and surface-based forms. You can start them two ways. The first way is to select Component ➢ Model In-place from the Home tab (Figure 9.4).

When you select this option, the dialog box in Figure 9.5 appears. Be sure to select the Mass category.

FIGURE 9.4
Selecting Model
In-Place

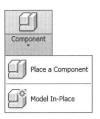

FIGURE 9.5
Selecting the Mass
category

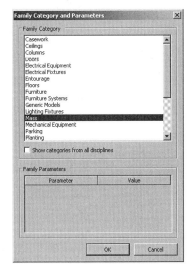

The other way is to select the Massing & Site tab, as shown in Figure 9.6. From the Conceptual Mass panel, select In-Place Mass. In either case, when you start to create the mass, you'll want to have the Mass category visible (it's turned off by default in all views).

FIGURE 9.6
Massing & Site tab

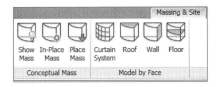

Rather than confuse you by allowing you to create objects that wouldn't be visible, Revit prompts you to turn the category on (Figure 9.7).

FIGURE 9.7
Revit enables the
Show Mass mode.

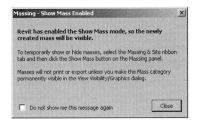

Once you close this dialog box, you'll be given the opportunity to name your in-place mass. In this case we're going to name the mass **Cube** (Figure 9.8).

FIGURE 9.8
Naming the mass

SIMPLE MASS CREATION

After you've named the mass from the previous steps and clicked OK, you'll be shown the contextually specific Massing toolset. The Home tab contains the tools that you'll use to create solid and void geometry as well as surface-generated masses, as shown in Figure 9.9.

FIGURE 9.9
Massing functionality

When you're finished creating your mass, you'll have to select Finish Mass (or Cancel Mass) in order to return to the regular project environment.

In Figure 9.10, we've created three masses: Cube, Pyramid, and Sphere.

FIGURE 9.10
Cube, Pyramid, and Sphere

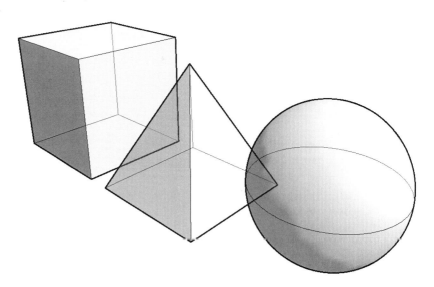

All three of these shapes have been created as completely different masses, not within the same in-place session. As each form was finished, the mass was completed and the process was repeated for each mass. The difference is that in your Family Browser, each mass will show up as a separate line item (Figure 9.11).

FIGURE 9.11
Separate masses in
the Family Browser

Starting with the cube, its dimensions are 100' × 100' × 100' (about 30m × 30m × 30m). The base of the pyramid is the same size as the cube with equal sides tapering to the same height. And the sphere is the same width as the cube.

FLOOR AREA FACES

Once each shape is complete, it's important to understand how to create floor area faces. Keep in mind that the process would be the same for in-place masses as those created in the Family Editor.

To create floor area faces, follow these steps:

1. Create more levels above the two default levels. Do this as shown in Figure 9.12. This will give you a total of 10 levels.

FIGURE 9.12
Intersecting levels

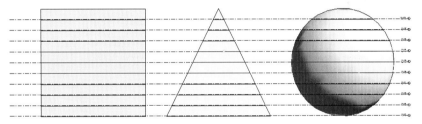

2. Now select all the masses and click the Mass Floors button in the contextual Model panel (Figure 9.13).

FIGURE 9.13
Mass Floors
command

3. Select all the levels, as shown in Figure 9.14.

FIGURE 9.14
Selecting all levels

The solid masses will be intersected by floor faces, as shown in Figure 9.15. Now the masses and floor faces can be calculated and scheduled.

FIGURE 9.15
Floor area faces

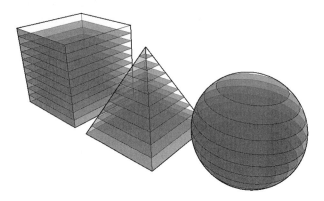

SCHEDULING MASSES

Select Schedules from the View tab, and you'll be given the option to schedule both Mass and Mass Floor (Figure 9.16). In this case we'll schedule the masses so we can do a comparative analysis between the different mass types.

FIGURE 9.16
Creating a
schedule

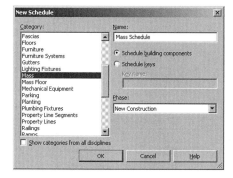

Select the categories as shown in Figure 9.17 and add them to the scheduled fields.

FIGURE 9.17
Scheduled fields

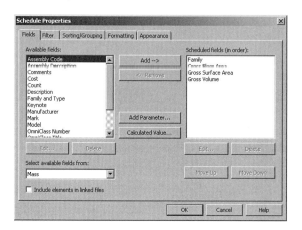

For this example, we'll also show you how to create two calculated values. This will allow you to calculate the overall volume compared to the floor area, as well as the overall surface area compared to the floor area. Schedules like this will be helpful during the early design process to help you understand how efficient the space of your design is compared to the volume and surface area required to contain that space.

1. Create the volume-to-floor ratio. Note the formula as shown in Figure 9.18. To keep the units consistent, you divide the gross volume by 1 before dividing by the gross floor area.

FIGURE 9.18
Volume-to-floor ratio

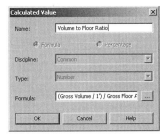

2. Create the calculated value to compare the surface-to-floor ratio, as shown in Figure 9.19.

FIGURE 9.19
Surface-to-floor ratio

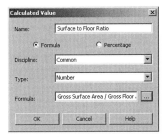

3. Finish both calculated values and finish the schedule. You'll see the Mass Schedule as shown in Figure 9.20. Notice that proportionally, a sphere and a cube have efficient floor areas compared to their required surface area and volume.

FIGURE 9.20
Completed schedule

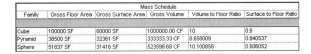

Mass Schedule					
Family	Gross Floor Area	Gross Surface Area	Gross Volume	Volume to Floor Ratio	Surface to Floor Ratio
Cube	100000 SF	60000 SF	1000000.00 CF	10	0.6
Pyramid	38500 SF	32361 SF	333333.33 CF	8.658009	0.840537
Sphere	51837 SF	31416 SF	523598.68 CF	10.100858	0.606052

On the other hand, the pyramid mass will require significantly more surface and volume to create the same relative surface area as a cube or a sphere; as a result, it takes far more surface area than a cube to contain the same space. Perhaps this is why pyramids aren't a common building mass—it's too expensive. Pyramids only pay for themselves if the labor is cheap or the owner has a lot of money to spend.

If you want to download this file, it's in the Chapter 9 folder and is named c09_Mass_Schedules.rvt.

CREATING MASSES

How you create masses (surface or form) differs significantly from the UI used to create other standard content in Revit. When you're creating standard project content, you tend to think of the form that you're creating and then start to create that form in a discrete mode that isolates you from doing anything else until the form making is complete (Figure 9.21). In some ways, this is Noun > Verb approach: you know the form that you want to create and then you create it.

FIGURE 9.21
Nonmassing form creation

Creating massing in Revit still requires that you know the form that you intend to create, but you're not required to select a particular Noun-type to get started. Rather, you simply start by creating the sketch-based elements that would define your shape. Then you select them as a group and choose the Create Form option (Figure 9.22). This will allow you to create both solids and voids.

FIGURE 9.22
Create Form option

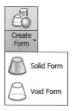

In the event that you don't select enough information for the Create Form command to make sense, you'll get the warning shown in Figure 9.23.

FIGURE 9.23
Create Form warning

Both solid and surface may be created from model lines or reference lines (Figure 9.24). But the differences are important. Keep in mind that your ability to further iterate the form that you create depends on whether you use model or reference lines to generate the form, even though the forms created may at first look exactly the same.

FIGURE 9.24
Draw panel for both model and reference lines

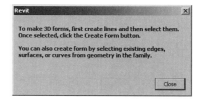

If your intent is to simply create a form that is not likely to require further iteration or rule-based parameterization, using model lines is fine. But if you intend to parameterize the form with formulas and other rules, it's best to start with reference lines. Figure 9.25 shows the subtle graphic difference between the two line types. The model line is on the left, and the green reference line is on the right.

FIGURE 9.25
Model lines and
reference lines

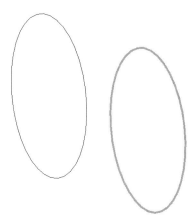

Since the difference is so subtle on the screen, we recommend that you give your reference lines more thickness and lighten the default green color so that they stand out better. This can be done from the Object Styles settings (Figure 9.26).

FIGURE 9.26
Object styles for
reference lines

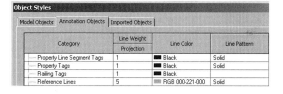

Because reference lines allow for more flexibility, we recommend that you use reference lines (even when you don't think you need to). Another reason is because you can create faces from closed loops if you use reference lines (Figure 9.27). This option isn't available when you select model lines. Selecting a closed loop of model lines will only create a form (solid or void), never a face.

FIGURE 9.27
Option to create
face or solid from
reference lines

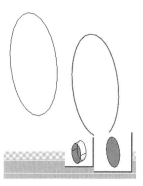

Massing Surfaces

All of the shapes that you'll create in this chapter are going to be done using reference objects. Figure 9.28 shows a number of line types: Spline Through Points, Spline, Curve, and Line.

FIGURE 9.28
Reference line
segment types

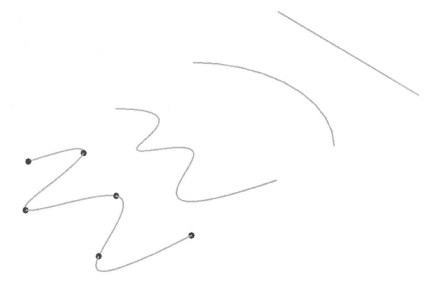

As you can see in Figure 9.29, each of these reference lines have different control points that allow for further control.

FIGURE 9.29
Reference line
control points

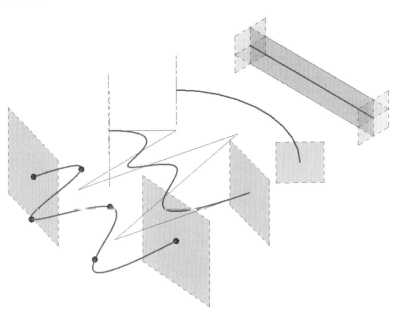

Since these are not closed loops, the form that will generate from each of these segments will only be face or surface (Figure 9.30). This is done by selecting each of the lines (one at a time, not together) and then selecting Create Form.

FIGURE 9.30
Surface forms

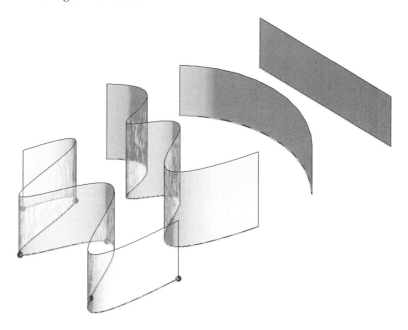

You can also create surface-based forms from more than one line at a time. The result is a surface that can be controlled in more complex ways than a single line.

For example, we'll take the Spline Through Points. The form on the left creates a face that is controlled by a single reference line, whereas the form on the right is a face controlled by two (and it could be more) reference lines (Figure 9.31).

FIGURE 9.31
Surfaces based on
multiple splines

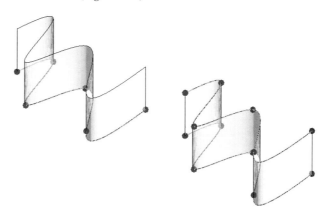

Moving the location of the control points on the form on the left maintains a consistent height to the top of the surface previously generated, whereas moving the control points of the surface on the right will create a surface that varies in height (Figure 9.32).

FIGURE 9.32
Single and multi-spline surfaces

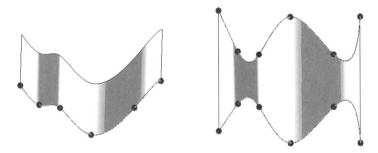

After a surface is generated, it's also possible to add more profiles, as illustrated by Figure 9.33.

FIGURE 9.33
Adding a profile

After the profile was added, the location of the profile was moved in order to create a bulge in the surface (Figure 9.34).

FIGURE 9.34
Moved Profile

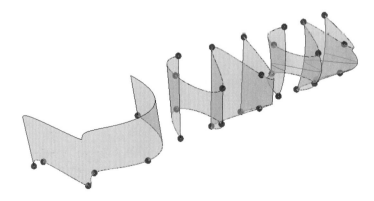

The fourth iteration of the form has been created by selecting the surface and then selecting the Dissolve tool (Figure 9.35). This will remove the surface (or solid form) but leave you with all the references used to create the form.

FIGURE 9.35
Using the
Dissolve tool

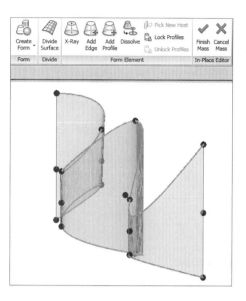

Once the face has been dissolved, another reference Spline Through Points was added between the upper and lower reference splines. The result is shown in Figure 9.36.

FIGURE 9.36
Additional
spline added

Selecting all three references and then selecting the Create Form tool will stitch them all into a new single surface (Figure 9.37).

FIGURE 9.37
New surface form

Selecting the points within the middle reference will allow for even more complex surface control (Figure 9.38).

FIGURE 9.38
Edited center spline

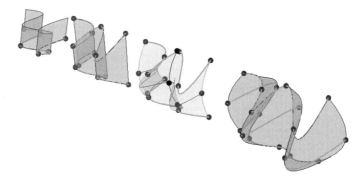

Keep in mind selecting all the splines and then creating the surface will result in very different forms than if you were to sequentially select only adjacent splines (Figure 9.39). The result is that the surface form isn't interpolated as smooth between the upper and lower splines. Instead, a distinct edge is created between the two splines.

FIGURE 9.39
Spline-based surfaces

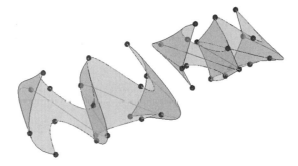

As you can see, it's easy to create complex surface forms in Revit using reference lines. Now let's begin to create complex forms using reference planes.

Massing Forms

As discussed earlier, creating solid masses isn't done by creating a particular type of form and then entering Sketch mode. Creating the necessary references and then evoking the Create Form tool creates mass forms.

First, you don't have to create solid forms. You can also create surfaces, not only from lines but also from closed loops. Figure 9.40 illustrates this.

FIGURE 9.40
Surface or
form option

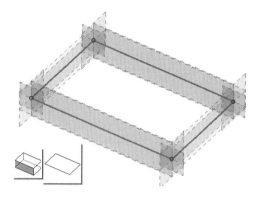

Even if you create a surface, you'd still have the option to convert it into a solid mass (Figure 9.41) by selecting the surface and using the control arrows to pull the surface into a three-dimensional shape.

FIGURE 9.41
Creating solid from
surface

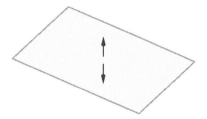

Now let's create each of the reference shapes necessary to create each of the familiar forms in Revit (Figure 9.42). From left to right, these shapes will create Extrusions, Blends, Sweeps, Revolves, and Swept Blends.

FIGURE 9.42
Using reference
shapes to create
forms

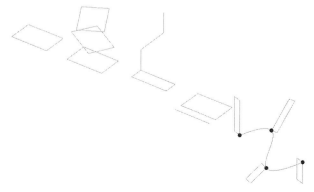

Figure 9.43 shows the resulting forms that are created from each of the references. You would also create voids from the same reference shapes. If you want to download this file for further investigation, it's named cO9_Massing_Types.rvt.

FIGURE 9.43
Resulting mass forms

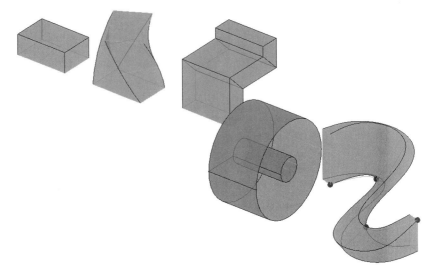

FIGURE 9.43
Resulting mass
forms

All of these mass forms contain parameters and controls relative to their form. We'll now explain how to create surface and solid forms intuitively in the project environment.

Intuitive Massing

Since this is an intuitive mass form, we'll cover how to create a surface and then assign host elements to the surface. This is a great way to create complex walls and roofs. Then we'll explain how to assign patterns to the surface. Start by opening a new project, and create a third level, as shown in Figure 9.44. We'll use these levels as controls for the Spline Through Points that will generate our first surface.

FIGURE 9.44
Creating an additional level

Select In-Place Mass and go to a top 3D view. Then create a Spline Through Points as shown on Level 1 (Figure 9.45). Although this might seem like a simple shape, the resulting form will be quite complex—just be patient!

FIGURE 9.45
Spline Through
Points

FIGURE 9.45
Spline Through
Points

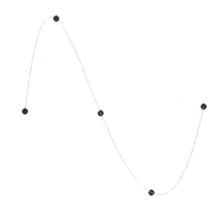

In-Place Surface

Now create another Spline Through Points using Level 3 as a reference, as shown in Figure 9.46.
Since you're working in a 3D view, you'll be able to see both splines at the same time.

FIGURE 9.46
Second Spline
Through Points

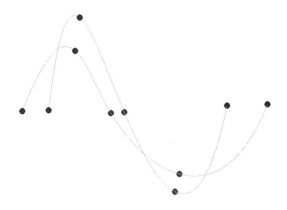

Now rotate the view so that you can see both splines. Select them both and then select Create
Form, as shown in Figure 9.47.

FIGURE 9.47
Selecting
Create Form

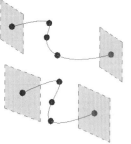

Figure 9.48 shows the resulting surface.

FIGURE 9.48
Resulting surface

WALL BY FACE

Now you'll create a wall by face and assign it to this form. Go to the Home tab and select Wall By Face, as shown in Figure 9.49.

FIGURE 9.49
Wall By Face

Figure 9.50 shows the resulting wall. The mass surface has been turned off in order to show only the wall.

Now let's return to the in-place mass and change the references. Before you do this, you may want to hide the wall so that only the mass and its references are shown.

By selecting each of the controls, you'll notice you can move them in x-, y-, and z-directions. Go ahead and adjust the controls as shown in Figure 9.51.

FIGURE 9.50
Resulting wall

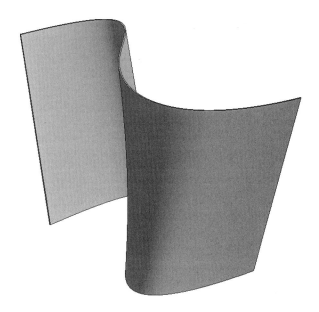

FIGURE 9.51
Modified surface

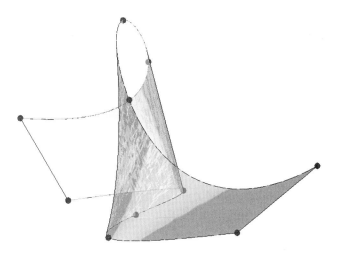

Now finish the mass and unhide your wall in the view. Select the wall and then choose the Update To Face option (Figure 9.52).

FIGURE 9.52
Update To Face

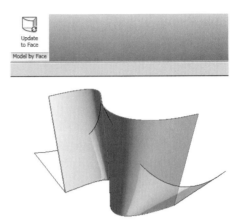

The wall will update to conform itself to the modified face, as shown in Figure 9.53.

FIGURE 9.53
Updated wall

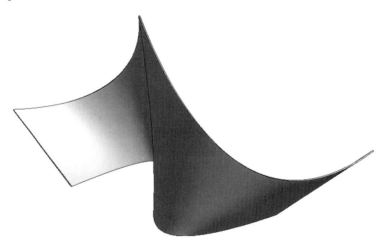

Now hide the wall, select the mass surface, and return to editing in place. Add another Spline Through Points using Level 2 as a reference, as shown in Figure 9.54.

Select the surface and you have the option to dissolve the surface (Figure 9.55). Go ahead and do this. Then select all three splines and re-create the surface.

Once the surface has been revised, finish the family and update the wall as done previously. Your updated wall will not look exactly like Figure 9.56. What's important is that you grasp the principles and the process. If the changes you made were so complex that the wall can't be updated to match the new face, just delete it and re-create it.

FIGURE 9.54
Adding another
Spline Through
Points

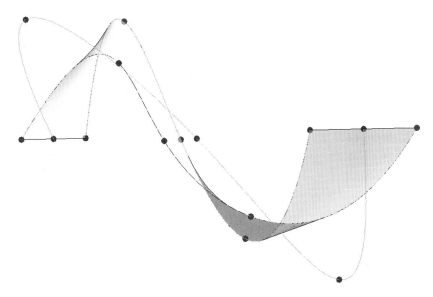

FIGURE 9.55
Dissolving the
surface

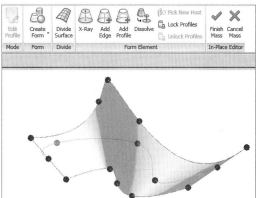

FIGURE 9.56
Finishing the fam-
ily and updating
the wall

PATTERN-BASED SYSTEM

Three steps are involved in assigning a pattern to a mass surface. First you divide the surface, then you assign a pattern to the surface, and finally you assign a component to the pattern.

1. Rather than start from scratch, create a copy of the surface previously created. Now select the mass surface and enter Edit In-Place mode. Select the surface. Be sure to delete the wall from the copied mass since you'll only need the surface.

2. While in Edit In-Place mode, select the surface and choose Divide Surface from the contextual menu (Figure 9.57).

FIGURE 9.57
Divide Surface tool

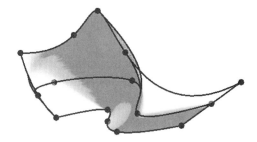

The default divided surface will look like Figure 9.58.

FIGURE 9.58
Divided surface

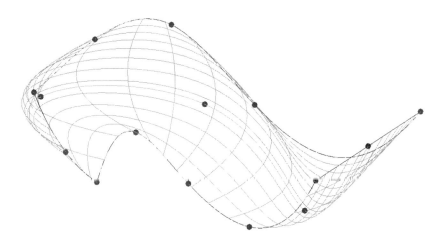

3. Once the surface has been divided, you can assign a pattern to the surface. The pattern will not contain any geometry; it's a lightweight method of resolving the eventual surface that will be replaced with more resolved geometry.

4. Select the surface and you'll see that no pattern has been applied, as shown in Figure 9.59. Go ahead and experiment with assigning different patterns from the Properties pull-down list.

FIGURE 9.59
Selecting
No Pattern

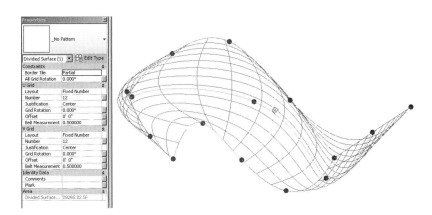

5. Eventually, select the Triangle (Flat) pattern (Figure 9.60).

FIGURE 9.60
Selecting the
Triangle (Flat)
surface pattern

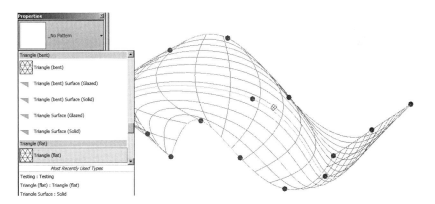

6. The resulting surface will be faceted with an analytic triangular pattern (Figure 9.61).

FIGURE 9.61
The result of
choosing the
Triangle (Flat)
pattern

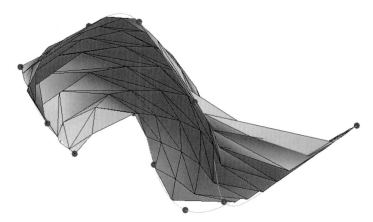

7. Take a moment to investigate the edge conditions of your analytic surface. There are three options: Partial, Empty, and Overhanging. Select the surface and enter Edit In-Place mode to investigate these three options.

The Partial option allows the triangulated surface to align with the edge of the mass surface (Figure 9.62).

FIGURE 9.62
Partial option

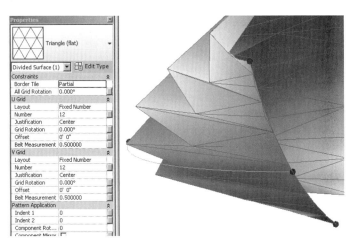

The Empty option doesn't allow the partial panel to be created (Figure 9.63).

FIGURE 9.63
Empty option

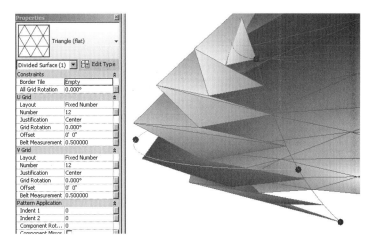

The Overhanging option completes the partial panels to extend beyond the mass surface (Figure 9.64).

FIGURE 9.64
Overhanging
option

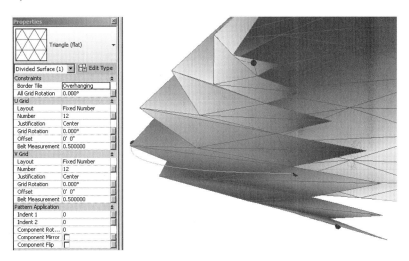

8. Select the Overhanging option. Now exit Edit In-Place mode.

PATTERN-BASED SYSTEM

Now you're going to create a pattern-based panel. Start a new family component and open the Curtain Panel Pattern Based (Figure 9.65).

FIGURE 9.65
Curtain Panel Pattern Based option

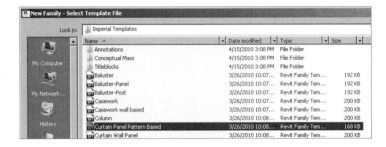

Then follow these steps:

1. To keep things simple, every pattern-based family that you'll need to create is in this family template. Just select the grid that contains the reference lines and you'll be able to select from all the panel options in the Properties tab (Figure 9.66).

FIGURE 9.66
Panel options in the Properties tab

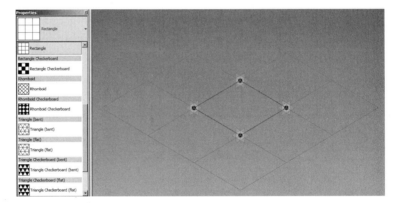

2. Select a few different options from the pull-down menu and you'll notice that the patterns will change accordingly. Eventually you'll want to select the Triangle (Flat) type, as shown in Figure 9.67.

FIGURE 9.67
Triangular (Flat) template

3. Apply the template and then update the panel and reload it into your project. This process is important, because if something breaks you'll know which step to reconsider.

4. Select the reference planes and then select Create Form. Again, only create the surface, not the geometry (Figure 9.68). Save the family (we've called it **Testing.rfa**) and then load it into your massing project.

FIGURE 9.68
Creating only the surface form

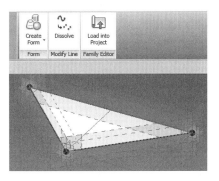

5. To assign the panel that you just created to the massing form, you need to select the mass and enter Edit In-Place mode. Once you've done this, select the mass again and open the Properties pull-down menu for your mass surface. Notice that in addition to the options for assigning a pattern, you can now assign geometry (Figure 9.69).

FIGURE 9.69
Options for assigning geometry

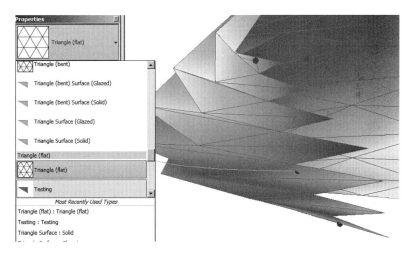

6. Assign this component to the mass. Then exit Edit In-Place mode. Now hide the mass so that only your panel will show (Figure 9.70).

FIGURE 9.70
Panel assigned to
mass surface

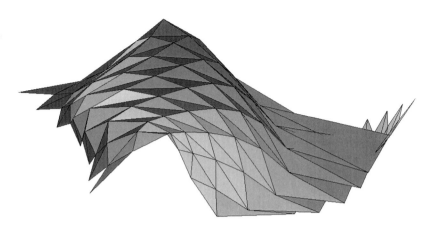

7. Return to the panel family. It's about to get very interesting!

   Select all three reference points and copy above the work surface, as shown in Figure 9.71. You can use graphic display options to turn off the gradient background.

8. Go to a top view and move the points similar to Figure 9.72.

9. Join the reference points with new reference lines, as shown in Figure 9.73.

10. Select all the reference lines and create a new form. This will result in a blended form, as shown in Figure 9.74.

11. Reload the family into the project. Your components will update, creating a surprisingly complex form (Figure 9.75).

FIGURE 9.71
Copying the three
reference points

FIGURE 9.72
Moving the refer-
ence points

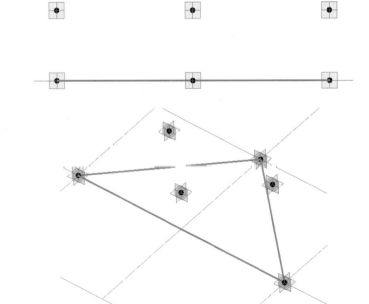

FIGURE 9.73
Joining the refer-
ence points with
new reference lines

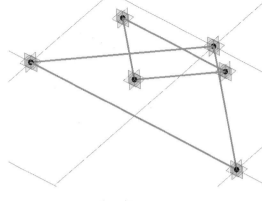

FIGURE 9.74
Blended form

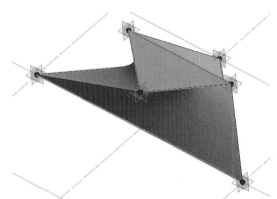

FIGURE 9.75
The updated com-
ponents, resulting
in a complex form

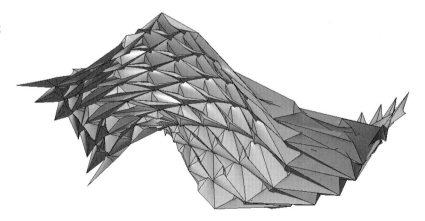

By revisiting the family and updating in the project, you can create interesting and complex forms. In Figure 9.76, the panels were created by associating a simple extrusion with a series of reference lines that were offset from the original sketch.

FIGURE 9.76
Voided blended panels

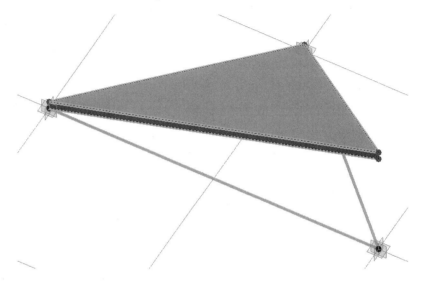

Figure 9.77 shows the resulting family, which has been assigned to a newly created blended surface. If you want to further investigate this project, download the c09_Intuitive_Massing_ Surface.rvt file in the Chapter 9 folder.

FIGURE 9.77
Revised form

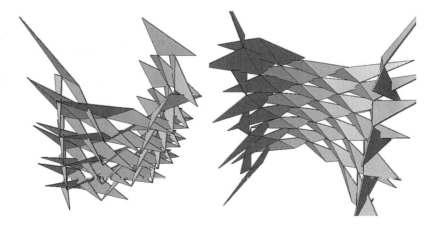

Of course, creating complex form-driven systems isn't for everyone or every project. But we think that CNC and other forms of rapid prototyping are going to make mass customization increasingly approachable over the next few years.

And if you are interested in generative form making, head over to Zachary Kron's blog. He works in the Revit factory as a software analyst. His blog is at `http://buildz.blogspot.com/` and his YouTube channel is `www.youtube.com/user/zachkron`. He's a great source of geometry, rule-based customization, and in some cases, API-driven customization.

In-Place Solids

Creating in-place mass solids is quite easy once you understand the process of creating and modifying the various forms in Revit. Let's start by entering in-place massing mode and select a rectilinear shape created from model lines (Figure 9.78). You should also select the option to make a surface from the closed loops that are being created. The other option would be to not make a closed loop, but you're creating a simple extrusion (initially), so this will save a step.

FIGURE 9.78
Rectilinear form

1. Sketch a form similar to the one shown in Figure 9.79. Specific dimensions are not important; it's really more about the proportions.

FIGURE 9.79
Plan view of sketch

2. Open the default 3D view and select the face of the surface that you just created. When you select this surface, controls become available that allow you to pull the surface into a solid (Figure 9.80).

FIGURE 9.80
Creating a
solid form

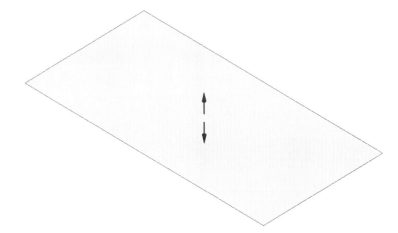

3. Pull the surface up until it resembles the form shown in Figure 9.81. Again, it's more about proportion than dimensions.

FIGURE 9.81
Resulting form

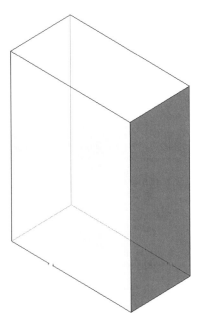

There are a number of shape handles that allow you to modify each face, edge, and intersection. Simply hovering over each face, edge, and vertex will highlight the appropriate control. You may also find it useful to tab through to select the desired control.

If you select a face, you'll be given the control shown in Figure 9.82.

FIGURE 9.82
Face control

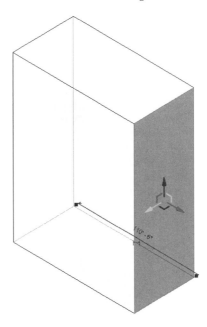

Selecting an edge will give you the ability to modify the edge of a form (Figure 9.83).

FIGURE 9.83
Edge control

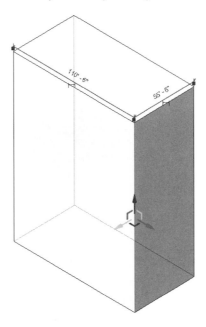

Selecting the intersection allows you to modify the location of a vertex (Figure 9.84).

FIGURE 9.84
Vertex control

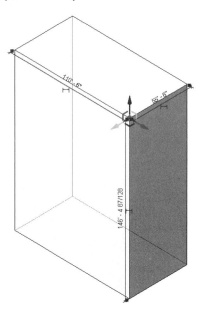

The control arrow allows you to modify the selected element parallel in the direction of the arrow, while the angled indicators of the same colors as their corresponding arrow will allow you to modify the location of the selected element perpendicular to the arrow (Figure 9.85).

FIGURE 9.85
Parallel and per-
pendicular control

First, let's turn on X-ray mode so we can see any of the profiles and controls (Figure 9.86). X-ray mode is helpful for seeing all of the controls that are available as well as the trajectory control of the extrusion.

Now that X-ray mode has been enabled, let's look at the options that Revit provides for turning a rather simple, extruded form into something complex. An edge (Figure 9.87) may be added to an existing form that is from vertex to vertex or parallel with the trajectory of the form (shown as a dotted line from the upper to the lower face).

FIGURE 9.86
X-ray mode

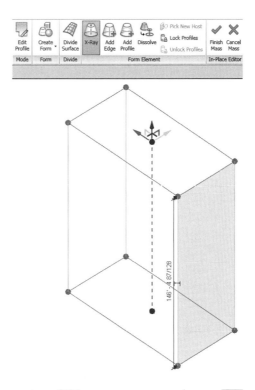

FIGURE 9.87
Adding an edge

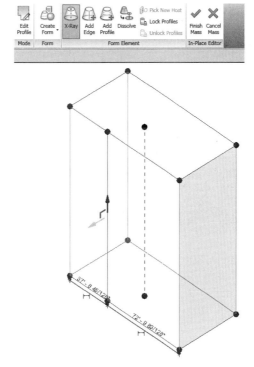

Once the edge has been added, you may push or pull the face adjacent to the new edge, as shown in Figure 9.88.

FIGURE 9.88
Pushing the face

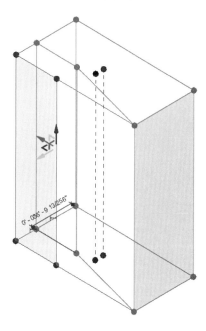

You may also push or pull the edge that has just been created, which will stretch both adjacent faces (Figure 9.89).

FIGURE 9.89
Pushing the edge

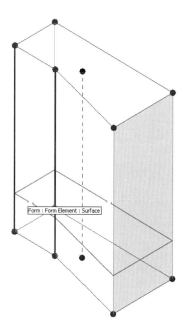

Pushing or pulling the edge that is perpendicular to the edge previously created will create curved and warped surfaces (Figure 9.90). This is fine, since the form that we're creating can be rationalized later when adding a pattern to the surface.

FIGURE 9.90
Pulling the edge

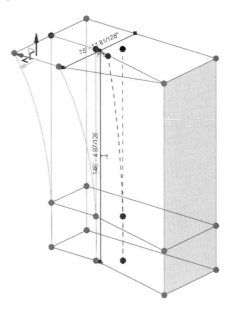

But if you'd rather rationalize the form now (and in doing so remove any warped surfaces), then add another edge from vertex to vertex, as shown in Figure 9.91. This will force the faces to become triangulated and planar, as three points define a plane.

FIGURE 9.91
Adding more edges

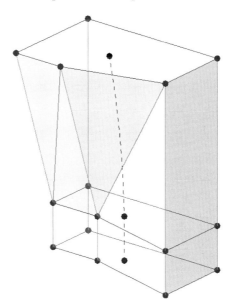

Pulling the top edge away from the vertical plane of the form results in a more dramatic form, as shown in Figure 9.92. Again, it's not necessary to maintain the exact dimensions; it's about trying to keep the proportions appropriate. This is what intuitive form making is all about!

FIGURE 9.92
Pulling the
upper edge

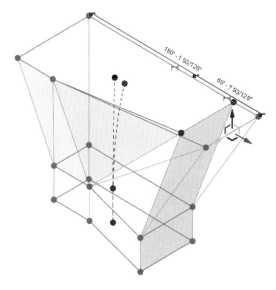

Using the Dissolve function (Figure 9.93) will remove the mass solid and leave behind the analytic profiles that define the solid. The dot in the center of each plane is a control that will allow you to edit the elevation, rotation, and location of the shape.

FIGURE 9.93
Using Dissolve
to remove the
mass solid

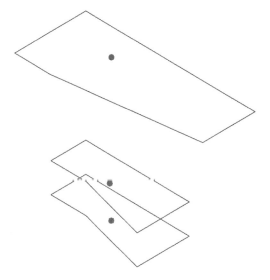

Selecting the profiles together and then choosing the Create Form command will stitch the form back together in a way that interpolates the shape as more of a lofted blend (Figure 9.94). You could also add more profiles to the shape.

FIGURE 9.94
Making a swept blend from three profiles

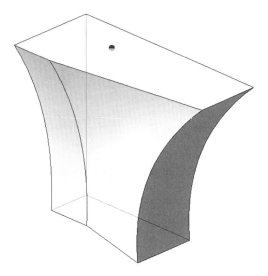

However, if you select only two profiles at a time, then the following occurs (Figure 9.95). This form was created by first selecting the two bottom and middle profile and then creating the form. Then the middle and upper profiles were selected and another form was created. The result is straight—rather than curved—interpolation between the profiles.

FIGURE 9.95
Making a blend from two profiles

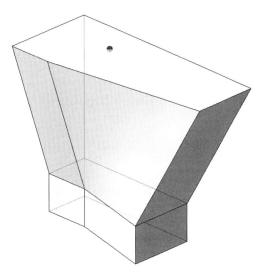

Rather than select either of the two previous options, let's alter the front edge of all three profiles. Start by deleting the existing edge (you'll have to tab to select just this edge) and then delete as shown in Figure 9.96.

FIGURE 9.96
Deleting the edge

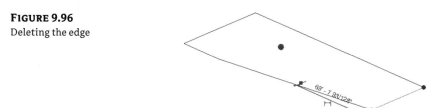

Now you'll want to draw a fillet arch on to rejoin the two remaining edges. To do this you'll have to set the work plane of the shape as shown in Figure 9.97. Just tab through until the horizontal work plane is highlighted and then select it.

FIGURE 9.97
Selecting the
work plane

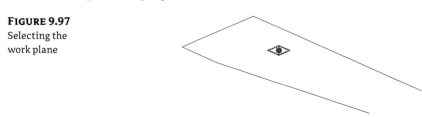

Once the work plane is selected, you'll be able to draw additional model lines. In this example, we're using a fillet arch to connect the lines (Figure 9.98). We'll do the same thing for the other two shapes.

FIGURE 9.98
Completing the
profile

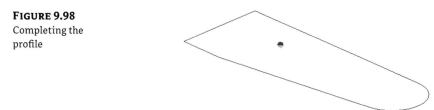

Now select the lower two profiles and choose Create Form. Then do the same with the upper two profiles. Finally, you'll want to remove any blends by adding an edge to the opposing edges.

Creating additional mass solids is easy. You can select an existing face and then select the Create Form command, as shown in Figure 9.99.

The same Create Form command was used to create the form shown in Figure 9.100.

In Figure 9.101, we've extended both faces considerably from their initial depth after using the Create Form option. Notice the locked relationship, which will only allow the faces of the form, not the edges or vertices, to be manipulated. In other words, you wouldn't be able to push or pull the top of the form up. This restriction can be removed by clicking the lock icon.

FIGURE 9.99
Creating the form

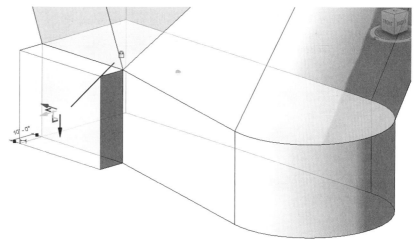

FIGURE 9.100
Creating
another form

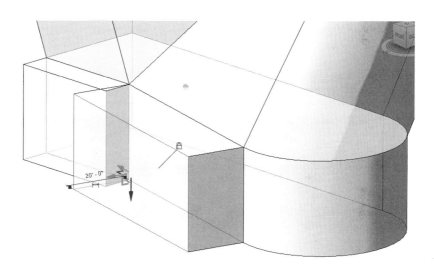

FIGURE 9.101
Unlocking a
reference

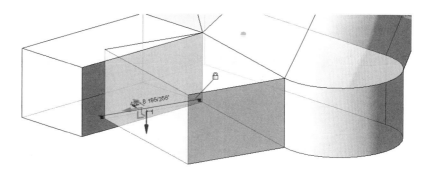

Once unlocked, the edge of the face is easily moved down to give a slope to the edge at the front of the form (Figure 9.102).

FIGURE 9.102
Modifying the edge

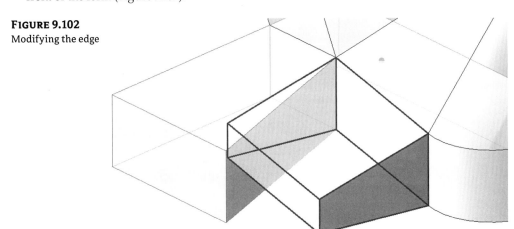

There will be many cases when creating existing geometry from an existing face will give you more mass than you need in your model. In these cases, it's simply a matter of drawing more model lines on the surface of the existing form. Then you'll be able to quickly and easily push and pull the faces, edges, and vertices of the resulting form (Figure 9.103).

FIGURE 9.103
Adding a profile

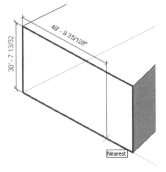

The in-place solid mass is finished, and the masses from Figure 9.102 have been joined so that the edge between the two masses is now visible (Figure 9.104). Go ahead and finish the in-place solid mass and return to the regular project environment.

FIGURE 9.104
Completed mass

FIGURE 9.104
Completed mass

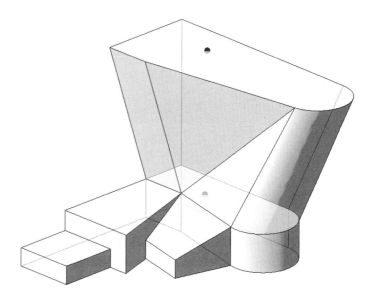

Once you're out of In-Place Massing mode, you'll notice that if you select the model, many shape handles simultaneously appear in the form of solid blue arrowheads (Figure 9.105). You can use shape handles to push and pull your solid mass, but you won't be able to modify edges or vertices without reentering In-Place Massing mode.

FIGURE 9.105
Using shape
handles

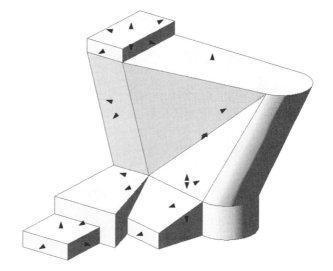

Figure 9.106 shows the finished mass in a perspective view. Both solids and voids can be used to complete a mass form. Whereas solids will add more geometry, voids will remove geometry from your mass.

FIGURE 9.106
Finished form

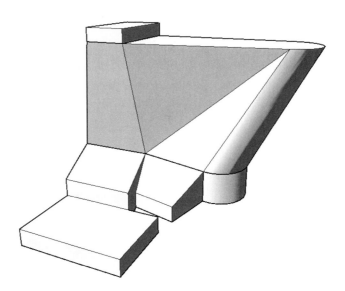

To demonstrate this, we'll return to In-Place Massing mode and create another face on the top of the existing form (Figure 9.107).

FIGURE 9.107
Adding a solid

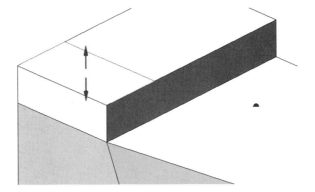

STARTING VOIDS AS SOLIDS

If you create the void as a void, it will immediately cut the solid mass and become invisible. This can be really annoying when you're trying to resolve your design and want to selectively cut after you've intuitively resolved a design idea. Fortunately, there's a better way, as described in the following exercise.

Follow these steps:

1. Rather than create a void, start by creating a solid, even a solid of a different color and category (if necessary) to keep things clear during your design iteration.

2. Select the solid mass and convert it to a void, as shown in Figure 9.108.

FIGURE 9.108
Converting a solid
to a void

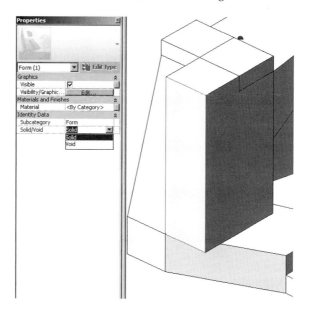

Figure 9.109 shows the result of the void cutting the solid. Keep in mind that if you want to convert the void back to a solid, you'll have to un-cut any geometry that was being cut by the void. But the nice thing about this technique (converting solids to voids and then cutting) is that you've selectively cut only the solids that you wanted to cut. Had you modeled the void as a void, you would have found that the void was cutting many solids and you'd have to un-cut solids that weren't even overlapping with the void!

FIGURE 9.109
Cutting the void

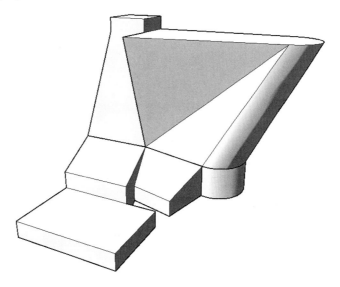

Overall, creating solids masses intuitively is a great way to establish, analyze, and visualize your overall design idea. As you saw earlier in the chapter, mass floors allow you to even quantify gross floor areas before you've committed to geometry.

Furthermore, it's possible to put different intuitive massing ideas inside different design options (covered in Chapter 11), so that many ideas can live in a single Revit project file. Simply initiate worksharing and create worksets for each study mass. Multiple team members will be able to see one another's work at the same time and in context with their design ideas. This is the holistic kind of team approach to design information that makes massing in Revit a unique and valuable design tool. If you'd like to investigate this file further, you can download the file c09_Intuitive_Massing_Solid.rvt from the Chapter 9 folder.

Next we'll investigate parametric and formulaic solid mass creation in the Family Editor.

Formula-Driven Massing

Formula-driven massing can be done in the project environment. But the challenge is that you have to work in context of the project, and all the parameters, formulas, reference planes, and lines can start to get in the way. Therefore, having the option of creating form-driven masses in the Family Editor without the clutter of the project environment can help you focus on what you're trying to accomplish.

You'll want to make sure that you open the right family template. The mass template is in the conceptual mass folder (Figure 9.110). Don't start with generic model or some other template.

FIGURE 9.110
Starting with the mass template

Also, turn off the gradient background that's on by default in the graphic display options (Figure 9.111). You can keep this on if you like, but the images will print better with the option turned off.

FIGURE 9.111
Graphic display options

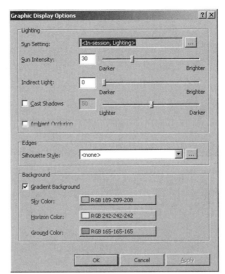

Overall, the UI is not too dissimilar from the project environment. It's like you're creating masses in-place—except that you're not in the project environment, you're in the Family Editor. One significant difference that you can see is that there is a single level and two reference planes, which also define the origin for massing family (Figure 9.112). So, keep in mind that when you reload this family into your project it will update relative to the origin in the family.

FIGURE 9.112
Massing UI

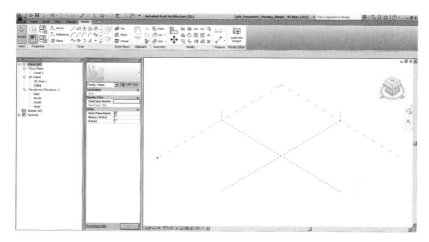

Simple Mass Family

In this example, you'll start by creating a simple mass and then add parameters and test the results. Follow these steps:

1. Create this simple mass using model lines on level one (Figure 9.113). You can save an extra step by selecting the Make Surface From Closed Loops option.

FIGURE 9.113
Selecting the Make Surface From Closed Loops option

2. Once you've created the surface in plan, go to the default 3D view and then pull the surface, as shown in Figure 9.114. Again, don't worry about the actual dimensions. Just get the overall proportions close.

FIGURE 9.114
Creating the mass

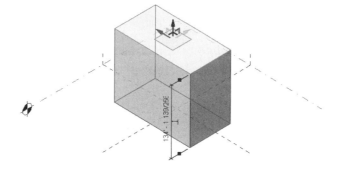

3. Now you'll dimension the form. Be sure to maintain a relationship to the insertion point of the mass template by using a continuous dimension string set to equal (Figure 9.115). Then dimension the overall dimensions in x, y, and z directions.

FIGURE 9.115
Add dimensions

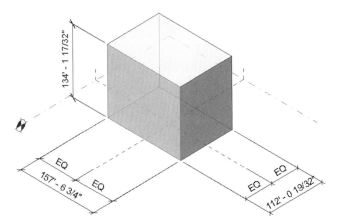

4. Now you'll add parameters to the overall dimensions. Simply select a dimension and you'll be shown a contextual menu that allows you to associate a parameter with the dimension you've just selected (Figure 9.116).

FIGURE 9.116
Associating parameters

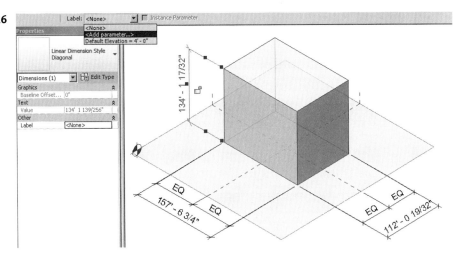

5. Label this dimension **height**, and make it an instance parameter (Figure 9.117). If you had many massing elements of the same type loaded into your project and you wanted to control all of them with the same value, this could be a type parameter. But for this example, an instance parameter is fine.

FIGURE 9.117
Creating parameters

Once you have all your dimensions associated with parameters, your project should look similar to Figure 9.118. That's because as you associate parameter values with your dimensions, the parameter name will display along with the dimension. This is helpful when you need to know which parameter is associated with which dimension.

FIGURE 9.118
Completed parameters

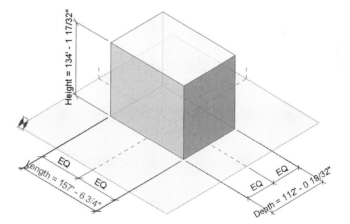

Now it's going to start to get interesting. Rather than maintain independent instance parameters for each dimension, we're going to associate formulas with the length and the depth values. Go ahead and do this as shown in Figure 9.119.

FIGURE 9.119
Creating formulas

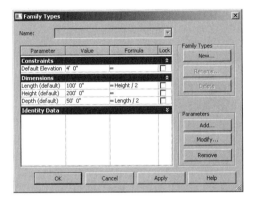

Now your entire mass family can be proportionally controlled simply by adjusting the height parameter (Figure 9.120).

FIGURE 9.120
Proportional form

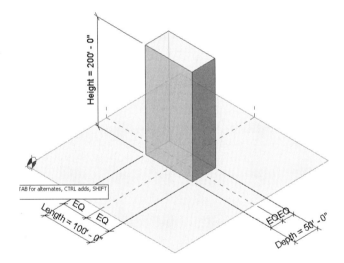

This proportional control can be accomplished in one of two ways. First, you can select the height dimensional value and change the dimension (Figure 9.121). This is desirable when you want to edit a value to an exact amount.

FIGURE 9.121
Adjusting the
height numerically

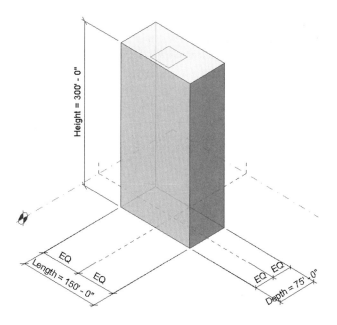

But in many cases, you'll still want to intuitively control the shape of the form first, and then when you get an idea of what looks right, set the resulting dimensional value to a more reasonable figure. This is done by selecting the top face of the form and pushing or pulling the control arrows until you get it close (Figure 9.122). Notice that each time you release the arrow the form adjusts in all dimensions (since the other dimensions are being controlled by formulas related to the height dimension).

FIGURE 9.122
Adjusting the
height intuitively

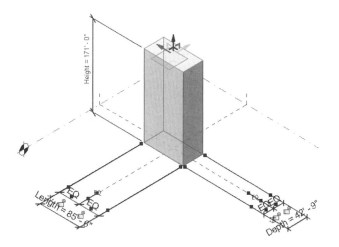

You can experiment further by creating more geometry at the base of the initial mass:

1. Dimension the form as shown in Figure 9.123.

FIGURE 9.123
Adding a
second form

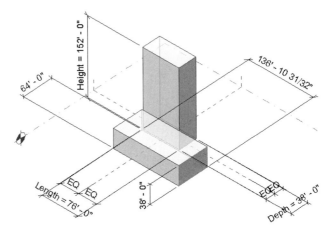

2. Associate the dimensions of this second form to the dimensions that you already created (Figure 9.124). What's terrific about this is that as you change a single value, the overall form will proportionally grow or shrink.

FIGURE 9.124
Associative
parameters

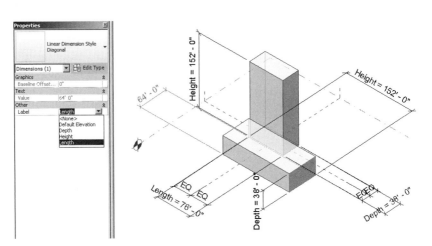

Ultimately this technique of associating parameters with other parameters is a great way to quickly and easily maintain important and interesting formal relationships between masses. Notice how the two masses in Figure 9.125 are barely intersecting near the base of the horizontal form.

FIGURE 9.125
Proportional forms

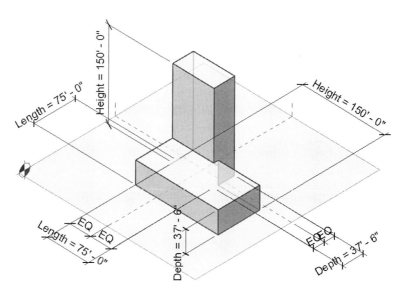

But when you modify the height of the vertical element, both forms grow accordingly (Figure 9.126). The intersection becomes much more noticeable, and if you continued to increase the height of the vertical mass, the intersection would eventually move beyond the face of the horizontal mass. If you want to download this family, look in the Chapter 9 folder for the file c09_Parametric_Massing_Simple.rfa.

FIGURE 9.126
Modifying
parameters

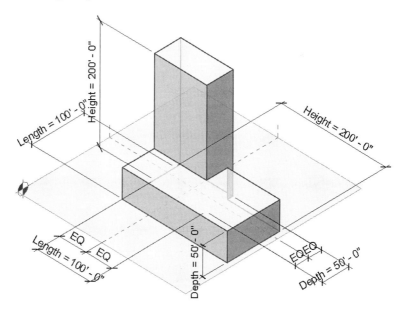

Overall, simple parametric masses can be created quickly and easily in the Family Editor as a mass. But in some cases having access to the old, pre-2010 geometry tools would be great. As you may be aware, there's a built-in solution for this. But since this book is about *mastering* Revit, we're going to show you how right now!

Generic Model Mass Family

A lot of users (the authors included) really miss the ability to use the old geometry tools to create masses. Although it's possible to create parametric generic forms in the Family Editor, when you place them in the project they're still generic elements. You can assign standard walls, curtain walls, and roofs to the faces. But you can't add patterns, create mass floors, or even schedule the results as a mass. We think this is unfortunate! Yes, being able to modify the edge and vertex of a new massing element has some advantages. But many of us early adopters knew how to create the same resulting shape using the old, familiar toolset! So, if you like the old pre-2010 tools, here's how to use them to create project masses in Revit 2011:

1. Open a generic model template (Figure 9.127). We're going to create a flexible, parametric form and then "trick" Revit into thinking that this generic family is a mass.

FIGURE 9.127
Generic model template

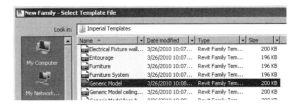

You won't be able to trick Revit by creating a generic model family and then convert it to a mass by changing the family category (Figure 9.128). But there's another way, so just hang in there!

FIGURE 9.128
Message box explaining you can't change the category

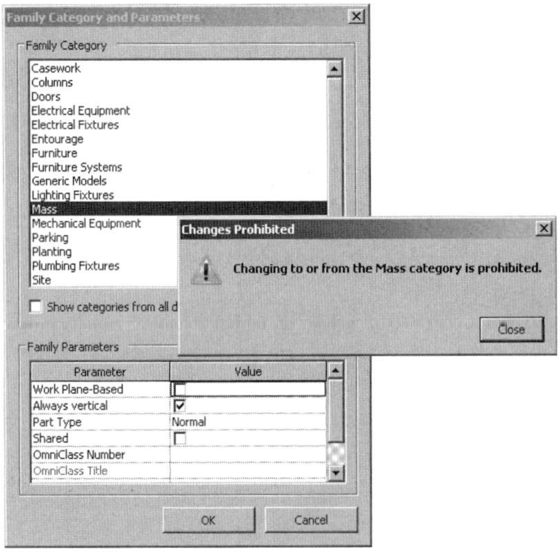

2. Go to a floor plan reference level view in your family. Begin by creating a reference line (not a reference plane), as shown in Figure 9.129. Note that the reference line is drawn from the intersection of the reference planes in an upward direction.

FIGURE 9.129
First reference line

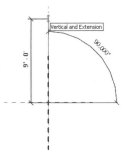

3. Draw another reference line in a downward direction (Figure 9.130). These reference lines will control the angular "twist" in our eventual family.

FIGURE 9.130
Second
reference line

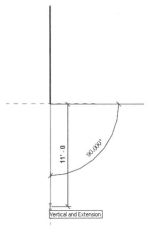

Now you're going to create a blend (Figure 9.131) that is associated with the reference lines you just created. The bottom of the blend will be associated with the first reference line and the top of the blend will be associated with the second reference line.

FIGURE 9.131
Creating a blend

4. Before you start to sketch the bottom shape for the blend, it's important that you select the reference line as your work plane (Figure 9.132).

FIGURE 9.132
Setting the
work plane

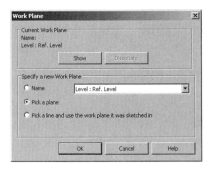

5. Select the upper reference line as shown in Figure 9.133.

FIGURE 9.133
Selecting the upper
reference line

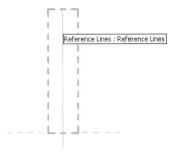

6. Sketch a rectilinear form as shown in Figure 9.134. The exact dimensions aren't important. What is important is that the dimensions are equally distributed between the reference lines. You also want to give parameters to the overall dimensions. We've called the instance parameter **BW** (for bottom width) and assigned the parameter to both the overall dimensions.

FIGURE 9.134
Bottom with
dimensions

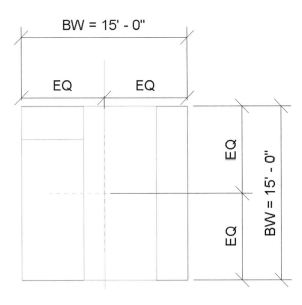

7. When you add the parameter, assign the settings shown in Figure 9.135.

FIGURE 9.135
Use these instance
parameters.

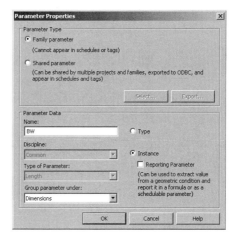

8. Select Edit to sketch the top of the blend. But make sure that you set the bottom reference line as the work plane (Figure 9.136). This will allow you to control the angular twist of the blend when it's complete.

FIGURE 9.136
Setting the
work plane

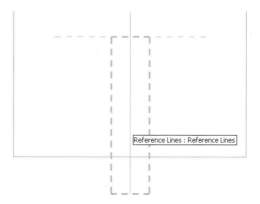

9. Essentially we're going to repeat the previous step for the lower sketch for this upper sketch. Equally distribute the overall dimensions and give the parameters as shown in Figure 9.137. We've called these parameters **TW** (for top width).

FIGURE 9.137
Top width param-
eters and sketch

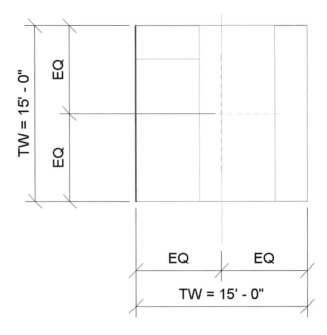

10. Now that the base and top width parameters have been set, you can add parameters to control the height of the blend. Do this by selecting the button to the right of the second end constraints (Figure 9.138).

FIGURE 9.138
Adding the height
parameter

11. Add the parameter **H** (for height), as shown in Figure 9.139. Now select Finish Family to complete the blended form.

12. You should take a moment to test that the reference lines control the top and bottom sketch of the blend (Figure 9.140). Simply select the reference line to highlight it and then

move the end of the reference line. The other end remains associated with the intersection of the insertion point and the top and bottom sketch rotate.

FIGURE 9.139
Instance parameter for the height

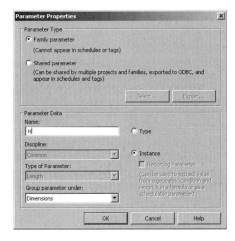

FIGURE 9.140
Twisting the blend with reference lines

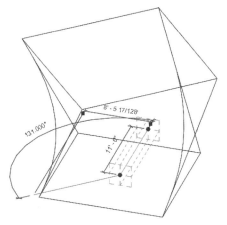

13. From a plan view, move the reference lines so that they're no longer on top of the reference planes. Now you can add angular dimensions between the reference line and the reference plane (Figure 9.141). Furthermore, you can add parameters to control the top and bottom angles of the blend. We've called these instance parameters **BA** and **TA** (for bottom angle and top angle, respectively). Figure 9.141 also shows all the parameters that control this blend. Go ahead and test them.

FIGURE 9.141
Angular
parameters

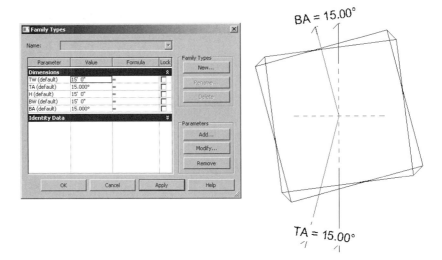

14. You're going to use the edges of this blend to drive the geometry that we're going to create. But since we don't want to see this blend, we'll turn it into a void (Figure 9.142).

FIGURE 9.142
Turning a solid
into a void

15. After you change the solid blend into a void, it will look similar to Figure 9.143.

FIGURE 9.143
The resulting
void blend

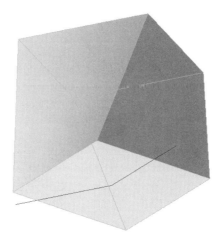

16. You'll begin to create the sweep that will create our building mass in the project environment. That's right—the building mass is going to be based on a circuitous sweep! Select the Sweep function from the Forms tab (Figure 9.144).

FIGURE 9.144
Selecting the
Sweep function

17. Now select Pick Path (not Sketch Path) in order to select the edges of the blend previously created (Figure 9.145).

FIGURE 9.145
Using the Pick
Path tool

18. Pick the edges of the blend, as shown in Figure 9.146. Note the location of the sketch plane along the lower rear edge. This is because this is first edge selected.

FIGURE 9.146
Selecting the edges
of the blend

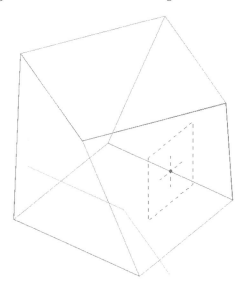

19. Once you have selected the edges of the blend, click the Select Profile option and select Edit Profile (Figure 9.147). This will allow you to sketch the profile in direct context of the selected edges.

FIGURE 9.147
Selecting the Edit
Profile option

20. After you've sketched the profile as shown, be sure to add parameters to the profile width and height. We've called the instance parameters **PW** and **PH**, respectively (Figure 9.148).

FIGURE 9.148
Adding parameters
to the profile width
and height

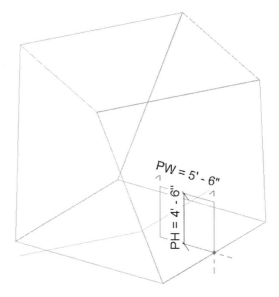

21. Finish the sketch and the sweep, and the profile will generate as shown in Figure 9.149.

FIGURE 9.149
Finished mass

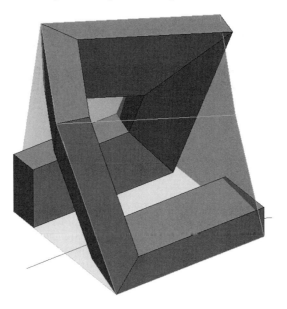

Now it's going to start to get really interesting! We'll use this generic model family in the project environment and Revit will think it's a mass:

1. Open a new project and begin by creating an in-place mass. We've named the mass as shown in Figure 9.150.

FIGURE 9.150
Naming the mass

2. While still in the In-Place Mass mode, go back to your family and load the generic model into your project environment. Go ahead and place the generic family as a component into your project. Again, this is being done during In-Place Mass mode.

3. Flex the parameters as shown in Figure 9.151. What started as a small parametric form the size of a room is now over 100′ (30m) tall!

FIGURE 9.151
Changing parameter values

4. Now finish the in-place mass. Even though this is a generic model family, because you've placed it during In-Place Mass mode, Revit treats it as a mass.

5. Add the levels as shown in Figure 9.152 so that there are levels that extend across the entire elevation of your massing.

FIGURE 9.152
Adding levels that
extend across the
elevation of your
massing

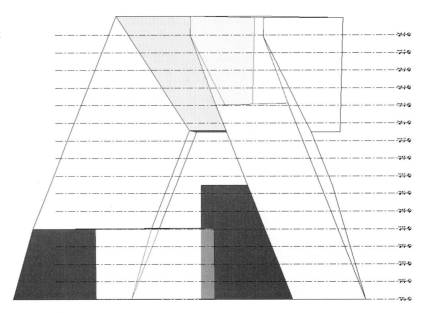

6. Return to In-Place Mass mode and select the generic mass, and you'll be able to add floor area faces to your massing (Figure 9.153).

FIGURE 9.153
Floor area faces

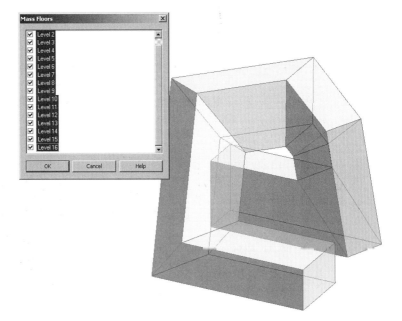

7. If you hover over the face and tab to select it, you'll also be able to associate patterns and pattern-based components with your generic massing family (Figure 9.154). This is because Revit is now treating it as a massing element in the Mass category.

FIGURE 9.154
Adding pattern-
based components

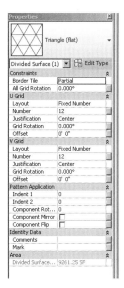
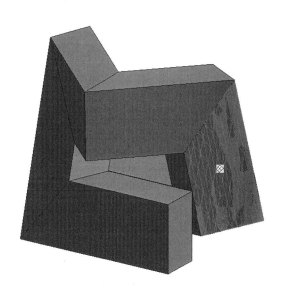

FIGURE 9.154
Adding pattern-
based components

Figure 9.155 shows four perspective views of the completed massing study, all created with the familiar geometry toolset.

FIGURE 9.155
Perspective views

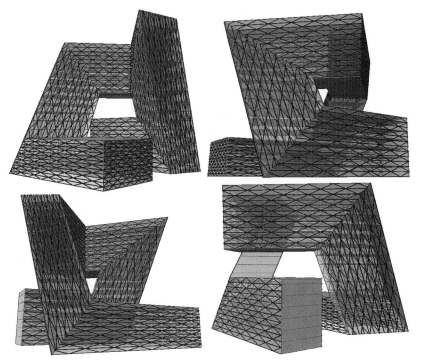

We've also rendered the model as shown in Figure 9.156. The results are quite interesting, and you'd still have the ability to modify the underlying parametric family and then rehost the faces. You'll also be able to schedule the volume, surface, and floor area of the mass.

FIGURE 9.156
Rendering of the generic massing project

You can download and further investigate the files that were used to create this exercise in the Chapter 9 folder. Simply download the project file c09_Parametric_Generic_Massing.rvt, which contains the in-place massing and the loaded generic element.

Now let's begin to investigate how to create parametric massing in the Family Editor using the conventional massing tools.

Complex Mass Family

Let's start by opening a conceptual massing family template, as shown in Figure 9.157. You'll also turn off the gradient background in this section.

FIGURE 9.157
Conceptual massing template

In the past, the ability to parametrically control objects in the massing editor was done using reference planes and reference lines. What was great is that Revit introduced reference point elements in 2010. Point elements allow for Cartesian x, y, z as well as rotational control.

With all complex and parametrically controlled families, we think it's best to get the rules down first. In this case, the rules are the parameters and formulas that will control a twisting, tapering tower. Open the Family Types dialog box and enter the values and formulas shown in Figure 9.158. Doing this first will save a lot of time and frustration from having to name parameters. You'll only need to assign parameters as necessary.

FIGURE 9.158
Family Types
dialog box

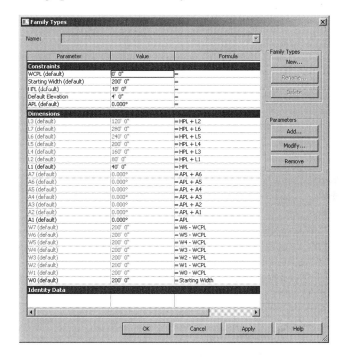

We're going to create the first rectilinear form on the first reference level. As you do this, be sure to use reference (not model) lines (Figure 9.159).

FIGURE 9.159
Using reference
lines

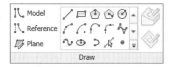

Dimension the sketch twice, making sure to use the EQ function to evenly distribute the sketch at the center of the reference lines at the origin. When finished, associate both overall dimensions with the W0 parameter that you've already created (Figure 9.160). W0 is shorthand for the width dimension on the 0 level.

FIGURE 9.160
Dimensioned
reference lines

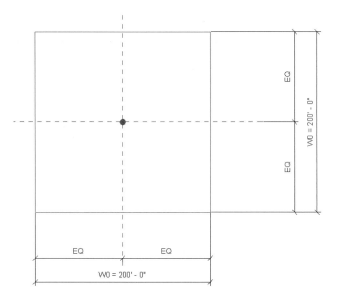

While in the same view, place seven point elements at the intersection of the default reference places. Each time you place a point element, you'll get a warning about overlapping point elements, as shown in Figure 9.161. Go ahead and ignore these warnings.

FIGURE 9.161
Ignore this
warning.

Now go to your south elevation and select just one of the point elements that you placed in plan. You can elevate it manually by dragging the up arrow to move it away from the other overlapping point elements (Figure 9.162).

FIGURE 9.162
Moving the point
element

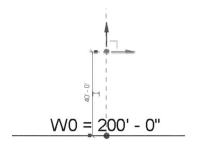

But when you select the arrow, you'll also have the option to parametrically associate the point element with one of the seven instance parameters that you've just created (Figure 9.163). The L parameters refer to the level number of each of your point elements. The first point element is L1 since it is reference level 1.

FIGURE 9.163
Adding a parameter to the point element

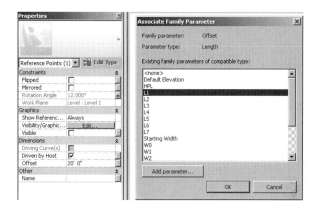

Now go ahead and do this for all your point elements. When you are finished, the south elevation will look similar to Figure 9.164.

FIGURE 9.164
The south elevation will look like this.

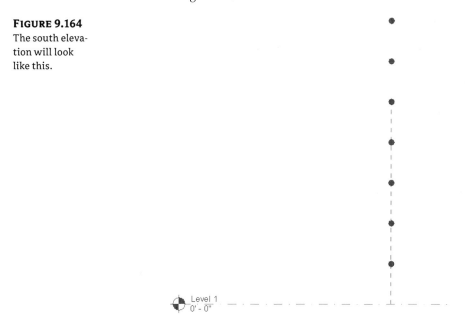

Right now the point elements are just spherical nodes. Their reference planes are not visible. Let's change that by selecting all of them and then selecting Always next to the Show Reference option in the Graphics panel of the Properties dialog box (Figure 9.165).

FIGURE 9.165
Selecting Always
next to Show
Reference

The reference planes of your point elements will now be visible, as shown in Figure 9.166.

FIGURE 9.166
The reference
planes will now
be visible.

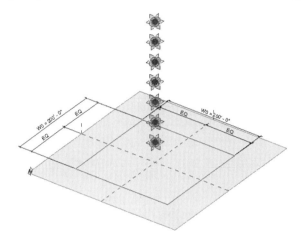

Select the lowest point element and associate it with the parameter that will control its angular rotation (Figure 9.167). Select the button next to the rotation angle and associate it with the A1 instance parameter.

FIGURE 9.167
Setting the
rotation angle

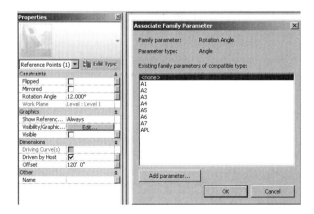

Now set the active work plane to the point element, as shown in Figure 9.168. Then sketch a rectilinear shape as shown. Dimension it just like we did for the sketch at level 0. Dimension both directions with an overall dimension as well as an EQ dimension. Finally, associate the overall dimensions with the W1 parameter, which will control the width of the sketch.

FIGURE 9.168
Creating the
second sketch

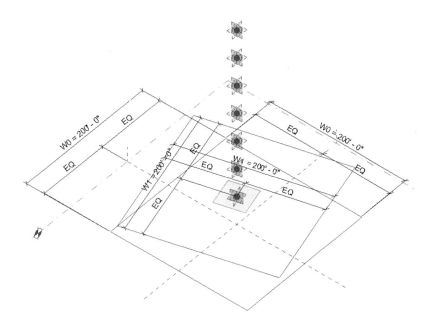

Systematically do this for each of the point elements, making sure to set the respective reference plane before you sketch the shape with reference lines. When you have finished this for all seven point elements that you created, your view will resemble Figure 9.169.

For clarity, we've hidden the dimensions in the view, so that you can see all the reference lines and point elements.

FIGURE 9.169
Reference lines and
point elements

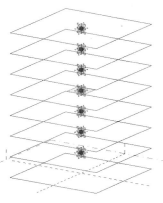

Now select all the reference lines and select Create Form. Although this will look like a simple extrusion, it's actually a blend with many profiles. Let's open the Family Types dialog box and begin to test the results before loading into the project (Figure 9. 170).

Test the parameter that controls the distance between levels by increasing the HPL instance parameter (which stands for height per level).

FIGURE 9.170
Testing our form and instance parameters

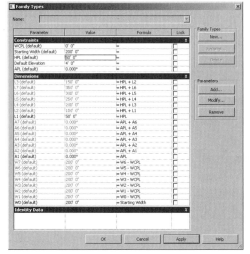
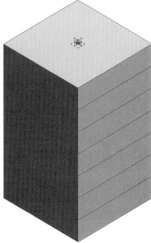

Now let's test the ability of the shape to taper (Figure 9.171). Do this by increasing the WCPL instance parameter (which stands for width control per level).

FIGURE 9.171
Increasing the WCPL instance parameter

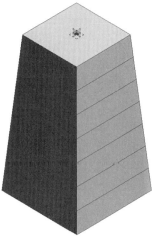

Now let's test the parameters that control the amount of angular twist per level (Figure 9.172). Do this by increasing the APL parameter (which stands for angle per level).

FIGURE 9.172
Increasing the APL
parameter

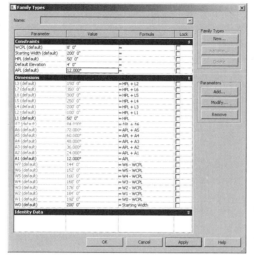

Now that we've tested the massing in the family environment, go ahead and open a new project and start to create a new, in-place mass. Then place this family into the project during In-Place Mass mode. When you select the massing family, you'll be given access to all of its parameters in the Properties dialog box, as shown in Figure 9.173. You can quickly and easily test the massing parameters in order to significantly increase the height, width, taper, and incremental rotation of the massing family.

FIGURE 9.173
Flexing the
parameters

Adding patterns to the face of your mass should be second nature if you've been doing all the exercises in this book. Simply tab to select the face, and then apply the pattern as shown in Figure 9.174.

FIGURE 9.174
Adding patterns
to the face of
your mass

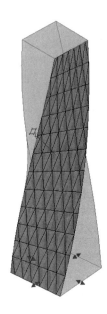

Floor area faces are another simple matter. Provided you have enough levels in your project, simply select the mass and then select the levels that you want to associate with the floor faces (Figure 9.175).

FIGURE 9.175
Floor area faces

Creating interesting and complex massing studies that can be parametrically controlled isn't just a skill developed over time. The rules that you develop to make and reiterate your design are also carefully considered aesthetic choices to make decisions rather than blobs! To see this file, go to the Chapter 9 folder and download c09_Parametric_Massing_Complex_Project.rvt.

The Bottom Line

Create and schedule massing studies.   Starting the design process with actual building elements can lead to a lot of unexpected frustration. Walls lead to rooms, which get room tags and eventually scheduled. But if you've failed to fulfill the program, you'll wonder where to start over!

Master It   You're faced with creating some design studies of a large hospital complex. How would you go about creating a Revit project that would allow you to create a massing study and schedule it against the design program?

Know when to use solid and surface masses.   While solid masses and surface masses can both be used to maintain relationships to host geometry like walls and roofs, surface masses can't be volumetrically scheduled or contain floor area faces.

Master It   You've been asked to create a complex canopy system for the entry to a hotel project. The system will consist of a complex wave of triangular panels. What kind of mass would you create?

Use mathematical formulas for massing.   Not all massing is going to be intuitive, in-the-moment decision making. By discovering the underlying rules that express a form, it is possible to create the formulas that can iterate and manipulate your massing study. So rather than manually manipulate the mass, you simply manipulate the formulas related to your mass.

Master It   What's the best way to discover and create these formulas?

Chapter 10

Conceptual Design and Sustainability

In this chapter, we will take a further look at Revit's Conceptual Design tool and how you can leverage it for sustainable design analysis. We'll also explore some tools with Revit and some that use Revit's BIM geometry to support sustainable design analysis.

Revit has a number of tools that support sustainable design processes and analysis, ranging from accurate material takeoffs to energy analysis to daylighting. As you move from a more traditional design workflow to Revit, you will see more opportunities to engage environmental simulations within the Revit model. This ability to see the model from different points of view makes a BIM project perfect for exploring sustainable design strategies. We will explore how Revit can help support those strategies.

In this chapter, you'll learn to:

◆ Embrace sustainable design concepts

◆ Leverage schedules

◆ Use sun shading and solar paths

◆ Prepare and export your model for energy analysis

◆ Analyze your project for daylighting

Sustainable Design Concepts

Environmentally thoughtful design strategies have been around for millennium, but the practice of sustainable design has seen substantial growth over the past few years. Sustainable design practices can help address many issues, among them energy use, access to natural daylight, human health and productivity, and resource conversation. One of the principal goals of sustainable design is to reduce a building's overall resource use. This can be measured in the building's carbon footprint (http://greenfootstep.org), or the net amount of carbon dioxide emitted by a building through its energy use.

An important factor in sustainable design is the large effect that the construction industry has on the environment. The United States, for example, uses 25 percent of the world's energy, and the U.S. building industry uses 40 percent of global energy. Buildings, taken together, are the largest single resource consumer in the world. To solve the problem of global warming, you need to look at the low-hanging fruit of the architecture, engineering, and construction (AEC) industry and work toward a more efficient, more sustainable building practice.

Before we delve into discussing any specific workflows involving BIM and sustainability, it's important to recognize that many concepts are both interdependent and cumulative. The more sustainable methodologies you can incorporate into a project, the "greener" the project becomes.

Take the example of building orientation, glazing, and daylighting. Rotating your building in the proper direction, using the right glass in the correct amount and location, and integrating sun shading into the project to optimize the use of natural light all build upon each other. Using these three strategies together makes a building operate more efficiently while allowing occupants access to plenty of natural light. The amount of usable daylight you might capture will be greatly reduced with highly reflective glass or if the building faces the wrong orientation. The appropriateness any of these individual strategies and the benefits depend on building type and climate.

Revit has similar characteristics. Because it is a parametric modeler, all the parts are interrelated. Understanding and capitalizing on these interrelationships typically take numerous iterations that span multiple projects. Optimizing the integrated strategies and technologies for a high-performance green design requires a continual look at understanding of how they work together to deliver the best potential. That is where Revit comes in—allowing the ability to iterate and analyze faster than in a more traditional process. The process is built on the following methodology for reducing the energy consumption of buildings:

1. Understand climate.

2. Reduce loads.

3. Use free energy.

4. Use efficient systems.

🌐 Real World Scenario

BAD MODELING HAS BAD DOWNSTREAM EFFECTS

Like poor ecology, poor BIM modeling can have a negative impact downstream on team members and project stakeholders. If you are choosing to use your model for sustainable design analysis, remember that the more accurate you are in your modeling, the more accurate your results will be.

Conversely, a poorly assembled model will deliver inaccurate results. If you do not establish the proper materials in a daylighting model, for instance, you will not get the right reflectivity and therefore your daylighting results will be inaccurate. If rooms and volumes are not established properly within the Revit model, your energy performance will be off. These faulty results can prompt you to make changes in your design that are incorrect or unnecessary.

It is a good idea to establish early on in your modeling process which sustainable design analyses you will be performing based on your Revit model geometry. It is much easier to set the model up for successful analysis when you begin than it is to go back and have to make significant changes to the model midstream to perform analysis.

Using Schedules

You can repurpose many tools in Revit for other uses. Schedules are a great example of this. In Chapter 5, we discussed how to use schedules to track quality control of the model. Schedules are also a useful tool in sustainable design. Schedules can help track the amount of materials in the design process. If the design is looking to achieve a Leadership in Energy and Environmental Design (LEED) certification (www.usgbc.org/leed), one of the possible points is for the use of recycled materials. Based on how LEED calculates their recycled content requirements (by volume and cost), some of the key materials for recycled content tend to be steel and concrete. Although the schedules created in Revit are not usable for LEED credit submissions in this case, knowing how to calculate recycled content within a project can help steer the project goals during the design phase.

Calculating Recycled Content

In this section's project, pretend you want to use fly ash, a by-product of steel manufacturing, in your project as recycled content. Fly ash was first used as a concrete additive in 1929 in the Hoover Dam. Since your building has a primarily concrete structure, you can easily calculate the amounts of fly ash using schedules.

To create this schedule, open the Chapter 10 Jenkins.rvt file. You can download this file from the book's companion website (www.sybex.com/go/masteringrevit2011).

1. Select the View tab and choose the Schedules fly-out. In this menu, select Material Takeoff, as shown in Figure 10.1.

FIGURE 10.1
Selecting Material Takeoff from the Schedule fly-out

2. The New Material Takeoff dialog box shown in Figure 10.2 appears. Rename the default schedule name to **Concrete Take-off**.

FIGURE 10.2
Naming the new schedule

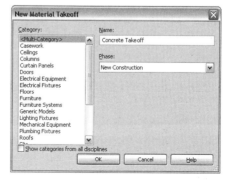

3. Now you want to add a couple of fields. Choose Material: Name and Material: Volume from the list on the left. Using the Add button, add them to the column on the right (Figure 10.3).

FIGURE 10.3
Adding fields to the schedule

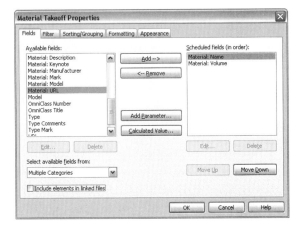

4. Now, still on the Fields tab, click the Calculated Value button. Clicking this button opens the Calculated Value dialog box, which allows you to add custom fields that contain equations. You cannot only leverage some of the features of Revit's database structure, but also create fields in your schedules that are formulaically based on other content. In this dialog box, name the value **Recycled Content** and change the type to Volume, as shown in Figure 10.4.

FIGURE 10.4
Setting up the calculated value

5. At the bottom of the Calculated Value dialog box is a blank field for the formula. This field directs Revit on how to perform the calculations. In this project, you want to calculate the volume of fly ash in the model. So, in Revit terminology, you want to create a formula using the Material: Volume and multiply that against the amount of fly ash you want to use in the construction. To create this formula, you can either type the formula in directly or select the fields you want to perform calculations against using the field selection button . If you choose to type your formula in directly, remember that schedules are case sensitive and the values will need to be entered that way. For this example, choose the selection button. This will open another dialog box (Figure 10.5), allowing you to select the Material: Volume field.

FIGURE 10.5
Adding the formula

6. For this project, your goal is to include 25 percent fly ash in our concrete mixture. Since you have just selected the Material: Volume field, you need to finish the equation. To do this, multiply by 0.25 so your final equation will look like Figure 10.6. Click OK.

FIGURE 10.6
Finishing the calculated value

7. Now that you have your fields defined, you need to visit the rest of the tabs to define your schedule. The next tab is Filter tab. So far, you haven't defined what materials you want to see in your schedule—you are currently showing all of them. In this example, you want to filter out all but concrete as a material. In the Filter By field, select Material: Name. In the drop-down next to that, select Begins With and in the field below the Material: Name, type **Concrete**. Your filtered schedule should look like Figure 10.7. This will schedule only materials that begin with the name Concrete. Filtering in this way can be more effective than filtering for an exact name because it allows for some variety in the material names. If you are working on a project team and one team member has called the material Concrete – Cast in Place and another team member has created a material called Concrete – CIP, this schedule will include both.

FIGURE 10.7
Adding filters to
the schedule

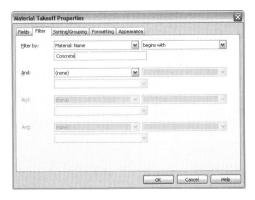

8. After you complete the Filter tab, select the Sorting/Grouping tab. In this tab, choose to sort by Material: Name (Figure 10.8). You also want to select the Grand Totals checkbox at the bottom of this tab.

FIGURE 10.8
Sorting the
schedule

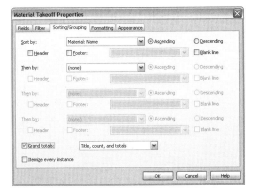

9. The last tab you'll need to adjust is the Formatting tab. Select this tab and highlight Material: Volume in the column on the left. Here you can adjust the alignment of the Material: Volume field. From the Alignment drop-down, choose Right. You want to see the columns calculate their totals. To do this, choose the Calculate Totals checkbox. This checkbox is activated individually for each column. You want to make the same adjustments for the Recycled Content field (Figure 10.9), both right-justification and calculating the totals.

FIGURE 10.9
Modifying the
format

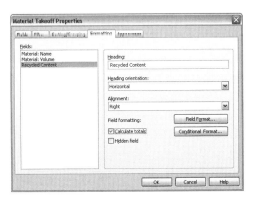

10. Now that you've completed all of the formatting and calculations, you can see the results of the schedule. Click OK, and the schedule will generate a single line, as shown in Figure 10.10. The new Concrete Take-off schedule shows the name of the material, the cubic feet of concrete in the project, and how much fly ash would be (calculated in cubic feet) if you use 25 percent of the volume of the concrete. This schedule will continue to dynamically update as you add or subtract concrete from the overall design, giving you an up-to-date amount of fly ash.

FIGURE 10.10

The Concrete Takeoff schedule

Concrete Takeoff		
Material: Name	Material: Volume	Recycled Content
Concrete - Cast-in-Place Concrete	24424.35 CF	6106.09 CF
Grand total: 18	24424.35 CF	6106.09 CF

Calculating the Window-to-Wall Ratio

The window-to-wall ratio (WWR) is the percent of glazing you have on any given façade versus the amount of unglazed area. Knowing this percentage can help determine the ideal amount of glazing you will want on each façade to maximize the efficiency of your HVAC system coupled with your glazing area. The exact percentage of this number will vary depending on your building use, longitude, and façade orientation. Working directly with your mechanical consultant, you can arrive at a goal percentage for each primary building façade.

As a general rule of thumb, it's best to minimize east/west exposure and maximize the north/south exposures if the building site allows. With south exposures, it's easier to control the amount of daylight entering the building with the use of sun shading. North exposures have limited, if any, direct solar exposure. Since the sun rises and sets on the east/west sides of the building, there is a full arc of daylight (from the peak of the azimuth to the horizon) over the course of the day, making those exposures the most challenging to moderate.

In the sample Jenkins building project, you have an adjacent building proposed next to the existing one. In this scenario, you have been modeling a proposed new building form in Revit's conceptual massing. While doing so, say you've been working with your mechanical engineer to establish the ideal WWR for your primary façade. You now need to calculate the amount of façade you have per floor so you can begin to add glazing to the design.

During conceptual design, the focus was more on the building form than the exact locations of the floors relative to the existing building. Since the form was created as a conceptual mass, the only datum established was the ground plane. To view the sample building addition, open the JenkinsAddition.rfa file located on the book's companion web page (www.sybex.com/go/masteringrevit2011). Open the Jenkins Building model and load the JenkinsAddition.rfa family into the file, placing it to the right of the primary façade (Figure 10.11). Now you're ready to create a quick schedule to run these calculations.

FIGURE 10.11
Adding the conceptual mass to the Jenkins model

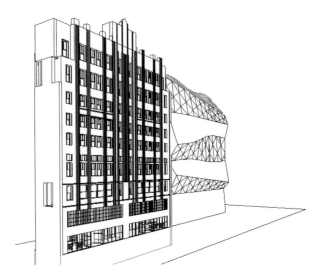

1. The first thing you might notice when inserting the mass into the model is that the mass isn't visible in each of the views. You need to turn on the visibility of the mass so you can see it in all the views. On the Massing & Site tab, click the Show Mass button. This will highlight and stay highlighted until turned off and allow you to see the inserted mass family in all the views (Figure 10.12). This is a unique feature for masses; activating this button will allow you to see the masses, but remember that if you don't select Mass in the Visibility/Graphic Overrides dialog box, it won't show up when you print the views, even though you'll see it on the screen.

FIGURE 10.12
Making the mass visible

2. Since you didn't add any levels to the mass, you need to project the levels of the original building into the addition and create floors. You want to ultimately create a schedule showing WWR by floor so you have more control over glazing areas. But first you need the floors projected into your mass. To do this, select and highlight the mass. The Modify | Mass tab will appear, Click the Mass Floors button (Figure 10.13).

FIGURE 10.13
Clicking the Mass Floors button

3. Selecting this tool will open the Mass Floors dialog box. Since you want one floor in the addition for each floor in the main model, select Levels 1–8, as shown in Figure 10.14. In addition, you're choosing to incorporate a double-height lobby space, so do not select the mezzanine level.

FIGURE 10.14
Selecting floors

4. Click OK to populate the mass family with floors, similar to Figure 10.15.

FIGURE 10.15
Floors have been added to the mass.

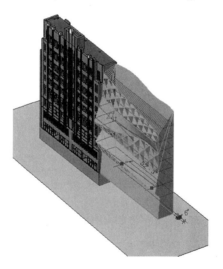

5. Now that the floors are established, you can create a schedule that will report some key information about the mass and the new floors. You can use scheduling to not only help you find the wall-to-floor ratio (so you can establish WWR) but also the actual area of each new floor plate. To start this, choose Schedule/Quantities from the View tab (Figure 10.16).

FIGURE 10.16
Creating a sched-
ule for the wall-to-
floor ratio

6. From the list of schedule categories, choose Mass Floor and give the new schedule a distinctive name (Figure 10.17).

FIGURE 10.17
Selecting the Mass
Floor schedule

7. Similar to the last schedule you created, you need to select some fields to populate the
schedule. Choose the following fields:

◆ Level

◆ Floor Area

◆ Exterior Surface Area

You also want to create a new Calculated Value. Click the Calculated Value button and
name the new field **Exterior Surface Area %**. Select Percentage from the radio buttons
and from the Of drop-down, select Exterior Surface Area (Figure 10.18).

FIGURE 10.18
Creating the new
calculated value

8. The finished Fields tab will look like Figure 10.19. Now, select the Sorting/Grouping tab.

FIGURE 10.19
The finished
Fields tab

9. On the Sorting/Grouping tab, you want to see the floors in order, so choose Level from the Sort By drop-down (Figure 10.20).

FIGURE 10.20
Sorting by Level

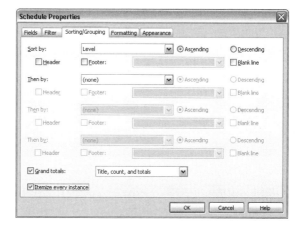

10. As a final adjustment to our schedule, you want to select the Formatting tab. For the following fields, change Alignment to Right and select the Calculate Values box (Figure 10.21).

◆ Floor Area

◆ Exterior Surface Area

◆ Exterior Surface Area %

FIGURE 10.21
Modifying
the schedule
formatting

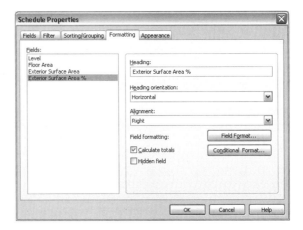

11. The finished schedule for this mass will look like Figure 10.22. You will see you were able to quickly calculate the floor area available by level in the mass as well as the exterior wall area. The Exterior Surface Area % tells you how much of the existing wall area each floor occupies. Using this, you can work with your mechanical consultant to better determine how much glazing you should have by façade and floor.

FIGURE 10.22
The finished
schedule

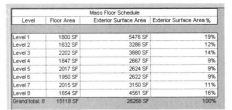

Mass Floor Schedule			
Level	Floor Area	Exterior Surface Area	Exterior Surface Area %
Level 1	1800 SF	5476 SF	19%
Level 2	1632 SF	3286 SF	12%
Level 3	2202 SF	3880 SF	14%
Level 4	1847 SF	2667 SF	9%
Level 5	2017 SF	2624 SF	9%
Level 6	1950 SF	2622 SF	9%
Level 7	2015 SF	3150 SF	11%
Level 8	1654 SF	4561 SF	16%
Grand total: 8	15118 SF	28266 SF	100%

Sun Shading and Solar Paths

Good sustainable design optimizes the use of natural daylight within the building, thereby minimizing the need for artificial lighting. While letting in the natural daylight, it's good to mitigate the amount of direct light coming into the building because sunlight directly entering a building becomes heat and that heat then needs to be conditioned or taken into account for HVAC loads.

You can see even in this project the difference in direct sun exposure on the glazing at different times of year. Figure 10.23 shows the sun striking the building at noon on the equinox, while Figure 10.24 shows the sun hitting the building façade during the summer solstice. The deeper windows in this façade help to add some shading to the glazing.

FIGURE 10.23
The Jenkins
building during
the equinox

FIGURE 10.24
The Jenkins
building during the
summer solstice

Sun Studies

Sun studies are views that can be stills or animated that help you visualize the solar exposure and sun shading on the building. These views can be created in interior or exterior conditions and help to demonstrate the course of the sun over the length of the year. By creating camera views at key locations within your model, you can see the resulting sun and shadows over the course of the day or year. In Figure 10.25, you can see the difference in the sun between the summer and winter solstices (June 21 and December 21, respectively).

FIGURE 10.25
Summer solstice (left) and winter solstice (right)

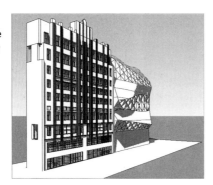 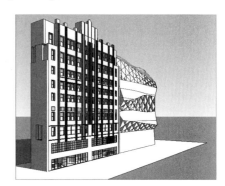

Remember that once the views are established, you will be able to revisit those same views as the design evolves so you can regularly see how the sun affects the new building form from the same angle.

Creating a Solar Study

Open the Jenkins building model in the Chapter 10 folder on the book's companion web page (www.sybex.com/go/masteringrevit2011), and let's create a few views to study the sun on the building interior and exterior. First, you need to establish a view in which to see the building.

1. Set up a camera view by selecting Level 3 and creating a camera view. Click at the lower left of the plan, then the upper right. This will create a camera view with a similar view angle to Figure 10.26. Name the view **Solar Study from the North**.

FIGURE 10.26
The default camera view

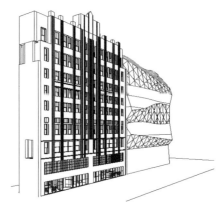

2. Before you turn on the sun, you need to turn on our mass. By default, the mass you placed earlier is not visible. Open the Visibility/Graphic Overrides dialog box by pressing VG on the keyboard and on the Model tab, select the Mass checkbox (Figure 10.27). This will allow you to see both the existing building and the new mass form.

3. By default, this view will look like a colorless perspective. You will adjust this as you add shade and shadow to the perspective. Now that you have a view established, click Graphic Display Options in the status bar at the bottom of the screen (Figure 10.28).

FIGURE 10.27
Selecting the Mass checkbox

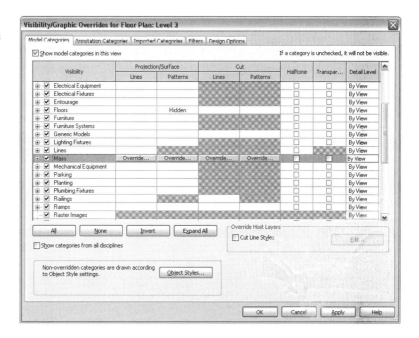

FIGURE 10.28
Clicking Graphic Display Options

4. In the dialog box that opens (see Figure 10.29), we're going to adjust some settings, but to get started, click the ... button at the top.

FIGURE 10.29
The Graphic
Display Options
dialog box

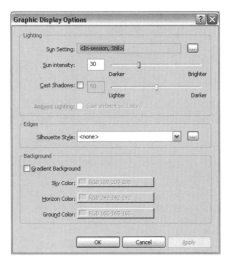

5. This will open a new dialog box that will control the sun settings (Figure 10.30). In this dialog box, you can control time of day, direction of the sun, and location of your project (longitude and latitude), among other settings. You can also control if you are going to see the sun placed at a single time of day or multiple times over a day, week, or year in an animation. There are four settings to choose from:

◆ Still casts the sun at a specific time of day based on the parameters you choose.

◆ Single-Day allows you to animate the sun and export the animation to an AVI file to show it over the course of a single day.

◆ Multi-Day casts the sun in the same position (same time of day) over the course of multiple days and can also be exported to an AVI.

◆ Lighting uses Revit's lighting families. The other families are sun based and will not activate any inserted lighting.

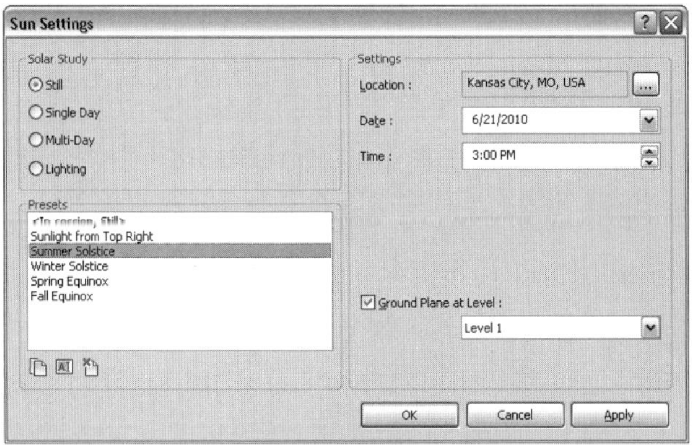

FIGURE 10.30
The Sun Settings
dialog box

You'll get to the animation in a bit, so let's start with a single view first. You're going to choose to see the sun and shadows on the summer solstice to begin.

6. Click the Still radio button.

7. Choose Summer Solstice from the Presets. This won't have all the settings correct, but once you put them in place, it will be set correctly for our location.

8. For the building location, choose your area. We have chosen Kansas City, MO.

9. The date and time for the solstice is June 21, 2010, and we'll set the time of day to 3 p.m.

10. By default, there is no ground plane selected. Without a ground plane, there's nowhere for the shadows to fall on the ground (sometimes you might not want to see those shadows). For our setting, choose Level 1. Click OK.

11. Now you are back in the Graphic Display Options dialog box. There are a couple more options you'll want to select. First, select the Cast Shadows checkbox. This will turn the shadows on and they will fall based on the settings you just established. The other checkbox you want to select is Gradient Background. This controls the color of the ground plane and the horizon in 3D views and helps to add a bit of visual depth to the images. It also helps to make them not "float" by applying a ground plane for them to rest on (Figure 10.31). Once this is done, click OK.

FIGURE 10.31
Turning on the shadows and the background

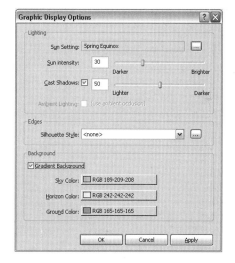

The finished view will look like Figure 10.32. After you create these settings, you can quickly toggle the shadows on and off using the other two selections from the Graphics Display options in the status bar. Remember, turning the shadows off will allow the view to render more quickly if you make any modifications to the model.

FIGURE 10.32
The finished view

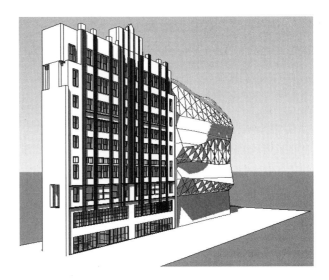

Once this view is complete, it's quick work to make other views using the same settings and visualize the building shading from various angles. In our model, let's choose two other angles: one from the third floor again looking from the south to the north (Figure 10.33) and one from the third floor inside the kitchen (Figure 10.34).

Adding shading to the view is not much easier to establish. Since you've already applied the settings to a previous view, all you need to do is select Shadows On from the View Control menu, and Revit will apply shadows to the view from the previously used shadow settings. Our exterior view will now look like Figure 10.35.

FIGURE 10.33
View from the
south looking
north

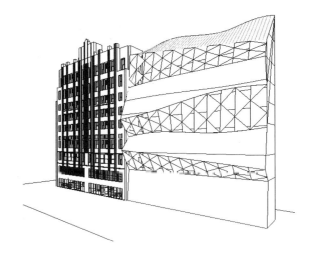

FIGURE 10.34
View from inside

FIGURE 10.35
Shaded view look-
ing north

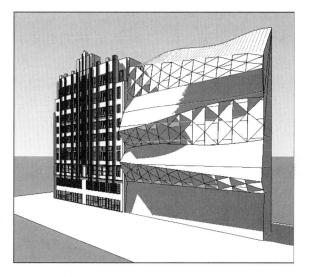

Apply this same setting to the interior view, and it will deliver some odd results—your windows won't be clear; they'll be solid. Whenever you are working in Revit views, it's important to know what phase you are working in as well as how phasing will affect visibility. Since the original building was created in an Existing phase, those materials render as solid in 3D views. To change this, select the view crop region and scroll down in the Properties Palette on the left. Change Phase Filter to Show Complete, as shown in Figure 10.36.

FIGURE 10.36
Changing the view
settings to Show
Complete

This will put all the materials shown within the view in the same state (a current or finished one). Now the finished view should have transparent glazing and look like Figure 10.37. You can see that even in this view, sunlight inside the space at this time of day is somewhat limited.

FIGURE 10.37
Shaded view
looking north

Creating an Animated Solar Study

Creating a solar study is a great tool to visualize the effects of the sun at various times of day on a building. But what about being able to watch the progress of the sun over the course of the day, week, or year? Fortunately, Revit has the ability to animate the solar studies so you can see the progress of the sun and its impact on the building.

Any view with Shade and Shadows turned on can be animated to show the sun over time. To access these settings, choose Graphic Display Options in the status bar (Figure 10.38).

FIGURE 10.38

Selecting Graphic
Display Options

Using the same method you used for the still solar study, choose Sun Settings in the Graphic
Display Options dialog box. This will bring you back to the Sun Settings dialog box you used
for the still. This time, let's select one of the other options. You can choose one of the following:

Single Day   Create single-day studies with the settings on the Single-Day tab. These settings
will show the effect of sun on a specific day at various intervals (15, 30, 45, or 60 minutes). By
setting the date and checking the Sunrise To Sunset box, you'll be able to animate the effect of
sun on your model.

Multi-Day   The settings on the Multi-Day tab are just like the settings on the Single-Day tab,
but the interval is days, weeks, or months, and you can see the effect of sun over the course
of an entire year. To create a multi-day sun study, we will follow steps very similar to a single
day study. Figure 10.39 shows the configured Sun Settings dialog box.

1. For this exercise, let's choose the Single Day study. We'll work with the solstice again, but
   you need to modify some of the settings from the last solar study.

2. Choose the Single Day radio button.

3. For the building location, choose your area. We have chosen Kansas City, MO.

4. The date and time for the solstice is June 21, 2010, and we'll set the time of day to range
   from 5 a.m. until 9 p.m.

5. Set the ground plane to Level 1. Click OK.

FIGURE 10.39

Animated solar
study settings

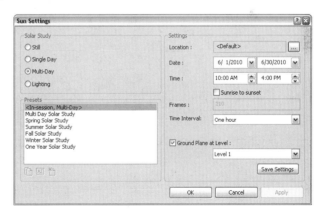

PREVIEWING A SOLAR STUDY

Your solar study will now look like a still; however, you will have a new tool available in the
status bar. Select the Graphic Display Options button from the status bar, and you'll see a new
option: Preview Solar Study (Figure 10.40). Selecting this will give you tools for video playback,
similar to your DVR or iTunes, under the Ribbon.

FIGURE 10.40
Preview
Solar Study

FIGURE 10.40
Preview
Solar Study

Using this method for playback will be choppy because Revit will need to render each of the frames. A more fluid way to view the animation is to export it as an AVI and view the animation in its totality.

EXPORTING THE ANIMATION

The solar study is easy and quick to export. To do so, click the Application button and select Export ➢ Images And Animations ➢ Solar Study, as shown in Figure 10.41.

Choosing this option will give you a standard Save As dialog box, allowing you to name and place the animation. Clicking the Options button in this box will provide you with some more advanced controls over the video output. Let's look at the Length/Format dialog box, shown in Figure 10.42, in a bit more detail.

FIGURE 10.41
Exporting the
animation

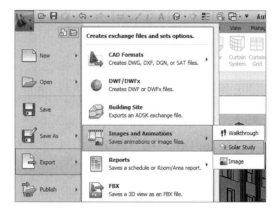

FIGURE 10.42
Length/Format
dialog box

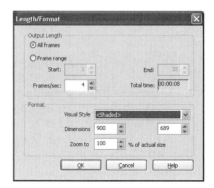

This dialog box gives you the option to export all the frames or just partial frame sets. You might want to include partial frames if you're looking for a visualization that is only summer months or only the afternoon in a Single Day sequence. You also have the ability to change the frame rate. By default, the frame rate is set to 15 frames per second. This is a good frame rate for video but tends to move pretty fast for a sun shading animation. We recommend reducing the frame rate to 4, which will allow you more time to absorb how the shading changes across the building over time but still moves quickly enough so the video isn't stagnant. Notice that changing the frame rate from 15 to 4 has increased the Total time from 3 seconds to 8.

The other element you can edit in this dialog box is the format. You can change the output of the video size and how it is rendered. Rendered video options are similar to the view settings (Shaded, Hidden Line, etc). Change the settings and click OK.

Now, click OK in the Save As dialog box. You'll be presented with one last set of options before the video exports: the Video Compression dialog box (Figure 10.43). This dialog box will allow you to use a variety of video codecs to compress the video for a smaller file size. Once you've chosen the appropriate compressor, click OK.

FIGURE 10.43
Compressing
the video

You'll see the Revit model reappear and render its way through the various animation times. Depending on the speed of your computer and the number of frames you're rendering, this could take several minutes. Once it's finished, you'll be able to view your final animation. Since it's not possible for us to embed a copy of the video within this book, you can download a copy of this animation from the book's companion website. Figure 10.44 shows a still of the video viewed in the VLC viewer.

FIGURE 10.44
The final video
viewed in the
VLC Viewer

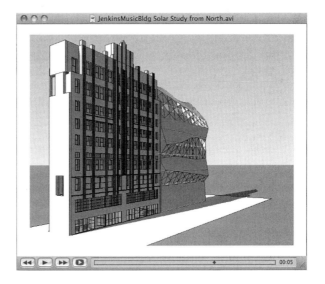

Creating a Solar Path

New to Revit 2011 is the ability to visualize the path of the sun across the model's sky. This is a feature recently ported to Revit from Ecotect. To activate this feature, open the Jenkins Building model in the Chapter 10 folder on the book's companion web page (www.sybex.com/go/masteringrevit2011) and open the default 3D view.

In the status bar at the bottom of the screen is a new icon, Sun Path. Click this icon and you'll see you have the option to turn the sun path on or off and go directly to the Sun Settings dialog box (Figure 10.45). Selecting this option will open the dialog box you had previously accessed through the Graphic Display Options dialog box. Here, you can access that dialog box directly and modify the Sun Settings (Figure 10.46).

FIGURE 10.45

The Sun Path tool

FIGURE 10.46

Sun Settings dialog box

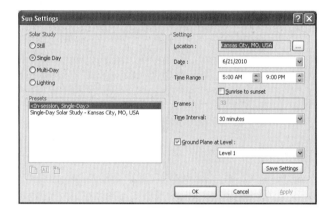

The settings here should reflect the Single Day animation you just completed. Let's leave these settings for now. Click OK to close this dialog box. Now, in Sun Settings, choose Sun Path On. You'll see a sun shown as a yellow ball placed in the sky and a compass rose placed under the building. The sun will have an arc displaying the path across the sky, reflecting its position at the day you chose, and nodes on this path, reflecting the time intervals you had preset (Figure 10.47).

Click and hold on the sun; this will activate the entire solar path across the range of the entire year (Figure 10.48). You can now drag the sun to any position within this solar range. Note that the time will be reflected just above sun itself and the date ranges are shown next to the compass rose.

FIGURE 10.47
Activating the
sun path

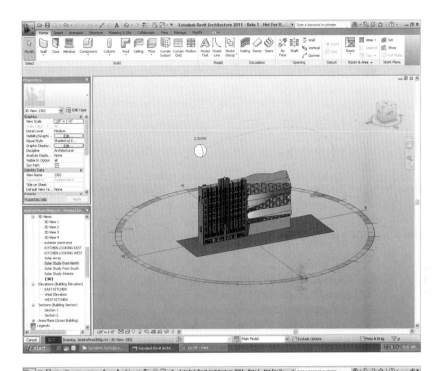

FIGURE 10.48
Dynamically
modifying the
sun path

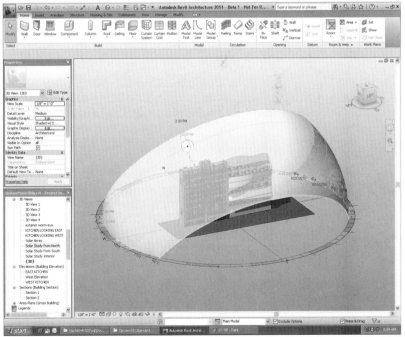

Energy Modeling

Understanding a building's energy needs is paramount to helping the project become more sustainable. According to the U.S. Energy Information Administration, buildings in the United States account for 30 percent of the world's energy and 60 percent of the world's electricity, making the United States the primary consumer of energy in the world and the built form the largest consumer (Figure 10.49). That gives you a large burden to build responsibly and to think about your choices before you implement them.

FIGURE 10.49
United States
Energy Use

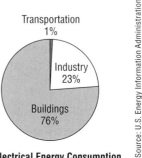

U.S. Electrical Energy Consumption

Source: U.S. Energy Information Administration

The energy needs of a building depend on a number of issues that are not simply related to leaving the lights on in a room that you are no longer using or turning down the heat or upping the air conditioning. Many of the systems within a building revolve around the energy use. For instance, if you increase the windows on the south façade, you allow in more natural light and lower your need for electric illumination. However, without proper sun shading, you are also letting in additional solar heat gain, with those larger windows increasing your need for more air conditioning and potentially negating the energy savings from lighting.

In exploring the use of energy in a building, you must consider all energy-related issues, which is why you can use energy simulation. These computer-based models use climatic data coupled with building loads, such as the following:

- The heating, ventilation, and air conditioning system (HVAC)
- Solar heat gain
- The number of occupants and their activity levels
- Sun shading devices
- Daylight dimming
- Lighting levels
- And a number of other variables

The energy model combines these factors to predict the building's energy demands to help size the building's HVAC system and parameters of other components properly so you are not using a system larger than what you need and so you can understand the impact of our design on the global environment. By keeping the energy model updated with the current design, you can begin to understand how building massing, building envelope, window locations, building orientation, and other parameters affect energy demands.

Using Revit for Energy Analysis

For energy modeling to be successful, you first need a solid, well-built model. This does not mean you need all the materials and details figured out, but you do have to establish some basic conditions. To ensure your model is correctly constructed to work with an energy modeling application, there are a few things that you need to do within the model to get the proper results. Some of this might sound like common sense, but it is important to ensure that you have the following elements properly modeled or you can have adverse results:

◆ The model must have roofs and floors.

◆ Walls inside and outside need to touch the roofs and floors.

◆ All areas within the analysis should be bound by building geometry (no unbound building geometry allowed).

The energy analysis won't be accurate without all the building elements in place.

To perform an energy analysis, you need to take portions of the Revit file and export them using gbXML to an energy analysis application. The following are the energy modeling applications commonly used within the design industry. Each varies in price, ease of use, and interoperability with a gbXML model. Choosing the correct application for your office or workflow will depend on a balance of those variables.

IES <VE>   IES <VE> (`www.iesve.com`) is a robust energy analysis tool that offers a high degree of accuracy and interoperability with a BIM model. The application can run the whole gamut of building environmental analysis from energy to daylighting to Computational Fluid Dynamics (CFDs) used to study airflow for mechanical systems. Cons to this application are its current complexity for the user and the relatively expensive cost of the tool suite.

Autodesk Ecotect   This application (`www.autodesk.com/ecotect-analysis`) has a great graphical interface and is easy to use and operate. The creators of this application also have a number of other tools, including a daylighting and weather tool. While easy to use, it can be challenging to import model geometry depending on what specific application you are using for your BIM model. As an example, SketchUp and Vectorworks can import directly, whereas applications like Revit can be more of a challenge.

eQuest   The name stands for the Quick Energy Simulation Tool (`www.doe2.com/equest`). This application is a free tool created by the Lawrence Berkeley National Laboratory (LBNL). Although robust, it contains a series of wizards to help you define your energy parameters for a building. Like Ecotect, it can be a challenge to import BIM model data smoothly depending on the complexity of the design, although it will directly import SketchUp models by using a free plug-in.

Autodesk Green Building Studio   Green Building Studio (`www.greenbuildingstudio.com`) is an online service that allows you to upload a gbXML file for a free energy analysis. The service provides quick and graphical feedback of the buildings' energy performance based on a survey of building use and loads. The survey is not highly detailed, so if your building type or use does not fit into the limited choices available, the results might not be accurate.

Exporting to gbXML

Before you can export the model to gbXML and run your energy analysis, you need to create several settings within Revit so you can export the proper information. It isn't important which order these get set, but it is important to check that they are set before exporting to gbXML. If the information within the model is not properly created, the results of the energy analysis will be incorrect.

PROJECT LOCATION

The physical location of the project on the globe is an important factor in energy use. In Revit, you can give your building a location a couple of ways. One is to choose the Manage tab and click the Location button (Figure 10.50).

FIGURE 10.50
Setting location

Another way to get to this same dialog box is through the Graphic Display Options you used for solar shading earlier in this chapter. Once in the Local Weather And Site dialog box (Figure 10.51), you can either select your location using the map in the lower portion of the window or type in your city and state and then click Search. This map will link to Google Maps, giving you a way to pinpoint the exact longitude and latitude of your project address.

FIGURE 10.51
The Local Weather and Site dialog box

BUILDING ENVELOPE

Although this might seem obvious in concept, a building without walls cannot have an accurate energy analysis run on it. Although the specific wall or roof composition won't be taken into account, each room needs to be bound by a wall, floor, or roof. These elements are critical in creating the gbXML file and defining the spaces or rooms within the building. These spaces can in turn be defined as different activity zones in the energy analysis application. Before you export, verify that you have a building envelope free of unwanted openings. This means all your walls meet floors and roofs and there are no "holes" in the building (Figure 10.52).

FIGURE 10.52
Make sure your building envelope is fully enclosed.

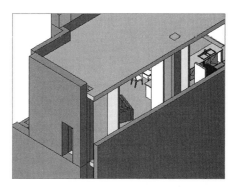

ROOMS AND VOLUMES

When Revit exports to a gbXML file, it is actually exporting the room volumes as they are constrained by the building geometry. This is what will define the zones within the energy analysis application. There are several steps you will need to verify to make sure your rooms and room volumes are properly in place.

All Spaces Need a Room Element

Each area within the Revit model that will be affected by the mechanical system will need to have a room element added to it. To add rooms, select the Room tool from the Home tab. Placed rooms within the model will look like Figure 10.53.

FIGURE 10.53
Placing rooms

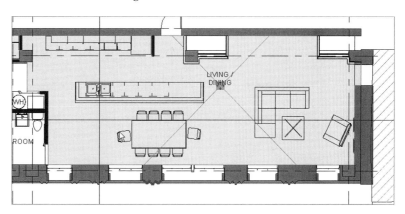

Setting Room Heights

Once all the rooms are placed, each room's properties should be redefined to reflect its height. The height of the room should extend to the bottom of the room above (in a multistory building), or if it is the top/only floor of a building, the room must fully extend through the roof plane. When you extend the room through the roof plane, Revit will use the Roof geometry to limit the height of the room element and conform it to the bottom of the roof. Rooms should never overlap either in plan (horizontally) or vertically (between floors) as this will give you inaccurate results.

An easy way to set the room heights is to open each level and select everything on the level. Using the Filter tool (Figure 10.54), you can unselect all the elements and choose to only keep the rooms selected. In this way, you can edit all the rooms on a given floor at one time.

FIGURE 10.54
Selecting the rooms

Once the rooms are selected, go to the Properties Palette and modify the room heights. By default, rooms are inserted at 8'-0" high. You have the option to set a room height directly, or you can modify the room height settings to go to the bottom of the floor above. This second option is what you have set for our rooms and is shown in Figure 10.55. Note that you'll need to set Upper Limit to the floor above and delete the value (8'-0" by default) in the offset. Repeat this same workflow for every floor of the building.

FIGURE 10.55
Modifying the room height

Turning on Room Volumes

Now that all the heights are defined, you have to tell Revit to calculate the volumes of the spaces. By default, Revit does not perform this calculation. Depending on the size of your file, leaving this setting on can hinder performance. Make sure that after you export to gbXML you come back to this dialog box and change the setting back to Areas Only.

To turn on room volumes, select the fly-out menu from the Room panel on the Home tab (Figure 10.56) and select Area And Volume Computations.

FIGURE 10.56
Opening Area
And Volume
Computations

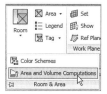

This will open the Area And Volume Computations dialog box. There are a couple of simple settings here that will allow you to activate the volume calculations within Revit (Figure 10.57). You'll want to select the radio button Areas And Volumes so that Revit will calculate in the vertical dimension as well as the horizontal for your room elements.

FIGURE 10.57
Enabling volume
calculations

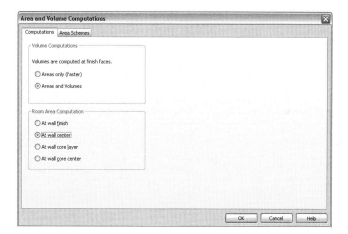

The second setting tells Revit where to calculate the rooms from. By choosing Wall Finish, Revit will not calculate any of the space a wall actually takes up with the model. Arguably, this is also conditioned space. Technically, what you would want is to calculate from the wall centers on interior partitions and the interior face of wall on exterior walls. However, Revit does not allow you that option, so you have chosen to calculate from At Wall Center. Once you've modified those settings, click OK.

EXPORTING TO GBXML

Now that you have all the room settings in place, we're ready to export to gbXML. To start this process, click the Application button and select Export ➤ gbXML. You will open a dialog box that looks like Figure 10.58.

FIGURE 10.58
Export gbXML
Settings

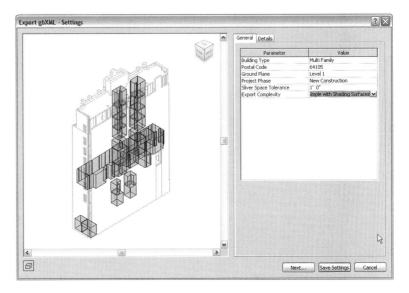

There are a few things to take note of in this dialog box. First, you'll see a 3D image of the building showing all the room volumes and bounded by the exterior building geometry. You can see in our building visualization that the boundary for the building is not completely full of room elements and that some of the room elements do not visually extend to the floor above. This would be your first clue that all your rooms do not have room elements placed or set properly, and you'll want to dismiss this dialog box to change those settings.

Second, you'll note the ViewCube at the upper right of the 3D view window. This window will respond to all the same commands as a default 3D view will directly in Revit, allowing you to turn, pan, and zoom the visualization.

There are also two tabs on the right of this dialog box. The General tab will contain general information about your building and you'll want to verify it is filled out properly. Some of this information is Building Type, Postal Code (Zip Code), Ground Plane, and Project Phase. These settings will help determine the building use type (for conceptual-level energy modeling) and the location of your building in the world. There are two other settings: Sliver Space Tolerance and Export Complexity. Sliver Space Tolerance will help take into account that you might not have fully buttoned up your Revit building geometry. This will allow you a gap of up to a foot and Revit will assume that those gaps (12″ or less) are not meant to be there. The Export Complexity setting allows you to modify the complexity of the gbXML export. There are several choices (Figure 10.59) based on the complexity of your model and the export.

FIGURE 10.59
Exporting com-
plexity settings

The Details tab will give you a room-by-room breakdown of all the room elements that will be exported in the gbXML model. Figure 10.60 shows the expanded Details tab. This is an important place to check as you'll also notice that this dialog box will report errors or warnings with those room elements. Selecting the warning triangle will give you a list of the errors and warnings associated with your rooms. You'll want to make sure your gbXML export is free of any errors or warnings before completing the export.

FIGURE 10.60
The Details tab

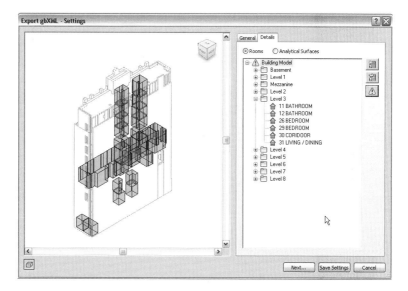

Once you're ready to finish the export, click Next. This will give you the standard Save As dialog box, allowing you to locate and name your gbXML file. Depending on the size and complexity of your building, a gbXML export can take several minutes and the resulting file size can be tens of megabytes.

You're now ready to import the gbXML file into your energy analysis application to begin computing your energy loads.

Daylighting

Daylighting is the use of natural light for primary interior illumination. This reduces your need for artificial light within the space, reducing internal heat gain and energy use. Natural light is the highest quality and most efficient light source available today, and the source is free.

An effective daylighting design relies heavily on proper building orientation, massing, and envelope design. The proper combination of these strategies allows you to optimize your building's use of natural resources and minimize your dependency on artificial lighting. A fully integrated daylighting system can enhance the visual acuity, comfort, and beauty of a space while controlling external heat gain and glare.

Some common terms that are associated with daylighting are:

◆ A footcandle, which is a measure of light intensity. A footcandle is defined as the amount of light received by 1 square foot of a surface that is 1 foot from a point source of light equivalent to one candle of a certain type. Depending on the sky conditions, daylight can produce anywhere from 2,000 to 10,000 footcandles.

◆ Illuminance, which is the luminous flux per unit area on an intercepting surface at any given point, expressed in footcandles. Commonly described as the amount of light on a surface.

◆ Luminance, which is the luminous intensity of a surface in a given direction per unit of projected area, expressed in footcandles. Commonly described as the amount of light leaving a surface.

◆ Glare, which is the sensation produced by luminance within the visual field that is sufficiently greater than the luminance to which the eyes have adapted to cause annoyance, discomfort, or visibility difficulty.

Not only does natural daylight help to light our workplaces and homes, but it also supplies us with a connection to the outdoors. Providing occupants with natural light and ties to the outside has been proven in a number of cases to have a positive effect on human health and productivity. Studies have shown that buildings with good daylighting design have positive effects on their occupants:

◆ Increased productivity levels

◆ Low absentee rates

◆ Better grades

◆ Retail sale increases

◆ Improved dental records

◆ Healthier occupants

Revit itself does not perform daylighting analysis. To get accurate daylighting results, you need to use other applications in the same way you did with energy analysis. Daylighting, however, is much easier to evaluate for accurate results and doesn't require several years of school to perfect. There are several tools on the market that will do daylighting analysis:

DaySIM DaySIM (http://apps1.eere.energy.gov/buildings/tools_directory/software.cfm/ID=428/pagename=alpha_list) is a free application supported by the U.S. Department of Energy. It is built from the Radiance engine, one of the most accurate and trusted currently available, but requires a working knowledge of the Radiance engine to be properly proficient.

Ecotect Ecotect offers its own flavor of daylighting analysis (www.autodesk.com/ecotect-analysis). Ecotect is powerful as a one-stop shop for sustainable design analysis (as it also performs energy analysis as well as other building analysis) but has been noted to be clunky and difficult to use.

3ds Max Design 3ds Max Design is a rendering application (www.autodesk.com/3dsmax) that in 2008 added a daylighting package. The daylighting engine is Radiance based but is easy to use and will directly import Revit model geometry through the use of an FBX translator.

For the purposes of this exercise, we'll focus on the 3ds Max Design daylighting tool because we think this allows the most speed and versatility for daylighting analysis.

Setting Up for Daylighting Analysis

As in energy modeling, you must perform several steps in order to successfully analyze a building for daylight. If all the steps are not performed, your analysis will be inaccurate and not trustworthy. Let's step through the specific settings needed to perform daylighting. In this analysis, we used the same Jenkins model we used for other exercises in this project to better emulate a real-life workflow.

BUILD A GOOD MODEL

As in energy modeling, if your building model is missing walls or has holes in the exterior (that aren't supposed to be there), it will leak light into the space and invalidate your results. Make sure your model is properly created; that there are roofs, floors, and walls in place; and that those elements meet properly in their corners.

Proper building phasing is also important. Your building model will be exported from a perspective or 3D view. Make sure that you have the view phase set to Show Complete.

MATERIALS

CERT
OBJECTIVE

Materiality is an important part of daylighting as the nature of the materials will allow light transmittance (in the case of glazing) or allow light reflectance (in the case of flooring, wall paint, etc.). You'll want to have all your materials properly defined in the view from which you want to create the daylighting simulation. To set your materials, navigate to the Manage tab and choose the Materials button. It will open the Materials dialog box (Figure 10.61). All of your elements within the model, even Generic elements (such as generic walls), should have materials defined. Let's look at some of these materials in more detail.

FIGURE 10.61
Materials
dialog box

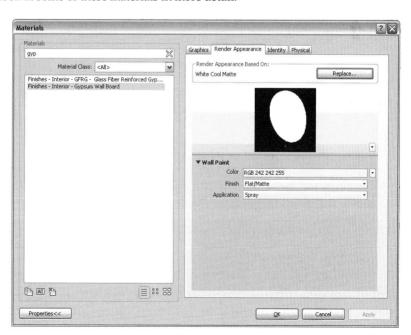

One common material will be paint (shown in Figure 10.61). Here, we have applied paint as the finish type (called Cool White Matte) to describe the finish type for Gypsum Wall Board, one of our more common building materials. As you can see on the Render Appearance tab, you have the ability to change some of the properties of the paint. You can alter the reflectance (flat, eggshell, semi-gloss, gloss, and so on) and how the paint is applied to the wall (rolled, sprayed, and so on). Each of these will affect the reflectance of the paint in a different way.

Another material you should look at is glazing. Getting the proper glazing settings will determine how much daylight you are getting inside the space. On the Render Appearance tab, shown in Figure 10.62, there are a few critical settings for glazing:

Color   The color of the glazing will partially determine light transmittance. Set your glazing color to reflect the color you will have in your design. Revit supplies several common glazing colors.

Reflectance   As with different colors, reflectance will also help determine how much light you will get inside a space. You will see that if you use the Replace feature at the top to select one of Revit's preset glazing colors, it will also give you a default value for reflectance.

Sheets Of Glass   The number of sheets of glass will determine how the light will be refracted as it moves from outside the building to the inside. Typically, in a Revit window family, you model glass as a 1" single pane for ease of modeling. Modifying the number of panes in this location will allow us to keep our modeling easy but still maintain a level of accuracy in the daylighting analysis.

FIGURE 10.62
Glazing material

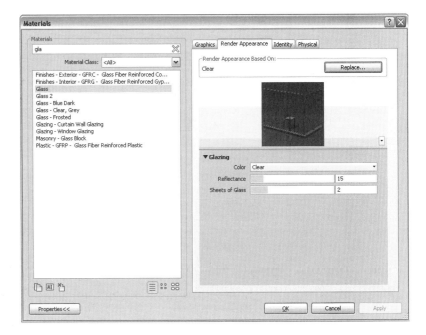

Depending on the stage of design you are in, you might not know what your final material is, but you want to apply some defaults to the material types so you can perform some preliminary lighting analysis. When in doubt, here are some default reflectance values you can apply to the Generic materials:

◆ Floors: 20% reflectance

◆ Walls: 50% reflectance

◆ Ceilings: 85% reflectance

EXPORTING TO 3DS MAX DESIGN

Once you have your materials defined and the model is ready to go, you need to define the view from which you want to export. To do this, select the camera tool from the View tab and create a perspective view of the area you want to analyze (Figure 10.63).

Now you are ready to export this view to FBX. To do so, click the Application button and select Export ➢ FBX. Once this is done, you can open 3ds Max Design and import the model.

FIGURE 10.63
Defining a view

Although this is a Revit book, we recognize that in today's design workflow not everything can happen within one application. Because of the general ease of performing daylighting in 3ds Max Design, you are going to finish the analysis in the other application. Before you begin in 3ds Max Design, there are a couple of things to note. First, you need to have a copy of Max Design, not Max. They are similar applications but the Design flavor of Max allows you to perform daylighting. Regular Max does not have this feature. Second, keep in mind that daylighting is science. The more accurate you are in following the steps, the more accurate your final results will be. These steps will be similar between Max Design 2009 and 2010.

1. Open 3ds Max Design. From the Customize drop-down, choose Units Setup. Set your units to American, as shown in Figure 10.64. This will report your analysis in footcandles. You'll need to specify this setting only once.

FIGURE 10.64
Changing your settings

2. Click the Application button, select Import ➢ FBX, and browse to your file. Select the file and click OK. You'll get the dialog box shown in Figure 10.65. Here, you'll want to make sure that the drop-down menu at the top is set to Autodesk Architectural (Revit). This dialog box also has a button at the bottom called Web Updates. From time to time, Autodesk updates the FBX importing routine that will help get a more accurate import. Periodically click this button to make sure your FBX import is current. Otherwise, click OK.

FIGURE 10.65
Defining a view

3. From this point, you'll have the imported Revit model in Max. It should look like the generic 3D view from Revit. To get to the view you exported from, right-click the white text in the upper-right corner of your view window and choose Default 3D View (if you didn't rename the view in Revit prior to export) or the view name you exported. This should bring you back to the familiar view you created in Revit.

4. Now, we're going to step through some settings in the Max dialog boxes and drop-downs. You should notice the Lighting Analysis menu at the top of the screen (if you don't have this, you don't have the right flavor of Max). Click the Lighting Analysis menu and choose Lighting Analysis Assistant (Figure 10.66).

FIGURE 10.66
Select Lighting Analysis Assistant.

5. The Lighting Analysis Assistant has four tabs. By default, it opens on the General tab (Figure 10.67). This tab allows you to load some presets for daylighting analysis. Choose the Load Lighting Analysis Render Preset from this tab. You should also notice the lighting scale at the bottom of the dialog box. This will give you minimum and maximum color values for your daylighting simulation. Feel free to play with these values to achieve a desired graphic during this process.

FIGURE 10.67
Settings on the General tab

6. Next is the Materials tab (Figure 10.68). This tab will show you if you have any materials in the import that are invalid and will therefore not reflect light properly. If you have invalid materials, it's probably a good idea to go back to Revit and fix them. This will not only make sure they are valid in the daylighting analysis, but if you alter them in 3ds Max Design, you'll need to alter them every time you perform another daylighting analysis. If you need to locate the materials that are invalid, you can select the pick button and it will highlight all the invalid materials in the project. At this point, you can also choose to ignore them as they might not be visible within your view and therefore not necessary to correct.

FIGURE 10.68
Materials tab

7. Now, let's jump back to the Lighting tab (Figure 10.69). On this tab, we're going to set the building location, time of day, and the rendering engine you want to use to perform the daylighting analysis. All of these settings will be created in other dialog boxes that are spawned from this dialog box. Don't worry—we'll step through them one at a time.

8. To begin, select the top Select & Edit button. This will activate the sidebar menu and allow you to modify the position of the sun (Figure 10.70). We're going to want to change the Orbital Scale value at the bottom of this menu to something like 1500. This doesn't affect any analysis, but it will move the visualization of the sun off the ground plane and up into the sky. The other thing you want to do is select the Weather Data File radio button. This will activate the setup button right next to this selection.

FIGURE 10.69
The Lighting tab

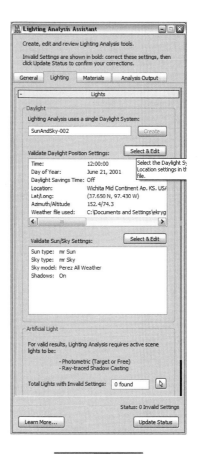

FIGURE 10.70
Using the Weather
Data file

9. By clicking the Setup button, you will open yet another dialog box called Configure Weather Data. Here you can set the building location and time of day. 3ds Max works off TMY2 weather data files created by the department of energy. You'll need to navigate to their website (`http://apps1.eere.energy.gov/buildings/energyplus/cfm/weather_data2.cfm/region=4_north_and_central_america_wmo_region_4`) and download an EPW file. This file contains the average weather for your given location over a 30-year interval. Once you've downloaded the EPW file, click the Load Weather Data button (shown in Figure 10.71) and browse to the file, select it, and click OK.

FIGURE 10.71
Loading the
weather file

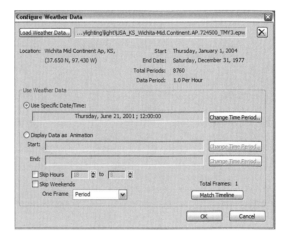

10. Now, click the Change Time Period button. This will pull up another dialog box (yes, you're now four deep) and give you a slider to change the date and time of your analysis (Figure 10.72). If you're performing an analysis for LEED EQ 8.1, you'll want to set it to June 21 at noon. You might notice that as you move the slider back and forth, the dates jump forward and backward over time. This happens by design. Over the 30-year span contained in the EPW file, it is displaying the specific day and year of the weather file that had weather that most closely reflected the average conditions over that 30-year span. Set your time and date and click OK. Click OK again to exit the other dialog box.

FIGURE 10.72
Setting the date
and time

11. Still on the Lighting tab, click the bottom Select & Edit. This will activate the sidebar menu. From this menu, choose Perez All Weather from the Sky Model drop-down (Figure 10.73).

FIGURE 10.73
Choose Perez
All Weather as a
sky model.

12. OK, nearly done with the settings. Choose the last tab, Analysis Output. You need to create a light meter in which to calculate the daylight (Figure 10.74). Click the Create Light Meter button, and in a plan view of your model, drag two points to create a grid.

FIGURE 10.74
Creating a
light meter

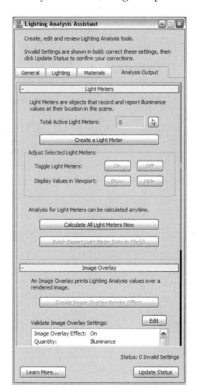

13. This will also active the sidebar menu and give you the option to add node points to the light grid. If you're after your LEED analysis, you'll need to relocate the grid to 30″ above the floor line and have meters every 2′ in both directions. Your final grid will look like Figure 10.75. Once that is set, click OK to dismiss this dialog box.

FIGURE 10.75
Creating the light meter grid

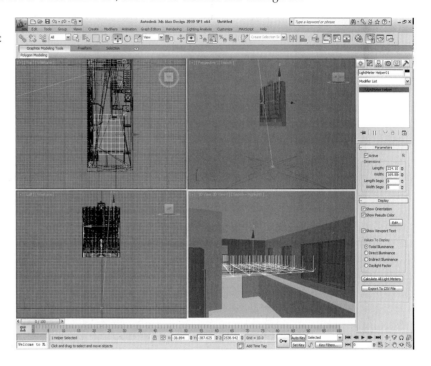

14. From the Render drop-down, choose Render Setup and select the Indirect Illumination tab. On this tab, you want to set Final Gather to 3 (Figure 10.76). Final Gather will calculate the number of times light will bounce within the space. A setting of 0 means no light bounces and will give an inaccurate reading. A setting of 7 will be highly accurate, but will take considerably more processing power to create as the light bounces calculate exponentially. A setting of 3 optimizes the accuracy and speed for your output.

FIGURE 10.76
Set Final Gather to 3.

15. You're now ready to perform the analysis. On the Analysis Output tab of the Lighting Assistant, click the Calculate All Light Meters Now button. This will render the light meters to give you a final image, like Figure 10.77. You'll be able to get a footcandle reading for each of the light meters as well as a color gradation showing you light and dark spots within the view.

FIGURE 10.77
The final analysis

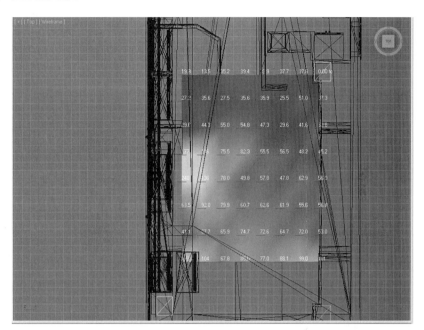

Once you've mastered the ability to perform these types of daylighting analyses, you'll find it is fairly quick and easy to iterate several designs and images. With a few more steps, you can render the final scene with a daylighting grid overlay (Figure 10.78).

FIGURE 10.78
A rendered day-lighting scene

In each of these scenarios, it's important to vet your results. Don't take the values at their face values; review them to make sure they are accurate. So that you have a scale in which to value your results, Table 10.1 gives you some footcandle readings that you can use to figure out how much light is a proper amount based on the tasks you are performing within that space.

TABLE 10.1: Footcandle Readings

ACTIVITY	CATEGORY	LUX	FOOTCANDLES
Public spaces with dark surroundings	A	20-30-50	2-3-5
Simple orientation for short temporary visits	B	50-75-100	5-7.5-10
Working spaces where visual tasks are only occasionally performed	C	100-150-200	10-15-20
Performance of visual tasks of high contrast or large size	D	200-300-500	20-30-50
Performance of visual tasks of medium contrast or small size	E	500-750-1000	50-75-100
Performance of visual tasks of low contrast or very small size	F	1000-1500-2000	100-150-200
Performance of visual tasks of low contrast or very small size over a prolonged period	G	2000-3000-5000	200-300-500
Performance of prolonged and exacting visual tasks	H	5000-7500-10000	500-750-1000
Performance of special visual tasks of extremely low contrast	I	10000-15000-20000	1000-1500-2000

A–C   for illuminances over a large area (such as lobby space)
D–F   for localized tasks
G–I   for extremely difficult visual tasks

The Bottom Line

Embrace sustainable design concepts.   Understanding the concepts behind sustainable design is an important part of being able to perform analysis within the Revit model and a critical factor in today's design environment.

Master It   What are four key methods for a holistic sustainable design?

Leverage schedules.   Using schedules in Revit helps you track many of your design elements throughout the whole design process. These schedules can also be used to validate programmatic information during conceptual design.

> **Master It**   Explain how to create a schedule from a conceptual mass that will show the programmatic areas for each floor level.

Use sun shading and solar paths.   Understanding the effects of the sun on a building design is a critical way to create and form space. Revit has tools to help you identify how the sun will affect the design and where shade and shadow will fall inside and outside the building over the course of the year.

> **Master It**   How can you use the tools in Revit to produce still and animated solar studies from interior and exterior views in order to understand shading and the sun's effect on the building and space?

Prepare and export your model for energy analysis.   Being able to predict a building's energy performance is a necessary part of designing sustainably. Although Revit doesn't have an energy modeling application built into it, it does have interoperability with many applications that have that functionality.

> **Master It**   Explain the steps you need to take to get a Revit model ready for energy analysis.

Analyze your project for daylighting.   Not only can proper daylighting in a building save energy, but it can make the inhabitants happier and healthier. Through analysis, you can now quantify the amount of light you're getting in any space and measure the footcandle readings before you begin building. This allows you to iterate the design-making modifications to maximize your daylight while balancing the amount of glazing against solar heat gain and mechanical needs.

> **Master It**   Understand how much daylight you need to perform certain tasks. How much daylighting is needed for the following:
>
> ◆ Working in an office
>
> ◆ Reading a book
>
> ◆ Working on or reading something small for an extended period of time

Chapter 11

Phasing, Groups, and Design Options

The ability to design a building in the computer used to be a differentiator. Computers were expensive, applications were expensive, and the people who knew how to use those applications were often expensive specialists who would take other people's work and re-create it digitally.

But now, designing in the computer is a commodity; just about anyone can do it to a reasonable level of proficiency. What has changed?

Well, many projects go through stages and phases. As a result, it's necessary to distinguish the element of time in your project: how something exists, how it will change, and what it will look like when the project is complete. In addition, design is about maintaining relationships between repetitive elements. Sometimes this repetitive element could be a single component in your project, such as a light or a piece of furniture. But it could also be an entire collection of elements, such as a hotel or hospital room.

Finally, one digital design at a time isn't enough. You need to be able to see many ideas simultaneously and in context with other ideas. The client and contractor need to see options and alternates. And it's important that these options not be fully independent, separate files so that the results can be analyzed and compared to each other.

This chapter focuses on these three concepts: time, relationships, and iteration. In Revit, they're addressed with phasing, groups, and design options. In this chapter, you'll learn to:

◆ Use the Phasing tools to create, demolish, and propose a new design

◆ Create and use Groups to manage big design ideas

◆ Make design options for design iteration

Associating Phasing to Geometry, Views, and Project Settings

The design of a project often goes through phases traditionally marked by level of detail and specificity. One of the earliest phases, schematic design, eventually evolves into construction documentation. This liner progression makes a lot of sense when drawings are discrete and moved through their own linear progression.

First plans, then elevations, then sections—each drawing relied on the information of the one that came before it and were often adjacent to each other on the same sheet of linen for faster reference.

Revit can be used much the same way as the traditional design processes described in the previous paragraph. But don't be surprised if you're quickly frustrated. The information gathered the first moment of design seems specific and fixed, having been automatically generated in a schedule that's just waiting to be immediately updated with an answer that isn't the one you were hoping to see.

Revit doesn't give you the benefit of working almost myopically focused on a particular task at a time and being accountable for only that task. Everything you do is influencing the entire project. If you're working on the plans, you're accountable for the elevations. If you're working on the sections, you're accountable for the schedules. And at first, understanding the holistic implications of your design decisions seems like too much information too soon—and results in circular errors from which you can't seem to escape.

Of course, the same thing happened in traditional 2D drawing and CAD environments. But by the time the circular conflict was discovered, the project was already in construction, and it was the challenge of the contractor to figure it out. And the designer often remained blissfully ignorant.

Revit will confront you with these design conflicts very, very quickly. One of the earliest marketing slogans for Revit was "If it's right anywhere, it's right everywhere." Well, the inverse was also true: if it was wrong anywhere, it was wrong everywhere. This is great on one hand because you're able to resolve design conflicts well in advance. But it's also a very unfamiliar way of working if you're not used to resolving design conflict so far in advance, because it interrupts your familiar design workflow.

We want to help you avoid these conflicts and roadblocks, or at least learn to be at peace with them until you're ready to address them. First, you need to stop thinking about Revit as a new tool to do an old thing. At first you can't avoid this. It's natural to see Revit through the patterns and principles of what you're familiar with in 2D and CAD. But it's not enough to see Revit as not being what it *isn't*. You need to start seeing it for what it *is*.

You need to embrace a new way of working that, for better or worse, allows you to approach design *concurrently*. This is not automatic, and it's going to take time, but you really don't have a choice. Working concurrently is simply not possible with the traditional, 2D CAD and task-centric tools. As hard as you might try, there's always something important that would be missed along the linear progression that those tools forced you to follow.

One of the biggest mistakes when trying to use Revit, a tool that allows you to work *concurrently*, is to expect it to conform to a design process that forces you to work *linearly*. And by the time you start working with phasing, groups, design options, and links, if you're still working in a linear mind-set but Revit is coming at you fast and furious with unexpected and completely concurrent information, you'll feel almost paralyzed.

If the old 2D CAD process was a linear progression of predesign, schematic design, design development, and construction documentation that all the while was intent on resolving plan, elevation, section, and detail, what's the new Revit process? Well, it's also in two parts:

◆ Instead of Pre-Design, Schematic Design, Design Development, to Construction Documentation, you're going to think along the lines of restrictions, relationships, repetition, and representations. You can't think about predesign in Revit. You need discover what you should and shouldn't do. Restrictions are not limiting—they're freeing! Once you resolve your restrictions, you'll know where to focus. You can't think about schematic design in Revit. You need to think about the core relationships that you're trying to create and maintain. You can't think about design development. You need to think about the repetition of an idea and a theme and how the repetition will need to flex when it encounters a unique condition. And you can't think about construction documentation. You need to think about the representations of your project that communicate far more than 2D information.

◆ Instead of plans, elevations, sections, and details, you need to think along the lines of intent to content. A wall is not a *thing* in a plan. It's an *idea* that exists everywhere. It's got intent, and the same goes for floors, furniture, lighting, and curtain walls. You don't know exactly what they are, but you understand the intent of what they are.

So get the idea of a wall as something in plan or elevation or section out of your mind and think about the "wallness." You don't know what it's made from (yet), but you do have a fairly good idea about what it's supposed to do and about where it is. Later, the intent of your design will evolve into specific content. The wall will have structure, finishes, and performance requirements.

The same goes for the other elements in your building. The intent of what they are and where they are will give way to manufactured specific content. And this content will maintain the intent of your design to locate and resolve your design intent far beyond the traditional resolution of a 2D detail. This specific content will have energy requirements, give off heat, be made of sustainable materials (or not), and so on. How can all this information possibly be contained in a traditional detail? It can't!

So, stop using Revit to do an old thing, and embrace the future of meaningful and concurrent information. As a designer, you owe it to your contractor, your owner, and your future!

Using Phasing to Give the Element of Time

Phasing is Revit's method of allowing you to add the element of time to objects in your project. It's easy to think of an architectural design in terms of what something is, where something is, and how it will be assembled. Phasing adds the dimension of "when" something is, which is incredibly useful and powerful.

Phases are most useful for doing the kinds of tasks that require you to show when elements are being introduced into your design. But a few words of caution and clarification: we don't recommend using extensive phasing to simulate construction sequencing, or "4D." It might seem like a great idea at first, but ultimately it'll break your model and lead to a lot of confusion across your project team.

The reason is threefold. First, using phasing to illustrate construction sequencing will not allow you to use phasing for its intended use. So if you need to show stages of existing, demolition, new construction, and so on, you'll find yourself having to work around sequences of Week 1, Week 2, Week 3, and so on. You will have traded more functionality in one area for limited functionality in another area.

The second reason is that it will break connections between elements that are normally joined. For example, in Figure 11.1, two walls intersect that belong to the same phase. The fact that they are graphically and geometrically joined is the desired condition.

FIGURE 11.1
Wall joins in the same phas

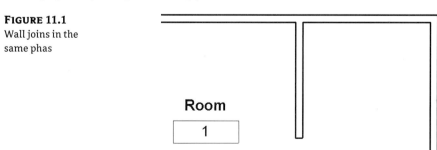

Room

1

But when walls are not from the same phase, their join condition may not clean up as intended, as shown in Figure 11.2. This can create a lot of tedious cleanup that isn't the best use of your time.

FIGURE 11.2
Joins across different phases may not always clean up as intended.

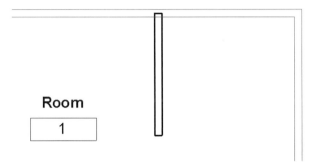

Finally, the best reason not to use phasing as a construction sequencing tool is that there's a better way! It will allow elements of various sequence properties to be scheduled, viewed, and even color-coded based on the sequence value that you define.

By using project parameters, you're able to create and assign an instance parameter value to everything in your project that you'd want to assign a construction sequence, as shown in Figure 11.3.

FIGURE 11.3
Creating a construction sequence instance parameter for project geometry

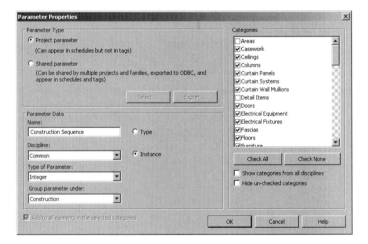

Once you've created this instance parameter, you'll be able to create view filters and filter rules that override the default condition of an object based on your parameter, as shown in Figure 11.4. Each Construction Week value is being given its own rule.

Combined with Visibility and Graphic Overrides, you're able to create a filter that modifies the graphics based on a parameter, as shown in Figure 11.5.

FIGURE 11.4
Applying filters by parameter

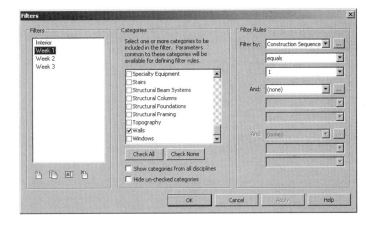

FIGURE 11.5
View filters and Graphic Overrides settings

The result is being able to modify the graphics of a view to illustrate some metadata about the objects in a far more flexible and predictable way than mere phasing, as shown in Figure 11.6. The other benefit is that this technique is not limited to views of geometry. View filters can be applied to any view, including schedules, which will allow you to group and filter schedules based on your unique project parameter.

Now that you understand a better way to create sequencing in Revit using parameters and filters, we'll discuss how phasing is used.

FIGURE 11.6
Using parameters and view filters to override graphics

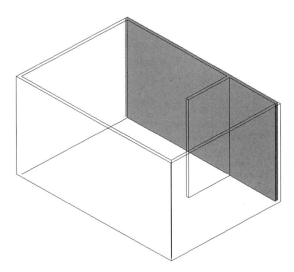

What Can Be Phased?

At a high level, only three types of elements can be associated with a phase in Revit: geometry, rooms, and views. Geometry is anything that you would use to build your design, like host components such as walls, floors, ceilings, and so on, as well as family components such as doors, windows, furniture, lighting, and so on. Once an element is placed in the project, the phase may be changed, as shown in Figure 11.7.

FIGURE 11.7
Changing the
phase of geometry

Rooms are also given phase properties, but there is an important difference: the phase of a building geometry may be changed after placement. The phase of a room may not, as shown in Figure 11.8. If you want to change the phase of a room, you'll need to delete and re-create it in the proper phase. You'll also find it faster to press Ctrl+X to cut the rooms from one view and then press Ctrl+V to paste them into a view of the desired phase.

FIGURE 11.8
The phase of a
room may not
be changed after
placement.

The phase of an element when initially placed is often confusing to a new user, but it's quite simple: the phase of the view that you're placing the element into determines its phase, as shown in Figure 11.9. Again, this is not as critical for geometry, since the phase of a building element can be changed after placement. But there are occasions when you're placing a lot of elements that you intend to be in a particular phase, and you'll want to create a view with that phase as active. Then you can place the elements in that view and not worry about having to change them later.

However, a view's phase is critical when you're placing rooms since you can't modify the phase of a room after placement. So be sure to verify the phase of the view before placing rooms.

FIGURE 11.9
Changing the phase of a view

Phase Settings

Let's get into the details of phase settings. Once you understand what each of the dialog boxes do (as well as what they don't do), the rest of phasing becomes clear.

On the Manage tab, click the Phases button, which will open the Phases dialog box, as shown in Figure 11.10. You'll notice that there are three tabs. The first tab is for your project phases.

FIGURE 11.10
Changing the phase of a view

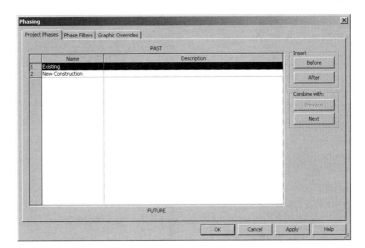

Right away, this is where people get confused, because they think that they need a phase for every different view that they'll be creating. And in the most common of phased projects, you'll have views to illustrate Existing, Demolition, and Proposed conditions. But since this dialog box only shows Existing and New Construction, people will in error create a new phase for Demolition.

If your project is a simple, three-phase kind of project (like a tenant upfit showing three phases), this extra phase isn't necessary. Just trust us! Basically, the Project Phase tab is for determining when the geometry is being created (*not* demolished). When would you want to create more phases? When you need to *create* geometry in more than these two phases.

For example, think of a staged construction project that will happen in two new phases. In this scenario, you need to move an entire office floor to one side of the building—all the staff, furniture, and so on. While everyone is working in half the building, you begin to design a phase that demolishes the other half and begins to reconfigure the proposed floor layout. This might be "New Construction – Phase 1."

Once that phase is complete and everything is cleaned up, you move everyone into the new space, and start the same process on the other half of the building. This phase might be "New Construction – Phase 2." Do you notice that we're still not creating a Demolition phase? Again, that's because the Project phases allow you to set when geometry is being created—not demolished.

Go ahead and create the two phases as just described (see Figure 11.11). We'll use this in a sample exercise in a moment.

FIGURE 11.11
Creating additional Project phases

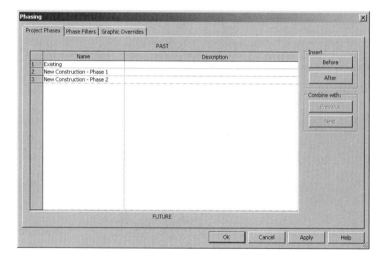

Once you've created these additional Project phases, pick any project geometry and look at its instance parameters. You'll notice that it can be assigned to any one of these three phases, as shown in Figure 11.12.

The next tab in your phasing dialog box is Phase Filters (Figure 11.13). There's seven predefined phases shown. All these phases can be deleted except for the Show All option.

FIGURE 11.12
Assigning available phases

FIGURE 11.13
The Phase Filters tab, with seven predefined phases

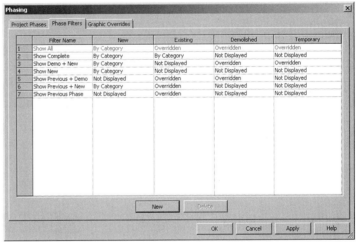

Don't be concerned if the filter names seem a bit cryptic at first. What's really important is the four graphic conditions that can be overridden: New, Existing, Demolished, and Temporary. Concentrate on these views for the moment, and the filter names will begin to make sense.

Select any of the drop-downs, as shown in Figure 11.14. You'll notice that the phase filter can override the graphics in one of three ways:

◆ The object can be shown by its category settings or *not* overridden. It will display in the project just like it does by default.

◆ The object can be overridden. That means that you can define a graphic override for that object. We'll get into the Graphic Overrides in a moment.

◆ The object can simply not be displayed.

FIGURE 11.14
Setting a filter
override

Once you understand how each of the phase filters displays objects, it all begins to make sense. For example, the Show Complete phase filter shows New and Existing elements by Category. But Existing and Temporary elements are not displayed at all. If you want to show the project when in the finished condition, when the dust has settled and everything is complete, this setting makes sense.

So to recap, things can be shown, not shown, or shown differently. Easy!

If there's any remaining confusion, it probably involves the naming convention of Show Previous + Demo. A better name might be Show Existing + Demolition but *Existing* is a bit misleading because this setting is showing the previous phase, which is not necessarily existing elements. It might be Temporary elements that need to be demolished. Therefore, Show Previous makes more sense.

The Graphic Overrides tab is the final tab in the Phasing dialog box (Figure 11.15). This dialog box relates back to the "Overridden" assignment of the previous tab.

FIGURE 11.15
The Graphic
Overrides tab

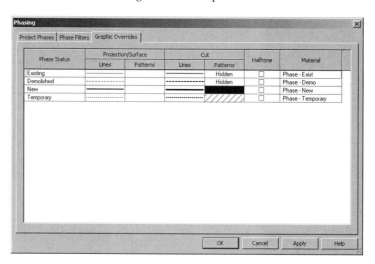

This dialog box allows you to override geometry in a few areas; the Line and Pattern characteristics of Projection/Surface and when Cut. You also have an option to just halftone the element. And finally, you can assign a unique Material setting when rendering. While this is helpful for illustrating actual rendering phase information, it can also be useful for rendering everything to a matte material, something we discuss in Chapter 15.

Now, if there's anything confusing about this dialog box, it's the lack of the ability to create a graphic override for "Future" elements. Such a feature would be helpful for showing future context in a phased construction, when you're trying to visualize the next condition. But as it is, phasing can show you where you are and where you're coming from, but not where you're going.

Why there's no Future phase in Revit is confusing to us; we hope to see this addressed in a future version.

Geometry Phase

Here's a simple exercise to illustrate each of the phases in a single view. First, open a new project using a default template. Next, draw four walls in parallel and then open a 3D view (Figure 11.16).

FIGURE 11.16
Four generic walls

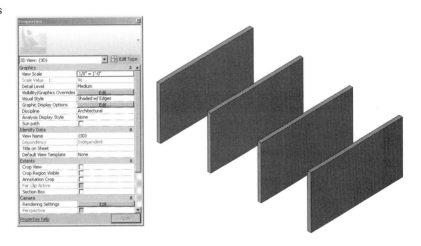

By default, all of these walls have been created in the New Construction phase because the phase of the view is New Construction.

Now, selecting each of the walls, associate them with each of the following phase settings:

Wall 1: Phase Created: Existing / Phase Demolished: None

Wall 2: Phase Created: Existing / Phase Demolished: New Construction

Wall 3: Phase Created: New Construction / Phase Demolished: New Construction

Wall 4: Phase Created: New Construction / Phase Demolished: New Construction

Figure 11.17 shows what you'll have when you're finished.

FIGURE 11.17
Default shaded overrides for phasing

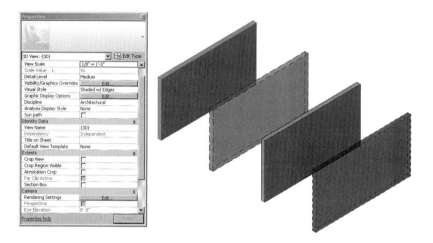

Right away you'll notice that the Existing (not Demolished) and the Proposed (not Demolished) look similar, except for the edge color. This isn't enough. So let's change the graphic properties of this wall so it's graphically more distinct.

Go to the Manage panel and select Phases; then click the Graphic Overrides tab (Figure 11.18).

FIGURE 11.18
Default Graphic Overrides settings

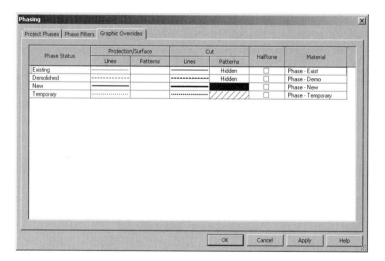

Next, select the option to open the Material setting for the Phase-Exist material (Figure 11.19).

FIGURE 11.19
Default shaded
override for exist-
ing materials

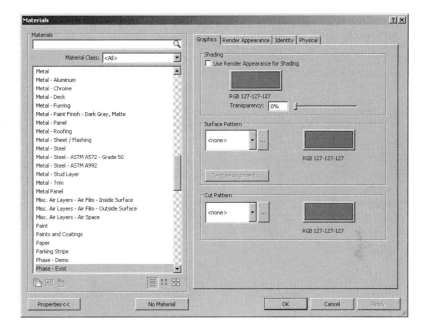

This is the setting we want to change. Select the Shading option, and you'll be able to assign a different shading value. We're selecting the lime greenish color along the top row (Figure 11.20).

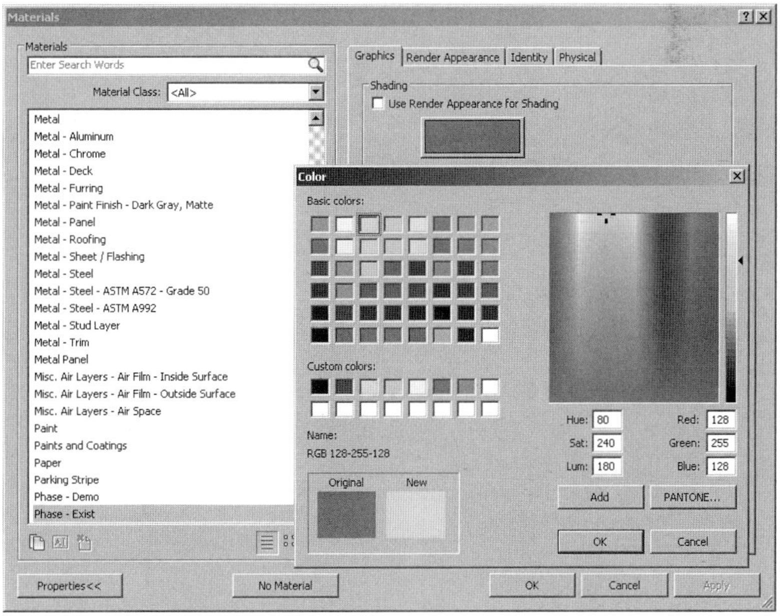

FIGURE 11.20
Overriding the
Shading value

When you finish changing these settings, you'll have the result shown in Figure 11.21.

FIGURE 11.21
Finished shading
values

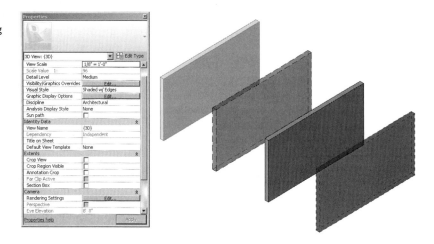

Now you can *really* graphically tell the phases apart. We think this particular setting should be part of the default Revit template. That way, new users would be able to distinguish the phase of an object far more clearly than in the default template.

View Phase

Now that we've talked about the phase properties of geometry, we'll cover the phase properties of views. Starting with the view from the previous example, select the View Properties. Selecting the space of the view, and then notice that the Properties dialog box automatically changes to reflect the properties of the view (Figure 11.22).

FIGURE 11.22
Phase filter options

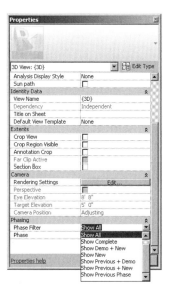

Applying each of these filters will help you understand the implications of how this will affect the properties of what will be shown in a view and how it will be shown.

First, let's start by changing the phase to New Construction and set the phase filter to Show All (Figure 11.23). This will show all the elements and override their graphic based on their construction phase and whether they're demolished. And it gives us a sense of all the elements as they exist in time.

FIGURE 11.23
Show All and New Construction

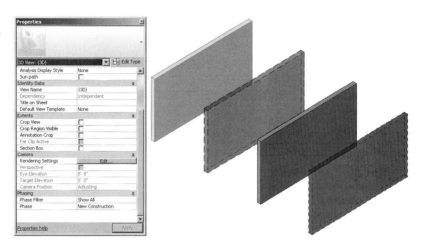

And although this is great for 3D views, where every phase has a distinct color, it's also wonderful for working in a plan, elevation, or section. Simply shade the view while working and you'll be able to clearly distinguish between objects in different phases, as shown in Figure 11.24.

FIGURE 11.24
Shaded plan view of phased elements

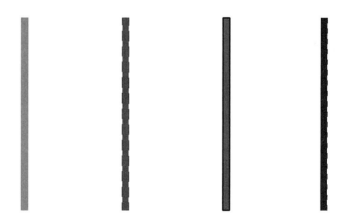

Now let's start moving through each of the sequences. But here's the important part. Rather than sequentially moving through the various phase filters from top to bottom, let's move through a sequence that makes *sequential* sense.

Let's begin by keeping the phase filter to Show All, but setting the phase *back* to Existing (Figure 11.25). This will only show the object created in the Existing phase—and their graphics are not overridden.

FIGURE 11.25
Existing
phase only

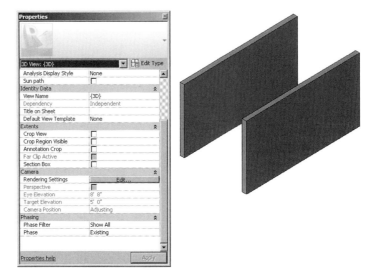

Keep in mind that it's impossible to see anything that's proposed from this present Existing phase. That's because there's no way to see beyond the present phase. We think you should be able to do this, but Revit just doesn't offer that functionality yet.

Now you need to set the phase to New Construction and select the Show Previous + Demo option (Figure 11.26). This shows both existing walls (the walls from the previous phase). And one of the walls is clearly being demolished. What's important to remember is that the graphic overrides that are being applied are relative to what you'd be seeing through the lens of the New Construction phase.

FIGURE 11.26
Show Previous
+ Demo

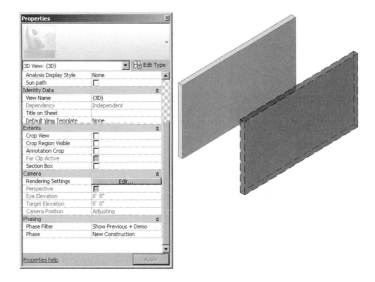

Now let's select the Show Previous Phase option in the phase filter, as shown in Figure 11.27. Maybe a better name would be Show Existing To Remain because the demolished elements are no longer shown.

FIGURE 11.27
Show Previous
Phase

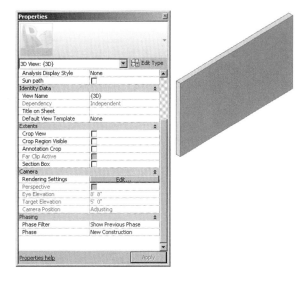

Now we'll move forward another moment in time and set the phase filter to Show Previous + New. This will show only the remaining elements (not any of the demolished content) from the present and previous view (Figure 11.28).

FIGURE 11.28
Show Previous +
New Elements

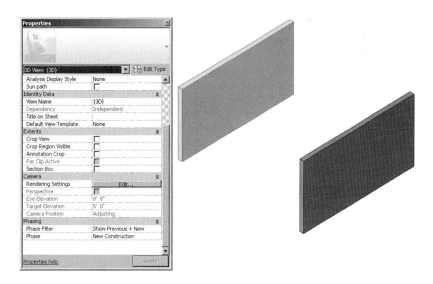

This brings up another interesting point. Why not show the Existing To Remain as well as the Proposed and Proposed Temporary elements? Although you could also create a new phase filter, for this example, we'll change the settings of the Show Previous + New Graphic override settings (Figure 11.29).

FIGURE 11.29
Showing
Existing and all
New elements

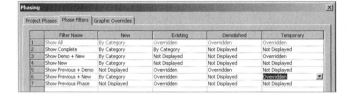

Figure 11.30 shows the result.

FIGURE 11.30
Existing To
Remain, Proposed,
and Temporarily
Proposed elements

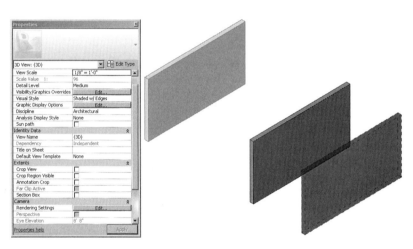

The next order of sequence will be to set the view to Show Demo + New, which would show demolished elements from the present and previous phase as well as any New elements from the present phase (see Figure 11.31).

FIGURE 11.31
Show Demo + New

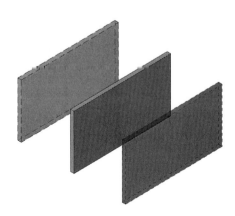

But this brings up another interesting point. If you want to show only the objects in the present phase (as well as demolition), then you'll want to modify the phase filters in the Phase Settings, as shown in Figure 11.32. We don't know how common it is to show demolition from a previous phase without showing the existing from the same phase. That's why we're just changing an existing setting rather than creating a new phase filter.

FIGURE 11.32
Turning Off demolished elements from a previous phase

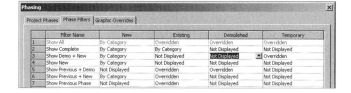

The result would be only the New and Temporary elements being shown in this view (Figure 11.33).

FIGURE 11.33
Showing only Proposed and Temporary elements

The next sequence, Show New, will only show the New elements in the present phase (Figure 11.34).

FIGURE 11.34
Showing New elements

Now comes the final setting, Show Complete (see Figure 11.35). This only shows the existing elements that remain from the previous phase (after demolition) and the new elements that are being proposed (minus the temporary construction that has also been demolished).

FIGURE 11.35
Showing finished conditions

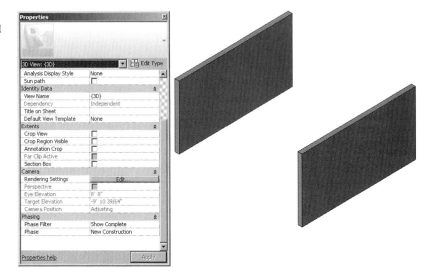

You can find the example file used in this section, called c11_Phases.rvt, in the Chapter 11 folder.

Creating, Distributing, and Updating Groups

It's easy to think of groups kind of like blocks (if you have an AutoCAD background) or cells (if you have a MicroStation background). But groups are much more than this. Yes, they're great at maintaining repetition within your Revit project. But there are some major differences:

◆ Creating groups is quite easy. And whether it's a 2D or 3D group, the insertion point for the group is easily defined and modified. The same can't be said of simple 2D blocks.

◆ Updating groups is a breeze. It's easy and intuitive to modify a group after it's been created. Practically anyone on your team can do it, which means that design workflow will not bottleneck in your project team.

◆ Copying groups throughout your project is also a breeze. Groups can be copied across different levels, rotated, and even mirrored (although mirroring isn't such a good idea, but more on that later).

There are a few good practices that you'll want to keep in mind when using groups. But they're so straightforward that you'll wonder how you've ever worked without them.

Creating Groups

You can create two kinds of groups in Revit. One is just for geometry, and they're called *model groups*. The other is just for view-specific content like text, tags, dimensions, and so on, and they're called *detail groups*. You can create one kind of group or the other explicitly. But if you try to create a group with both model and detail elements, Revit is smart enough to create a detail group that's associated with the model group.

To demonstrate this, open a new project and start with drawing four walls, as shown in Figure 11.36. Don't forget to dimension the length and width conditions.

FIGURE 11.36

Four walls and dimensions

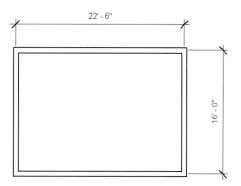

Now select the Create Group function under the Modify | Multiselect tab. Go ahead and keep the default name Group 1 for both Model Group and Attached Detail Group (Figure 11.37).

FIGURE 11.37

Creating the model and attached detail group

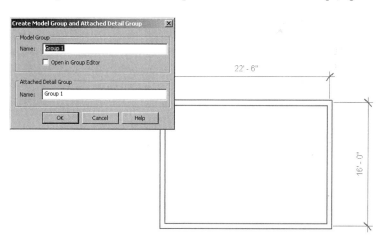

Now select the group and copy it to the side of your original group. You'll notice that only the geometry is copied, which is fine (Figure 11.38).

FIGURE 11.38
Copied group

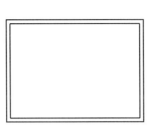
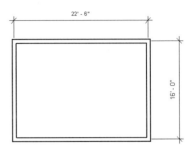

Associating the detail group is really simple. Just select the group and then select the Attached Detail Groups option, and you'll see the dialog box shown in Figure 11.39.

FIGURE 11.39
Attached Detail
Group Placement
dialog box

The results are fairly straightforward (Figure 11.40). Both groups are now identical with geometry and dimensions.

FIGURE 11.40
Identical groups

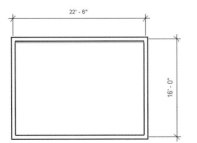
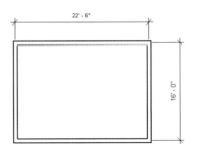

Modifying Groups

Now that you've created two identical groups, you'll add a door to one of the walls that belong to the group, as shown in Figure 11.41. But don't add it to the group—just place it in one of the walls.

FIGURE 11.41
Adding a door outside of Group mode

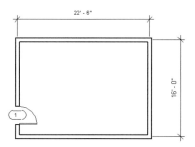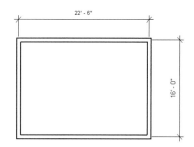

Now you can select the group to the left and select Edit Group. You'll enter a special editing environment, as shown in Figure 11.42. Everything in the view becomes a sepia tone and you're able to add, remove, and attach other elements to your group.

FIGURE 11.42
Group Edit mode

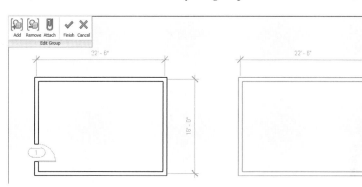

Now add the door to the group by selecting the Add function. You'll notice that you can't add the door numbers. This is fine, because you'll add them later when numbering. Now finish the group and you'll notice that both groups have a door in the same location (Figure 11.43).

FIGURE 11.43
Finished group

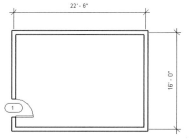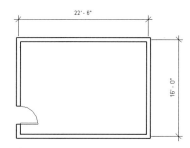

The process is essentially the same for modifying groups: enter Group mode, make the changes and/or additions, and then finish the group. Be careful when you're duplicating and swapping one group for another one, which is common during design iteration.

Copying Groups

First, duplicate the group. The easiest way to do this is to right-click the group name that you want to duplicate in the Project Browser, as shown in Figure 11.44.

FIGURE 11.44
Duplicating a
group

Now you can select any of your groups and swap it for this new group. Go ahead and exchange Group 1 for Group 2.

Now enter Group Edit mode for this second group, and edit it as shown in Figure 11.45; then finish the group.

FIGURE 11.45
Modifying the
second group

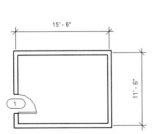
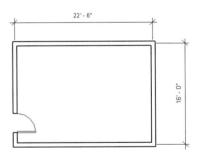

This brings up an important point of discussion. Groups have insertion points that need to be considered before you exchange one group for another. When you create a group in Revit, the insertion point is initially at the geometric center of all the stuff in the group, which is fine if you're trying to find it.

But keep in mind that as you edit the group, the insertion Apoint doesn't move until you deliberately move it. This can be seen in Figure 11.46, as editing the geometry for Group 2 retains the same insertion point that was active when the group was created.

FIGURE 11.46

Insertion points in different groups

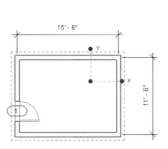
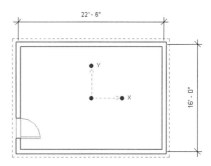

Moving the insertion point is an easy matter of dragging (and if necessary, rotating) the Insertion Point icon to a common location before swapping one group for another (Figure 11.47).

FIGURE 11.47

Relocating insertion points

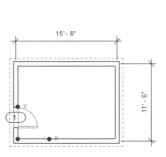
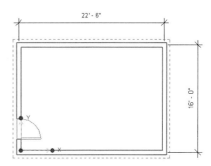

Once you've done this, swapping groups occurs at the same relative location. Figure 11.48 illustrates Group 1 being swapped for Group 2, and vice versa. But common insertion points are being maintained.

FIGURE 11.48

Exchanged groups

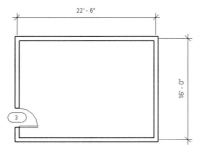
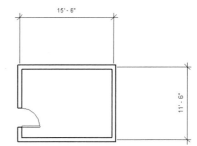

Excluding Elements Within Groups

Of course there will be occasions where everything in a group works great. And it works throughout the project, except for that one particular condition. This is really frustrating. And in the past, you had to create new groups for each slight exception, which might have been conceptually consistent, but often led to an exponentially growing list of group variants.

This is now deftly handled by excluding elements from groups. The rest of the groups are intact, and scheduling is aware of excluded elements. Figure 11.49 shows an example. We've copied the group above the first one. But in this condition, there's a column right in the middle of the door.

FIGURE 11.49
Group conflicts

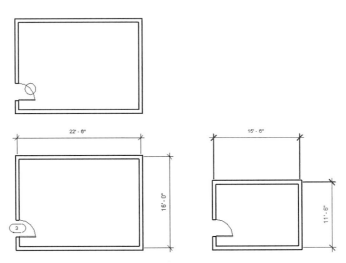

First, select the door and select Create Similar to place a new door where you want it to go. This door will not be part of the group (you can't place elements as exceptions). In this case, the new door has been placed above the grouped door, and its swing direction has been flipped (Figure 11.50).

FIGURE 11.50
Adding a new door

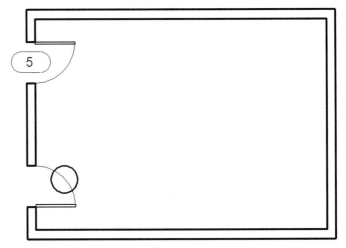

Now you can exclude the door that conflicts with the column as an exception to the rest of all the other groups. This can be a bit confusing at first, because you don't enter Group Edit mode to exclude members from groups. Simply hover over the group and tab through until the door is highlighted. Then select the door, as shown in Figure 11.51.

FIGURE 11.51
Selecting elements in groups

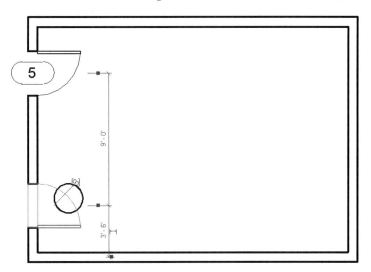

Once this is done, you'll notice an icon to the upper left of the door (Figure 11.52).

FIGURE 11.52
Selecting the door in the group

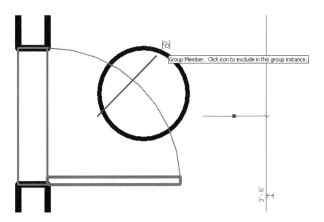

Selecting this icon will allow you to exclude the door as an exception to the group, and the wall will heal itself as if the door is not there (Figure 11.53).

FIGURE 11.53
Excluded elements
from groups

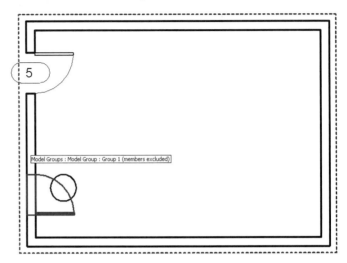

Hovering your mouse over the group will reveal any hidden elements in the group (Figure 11.54). Just tab through to select the hidden door to include the component back into the group.

FIGURE 11.53
Excluded elements
not shown

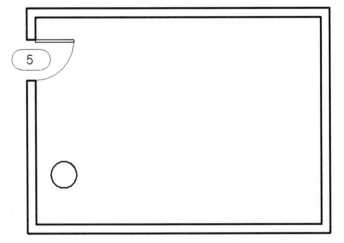

Saving and Loading Groups

Even though we consider Revit to be the only whole building BIM (WBB) application in the world (by integrating the building, content, documentation, and multiuser workflow into one database), there are times when you'll want to share the data across many files.

And just like you wouldn't want your family components locked up inside a project file, there are good reasons to keep commonly used groups outside your project. You might even want to keep them in a folder just like your custom content. This can be accomplished by saving groups outside your projects.

Saving groups is a simple matter of right-clicking the group name in your Project Browser and selecting Save Group (Figure 11.55).

FIGURE 11.55
Saving groups

You'll then be prompted to save the group as an RVT file (not an RVG file as in the past). You can open this file like any other RVT file and then reload the group into the project in order to update all the instances.

Be aware that when you load the group in a project, if the group name already exists, you'll be given a warning. You can overwrite the existing group (by selecting Yes) or load with the option to rename the group that's being loaded (by selecting No). Or you can cancel the operation altogether (Figure 11.56).

FIGURE 11.56
Loading modified
groups

What's really great is that when you reload the group Revit even remembers to exclude previously excluded elements from the group that's been modified in another session of Revit. Figure 11.57 shows a desk and chair have been added to the group. The group has been reloaded, overwriting the original group, but the exclusion remains intact.

FIGURE 11.57
Retaining excluded
group elements

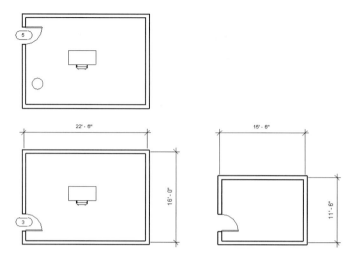

Creating Groups from Links

Because groups are also RVT files, they can be linked into the project environment as well.
While you can't edit a link in place (as with a group), there's some excellent reasons you might
want to start a group as a link and then bind the link at a later time, which will convert it to
a group. Groups and links can also exist within design options (more on design options in a
moment).

Simply select Link Revit from the Insert tab (Figure 11.58).

FIGURE 11.58
Adding groups
as links

Then browse to your group and click Open, as shown in Figure 11.59.

FIGURE 11.59
Select the group
and click Open.

After the link has been placed, you can copy it throughout your project. Keep in mind that all the functionality between groups and nongrouped elements will not behave the same as links and the rest of your project. For example, in Figure 11.60, the upper-right collection of walls and furniture is a link, not a group. And as a result, walls are not cleaning up between links and groups in the same way as they are between groups and groups or other walls.

FIGURE 11.60
Wall joins between links vs. groups

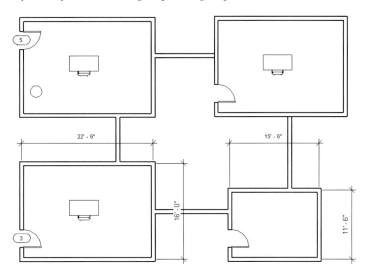

But this graphic restriction may not be a concern during programming and predesign, when links allow for a lot of rapid flexibility.

After you've resolved your design using links, you can bind them into the project environment (Figure 11.61).

FIGURE 11.61
Binding links

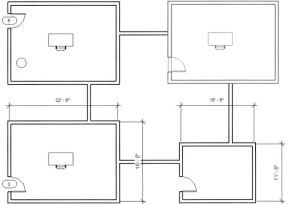

But rather than "explode" the link into separate and unrelated elements, Revit converts the link to a group. Once this happens, the previous graphic issue is resolved as walls easily join across groups, as shown in Figure 11.62.

FIGURE 11.62
Resolved wall
graphics

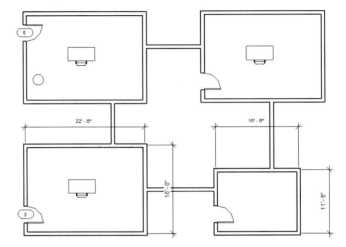

Best Practices for Groups

Groups are great for creating and maintaining design iteration within a single project. And they're also great for maintaining consistency across multiple projects, since groups can be saved and loaded across multiple files. They can even be linked as separate RVT files and then converted to groups at a later time.

But like everything in Revit (and in life), there are some important exceptions that you want to be aware of. Nearly every time there's been a problem with groups we've noticed that it's the result of doing one of the following five things. Not that doing any of these things will kill your project—they may be completely technically feasible. But they may put your project into a world of hurt that you'll wish you could have avoided:

Avoid putting datum in your group.   You should avoid putting datum (levels and grids) inside your group. First, you can't manage the extents of the datum unless you're in Group Edit mode, which can create conflicts elsewhere in your project. Of course you will have the option to *not* include the datum when you bind your link. Again, this doesn't necessarily create a technical hurdle. But it can create a lot of confusion. We've seen situations where duplicate levels are deleted, only to find out that those levels were hosting content in the project.

Don't nest groups.   You should take care to avoid nesting groups. Although nesting can save time in some situations when the design is preliminary and your team is trying to distribute content and design ideas quickly, you'll likely find a point of diminishing returns as the design evolves. You can't get to all the features and functionality of Revit when you're in Group Edit mode. And if you're nested deep into groups and trying to modify project properties, you'll get quickly frustrated digging in, out, and across nested groups to go back and forth between your group and project.

Group hosted elements and their hosts together. You want to keep your hosted elements and hosts together. For example, try not to group doors and windows without their host walls. Technically, nothing keeps you from creating a group from windows without their host. But if any of your windows become unhosted and then deleted, this will delete other windows that are properly hosted. This also goes to the heart of what needs to be hosted in a Revit project. Another example is that elements such as plumbing fixtures that don't need to cut their host shouldn't be hosted. Instead, they should be face-based (or assigned the option Moves With Nearby).

Don't use attached relationships in groups. Avoid attached relationships within groups. In other words, give walls explicit heights rather than Attaching Top/Bottom to levels or other hosts (like floors and roofs). If you manipulate the datum or attached host and the relationship creates inconsistent conditions, you'll get a warning asking you to fix the groups (Figure 11.63).

FIGURE 11.63
Avoid attaching
with groups

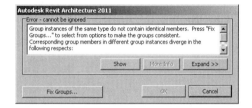

Fixing the group really doesn't fix the group. It actually explodes it or creates a new group (Figure 11.64).

FIGURE 11.64
Resolving attach-
ments warning

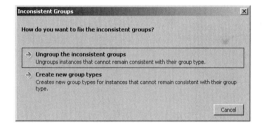

Don't mirror groups. Finally, and maybe most importantly: don't mirror groups. Instead, it's better to create left and right versions. Does mirroring work in concept? Yes. Does it work in the real world? Not really. Sorry.

Think about it. You'd love to be able to mirror that precious prototype coffee shop, right? Well, Revit doesn't disallow mirroring of content as a parameter (which still wouldn't solve the problem, but that's another matter). Mirror the coffee shop and now the baristas are foaming milk on the right rather than the left. This might look great in a rendering, but it doesn't make sense for the company that manufactures espresso machines.

And now the display cases have power supplies on the wrong side. The cash register has keys on the wrong side. The desk in the managers' office now has drawers on the left and filing cabinets on the right. And to make matters worse, the sink in the bathroom now has hot water coming from the wrong faucet. Again, it makes all the conceptual sense in the world to be able to mirror a building…and a group. But the implementation of trying to make this work can cost a lot of time and money trying to repair. And that's just a coffee shop. If you think it's a good idea to mirror a hospital room or a surgical theater or some other mission-critical building or civil construct, well…someone could die. Or you will have to work very, very late.

If you'd like to download the file that has been created during the examples, you can find it in the Chapter 11 folder; it's called `c11_Groups.rvt`.

Making Design Options for Design Iteration

Design options are great when you work within the rules of how design options work. It's kind of like the rules with mirroring groups. What you think might make sense conceptually doesn't always work in the practice.

Design options are great for iteration within the walls of a building or a single Revit project. Interior renovations can go off without a problem. Iteration of spaces or functions within well-defined boundaries is also not a problem.

But one of the first and most important rules to remember is that an object that is being hosted can't be in a design option unless the host is also in the design option (Figure 11.65). That means if you want to show a door in two possible locations as an option in your design, you'll have to create two walls to host those two doors in your two options.

FIGURE 11.65
The hosted and host must exist in the same design options.

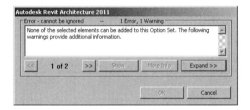

Second, design options are not for "whole building" iteration. If you're not sure about which direction your big design idea is headed, don't put both buildings in the same file and think you're going to save yourself any time. You'll be better off starting another file (and if necessary, starting another file). Even if you're trying to resolve just a big part of a bigger building, put that big part of the building in a separate file and link the results. You can even put each of the links in their own design option. For example, if you have a couple of different ideas for your curtain wall, put that part of the design in a separate file and link them all into your main project file, assigning each of the links to a different design option.

With those two suggestions out of the way, we'll show you how to use design options as intended.

Creating Design Options

Again, let's start simple, establish the principle, and then add complexity later. Create four simple walls with a wall down the middle of the space both as shown in Figure 11.66.

FIGURE 11.66
Starting design
options

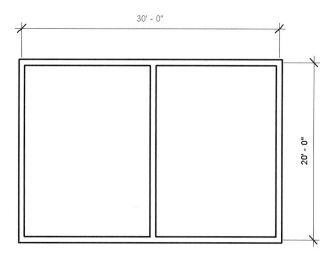

We're going to configure this simple space into a design option that divides the space vertically in one option and horizontally in the other:

1. Select your Manage tab in order to initiate design options. Select the Design Options tab
   (Figure 11.67).

FIGURE 11.67
Design Options tab

2. Create a new option set (which will automatically create one design option) and then create another option as shown in Figure 11.68. Click Close to dismiss the dialog box.

FIGURE 11.68
Creating an
option set and
two options

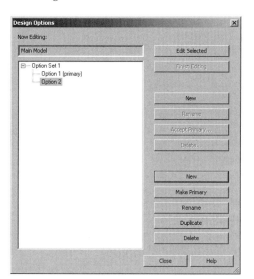

Now that you've started design options, everything in the project (which, admittedly isn't a lot) is now in the Main Model. Let's start adding elements to one of the two options.

3. In a process that might at first to appear to be a bit confusing, select the center vertical wall and add it to Option Set 1/Option 1 (Figure 11.69).

FIGURE 11.69
Adding elements to options

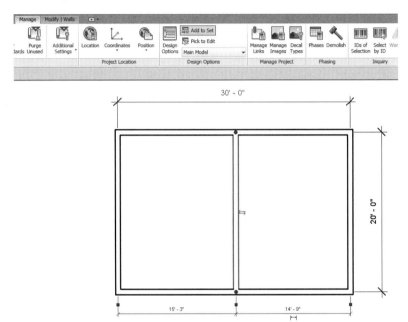

4. You'll do this by selecting the wall, which you notice will immediately initiate the Modify | Walls tab. But you can get around this limitation by simply and easily *reselecting* the Manage tab (that was just visible a moment ago before you selected the middle wall). Now select the Add To Set option and add the wall to the first option but not the second one, as shown in Figure 11.70.

FIGURE 11.70
Selecting the option

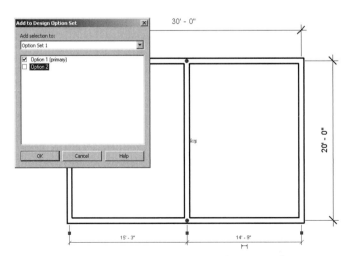

Just as a side note, you'll need to do this every time you select elements in the Main Model and you need to add to a design option. But you'll get used to this convoluted and time-consuming process over time. You could create a keyboard shortcut or menu item to the Quick Access toolbar. But of course this would defeat the purpose of using the new user interface.

Editing Design Options

You can also add elements to a specific design option by selecting the option from the Design Options panel (Figure 11.71).

FIGURE 11.71

Selecting an option
to edit

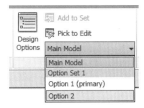

Another, faster option is to use the Active Design Option selector at the bottom of the screen (Figure 11.72).

FIGURE 11.72

Active Design
Option selector

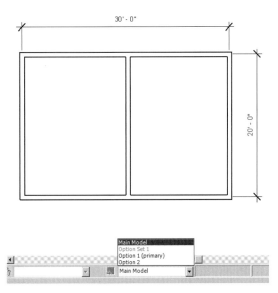

This will allow you to enter a special mode where you can add elements from outside the option, or create them from within the option. Everything that is not inside this option will turn light gray, indicating that it is not inside the presently editable option. Now you can add another wall as shown (Figure 11.73).

FIGURE 11.73
Edit Option mode

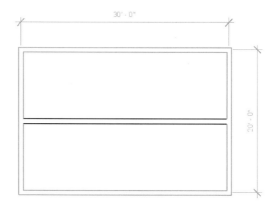

Viewing and Scheduling Design Options

You notice that whenever you switch between Option 1 and Option 2, the view automatically changes to show the option that you've selected. This is because initiating design options automatically creates another tab in the Visibility/Graphic Overrides dialog box. By default, the Design Options tab shows Automatic (Figure 11.74). This means that the primary design option (in this case, Option Set 1) will be shown in the view.

This tab is available for any view, even for schedules, as shown in Figure 11.75. Selecting the Visibility Graphics settings in the View Properties of a schedule filters the schedule according to the desired design option.

Of course, if you want to specify or lock a view to a particular design option, simply specify this in the Visibility/Graphic Overrides dialog box (Figure 11.76).

FIGURE 11.74
The Design Options tab displays Automatic.

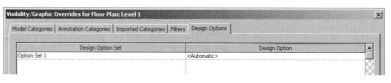

FIGURE 11.75
Design Options in the View Properties of a schedule

FIGURE 11.76
Locking the view to a design option

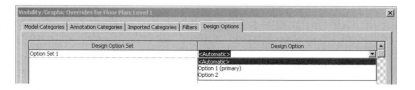

This can be particularly useful for views that are being placed on sheets. For working views, it's fine to leave the View Properties set to Automatic, so the view switches to actively show the desired design option.

Deleting Design Options

As your project grows and begins to resolve more detail, it may be necessary to delete an option set, accept the primary design option, or delete a single design option. While some of these options might at create somewhat similar outcomes, there are important differences.

First, deleting an option deletes the option set and all of its associated options. You delete an option set by selecting it in the Design Options dialog box and clicking the Delete button (Figure 11.77).

FIGURE 11.77
Select the option set and click Delete.

You'll see the following warning indicating that you're about to delete all the geometry associated with the option set (Figure 11.78). Click Yes.

FIGURE 11.78
Click Yes at this warning.

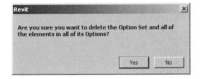

Additionally, any views that are associated with the option set will be deleted by default, but you're given the option to uncheck views that you want to retain, as shown in Figure 11.79.

FIGURE 11.79
You can uncheck views that you want to retain.

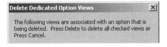

Yes, this is a lot of warnings, but for good reason! All your related geometry, plans, elevations, sections, schedules, 3D views, and so on are about to be deleted. You do have the option to keep the views, but they'll only show what's left in the Main Model. And the Main Model may or may not technically exist. That's because if you only have one option set in your project, then design options will no longer exist. There's no longer a distinction between the Main Model and anything else.

Second, accepting the primary design option ultimately removes the option set, but it also retains the geometry associated with the primary option, as shown in Figure 11.80.

FIGURE 11.80
Delete option set warning

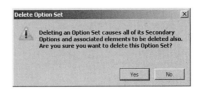

You do this by selecting the desired option set and then clicking the Accept Primary button in the Design Options dialog box. Accepting the primary option also deletes any of the other options associated with the option set. And finally, the design option set is removed and all and all of the geometry associated with the primary option is moved into the Main Model.

Finally, you can delete a single design option within an option set. However, you may not delete a primary option. You'll first have to assign a new primary option. Do this by selecting the desired option and then clicking the Make Primary button, as shown in Figure 11.81. Once this is done you can delete the formerly Primary Option.

FIGURE 11.81
Make Primary
option

Just remember that all of the previous warnings will apply. Deleting a design option will delete all the geometry and associated views.

 Real World Scenario

PUTTING IT ALL TOGETHER

Now it's time to bring it all together—phasing, groups, and design options. Let's create a tenant upfit in two phases. The first phase will resolve construction on one side of the space, and then we'll turn to the other side of the space to complete the renovation. We'll also rely on groups for collections of components. Finally, we'll create a design option for the second space. Ultimately, you need to visualize the exercise in plan, perspective, and schedule.

Here's the existing condition of the space from the previous exercise. If you haven't created the file to this point, go ahead and download that file to get started. Before you create your facsimile, remember that this will be the existing condition. So rather than create the existing walls and then change their phase, let's start by duplicating a view and changing the view of that phase so that the walls and other content are already on the existing phase.

Duplicate Level 1 and rename it **to LEVEL 1, EXISTING**, as shown here.

Then click inside the view to activate the view's properties; make sure that the phase is set to Existing.

EXISTING PLAN

Leave the phase filter to Show All for now. Don't be concerned that the elevation tags have disappeared in the view. View tags are also phase aware, and they're in the New Construction phase. The overall space is 80′ × 80′. We've also added some exterior dimensions as a reference. The finished exterior plan is shown here:

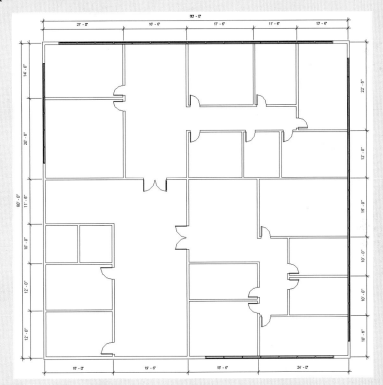

As you can see, the finished existing space is really two areas. In this scenario, the tenant in the lower-left space is expanding and will be taking over the upper space.

The idea is that we're going to demolish the space in stages. We don't want to upset the existing tenants to complete the phased work.

PHASE ONE: DEMOLITION

Some of the existing walls will remain. But you don't want to demolish them in this view. That's because the demolition should take place at the start of New Construction. But there's going to be two construction phases (so there will also be two demolition phases). If you haven't created those two phases, do so now, as shown here.

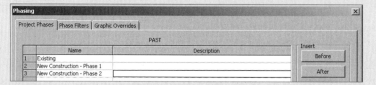

Now let's duplicate Level 1 again and rename as shown here. This will be the view that contains the demolition.

Now go to that view and be sure to change the phase and phase filter, as shown here.

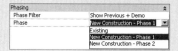

Now demolish the walls as shown here. As a shortcut, you don't have to demolish the doors if you demolish the walls that host them.

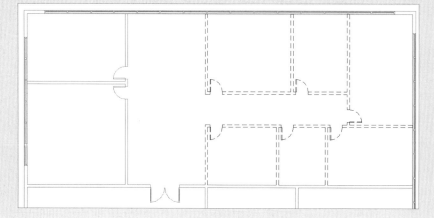

Now let's add the new elements. First, we'll replace a portion of the walls around the upper-left spaces with storefront. Since this is proposed, and the walls exist, it will automatically demolish the openings. The graphic shown here is a perspective of the work thus far. Recall that we've shaded the existing walls so that they'll stand out more from the proposed walls and the demolished walls are in shown in red.

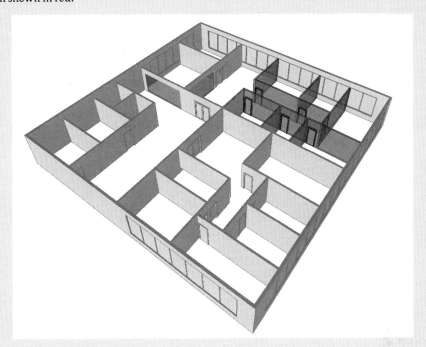

PHASE 1: PROPOSED

First, let's duplicate Level 1 and rename as shown here:

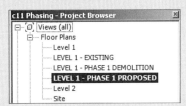

Make sure that the phase and phase filter are set as shown here. This view will only show the existing elements that remain after demolition and the proposed content.

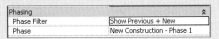

Now we'll start adding furniture to the space. We'll add a reception area and other office furniture. Add desks, tables, shelving, and chairs, as shown here:

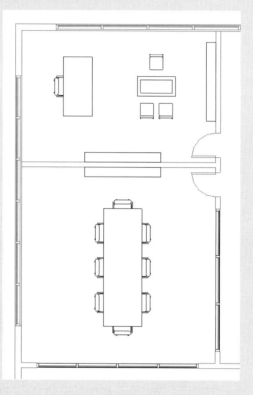

Now let's start adding open office furniture. But let's group the assembly before we start copying through the office space.

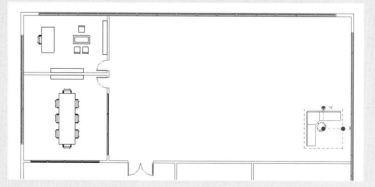

The graphic shown here is the completed space in a plan view:

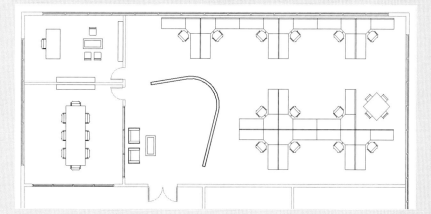

The graphic shown here is the space in a perspective view. Note that the demolished walls are not being shown. To give some graphic clarity and allow you to see through the context of the existing walls, we've temporarily set the transparency value of the existing material (in the phase properties) to 50%.

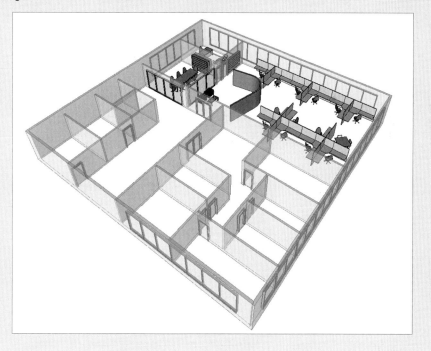

PHASE 2: DEMOLITION

Let's start by duplicating Level 1. Then rename the view to **LEVEL 1, PHASE 2 DEMOLITION** and set the phase and phase filters as shown here:

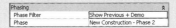

Now demolish the existing walls as shown here. Note that you'll have to split the long wall between Phase 1 Proposed and Phase 2 Proposed in order to allow only a portion of the wall to be demolished.

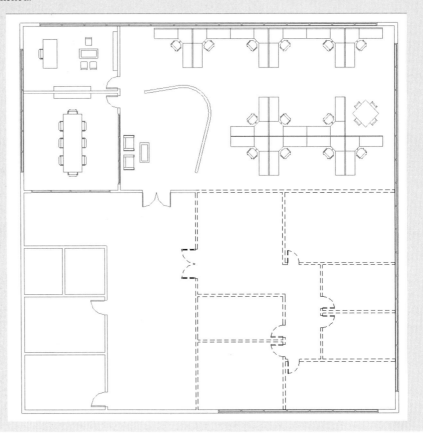

The graphic shown here is a perspective view showing the proposed demolition for the second phase. Don't be confused by the proposed content from the previous phase showing as existing. This is correct, since that content is now considered existing when seen through the lens of the second phase.

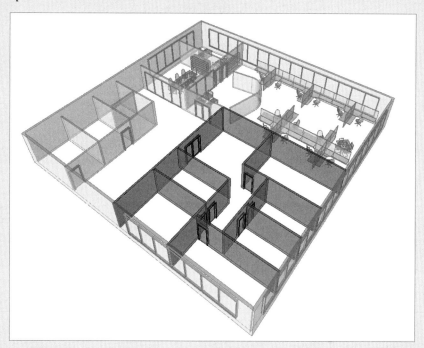

PHASE 2: PROPOSED

Now let's duplicate the view again for the start of proposed work. Duplicate Level 1 and rename it to **LEVEL 1, PHASE 2 PROPOSED**. Set the phase and phase filter as shown here:

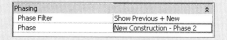

Start working in your new plan view, adding proposed elements as shown. Don't worry about getting the design right—just get the idea right. Here's the plan view:

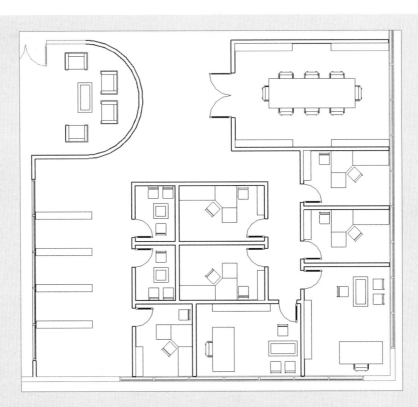

Just remember, adding elements in the view with the appropriate phase and phase filter settings is the easiest way to avoid confusion. Here's a perspective of the same view:

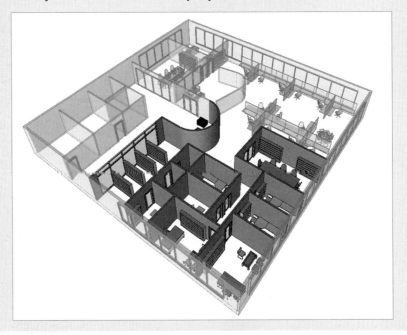

Now that you're finished with the demolition and proposed work in both phases, take a moment to set up a perspective and then duplicate it three more times. Each of the views will show each phase sequence. Your Project Browser should look similar to this:

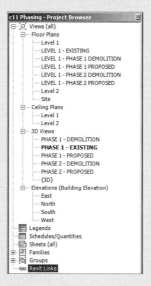

Except for the existing perspective, here are all of the tiled views thus far:

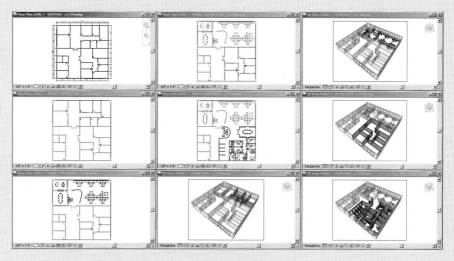

SCHEDULING

Now let's create a schedule for walls that will quantify demolition for each phase. As a side note, we believe it would be helpful to be able to create Multi-Category schedules that would allow both host and component categories to be scheduled at the same time—for example, being able to schedule demolition for both walls and doors in the same demolition schedule. But this is not presently possible. So we'll create the schedules individually.

First, there's no phase filter to show only demolished elements. We'll need to create this filter, as shown here:

You can visually confirm what it will show by applying it to a working view:

Now let's start by creating a schedule for walls that are being demolished by volume. We also need to estimate the cost of disposal for each phase. Create the schedule as shown here:

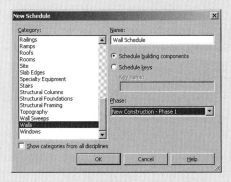

The following graphic shows the schedule fields that you'll need to create. You'll only be able to select the Type and Volume fields from the Available Fields selection.

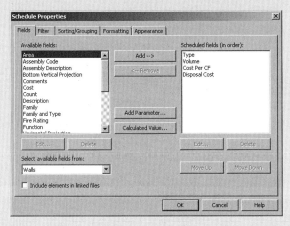

We'll also need to create a project parameter for the cost per unit volume (CF) per wall type. Click Add Parameter and fill out the resulting dialog box as shown here. Choose Type Parameter because we want to be able to add one value per wall type, not per each instance.

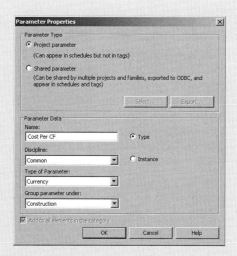

You'll need to add a Calculated Value in order to multiply the demolished units' volume by the cost per units and get the total. We've divided the Volume value by 1 in order to keep the units consistent, as shown here:

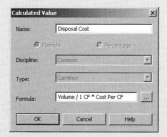

The Sorting/Grouping settings are shown here:

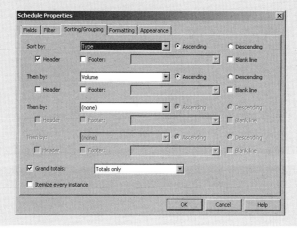

The Formatting settings are shown here:

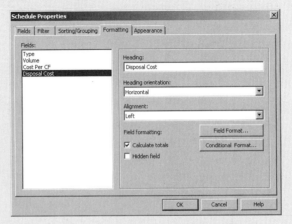

Here's the Formatting for the Disposal Cost Calculated value:

When you're finished, the schedule will appear showing with the following values. Your schedule will not be exactly the same because the amount of demolition will vary between this example project and your project.

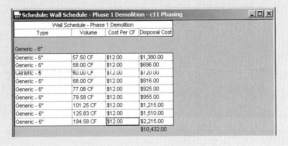

For the Phase 2 demolition schedule, don't start over. Duplicate the previously created schedule and just change the phase, as shown here:

All that's left is to assemble the views on sheets. We'll only need to use two sheets. Each sheet will show a combined Phase 1 Demolition and Proposed views (plans, perspective, and schedules):

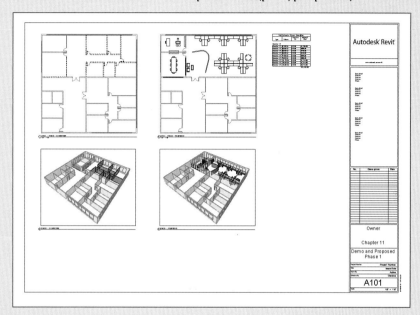

DESIGN OPTIONS

Everything looks great, but as to be expected, you need to show another option for Phase 2. This is really easily done!

First, create a new design option set and two options, as shown here. Notice that we've renamed the set for clarity.

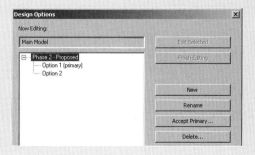

Here's a great tip. To isolate what you need to assign to Option 1, set the phase filter to Show New elements. This will turn off any existing conditions from the previous phase.

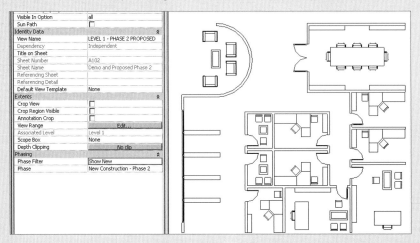

Now select everything in the view, return to the Manage tab, and click Add To Set. Deselect Option 2, as shown here, and click OK. This will add everything to the Option 1 (primary) design option. Then set the phase filter back to Show Previous + New.

Now duplicate LEVEL 1 - PHASE 2 PROPOSED, and rename it to **LEVEL 1 - PHASE 2 PROPOSED - OPTION 2**. This will be your working view for the second design option.

Next, set the View Properties to show the second option:

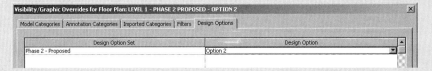

Now make Option 2 active and create another design iteration, as shown here:

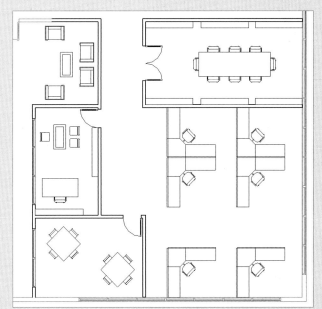

Now place this design option on the sheet next to the Phase 2 demolition and first option. You can also duplicate the perspective view of the first option; remember to change its Visibility Graphics to show Option 2, as shown here:

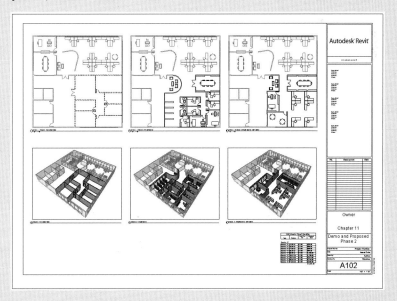

If you'd like to download the file used in this example, you can find it in the Chapter 11 folder; it's called c11_Exercise.rvt.

The Bottom Line

Use phasing.   Time is such an important element to the design process and nearly impossible to capture with traditional CAD tools. Don't use phasing for construction sequencing (there's a better way). Embrace phasing for *communication*, not just *illustration*.

Master It   How can you use phasing to communicate your design across a series of key stages? What kind of project is best suited to phasing?

Know why you shouldn't mirror groups.   Groups are great for creating collections of both host and family component geometry. Just remember to use best practices and you'll avoid a lot of common roadblocks. Everything still schedules, as you'd expect. And creating exceptions in groups allows you to make subtle changes without creating a new group.

Master It   Why shouldn't you mirror groups?

Make design options for design iteration.   Like groups, design options work great when you work within the rules. Design options are intended for design iteration that is bounded and well defined—not for putting multiple buildings in one project file. Remember that links, groups, and phasing can exist within design options. Always keep hosted elements with their host when using design options.

Master It   Suppose you have a multistory tower. How could you show repetitive curtain wall options?

Chapter 12

Visualization

Visualization in Revit—or with any tool (even a pencil)—isn't an exact science. It still requires a patient, aesthetic eye. The computer just does what you tell it to do, so many times users become frustrated because they don't know what they're trying to accomplish. But inexperienced users are often doubly frustrated because they don't know how to accomplish something. And so they set about trying to learn how to do a particular task.

Learning how to do a particular thing with a rendering tool is fine; it's part of a successful process. But we often find that people believe that the key to creating successful visualizations is the ability to make something seem "real"—or even "hyper-real"—and this is the goal of their learning process. Unfortunately, this is the first mistake (of many). If your goal is to make your renderings more realistic and believable, you'll quickly come to a dead end.

The most important thing you can do to successfully visualize your work starts first with one thing: listen. That's right—it's your ears that make you a great artist! You need to be able to understand what your client is trying to accomplish. Because you're not really trying to visualize something; you're trying to communicate something *for someone else*. First learn to listen, and you'll understand what your client needs to communicate. And you'll be far more successful!

In this chapter, you'll learn to:

◆ Create real-time and rendered analytic visualizations

◆ Render emotive photorealistic visualizations

◆ Understand the importance of sequencing your visualization workflow

The Role of Visualization

We believe that anyone can use Revit to create compelling, emotive visualizations. And what's really great is that your visualizations are based on the same coordinated design information that you're depending on to document to complete your project. But there are a few challenges:

◆ Creating emotive visualization is usually such a small part of your project's overall workflow that it's hard to spend the time necessary to hone your rendering skills. This is the reason that photorealistic renderings, both still and moving image, are often the realm of a specialist who deeply understands the techniques and workflow needed to create compelling imagery.

◆ The reality is that visualization is both art and science, but especially art. You'll never be able to just push a button and get a beautiful image. There's a world of difference between something that's photorealistic and something that emotive and compelling. In other words, the button says Render, not Beautiful.

◆ Most importantly, visualization is about communication, something that many people forget to take into account. Don't ever create a rendering until you know what you're trying to accomplish. You must know your audience and understand what needs to be communicated (keeping in mind that the person requesting the rendering isn't always the intended audience). Otherwise, you'll likely spend hours of time doing something that is perfectly and exactly *wrong*.

We've learned this the hard way. Imagine the disappointment after spending hours creating what we thought was an amazing rendering, only to find out that the client wanted something more gestural and sketchy. Or imagine our frustration after we created something unresolved and fuzzy, only to find out that the client needed images that are polished and resolved, something more suitable for finished marketing materials. Rendering is about more than visualization. It's about communication. What you may need to communicate may be completely opposed to emotively well-lit, photorealistic material and entourage.

This brings up two important points about where you'll likely struggle with rendering in Revit, and why unfortunately there's very little that you can do about it:

◆ Although engineers often analyze in order to design, architects often visualize in order to design. But if your intent is to put all of this visual iteration into Revit just to render it, you'll probably get frustrated over all the chaff you're putting into a database that you want to keep light and flexible (particularly during early design). The reality is that Revit is most useful during early design to communicate analytic rather than photorealistic information. But this isn't going to help create highly polished, wouldn't-it-be-great-if kind of renderings when Revit is best suited during early design to answer massing, relationships, adjacencies, and other analytic questions.

◆ You'll never be able to render out of Revit more than you put into it. The level of detail required to create deeply emotive and detailed visualizations is not very likely the level of detail required to create accurate documentation. As a matter of fact, creating, changing, and resolving that level of detail may bring your project documentation to a grinding halt!

For example, the next time you're in your favorite coffee shop, take a moment and look at the espresso machine. Examine the detail of materials, hardware, and parts—the knobs, switches, and valves. Is this the level of detail that you want to have in your Revit project? Probably not! In fact, it's more likely that the documentation of a coffee shop simply requires a believable placeholder for an espresso machine; it needs to properly schedule and only be generally believable across all your project views.

But deeply emotive renderings often require specific detail and design resolution. In other words, not just "any" espresso machine will do! It needs to be a particular make, model, and manufacturer. Yet, if you're resolving this level of detail for visualization, it's likely that you're too deep into the weeds if you're spending valuable project time carefully modeling the valves on espresso machines.

So even though Revit has the ability to help you create great renderings, the level of detail required at the beginning of a project (when analytical relationships are still being resolved) is too much detail for that particular stage of design. Even when the project is well resolved and established, the level of detail required for a highly finished and photorealistic visualization is far beyond what's required to complete your project documentation. So, what is the point of this chapter?

Our focus is to get you somewhere in the middle. You need to deeply understand how Revit works, but you also need to understand that although something may be technically feasible, it may not be practicable from a workflow standpoint. Overall, our goal is to help you focus on communication, not just visualization. So if you're happy with visualizing your project at its current level of development (not too far ahead and not overly detailed), you're going to have a lot of success rendering inside Revit.

Analytic Visualization

There are two key models of communication: analytic and photorealistic. Think for a moment about Google Maps: there's an option to view both Map and Satellite modes. Think of the Map mode as your analytic view and the Satellite mode as your photorealistic view. Both views are important depending on what you're trying to communicate. If you're simply trying to understand directional information, the Maps view is better. But if you're trying to show someone what something looks like with regard to trees and other real-world features, the Satellite view has obvious advantages.

It's also interesting to note that real-time information is easier to maintain in analytic views. For example, Google Maps has the option to show live traffic data. But this doesn't mean that they're showing actual cars moving on actual streets in photorealistic mode. Rather, they're color-coding the streets based on overall traffic patterns and movement.

The same is going to be true when you're visualizing your project in Revit. More often than not, you'll have the ability to show analytic information in real time. But showing photorealistic renderings of your project will require additional time (perhaps even days) in order to render your views.

Therefore, *analytic visualization* abstracts your model to communicate information that is not available by viewing the project literally. For example, massing studies are analytic representations of the building's overall form during the earliest design stages. Massing is useful in order to visualize geometric proportion and site context, and also for creating sun and shadow studies as well as preliminary energy analysis.

Even as you get into more of the project development and detail, materials may be a distraction whereas textures may not. Keeping your materials abstract and analytic allows you to help keep your focus on communicating the big ideas of your project. For example, does the spatial arrangement elegantly fulfill the design requirements? How is the vertical/horizontal stacking? We'll show you how to communicate these ideas in the following sections.

Monochromatic Views

Traditionally, architects built monochromatic, physical models that communicated the essence of the design without being too literal too soon. You can accomplish this same technique in Revit.

For example, take a look at the rendering in Figure 12.1, which has been created by rendering the view with all the default materials active.

FIGURE 12.1
Default material
rendering

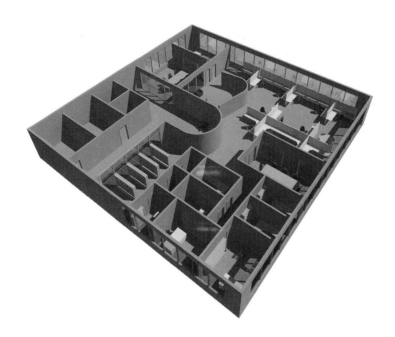

The challenge is that in order to get the materials correct, you'll have to commit a significant amount of time to select, test, edit, and refine many material selections for an otherwise simple view that's quite early in the design stage. You don't have time for resolving all this specificity when doing so might result in something having the right material but in the wrong location.

Figure 12.2 shows the same view rendered analytically, with all the materials set to an abstract matte white setting.

FIGURE 12.2
Abstract rendering

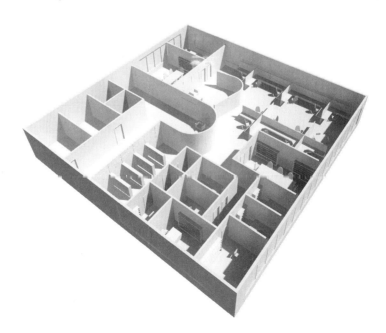

By selecting a matte material for everything in the view, you're able to focus on form–space and light–shadow relationships. Using the graphic overrides that are available with the Phasing tool can create a rendering like this quickly and easily. This is much faster than trying to select neutral materials for everything in your view. Here are the steps to create a matte rendering using the material overrides in Phasing:

1. Open the Phasing settings and select the Phase Filters tab (Figure 12.3).

FIGURE 12.3
Phase settings

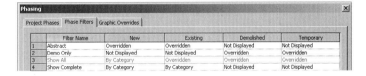

2. Create a new phase filter called **Abstract**. Set the New and Existing material assignments to Overridden.

CERT OBJECTIVE

3. Go to the Graphic Overrides tab and create a new material assignment called **Abstract** (Figure 12.4). We've used a matte white material.

FIGURE 12.4
Material assignments

4. Now assign this material to your New and Existing objects (Figure 12.5).

FIGURE 12.5
Assigning abstract material

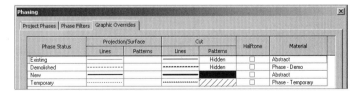

That's it! When you want to render a project view with this abstract material assignment, simply assign the phase filter and phase, and you'll get an abstract, matte rendering as a result (Figure 12.6).

FIGURE 12.6
Phase and phase filter

The previous example was an analytic rendering of a 3D view. But you can also see analytic information in a number of view types, not just 3D but also in 2D views. For example, color-filled room and area plans illustrate information about your project's spaces that are a representation of the space type.

Project Parameters

Viewing information about your project is easy and it has to do with view filters. In this section, first you'll create a view filter based on a project parameter, and then you'll create one to illustrate a user-defined project parameter. A filter can be used to alter the default display properties of elements on a per-view basis. As you can see from the Filters dialog box in Figure 12.7, you can apply up to three filters to a single view to override the graphic values of 2D and 3D content as well as spaces.

FIGURE 12.7
Filters dialog box

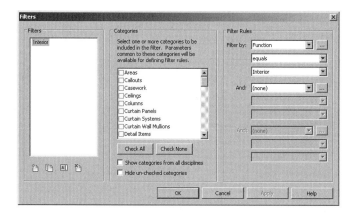

Figure 12.8 shows a simple example of how this works. In the view, there are walls that are two-hour rated. You'd be able to see this in a schedule, but how would you see this in a project view (2D or 3D)?

FIGURE 12.8
Default view

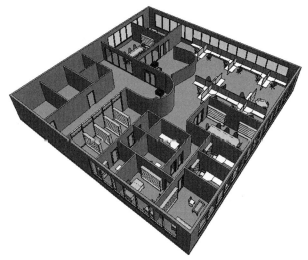

1. First, open the Filters tab in the Visibility/Graphic Overrides dialog box (Figure 12.9). Click Add to begin the process of creating and applying a new filter.

FIGURE 12.9
Selecting the
Filters tab

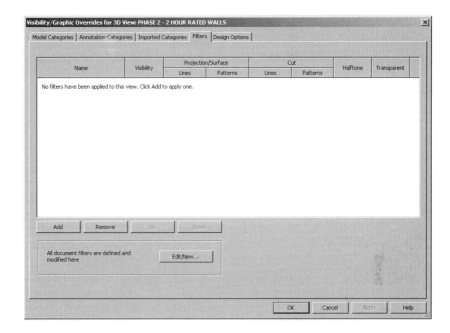

2. Create a new filter called **Rated Walls**, as shown in Figure 12.10. Click OK and be sure to select Walls in the Categories option and then Filter Rules, so that the graphic override will only be applied to walls when the rating equals a value of 2.

FIGURE 12.10
Creating the filter,
category, and
filter rules

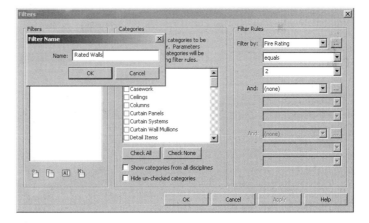

3. When you return to the Visibility/Graphic Overrides dialog box, you'll see the filter is ready to be applied (Figure 12.11).

FIGURE 12.11
Our added filter

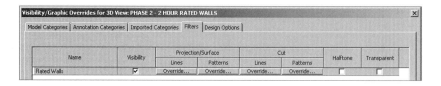

4. Override the Projection, Surface, and Cut patterns, as shown in Figure 12.12.

FIGURE 12.12
Graphic overrides

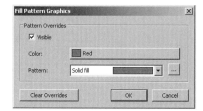

5. When you're finished, click OK twice to return to the view of the project. You'll see that the filter is overriding the project-defined graphics of the two-hour rated walls (Figure 12.13).

FIGURE 12.13
Applied filter in
Shaded view

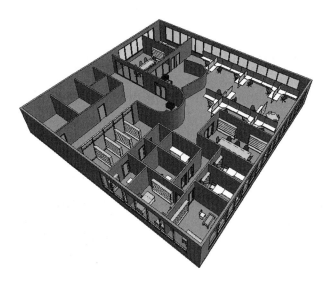

What's wonderful about this is that you're able to visually coordinate and verify your project schedules with project views that confirm what is being described in the schedules. This even works in Hidden Line view, as shown in Figure 12.14. Changing elements in the schedule or from the project environment will immediately update in all views of your project.

FIGURE 12.14
Applied filter in
Hidden Line view

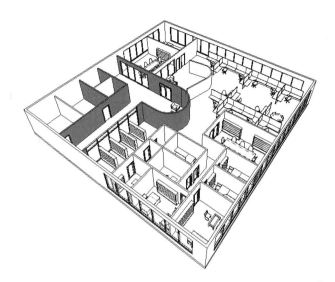

User-Defined Parameters

Now let's look at another example where a particular parameter is not in the default project environment. In this example, we need to show the space as functionally complete, but a lot of the content that is shown isn't actually in the scope of work or contract. There are two particular challenges.

First, this kind of parameter might need to be applied across many categories of elements—not just furniture, equipment, and so on. Second, it may apply to one element, but not apply to another element in the very same category, name, and type. So, you'll want to make sure we're using an instance parameter (not a type parameter). Here are the steps:

1. Return to your Filters dialog box as before and create a new filter named **Not In Contract**.

2. Make sure that you select numerous categories of elements that you want to be able to distinguish as Not In Contract, as shown in Figure 12.15. When you're done, select More Parameters from the Filter Rules pull-down list.

FIGURE 12.15
Multicategory
selection

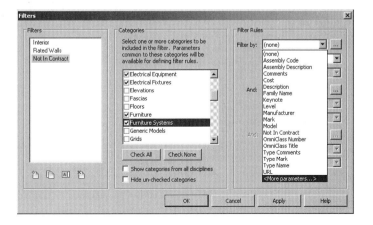

3. Now select the same categories as shown in Figure 12.16. This user-defined project parameter will allow you to distinguish elements across a number of categories.

FIGURE 12.16
User-defined
instance
parameters

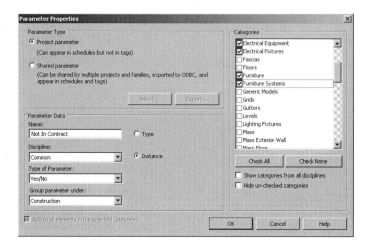

4. Apply your parameter to the filter. In this case, you're instructing Revit to override the graphics when the value of Not In Contract equals Yes (Figure 12.17).

FIGURE 12.17
Filter parameters

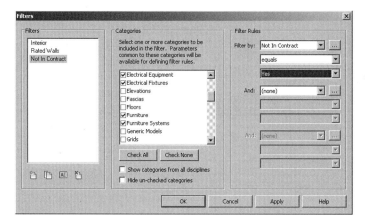

5. Returning to the Filter tab in the Visibility/Graphic Overrides dialog box, you'll define how the graphics will be overridden. Once again, you're overriding the surface pattern with a solid color, this time yellow (Figure 12.18).

FIGURE 12.18
Graphic overrides
for the Not In
Contract filter

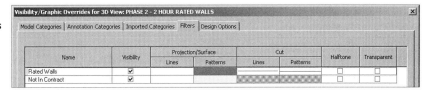

6. Select elements from the categories that you've just created a filter for. You'll notice that as you select the object in your file, the instance parameter is highlighted (Figure 12.19).

FIGURE 12.19
Instance
parameters

Select this value. As you do, the components will have the solid color applied, as shown in Figure 12.20, because the filter that you created now applies to the elements that you've selected, even in Hidden Line views!

FIGURE 12.20
Not In Contract
graphic override

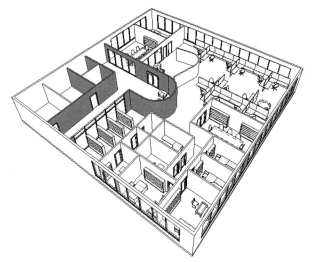

Identifying Design Elements

Finally, this process can be valuable for identifying "generic" host design elements as you move between design iteration and design resolution. Figure 12.21 shows a filter that has been applied to a view to highlight any walls, floors, ceilings, or roofs that have the term Generic in their family name.

FIGURE 12.21
Identifying generic
elements

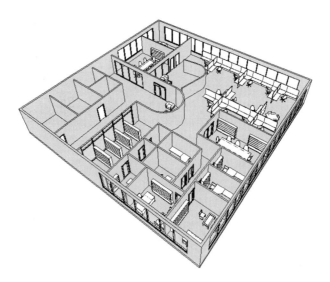

Now you can quickly identify what needs more detail from within your project. Revit's default template already uses the term Generic to describe basic design host elements, which makes them easy to filter, as shown in Figure 12.22.

FIGURE 12.22
Generic host
element filter

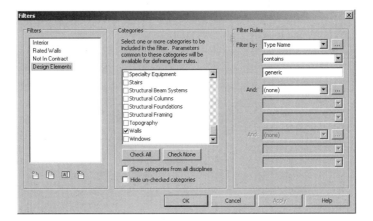

Solar and Shadow Studies

Sun and shadow studies are another analytic visual style that allows you to communicate natural lighting based on your project's location, orientation, and time of year. The sun's path is also displayed (Figure 12.23), and you can edit the path of the sun both directly and indirectly.

FIGURE 12.23
Visual sun path

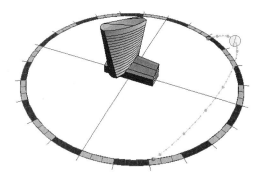

The size of the sun's path may need to be relatively larger or smaller depending on the size of your project or project context. To modify the size of the path, select the sun path and then select the Properties menu. Figure 12.24 shows the path at 100 percent.

FIGURE 12.24
Sun path proper-
ties at 100 percent

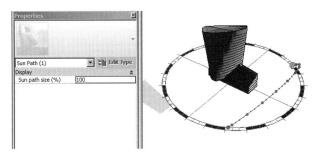

This would be fine for a sun and shadow study of the massing study with no context. But if you need to show additional context, you'll want to increase the size of the sun path. This is shown in Figure 12.25. The path has increased to 200 percent. The building seems relatively smaller, but the size of the sun path has increased.

FIGURE 12.25
Sun path proper-
ties at 200 percent

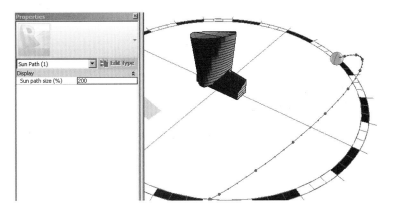

The sun path can be activated from the View Control bar (Figure 12.26) as well as the Lighting menu in the Rendering window.

FIGURE 12.26
Activating the
sun path

Selecting the sun path directly in the view will allow you to edit the path by dragging to change the date (Figure 12.27).

FIGURE 12.27
Editing the
sun path

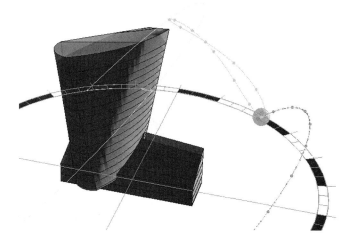

The other option for editing the sun path is to open the sun settings. Opening the sun settings (Figure 12.28) allows you to more specifically select the settings for your particular view and solar study type.

FIGURE 12.28
Sun settings

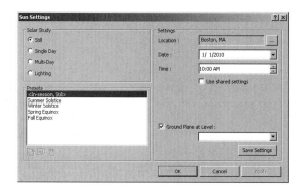

There are four different types of solar studies that can be created within Revit:

◆ The Still setting allows you to create a study of a particular time, date, and location.

◆ Single Day allows you to create a study over an entire day at intervals of 15, 30, 45, and 60 minutes.

◆ Multi-Day allows you to create a sun study over a range of dates at intervals of an hour, a day, a week, and a month.

◆ A Lighting study is not related to a particular time, date, or place. It's more useful for adding graphic depth and texture with "Sunlight" from an analytic top right or top left.

Single images are created using the Rendering dialog box. However, animations of single and multi-day solar studies are created by clicking the Application button and selecting Export ➢ Images And Animations ➢ Solar Study (Figure 12.29).

FIGURE 12.29
Animation
export path

You'll then be given an option to export the animated solar study using a number of graphic styles (Figure 12.30). Selecting the Rendering option will sequentially render all the frames. This will take considerably longer than any of the other options, which are effectively taking sequential screen captures.

FIGURE 12.30
Animation length
and format

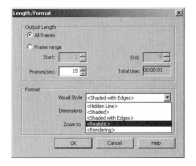

The difference in time needed to render a view compared to exporting screen captures can be quite considerable. For example, exporting a single day consisting of 36 frames (15-minute intervals) as screen captures can take as little as 1 minute (at a rate of 1 frame every 2 seconds). Yet rendering the same number of frames could easily take 3 hours (at a rate of 5 minutes per frame and a total time of 180 minutes)!

Analytic visualization is incredibly useful for quickly communicating information about your project in a way that isn't literally associated with the actual real-world material assignments of your project elements. While photorealistic visualization would render wood as "wood," an analytic visualization could be used to identify which wood materials were sustainably harvested, recycled, or LEED certified. Analytic visualization is concerned about what something *means*, not just what it looks like. Because analytic visualizations can often be viewed in real time, your project information remains visually concurrent and up-to-date.

Photorealistic Visualization

When compared to analytic visualization, *photorealistic visualization* is more concerned with the emotive, experiential qualities of your space and content. Materials are carefully selected for accuracy and real-world simulation. But quite often, real-world isn't enough. Put another way, if analytic visualization is about what something *means*, photorealistic visualization is about how something *feels* or is experienced.

In many cases you'll find yourself tweaking materials and lighting in order to "theatrically" increase the nature of the space. Embellishing your project with nonproject entourage is probably essential, and we'll cover important techniques to keep that content from cluttering up the views that are necessary for documentation. In addition, lighting is key, which means you'll have to contend with considerably longer rendering times.

Visual Styles

In this section, we'll describe the various visual styles that are available in the View Control bar with regard to rendering. Even though these settings create photorealistic renderings, their settings affect the outcome of renderings. Figure 12.31 shows the View Control bar of an orthographic view. Figure 12.32 shows the View Control bar of a perspective view. The major difference is that orthographic views are set to a scale.

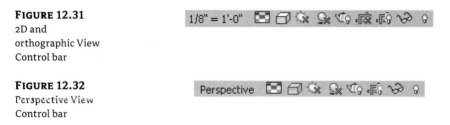

FIGURE 12.31
2D and orthographic View Control bar

FIGURE 12.32
Perspective View Control bar

Note that 2D project views can't be rendered. But you can orient an orthographic view to a 2D orientation and render.

LEVEL OF DETAIL

The first option controls the level of detail in the view (Figure 12.33).

FIGURE 12.33
Level of detail

What is visible by default in a view is initially determined by the scale of the view, as shown by selecting Manage ➢ Additional Settings ➢ Detail Level. Figure 12.34 shows the default settings.

FIGURE 12.34
View scale-to-detail level

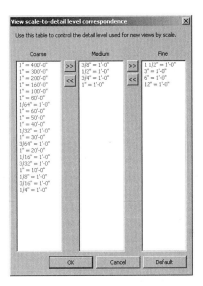

But this level of detail setting can be overridden after the view is created. This is important for two reasons. First, changing the scale after the view is created will not automatically reset the level of detail, and second, rendering a view with a more granular detail level will (generally speaking) take more time. Even though the results will not be visible to the naked eye, the calculations required to render what you won't be able to discern (because the objects are so small) will still be computed.

So, it's very important that you render at the appropriate level of detail.

To illustrate this, look at the two perspectives in Figure 12.35. Although these two views look identical, one will rotate, refresh, and render faster than the other. This is because they're also set to different levels of detail.

FIGURE 12.35
Nonidentical views

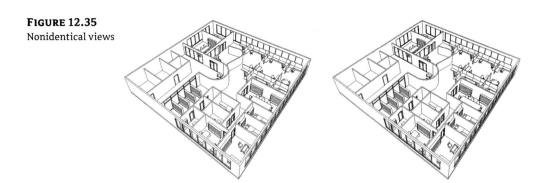

The reason is not discernable at this scale because the differences are barely a pixel in size. The view on the left is set to a Coarse level of detail. But the view on the right is set to a Fine level of detail. While this different detail level doesn't have much of an effect on the content in either view, there is a critical difference.

The Executive Chair family has been modified so that the casters at the base of the chair only display at a Fine level of detail. The results are shown in Figure 12.36.

FIGURE 12.36
Detail level of chair

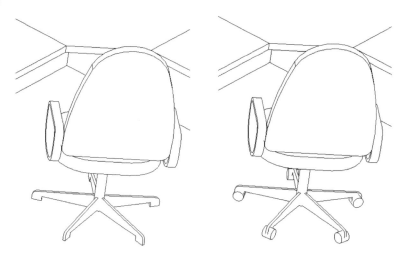

And although this difference may not have a large effect on a small project, it can have a significant effect on your project when you render (not to mention the additional time it will take when you export and print). So, be sure that before you render a view, the level of detail is appropriately set. If you're far away from the building or your view is quite broad, a Coarse detail level is quite sufficient. But if you're zoomed in on a particular detail or part of the building (or just a single office or room), then a Fine detail level might be more appropriate.

VISUAL STYLE

The visual style of your view can be one of six settings (Figure 12.37).

FIGURE 12.37
Visual styles

The Wireframe view (Figure 12.38) maintains only the edges of objects. Faces are hidden.

FIGURE 12.38
Wireframe view

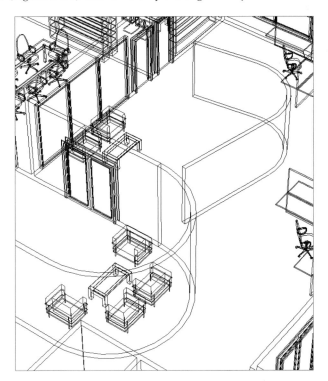

Hidden Line keeps both the edges and faces visible (Figure 12.39).

FIGURE 12.39
Hidden Line view

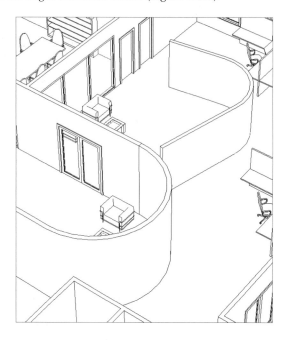

The Shaded view shows faces in their shaded value without accentuated edges (Figure 12.40). Note the change in color depending on an object's orientation. This is particularly pronounced on curved surfaces.

FIGURE 12.40
Shaded view

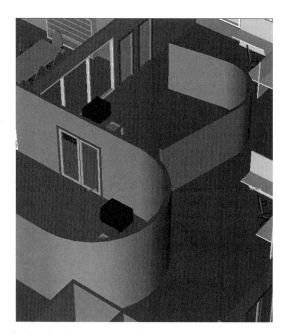

Shaded With Edges is simply the Shaded view but with edges shown (Figure 12.41). Again, the color of the object is the shaded value but relative to the orientation of the object to the viewer.

FIGURE 12.41
Shaded With
Edges view

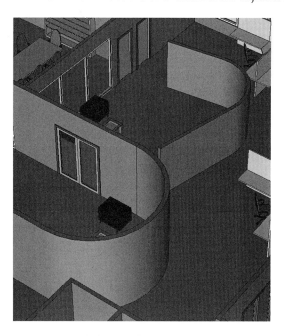

Consistent Colors view removes the color variation based on an object's orientation to the viewer. Colors are strict interpolations of the shaded value (Figure 12.42) and therefore have a flatter yet more consistent appearance.

FIGURE 12.42
Consistent
Colors view

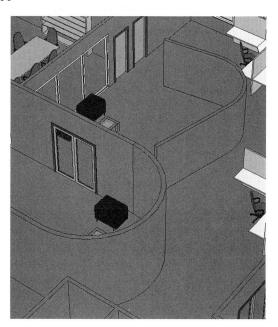

The Realistic setting provides real-time overlays of geometry with the material that will be used during a photorealistic rendering, as shown in Figure 12.43.

FIGURE 12.43
Realistic view

SHADOWS AND GRAPHIC DISPLAY

We've already discussed the sun settings, so in this section we'll move ahead to the Shadows On/Off settings (Figure 12.44).

FIGURE 12.44
Shadows On/Off

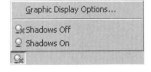

The ability to turn shadows on in real time is a terrific feature that helps you add an improved sense of depth to your view (Figure 12.45).

FIGURE 12.45
Default
Shadows On

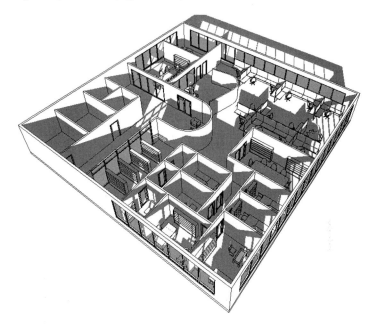

There are a couple of things to keep in mind when turning on shadows. For example, screen refreshing takes a bit longer when shadows are turned on. So, you'll probably want to keep shadows off in your working views as you zoom in, zoom out, and rotate.

In addition, the default settings could use some adjusting. To do this, open the Graphic Display Options dialog box, as shown in Figure 12.46.

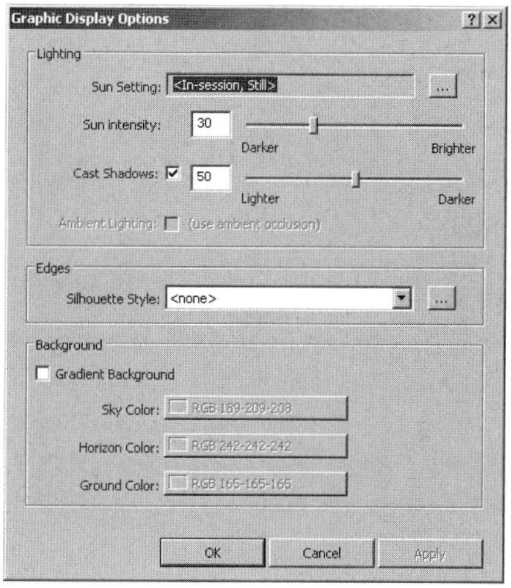

FIGURE 12.46
Graphic Display
Options dialog box

Unless you're doing a solar study, the default sun setting should probably be set to Sunlight From Top Right or Sunlight From Top Left (Figure 12.47).

FIGURE 12.47
Sunlight From
Top Left

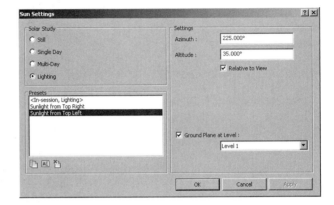

The more that you increase the Sun Intensity setting (Figure 12.48), the more washed out your view's appearance.

FIGURE 12.48
Increased Sun
Intensity setting

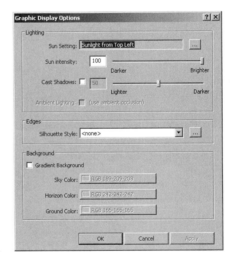

Turning the shadows off can have an appealing effect that softens the shaded materials in your view considerably (Figure 12.49).

FIGURE 12.49
Softened view

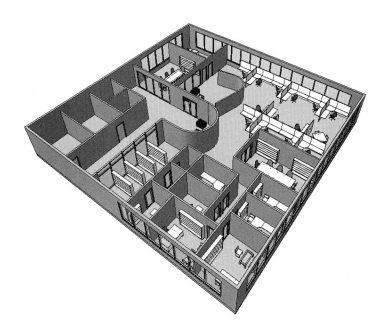

If you're going to turn shadows on, experiment by decreasing the default Cast Shadows value (Figure 12.50).

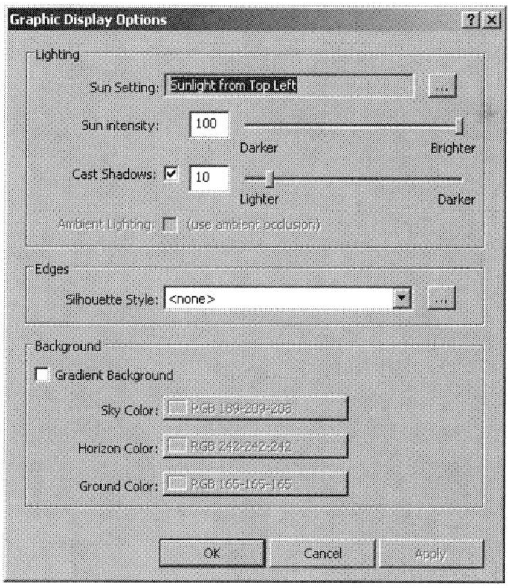

FIGURE 12.50
Decreased Cast
Shadows value

This will keep the shadows on in your view but not overwhelm it with dramatic changes in lit and nonlit areas (Figure 12.51).

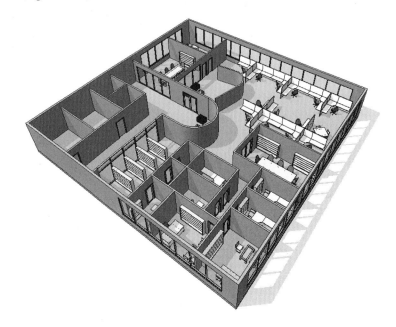

The Silhouette Style option allows you to override the edges of objects when that edge is defined by space (Figure 12.52).

In Figure 12.53, the image on the left illustrates the view without silhouettes, and the image on the right shows the view with Wide Lines enabled.

Selecting the Background option will allow you to simulate a horizon without rendering. Figure 12.54 shows the default settings.

FIGURE 12.53
No silhouettes
vs. Wide Lines
silhouettes

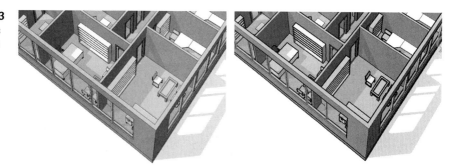

FIGURE 12.54
Background
settings

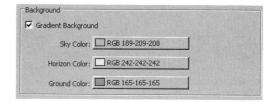

Ambient Lighting

The ambient lighting option is new in Revit 2011, and combined with other graphic options such as real-time shadows, edge enhancements, and real-time materials, it allows you to create emotive, real-time views of your project that do not require renderings.

To activate ambient lighting, open the Graphic Display Options dialog box and select the Ambient Lighting check box, as shown in Figure 12.55. The results are subtle but noticeable, particularly around the intersections of like objects. Shaded elements are embellished by highlights in the center of objects and deeper shading at the edges, as shown in Figure 12.56. The result is almost a water-colored effect that considerably softens the shaded view.

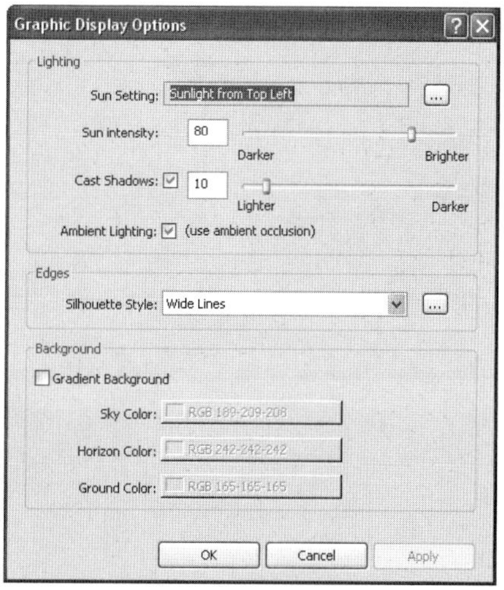

FIGURE 12.55
Activating ambi-
ent lighting

FIGURE 12.56
Ambient lighting

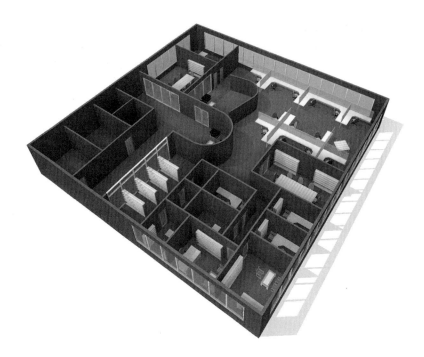

The effect can be accentuated when combined with the option to enhance the silhouette of edges for even more real-time effects (Figure 12.57). We expect this feature to be one of the most used communication and visualization tools in Revit 2011.

FIGURE 12.57
Ambient lighting
with edges

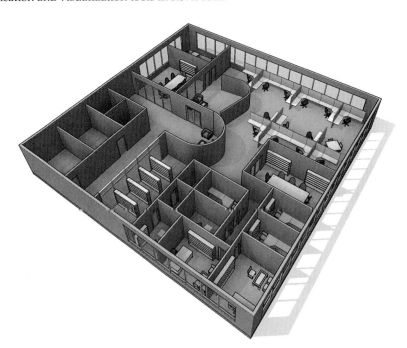

Section Box

Before we get into the rendering process, let's discuss the section box. By selecting the Section Box option, as shown in Figure 12.58, you create a rectilinear matrix around your project that may be pushed and pulled to isolate a portion of your project.

FIGURE 12.58

Activating the section box

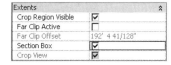

In Figure 12.59, the section box has been pulled to isolate a portion of the project. This technique is helpful for isolating a smaller portion of a larger project. But a word of warning: be careful turning the section box off and on. The extents of the section box will reset and you'll have to pull them back into place. Very frustrating!

FIGURE 12.59

Pulling the section box to isolate a portion of the project

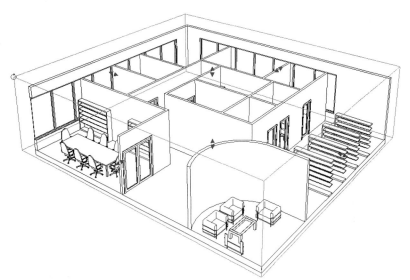

If you select the Type Properties of the view, you'll notice that there's a setting to determine the color of the poche (Figure 12.60).

FIGURE 12.60

Poche settings

The poche can be seen in all display types (Wireframe through Realistic), but it is only displayed in a view that is set to the Coarse level of detail. We recommend that you set the default color to black.

Here's why. As shown in Figure 12.61, the regions between host elements (like the walls and floors) are shown as discrete geometries. Yet it's often more desirable to show the poche as solid across these boundaries.

FIGURE 12.61
Regions between host elements are shown as discrete geometries.

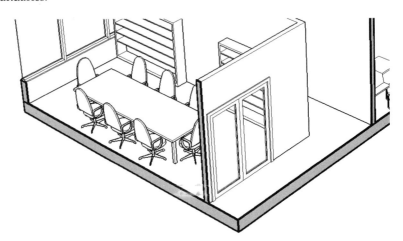

On the one hand, you can use the Join Geometry option to clean up the lines between elements. But this is very time-consuming and often leads to other problems in your file when a lot of things get "joined" just to create graphic impression.

Ideally, we'd like to have the option to "graphically" join the regions between these elements so that they appear monolithic without using the Join Geometry tool. That way, we could select a nice color that would stand out from the rest of the model and communicate the cut plane. Maybe in the next release!

In the meantime, one simple way to clean this up graphically is to select a poche color that is the same as the color of the lines between elements: black. Again, it's not the most desirable result, but it's very fast, doesn't require manual joining of geometry, and reads well (Figure 12.62).

FIGURE 12.62
Solid poche black

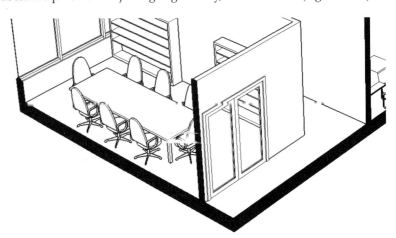

Rendering Settings

You can access the Rendering dialog box by clicking the teapot icon on the View tab or at the base of the view in the Visual Styles bar. Figure 12.63 shows the Rendering dialog box.

FIGURE 12.63
Rendering
dialog box

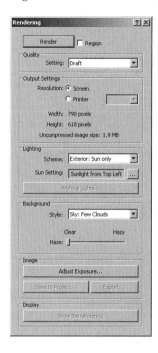

An important setting in this dialog box is the resolution. It's easy to spend far too much time creating a rendered view, because rendering times increase exponentially when the resolution doubles. Think of it this way. If you're rendering a view at 150 dots per inch (dpi) and then you render the same view at 300dpi, the image is now four times larger, not twice as large ($1 \times 1 = 1$ and $2 \times 2 = 4$). If you were to render the view at 600dpi, it would be 16 times larger ($4 \times 4 = 16$) and you could reasonably expect the 150dpi image that rendered in a few minutes to take considerably longer at 600dpi.

How large you need to render something depends on what you're going to use it for: screen or print. Don't expect a rendering the size of a 3″ × 5″ postcard to work for a 3′ × 5′ banner.

So, what resolution is big enough? Well, it's probably better to render things a bit larger, which will give you some flexibility if you need to increase the size of your image later.

Revit provides five present quality settings (Figure 12.64).

FIGURE 12.64
Quality settings

Figure 12.65 and Figure 12.66 illustrate the range between the Draft and the Best settings.

FIGURE 12.65
Draft settings

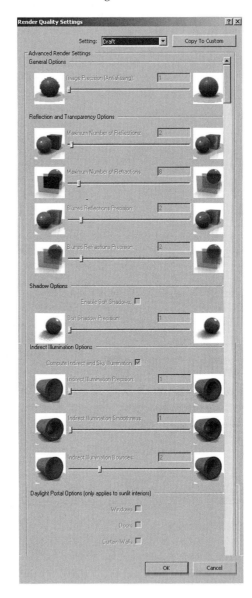

FIGURE 12.66
Best settings

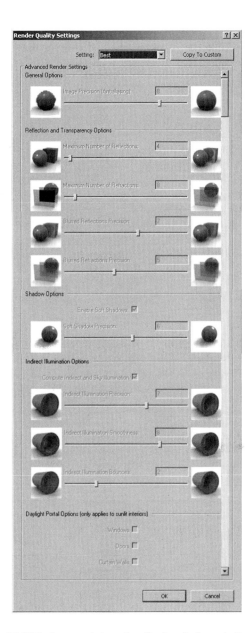

FIGURE 12.66
Best settings

The output settings (Figure 12.67) help you determine the level of resolution that your image can be saved at when rendered. The screen resolution is simply the resolution of the view on your monitor.

FIGURE 12.67
Output Settings

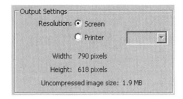

You should be much more interested in the printer settings because of the likelihood that you'll need to print your views. Again, the resolution is important, because you're printing for something that will be viewed at some distance (arm's length or a few feet away) with the naked eye. Rendering beyond what can reasonably be seen will add a lot of time to your renderings. While the default printer resolutions are shown in Figure 12.68, you can input other values by typing them in the dialog box.

FIGURE 12.68
Printer settings

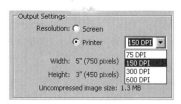

Estimating your image resolution is easy. If the image is going to be viewed on a screen, 150dpi is likely sufficient and even gives you some flexibility if the image has to be slightly larger. If you need to print the image, 300dpi will work the vast majority of the time. Now take the longest dimension of your image (height or width) and multiply the dimension by the needed resolution. That's it!

Here's a test. Figure 12.69 was rendered at each default setting of the screen resolution. The image size was *only* 3″ × 2″—very small to be practical, but it was sufficient to chart render times rendering at 150dpi and 300dpi.

FIGURE 12.69
Rendered project

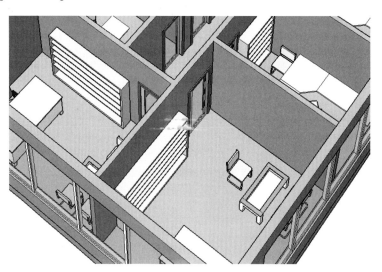

We kept the image small so the renderings could compute faster, and we left the lighting scheme to Exterior: Sun only and set the background color to solid white. As you can see in Figure 12.70, the time to complete each setting does not increase linearly. This is important to keep in mind as you change your quality settings and resolution, especially between High and Best, as there is a greater than six times increase in rendering time! Make sure the increase in time is worth the effort.

FIGURE 12.70
Quality render
times

	Total Rendering Time in Seconds	
	150dpi	**300dpi**
Draft	32	112
Low	42	121
Medium	99	309
High	423	1338
Best	2646	8318

Creating Your View

Creating and modifying your camera controls is almost as important as what you're creating. If you're not careful, you can easily under-impress the viewer by selecting the wrong view and aspect ratio of camera and controls.

Perspective views communicate far more depth than orthographic views (Figure 12.71). Unless the view needs to be at dimensioned scales, we prefer to use perspective views of the project.

FIGURE 12.71
Orthographic vs.
perspective view

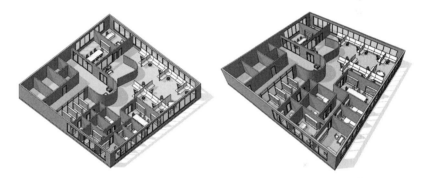

Still Image Camera

When you create your camera view, the first point to select is your eye elevation, and the second point is the target elevation. Keep in mind that when you rotate your view, the rotation is centered on the target elevation (Figure 12.72).

FIGURE 12.72
Placing the camera

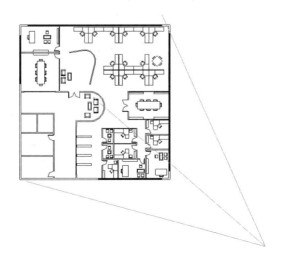

Also, realize is that there is effectively a boundary box, which defines the extents of your camera view. This can be seen by going to another view, like a plan, and then selecting the camera from your Project Browser, as shown in Figure 12.73.

FIGURE 12.73
Selecting Show Camera

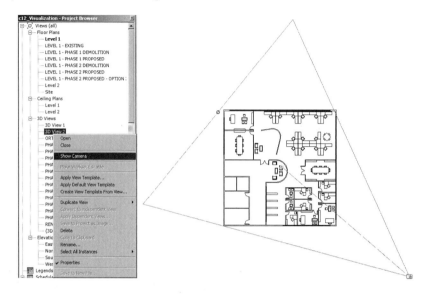

Once you can see your camera, you can select and move your camera around your project. This will allow you to move your camera closer and farther. It will also allow you to select the clipping planes of your camera and edit the front and back planes of your camera's view.

The aspect ratio of your camera is also very important. For example, a television ratio of 4:3 seems far less expansive and dramatic than a 16:9 wide screen ratio. Figure 12.74 illustrates this; the image on the left is 4:3 and the image on the right is 16:9. The result is that the view on the left seems too tight and constrained, whereas the view on the right is far more natural.

FIGURE 12.74
Aspect ratio

To change the aspect ratio, select the view boundary and then select the Size Crop option on the Modify Camera tab. In the resulting dialog box, you can change the aspect proportionally or nonproportionally (Figure 12.75). Keep in mind this doesn't zoom your camera forward and backward; it simply changes the relative height and width of the view.

FIGURE 12.75
Crop Region Size
dialog box

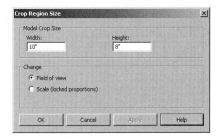

To dolly your camera, simply activate the Navigational Wheel (Figure 12.76). You'll be able to zoom, pan, and orbit as well as control other view features.

FIGURE 12.76
Navigational
Wheel

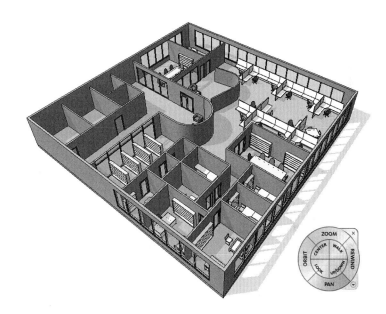

Animation Path

Creating an animation path is much like creating a series of cameras. To create a camera path, select the Walkthrough option from the View tab (Figure 12.77).

FIGURE 12.77
Creating the
walkthrough

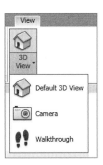

From your plan view, start placing a series of cameras. Note that each time you pick a location, these cameras will become the key frames in your animation. When you have placed the last camera, press the Esc key, and your finished path will appear (Figure 12.78).

FIGURE 12.78
Finished
camera path

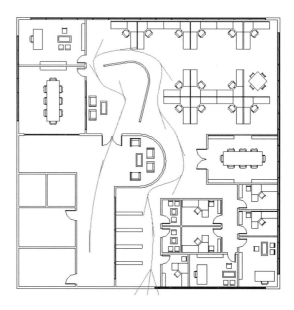

Right-clicking the path will allow you to go the series of views that you just created (Figure 12.79).

FIGURE 12.79
Going to the
camera view

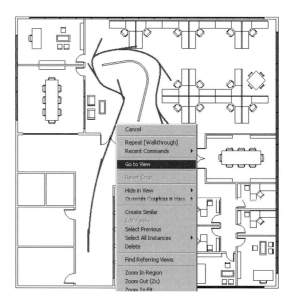

We'll be the first to admit that the walkthrough tools are not very intuitive. Figure 12.80 shows the first view in the path that we've just created along with the Walkthrough View Properties.

FIGURE 12.80
Walkthrough properties

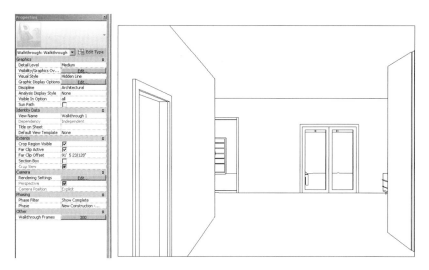

Let's modify the aspect ratio to 16:9. Select the view boundary and select Size Crop. By default, the view is 6″ × 4½″. An 8″ × 4½″ ratio is proportionally 16:9 (Figure 12.81). The view is now wider and less constrained.

FIGURE 12.81
Setting the aspect ratio

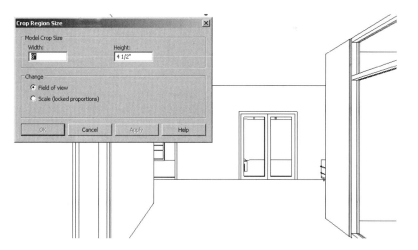

We're going to export a Hidden Line view for testing (especially before rendering), but we want to give the walkthrough more depth. So change the silhouette edge style to wide lines (Figure 12.82).

FIGURE 12.82
Setting the graphic
display options

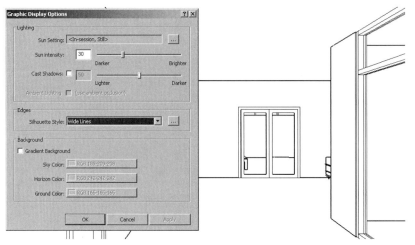

It's not desirable to simply walk with the camera facing the same direction that you're walking. So we're going to modify the camera. But this will require that you open a couple of views, as shown in Figure 12.83. This way, you'll be able to see the results of your work in one view in other views.

FIGURE 12.83
Tiled camera
and views

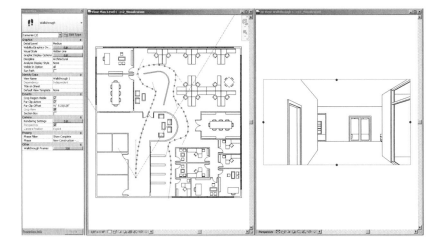

A couple of important points should be noted. First of all, we're showing the plan and the camera view at the same time. This allows us to see both the graphic and analytic camera, which is important for modifying views. As you can see, when you select the boundary of the view on the right, the camera path highlights in the view on the left.

Since the view is selected, you have the option of editing the crop size just like any other camera. But you also have the option of editing the walkthrough, as shown in Figure 12.84.

FIGURE 12.84
Edit Walkthrough
option

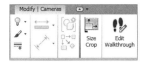

Click the Edit Walkthrough option, and you'll be given the contextual toolbar shown in Figure 12.85.

FIGURE 12.85
Key Frame Editor

After you open the Key Frame Editor, the camera path now shows important controls (Figure 12.86).

FIGURE 12.86
Camera path and
controls

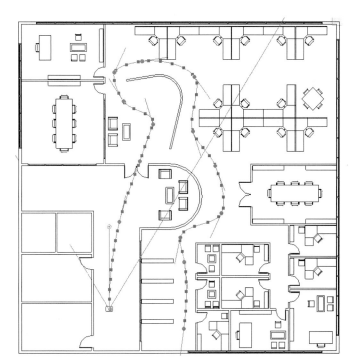

The red dots along the path represent key frame locations (when you placed your camera, remember?) and the red dot directly in front of the camera will allow you to control the rotational direction. By default all the cameras face ahead relative to their location on the path. But you can edit this so that the camera can follow one direction but face another direction.

Since the default path is 300 frames in length, it would take a long time to go to each frame and edit what you see. It's better to jump ahead from key frame to key frame, editing fewer locations. When you do this, Revit will interpolate the frames between the key frames for you. As you jump ahead key frame to key frame, try to experiment rotating the camera to the left and right as well as glancing up and down. This can be done from the plan view on the left, or from the camera view on the right.

Once you've edited your key frames, you can export the animation from the Export menu, as shown in Figure 12.87.

You'll be given options to export an AVI with all the rendering options that you're given for still images (Figure 12.88).

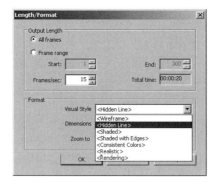

A 15 frame-per-second (fps) frame rate is minimal to keep the animation smooth. But if you increased the frame rate, the animation length would shorten and it would seem like you were running (rather than walking) through the scene. What can you do? Simply add more frames to your animation.

At the bottom of the camera properties, open the Walkthrough Frames dialog box (Figure 12.89). By increasing the total frames, you can also adjust the relative fps in order to maintain the desired speed.

FIGURE 12.89
Default frame count

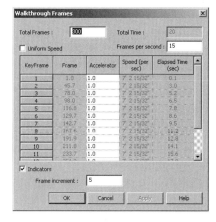

So for example, if you wanted to increase the fps to 30 but maintain the same travel speed, you would also increase the Total Frames setting to 600 (see Figure 12.90). Simple!

FIGURE 12.90
Increasing the frame count

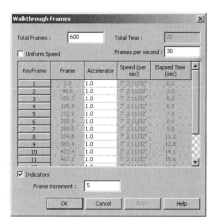

Finally, where a lot of people struggle is with the speed of their animation. Unless you're breaking up your animation into separate paths (which will be combined later into a single sequence), it's necessary to be able to speed up or slow down your camera's movement. In Revit, you can uncheck the Uniform Speed option in order to speed up or slow down the camera during a single animation study.

Although there's no exact rule for this, you can imagine the results. Think about how a plane seems to speed up relative to the ground as it approaches to land. In fact, it's slowing down. Yet your relative distance to the ground influences the perception of how fast you're moving. So even though you're slowing down, as you get closer to the ground, it seems like you're moving faster. And when you're at 30,000 feet it seemed like you were barely moving at all. Just imagine how the astronauts feel in space. While it might seem like they're barely moving at all and the earth slowly spins below, in fact they're orbiting at over 17,000 miles per hour. Don't hit any space junk!

The same visual effect plays a part in your renderings. The farther you are from something, the faster your camera can move as you fly by and still seem smooth and fluid. But you will need to slow down considerably if you're walking through the building, where a comfortable pace is 6–8 feet a second.

We've exported the animation from this portion of the chapter. If you want to investigate the file or animation, you can download the c12_Visualization.rvt file or the c12_Visualization_Animation.avi from the Chapter 12 folder.

Visualization Sequence and Workflow

You'd be surprised, but many people actually render in the wrong sequence. The workflow for creating compelling renderings is not the same workflow that you use to resolve your design process. If you try to do one like the other, the result is a lot of wasted time and frustration. Trial and error takes too long, and you won't get the desired results (and may even conclude that Revit "can't render").

Consider a reasonable design process to create a building that moves from intent to content:

1. Host components (walls, floors, stair, railings, and so on)

2. Family components (doors, windows, and so on)

3. Furniture, fixtures, and equipment

4. Assembly details and documentation

But if you're rendering in the order of the previous process, your results will be skewed. That's because in order to create photorealistic renderings, you're probably modifying your views in the following order:

1. Geometry (host and family components)

2. Materials (host and family components)

3. Cameras (setting up your views)

4. Lighting (lots of errors and rendering, adjusting, rendering, and so on)

5. Render (final renderings)

The challenge is that this is not the workflow for creating great renderings. If you're focused on the design process of *visualization*, the intent to content workflow is more along the lines of the following:

1. Geometry (host and family components)

2. Cameras (setting up your views)

3. Lighting (using matte materials)

4. Materials (host and family components)

Yes, this is this is as simple as it gets: cameras, then lights, and then materials. But in Revit, lights don't usually show up until the building is well resolved, because you're placing lights meant to be the lights in the building, not just for "rendering." So, the design process is simply out of sequence with the visualization process.

Furthermore, you need to evaluate the lighting neutrally, not with materials to distract you. But as you're placing your content, a lot of stuff already has material assignments. You need to find a way to neutralize the material settings while you figure out lighting. The great thing is that we've already got all the parts to do this from earlier in the chapter. Now we just need to put it all together!

Geometry and Cameras

Geometry and cameras are the first step. You don't want to wait to see your project in perspective until after you've designed it. Unfortunately, you still can't design in perspective views in Revit, but ideally this will change. The point is that you need to be able to experience the space as you're designing, so go ahead and create perspective views of your project so that as you design you can see the results in real time.

You can either use the project c12_Rendering Workflow.rvt in the Chapter 12 folder or your own file. The workflow is what's important. If you're using the file that we've created, you'll want to start in the RENDER - CONFERENCE ROOM 3D view. As you can see in Figure 12.91, we've already adjusted the shadows and sunlight as well as applied silhouette edges to the view.

FIGURE 12.91
Viewing our project in Hidden Line view

Right away, this isn't a bad view to have in your document set. The linework, subtle shadows, transparency of the glazing, and 16:9 aspect ratio help create a balanced view that doesn't require rendering. So don't be afraid to put these live views into your document set for quick reference.

Another option that you have is to use the graphic overrides that we created using phasing. By setting the view phase to Abstract and increasing the transparency of the Shaded value (Figure 12.92), you'll be able to see through solid objects and beyond the immediate space.

FIGURE 12.92
X-ray view

This is helpful when you're visualizing a space yet want to give context to the other adjacent spaces (Figure 12.93).

FIGURE 12.93
Abstract Phase
setting

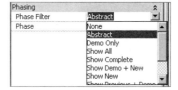

Sunlight

Now let's render the view. Keep in mind that the rendered material applied to the Abstract phase override is solid white, so you'll want to turn off the visibility of your curtain panels if you want see through the glazing. The rendering settings for this view are shown in Figure 12.94.

The reason that we're using Printer as the Output setting is because 300dpi is sufficient for the printing of this page. And an 8″ wide image will suffice for the anticipated width of this book. Low quality is also sufficient based on our experience, because it's not worth the extra jump in time to render much higher than this first pass.

Figure 12.95 shows the results of the rendering. The scene can be viewed beyond the immediate space of the conference room. Take particular note of the shadows and how the lighting drops off from the edge of a shadow.

FIGURE 12.94
Rendering settings
for our view

FIGURE 12.95
Sun Only
rendering

Of course this image is being rendered with the sun, which doesn't count for interior renderings; it's just a benchmark. So let's turn off the sun and start placing some artificial lights.

Since we're rendering abstractly using a phase override, everything is going to be solid white. But if your "light" source is behind a solid lens, it's not going to render very well.

The best way we've found to handle this (until Revit allows for more analytic rendering) is to create an Object subcategory for the lens that surrounds the light source. This will allow you to control the visibility of the lens of lighting fixture and allow the light to seemingly pass through the object. Unfortunately, this will not give the most realistic effect since many lighting effects result from light passing through translucent objects (like lenses or shades). But it's the best you'll be able to do for now to resolve lighting *before* you resolve materials.

You need to add a ceiling to the spaces. To keep things generic, we've added a compound ceiling to all the spaces (Figure 12.96). It's just a placeholder for your ceiling that will change later. But the important thing is that you don't get hung up centering ceiling tiles during your design process. Rooms will change dimensions, and all that time spent centering will go to waste.

FIGURE 12.96
Ceiling settings

Figure 12.97 shows a Hidden Line view of the space with the materials set to 0 percent transparency. We've also turned the shadows off since it'll just distract us from not having the sunlight influence the view.

FIGURE 12.97
Ceilings added

Now go ahead and render the view with the settings shown in Figure 12.98. Notice that we've set the Lighting to Interior: Artificial Only. We haven't placed any lights yet, but the reason that you want to render is to make sure that you don't have any light leaks and to benchmark your rendering. It should be completely black when the rendering completes.

FIGURE 12.98
Rendering Settings
dialog box

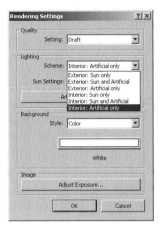

Artificial Lighting

Now load the family `Downlight - Recessed Can.rfa` and place it in the ceiling and along the two walls, as shown in the reflected ceiling plan (Figure 12.99). The exact dimensions aren't important—just get the idea right.

FIGURE 12.99
Lights in ceiling

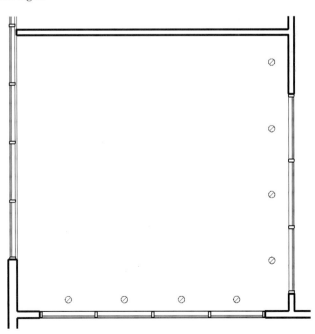

This light family doesn't have a lens, so you don't have to create an Object subcategory for the lens. But before you start to render these artificial lights, we need to explain the process and technique of using light groups.

Light Groups

Sometimes you'll want to isolate the lights that are being calculated and rendered in a particular view. You might want to test the lighting that will result from having certain lights on and others off, just like in a real space. Revit allows you to create light groups for this purpose. This saves you a lot of time compared to turning individual lights off and on manually.

By default, whenever you place a light in your project, they're not in any group. They're "unassigned" just like the lights shown in Figure 12.100.

FIGURE 12.100
Light groups

Besides the assignment for the light group, you also have the option of turning down the Dimming value. This is great for giving your space a half-lit effect.

Now let's create two light groups for this space. Simply select New and then create the two groups as shown in Figure 12.101. We're also working from a 3D axonometric view, which will allow you to see the ceiling plan from above. This will be helpful for selecting lights from above if necessary.

FIGURE 12.101
Creating light groups

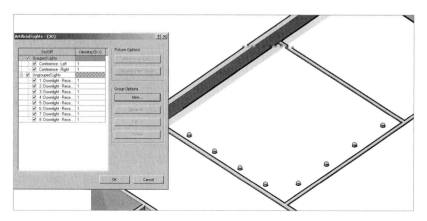

Now let's assign the lights to the groups. Just select the lights and then assign to the light group from the contextual pull-down menu, as shown in Figure 12.102. Then do the same thing for the lights along the other wall.

FIGURE 12.102
Assigning light groups

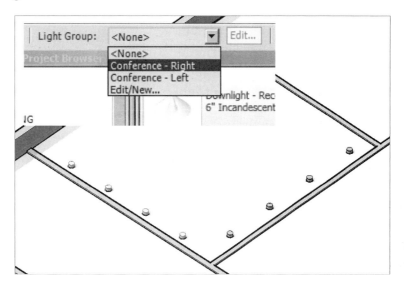

Now return to the interior perspective. Before you start to render the view, let's test the light groups by only rendering the lights in the right group. Figure 12.103 shows the results.

FIGURE 12.103
Rendering light groups

With that successful, let's complete the rendering of the space with the other light group turned on. Keep in mind that the more lights you have turned on in your view, the longer the calculations will take, and therefore the longer it'll take to render your view. Figure 12.104 shows the results of this second rendering. This figure also illustrates the ability to adjust the exposure in a completed rendering.

FIGURE 12.104
Rendering both light groups

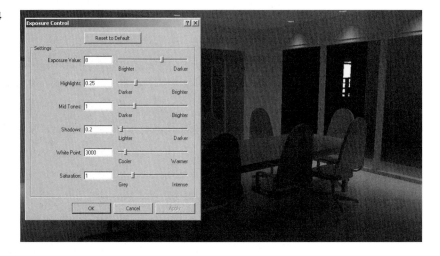

By default, the image will have a rather sepia tone. But removing the sepia tone can be controlled by adjusting the White Point value.

Keep in mind that what you're looking for is how the lighting affects the space. Are the lights too close or too far apart? Go ahead and add more lights, as shown in Figure 12.105.

FIGURE 12.105
Adding more lights

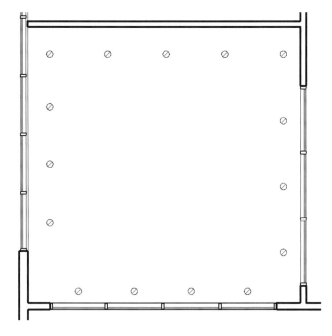

After rendering the space with all the lights, it's becoming apparent is that the lights aren't illuminating the conference table (Figure 12.106). You need to add a nice linear lighting source above the table in order to understand the effect that light will have on the space. Again, it's important that you do this without the distraction of materials.

FIGURE 12.106
Rendering without center lights

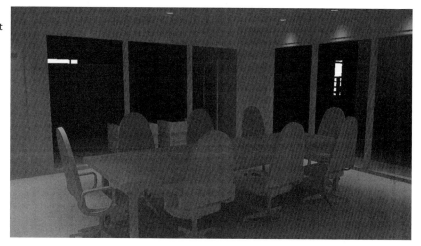

Use the Revit family `Pendant Light - Linear - 1 Lamp` and place it as shown in Figure 12.107. A great technique is to use a 3D view that's oriented to the top and then set the view to Wireframe.

FIGURE 12.107
Placing the light
in top-oriented 3D
Wireframe view

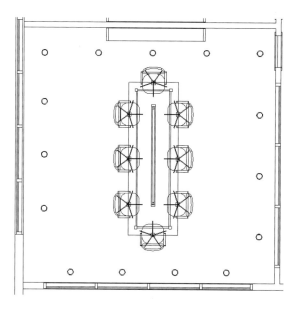

This will allow you to place elements in the ceiling but also see their context and center the light properly with regard to the conference table and chairs. This time we'll have to put the lens on an Object subcategory. Figure 12.108 shows the light in 3D. The Type Properties of the light have also been adjusted to allow the light to hang down from the ceiling as shown.

FIGURE 12.108
Conference
table light

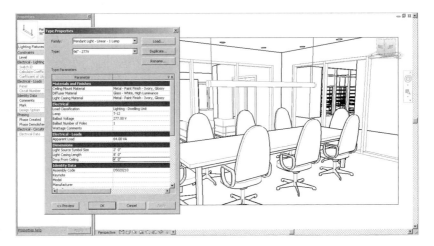

The light doesn't have a lens, but you'll go ahead and make one and then assign it to a subcategory in order to test a rendering with the lens turned off and on. First, go ahead and check the visibility settings of Lighting Fixtures as shown in Figure 12.109. Notice the Object subcategories are only Hidden Lines and Light Source. This will change in a moment when you add Lens to the list.

FIGURE 12.109
Lighting Fixtures
categories and
subcategories

Open the linear light family and go the Right elevation. Then create an extrusion as shown in Figure 12.110.

FIGURE 12.110
Extrusion sketch

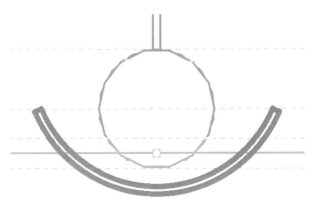

You'll be prompted to select a work plane. Select the work plane shown in Figure 12.111.

FIGURE 12.111
Selecting work
plane

Don't forget to align and lock the finished extrusion as shown in the front elevation (Figure 12.112).

FIGURE 12.112
Align and lock

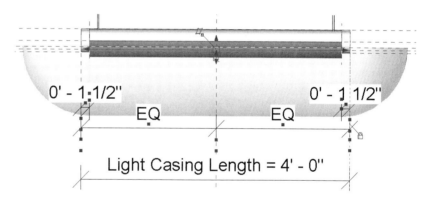

Also, it is important to note that there's a lens of sorts in the light fixture (Figure 12.113). Go ahead and delete this geometry from your light, since we've already created a new lens.

FIGURE 12.113
Delete the original
lens geometry.

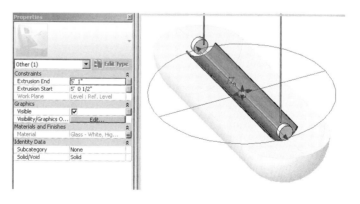

Now reload the light into your project. It will update as shown in Figure 12.114.

FIGURE 12.114
Updated light

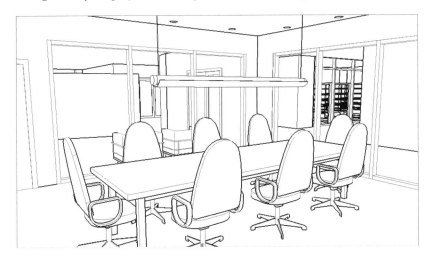

If you render the view, you'll notice that light can't make it past the lens, as shown in Figure 12.115.

Eventually the lens will have a translucent material that will allow the light to shine through. But for rendering matte images, we may not want the light blocked so severely. We'll control this by assigning a subcategory to the lens geometry that will allow us to turn off all the lenses in the view at one time, particularly if you use the same naming convention for all the lenses that you put in your lighting fixtures.

FIGURE 12.115
Rendering with
a lens

Now return to the light family and create a parameter to control the material of the lens. We'll also create and assign the lens to an Object subcategory.

First, select Object Styles from the Modify tab. Then create the Object subcategory as shown in Figure 12.116.

FIGURE 12.116
Creating the subcategory

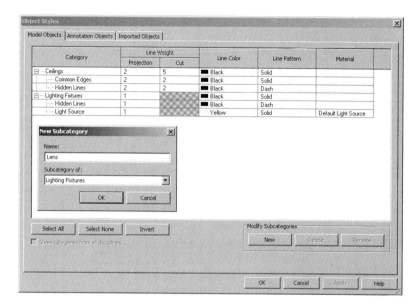

Close the dialog box and then select the lens. Now you can assign this geometry to the sub-category that you just created (Figure 12.117).

FIGURE 12.117
Assigning the subcategory

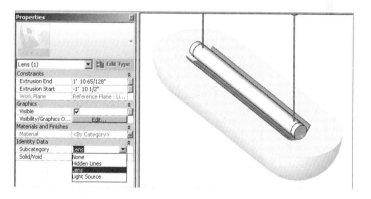

Now that you've created and assigned the subcategory, let's assign the material parameter. You already have the material parameter Diffuser Material from the geometry that you deleted in Figure 12.116. So just assign this as shown in Figure 12.118 to the new lens.

FIGURE 12.118

Creating and
assigning
the material
parameter

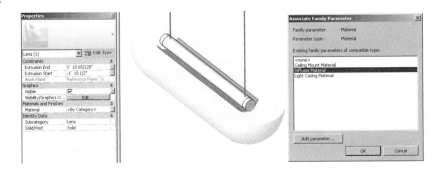

Don't worry about assigning an actual material for now. In practice, it'll only change in the project. So you'll wait to assign it in the project environment rather in the Family Editor.

Now reload the light into the project and go to the visibility settings of the view. There's a subcategory for the Lens part of the lighting fixture. Uncheck this value, as shown in Figure 12.119. The lens is turned off, which is perfect!

FIGURE 12.119

Deselecting the
Lens subcategory

		Lighting Fixtures
	☑	Hidden Lines
	☐	Lens
	☐	Light Source

Now re-render the view. The results will look like Figure 12.120. Note that the lens for the linear light isn't showing, but this is fine. You're after the lighting effect of the lighting fixture. The lens will come back on when you render with all the materials showing. But before rendering with materials, you need to add some entourage.

FIGURE 12.120

Rendered view

If you want your rendering to seem more complete than just a rendering of the building elements, you'll have to add entourage. But you don't want to clutter all your views with the kinds of things that you want to add that will not be part of your document set.

Worksets are great for controlling this part of your project. By creating a workset called Entourage, you'll be able to place your project content on a workset where all of its visibility can be quickly and easily controlled. But before creating and assigning elements to this workset, make sure the workset is turned off by default in other views (Figure 12.121).

FIGURE 12.121
The workset should be turned off in other views.

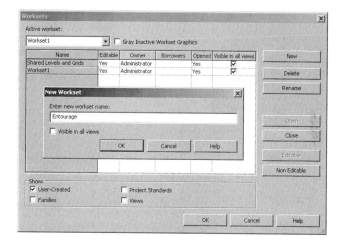

This means that the entourage will not show up in existing or new views until you turn them on, rather than having to turn this workset off in all present and future views. This will save you a lot of time as you add entourage to your project.

In this case, we're going to add some laptops to the conference table; we'll be sure to place them on the Entourage workset (Figure 12.122).

FIGURE 12.122
Adding entourage

Materials

Now that you have determined the right lighting effects using matte materials, you can set the phase back to Show Complete (Figure 12.123). You'll also want to turn on the visibility for the curtain wall panels as well as the lens in the linear lighting fixture and render the view. Keep in mind that with all the new materials, transparency, and reflectivity, it will take quite a bit longer to re-render the view.

FIGURE 12.123
Rendering with material.

Once you render the view and you can start to see the transparency and reflectivity in the curtain panels, the rendering takes on a much more realistic effect. You can also see the materials in the table and chairs, as well as the lens for the linear light above the conference table.

The Bottom Line

Create real-time and rendered analytic visualizations.   Analytic visualization is about communicating information about your project in a nonliteral way, and it's very important! It's not about showing real materials in the project but using filters to visualize important metadata.

Master It   During the renovation of a space, you want to reuse the doors rather than throw them away. How would you illustrate this?

Render emotive photorealistic visualizations.   Photorealistic visualization is also about communicating design ideas but in emotive ways that are much closer to how the space will be experienced, including real lighting, materials, and entourage. Just remember that the time it takes to calculate and render your views will change dramatically based on the quality and resolution of your views.

Master It   Would the rendering for a PowerPoint presentation differ from a rendering being printed for a marketing brochure?

Understand the importance of sequencing your visualization workflow. The sequence of design—building, content, materials, and cameras—is not the same as the sequence for visualization (geometry/cameras, lighting, materials). Lighting is far more important than materials of actual objects. Get the lighting right, and the materials will look great, but not the other way around.

Master It How do you create a rendering environment that replaces the actual materials with matte materials in order to study the effects of lighting on your design?

Part 4

Extended Modeling Techniques

In Part 3 we covered a variety of topics that are primarily useful in—although not exclusive to—the earlier design phases of a project. As you continue to develop your designs, there will be an increased specificity to the elements required in the building information model. You will need to expand your knowledge of the fundamental components of a building model, including walls, floors, roofs, stairs, and railings. In addition, you will likely be required to understand and create your own Revit families. This part will dig deep into rich component-building skills necessary for mastering Revit Architecture.

Chapter 13

Walls and Curtain Walls

According to the AIA document E202 BIM Protocol Exhibit, there are five levels of model development ranging from 100 to 500. If you examine excerpts from the Model Content Requirements describing each level of development (LOD) for the design professions—LOD 100, LOD 200, and LOD 300—the evolution of modeling granularity becomes apparent. Although LOD 100 represents a conceptual level of information defined as "overall building massing," LOD 200 and LOD 300 are represented by "generalized systems or assemblies" and "specific assemblies," respectively. This chapter will help you create walls that comply with both LOD 200 and LOD 300.

Walls in Revit can be created in four different ways: basic walls, stacked walls, curtain walls, and in-place walls. In this chapter, you'll explore the skills you'll need to create and customize walls to meet the needs of your design. You will also dive into the new and exciting realm of complex curtain wall and panel generation made possible with Revit's conceptual massing tools.

In this chapter, you'll learn to:

- ◆ Use extended modeling techniques for basic walls
- ◆ Create stacked walls
- ◆ Create simple curtain walls
- ◆ Create complex curtain walls

Using Extended Modeling Techniques for Basic Walls

As you might already know, walls in Revit are made from layers of materials that can represent generic placeholders for design layouts to complete assemblies representative of actual construction. These layers are assigned functions that allow them to react to similar layers in other walls as well as in floors and roofs. The function assignments within object assemblies give you a predictable graphic representation when you join these types of overlapping elements.

After you have become familiar with the basic modeling functions for walls, you'll probably need to create your own wall types to achieve more complex designs. As you also add more information into the source of your building model, you will be able to extract more useful results through intelligent tagging and schedules. In this section we'll show you how to get the most out of your basic wall types in Revit.

Creating Basic Wall Types

Walls and curtain walls are *system families* in Revit, which means they exist in a project but cannot be saved as individual families (RFA files). Other system families in Revit include floors, ceilings, roofs, stairs, railings, and mullions. There are only three ways to create or add new system families to your project:

◆ Duplicate a type from one that already exists and modify its properties

◆ Copy and paste them in as objects from one project to another

◆ Use the Transfer Project Standards tool

In Chapter 4 we discussed different strategies for managing standard content through the use of templates. If you have a series of standard wall types you use on every project, you have the option of either storing such wall types in your main project template using the *subtractive method* or storing them in separate container project files in an *additive method*. If you need to make new, custom types that are not part of your template, you can create new wall types on the fly at any stage of a project by duplicating existing types, adding or removing wall layers, and adjusting the parameters to meet your requirements. Regardless of which method you employ to manage templates and standard system families, we will show you how to create and customize your own wall types in the following sections.

Within a project file, you can access and edit a wall type in one of two ways:

◆ In the Project Browser, scroll down to the Families category, locate any wall type, right-click it, and select Properties, or simply double-click the wall type name.

◆ Select a wall in the model or start the Wall command, open the Properties Palette, and click Edit Type.

The Type Properties dialog box will appear as shown in Figure 13.1. If you don't see the graphic preview to the left, click the Preview button at the bottom of the dialog box.

FIGURE 13.1
The Type Properties dialog box for a wall

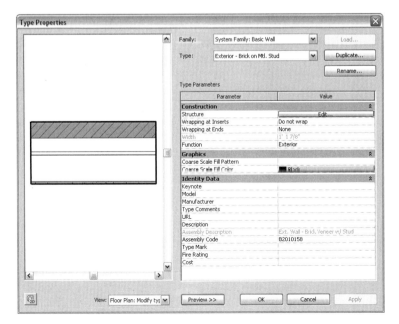

EDITING WALL STRUCTURE

The first aspect we will discuss is the editing of a wall type's structure. To access these settings, select Structure as the parameter to edit. This will open the Edit Assembly dialog box, as shown in Figure 13.2. From here you can add or delete wall layers, define their materials, move layers in and out of the core boundaries, and assign functions to each layer. You can also add sweeps and reveals or modify the vertical constraints of the layers.

FIGURE 13.2
The Edit Assembly dialog box lets you define the construction layers of a wall type.

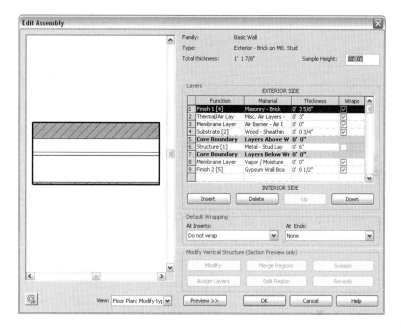

This dialog box is divided into four zones: the Preview window, the Layers table, the Default Wrapping option, and the Modify Vertical Structure options (which are active only when the preview is set to section display).

Preview Window   On the left side of the dialog box, you will see a graphic preview of the wall structure in plan or section. If you didn't activate it in the Type Properties dialog box, click the Preview button at the bottom of the dialog box. To switch from the default plan view to the section view or vice versa, click the drop-down list under View to choose an alternate viewing option. In the preview, the core boundaries of the wall are shown with green lines. Note that in the section preview, each wall layer is highlighted in blue when you select a row in the Layers table. Also note that you can change the height of the wall shown in the section preview by modifying the Sample Height value in the upper-right part of the dialog box. You can use any mouse-based navigation method to adjust the preview as well as activate the Steering Wheel by clicking the button at the bottom right of the dialog box.

Layers Table   The Layers table is where you add, delete, move, and define layers of the wall structure. Each wall layer is represented as a separate row of information. Two of the rows are gray, representing the core boundaries of the wall (which will be discussed in greater detail later in the "Wall Core" section of this chapter). The table is divided into four columns:

Function   This column provides six choices for wall layer functions that relate to the purpose of the material in the assembly. Each of these functions defines a priority that determines how it joins with other walls, floors, and roofs. Note that the numeric priority is more important to understand than the name of the function itself.

◆ Structure [1] defines the structural components of the wall that should support the rest of the wall layers. This function gives the highest priority to a wall layer and allows it to join with other structural layers by cutting through lower-priority layers.

◆ Substrate [2] defines continuous board materials such as plywood, particle, or gypsum board.

◆ Thermal/Air [3] defines the wall's thermal insulation layer and/or an air gap.

◆ The Membrane Layer is a zero-thickness material usually represents vapor prevention.

◆ Finish 1 [4] specifies a finish layer to use if you have only one layer of finish.

◆ Finish 2 [5] specifies a secondary, weaker finish layer.

With the exception of the Membrane Layer, which has no priority assigned, all the other layers have a priority value from 1 to 5. Revit uses these priorities to determine how to clean up the intersections between various layers when two or more walls are joined. The principle is simply explained: priority 1 is the highest and 5 is the lowest. A layer that has a priority of 1 will cut through any other layer with a lower priority (2, 3, 4, or 5). A layer with priority 2 will cut through layers with priority 3, 4, or 5, and so on. In Figure 13.3, layers with the same priority clean up when the two intersecting walls are joined. Notice the way the finish layers don't join on the right side of the vertical wall because one has a priority 4 and the other is priority 5.

FIGURE 13.3
Layers with the same priority clean up when joined.

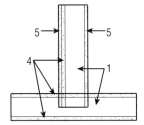 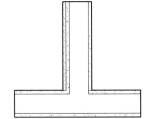

Material Associating a material to a wall layer provides graphic (color, cut/surface patterns, and render appearance), identity (mark, keynote, description, and so on) and physical characteristics (for analysis purposes) for each wall layer. Using material takeoffs, you can calculate quantities of individual materials used in wall assemblies throughout your project. Keynoting and material tagging functionality is also supported through wall layers and is discussed in greater detail in Chapter 19, "Annotating Your Design."

A material definition also affects cleanup between layers of joined walls. If the priority of the layers is the same and the material is the same, Revit cleans up the join between these two layers. If the priority of the layers is the same but the materials are different, Revit separates the two layers graphically with a thin line. In Figure 13.4 the structure layer of one of the joined walls was simply changed from Metal – Stud Layer to Metal – Stud Layer 2.

FIGURE 13.4
Two layers with the same priority but different materials. The separation between the two layers is indicated with a thin line.

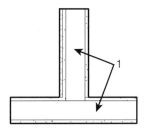

Thickness   This value represents the actual thickness of the material. Note that the membrane layer is the only layer that can have a thickness of zero.

Wraps   Wall layers rarely end with exposed edges at wall ends or wall openings, windows, or doors. This option allows a layer to wrap around other layers when an opening or wall end is encountered. Figure 13.5 illustrates the layer wrapping of the outer wall layer based on the closure plane defined in the window family. Layer wrapping will be covered in greater detail later in this chapter.

FIGURE 13.5
Layer wrapping is a result of a coordinated approach between wall layers and hosted families such as windows.

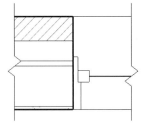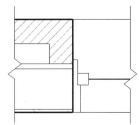

Default Wrapping   Although you can specify whether each wall layer will wrap in the Layers table, you must also specify whether these options are activated at all in the wall type. To activate this option, you must decide whether the wrapping should occur at openings or wall ends or both. For inserts, you can choose Do Not Wrap, Exterior, Interior, or Both. Similarly, for wall ends the options are None, Exterior, and Interior. The default wrapping parameters appear in both the Edit Assembly dialog box and the wall's Type Properties dialog box.

Modify Vertical Structure   These settings are available only when you enable the section view in the Preview window. In this area of the Edit Assembly dialog box, you can add articulation to the wall type using any combination of cornices, reveals, trims and panels. We will discuss these in the "Adding Wall Articulation" section later in this chapter.

In summary, editing a wall type's structure begins with adding or deleting wall layers. Each layer is assigned a priority, material, thickness, and wrapping option. To move layers up and down in the table or to add and remove layers, use the buttons at the bottom of the Layers table. Next we will cover some more complex aspects of wall structure in greater detail: *wall cores, function*, and *layer wrapping*.

WALL CORE

One of the unique functions of a basic wall in Revit is its ability to identify a core. The wall core is more than a layer of material; in fact, it can comprise several material layers. It defines the structural part of the wall and influences the behavior of the wall and how it interacts with other elements in the model. The core boundaries are references to which you can dimension or constrain sketch lines when you use the Pick Walls selection option for floors, ceilings, or roofs.

The example shown in Figure 13.6 illustrates a sample floor in Sketch mode where the outer core boundary of the wall was selected using the Pick Walls method. Note that the core boundaries of the wall are shown as dashed lines for clarity.

FIGURE 13.6
A wall's outer core boundary is used to define an edge of the floor.

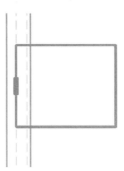

When floors generated with the Pick Walls method intersect the walls that were picked during Sketch mode, you will receive a prompt to automatically join the geometry and cut the overlapping volume out of the wall:

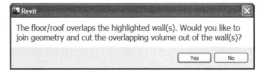

If you click Yes to this message and examine the intersection of the wall and floor in a section view, you will see the result of the joined elements (Figure 13.7). Note that you can get the joining prompt to appear again simply by selecting the floor, clicking the Edit Boundary button in the ribbon, and then clicking Finish Edit Mode (green check icon). If any portion of the selected floor and related walls still overlap but are not joined, the prompt will be displayed.

FIGURE 13.7
Section detail of joined wall and floor slab

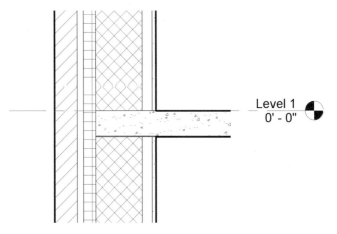

FUNCTION

The Function type property of walls is a simple list of values, but it can be used in very powerful ways. A wall's function can be used to filter schedules or as view filters—for example, if you wanted to hide interior walls for a series of drawings only showing core and shell (exterior) elements. The function property also affects the default placement behavior when you create new walls. The behaviors associated with each function are as follows:

- Interior (default height for new walls is set to the level above the active level)

- Exterior (default height is Unconnected: 20'-0" [8000mm])

- Foundation (default height is determined as *Depth*, specified down from the active level)

- Retaining (default height is Unconnected: 6'-0" [2000mm])

- Soffit (default height is Unconnected: 1'-0" [250mm])

- Core-shaft

The Function type property can also be used when exporting from Revit to CAD formats. You can export walls of different functions to specific layers assigned in the Export Layers dialog box shown in Figure 13.8.

FIGURE 13.8
Wall functions can be assigned to different layers for exported CAD files.

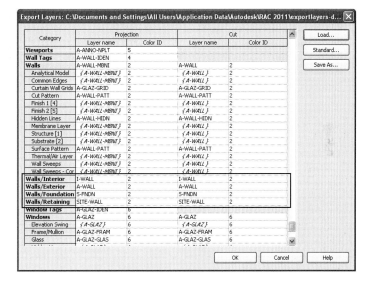

LAYER WRAPPING

To create a layer wrapping solution for openings that reflect real-world conditions, you must define two settings. First, select the layer(s) of the wall structure you want to wrap and check the boxes in the Wraps column of the Edit Assembly dialog box. You must then specify the default wrapping behavior for the wall type. These default settings can be set in either the Edit Assembly or Type Properties dialog box, as shown in Figure 13.9.

FIGURE 13.9

Default wrapping options can be set in Edit Assembly or Type Properties.

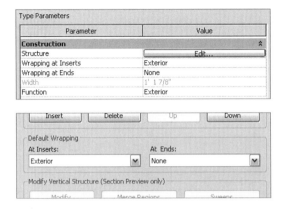

Specifying the layer wrap settings in the wall type alone may not be sufficient to generate the graphic results you desire. Another set of rules established in hosted families allows you to further customize how layers in a wall will wrap to inserted objects. The following exercise will illustrate this functionality.

Begin by opening the file c13-Wall-Wrapping.rvt from this book's web page: www.sybex .com/go/masteringrevit2011. Activate the Level 1 floor plan, and you should see a wall with an inserted window as shown here:

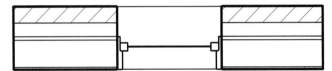

1. To begin the exercise, select the wall, open the Properties Palette, and click Edit Type. Notice the setting for Wrapping At Inserts is set to Do Not Wrap and the setting for Wrapping At Ends is set to None.

2. Click OK to close the Type Properties dialog box.

3. Select the inserted window and click Edit Family on the Modify | Windows tab in the ribbon.

4. When the window family opens, go to the Project Browser and activate the floor plan named Floor Line.

   You will notice that this window family has been slightly modified from the original Fixed window family in Revit's default library. Two reference planes have been added that allow the depth of the window frame and the wall wrapping to be customized.

5. Find the reference plane named Closure, select it, and open the Properties Palette. Find the parameter named Wall Closure and make sure the option is checked, as shown in Figure 13.10.

FIGURE 13.10
Assign the Wall
Closure param-
eter to a reference
plane.

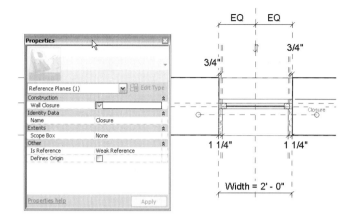

6. Create a dimension between the exterior face of the sample wall and the Closure reference plane. Note that you may need to use the Tab key to ensure you have selected the
   wall reference and not the centerline of the wall or any other extraneous reference plane.

7. Click the Esc key or the Modify button to exit the dimension command and select the
   dimension you just created.

8. On the Options Bar, find the Label drop-down list and choose <Add Parameter…>.

9. In the Parameter Properties dialog box, type **Exterior Wall Closure** in the Name field and
   click OK to close the dialog box.

10. Click Load Into Project from the Family Editor panel in the ribbon. Note that you may
    be prompted to select a project or family if you have more than the two sample files
    open. When prompted with the Family Already Exists dialog box, select Overwrite The
    Existing Version.

11. In the Level 1 floor plan of the example project, select the wall and click Edit Type from
    the Properties Palette. From the Structure parameter, click Edit.

12. In the Edit Assembly dialog box, find row 1, which will have a function of Finish 1 [4],
    and the material Masonry - Brick. Make sure the Wraps option is checked.

13. Set the Wrapping At Inserts option to Exterior and click OK to close both dialog boxes.

    You should now see the masonry layer wrapping into the opening in the wall created by
    the inserted window. You can now customize the depth at which the brick will wrap.

14. Select the window and click Edit Type from the Properties Palette. Find the Exterior Wall
    Closure parameter and change the value to 0′-6⅝″.

15. Click OK to close the Type Properties dialog box. Notice how the depth of the wrapped masonry layer changes in the plan view:

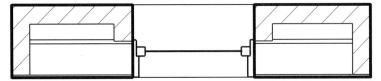

Adding Wall Articulation

If you need to develop more complex and articulated finishes expressed horizontally along the vertical surfaces of certain walls, you can customize wall types in a variety of ways within Revit to achieve just about any aesthetic effect. Reveals and sweeps can be added to a wall type, and you can edit the vertical extents of material layers. You can find a good example of this kind of wall in the default project template. The wall type Exterior - Brick and CMU on MTL. Stud (Figure 13.11) contains a variety of sweeps, reveals, and vertical modification of material layers.

FIGURE 13.11
Sample wall with added articulation

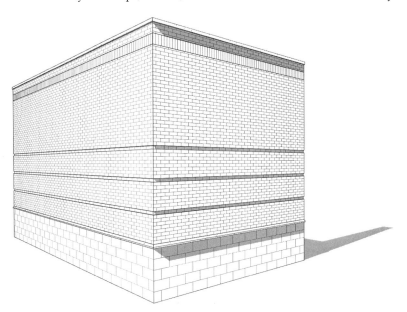

To access these settings, select any wall in your project and click Edit Type in the Properties Palette. You can also find the wall type in the Project Browser and double-click it to open the Type Properties dialog box. Once it is open, make sure the preview pane is open and the view in the preview is set to Section. Within the Type Parameters, click the Edit button in the Structure field to open the Edit Assembly dialog box and begin modifying the layers and vertical articulation of the wall type, as shown in Figure 13.12.

FIGURE 13.12
With section view active, tools for modifying the vertical structure become active.

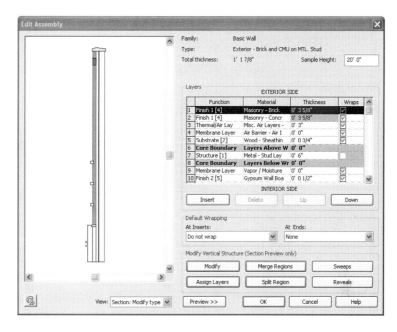

In the following sections, we'll examine how to create these types of articulation in your wall type. To begin the exercises, create a new project using Revit's `default.rte` or `DefaultMetric.rte` template. Create a single wall segment using the type Exterior – Brick On Mtl. Stud. You will create a new wall type based on this wall throughout the following exercises.

ASSIGNING TWO DIFFERENT MATERIALS ON THE FINISH FACE OF A WALL

We will begin our series of exercises by creating a new wall type based on an existing layered wall structure. Select the wall segment you created using the type Exterior – Brick On Mtl. Stud and open the Type Properties dialog box. Click the Duplicate button and create a new wall type named **Mastering - Wall Exercise**.

Now let's assume that you need to create a partial region of the finish face where the material is different. For example, you might want to use split-face concrete block at the base of the wall instead of brick.

1. With the Type Properties dialog box open, click the Edit button in the Structure field to open the Edit Assembly dialog box. Make sure the preview window is open and the view is set to Section.

2. In the upper right of the Edit Assembly dialog box, change the Sample Height value to 6'-0" [2000mm]. Use either the Steering Wheel button at the lower left of the dialog box or your mouse to zoom into the shorter segment of wall in the preview window.

3. Click the Split Region button under Modify Vertical Structure and move your mouse pointer along the inside face of the brick layer to a point 4'-0" [1200mm] above the bottom of the sample as shown in Figure 13.13. Note that when you split the layer, the thickness value of the layer indicates it is *Variable*.

FIGURE 13.13
Splitting the exterior finish into two materials

Layers

	Function	Material	Thickness	Wraps
		EXTERIOR SIDE		
1	Finish 1 [4]	Masonry - Brick	Variable	☑
2	Thermal/Air Lay	Misc. Air Layers -	0' 3"	☑
3	Membrane Layer	Air Barrier - Air I	0' 0"	☑
4	Substrate [2]	Wood - Sheathin	0' 0 3/4"	☑
5	**Core Boundary**	**Layers Above W**	0' 0"	
6	Structure [1]	Metal - Stud Lay	0' 6"	☐
7	**Core Boundary**	**Layers Below Wr**	0' 0"	
8	Membrane Layer	Vapor / Moisture	0' 0"	☑
9	Finish 2 [5]	Gypsum Wall Boa	0' 0 1/2"	☑

INTERIOR SIDE

Insert	Delete	Up	Down

4. Click the Insert button to add another row immediately below the first exterior layer. Change its function to Finish 1, its material to Masonry - Split Face Block, and its thickness to 0'-0".

5. Click the Assign Layer button, select the new row you created in the previous step, and then click the lower portion of the split region in the section preview.

6. Click OK to close all open dialog boxes and save your project for additional exercises in this chapter.

After you assign a material row to a split layer, you'll notice that the thickness values of the two layers are linked but you can't change them in the table. To change the thickness of a split wall layer, click the Modify button and select one of the faces in the section preview. Edit the temporary dimensions to change the thickness of the layer.

You may also notice that once a layer is split and an additional layer is assigned to the split portion, the resulting portions can only be the same thickness. To create a similar result with a layer of varying thickness, you will need to create a stacked wall. We will discuss this later in "Creating Stacked Walls."

If you encounter a situation where you need to merge horizontal or vertical layers that already exist in a wall type, use the Merge Regions button and select a line in the section preview between two layers. Once the mouse pointer is over a line between two layers, an arrow indicating which layer will override the other appears as shown in Figure 13.14.

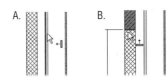

SWEEPS AND REVEALS

Many walls have horizontal articulations that are either attached to or embedded in the wall assembly. Cornices, soldier courses, and reveals are examples of elements that can be incorporated into wall types in Revit. To begin adding these, we will continue our previous exercise of creating a new wall type named Mastering - Wall Exercise. In the following exercise, you will add a bullnose sweep to the wall.

1. Return to the wall's type properties and open the Edit Assembly dialog box.

2. Click the Sweeps button to open the Wall Sweeps dialog box. Click the Load Profile button and open the file `c13-Profile-Bullnose.rfa`, which can be downloaded from this book's companion web page (`www.sybex.com/go/masteringrevit2011`).

3. Click the Add button to insert a sweep row. Change the values in the row as follows:

   ◆ Profile: c13-Profile-Bullnose: 3⅜″ D × 4″ H

   ◆ Material: Concrete - Precast Concrete

   ◆ Distance: 4′-0″ [1200mm]

   ◆ From: Base

   ◆ Side: Exterior

   ◆ Cuts Wall: Checked

   ◆ Cuttable: Checked

4. Click Apply and you should see the sweep appear just above the split region, as shown in Figure 13.15.

FIGURE 13.15
Bullnose sweep added to wall assembly

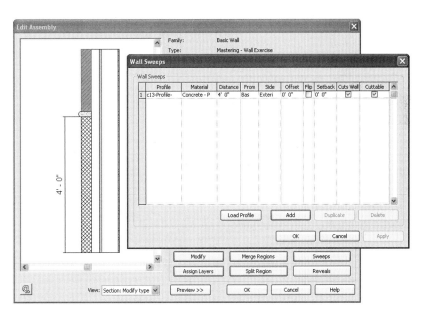

Notice that the loaded profile was created for predictable results when placed in a wall assembly. For your own wall you may need to adjust the offset, flip, and setback values to achieve the desired results. Next, you'll add a different profile to the same assembly.

5. Click OK to close the Wall Sweeps dialog box. In the Edit Assembly dialog box, change the Sample Height value to 12'-0" so that the next sweep addition won't conflict with the one you just added. Adjust the section view as required to see the whole wall.

6. Click Sweeps to reopen the Wall Sweeps dialog box. Click Load Profile again and navigate to Revit's default library. From the Profiles folder, select either `Cornice-Precast.rfa` or `M_Cornice-Precast.rfa`.

7. Click Add to create another new row and change the values in the row as follows:

   ◆ Profile: Cornice-Precast

   ◆ Material: Concrete - Precast Concrete

   ◆ Distance: 0'-0"

   ◆ From: Top

   ◆ Side: Exterior

   ◆ Offset: −0'-3 5/8"

8. Notice that the order of the rows is automatically adjusted based on the vertical relationship of the sweeps added to the wall. Click OK to close the Wall Sweeps dialog box.

   Notice that a negative value for Offset was specified to bring the cornice sweep into the exterior finish layer. Vertical adjustments can be made by assigning positive or negative values in the Distance column.

9. Click OK to close all open dialog boxes and save the project file for additional exercises in this chapter.

The process to create reveals is almost identical to that used to create sweeps. Simply click the Reveals button to open the Reveals dialog box. Experiment with adding your own reveals to the wall type you're creating throughout this chapter's exercises. We've added two reveals to the wall assembly (Figure 13.16) using the default Reveal-Brick Course profile family.

FIGURE 13.16
Reveals have been added to the compound wall assembly.

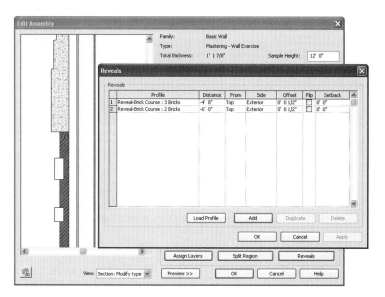

If you create two or more walls using your new compound wall type, you'll see how nicely the sweeps wrap around corners in a 3D or camera view, as shown in Figure 13.17.

FIGURE 13.17
Camera view of compound wall with reveals and sweeps

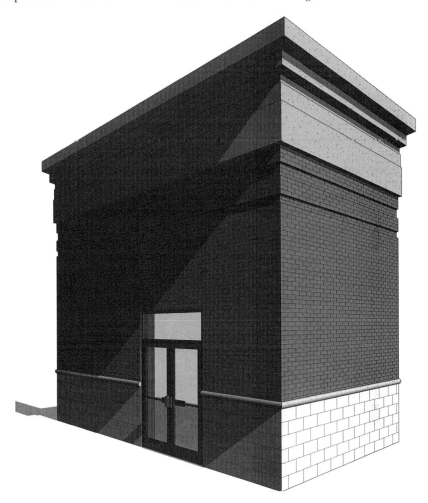

MODIFYING WALL SWEEP RETURNS

In the previous exercises, you learned how to include sweeps and reveals in the assembly of a wall type; however, you can also apply a sweep to a wall if it's only needed in a limited location. For example, you might need to create a fancy wainscot molding in one special room. To accomplish this, go to the Home tab in the ribbon and click Wall and then Wall Sweep. Note that a sweep can be placed on a wall vertically or horizontally by changing the placement option in the ribbon while the Wall Sweep tool is active. Select a wall sweep type from the Properties Palette and pick the wall faces to which you'd like to apply the sweep. If necessary, the sweep can be adjusted vertically in an elevation or section view.

Although profile families can be used in them, a wall sweep is a system family that only exists in a Revit project. New sweep types can only be created by using the Transfer Project Standards tool or by duplicating existing types within your active project. You can now also schedule wall sweeps in Revit 2011.

Let's take a look at how to customize the returns of a wall sweep:

1. Select the sweep and it will display grips at each end. You can simply drag either end of the sweep as required.

2. To change the way the sweep returns or turns a corner, click the Modify Returns button in the Modify | Wall Sweeps contextual ribbon. Notice that there are some additional settings in the Options Bar.

You can change the angle of the return or return it to a straight cut, but for now leave the options as Return and Angle = 90°.

3. The mouse pointer changes to a knife symbol, and when you click somewhere on the end of the sweep, it creates a new segment that can be wrapped around the edge of a wall or opening.

4. After picking one of the ends of the sweep, press Esc or use the Modify tool to exit the command.

5. Select the sweep again and drag the control to adjust the length of the sweep return around the corner of the wall. Figure 13.18 shows how the return can be wrapped around the edge of a wall.

FIGURE 13.18
Modified wall sweep returns

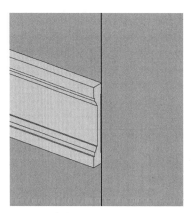
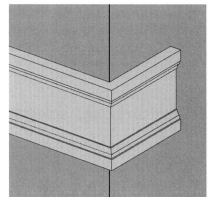

Modeling Techniques for Basic Walls

In the previous sections, we explored different methods to create a variety of basic wall types. When you begin to use these types to assemble your building model, there are still more methods at your disposal to further customize how walls are applied. Let's take a look at some techniques you can use for modeling basic walls. Note that some of these techniques can be used for stacked walls and curtain wall as well.

EXTENDING WALL LAYERS

In many types of construction, you'll need layers of materials to extend within or beyond the constraints of the wall. Some common examples include the extension of sheathing and siding on an exterior wall or gypsum wallboard extending only slightly above the ceiling for interior partitions (Figure 13.19).

FIGURE 13.19
Examples of wall layers extending past or within the constraints of the wall

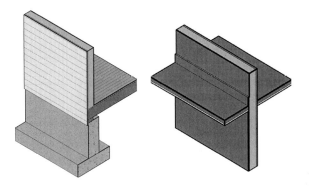

Enabling the extension of layers within a wall assembly requires you to unlock specific edges in the section preview of the Edit Assembly dialog box. Once layers have been unlocked, an instance parameter of the wall becomes active; either Base Extension Distance or Top Extension Distance (depending on which edges you unlocked). This value can be entered directly in the Properties Palette or adjusted graphically in a section view by dragging the small blue triangle control at the edge of the unlocked layer. Let's go through an exercise to explore this functionality:

1. From the Home tab of the ribbon, select the Wall tool to create a new wall using any generic type. Select it and duplicate it by editing the type. Name the new type **Exterior Siding**.

2. Click Edit in the Structure field to open the Edit Assembly dialog box.

3. Add a new layer to the exterior of the wall, set its function to Finish (4), use the material Siding - Clapboard, and assign a thickness of ¾" [18mm].

4. Open the preview pane and switch to section view. Zoom into the bottom of the wall.

5. Select the Modify button and click the bottom edge of the exterior siding layer. Click the padlock icon to unlock the layer (Figure 13.20). Note that you can unlock as many layers as you like; however, the unlocked layers all need to be adjacent. For example, you cannot unlock wallboard layers on both sides of a framing layer.

FIGURE 13.20
Using the Modify button, click the padlock icon to unlock layers.

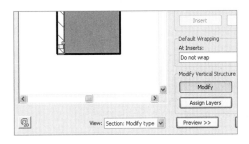

6. The siding layer is now unlocked. Click OK to close all open dialog boxes. Make sure the wall segment you created is still selected and the Properties Palette is open. You'll see that the Base Extension Distance parameter is now enabled. Change the value to –10″ [–250mm] for this parameter and check the wall in 3D. You'll see that the siding layer is now extending 10″ [250mm] below the base of the wall, as shown in Figure 13.21.

FIGURE 13.21
Modifying the wall layer to have a base extension.

7. If you switch to a section view and set the Detail Level to Medium or Fine, select the wall and you will see small blue triangles at the edges of the layers that can be modified (Figure 13.22). You can drag the controls to the required offset or use the Align tool to set the unlocked edge to another reference object. If you Tab-select the edge, you can use the Move tool to set a precise distance as well.

FIGURE 13.22
Unlocked layers can be modified in a section view by dragging or with the Align or Move tool.

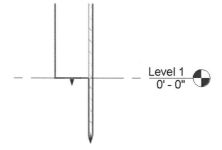

Notice that there are also controls for layers that are locked. Editing the wall with a control of a locked layer changes the Base Offset or Top Offset value and will automatically adjust any Base Extension or Top Extension distances you previously established.

EDITING WALL JOINS

In another common design and construction scenario, you may need to specifically control how two or more walls behave when they intersect. There are a number of ways to customize these occurrences. Let's examine two scenarios where wall joins may need to be edited: phasing conditions and acute angled corners.

When you create a model for a renovation of an existing building, you will likely create elements that are existing, demolished and new. In the example shown in Figure 13.23, a new wall and a wall to be demolished are intersecting an existing wall. Notice that the walls are cleaning up with each other as they normally would if they were all in the same phase.

FIGURE 13.23
Wall joins will clean up by default regardless of phasing.

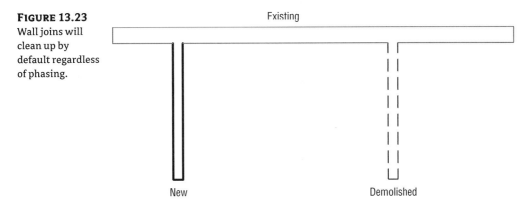

If you would like to change the graphic behavior of the new and demolished walls when they intersect the existing wall, follow these steps:

1. Select the new or demolished wall. Right-click the grip control at the end of the wall you'd like to modify and select Disallow Join.

2. This will cause the walls to overlap, as shown in Figure 13.24.

FIGURE 13.24
Walls with disallowed joins will overlap.

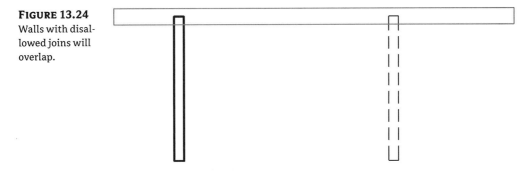

3. To complete the operation, you can use the Trim/Extend Single Element or Trim/Extend Multiple Elements tool or simply drag the endpoints of the walls to create the most appropriate intersecting condition (Figure 13.25).

FIGURE 13.25
Use Trim/Extend or drag wall endpoints to complete the modification.

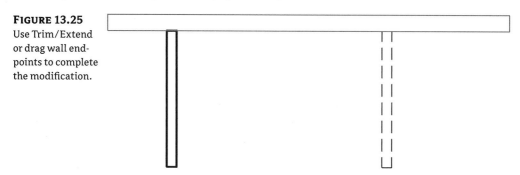

For walls that meet at an acute angle, you can use the Edit Wall Joins tool to control the resolution of the intersection.

1. From the Modify tab in the ribbon, locate the Geometry panel and select the Wall Joins tool.

2. Hover your mouse pointer over an intersection of two walls at an acute angle. You will see a box appear around conditions that can be modified with this tool (Figure 13.26).

FIGURE 13.26
Use the Wall Joins tool to modify intersecting wall conditions.

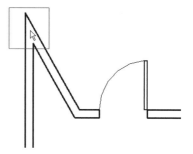

3. In the Options Bar, you will see a number of choices to help you customize the joining condition between the walls related to the selection.

4. To cycle through the available options, choose one of the joining types (Butt, Miter, or Square Off) and then click the Previous or Next button. Some options are shown in Figure 13.27.

FIGURE 13.27
Various corner conditions can be chosen with the Wall Joins tool.

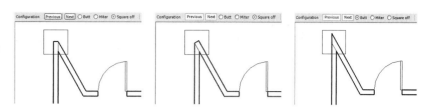

MODIFYING WALL PROFILES

CERT OBJECTIVE

An important extended modeling technique for walls is the ability to customize the elevation profile of a wall segment. There are two ways you can accomplish this: by attaching the wall's top or base to another element or by editing the sketch profile of the wall. You can apply these methods to basic walls, stacked walls, and curtain walls.

To attach a wall to another element, simply select a wall segment, and you will see the Attach Top/Base button in the contextual Modify ribbon. Once this command is activated, select either Top or Base in the Options Bar and then pick an object. Walls can be attached to roofs, ceilings, floors, reference planes, and even other walls. Figure 13.28 shows a stacked wall that has been attached to a curvilinear roof by extrusion.

FIGURE 13.28
Stacked wall attached to an extruded roof

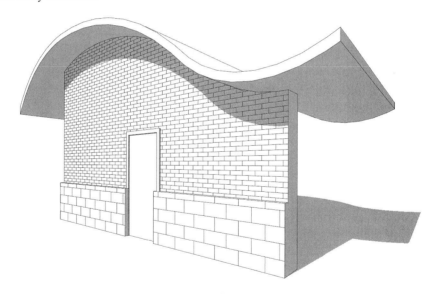

When you use the attach method, be mindful of how Revit treats walls that are attached to other objects. After using this method, the instance parameters Top Is Attached and Base Is Attached will show the status of the selected wall's attachment. These are read-only parameters and are for information only. Be aware that the top constraint and any other offset or height value will not display the actual height of the wall when it is attached to something. For example, if a wall whose base constraint is Level 1 and top constraint is Level 4 is attached to a floor slab on Level 2, the wall's top constraint will still be listed as Level 4 in the Properties Palette. This anomaly does not affect other calculations such as wall length, area, and volume.

AUTOMATICALLY ATTACHING WALLS TO FLOORS

When you create a standard floor by sketching a boundary, the floor is hosted on a specific level. After you complete the boundary sketch and finish the editing mode, Revit offers you some help to attach walls to the floor. Any wall whose top constraint is the level on which the floor is hosted can be automatically attached to the bottom of the floor.

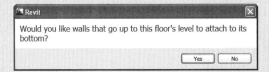

As a bonus, you can access this functionality at any time—not just when you create a floor. If you forgot to attach the walls to the floor when you first modeled the floor, simply select the floor and then click Edit Boundary. Click the Finish Edit Mode button and you should be prompted to attach walls to the floor.

The second method of modifying wall profiles is to edit the sketch profile of the wall. To do this, select a wall and click the Edit Boundary button in the contextual Modify ribbon. This will open a Sketch mode in which you can draw a new boundary for any edge of the wall shape, as shown in Figure 13.29. Click Finish Edit Mode to complete the operation.

FIGURE 13.29
The sketch elevation boundary for a stacked wall instance is edited.

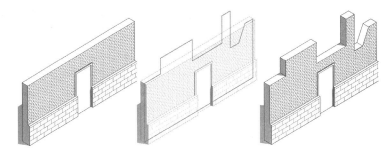

Creating Custom In-Place Walls

Whether you are working on traditional architecture, restoration of historic buildings, or free form design, you may need to create walls that are irregular in shape. The Model In-Place tool, found in the Component drop-down on the Home tab, lets you create any wall style independent of the constraints of the layer structure described in the previous sections of this chapter. Figure 13.30 shows an example of such a wall created with the solid geometry tools also found in the Family Editor.

FIGURE 13.30
Manually con-
structed wall used
to create nonverti-
cal surfaces.

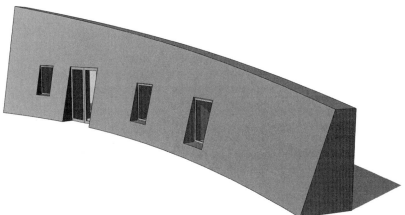

You can refer to Chapter 15, "Family Editor," to explore the various modeling techniques available in the Model In-Place mode. Remember that the selection of the family category is important to the behavior of the custom geometry. Select the Walls category to allow your custom elements to be scheduled with other walls and for hosted elements such as doors and windows to be placed.

Creating Stacked Walls

Walls in a building—especially exterior walls—are often composed of several wall types made out of different material combinations and with different widths that stack one on top of another over the height of the façade. Because these walls usually sit on top of a foundation wall, you would likely want to establish an intelligent relationship among these different wall assemblies so the entire façade acts as one wall (for example, when the foundation wall moves and you expect walls on top of the foundation to also move). This is where stacked walls can help.

Stacked walls allow you to create a single wall entity composed of different wall types stacked on top of each other. Before you can create a stacked wall, some basic wall types need to be preloaded in your project. To help you understand how stacked walls work and how to modify one, follow these steps:

1. Open a new session of Revit and make sure at least three levels are defined. If you don't have three levels, switch to an elevation view, add a few levels, and then go back to the Level 1 floor plan view.

2. From the Home tab on the ribbon, pick the Wall tool and select Stacked Wall: Exterior—Brick Over CMU w Metal Stud (you can find stacked wall types at the bottom of the list in the Type Selector). Draw a segment of wall in the Level 1 floor plan.

3. Select the wall segment. In the Properties Palette, click the Edit Type button and then duplicate the wall type to create a new stacked wall called **Mastering Stacked Wall**.

4. Click the Edit button in the Structure field to open the Edit Assembly dialog box. Open the preview pane and set the view to Section. When you're editing the stacked wall type,

you'll notice that the Edit Assembly dialog box (Figure 13.31) is slightly different from when you're working with a basic wall. Rather than editing individual layers, in this dialog box you are editing stacked wall types and their relationships to each other.

FIGURE 13.31

The Edit Assembly dialog box for stacked walls

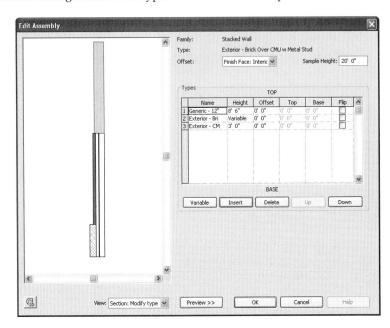

5. Click the Insert button to add a new wall to the stacked wall assembly. A new row appears in the list and allows you to define a new wall. Select the Generic - 12" [300mm] wall type from the Name list and enter a Height of 10'-0" [3000mm] (the height value is not important in this exercise).

6. At the top of the dialog box, find the Offset drop-down list and change the setting to Finish Face: Interior. This will align the interior faces of the stacked walls and allows you to use the Offset field in the Types table to adjust each stacked wall type in a predictable manner.

7. Select the row of the generic wall type by clicking the row's number label at the left side of the table. Click the Variable button to allow the wall to vary in height to adjust with varying level heights. Note that one row must have a variable height, but only one row in the assembly can be assigned as such. All others must have a specific height value.

8. Go back to the Level 1 floor plan and draw a new wall with the Mastering Stacked Wall type, setting its top constraint to Level 3 in the Options Bar.

9. Cut a section through the model and change the heights of Level 1 and Level 3 to see the effect this has on the wall (make sure the level of detail in the section is set to Medium so you can see the layers of the wall). You'll see that changing Level 2 does not change the bottom walls because they are of a fixed height; however, changing the height of Level 3 changes the height of the variable wall.

At any time, you can break down a stacked wall into its individual wall types. To do this, select a stacked wall and from the right-click menu select Break Up. Once a stacked wall is broken up, the walls become independent and there is no way to reassemble them back to a stacked wall. The base constraint and base offset of each subwall are the same as the stacked wall. For example, if the stacked wall was placed on Level 1, the base constraint for an upper subwall would still be Level 1, with the height difference accounted for in the wall's Base Offset parameter. This can be modified in the Properties Palette if necessary.

The following are some important notes about stacked walls from the Revit User's Guide (from its "Vertically Stacked Wall Notes" section):

◆ When you create a wall schedule, vertically stacked walls do not schedule, but their subwalls do.

◆ When you edit the elevation profile of a stacked wall, you edit one main profile. If you break up the stacked wall, each subwall retains its edited profile.

◆ Subwalls can host sweeps; stacked walls cannot.

◆ Subwalls cannot be in different phases, worksets, or design options from that of the stacked wall.

◆ To place inserts such as doors and windows in a stacked wall, you may need to use the Pick Primary Host tool to switch between subwalls composing the stacked wall. For example, the door shown in Figure 13.32 is outside the upper wall because the main host of the door is the bottom subwall.

FIGURE 13.32
Inserts may not host correctly in vertically stacked walls.

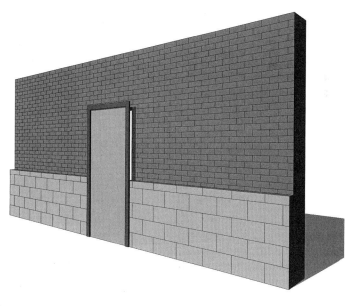

To place the door properly, select it and then click Pick Primary Host from the Modify | Doors tab in the Host panel. Place your mouse pointer over the wall and select the upper subwall (you may need to press the Tab key to select the correct component). The door will then be properly hosted in the upper wall, as shown in Figure 13.33.

FIGURE 13.33
Use the Pick Primary Host tool to adjust inserts in stacked walls.

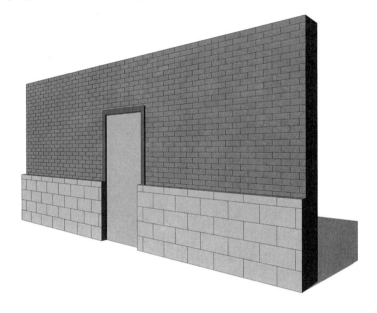

Creating Simple Curtain Walls

Curtain walls and curtain systems in Revit are unique wall types that allow you to embed divisions, mullions, and panels directly into the wall. They have a distinct set of properties, yet still share many characteristics of basic walls. A *curtain system* has the same inherent properties of a curtain wall, but it is used when you need to apply a curtain wall to a face. Curtain systems are usually nonrectangular in shape, such as the glazed dome shown in Figure 13.34.

FIGURE 13.34
Glazed dome created with a curtain system

A curtain wall is defined by the following elements and subcomponents:

The Curtain Wall   A curtain wall is drawn like a basic wall and is available in the Type Selector when the Wall tool is activated. It has top and bottom constraints, can be attached to roofs or reference planes, can have its elevation profile edited, and is scheduled as a wall type. When a curtain wall is selected in a model, the overall curtain wall definition is displayed as a dashed line with extensions at both ends of the segment:

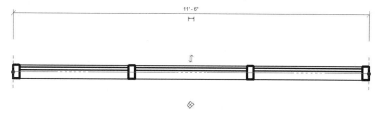

The dashed line of the overall curtain wall definition represents the location line of the wall. This is important if you are placing a curtain system on a face because the placement will be based on the location line. The location line of a curtain wall also determines the measurement of room area. Even if the Room Area Computation option is set At Wall Finish, a room's area will be measured to a curtain wall's location line. For more information, refer to a post on the Do U Revit blog (`http://do-u-revit.blogspot.com/2010/04/room-area-and-curtain-walls.html`).

So, how do you adjust the location line of a curtain wall? This is accomplished by modifying the offsets in the mullions and panels you assign to a curtain wall or system. We'll cover this process in the section "Customizing Curtain Wall Types," later in this chapter.

Curtain Grids   These are used to lay out a grid, defining the physical divisions of the curtain wall. You can lay out grids freely as a combination of horizontal and vertical segments, or they can be predefined in a curtain wall's Type Properties in regular spacing intervals. Figure 13.35 shows a freely designed layout of curtain grids and expressive curtain panels in between.

Mullions   These represent the structural profiles on a glass façade and in Revit they follow the curtain grid geometry. Mullions can be vertical or horizontal and can be customized to any shape based on a mullion profile family. Offsets specified in a mullion's Type Properties affect how the mullion is placed relative to the curtain wall's location line.

Curtain Panels   These fill in the space between the curtain grids. Offsets in a curtain panel's Type Properties determine how the panel is placed relative to the curtain wall's location line. Curtain panels are always one of the following:

Empty Panels   No panel is placed between the grids.

Glazed Panels   These can be made out of different types of glass that can have any color or transparency.

Solid Panels   Panels can be created with custom geometry in the Family Editor and can include anything from doors to spandrels to shadow boxes to solar fins.

Wall Types as Infill   When you have a panel selected, you can also choose a basic wall type from the Type Selector to fill the space between the curtain grids. All wall types in the project will be available for your selection. An example of this application would be interior office partitions in which the lower portion is a standard wall and glass panels fill the upper portion.

FIGURE 13.35
Curtain wall with
regular orthogonal
grids and expres-
sive curtain panels

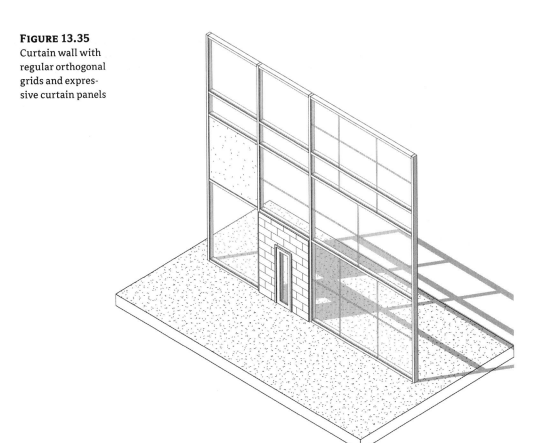

Designing a Curtain Wall

Let's go through a quick exercise to become familiar with the creation of a simple curtain wall. To create a curtain wall, you can either model a standard wall, then change its type to Curtain Wall, or select a curtain wall type from the Type Selector when the Wall tool is active.

1. From the Home tab in the ribbon, select the Wall tool. From the Type Selector (in the Properties Palette) select Curtain Wall 1.

2. In the Level 1 floor plan, draw a single curtain wall. Go to a 3D view to see the result.

   The basic curtain wall definition has no predefined grids or mullions. The wall segment you see is actually just one big system panel that you will need to divide. Note that if you create a curved segment for a curtain wall, the panels are always straight segments. Thus, if you try to make a curved segment with Curtain Wall 1, there will only be one straight panel segment between the endpoints of the curve until you start to divide it up with curtain grids.

3. Divide the wall into panels using the Curtain Grid tool from the Home tab. Position your mouse pointer over the edges of the wall to get a preview of where the grid will be placed (select a vertical edge to place a horizontal grid or select a horizontal edge to place a vertical grid).

Revit offers some snapping options when you are placing curtain grids that will help you divide the panels and subsequent divisions at midpoints and thirds. Watch the status bar for snapping prompts because there are no graphic indicators of the snapped positions other than the mouse pointer pausing. Place grids on the wall segment so that you get something like the wall shown in Figure 13.36.

FIGURE 13.36
Curtain wall with a few manually applied grids

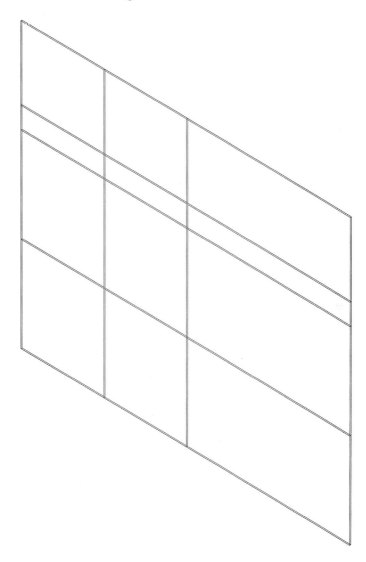

4. From the Home tab, select the Mullion tool. Notice that you can select from a variety of mullion types in the Type Selector; however, the default choice is adequate for this exercise. At the right end of the ribbon, you will see the Placement panel with three options for placing mullions: Grid Line, Grid Line Segment, and All Grid Lines. You can place mullions on the curtain wall using any of these methods. Give each a try to see how they work.

MODIFYING PANELS AND MULLIONS

Next you'll replace panels in the wall you just created. As we explained earlier, panels are subcomponents of the overall curtain wall, so you may need to press the Tab key to select a panel and view its properties. Revit has special selection tools for curtain walls that are available in the right-click context menu when you highlight a mullion or a panel. In the following exercise, you will replace the narrow band of glazing panels with solid panels.

1. In a 3D view, select one of the glazing panels in the narrow horizontal band (press the Tab key to select it if necessary).

2. From the right-click context menu, choose Select Panels ➤ Along Horizontal Grid, as shown in Figure 13.37.

FIGURE 13.37
Select multiple curtain panels along a grid with commands in the right-click menu.

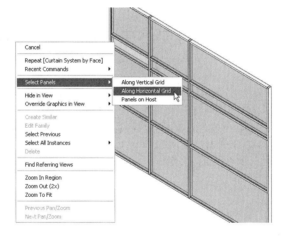

3. With all the glazing panels selected along the horizontal grid, go to the Type Selector and find the type named Solid under the family System Panel (note that the Glazing panel type is in the same family as the Solid panel).

CUSTOMIZING CURTAIN GRID SEGMENTS

Finally, you will practice the techniques to add or remove segments of curtain grids to refine our curtain wall design. One important fact to remember when working with curtain grids is that they are always *implied* across the extents of the curtain wall. When we say they are implied, we mean they are not necessarily expressed on all panel segments. To further elaborate, you will add a curtain grid to the midpoint of the right, center panel and delete the division between the two panels to the left of the added grid as shown in Figure 13.38.

FIGURE 13.38
Individual grid lines are added or deleted to further customize the design.

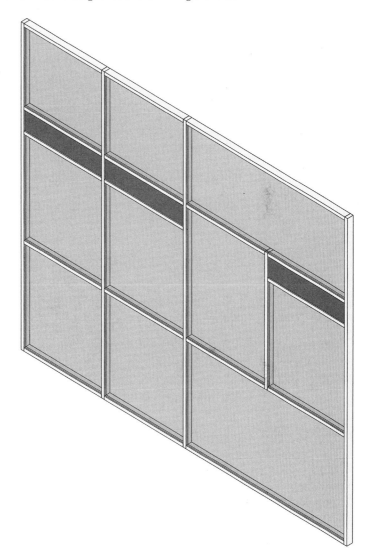

1. Begin by activating the Curtain Grid tool from the Home tab. In the Placement panel at the right end of the ribbon, click the One Segment button. Hover your mouse pointer over the bottom edge of the right-center panel, snapping to the midpoint of the panel (Figure 13.39).

FIGURE 13.39
A single segment is added to the center panel of the curtain wall.

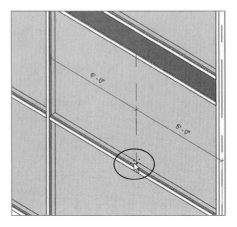

2. The second step is tricky. You *do not* continue creating another division in the short panel above the center panel. Instead, press the Esc key or click the Modify tool to exit the Curtain Grid command. Select the vertical grid line you created in step 1 (you may need to press the Tab key until you see the dashed line indicating the curtain grid). Notice that the grid extends the entire height of the wall (Figure 13.40).

FIGURE 13.40
Select the curtain grid in order to add or remove individual segments along the grid.

3. With the curtain grid selected, click the Add/Remove Segments button in the Modify | Curtain Grids panel of the ribbon. Pick the segment of the curtain grid that passes through the short panel. Press the Esc key and you should see that the short panel is also split in half.

4. Activate the Mullion tool and place mullions on the division between the two center panels, as shown in Figure 13.41.

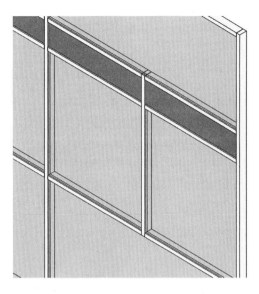

5. Press the Esc key or click Modify. Select and delete the horizontal mullion between the two left panels (this step is optional).

6. Similar to the process of adding grid segments, select the horizontal curtain grid below the narrow band and click the Add/Remove Segments button in the ribbon. Click the segment in the left-center panel. If you did not delete the mullion in step 5, a warning will appear prompting you to delete the mullion segment. The result should look like the wall shown in Figure 13.42.

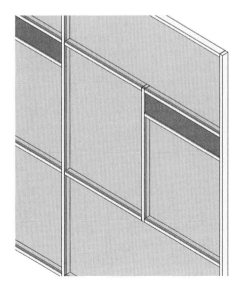

PLACING DOORS IN CURTAIN WALLS

In the final exercise of this section, you will swap one of the curtain panels for a door panel. Door families for curtain walls can be found in the Doors folder of Revit's default library, but they behave differently than regular doors. The height and width of the curtain wall door is driven by the curtain grids—not the Type Properties of the door.

1. From the Insert tab on the ribbon, locate the Load From Library panel and click the Load Family button. Navigate to the Doors folder of Revit's default library and load the Curtain Wall Dbl Glass.rfa family.

2. Zoom into the bottom-middle panel in your curtain wall. Delete the mullion under this segment as shown in Figure 13.43 (you don't want to have a tripping hazard at your door!). Remember, you may have to press the Tab key to select the mullion.

FIGURE 13.43
Delete the mullion below the panel where the door will be placed.

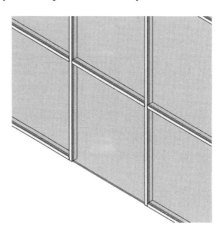

3. Select the bottom-middle panel and go to the Type Selector. Find the Curtain Wall Dbl Glass.rfa family and select it from the list so the results look like the wall in Figure 13.44. The door swing can be adjusted in plan as any other door in Revit.

FIGURE 13.44
System glazing panel has been swapped for a double door panel family.

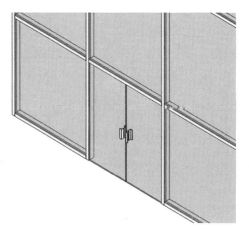

PLACING CORNER MULLIONS

Revit includes special mullions to be used at the corners of two curtain walls. These mullion types are unique in that only one is needed to connect two wall segments. In the default project template you will find four corner mullion types, as shown in Figure 13.45: (a) V Corner Mullion, (b) Quad Corner Mullion, (c) L Corner Mullion, and (d) Trapezoid Corner Mullion.

FIGURE 13.45
Available curtain wall corner mullions

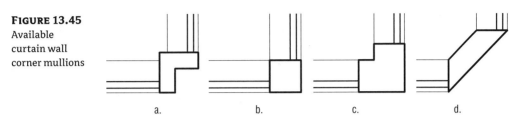

a.   b.   c.   d.

Corner mullions cannot be customized beyond the shapes included in the Revit project template; however, you can modify the material assigned to the mullions as well as the offset and depth dimensions in the Type Properties. When you use corner mullions between two segments of curtain wall, they will automatically adjust to the angle between the segments, as shown in Figure 13.46.

FIGURE 13.46
Corner mullions adapt to angles between curtain wall segments.

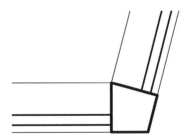

Before you place a corner mullion, make sure that the endpoints of the two curtain wall segments are cleanly connected. You can drag the endpoint controls of the walls or use the Trim/Extend To Corner tool. To place a corner mullion, simply use the Mullion tool and select one of the corner edges of either one of the wall segments. If you have already placed a regular mullion at the end of a curtain wall segment, select the mullions along the vertical edge and then use the Type Selector to choose a corner mullion type. Remember you can use the right-click menu (select Mullions ➤ On Gridline) to make the selection easy.

Customizing Curtain Wall Types

In the previous exercises you learned the fundamental techniques of building a simple but custom curtain wall design. To reap some additional productivity from the curtain wall tool, you can predefine almost all the properties necessary to generate a complete curtain wall assembly simply by placing the wall in your project. In the following sections we will examine one of the curtain wall types included with Revit's default project template.

Begin a new project with the Default.rte or MetricDefault.rte template and create a wall segment 30′ [9000mm] long using the type Curtain Wall: Storefront. Switch to a 3D view and you will see the wall already has vertical and horizontal divisions along with mullions placed on the divisions. In the example shown in Figure 13.47, we have placed an additional curtain grid and swapped one of the panels for a door type.

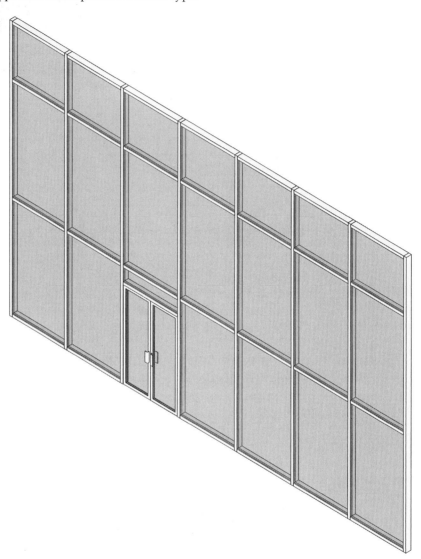

Select the sample of Storefront wall you had previously created and click the Edit Type button in the Properties Palette. The settings that drive the generation of this type of wall are relatively easy to understand. Let's review some of the more important options related to these properties:

Automatically Embed When this option is enabled, any instance of this curtain wall type will embed itself inside other wall segments. This is useful for modeling extended areas of ribbon or strip glazing (Figure 13.48) instead of using a window family.

Figure 13.48
The Automatically Embed option allows curtain walls to be placed inside basic walls.

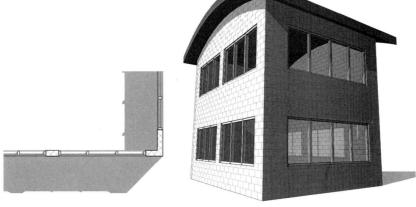

Join Condition   This defines the behavior of the mullion joins. It can be one of the following:

- ◆ Not Defined (join conditions can be overridden as necessary)
- ◆ Vertical Grid Continuous
- ◆ Horizontal Grid Continuous
- ◆ Border and Vertical Grid Continuous
- ◆ Border and Horizontal Grid Continuous

Grid Pattern: Layout   There are four options to define how the vertical and horizontal grids will be arranged in your curtain wall.

Fixed Distance   The most common setting, which allows you to specify spacing between gridlines. Leftover panel segments must be accounted for in the overall length of the wall.

Fixed Number   Divides the wall segment into equally spaced panels. When you select this option, the Spacing parameter becomes disabled. In its place, a new integer parameter named Number will appear in the Instance Properties.

Maximum Spacing   Indicates the maximum spacing distance. Curtain panels will be equally divided over the length of the wall segment, not to exceed the Spacing value.

Minimum Spacing   Indicates the minimum spacing distance. Curtain panels will be equally divided over the length of the wall segment, no smaller than the Spacing value.

Mullions   This allows you to specify the mullions that will be automatically applied to the curtain wall. Corner mullions can be applied to either Border 1 or Border 2 for the vertical mullions, but use them carefully as their resolution at corners of will depend on how you construct your wall segments.

MODIFYING PINNED PANELS AND MULLIONS

You may have already noticed when a panel or mullion is selected from a predefined curtain wall type that they appear with a pushpin icon. This indicates that these elements are part of a system and cannot be changed without additional action.

To change or delete a predefined panel or mullion in a curtain wall instance, select the element and click the pushpin icon. The icon will change to a pushpin with a red X next to it. At this point, you can change the element using the Type Selector or delete it (only mullions can be deleted). Be careful when you attempt to unpin elements from a curtain wall as you cannot repin back to the predefined system. Within the active session of Revit, you may be able to return to an unpinned curtain wall element and still find the unpinned icon. This allows you to fix any accidental unpinning, but once your project is closed and reopened, you can no longer reassociate the unpinned elements.

CREATING CUSTOM CURTAIN PANELS

A curtain panel does not have to be confined to a simple extrusion of glass or solid material. You can create any kind of panel family to satisfy your design requirements. When creating a new panel, be sure to select the `Curtain Wall Panel.rft` or `Metric Curtain Wall Panel.rft` family template file. The width and height of the panel are not explicitly specified in the family; instead, the outermost reference planes will adapt to the divisions in the curtain wall into which the panel is embedded. If required, you can adjust the panel geometry to offset within or beyond the reference plane boundaries in the family. This is useful for creating butt-glazed curtain wall assemblies.

COMPLEX CURTAIN WALL APPLICATIONS

Although covering several specific examples in detail is outside the scope of this chapter, we will offer some real-world examples of creating your own custom curtain panels. Refer to Chapter 15 for guidance on creating your own families. These examples are included in a sample file named `c13-Curtain-Wall-Samples.rvt` on this book's companion website (`www.sybex.com/go/masteringrevit2011`).

Spider Fittings and Sunshades   Generic models can be nested in a curtain panel family. In the example shown here, two instances of the spider component are placed on one edge of the panel. Visibility parameters are assigned to the two spider fittings that enable either the top or bottom spider to be displayed as needed. The spider fittings were downloaded from RevitCity.com and the sunshade is a Kawneer model 1600 SunShade – Planar downloaded from Autodesk Seek (`http://seek.autodesk.com`).

Spandrel and Shadowbox   Often in glazing applications, the spacing of horizontal members will consist of a pattern including a narrow band or spandrel to mask the floor and ceiling sandwich. Revit does not currently have the ability to define two spacing values, but you can create the spandrel or shadowbox in a single panel family. In the example shown here, the spandrel height is a type property of the custom panel family. Standard mullions are applied to the wall.

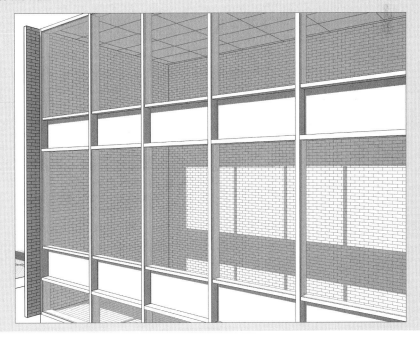

Louvers   Our last example shows how metal louvers can be embedded in a curtain panel family. The image shown here is a panel developed with a nested generic model. The louver fins are arranged in a parametric array within the generic model, and then the generic model is placed in the panel. The edges of the louver array are constrained to the reference planes in the panel. This parametric louver curtain panel was downloaded from RevitCity.com.

Creating Complex Curtain Walls

Often at the early stages of design, as an architect or designer, you need to be able to model curtain wall systems that indicate design intent. These systems need to be flexible and robust enough to allow us to explore design iteration, but they also need to be useful enough downstream as your project moves from concept to design development and then on to fabrication.

In Revit Architecture 2011 you can build Concept Curtain Walls utilizing Revit conceptual massing tools. There are two potential workflows, and it's important to understand the differences. You can model your curtain wall system directly within the project environment from massing forms; or you can build it as a family within a conceptual design environment.

Project Environment   You can build your forms directly within your project environment using the in-place massing tools. When constructing concept curtain walls through the In-Place Mass tool, the conceptual design environment does not have 3D reference planes and 3D levels.

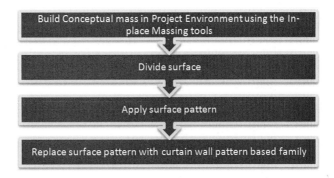

Conceptual Design Environment (CDE)   You create your concept curtain wall designs in the Revit Conceptual Design Environment (CDE), which is a type of family editor. These forms reside outside the project environment. You can then reference these massing families into a project environment, allowing you to explore contextual relationships with the building form.

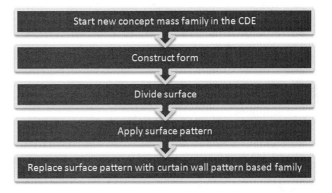

You start by designing your conceptual form that will represent the shape and form of the surface of the curtain wall. You are then able to subdivide the surface of this form using a grid system, referred to as a UV grid. As surfaces are not always planar (flat), a UVW coordinate system is used to plot location across the surface. This grid system automatically adjusts following the natural contours of a non-planar surface or form. The UV grid is then used as a guide for patterning the surface. You can investigate how you might panelize the surface to make it constructible by applying a geometric pattern to the surface. This pattern provides a basic graphically representation of how the panel may look. These graphic patterns can then be replaced with parametric components that automatically conform to the divided surface.

Dividing the Surface

Let's take a look at the basic tools that will allow you to divide the surface of a conceptual form:

1. Start by opening c13-Square-Panel.rfa from this book's companion web page at www.sybex.com/go/masteringrevit2011. This file represents a simple conceptual shape for a curtain wall design (Figure 13.49).

FIGURE 13.49
Conceptual shape
to be used as a
basis for a complex
curtain wall design

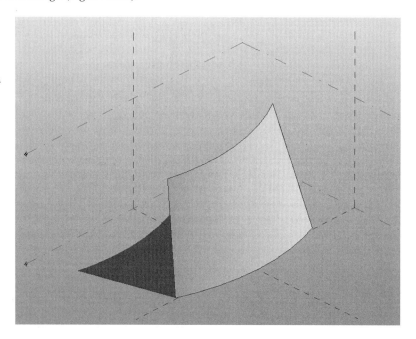

2. Select the form and then click Divide Surface on the Modify | Form tab in the ribbon. This will divide the surface of the form and you will see horizontal and vertical grids displayed. This is the *UV grid*.

   Note that you can control the display of the UV grid when it is selected (Figure 13.50). To modify the display, click the U Grid or V Grid button in the UV Grids And Intersects panel on the Modify | Divided Surface tab of the ribbon.

3. Make sure UV grids are both displayed and the surface is selected. Notice how the Options Bar provides a number of settings for you to modify the divided surface. You can control the U grid and V grid by a number or with a specific distance. If you select the Number option, you can enter a number of divisions that will distribute evenly across the surface.

4. Select Distance, which will allow you to enter a specific absolute distance between grids across the divided surface. Under the Distance setting, there is also a drop-down menu that also allows you to specify a Maximum Distance or a Minimum Distance, which are similar to the constraints described earlier in this chapter for basic curtain walls. Make sure the surface is divided by Number, with a U grid of 10 and a V grid of 10.

FIGURE 13.50
A surface of the
conceptual form
has been divided
and the UV grid is
displayed.

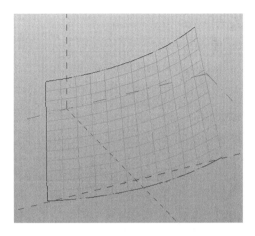

5. With the UV grid selected, you will see a 3D control (XYZ axis arrows), and an icon appears in the center of the surface. Click the icon to enable the Configure UV Grid Layout command. The display will change (Figure 13.51) and you can now apply specific settings to control the UV grid even further. You have the ability to alter the rotation of the grid, the UV grid belt, and justification of the UV grids at the surface borders. These grid configuration parameters can also be found and modified in the Properties Palette.

FIGURE 13.51
The UV grid can
be configured by
clicking the icon
at the center of the
surface.

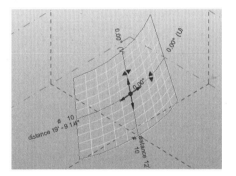

6. In the Properties Palette, set the U Grid Rotation value to 45 degrees, and set the V Grid Rotation value to 45 degrees; then click Apply. Notice how the modified values are updated in the 3D view with the Configure UV Grid Layout command activated.

In the Configure UV Grid Layout mode (Figure 13.52), you will see a number of controls—all of which relate to parameters you can also access in the Properties Palette. The arrow cross in the middle of the grid is the *grid justification* marker. You can drag it to any side, corner, or center of the grid, which will adjust the value of the Justification property of both U and V grids.

The *belts* represent the lines along the surface from which the distance between grids is measured. The distance is measured by chords, not curve lengths, and can be seen in the Properties Palette as the Belt Measurement parameter for both U and V grids.

FIGURE 13.52
The UV grid can be modified directly or via the values in the Properties Palette.

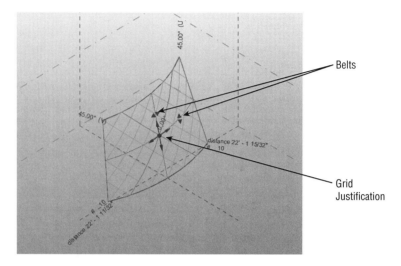

Dividing the Surface with Intersects

As you have seen in the previous exercise, the Divide Surface tool allows you to divide the surface of a form using the natural UVW grid of the surface. However, what if we want to divide the surface with a customized grid pattern? New to Revit Architecture 2011 is the ability to divide a surface by intersecting geometry. By using the Intersect feature you can divide the surface based on the following:

♦ Intersecting levels, reference planes, and even lines drawn on a reference plane

♦ A mixture of U or V grids and intersects

Let's take a look at an example based on our previous file, which will demonstrate how we can use a series of defined reference planes to divide a surface.

1. Start by opening the file `c13-Square-Panel-Intersects.rfa` from this book's companion web page at `www.sybex.com/go/masteringrevit2011`.

Notice that a series of reference lines have been drawn in the X plane; you will use these reference planes to divide the surface of the form.

2. Select the surface and choose Divide Surface from the ribbon. Click the U Grid tool on the ribbon to disable the display of the U grids.

3. With the surface still selected, click the Intersects button on the ribbon. Select all the reference planes in the X plane and then click the Finish icon in the Intersects panel on the ribbon. This will divide the surface based on where the reference planes intersect the surface of the form. Note that you could also choose Intersects ➤ Intersects List to choose named references such as levels or named reference planes instead of picking them in the model view.

4. Go to the Project Browser and open the 3D view named Surface Only to review the results (Figure 13.53).

FIGURE 13.53
The surface is divided by inter-secting planes and lines.

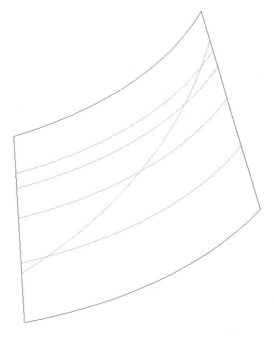

Applying Patterns

Surface patterns allow you to quickly preview in a graphical manner how a panel will work across the surface of the form. As you are not working with complex geometry at this stage, the editing and adjustment to the design concept is quick. Revit provides a number of predefined patterns that are available from the Properties Palette, and they can be applied to your divided surface. You will now apply a surface pattern to a form:

1. Start by opening c13-Square-Panel-Pattern.rfa from this book's companion web page at www.sybex.com/go/masteringrevit2011.

2. With the UV grid on the form selected, you will notice in the Type Selector that the default empty pattern named _No Pattern is applied to the surface. Open the Type Selector and you will see that you can apply one of a number of predefined patterns to the surface. Click the Rectangle Checkerboard Pattern type to apply it to your surface (Figure 13.54).

3. Experiment with the various predefined patterns and adjust the UV grid as required to play with the proportions of the patterns.

At any time, you can display both the underlying surface divisions along with the pattern display. With the grid selected, click the Surface button in the Surface Representation panel on the Modify | Divided Surface tab. This display should give you a better understanding of the relationship between the pattern definition and the spacing of the surface divisions.

FIGURE 13.54
Surface with Rectangle Checkerboard Pattern applied

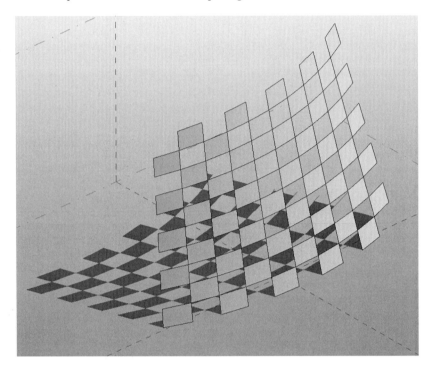

Editing the Pattern Surface

There will be situations where you will want to edit and control the border conditions for pattern surfaces. Patterned surfaces may have border tiles that intersect the edge of a surface, and they may not end up as complete tiles. You can control the border tile conditions by setting them to Partial, Overhanging, or Empty in the Border Tile instance property of the patterned surface. You will now modify a conceptual curtain wall to examine how the different border conditions affect the surface.

1. Start by opening c13-Square-Panel-Border.rfa from this book's companion web page at www.sybex.com/go/masteringrevit2011.

2. Select the surface and in the Properties Palette, locate the Border Tile parameter under Constraints. Set the value to Empty and click Apply. Notice that the tiles at the borders are no longer visible, as shown in Figure 13.55.

3. Next change the Border Tile parameter to Overhanging and click Apply. The border tiles will now show in their entirety, extending beyond the edge of the surface.

FIGURE 13.55
Border parameter
set to Empty

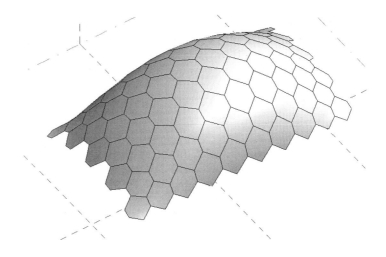

Surface Representation

When editing a surface in the conceptual design environment, you have the option to choose how surface elements will be displayed. A number of options are available to you, allowing you to customize how you show or hide the various elements that make up a divided surface in a view. If you select either the U or V Grid icon, this will enable or disable the UV grid in the view. The Surface icon allows you to display the original surface, nodes, or grid lines The Pattern icon allows you to hide or display the pattern lines or pattern fill applied to the surface. The Component icon allows you to hide or display the pattern component applied to the surface. If you decide to make any changes to the display using the Surface Representation tools, these changes will not carry through into the project environment. To globally show or hide surface elements you will have to alter this from the Visibility/Graphic Overrides dialog box.

In the Surface Representation panel, you will also notice a small arrow in the bottom-right corner. Clicking this arrow will open the Surface Presentation dialog box, where you will find additional display options for the surface, patterns, and components. You also have the ability to display nodes and override the surface material of the form. Let's practice controlling the surface representation of your form.

1. Start by opening `c13-Square-Panel-SurfaceRep.rfa` from this book's companion web page at `www.sybex.com/go/masteringrevit2011`.

2. With the surface selected, go to the Surface Representation panel in the ribbon and click the arrow in the bottom-left corner to open the Surface Representation dialog box (Figure 13.56).

FIGURE 13.56
Use the Surface Representation dialog box to further customize the display of your form.

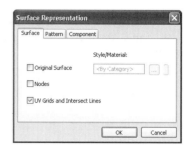

3. On the Surface tab, enable Nodes; this will display a node at each intersection of the UV grid, as shown in Figure 13.57.

FIGURE 13.57
Nodes are displayed at the intersection of the U grids and V grids.

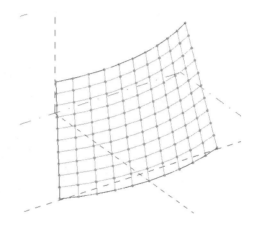

Adding Definition

So far, you have created a surface, subdivided it, and applied a graphical representation to the form. You can now begin to add actual component geometry similar to mullions and panels. Note that although the underlying graphic pattern will remain, the component geometry will take precedence. To begin this process, you will create special curtain panel families using the Curtain Panel Pattern Based.rft or M_Curtain Panel Pattern Based.rft family template. This type of panel family can be applied to the divided surface to populate it with architectural components, adding realistic definition to your conceptual curtain wall surface.

BUILDING A PATTERN-BASED PANEL FAMILY

In the following exercise, you will build a simple rectangular panel and apply it to your divided surface.

1. Click the Application button, choose New ➢ Family, and select the Curtain Panel Pattern Based.rft family template.

Figure 13.58 shows the pattern-based curtain wall family template, which consists of a grid, a series of reference lines, and adaptive points. The grid is used to lay out the pattern of the panel. The adaptive points and reference lines act as a rig, defining the layout of the panel. You can construct solid and planar geometry within and around the reference lines to form the panel.

When a panel is applied to a divided surface, the points in the panel adapt to the UV grid and the panel will then flex accordingly. As a general rule, the grid pattern in your curtain panel family should match the pattern on the divided surface to which it is applied. For example, if you have applied a hexagonal pattern to your divided surface, make sure that the curtain panel family is also using a hexagonal pattern.

FIGURE 13.58
The rig in the pattern-based curtain panel family

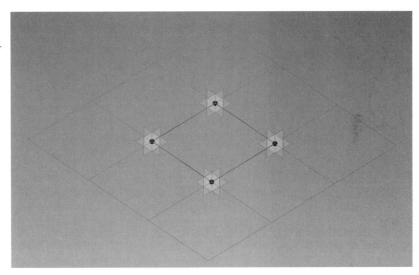

2. You now need to decide what pattern you will use for the component. To change the pattern, select the grid, go to the Type Selector, and change the pattern to Rhomboid. Notice how the adaptive points and reference lines update to reflect the change. Review the various patterns that are available to you. Revert back to the Rectangular pattern.

Modeling a pattern-based curtain panel is similar to how you would sketch and construct a form within the conceptual design environment. You use points, lines, and reference lines to construct geometry.

CHANGING PATTERNS WITH GEOMETRY

It is important to understand that if you decide to switch your curtain panel grid pattern after creating solid forms, the geometry will not automatically adapt to the new pattern you choose. The geometry will be left orphaned and you will need to delete any geometry and remodel, based on the new pattern.

---

3. Select one of the adaptive points and drag it. These points will not move horizontally, only vertically. As you move the point, the reference lines attached to the point will alter the shape. Therefore, as you build geometry on the defined reference lines and an adaptive point is moved or adjusted, the reference lines are altered and the geometry constructed along the reference lines updates to reflect the change.

4. To reset the adaptive points back to the grid, select the grid and you will notice a Reset Points To Grid button in the Options Bar. Click the button to reset the points.

5. Select the four reference lines and click the Create Form ➤ Solid Form button in the ribbon. You will see two icons appear in the middle of the model view (Figure 13.59), giving you the option to create an extruded form or a flat planar surface. Select the icon for the planar surface.

FIGURE 13.59
Geometry options are presented when using the Create Form tool.

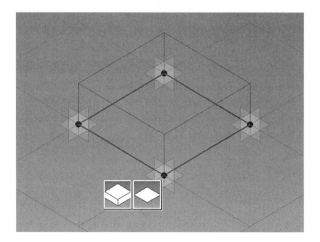

6. Next we will flex the geometry to test its consistency. Select one of the adaptive points and move it vertically. Observe how the geometry flexes, as shown in Figure 13.60, and then reset the points to grid.

7. Switch to the Home tab in the ribbon and from the Draw panel select the Point Element tool. Place a point on one of the reference planes, as shown in Figure 13.61. This point becomes a hosted point; observe how its symbol is smaller than the adaptive points. Select the point and from the Properties Palette, change the value of the Show Reference Planes parameter to Always. This will make it easier to build geometry using the hosted point in later steps.

8. From the Home tab and the Work Plane panel, click the Set button (Set Work Plane tool) and pick the work plane of the hosted point.

9. Draw a circle with a radius of 6 inches [150mm] on the work plane of the hosted point, as shown in Figure 13.62. It can be a little tricky drawing the circle onto the active work plane of the hosted point. Therefore, use the Show Workplane tool to display the active work plane for the point. This will make the process of sketching the circle easier.

FIGURE 13.60
The panel form will flex when the points are dragged vertically.

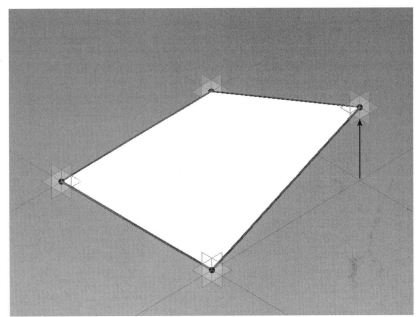

FIGURE 13.61
A reference point is placed on one of the reference lines.

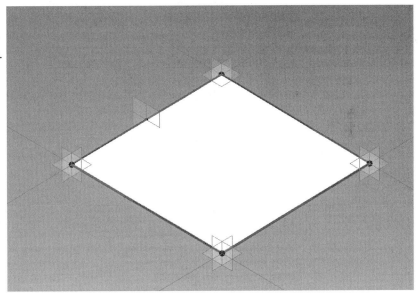

FIGURE 13.62
Draw a circle on
the vertical work
plane of the hosted
point.

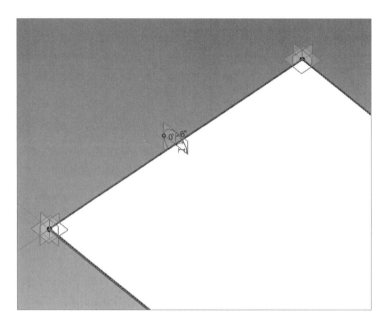

10. Select the circle and the four default reference planes, and then choose Create Form ➤ Solid Form. This will sweep the circle profile along the four reference planes, as shown in Figure 13.63.

When building your curtain panels, consider how you will assign geometry to appropriate subcategories. This will ensure you have full control over the elements from a visual and graphical point of view. For details on assigning geometry to subcategories, refer to Chapter 15.

11. Save the family as **Square-CWPanel.rfa**.

FIGURE 13.63
Creating a form
from a circle and
four reference lines

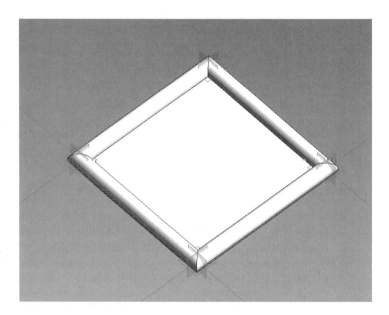

APPLYING COMPONENTS TO A DIVIDED SURFACE

Now that you have created a pattern-based curtain panel family, you'll need to load this family into your conceptual mass family and apply it to the divided surface, replacing the graphical pattern with the actual component.

1. Download and open the file c13-Square-CWSystem.rfa from this book's companion web page at www.sybex.com/go/masteringrevit2011.

2. Load the family file Square-CWPanel.rfa you created in the previous exercise into this file by clicking Load Family on the Insert tab of the ribbon, or switch to that file and click the Load Into Projects button.

3. In the conceptual mass file, select the pattern and divided surface. In the Properties Palette, click the Type Selector and scroll down the list until you find the name of your pattern-based curtain panel family. Note that your new panel family will be listed under the pattern within which it was designed. The component will now be applied to the patterned surface, as shown in Figure 13.64. Note that the more complex the surface and component, the longer it will take to load.

FIGURE 13.64
The pattern-based curtain panel component is applied to a surface in a conceptual mass family.

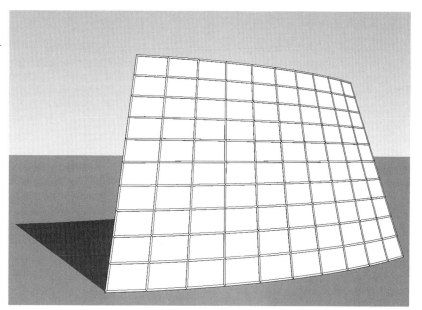

CREATING A PYRAMID CURTAIN WALL PATTERN-BASED FAMILY

Now that you have mastered the technique of constructing a simple planar curtain panel, let's take a look at how to create a pyramid type panel. You will add a type parameter to your pyramid curtain panel so that you can vary the apex of the panel.

1. Start a new family using the Curtain Panel Pattern Based.rft family template.

2. Place a reference point, ensuring it snaps to the middle of one of the reference lines included within the template. Place another reference point on the opposite reference line to the one you previously placed, as shown in Figure 13.65.

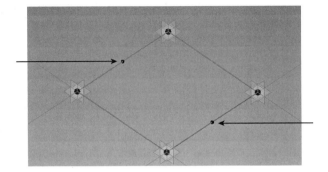

3. From the Home tab in the ribbon, click the Reference tool and ensure 3D Snapping is activated in the Options Bar. Draw a reference line between the two newly placed hosted reference points, as shown in Figure 13.66.

FIGURE 13.66
A reference line is drawn between two hosted points.

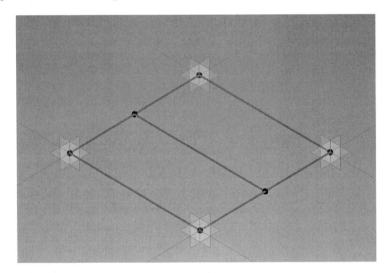

4. Place another reference point, so that it becomes hosted, at the midpoint of the previously created reference line (Figure 13.67). Select this reference point and from the Properties Palette make sure that Show Reference Planes is set to Always.

5. From the Home tab, choose the Set Work Plane tool and select the work plane of the hosted point at the middle of the previously drawn line. Activate the Reference Line tool and uncheck the 3D Snapping option. Draw a reference line vertically in the Z plane from the hosted point. Ensure that the start point of the reference line is locked to the hosted point. You may need to drag the end of reference line, nearest to the point, in the Z direction, before dragging it back to the hosted pointed. This will ensure the lock symbol will appear.

6. Select the vertical reference line to display the temporary dimension and turn this into a permanent dimension by clicking the dimension icon.

FIGURE 13.67
Place a hosted point at the midpoint of the reference line.

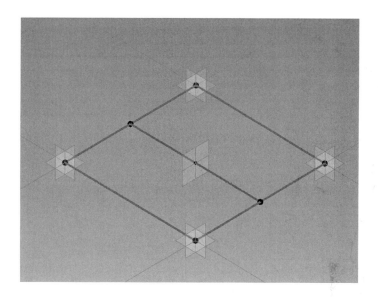

7. Select this dimension and then choose <Add New Parameter...> from the Label pull-down in the Options Bar. Assigning this dimension to a parameter will allow us to alter the apex of the pyramid panel as needed. In the Parameter Properties dialog box, name the parameter **Apex_Height**. Click OK to close all open dialog boxes.

8. Add a series of reference lines using the 3D Snapping option from the apex to the four points on the base of the pyramid, as shown in Figure 13.68.

FIGURE 13.68
Reference lines are created from the corners to the apex.

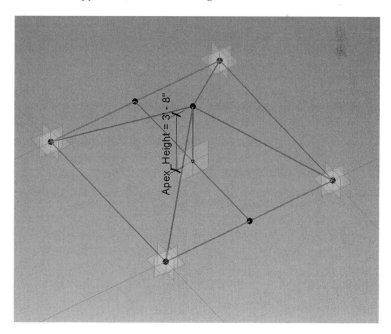

9. You will now create faces on each slope to complete the pyramid shape. To do this, select one reference line from the base and two reference lines on the sloping edges (use the Ctrl key to add lines to your selection) and click the Create Form button. Select the planar triangular face rather than the extrusion (Figure 13.69).

FIGURE 13.69
Select three reference planes, then use Create Form to generate each face of the pyramid.

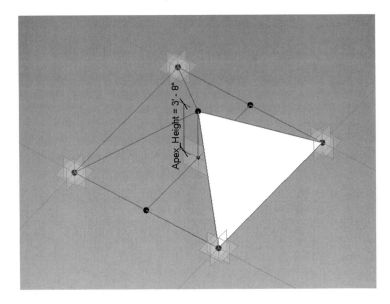

10. Repeat step 9 for the three remaining faces until you have a completed pyramid, as shown in Figure 13.70.

FIGURE 13.70
All four sides of the pyramid have been created.

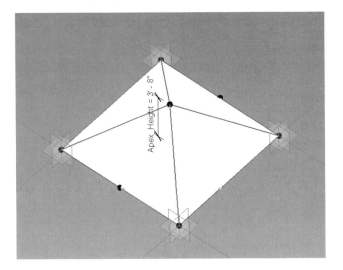

11. It is important that we flex the pyramid to check that you can control the height of the apex. Open the Type Properties dialog box and you will see the parameter named Apex_Height. Change the value a few times and click Apply after each change. The pyramid panel should change in height. Save your file as **Pyramid-Panel.rfa**.

12. Open the file c13-Pyramid-Project.rfa from this book's companion web page at www.sybex.com/go/masteringrevit2011. Load your Pyramid-Panel.rfa family into the c13-Pyramid-Project.rfa. Select the surface, go to the Type Selector, and choose Pyramid-Panel. Your pyramid shape curtain panel will now be populated across the divided surface, as shown in Figure 13.71.

FIGURE 13.71
The pyramid panel is populated across the entire surface.

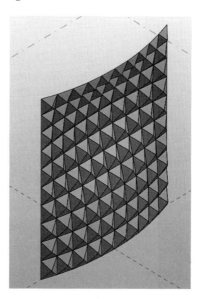

Creating Custom Patterns

Although Revit Architecture includes a variety of patterns you can use for conceptual curtain walls, at present there is no way to create your own pattern-based curtain panel template. The current patterns shipped with Revit Architecture are hardwired so there is no way to modify these either; however, with a bit of creative thinking you can utilize the provided templates to construct panels that will conform to a custom pattern concept. When you consider building a custom panel, it is important to take into account how it will repeat vertically and horizontally. You will need to break it down into to its smallest module. If you think about a repeating architectural pattern such as a masonry wall, its individual component can be broken down into the brick that forms that pattern, which is in essence a rectangle. An example of a hexagon-shaped panel, constructed within a rectangular pattern, is shown in Figure 13.72.

FIGURE 13.72
A hexagonal panel
is constructed
within a standard
rectangular
pattern.

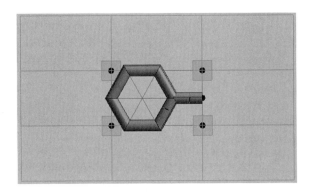

Once you have decided on the design for your panel, look at how the panel could be modularized. To do this, consider laying out the pattern utilizing graph paper. This will certainly help you better understand the layout before attempting to construct the panel using an appropriate template. In Figure 13.73, you will see the hexagonal panel applied across a divided surface.

FIGURE 13.73
The hexagonal
panel applied
across a divided
surface

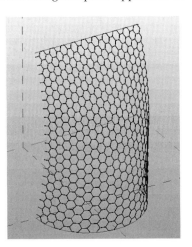

Limiting the Size of Pattern-Based Families

When designing complex curtain wall systems, the goal is to limit the variety of panels. The more variety you have, the higher the cost because you have to create a greater number of unique panels. When you divide a surface in Revit 2011, the panel sizes can vary quite dramatically. While Revit does not actually offer the ability to limit panel sizes, you can start to reduce the size and variety of panels by nesting curtain panels inside other panels. In the following exercise, you will learn how to nest panels to limit size variation.

1. Start by creating a simple pattern-based curtain panel family (use either `Curtain Panel Pattern Based.rft` or `M_Curtain Panel Pattern Based.rft`). Make sure the grid is set to the Rectangular type.

2. Select the four reference lines and use the Create Form tool to generate a planar surface.

3. Similar to the previous exercise, place a hosted point on one of the edges of the surface and then draw a circle with a 6″ [150mm] radius on the point's work plane. Use Create Form to generate a swept profile on two edges to represent a mullion as shown in Figure 13.74. Save this panel as **Limit-Panel-1.rfa**.

FIGURE 13.74
A panel with a swept profile is created to be nested into another panel family.

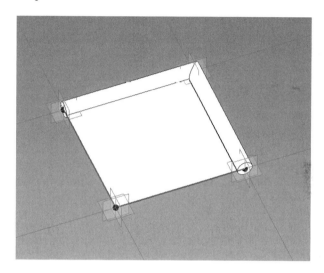

4. Start another new pattern-based curtain panel family, again using the Rectangular grid pattern. Select the four reference planes and use Create Form to generate a planar surface rather than an extrusion.

5. Select the planar surface and click the Divide Surface tool from the ribbon. You will divide this surface and set the UV grid by number, setting U Grid = 2 and V Grid = 2, as shown in Figure 13.75.

6. Load the Limit-Panel-1 family into the divided surface panel.

7. Select the divided surface and apply your panel to the divided surface by choosing Limit-Panel-1 from the Type Selector. This will nest the panel into the subdivisions of the divided surface (Figure 13.76). Save this panel as **Limit-Panel-2.rfa**.

You can now apply this nested panel into any divided surface. Download and open the file c13-Limit-Panel-Project.rfa from this book's companion web page at www.sybex.com/go/masteringrevit2011.

8. In the c13-Limit-Panel-Project.rfa file, select the pattern and divided surface. From the Type Selector, select the name Limit-Panel-2. Note that your new panel family will be listed under the pattern within which it was designed. It will take a few seconds for Revit to replace the pattern with the real geometry of the panel. But observe that by nesting the panel inside other panels you have been able to limit the size and variety of the panels (Figure 13.77).

FIGURE 13.75
Create another pattern-based family and divide the surface into a 2 × 2 grid.

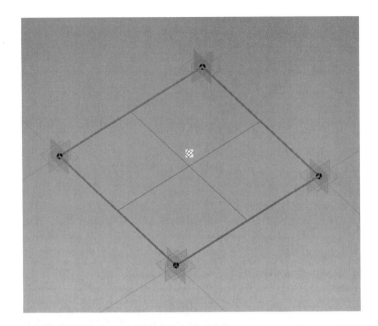

FIGURE 13.76
The simple panel is nested into the divided surface of the host panel.

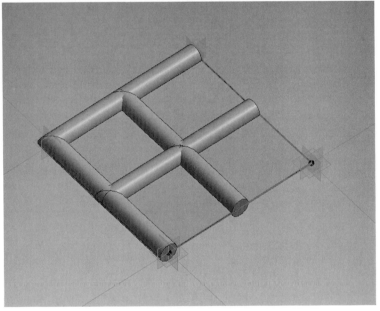

FIGURE 13.77
The host panel
containing the
nested panel is
populated on a
divided surface.

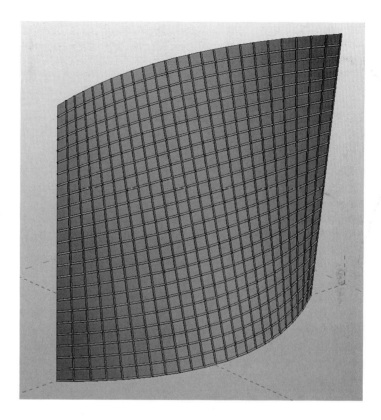

Using the Adaptive Component Family

So far the examples covered look at using the UV grid to nest in curtain wall pattern–based families; however, there will be situations where you may want to manually place a panel, specifically at border conditions where you may need to construct custom panels. In Revit Architecture 2011, you can use the new Adaptive Component functionality that is available to you in the pattern-based curtain panel. This functionality is designed to handle cases where components need to flexibly adapt to many unique related conditions. This new functionality also addresses the problems of creating and placing pattern component panels (triangular, pentagonal, hexagonal, and so on) on nonrectangular and irregularly spaced grids. In the following exercise, you will create an adaptive panel and manually place it along the border of a divided surface.

1. Create a simple pattern-based curtain panel family (Curtain Panel Pattern Based.rft or M_Curtain Panel Pattern Based.rft) and use the rectangular grid pattern. Select each of the four adaptive points and notice that each point has a number from 1 to 4.

2. Select one of the points; then from the Properties Palette change the Show Placement Number parameter to Always.

3. Select all the reference planes in the family and choose Create Form; select the Planar Surface option. Save this panel as **My Adaptive Panel.rfa**.

4. Download and open the file c13-StitchSurface-Project.rfa from this book's companion web page at www.sybex.com/go/masteringrevit2011.

5. Load the panel you previously created into c13-StitchSurface-Project.rfa.

Notice that in c13-StitchSurface-Project.rfa the UV grid has been enabled as well as the nodes at the intersections of the UV grid (Figure 13.78). It will be these nodes that you will use to snap your panel.

FIGURE 13.78
Sample surface with nodes displayed

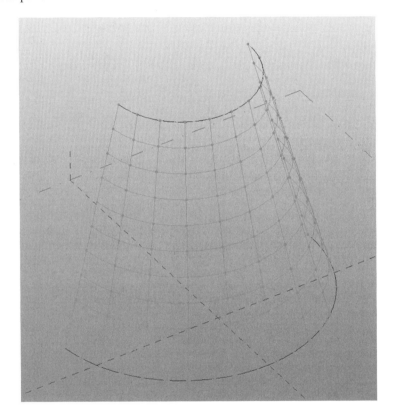

6. Locate the Families category in your Project Browser and expand the Curtain Panel tree. You will find the My Adaptive Panel type in this list. Drag it into the 3D view window.

7. With the panel attached at your mouse pointer, place the pointer onto one of the nodes on the subdivided surface to place the first point. Place the remaining points onto the corresponding nodes, as shown in Figure 13.79. Observe how the panel will adapt based on its placement in the surface division.

FIGURE 13.79
Placing an adaptive panel into a divided surface

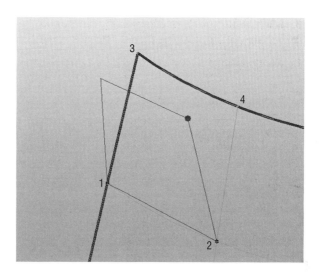

Scheduling Pattern-Based Panels

Now that you have completed the design of your pattern-based curtain wall families, you may want to use Revit's scheduling capabilities to assess the quantity and area of panels in your conceptual curtain wall system. This can be useful for calculating approximate costs at the early stages of design. You can schedule panels that have been applied to an in-place mass directly in the project environment; however, it is not possible to schedule panels in the conceptual design environment. You will first have to load your concept mass into a project, where you will then be able to schedule the panels. In this example, you will open a sample file, load it into a project, and then create a schedule, which will list all the panels that make up your conceptual curtain wall.

1. Download and open the file c13-Square-Panel-Schedule.rfa from this book's companion web page at www.sybex.com/go/masteringrevit2011.

2. Start a new project using either default.rte or MetricDefault.rte; then load the file c13-Square-Panel-Schedule.rfa into your new project.

3. From the Massing & Site tab in the ribbon, click the Place Mass button and select c13-Squre-Panel-Schedule from the Type Selector. Make sure that the Place On Workplane icon is selected in the Placement panel and place the massing component in the Level 1 floor plan.

4. Open the default 3D view to view your model (Figure 13.80).

5. From the View tab in the ribbon, click Schedules and then click Schedules/Quantities. This will open the New Schedule dialog box. Select Curtain Panels from the Category list and click OK.

6. You will now define the fields that will be included within your panel schedule. Choose Family in the left column and click the Add button to add this field to your schedule. Next add Area and then Count.

FIGURE 13.80
A conceptual curtain wall is loaded into a project and placed using Place Mass.

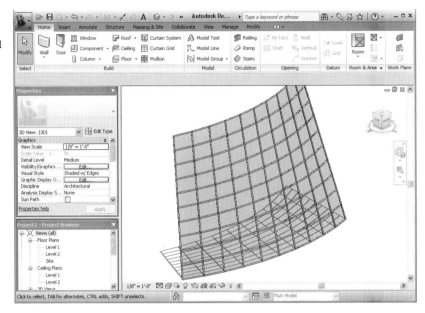

7. Click the Sorting/Grouping tab and check the options for Grand Totals and Itemize Every Instance.

8. Click the Formatting tab and select the Area field. Make sure the Calculate Totals option is selected. Do the same for Count.

9. Click OK and your schedule will be created. If you scroll down to the bottom of the schedule, the total area and the number of custom panels in your conceptual curtain wall will be listed.

A portion of this chapter was written with the help of David Light.

David Light is currently employed as the Revit Specialist for HOK London, focusing on Revit and BIM as well as helping to drive forward the firm's global buildingSMART principles. David was first introduced to Revit at version 4.5 just after the Autodesk acquisition and has had an unhealthy passion for the technology ever since. Before joining HOK, David worked for the UK's Autodesk Premier Solutions Center providing coaching, training and consultancy in Revit Architecture and Revit Structure. David has developed a reputation as one of the leading UK experts in Revit and is a popular speaker and blogger on all things Revit and BIM.

The Bottom Line

Use extended modeling techniques for basic walls.   Walls in Revit are made from layers of materials that can represent generic placeholders for design layouts to complete assemblies representative of actual construction.

Master It   How can you customize the profile of a wall?

Create stacked walls.   Exterior walls are usually composed of several combinations of materials with varying thicknesses. These various wall types can be combined into a single entity called a stacked wall.

Master It   How do you create a stacked wall?

Create simple curtain walls.   A curtain wall is an assembly of parts including curtain grids, panels, and mullions. They can be created in predefined types with regular horizontal and vertical spacing along with specific panel and mullion types.

Master It   How do you add a door to a curtain wall?

Create complex curtain walls.   Revit's conceptual massing environment can be used to create complex curtain wall configurations. Pattern-based panel families can be loaded into the massing environment and populated on a divided surface. These populated surfaces can then be loaded and placed in a project model for documentation and scheduling.

Master It   How do you create a complex divided surface?

Chapter 14

Floors, Ceilings, and Roofs

Floors, ceilings, and roofs, which may seem to be simple or common building components, can sometimes prove to be difficult to model and detail in your project designs. In previous chapters, you read about using conceptual design tools to create masses that help drive building elements. In this chapter, we expand on the development of these sketch-based objects.

In this chapter, you'll learn how to do the following:

- ◆ Understand floor modeling methods
- ◆ Model various floor finishes
- ◆ Create ceilings
- ◆ Understand roof modeling methods
- ◆ Work with advanced shape editing for floors and roofs

Understanding Floor Modeling Methods

Floors are likely to be one of the first sketch-based elements you will encounter in Revit. Many families in the default libraries are floor hosted, so you must first have a floor before placing such components. Consequently, these components will be deleted if the floor that hosts them is deleted. You can find a more detailed discussion on creating families in Chapter 15, but for now let's review the fundamental types of floors that can exist in a Revit project: a floor, a structural floor, a floor by face, and a pad.

Floor

The traditional floor object is a sketch-based element comprised of any number of material layers as defined by the user. The top of the floor object is its reference with respect to the level on which it was created. As such, changes to a floor's structure will affect its depth down and away from the level. You can start modeling floors with generic types, which are similar to generic walls containing a single layer, and then change the generic floors to more specific assemblies later in the development of your project. To do this, simply select one or more floors and choose a different wall type from the Type Selector in the Properties Palette. You can also use the Match Type Properties tool located in the Clipboard panel of the Modify tab of the ribbon.

You can use floors in a variety of ways to meet the needs of a specific phase of design. In early phases, for example, you can create a floor type to represent the combined floor, structure, plenum, and ceiling assemblies of a building. Commonly referred to as the *sandwich*, a sample is shown in Figure 14.1.

FIGURE 14.1
A single floor type
may be used to
show the entire
floor/ceiling
sandwich in early
design.

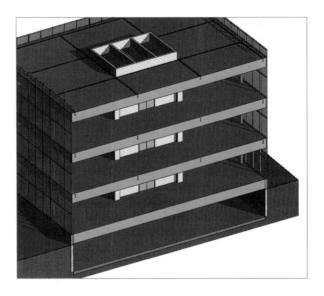

During intermediate phases of design, you can model ceilings so the floor types can include only the floor and a structural layer, as shown in Figure 14.2. Columns may be created, but more precise horizontal structural framing may not be modeled yet. The layer within the floor type represents an assumption of the maximum depth of structural framing.

FIGURE 14.2
This floor assem-
bly includes an
assumption for the
depth of structural
framing.

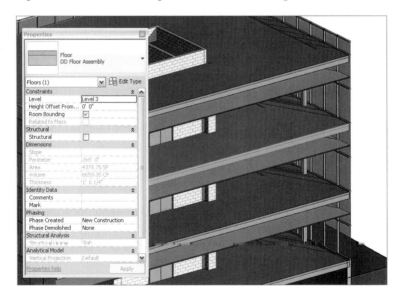

In later phases approaching and including construction, floors should be modeled as close to actual conditions as possible. You should accommodate detailed finish conditions for floors as well as coordination with a resolved structural system. Accurate modeling of these conditions will help support consistent quantity takeoffs and interference detection. Figure 14.3 illustrates an example of a more accurate floor slab.

FIGURE 14.3
Floor assemblies for construction should be accurate and separate from structural framing.

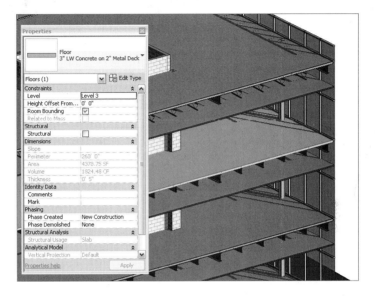

These floor assembly types are offered as suggestions for the sake of increased productivity. As such, they should be used with care, especially when performing quantity takeoffs for estimating. For example, the *area* of floor will be the only accurate value to be extracted from a floor sandwich model in early design, not a volumetric material takeoff. For more information on the use of models by others, we recommend referring to the AIA document E202 BIM Protocol Exhibit, which lists authorized uses of a model at various levels of development. You can download a sample of this document for free from www.aiacontractdocuments.org/bim.

 Real World Scenario

COLLABORATION AND THE OWNERSHIP OF FLOORS

Whether or not you are working under an integrated project delivery (IPD) contract, the so-called ownership of floors should be carefully considered for the collaboration process between an architect and a structural engineer. Floors can be one of the most contentious elements of a building design because they can be simultaneously construed as architecture and structure.

The model element author (MEA) for floors should be discussed and clearly defined for each phase in your project BIM execution plan. Remember that element ownership can pass between the architect and the structural engineer when it is appropriate for a given phase. For example, the architect may choose to be the MEA for floors in schematic design, but pass ownership to the structural engineer in design development and construction documentation.

Structural Floor

The structural floor is new to Revit Architecture 2011and is similar to a traditional floor but has structural functionality such as the ability to indicate span direction and to contain structural profiles. For example, you can specify a composite metal deck profile, which will display in sections and details generated within your project.

If you are working with a project file that has been upgraded from a previous version of Revit, the only way to create a new structural floor is to create a new one by going to the Home tab, locating the Build panel, and choosing Floor ➤ Structural Floor. This will create a floor with the instance property called Structural (Figure 14.4). Note that because the Structural parameter is an instance property, any floor type can become a structural floor.

FIGURE 14.4
Structural parameter in a floor's instance properties

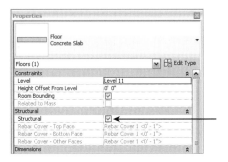

Once the Structural parameter check box has been selected for a floor, you can edit its type properties to add a structural decking layer. Let's create a new structural floor so you can explore how this is done:

1. Open the file c14-Floors.rvt from the book's companion web page (www.sybex.com/go/masteringrevit2011), and activate the Level 3 floor plan.

2. Go to the Home tab in the ribbon, and from the Build panel, select Floor ➤ Structural Floor.

3. In the Draw panel of the Modify | Create Floor Boundary ribbon, make sure your options are set to Boundary Lines with the Pick Walls tool as shown in Figure 14.5.

FIGURE 14.5
Use Pick Walls mode to draw boundary lines.

4. In the Options Bar, specify an offset of 0′-3″. This setting will place the floor boundary just within the inner face of the curtain wall mullions because the location line of the curtain wall is at the center of the mullions that are 5″ deep.

5. Begin picking the exterior curtain walls by selecting one of the north-south-oriented walls first. Note that the first wall you pick will determine the span direction of the structural floor. You can change this at any time by picking the Span Direction tool from

the Draw panel and then selecting one of the boundary lines in the floor sketch. Pick the remaining exterior walls to complete the floor boundary.

Properties

6. Once you have finished defining the boundary lines of the floor, open the Properties Palette by pressing Ctrl+1, typing **PP**, or clicking the Properties icon at the left end of the ribbon.

7. Click Edit Type in the Properties Palette. Select Generic 12″ as the active type and click Duplicate. Name the new type **Structural Slab**.

8. In the Edit Type dialog box, click the Edit button in the Structure row to open the Edit Assembly dialog box.

9. In the Edit Assembly dialog box, find the layer of the assembly that represented the generic floor you duplicated. This should be row 2. Change the material of this layer to Concrete – Cast-in-Place Concrete and change the thickness to 0′-6″.

10. Select row 3 and click the Insert button. There should now be four layers. Select the new row 3 and set its function to Structural Deck [1]. Note the new Structural DeckProperties that appear below the Layers as shown in Figure 14.6.

FIGURE 14.6
Setting a layer's function to Structural Deck exposes additional options.

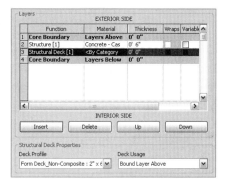

11. The value for Deck Profile should default to Form Deck_Non-Composite: 2″ x 6″, but this depends on having a structural deck profile loaded into your project.

If you don't have a structural deck profile loaded, finish the floor, go to the Insert tab of the ribbon, and select Load From Library. In your default Autodesk content library, find the Profiles folder and open the Structural subfolder. Pick an appropriate deck profile and click Open to load it. Select the Structural Slab floor and click Edit Type in the Properties Palette to continue the exercise.

12. Activate Wall Section 1, and you should see the completed slab at Level 3. Notice that you do not see the details of the structural decking when Detail Level is set to Coarse. If you activate the callout at Level 3 (Detail At Level 3), you will see the structural decking because the callout's Detail Level is set to Medium. This difference is illustrated in Figure 14.7.

FIGURE 14.7
Structural floor
as represented in
Coarse detail level
(left) and Medium
detail level (right)

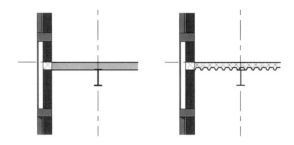

Floor By Face

This floor modeling method is used when you have generated an in-place mass or loaded a mass family. After you assign mass floors to a mass, you can use the floor by face method to assign and manage updates to floors, as shown in Figure 14.8. This type of floor modeling is discussed in greater detail in Chapter 9.

FIGURE 14.8
The Floor By Face
tool can be used
to manage slabs
in more complex
building designs.

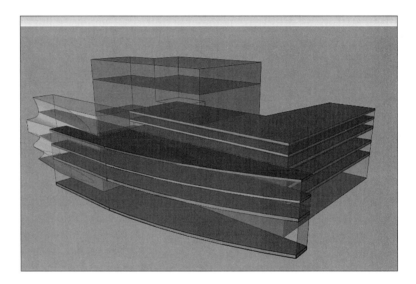

Pad

A pad is technically not a floor but has similar properties to a floor. What differentiates a pad is its ability to cut into a toposurface and define the lowest limits of a building's basement or cellar. If desired, the pad can be configured to represent a slab on grade, as shown in Figure 14.9.

FIGURE 14.9
A pad can be configured as a slab on grade for a basement.

FIGURE 14.9
A pad can be configured as a slab on grade for a basement.

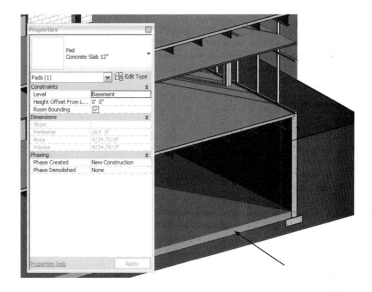

Slab Edge

Slab Edge is a tool that allows you to create thickened portions of slabs typically located at the boundaries of floors. A slab edge type is composed of a profile family and a material assignment. It is important that the material assignment of the slab edge match that of the floor to which you will apply the slab edge in order to ensure proper joining of geometry. Let's explore the application of a slab edge to a floor at grade:

1. Open the file c14-Design-Floor.rvt from the book's companion web page (www.sybex .com/go/masteringrevit2011) and activate the 3D view named Floors Only.

2. Click the Home tab in the ribbon and select Floor ➤ Slab Edge from the Build panel. Note that this tool is also available from the Structure tab.

3. If necessary, orbit the 3D view so that you can see the bottom of the lowest floor slab. Pick all four bottom edges of the floor slab at the level named Ground.

4. Activate the view Section 1, and you will see the slab edge applied to and joined with the floor, as shown in Figure 14.10. Remember that the material in the slab edge type must match the material in the floor type properties for the geometry to join properly.

FIGURE 14.10
Thickened slab edge applied to the bottom of a floor

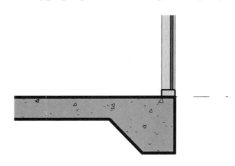

Creating a Custom Floor Edge

You can apply a great deal of flexibility to a floor assembly in early design. As we described earlier, you can create a floor for early design phases that accommodates the floor, structure, plenum, and ceiling in a single floor type. You can also apply a customized edge to this type of assembly for more creative soffit conditions at exterior walls, as shown in Figure 14.11.

FIGURE 14.11
Customized edge applied to a floor assembly in early design

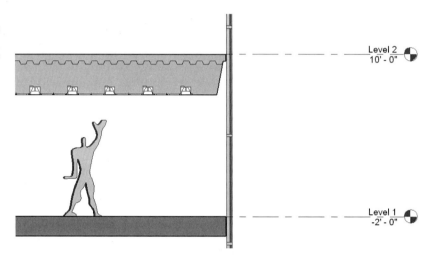

Level 2
10' - 0"

Level 1
-2' - 0"

Let's run through a short exercise so you can practice this skill:

1. Open the file c14-Design-Floor.rvt from the book's companion web page (www.sybex.com/go/masteringrevit2011) and activate the view Section 1.

2. Select the floor at Level 1 and open the Properties dialog box. Change the type to Design Floor Sandwich.

3. Begin a new in-place component by going to the Home tab and selecting Component ➢ Model In-Place from the Build panel.

4. Set the Family Category to Floors and specify the Name as **Floor Edge-L1**.

   Notice that you are now in family editing mode, and the ribbon will have different tabs and panels.

5. Click the Home tab and select Void Forms ➢ Void Sweep from the Forms panel.

6. Click the Pick Path tool from the Sweep panel and choose all four top edges at the perimeter of the floor at Level 1. You can activate the 3D view Floors Only to complete the picking of all four edges, as shown in Figure 14.12.

FIGURE 14.12
Pick edges of the
void sweep in a
3D view.

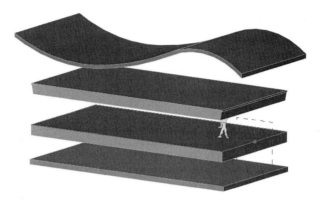

7. Click the Finish Edit Mode icon in the Mode panel when all four edges of the floor have been picked.

8. Open the Properties dialog box if it isn't already visible.

   Note that you might need to reactivate the Select Profile mode if the Properties dialog box only lists Family: Floors. To do this, click the Modify | Sweep tab in the ribbon and click Select Profile in the Sweep panel.

9. In the Profile parameter, select SD Sandwich Edge : 36″ w 6″ Slab from the drop-down list, as shown in Figure 14.13.

FIGURE 14.13
Select a loaded
profile family for
the void sweep.

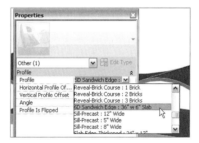

Note that the SD Sandwich Edge profile has been preloaded for the convenience of this exercise. If you would like to explore how this profile was created, expand the Families tree in the Project Browser and find Profiles ➤ SD Sandwich Edge. Right-click it and choose Edit from the context menu.

10. You may need to adjust the orientation of the profile so that it faces in toward the floor, as shown in Figure 14.14. To do so, make sure the profile is selected and click the Flip button in the Options Bar.

FIGURE 14.14
Make sure the sweep profile is facing toward the floor.

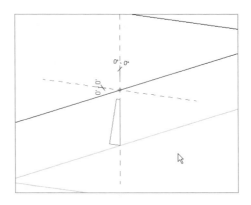

11. Go to the Modify | Sweep tab in the ribbon and click the Finish Edit Mode icon from the Mode panel.

12. Go to the Modify tab in the ribbon and select Cut ➤ Cut Geometry in the Geometry panel. Pick the void sweep, and then the floor at Level 1.

13. Click Finish Model in the In-Place Editor panel at the right end of the ribbon.

Activate the Section 1 view, and you should see that the floor sandwich assembly at Level 1 has been customized in a similar way to the floor at Level 2 (Figure 14.15). You can experiment with adding embellishing detail components as shown in the section.

FIGURE 14.15
The edge of the floor sandwich assembly for Level 1 has been customized.

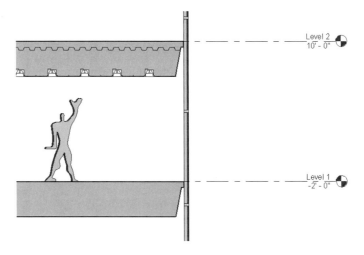

Sketching for Floors, Ceilings, and Roofs

Because floors, ceilings, and roofs are sketch-based objects, the method you use when creating the boundary lines is critical to the behavior of the element to those around it. The recommended method is to use the Pick Walls option, as shown previously in Figure 14.15.

Project Gallery

This gallery is a collection of some of the work being produced by architects and designers in the trenches using Revit. The work shown here is all real work for real clients, and the firms represent the full gamut of how they use Revit as a tool. Some firms are using it strictly for documentation and visualization, whereas others are pushing to sustainability or construction. Firm sizes also range from large firms of a few hundred architects to firms like Davison Architecture, which is a shop of merely four people. Regardless of the size of your office or your IT department, you can produce some truly elegant work using BIM.

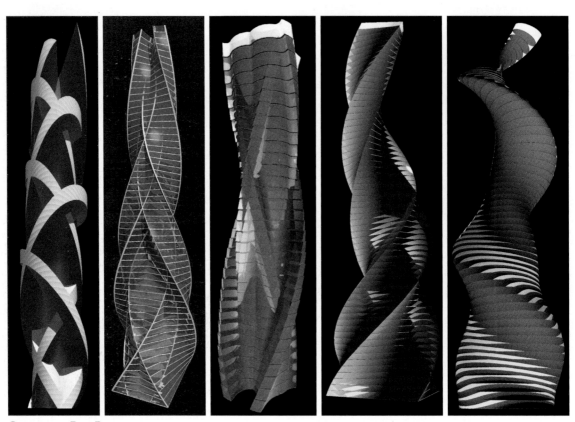

Parametric massing forms derived using formulaic geometric shapes.

HNTB Architecture

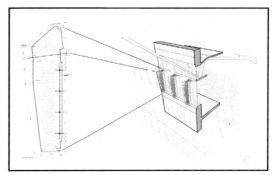

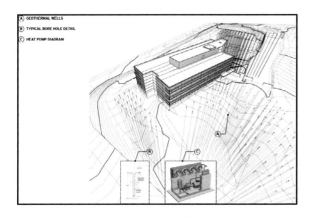

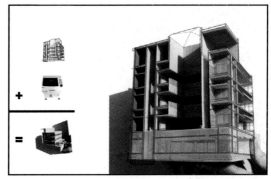

This tenant building was recently completed and occupied. The client requested LEED silver design, with the architecture, structure, and MEP work done using Revit. The Revit model was additionally used for energy and daylighting analysis.

HOK

The Salvador Dali Museum is the most visited museum in the Southeast United States because of its extensive collection of the work of the artist. A new structure is being designed to exhibit and protect the priceless collection.

The new museum will be on three floors, fronting a beautiful site in the St. Petersburg waterfront. It will include the permanent collection, a temporary exhibit space, curatorial and administration offices, a grand public entrance, the museum shop, art vaults, and library.

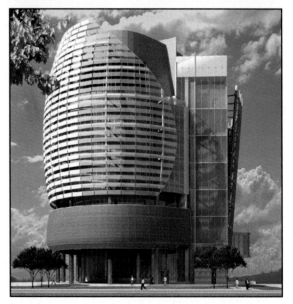

The Samsung Research and Development Facility is a multi-disciplined high-technology building located within the Samsung Global Engineering Center campus, also designed by HOK. The architectural solution is conceived around the idea that a seed and its progression through the germination process are analogous to the conception and maturation of ideas.

The building's skin is designed as a series of enclosing shells acting as shading and diffusing devices for sun and wind. These enclosure structures enhance utilization of natural daylight, as well as reduce the building's dependency on electromechanical systems by shading external summer heat sources and shield the building from cold winter wind.

King Abdullah University of Science and Technology (KAUST) is Saudi Arabia's first LEED certified project and the world's largest LEED-NC Platinum project. HOK designed the 6.5 million square foot campus on a highly visible 9,000 acre site along the Red Sea, 50 miles north of Jeddah.

This project has been selected as one of the 2010 "Top Ten Green Projects" by the American Institute of Architects (AIA) Committee on the Environment (COTE). The annual awards program honors sustainable projects resulting from an integrated approach to architecture, natural systems, and technology.

IMAGES IN THIS SECTION COURTESY OF HOK. SOURCE: hok.com

Bohlin
Cywinski
Jackson

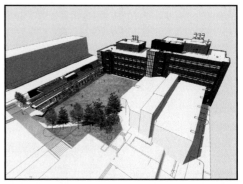

Lehigh University's STEPS Building.
(STEPS stands for Science Technology
Environment Policy Society.)

Bohlin Cywinski Jackson

Architecture Planning Interior Design

Wilkes-Barre / Pittsburgh / Philadelphia / Seattle / San Francisco

Davison
Architecture

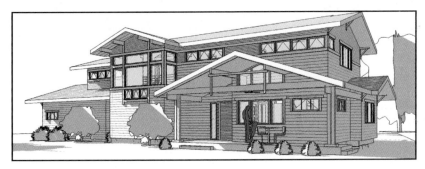

(Above) Timber Creek Hearth House, a contemplative retreat set in the woods of Missouri. The construction documents, renderings, and walkthrough were completed in Revit. (Below) Single-family residence completed in Prairie Village, Kansas.

DAVISON ARCHITECTURE
+ URBAN DESIGN LLC

Lake | Flato Architects

Camana Bay Project, Cayman Islands. Commercial mixed-use office and retail. The entire project was done in Revit (Arch, MEP, Structural). New construction: two wings and parking garage.

Pool pavilion for custom residence, Beaumont, Texas. Multibuilding residential compound. The architecture was done in Revit. New construction.

Ellerbe Becket,
an AECOM Company

For the Cheney Stadium design–build competition, we needed a versatile tool that could quickly express our ideas in real-world terms. Revit was able to organize concepts with its massing tool, easily translate masses into measurable building components, then quickly provide data to confirm program requirements and complete budget analyses. Collaborating with both the design and construction teams using Revit, design decisions were made with confidence, resulting in a compelling entry to the competition.

ELLERBE BECKET

RTKL Associates

(Above) This project is part of an ongoing, 1.6 million–square-foot campus for the consolidated headquarters of the Food and Drug Administration. The present phase accommodates 2,100 of the 9,000 employees who will occupy the site in 2012. (Below) This phase includes an atrium space between wings of the building that relates to a similar space across a central courtyard. All the design, documentation, and rendering were completed in Revit by the design team as part of the ongoing study and presentation process.

(Above) RTKL created a north-facing sawtooth skylight to cost-effectively direct daylight into the atrium and the surrounding spaces without glare or direct solar radiation. They used Ecotect to analyze the design and Revit to render the experience. (Below) With each successive phase of the design of the campus, RTKL has furthered their use of BIM technology to advance sustainability solutions and the process of collaborative design.

RTKL

SOM

Medical Facility, New Hyde Park, New York. The 300,000 sq. foot hospital consolidates women's services and birthing care while creating a new centerpiece and focal point to revitalize a fragmented 48-acre medical campus. Program requirements are organized to provide clear circulation using the convex building shape for exterior views and family spaces are located at the sunny ends of the building.

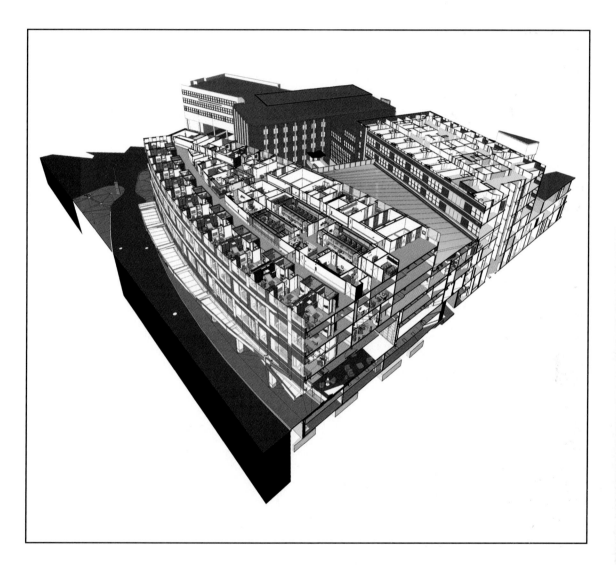

The level of detail and project organization required 12 separate architectural models. Linked with the MEP, FP, and Structural models, SOM provided a complete BIM project coordinated with all major disciplines.

Tower Project, Manila, Philippines. This multiuse tower responds to its site's street edge by expanding on its north side and contracting on its south, resulting in a "fan" shaped building plan. A pattern of ceramic frit applied to the exterior curtain wall panels lends reference to local organic motifs, reinforces the vertical proportions of the tower, and serves to supplement the shading capability of the glass.

The project was completed entirely in Revit, from the design phase through the production drawings. All renderings were also generated from Revit, making extensive use of Materials for design flexibility.

By selecting the walls to generate the sketch for the roof, you are creating an intelligent relationship between the walls and the roof. If the design of your building later changes and the wall position is modified, the roof will follow that change and adjust to the new wall position without any intervention from you (Figure 14.16).

FIGURE 14.16
Using the Pick method:
(A) original roof;
(B) the entrance wall position has changed, and the roof updates automatically;
(C) the angle of the wall to the right of the entrance has changed, and the roof changes to a new shape.

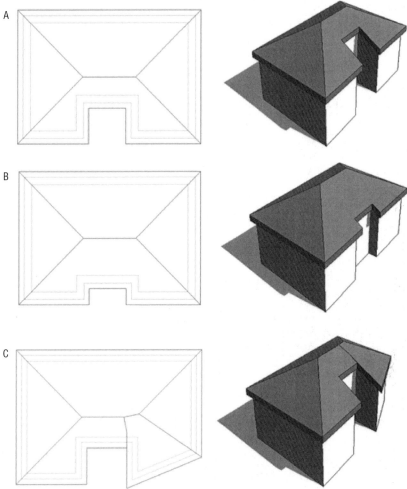

Also notice in Figure 14.16 that the illustrated roof was generated with overhangs beyond the exterior faces of the walls. You can specify an overhang or offset value for a floor, ceiling, or roof in the Options Bar *before* picking walls to define the sketch.

If your building design is using curtain walls, be careful with the location lines of these walls. The location line of a curtain wall is defined relative to the offsets specified in the mullion and panel families that comprise the curtain wall type. As discussed in Chapter 13, you have many options when defining the relative location line of your curtain wall types. Refer to the exercise in the "Structural Floor" section earlier in this chapter for an example of picking curtain walls with an offset based on a centered location line.

Modeling Floor Finishes

You can apply floor finishes in a variety of ways. Most methods are based on the thickness of the finish material. For example, a thin finish such as carpet might be applied with the Split Face and Paint tools, whereas a thicker finish such as mortar-set stone tile might be a separate floor type.

Split Face for Thin Finishes

One of the easiest ways to divide a floor surface for thin finishes is using the Split Face and Paint tools. This method will require a floor to be modeled and an appropriate material defined with at least a surface pattern. Note that you can only schedule finishes applied with the Paint tool through Material Takeoff schedules. Let's explore this method with a quick exercise.

1. Open the file `c14-Design-Floor.rvt` from the book's companion web page (`www.sybex.com/go/masteringrevit2011`) and activate the Level 1 floor plan. You will see an area of the floor that is bounded by a wall and two reference planes.

2. Click the Modify tab in the ribbon, activate the Split Face tool from the Geometry panel, and pick the floor in the Level 1 floor plan.

3. Draw a rectangle in front of the three interior walls, as shown in Figure 14.17.

FIGURE 14.17
Sketch a rectangular boundary with the Split Face tool.

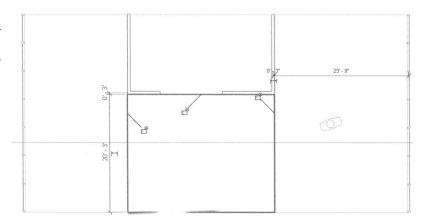

Note that you can constrain—or lock—the sketch lines to the interior walls, reference planes, and floor edge. You may do so in this exercise, but constraints should be used sparingly in larger projects to avoid slower model performance and updating calculation time.

Also note that you generated a complete rectangular sketch instead of only three bounding lines. You do not need to draw the boundary line at the edge of the floor; however, if you don't include that line and the floor shape is modified in the future, the split face may be deleted because it is no longer a closed-loop sketch.

4. Click the Finish Edit Mode icon in the Mode panel.

5. Return to the Modify tab in the ribbon and activate the Paint tool in the Geometry panel.

6. At the right end of the ribbon, choose Carpet Tile from the Material drop-down list.

7. In the Level 1 floor plan, click near the edge of the split face you created earlier to assign the material. The result should look like the sample shown in Figure 14.18.

FIGURE 14.18
Completed application of carpet tile material to a split face on a floor

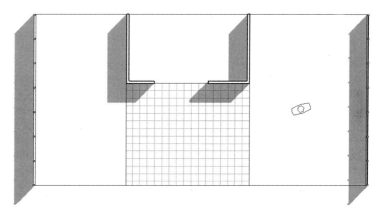

Modeling Thick Finishes

Thicker finish materials such as tile, stone pavers, or terrazzo can be applied as unique floor types and modeled where required. For large areas of finish such as a public atrium or airport terminal, you can simply assign these materials within the layers of a floor assembly. When you need to add smaller areas of thick floor finishes, there are two scenarios you may encounter: with a depressed floor and without.

In areas such as bathrooms, a thick-set tile floor may require the structural slab to be depressed in order to accommodate the thickness of the finish material. In the example illustrated in Figure 14.19, the main floor object has been cut with an opening at the inside face of the walls. Another floor has been modeled with a negative offset value to accommodate the thickness of the tile material, and the tile has been placed as a unique floor element.

If you don't need a finish but just a slab depression, you can create it with an in-place void extrusion. Simply click the Home tab on the ribbon and click Component ➤ Model In-Place. Choose the Floors category and create a void extrusion where you need a slab depression. Remember to use the Cut Geometry tool to cut the void from the floor before finishing the family. As an alternative, you can create a floor-based generic family that contains a parametric void extrusion. You can download the file c14-Slab-Depression.rfa as an example of this type of family from the book's companion web page: www.sybex.com/go/masteringrevit2011.

FIGURE 14.19
The thick tile fin-
ish and depressed
slab are modeled as
separate elements.

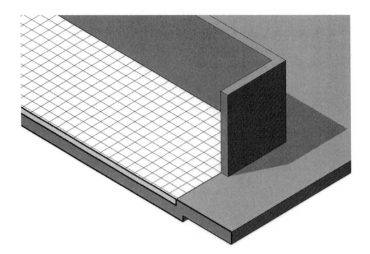

Finally, if the structural requirements allow a thick finish to be applied to a floor without dropping the structural slab, a finish floor element can be modeled directly in place within the structural slab. As shown in Figure 14.20, the tile floor has been graphically embedded in the structural floor using the Join Geometry tool. To do this, click the Modify tab on the ribbon and click Join Geometry. Make sure to pick the finish floor *before* the structural floor or you will get an error.

FIGURE 14.20
The thick tile fin-
ish floor has been
joined with the
structural floor.

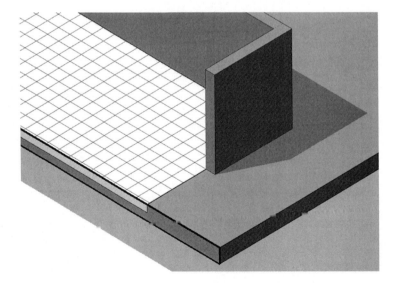

Creating Ceilings

Ceilings are system families composed of sketch-based elements that also serve as hosts for components such as light fixtures. Like other host elements such as floors and roofs, if a ceiling is deleted, hosted elements on that ceiling are also deleted. Ceilings in Revit are classified as either a Basic Ceiling or a Compound Ceiling. The Basic Ceiling family does not have a layered assembly and is represented in section as a single line; however, it does have a material parameter that can display surface patterns in reflected ceiling plans and 3D views. The Compound Ceiling family allows you to define a layered assembly of materials that are visible when displayed in a section view. As with floors, you can change ceiling types by selecting a ceiling in your project and choosing another type from the Type Selector in the Properties Palette or with the Match Type Properties tool.

Both the Basic Ceiling and Compound Ceiling types can serve as a host to hosted family components. Ceilings also serve as bounding elements for the volumetric calculation of rooms. This is critical when using environmental analysis programs such as Green Building Studio or Autodesk Ecotect Analysis. For more information about analysis for sustainable design, see Chapter 10, "Conceptual Design and Sustainability."

You can create a ceiling in one of two ways: automatically or by sketching a boundary. When you select the ceiling tool from the Home tab of the ribbon, you can switch between the Automatic Ceiling and Sketch Ceiling modes at the right end of the ribbon.

In Automatic Ceiling mode, Revit will try to determine the boundaries of a ceiling sketch when you place your cursor inside an enclosed space. If an enclosed space cannot be determined, your cursor will still indicate a circle/slash and you must switch to Sketch Ceiling mode. In this mode, you can use the Pick Walls method as discussed earlier in this chapter to create intelligent relationships with the bounding walls of the ceiling.

Ceilings are best modeled in ceiling plans even though they can be created in a floor plan. When you place a ceiling, its elevation will be based on the level of the current plan with an offset from that level. With the Properties dialog box open, the Height Offset From Level value can be modified as you create ceilings.

ROOM BOUNDING PERFORMANCE

Floors, ceilings, and roofs all have the ability to be room bounding elements. This parameter can be found in the instance properties of each object. If you are not using volume calculations for rooms or you don't intend to use the model for environmental analysis, you might consider turning off the Room Bounding parameter in horizontal objects. In larger Revit projects, unnecessary applications of the Room Bounding parameter may lead to reduced model performance.

Understanding Roof Modeling Methods

In today's construction environment, roofs come in a great number of shapes and sizes. They can be as simple as a pitched shed roof or can involve complex double-curved surfaces or intersecting vaults. Once you understand the fundamental concepts, tools, and logic pertaining to roofs in Revit, you will be able to design almost any roof shape.

Roofs are similar to floors and ceilings because they are sketch-based elements and can be defined in generic types or with specific material assemblies. You can also change a roof element from one type to another in the same manner as a floor or ceiling. A fundamental difference between floors and roofs is that a roof's thickness is generated *above* its referencing level, not below. You can also easily create slopes in roofs by defining slopes in the roof's sketch lines. In general, roofs in Revit can be constructed in four different ways: by footprint, by extrusion, by face, or modeled in-place. The following sections provide a closer look at these approaches and review their application to real-world scenarios.

Footprint Roofs

Use the roof by footprint method to create any standard roof that more or less follows the shape of the footprint of the building and is a simple combination of roof pitches (Figure 14.21).

FIGURE 14.21
A simple roof created using the roof by footprint method

These roofs are based on a sketched shape that you define in plan view at the soffit level and that can be edited at any time during the development of a project from plan and axon 3D views. The shape can be drawn as a simple loop of lines, using the Line tool, or can be created using the Pick Walls method that also should result in a closed loop of lines.

To guide you through the creation of a roof by footprint and explain some of the main principles and tools, here is a brief exercise demonstrating the steps:

1. In a new project, open a Level 1 plan view and create a building footprint similar to Figure 14.22. Make sure the height of the walls is set to Unconnected: 20'-0" [6000mm].

2. Activate the Level 2 plan; then select the Home tab in the ribbon and click Roof ➢ Roof By Footprint.

3. From the Draw panel in the Modify | Create Roof Footprint tab, select the Pick Walls tool (this should be the default).

FIGURE 14.22
Sample build-
ing outline to be
sketched on Level 1

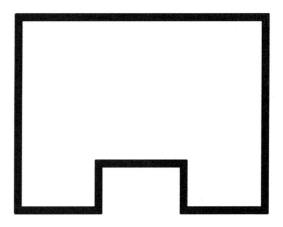

4. When you've chosen to create a roof by footprint, the Options Bar displays the following settings (change the Offset value to 1'-0" [300mm]:

To define whether you want a sloped or flat roof, use the Defines Slope check box in the Options Bar. The Overhang parameter allows you to define the value of the roof overhang beyond the wall. When the Extend Into Wall (To Core) option is checked, the overhang is measured from the wall core. If the option is deselected, the overhang is measured from the exterior face of the wall.

5. After defining these settings, place your cursor over one of the walls (don't click), and using the Tab key, select all connected walls. Your display should look like Figure 14.23.

FIGURE 14.23
Roof sketch lines
are automati-
cally drawn after
Tab-selecting the
bounding walls,
and they are offset
from the walls
by the value of
the overhang as
defined in the
Options Bar.

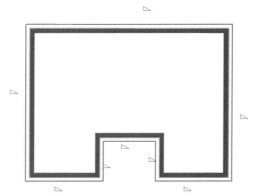

6. Select the two north-south walls within the alcove, open the Properties dialog box, and uncheck the Defines Slope parameter, as shown in Figure 14.24.

FIGURE 14.24
Uncheck the
Defines Slope
parameter for
two of the roof's
boundary lines.

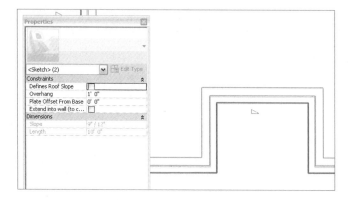

7. Click the Finish Edit Mode icon in the Mode panel of the ribbon. If you are prompted with the question, "Would you like to attach the highlighted walls to the roof?" click the Yes button. Activate a 3D view, and your roof should like the image in Figure 14.21.

If the shape of the roof doesn't correspond to your expectations, you can select the roof and select Edit Footprint from the Mode panel in the Modify | Roofs tab to return to Sketch mode, where you can edit lines, sketch new lines, pick new walls, or the modify the slope.

To change the slope definition or angle of individual portions of the roof while editing a roof's footprint, select the sketch line of the roof portion for which you wish to change the slope and toggle (check) the Defines Slope button in the Options Bar, toggle the Defines Slope parameter in the Properties dialog box, or right-click and choose Toggle Slope Defining. If you mistakenly made all roof sides with slope but wanted to make a flat roof, you can Tab-select all sketch lines that form the roof shape and clear the Defines Slope box in the Options Bar.

Roof slope can be measured in different ways: it can be set as an angle or percentage rise. All slope measuring options can be found in the Manage tab by selecting Project Units in the Project Settings panel and then selecting Slope to open the Format dialog box (see Figure 14.25). If the current slope value is not in units you wish to have (suppose it displays percentage but you want it to display an angle), change the slope units in the Format dialog box—you will not be able to do that while editing the roof slope. Setting it here means specifying the way you measure slopes for the entire project.

FIGURE 14.25
Format dialog box
for slopes

Here are some of the important Instance Properties you should be aware of and need to set properly; all are found in the Properties dialog box shown in Figure 14.26.

FIGURE 14.26
Roof instance
properties

Base Level　As in other Revit elements, this is the level at which the roof is placed. The roof moves with this level if the level changes height.

Room Bounding　When this is checked, the roof geometry has an effect on calculating room area and volume.

Related to Mass　This property is active only if a roof has been created with the roof by face method (Conceptual Mass tools).

Base Offset From Level　This option lowers or elevates the base of the roof relative to the base level.

Cutoff Level　Many roof shapes require a combination of several roofs on top of each other—for this you need to cut off the top of a lower roof to accommodate the creation of the next roof in the sequence. Figure 14.27 shows an excellent example of this technique.

FIGURE 14.27
The cutoff level
applied to the main
roof and a second-
ary roof built on
top of the main
roof using the cut-
off level as a base

Cutoff Offset When the Cutoff tool is applied, the Cutoff Offset value also becomes active and allows you to set the cutoff distance from the level indicated in the Cutoff Level parameter.

Rafter Cut This defines the eave shape. You can select from Plumb Cut, Two Plumb Cut, or Two Plumb Square. When Two Plumb Square is selected, the Fascia Depth parameter is activated, and you can set the value for the depth.

Rafter or Truss With Rafter, the offset of the base is measured from the inside of the wall. If you choose Truss, the plate offset from the base is measured from the outside of the wall. Figure 14.28 illustrates the difference between the rafter and truss settings.

FIGURE 14.28
Rafter setting (left) and truss setting (right) for roofs

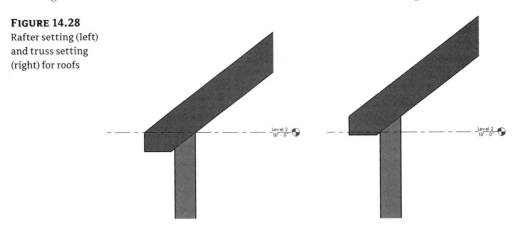

Roof by Extrusion

The roof by extrusion method is best applied for roof shapes that are generated by extrusion of a profile, such as sawtooth roofs, barrel vaults, and waveform roofs. Like the roof by footprint method, it is based on a sketch; however, the sketch that defines the shape of the roof is drawn in elevation or section view (not in plan view) and is then extruded along the plan of the building (see Figure 14.29).

FIGURE 14.29
An extruded spline-shaped roof

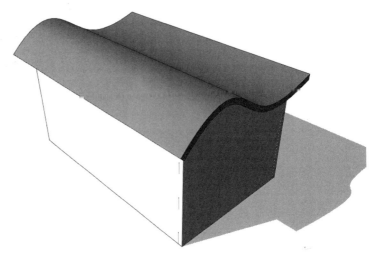

Roofs by extrusion do not have an option to follow the building footprint, but that is often needed to accommodate the requirements of the design. To accomplish this, the Vertical Opening tool can be used to trim the edges of an extruded roof relative to the building outline.

To briefly explain the concept: you create a roof by extrusion by defining a profile in elevation or 3D that is then extruded above the building. The extrusion is usually based on a work plane that is not perpendicular to the building footprint, as illustrated in Figure 14.30. If the shape of the building is nonrectangular in footprint or the shape of the roof you want to create is not to be rectangular, this tool will let you carve geometry from the roof to match the footprint of the building or get any plan shape you need using a plan sketch.

FIGURE 14.30
Extruded roof created at an angle to the building geometry

With sketch-based design, any closed loop of lines creates a positive shape, every loop inside it is negative, the next one inside that negative one will be positive, and so on. In Figure 14.31, a roof by extrusion was drawn at an angle to the underlying walls, but the final roof shape should be limited to a small offset from the walls. To clip the roof to the shape of the building footprint, the Vertical Opening tool was used to draw, in plan view of the roof, a negative shape that will remove the portions of the roof that extend beyond the walls.

FIGURE 14.31
The Vertical Opening tool with two sketch loops trims the roof to the inner loop.

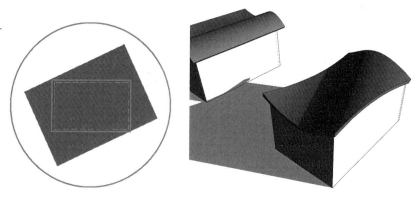

Roof In-Place

The roof in-place technique accommodates roof shapes that cannot be achieved with either of the previously mentioned methods. It is the usual way to model historic roof shapes or challenging roof geometries such as those illustrated in Figure 14.32. The figure shows a barrel roof with half dome (Extrusion + 1/2 Revolve), a dome roof (Revolve only or Revolve + Extrusion), and a traditional Russian onion dome (Revolve only).

FIGURE 14.32
Examples of modeled in-place roofs

To create an in-place roof, select the Home tab in the ribbon and click Component ➢ Model In-Place from the Build panel. Select Roofs from the Family Category list and click OK. While you remain in the In-Place Family editing mode, you can create any roof shape using solids and voids of extrusions, blends, revolves, sweeps, and swept blends (Figure 14.33). More advanced editing techniques are discussed later in this chapter, in the section "Advanced Shape Editing for Floors and Roofs."

FIGURE 14.33
Organic-shaped roof created using the Swept Blend modeling technique

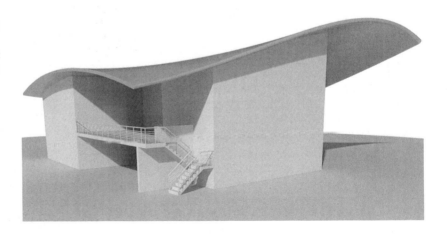

Roof By Face

The Roof By Face tool is to be used when you have created an in-place mass or loaded a mass family. These types of roofs are typically more integrated with the overall building geometry than the examples we've shown for in-place roofs. You can find more detailed information about using the roof by face method in Chapter 9, "Advanced Modeling and Massing."

Sloped Glazing

In Chapter 13, "Walls and Curtain Walls," you learned that a curtain wall is just another wall type made out of panels and mullions organized in a grid system. Similarly, sloped glazing is just another type of a roof that has glass as material and mullions for divisions. Using sloped glazing, you can make roof lights and shed lights and use them to design simple framing structures.

To create sloped glazing, make a simple pitched roof, select it, and use the Properties dialog box to change the type to Sloped Glazing. Once you have done that, activate a 3D view and use the Curtain Grid tool from the Build panel of the Home tab on the ribbon to start applying horizontal or vertical grids that define the panel sizes; then you can apply mullions using the Mullion tool in the Build panel. Figure 14.34 illustrates an example of a standard gable roof that has been converted to sloped glazing.

FIGURE 14.34
Sloped glazing is created by switching a standard roof to the Sloped Glazing type and assigning grids and mullions.

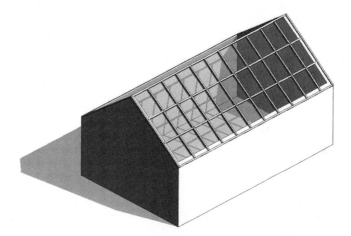

Slope Arrows

If your design calls for a sloped roof with an unusual footprint that does not easily lend itself to utilizing the Defines Slope property of boundary lines, slope arrows can be added within the sketch of the roof. First create the sketch lines to define the shape of a roof, but don't check Defines Slop in the Options Bar. Instead, choose the Slope Arrow tool from the Draw panel. Draw the slope arrow in the direction you want your roof to pitch. Select the arrow and in the Properties dialog box, you can set any of the parameters as shown in Figure 14.35. The Specify parameter can be set to either Height At Tail or Slope. If you choose Height At Tail, be sure to specify the Height Offset At Head parameter as the end result of the desired slope.

FIGURE 14.35
Defining the properties of a Slope Arrow added to an irregular footprint roof sketch

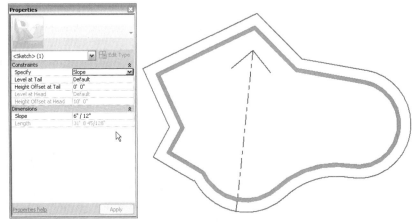

🌐 Real World Scenario

CREATING A DORMER STEP-BY-STEP

Roofs with dormers generally cause grief for architects, so we'll guide you through the creation of one:

1. Create the base of a building, set up three levels, and create a Roof By Footprint with Defines Slope checked for all sides.

2. Approximately in the position indicated below, on Level 2, create the four walls of a dormer. Set their height to a value that makes them extend above the roof. (For easier verification, create a cross-section through the dormer to check the height of the dormer walls and, if necessary, modify their height in the Element Properties so that they extend above the roof.)

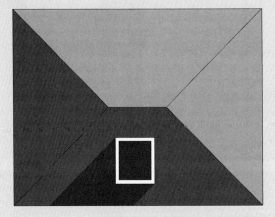

3. Using the Roof By Footprint tool, create a pitched roof on top of the dormer walls.

4. If you switch to a side elevation view, you will notice that the dormer roof probably does not extend to meet the main roof, so you will need to use the Join/Unjoin Roof tool, located in the Modify tab in the Edit Geometry panel, to join the main roof and the dormer. Select the Join/ Unjoin Roof tool, select the main roof as the target, and then select the edge of the dormer roof to extend.

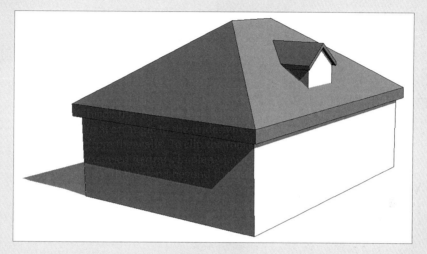

5. From the Opening panel on the Home tab, select Dormer. Now pick first the main roof, then the dormer roof, and then select the sides of the walls that define the dormer. Select the inside faces of the walls. Unlike most sketches, in this case you will not need to provide a closed loop of lines. Finish the dormer opening.

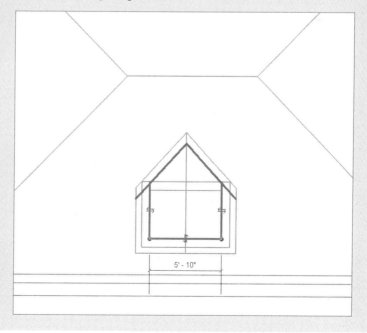

6. The last thing to do is to go back to the section view you previously created and edit the elevation profile of the side walls to make sure they don't extend below or above the roofs. Note that you should *not* use the Top/Base Attach tool; instead, select the wall and use the Edit Profile tool available in the Mode panel of the Modify | Walls tab to edit its elevation profile and manually resketch the edge lines of the walls to get the triangular elevation profile as shown.

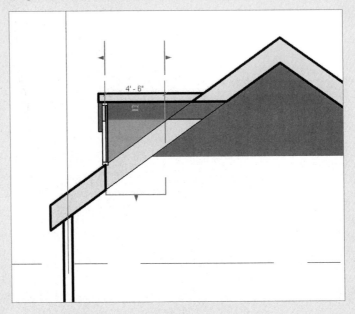

Your dormer opening is now correct. You will see that it has cut the roof in two directions, as a true dormer needs to.

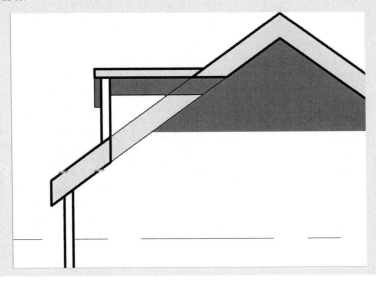

As a final option, you can convert the front wall of the dormer to a storefront wall type or add a window.

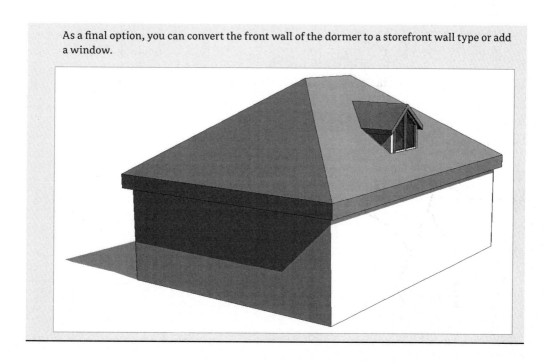

Advanced Shape Editing for Floors and Roofs

No flat roof is ever really flat! Revit is equipped with tools that allow for tapered insulation over a flat roof and similar conditions. A rich set of shape-editing tools for roofs and floors help create and modify such conditions quickly and accurately. These powerful tools are modifiers that are applicable to roofs and floors and will allow you to model concrete slabs with multiple slopes for sidewalks or roof assemblies with tapered insulation (see Figure 14.36).

FIGURE 14.36
Roof with sloped drainage layer

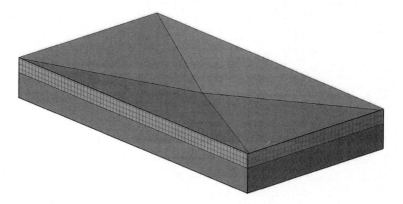

The set of tools available for editing floor and roof shapes appears in the ribbon when a flat floor or roof is selected.

Let's take a look at what each tool is designed to do:

Modify Sub Elements This tool allows you to directly edit element geometry by selecting and modifying points and edges. If you don't create any additional points or split lines before activating this tool, the object's outer edges and corners will be available for editing.

Add Point This tool allows you to add points on the top face of a roof or floor. Points can be added on edges or surfaces and can be modified after placement using the Modify Sub Elements tool.

Add Split Line This tool allows you to sketch directly on the top face of the element, which adds vertices so that hips and valleys can be created when the elevations of the lines are modified using the Modify Sub Elements tool.

Pick Supports This tool allows you to pick linear beams and walls in order to create new split edges and set the slope and/or elevation of the floor or roof automatically.

Once a floor or roof has been modified using any of these tools, the Reset Shape button will become active. When used, this tool will remove all modifications applied to the selected floor or roof.

Creating a Roof with a Sloped Topping

Let's do an exercise that shows you how to make a roof with a sloped topping like the one shown in Figure 14.37 (shown in plan view).

FIGURE 14.37
A roof plan showing a roof divided in segments, with drainage points

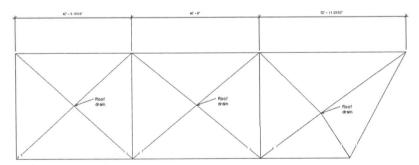

Follow these steps:

1. Open c14-Roof-Edit.rvt from the book's companion web page (www.sybex.com/go/masteringrevit2011).

2. Select the roof that has already been prepared for you.

3. Activate the Add Split Line tool (note that the color of the rest of the model grays out while the roof lines are dashed green).

4. Sketch two ridge lines to divide the roof into three areas that will be independently drained. The ridge lines will be drawn in blue color.

5. Using the same tool, draw diagonal lines within those areas to create the valleys. Make sure you zoom in closely when drawing the diagonal lines, so to be sure that you are snapping in the exact same dividing points. (If you notice that the split lines are not snapped to the correct points, select the Modify Sub Elements tool, pick the incorrect lines, delete them, and try again.)

You have split the roof surface into many regions, but they are still all at the same height and pitch. You should have a roof that looks like Figure 14.38. Press the Esc key or click the Modify button to stop the editing mode.

FIGURE 14.38
Using the Add Split Line tool, you can create ridges and valleys.

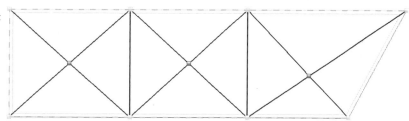

6. Switch to a 3D view.

7. To add a slope, you need to edit the height of the drainage points or the heights of the edges and ridges created by the split lines. For this exercise, you will raise the elevation of the boundary edges and ridges. Activate the Modify Sub Elements tool and select an edge of the roof (dashed green line). New controls that allow you to edit the text will appear, and you can either move the arrows up and down or type in a value for the height. Type in **1′ 0″** (13cm).

8. Repeat steps 1–7 for all boundary edges and the two north-south split lines forming the ridges between the drainage areas.

9. Make a section through the roof—if possible, somewhere through one of the drainage points. Open the section; change the detail level to Fine to see all layers. The entire roof structure is now sloped toward the drainage point.

Applying a Variable Thickness to a Roof Layer

What if you wanted the insulation to be tapered but not the structure? For that, the layers of the roofs can now have variable thickness. Let's see how to apply a variable thickness to a layer of the roof assembly.

1. Select the roof, open the Properties dialog box, and select Edit Type to view the roof's Type Properties. Click Edit in the Structure row to edit the layers of the roof assembly.

2. Activate the preview. You will notice that in the roof-structure preview, you do not see any slopes. That is correct and will not change. This preview is just a schematic preview of the structure and does not show the exact sloping. Look for the Variable column under Layers, as shown in Figure 14.39. This allows layers of the roof to vary in thickness when slopes are present. Check the Variable option for the insulation material.

FIGURE 14.39

Specify variable layers of material in the Edit Assembly dialog box.

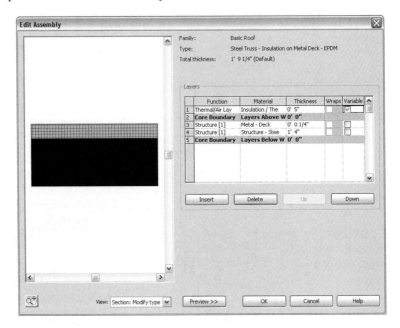

3. Go back to the section view and observe the changes in the roof assembly. As you can see, only the insulation is tapered, while the structure remains flat.

Note that you will only be able to modify an adjustable layer of a floor or roof with a negative value to the next nonadjustable layer of the assembly. In the earlier exercise, for example, if you modified the drainage points by more than –0'-5" (–13cm), an error would be generated, and the edits to the roof would be removed. You must think about the design requirements of your roof or floor assembly when planning how to model adjustable layers. An alternative approach to the previous exercise might have been to increase the thickness of the insulation layer in the roof assembly to that required at the high pitch points. The drainage points could then be lowered relative to the boundary edges and ridge lines.

The Bottom Line

Understand floor modeling methods.   Floors are one of the most fundamental, sketch-based system families used in a Revit model. You can customize them to accommodate a variety of assumptions at various stages of design.

Master It   How can you create a structural floor with integrated metal decking?

Model various floor finishes.   Thick and thin floor finishes can be created in Revit to support tagging, scheduling, and quantity takeoffs.

Master It   How would you represent a thin finish material in your project such as carpet?

Create ceilings.   Ceilings are sketch-based system families that can host objects such as light fixtures and HVAC diffusers.

Master It   What's the best way to model a ceiling within a space?

Understand roof modeling methods.   Roofs can be modeled as simple single-pitch shed roofs or complex extrusions of sinuous curves.

Master It   What is the best way to create a single vault roof?

Work with advanced shape editing for floors and roofs.   A small but powerful toolset is available for extended editing of floor and roof objects. These tools allow you to create warped floor slabs and tapered layers of roof assemblies.

Master It   How do you create a drainage point in a flat roof slab?

Chapter 15

Family Editor

If you're not designing or documenting a building, you're probably designing or placing the stuff that goes inside it: structural members, doors, furniture, lighting, equipment, and more. And if you think about it, this effort is a significant part of the design process. If the surrounding walls, floor, and roof or ceiling contain the space, it might be said that the content describes the function and utility of a space. In other words, content provides context. In many respects, it gives the space meaning. The rhythm of placement, orientation, and elevation of content can turn a mundane space into an elegant and memorable one.

In Revit, the Family Editor is where you'll model all the content that isn't built as part of the project. And if you're familiar with other 3D modeling applications, the good news is that it will be easy to get started. But the *really* great news is that if you've never modeled in 3D, you have nothing to lose.

The key isn't just being able to model; you can model in 3D in lots of applications. The Family Editor offers the ability to make content that will flex appropriately as your design changes; you can iterate your design without starting over. Sometimes you'll need to change the height, width, or length. Other times you'll need to modify the material. And in some cases you'll nest geometry into another family in order to create assembled options on the fly.

Creating content in Revit often involves assigning parameters. At first, parameters might seem new and scary. But parameters are just values that you assign to what you're making so that you can quickly and easily change it, and there's no programming involved. This is so much superior to how you're probably used to modeling in 3D in other applications, where changing a model often means storing and then manually recalling endless earlier versions.

So relax, and prepare yourself for getting excited about design. Once you get your mind around creating parametric content in the Family Editor, you'll probably realize you can do anything in Revit.

In this chapter, you'll learn to:

◆ Understand the Family Editor

◆ Choose the right family template

◆ Create and test parameters

◆ Know why formulas are important

Understanding the Family Editor

Plenty of generic 3D modeling applications allow you to create content that will be used in designing your buildings, and modeling in 3D is certainly a big part of the Family Editor. But the key to the Family Editor isn't that you're modeling "anything" but that you're modeling "something." Something specific. The thing that you're trying to design is meant to be a particular thing and behave in a particular way.

So when you're modeling in the Family Editor, you're not just trying to model how and what something is, you're also trying to predict how it might change. Anticipating change is key to creating great, flexible content that is able to quickly and easily change as your design changes.

For example, take a simple table. If you were to model this in something like SketchUp, what you'd have when you're done is exactly what you've modeled. But think about the design process and how something might need to change: height, length, width, and material. In the real world, each of these parameters is really important. Say, if you have only three options for each of these values, this results in 81 (3^4) permutations! Who has time to manually create each of these options? But this is what you'd have to do if you were using a generic modeler rather than something like Revit, where these options are simply driven by rules. And just imagine what would happen if you needed to create another set of options! In Revit, creating another option can be done on the fly.

As you probably know, your design is going to change. Being able to anticipate change will help you not only understand how best to approach Revit but also how to keep from becoming a frustrated designer, faced with what seems to be unpredictable whims and demands of your clients, consultants, and contractors.

Putting the Family Editor in Context

We'll start by putting the Family Editor in context. Without oversimplifying or complicating matters, think about how you'd organize a design problem: constraints, building, content, documentation, and workflow. Interestingly enough, this parallels how Revit also views the design process: data, host families, component families, views, and worksharing.

Data   Before you start designing in 3D, you're going to need some context! What are the likely levels in elevation or key structural locations in the plan? Data helps give context to almost all the building and project components. And without data (at least levels), it's impracticable to start designing your project. Fortunately, the default Revit template has two levels, and the default view is level 1.

Keep in mind that everything you create in the Family Editor needs to understand its relationship in the project. And even if it's not relating to geometry, it's relating to the data in the project: a grid or level. Knowing how your family component will respond to data in the project environment is critical.

Host Families   In Revit, the main building elements are called host or system families. Host and system families are all geometry, but it's geometry that's built within the project environment, not in the Family Editor (although some host families may contain component families). Walls, Floors, Roofs, and Ceilings are the most common host families.

After data, families often need to be hosted by system families (or at least need to maintain a particular relationship). You need to know whether your family will have to maintain some relationship to system families in your project.

Component Families Component families are created outside the project environment. They're loaded into the project and then distributed as needed. When you change the Type Properties of a component family, you're changing the properties of all components of the same type. But when you change the Instance Properties of a family component, you're changing only the instances that you've selected.

Views The views of your model include schedules, 2D views (plans, elevations, and sections), 3D views (orthographic and perspective), or even drafting views for drawing whatever you like and then associating it with the model.

Many views have scale- and detail-level properties. The detail level is particularly important to consider when creating a family component, because you often don't need to show every facet and detail in every view and scale. Fortunately, this view scale-to-detail level relationship is automatically defined in Revit. So, once you place your family component in Revit, it will automatically hide or reveal detail based on the scale of a view in your project (Figure 15.1).

FIGURE 15.1
Default view
scale detail

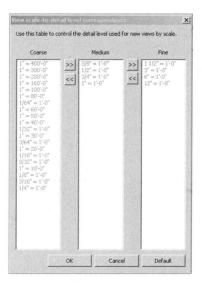

Worksharing Finally, worksharing allows all your team members to access the Revit project at the same time in a flexible, nonlinear manner. One moment you're moving a wall, the next moment you're adding a door, and the next you're adding a tag or changing the look of the schedule. Revit is able to handle this kind of nonlinear and unpredictable change quickly and easily.

Choosing the Right Family Template and Category

Now that you have a better understanding of where your component families sit in relation to your overall project, we'll discuss some specifics. If you attempt to create a new family (Revit ➤ New ➤ Family), you'll notice that there are a lot of different templates. Choosing the right template is important (Figure 15.2).

FIGURE 15.2
Template
categories

FIGURE 15.2
Template
categories

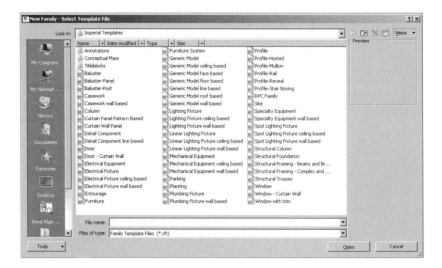

Selecting the right template determines a lot of behavior about the family. In some cases, you can change the category of the template that you've selected from one to another. For example, in Figure 15.3, a Generic Models family template is capable of being turned into another template. This is helpful if you need a family to schedule in a different category than one you might have initially selected. But in many cases, categories cannot be switched, and nonhosted or non-face-based components cannot be changed to hosted or face-based (and vice versa). That's why you need to choose the category carefully.

FIGURE 15.3
Switching between
family categories

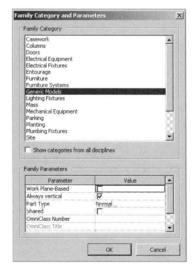

Some categories are hardwired for specific behavior, and if you change from that category to another, you can't go back. For example, if you start a family in one of the baluster templates, you can switch to another template. But after having done so, you cannot switch back to a baluster family.

Scheduling

In addition, keep in mind as you start a new component that the category you select ultimately controls how the family component will schedule. So, if you're trying to determine which template to select, it will be helpful to ask yourself or your team members how the family should schedule. Figure 15.4 illustrates all the schedule categories that are available in Revit.

FIGURE 15.4
New Schedule dialog box

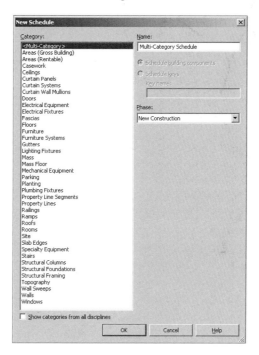

Projection and Cut Values

Another important characteristic of the family category is that it will control whether a family will "cut" when intersecting a view plane (plan, section, elevation, and so on). For example, convention dictates that when furniture encounters a cut plane, you should show a projected view.

Revit respects this convention by cutting some categories while not cutting others. You can figure out which categories cut or don't cut by going to the Manage tab and clicking Object Styles (Figure 15.5).

As you can see in Figure 15.5, categories such as Casework, Ceilings, and Columns cut, while categories such as Electrical Equipment, Electrical Fixtures, and Furniture do not.

FIGURE 15.5
Cut properties via
Object Styles

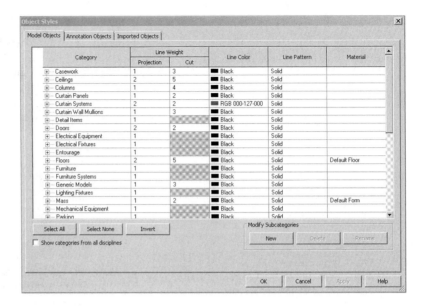

FIGURE 15.5
Cut properties via
Object Styles

Another important characteristic of the object properties is the default line weights given to objects when they're placed in a project. These line weights effect both projection and cut values. Just remember that it's probably best not to manipulate the Line Weights dialog box (Figure 15.6) unless you know what you're doing. If you intend to increase or decrease the line weight of a category of objects, use the object properties rather than the Line Weights dialog box.

FIGURE 15.6
Line Weights
dialog box

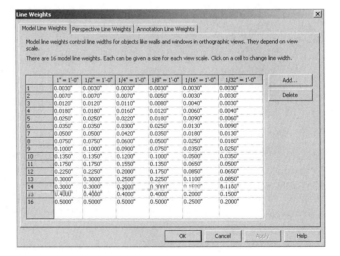

ASSIGNING PARAMETERS

As you start to get into the parameter that can control a family's geometry, material, or other value, keep in mind that it's not always necessary to create components as fully parametric. This is especially true of the first pass. The location and spacing of content is often more important than whether the family can flex geometrically.

Nonparametric families often occur when the component being modeled is specific and highly unique. It may have parameters that control materials or a few other values, but not much more. At this point, little more than selecting the right category and insertion point is necessary. It's often far more efficient to maintain design relationships by modifying the component in the Family Editor and then reloading it into the project—at least until more is known about the design. When more is known, you can open the family and embed more parameters.

Creating a Family Component

Now that we've discussed some of the basic definitions and rules of the Family Editor, we'll talk about the hierarchy of creating a family component. As previously discussed, not all families are created in the Family Editor. Host families, for example, such as walls, floors, and ceilings, are created directly in the project environment. It's possible to create component families in the project environment, but it's important, in most cases, that you not do this.

Creating "in-place" families is often a dead-end process that will rob you of hours of otherwise productive time for a number of reasons. First, an in-place family should be used only in cases where the object that you're making is not likely to be moved, rotated, or copied. Any attempt to move, rotate, or copy an in-place family can often have unintended consequences that are difficult to pinpoint. For example, if you model an in-place family and then create copies in your project, they may all initially look the same, but in fact you're copying new instances. So, modifying one of the instances is going to leave the others untouched, which can be frustrating if you've copied the instances thinking that later changes would ripple through the project.

Second, each copied instance will schedule independently from the other instances as separate line items. This is often not desirable, as you may want to group like elements together in a schedule.

Finally, there's no way to convert an in-place family into a component family. In some cases, you can copy and paste sketch lines or other 2D elements between the project and family environments. But if you try to copy and paste geometry from the project environment to the Family Editor, you'll get the warning shown in Figure 15.7. The only way to proceed is to start again in the Family Editor.

FIGURE 15.7

It's not possible to copy content from your project to the Family Editor.

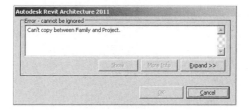

The bottom line is that if you're going to use more than a single, highly unique instance in a project or across projects, it's probably best to create the component in the Family Editor, not as an in-place family.

So, you need to consider the following criteria before you create a family component, particularly since some of the criteria can't easily be changed (if at all). You'll probably have to start over if you choose poorly. We've also tried to order the criteria for creating a family component from most to least restrictive. Most restrictive means you may have to start over. Least restrictive means you may get away with changing a parameter or value after you've already started the family.

Hosted vs. Nonhosted

The first and most important question you need to ask yourself as you select your template is whether the family is meant to be hosted or nonhosted. If you choose poorly here, you'll likely have to start over. For example, if you start a window as a nonhosted element and then want to make it hosted later, you'll probably be better off starting over.

First, keep in mind that hosted objects are meant to cut their host or create an opening or depression. Obviously a window (with few exceptions) needs to cut the wall that it will go into. Or a fire extinguisher case will often need to create a recess in the wall in which it will be placed. Second, if the component is to be hosted and you're certain that it needs to create an opening in its host, it can only cut one host. For example, a window that is wall hosted may not be hosted by a roof or ceiling.

Want to see a bad example of this? Open the Tub-Rectangular-3D family component in the Family Editor that comes with Revit (Figure 15.8).

What's wrong with this picture? Well, first, not all tubs need walls, so you'll have to make another family that has no host in order to place the tub where there is no wall. This seems a bit redundant, because one tub will do.

FIGURE 15.8
Wall-hosted
plumbing fixtures

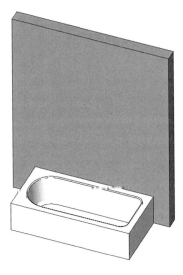

Second, if you delete a host, all the nested elements are deleted as well. This makes some sense when you delete a wall that contains a window. But it will certainly lead to a lot of frustration if you delete a wall that contains bathroom fixtures!

But what if you want the tub to move with the wall? There's a better way. Simply place the element and select the Moves With Nearby Elements option (Figure 15.9). When the host moves, the component will move as well.

FIGURE 15.9
Moves With
Nearby Elements
option

We can't stress enough: stay away from creating hosted relationships between objects that do not require hosting (that do not cut or otherwise modify the host). This brings up an interesting point of debate, though. Rather than use hosted elements, why not make elements face-based? There are some interesting advantages:

◆ You don't have to decide on a particular host. Any surface will do: Wall, Ceiling, Top Of Casework, anything that has a face. This is great if the lighting component you're creating needs to cut into a wall, floor, and ceiling!

◆ A face-based element can cut the face of geometry in both the project and family editing environment. So the light fixture that cuts a wall in a project can cut the face of a piece of casework in the Family Editor.

◆ Deleting the host will not delete the component. Is this always desirable? Well, maybe yes and maybe no. But what's important is that you have the option if the component is face-based. You won't have the option if the component is hosted.

This brings up one last point with regard to hosting and face-based elements. Why not simply model the elements, share the parameters, and then nest? This often gives the most flexibility.

Family Category

After you've chosen whether you're going hosted or nonhosted, you need to choose the correct family category. As mentioned earlier in the chapter, this is also critical. The reason you need to select the category carefully is because some categories can be switched after the fact, but this is not always the case. This is particularly true when the component has behavior that is specific or unique.

For example, lighting fixtures contain elements that allow the light to render once placed in the project environment. Balusters are another example of elements that have specific behaviors built in. If you don't select the appropriate category, you may find yourself starting over.

Insertion Point

Now that you've defined the hosting and family category, the rest is pretty flexible. If you choose poorly, you'll probably be able to recover most if not all of your work if something needs to change. But some considerations should come before others, which is why we believe that the insertion point is the next most critical criterion on your list of family creation.

The insertion point determines the location about which the family will geometrically flex—not just in plan view but also in elevation. The reference level in the Family Editor directly corresponds to the datum level in your project. Keep in mind that not only does this relate to the visibility of your component in a view, but it also relates to how the component will schedule. This is important for a couple of reasons. First, when the family expands or contracts geometrically, the insertion point will remain relatively fixed.

But second (and often more importantly), the insertion point is the point of reference when two family components are exchanged. This is critical if the "design" family that you've used as a placeholder is being swapped out for something more specific at a later date. If the insertion points are not concurrent, the location of the new family will not agree with the location of the old one.

For example, the default Desk.rfa file in the following example has the insertion point located at the center of the object (Figure 15.10). This means the desk will flex about this point. But this is not desirable if the desk, table, or furniture object has a different insertion point that you are about to swap out for this example or if the family needs to flex from a different location.

FIGURE 15.10
Default Desk.rfa
family component

Keep in mind that changing the insertion point is easy. As you would expect, you don't move the geometry to the insertion point. Rather, you simply select two reference planes and then make sure the Defines Origin option is selected. Based on our experience, we recommend that the insertion point for this particular family would best be located at the face of the desk, as shown in Figure 15.11. This would allow the desk to flex with respect to the seating, so that if the desk is larger or smaller you won't have to spend time relocating all the chairs.

FIGURE 15.11
Redefining the
insertion point

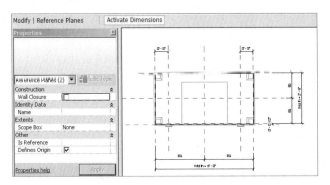

Reference Points, Planes, and Lines

If you're confident that what you're about to model in the Family Editor will need to flex (length, angle, location, and so on) from within the rules of the family (not just within the project), then it's important that you start modeling the geometry by first creating the rules that will allow the geometry to flex.

With little exception, you don't want to give parameters to the geometry itself. You'll want to create the necessary reference planes, lines, and points first. Then associate the parameters to these references and whenever possible test the parameters to make sure the references are flexing properly. Once you're confident the references are flexing, you can build the geometry in context to the references, again testing to make certain that when the references flex, the geometry is flexing as well.

Which reference you use is based on how you want the geometry to flex:

Reference Points   These have three planes that can be set to host sketch lines or geometry. You can also use a series of points to control a line or even a spline. Other objects such as reference lines or other geometric surfaces can also host reference points. You can select reference points from the dialog box shown in Figure 15.12.

FIGURE 15.12
Reference points
in the Draw
dialog box

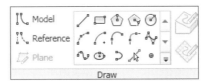

However, reference points are available only in the categories of certain families: Mass, Adaptive Mass, and Curtain Panel Pattern Based.

Reference Planes   These define a single plane that can be set to host sketch lines or geometry. They're best for controlling linear geometric relationships. Reference planes don't have endpoints. This is important because you don't want to use reference planes for controlling angular or directional relationships.

The linear relationships of length, width, and height are perfectly well suited for controlling the geometric parameters of the desk default `Desk.rfa` family component. All of the geometric options are parallel to one another (Figure 15.13).

Reference Lines   These by definition have endpoints and are great for controlling angular and directional relationships. They can have four points of reference, two along the length of the line (which are perpendicular to each other) and one at each end that is perpendicular to the line.

You can also create curved reference lines, but they only have planes that may be used for hosting at each end. There are no references along the curved line (Figure 15.14).

The great thing about reference lines is that because they contain endpoints, they're able to manage angular relationships.

FIGURE 15.13
Reference planes
controlling the
parameters of the
default Desk.rfa
family

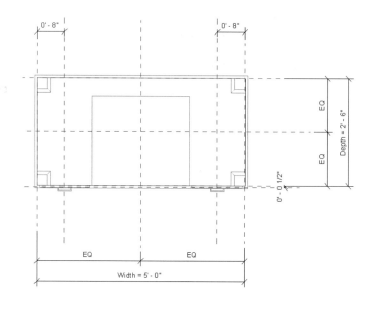

FIGURE 15.14
Straight and
curved reference
lines

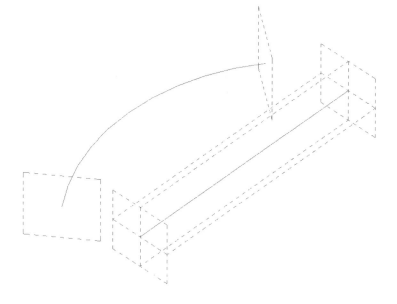

Real World Scenario

PARAMETERIZING REFERENCE LINES

Here's a simple tutorial for parameterizing reference lines. Don't even try this with reference planes. It would break—because by definition, "planes" don't have endpoints. So when you try to parameterize an angular value between two reference planes, they tend to lose their angular origin. Fortunately, lines have endpoints, so controlling them from an endpoint is far more predictable.

First, open a Generic Model template and draw a series of connected reference lines. If you are deliberate and make them all the same length and angle, it'll save some time. Here's what you should have when you're finished:

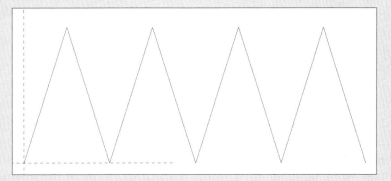

Now take a moment and add length and angle dimensions to each of the lines. Then parameterize all the length parameters together, and then do the same things for the angles. If you've drawn your reference lines carefully (all the same length and angle), you'll be able to parameterize them by selecting the dimensions all at once. If they're different, you'll need to select each length (and each angle) one at a time and associate with the appropriate parameter. When you're finished, it should look like this:

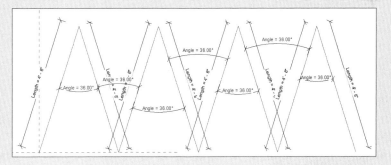

Now comes the interesting part: create a single swept form by picking each of the reference lines together. After you've finished your sweep, you'll realize that when you flex the angular and length parameters, the sweep will remain associated with the reference lines.

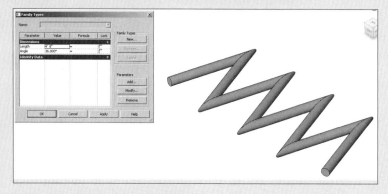

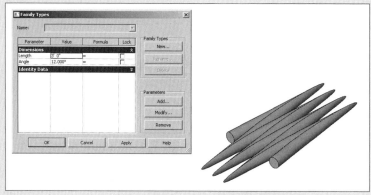

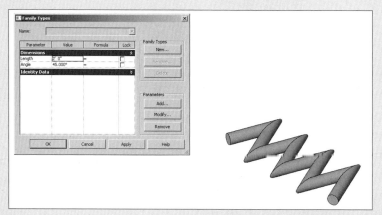

With this technique, you can imagine that modeling accordion panels shouldn't be a problem. You can show the panels as open or closed, driving the individual segment lengths from an "overall" length that is divided among the individual segments.

Visibility Settings

The time it takes for Revit to generate or regenerate a view depends on how much stuff in the view needs to be displayed. One of the great things about Revit is that it automatically assigns the level of detail based on the scale of the view (Figure 15.15).

FIGURE 15.15

View Scale-To-Detail Level Correspondence

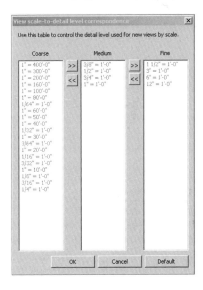

When you're building smaller parts of a larger component (or if the elements are not visible in certain orientations), you should assign those elements to only reveal themselves at a certain level of detail (or only certain orientations). This will keep Revit from having to manage more information than necessary. Here's a rule of thumb: once the separate lines that represent something print as a single, merged line, there's little point in having that element display in that view or at that scale. Although this was an entirely intuitive realization when drawing with a pencil (don't draw over the same line twice), unfortunately computers have allowed us to draw beyond a point of diminishing returns.

To see how to fix it, open the default `Desk.rfa` family, which is fairly well built. But if you look closely, you'll notice that orientation and detail level are not being fully specified. All of the drawer faces and hardware are showing up at every view in every section or elevation.

STARTING WITH EXISTING CONTENT

Let's face it, we've all downloaded content to get a first design pass at a piece of content. Autodesk Seek, Revit City, and the AUGI forums are all great places to start. When you do this, take a moment to make sure that the detail level and orientation of detail are appropriate.

In this `Desk.rfa` family, everything is showing up in every level of detail. This isn't necessarily a big deal with just a few objects. But multiply this by all the other elements that will make up your plans, reflected ceiling plans, elevations, and sections, and you'll notice that your views don't refresh, rotate, print, and export as fast as you'd expect. When this happens, one of the first things we look for is an object in a view that is being shown at a level of detail that is far too high. In some cases the object only prints as a small, black dot. But when you zoom in you'll notice that it's full of detail.

Controlling the detail parametrically is done through the Family Elements Visibility Settings dialog box (Figure 15.16).

FIGURE 15.16
Family Elements
Visibility Settings
dialog box

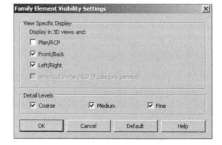

Notice that the box for the Plan/RCP option is unchecked? This is appropriate for the desk, because little more than the surface of the top of the desk needs to show up in plan. The legs, the hardware, and even the faces of the drawers don't need to show up in plan.

But what about the elevations? By turning off the Thin Lines option, you can see that all the geometry is showing up at every level of detail in a view that's set for ⅛″ = 1′-0″ (Figure 15.17).

FIGURE 15.17
Lines beginning
to merge

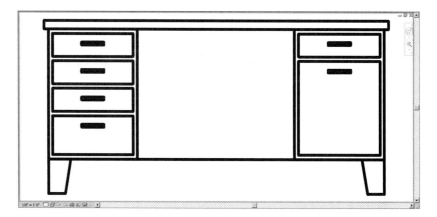

In these cases, Zoom To Sheet Size is your friend. Figure 15.18 shows the same desk in elevation when that option is active. It's obvious that we'd never need that level of detail at that scale.

It's pretty obvious that there's far more detail than necessary for this view and the solution is simple. Set the drawer faces to show up at a Medium detail level or finer, and set the hardware to only show up at a Fine detail level. Do this to all your content and performance should noticeably increase (Figure 15.19).

FIGURE 15.18
Zoom To
Sheet Size

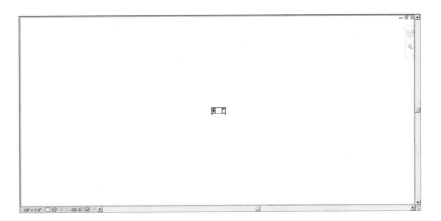

FIGURE 15.19
Adjusting detail
level

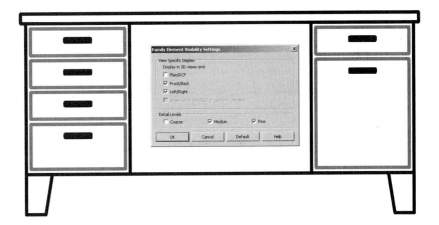

Materials

Materials are crucial to a family. But keep this in balance—don't obsess about the material that will display when a family is being rendered. What's more important is the Shading setting and the Transparency value of the material because they communicate much about the intent of your design in the early stages (Figure 15.20).

In addition, material options are often not easily created in Revit. Yes, a family can have a material parameter. But expressing many different parameters for visualization purposes is probably left to the visualization specialist who understands the subtleties of creating an emotive image, not just a "rendering"—and it's unlikely they'll be using Revit to iterate or emotively visualize your design.

FIGURE 15.20
Shading and
Transparency
in the Materials
dialog box

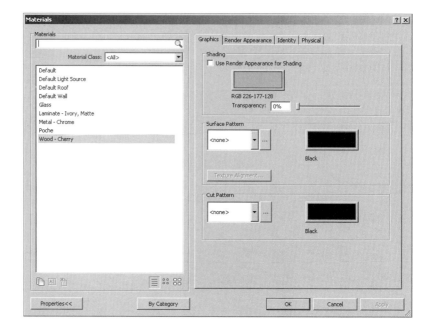

Dimensions

As mentioned earlier, dimensions are useful for controlling the geometry parameters of your families. But it's best to keep the dimensions outside of Sketch mode. Let's use the desk as an example. In plan view, you can see all the reference planes and dimensions (Figure 15.21).

FIGURE 15.21
Parameterized
dimensions

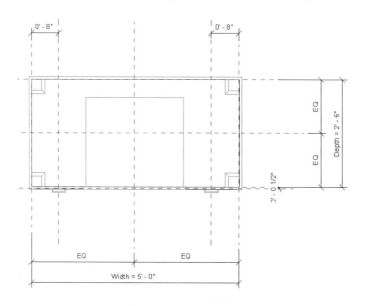

Now select the top of the desk and select the Edit Extrusion option. What you'll find are dimensions to the edge of the desktop (Figure 15.22).

FIGURE 15.22

Dimensions inside Sketch mode

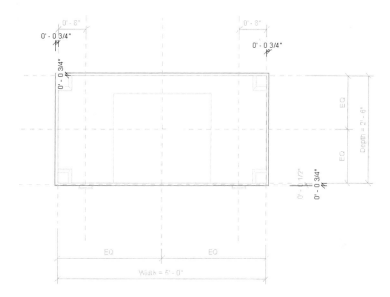

These dimensions are "inside" the Sketch mode of the desktop. This is fine in the sense that they'll work. But as a best practice, don't put parameterized dimensions inside Sketch mode. The reason is that when you complete the sketch, the dimensions will be hidden. Then when you're trying to troubleshoot or modify parameters, you won't be able to easily find the values that correspond to in the model view.

So whenever possible, keep all dimensions outside of Sketch mode.

Object Styles and Subcategories

Revit has predefined a number of hardwired family categories. These categories can't be modified or added. As mentioned earlier, they define how elements display, schedule, export, and so on. But within the default object categories, you can create subcategories for model, annotation, and imported objects (Figure 15.23).

FIGURE 15.23

Object Styles dialog box

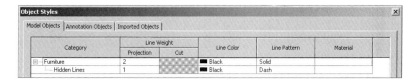

Although you can use subcategories to control the visibility of some part of the whole component, keep in mind that the detail level and visibility settings already manage visibility. The subcategories are most important when you're exporting your project, because each category and subcategory is permitted its own CAD layer (Figure 15.24).

FIGURE 15.24
Export options
for categories and
subcategories

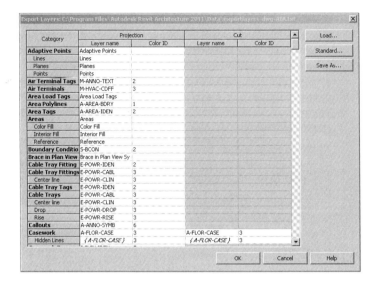

So if your project is being exported to CAD in such a way that you'll need to associate objects with granular layer settings, creating and assigning subcategories to elements is necessary. But don't rely on subcategories to manage visibility.

Type and Instance Parameters

CERT
OBJECTIVE

A lot of users new to Revit start to panic when they have to select between a type and an instance parameter. Just keep in mind that you can change these two items after you set them initially. When you reload the family into the project environment, the previous settings will be overwritten.

The key difference is that modifying a type parameter will always modify all the other components of the same time. On the other hand, an instance parameter will only modify the components that you have selected. Figure 15.25 shows the parameters of the default Desk.rfa family.

FIGURE 15.25
Parameters of the
Desk.rfa family

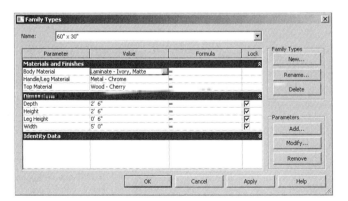

You can tell all these parameters are type parameters because any time you have an instance parameter, the text "(default)" appears after the parameter value. In this case, it's likely important that the dimensions are type parameters. You don't want users to create random or arbitrary Depth, Height, and Width values.

On the other hand, each new option can create a lot of new types. By default, loading a family into your project will also load all the types. If you want to create the potential for many types but be selective about which types are loaded, you can use a type catalog to load only specific types.

USE NESTING AND PATTERNS FOR QUICK TURNAROUND

Geometry from one family can be loaded into another family. This is called "nesting," and it allows you to create a single element that will be used many times in one or more families. This is much more desirable than creating an element and then grouping and copying it around the same family. Become accustomed to using nesting whenever possible because it'll save you a lot of time when your design changes.

First, it's much easier to change and control the location of a nested family. The nested family can also have references and parameters that can control it when nested.

But more importantly, the nested family can be controlled by a "Family Type" parameter, which will allow you to switch between nested families as another parameter. This is incredibly powerful for creating design iteration within families that are in your projects.

Second, as soon as you have a reasonable representation of your family, get it in the project. Don't be afraid to start simple and update it later. Users sometimes obsess about the details and hesitate to load the family into the project until it's "perfect." This tendency can hold up a project. So get the idea in the project first and make it ideal later. Just take care about the insertion point so that when you modify it (or exchange it with something more detailed) its relative location will remain the same.

Finally, look for opportunities to use model patterns in lieu of geometry. This is important in the project environment, but it's also important (and often overlooked) in the Family Editor. Model patterns graphically regenerate far faster than small geometric parts and pieces.

Using Advanced Modeling Techniques

Creating complex geometry isn't always as easy as opening the Family Editor and starting to model the shape that you think you're trying to create. Sometimes you need to model one form in order to create another form. And sometimes you need to model a complex, parameterized form in order to parameterize the actual shape that you're trying to create. So that you understand these advanced techniques, we'll first cover the available geometry types that can be created in Revit.

There are five discrete geometry types in the Family Editor: extrusions, blends, revolves, sweeps, and swept blends. Both solid and void forms can be modeled from these shapes (Figure 15.26).

FIGURE 15.26
Geometry types

Which one you select is important, but our advice is to use the simplest form that will express what you're trying to model, keeping in mind how the geometry is likely to change.

In other words, an extrusion, blend, sweep, and swept blend can be used to create initially similar forms. It's impossible to tell them apart (Figure 15.27).

FIGURE 15.27
Initially similar forms

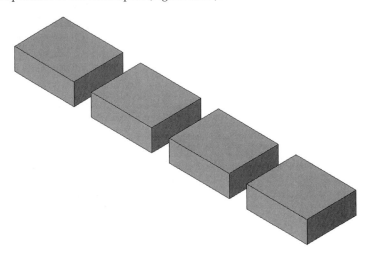

But once these forms change, you'll understand that they can iterate into very different shapes (Figure 15.28).

FIGURE 15.28
Left to right: extrusion, blend, sweep, and swept blend

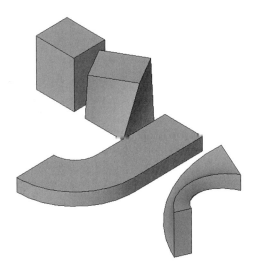

Creating Solid and Void Relationships

One of the great things in Revit is that the relationship between solid geometry and cutting void is nonlinear. Solids that are joined together may still maintain independent relationships. They're not locked together after they're joined.

Additionally, not all voids must cut all solids. The void may selectively cut one solid but not another solid, even though the two solids are joined together. For example, in Figure 15.29 we've joined the solids from the previous image and overlapped them with a single void. Notice how the void is cutting all of the joined solids.

FIGURE 15.29
Single extruded
void overlapping
all joined solids

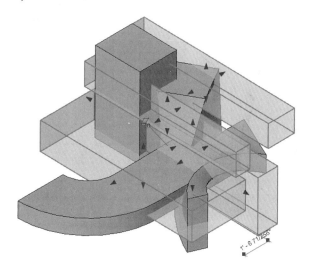

Figure 15.30 shows the results of finishing the sketch.

FIGURE 15.30
All joined
solids cut

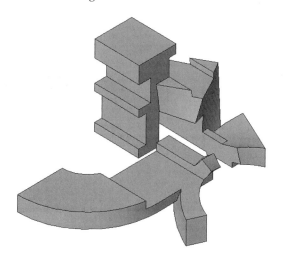

This is often not desirable because now you'll have to go back and "uncut" three of the four joined solids. So in many cases you'd rather model a void that only selectively cuts. The trick here is not to model the void as a void. If you do, then by default it will cut all the solids that came before it. Rather, model the geometry as a solid (Figure 15.31).

FIGURE 15.31
Initially modeling the desired void as a solid

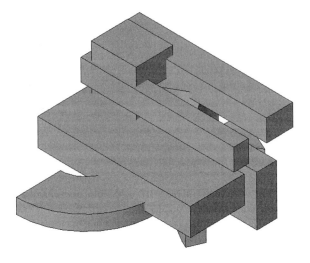

Now you can convert the solid to a void from the Properties dialog box, as shown in Figure 15.32.

FIGURE 15.32
Converting a solid to a void

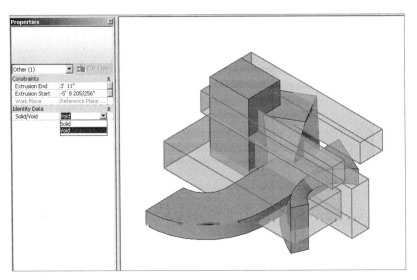

Figure 15.33 shows the results. The void doesn't cut any of the solids. This is desirable when you want to complete the void and still see it, because by default, once a void cuts a solid it becomes invisible, which makes it rather hard to find. This technique still shows the void for editing (Figure 15.33).

FIGURE 15.33
Noncutting voids remain visible.

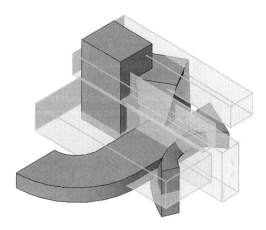

Now you can selectively cut only what you want to cut (Figure 15.34).

FIGURE 15.34
Selectively cutting forms

To review this file, you can download it from the Chapter 15 folder at the book's web page (www.sybex.com/go/masteringrevit2011); it's called Solid Void.rfa.

Carving Geometry

If you're really 3D savvy, creating complex geometry often involves creating what you need with complex modeling tools in order to reach some final result. The process in Revit is often different and has some wonderful benefits as well.

Think of a sculptural process as being additive or subtractive. Creating sculpture as an additive process means that you're casting the desired shape. Creating sculpture as a subtractive process means starting with more stuff than you need and then carving away until you have the final result.

Many complex geometry applications create complex forms as an additive process. In other words, you create a form and then manipulate that result with other tools; pushing, pulling, and twisting until you've morphed the final shape.

Think of Revit as more of a hybrid process that relies heavily on a subtractive approach that carves away what you don't need. Although this may seem a bit counterintuitive at first (because in many 3D modeling tools, cutting geometry is a linear process that doesn't lend itself well to parametric editing), in Revit the void is a live thing that can be quickly and easily modified.

For example, you may not believe that the form shown in Figure 15.35 has been created in Revit. If you're trying to create this form using an additive process, it's quite complicated. But if you create it using a subtractive approach, then it's quite easy, and the results can be surprisingly elegant.

FIGURE 15.35
Sculptural forms

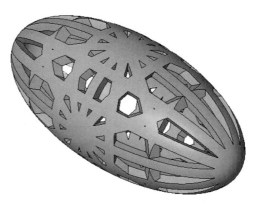

Furthermore, the form consists of only three (copied) extrusions and a single void. But it's easily done and with just a few steps.

Real World Scenario

COMPLEX FORMS MADE SIMPLE

Creating that sculptural form is not hard. Don't believe us? Follow these steps:

1. Create the extrusion sketch shown here in a Front/Back elevation. In this case, the overall height is 6'. The width is 0'-4".

2. When you finish the sketch, set the overall length to 9′-0″. This is the resulting shape.

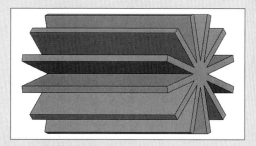

3. Go to your Left/Right elevation and use Copy/Rotate to move the form 90 degrees so that the copy is vertical. You'll also have to select the Disjoin option.

4. Go to the Top/Bottom view and use Copy/Rotate to move the original form 90 degrees to that the copy is facing left/right.

5. Use the Join Geometry tool and join all three forms together. When you're done, the form should look like this:

Now it gets really interesting! We'll show you how to cut multiple solids from a single void after you initially modeled the void as a solid. Here's the sketch of the solid revolve in the Front elevation:

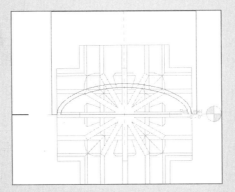

6. When you finish the form, you want to make certain that none of the geometry from the star form is showing outside the revolve that you've created, as shown here:

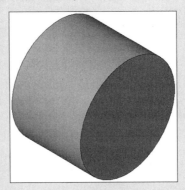

7. Change the solid revolve into a void. The void won't cut! This is what you want: the ability to model solids and voids with the flexibility to cut the void when you're ready, not before.

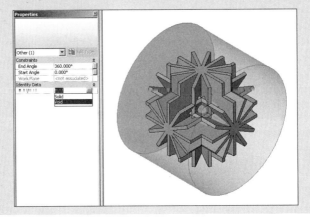

Here's a tip for cutting a lot of geometry with a void without having to select elements one by one. First, select the void and select Cut To Clipboard (or press Ctrl+X). This will remove the void! Don't worry.

8. Select Paste ➤ Aligned To Same Place. Another much less known option is to press Ctrl+V for paste. But when the form starts to hover, select 0, and then press Enter. This will paste the element at 0,0,0, the origin of the original element.

As a result, you should begin to understand that complex form making in Revit is quite often a subtractive process—you create more geometry than necessary and then use a void to carve away what you don't need.

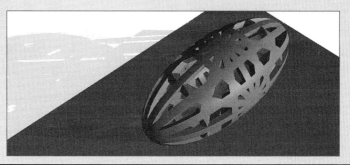

There are some great examples of creating sculptural forms in Chapter 26. Carving geometry is a technique that set designer Bryan Sutton (profiled in that chapter) uses extensively. If you want to explore this file further, just look in the Chapter 15 folder on the book's web page for the file Egg Sculpture.rvt.

Using Geometry to Drive Geometry

As discussed previously, reference planes, points, and lines are most often used to drive geometric form. If you've been using Revit for any length of time, you've been creating parametric content. But there will be some cases where these three options alone are just not enough. This is particularly difficult with linear or tubular forms, as shown in Figure 15.36.

To learn how to drive geometry with geometry, follow these steps:

1. Open a Furniture template, and add reference planes to control the height of the seatback and the seat. Figure 15.37 shows the reference planes and other locked dimensions.

2. Now you'll model the "negative space" that would define the centerlines of the tubular structure with a solid extrusion. Make the overall form 20″ wide. Once you finish the line of the inner sketch, simply offset about 1″ or so (Figure 15.38).

Figure 15.39 shows the finished form. Now you have to start adding the voids that will shape the back of the seat and backrest.

3. Create the two individual voids in the Front/Back elevation orientation (Figure 15.40).

When you're done, you've completed a path that represents the path of the structural tubing (Figure 15.41).

FIGURE 15.36
Chair with tubular
structure

FIGURE 15.37
Parameterized
reference plane

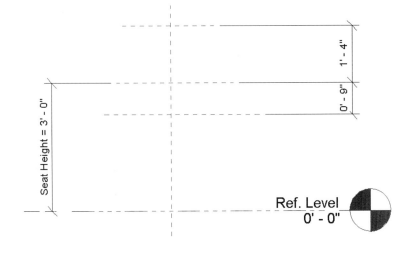

FIGURE 15.38
Extrusion sketch
in elevation

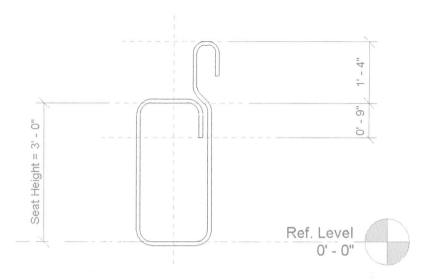

FIGURE 15.39
Finished extrusion

FIGURE 15.40
Voids that cut
the seat back
and seat rest

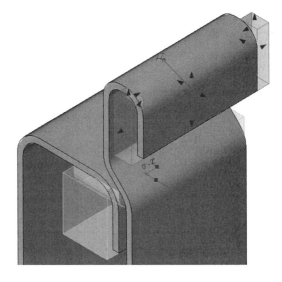

FIGURE 15.41
Complete path

4. Select the Solid Sweep tool and pick the edges that make up the centerline of the structural tubing. Then sketch the profile that you want to follow along this path (Figure 15.42).

CREATING SEPARATE PATHS FOR COMPLEX SWEEPS

You may find that you're unable to create the edge-based sweep with one continuous path because of the complex curves that happen at the back of the seat and seat rest. Simply create multiple paths where a singular path would break the sketch.

FIGURE 15.42
Picking edge-based
sweeps

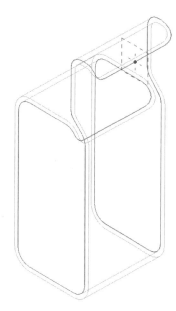

When you finish the path-based sweeps, you'll have the result shown in Figure 15.43.

FIGURE 15.43
Edge-based sweeps
with extrusion
hidden

5. Model the extrusions for the leather seat and seat back. We've also added some additional reference lines to control the vertical location of the leather seat rest (Figure 15.44).

6. Now the tubular geometry is being controlled by the extrusion. But of course you don't want to see the extrusion in the project environment. This is easily fixed. Just select the extrusion, and in the Properties dialog box, deselect the Visible option under Graphics (Figure 15.45).

FIGURE 15.44
Additional refer-
ence planes

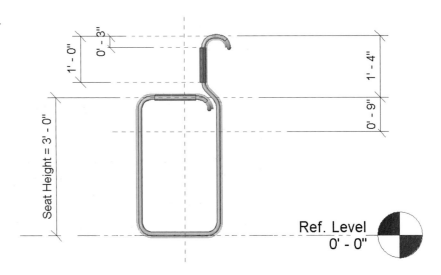

FIGURE 15.45
Deselect the Vis-
ible option to hide
the extrusion in
the project envi-
ronment.

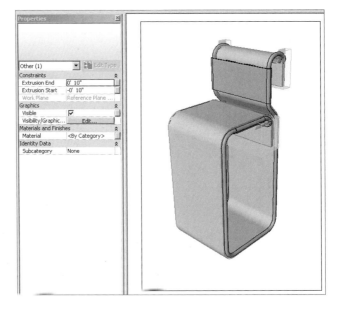

Once loaded into the project, the extrusion will be hidden, and because of the parameters that drive the extrusion, you can create new types (Figure 15.46).

If you want to explore this file further, just look in the Chapter 15 folder on the book's web page for the file Tube Chairs.rvt.

FIGURE 15.46
Final form in
the project
environment

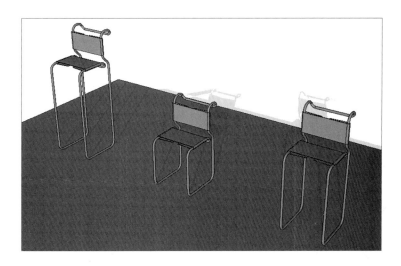

FIGURE 15.46
Final form in
the project
environment

Building a Shelf Using Formulas and Type Catalogs

The real challenge in modeling in 3D is being able to predict and elegantly maintain change and iteration. Once you're able to do this, you really start to work effectively.

To get to this point, you need to understand nesting, family types, formulas, and type catalogs, and in the following sections, we'll walk you through an exercise that includes these techniques. Specifically, you'll build a simple shelf. A shelf is something we're all familiar with, and designing a shelf that elegantly changes with your design is a wonderful thing. Once you learn these techniques, you can apply them to many other concepts in Revit when you're creating elegant content.

The shelf family you will create in the following exercises will contain many brackets, so the brackets will be nested. Which bracket is used will depend on Family Type parameters. Then, the number of brackets will be controlled by formulas that add brackets as the shelf increases in length. Finally, you'll use type catalogs to select only the desired permutations.

Figure 15.47 shows some possibilities for the final shelf.

FIGURE 15.47
Finished shelf
examples

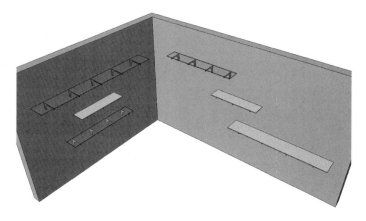

Modeling the Brackets

You'll start by building one of the two brackets.

1. Open a Generic Model template. Starting in the Left Elevation view, create a reference plane to the left of the Center Front/Back reference plane to control the support depth.

2. Add a dimension from the Center Front/Back Reference plane (which is also the insertion point) to your new reference plane.

3. Parameterize the Length value as a Type Parameter, calling it **Support Depth**. When you're done, you should have what looks like Figure 15.48.

FIGURE 15.48
Parameterized
reference planes

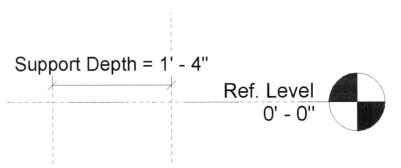

4. Sketch the extrusion shown in Figure 15.49. You won't need to lock any of the sketch lines. Their proximity to the reference planes will cause them to flex. We'll also change the overall thickness of the bracket to ¼", being careful to distribute half the bracket thickness to either side of the Center Left/Right reference plane.

FIGURE 15.49
Sketch and Proper-
ties settings

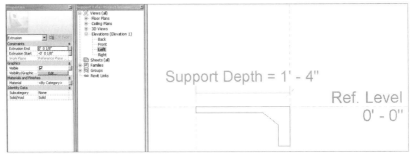

5. Save the bracket as **Support 1.rfa**. It should look like Figure 15.50.

As a general principle, if you have to model an iteration that is similar to an existing example, don't start from scratch. Instead, open the existing example and modify it.

6. Click Save As, and call this new family **Support 2.rfa**.

7. Go back to the Left elevation and edit the previous extrusion. Offset the sketch lines ¼", as shown in Figure 15.51. Generally speaking, try offsetting sketch lines to create openings rather than adding voids. The results are flexible and faster to model.

8. When you finish the sketch, your new bracket should look like Figure 15.52. Now save the family, and you're ready to nest these two brackets in your shelf family.

FIGURE 15.50
Completed bracket

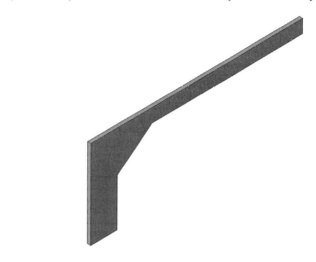

FIGURE 15.51
Offset and copy the sketch lines.

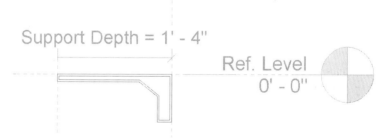

FIGURE 15.52
Support 2.rfa

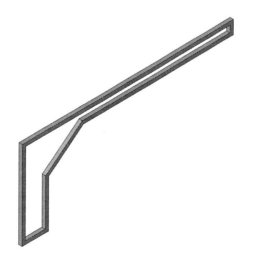

Nesting the Brackets

To nest these two brackets in your shelf family, follow these steps:

1. Open a Furniture template (this is a shelf after all) and go ahead and nest both brackets into this template. Don't place them—just load them for later.

2. Close the bracket families, leaving only the Furniture family open. Finally, go ahead and save this new family, calling it **Parametric Shelf.rfa**.

3. Lets start in a plan view. As a rule, try to create all your reference planes and associated parameters in as few views as possible. This will save you time later.

4. Now create the additional reference planes, dimensions, and type parameters as shown. For reference, I've put a temporary circle at the default insertion point. Also note that when the shelf flexes, it will distribute evenly to either side of the Center Left/Right reference plane because of the EQ dimension below the Shelf Width length parameter (Figure 15.53).

FIGURE 15.53
Parameterized
reference planes

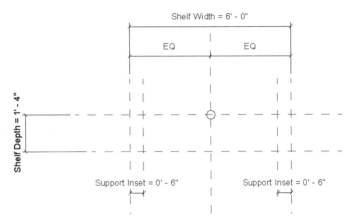

5. Now let's model the shelf geometry from this same view. Again, there's no need to lock any sketch lines to the reference planes. Also, note the Constraints in Figure 15.54. Extrusion Start is 0″ and Extrusion End is negative ½″. This means that the shelf is ½″ thick. As a result, the top of the shelf will initially be aligned with the level it's placed on in the Revit project.

FIGURE 15.54
Extrusion sketch
for shelf

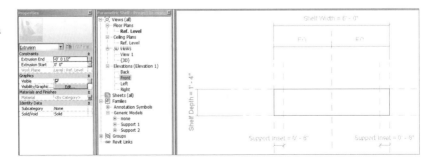

6. Return to your plan view and place the Support 1 bracket. Then go to the Right elevation and move the bracket into place, as shown in Figure 15.55, so that it's under the shelf. Just place one bracket. The rest will come later! Also, you don't need to apply Align/Lock to the bracket.

FIGURE 15.55

Support 1 bracket
under the shelf

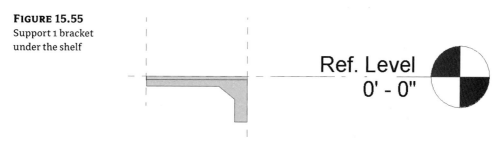

7. Now we'll associate the Bracket parameter with the parameter that controls the depth of the shelf. Select the bracket and then select Edit Type to bring up the dialog box shown in Figure 15.56. Note that the Support Depth value isn't associated with anything.

FIGURE 15.56

Nesting the sup-
port depth

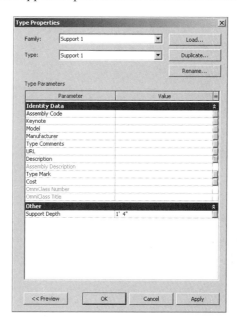

8. Click the square button to the far right of the Support Depth parameter. This will bring up another dialog box. Select the Shelf Depth parameter, as shown in Figure 15.57.

Now when the Shelf Depth length changes, the bracket will grow to match.

FIGURE 15.57
Parameterized
reference planes

Assigning Family Type Parameters

Now that you've nested the brackets and tested the parameters, you'll continue by adding
Family Type parameters, which will allow you to select between the nested bracket families.

1. Select the bracket and look toward the top of the view. There's a value called Label. Pull
   down the menu and select Add Parameter, which will open the dialog box shown in
   Figure 15.58. In the Name field, enter **Support Type**.

FIGURE 15.58
Parameterized
family type

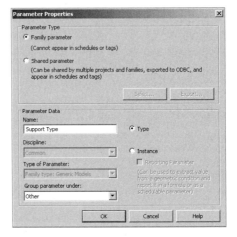

2. Select between brackets in the Family Types dialog box. Set the Bracket Support value to
   Support 2. It's already associated because both brackets are of the same Generic Model
   category (Figure 15.59).

3. While you're in this view, select the Edit Type option, associating the Support Depth
   value of Support 2 with the Shelf Depth of this family (just like you did a moment ago
   for Support 1).

FIGURE 15.59
Family type
Support 2.rfa

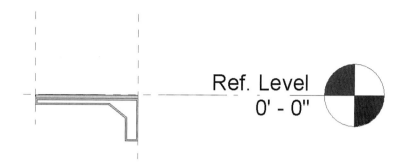

FIGURE 15.59
Family type
Support 2.rfa

Creating Parametric Arrays

Now that you've associated Family Type parameters to the brackets, you'll continue by creating a parametric array in order to control the number of brackets on a case-by-case basis once the family is loaded into the project environment.

1. Return to the Front Elevation. Select the bracket, then select the Array command, and make an array with the following settings (Figure 15.60). Put the second bracket on the right side of the Center Left/Right reference plane.

FIGURE 15.60
Creating the array

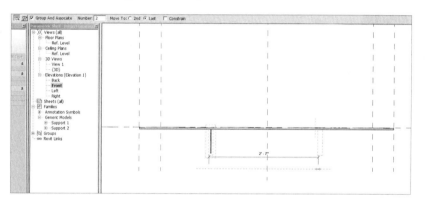

2. Now you're going to parameterize the array. Select either of the brackets, and you'll notice they're now in groups. Now select the line that extends above the shelf and extends to either side of the groups. When you select this line, you'll be given an option to parameterize the grouped array (Figure 15.61).

3. Select Add Parameter, and complete the dialog box as shown in Figure 15.62. By default, the array has two brackets, which is fine for now. You'll parameterize this later.

4. Go back to the Front elevation and align/lock the brackets to the reference plane that is associated with the support inset. If you'll remember, we modeled the bracket on the Center Left/Right reference plane in its family. This reference plane is now a reference that you can use when the family is nested. As a result, you'll be able to use this reference when aligning and locking to the reference plane in the shelf project (Figure 15.63).

FIGURE 15.61
You can parame-
terize the grouped
array.

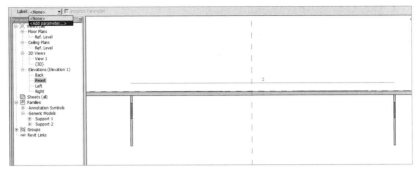

FIGURE 15.62
Parameterizing the
number of brackets

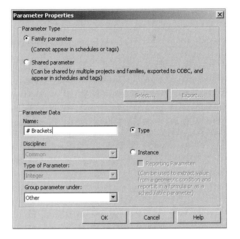

FIGURE 15.63
Be sure to lock the
shelf bracket when
aligning.

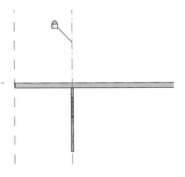

After you've aligned and locked both brackets, their locations should flex when you change
the Shelf Width parameter. Go ahead and test this now. In fact, as a best practice, it's a good idea
to test the parameters after every few steps.

Using Formulas

Now let's create a formula that adds brackets as the length of the shelf increases. We'll show how to do this simply at first, and then we'll add some complexity.

1. Open the Family Types dialog box. Rather than specify the number of brackets (# Brackets), add a formula to the right of this value under the Formula column:

(Shelf Width / 3') + 1

The reason that you add one to the end of the line is that if for some reason the width of the shelf is less than the specified width between brackets (3' in this example), then the number of brackets might result in one. But you're not permitted to have an array of less than two. A value of one would cause the formula to fail. And besides, a shelf with one bracket tends to be a bit unstable. And because we specified the first and last location of the array, this will guarantee a bracket at each end of the shelf.

Now that you've got down the basics, let's make the array more sophisticated.

2. Remove both the Support Inset values from the overall Shelf Width value:

(Shelf Width - (2 * Support Inset)) / 3' + 1

This is better. However, this formula also will lock the relative spacing between the brackets to 3'. If you want to keep the value flexible, you'll create a Length parameter that allows you to reiterate the bracket spacing.

3. Open the Family Types dialog box, and in the Parameters option select Add and then input the values shown in Figure 15.64.

FIGURE 15.64
Creating the Minimum Bracket Space parameter

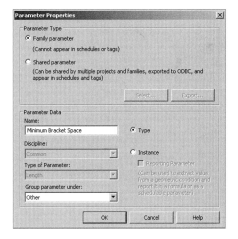

4. Click OK, and close the dialog (Figure 15.65).

FIGURE 15.65
Completed
dialog box

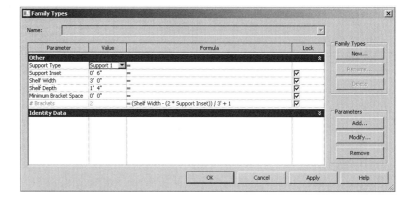

5. Reopen the Family Types dialog box, and use the parameter you've just created in place of the fixed 3' value. Give the Minimum Bracket Space parameter a value (or when you apply the formula it will not work). In this case, give it a value of 3'.

6. Substitute the text in the formula. Remember that spelling and case are important, so copy and paste will help (Figure 15.66).

FIGURE 15.66
Completed
formula

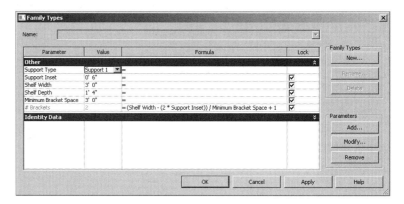

7. Flex the family and experiment with different bracket spacing, shelf width, and support inset values.

Finally, it's not possible (or desirable) to set the actual or real bracket spacing. But it may be helpful to know this value as real-time feedback. So now you'll create the formula that will report this value.

8. Open the Family Types dialog box, and click Add to create a new Length parameter, as shown in Figure 15.67.

9. Then add the following to the Actual Bracket Space formula field:

(Shelf Width - (2 * Support Inset)) / (# Brackets - 1)

This will report the real value of the bracket spacing, not just the minimum specified (Figure 15.68).

FIGURE 15.67
Creating the
Actual Bracket
Space parameter

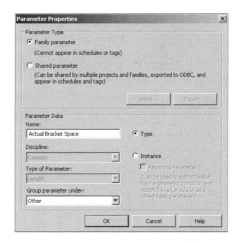

FIGURE 15.68
Creating the
Minimum Bracket
Space parameter

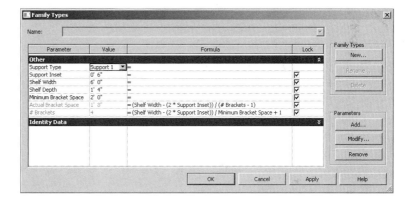

Associating Materials

Now let's associate the material of the shelf with a parameter to control the material.

1. Select the shelf and then click the button to the right of the Material row (Figure 15.69).

FIGURE 15.69
Selecting Material
properties

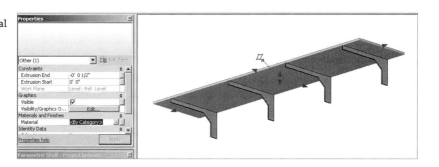

2. Click the Add Parameter button in the Associate Family Parameter dialog box (Figure 15.70).

FIGURE 15.70
Associate Family
Parameter
dialog box

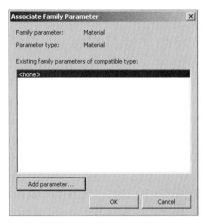

3. Add the Material parameter, as shown in Figure 15.71. In this case we've named the parameter "Shelf Material".

FIGURE 15.71
Adding the Mate-
rial parameter to
the shelf

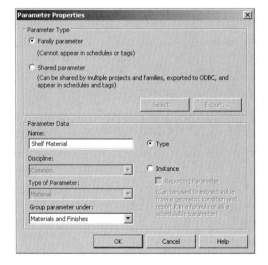

Now you can open the Family Types dialog box and see that the material of the shelf geometry has been parameterized to associate with a material (Figure 15.72). Once this family is loaded into the project environment, you can change the material of a shelf as a type. You'll also be able to specify the bracket, as well as the spacing of the bracket.

FIGURE 15.72
Material parame-
ter in Family Types
dialog box

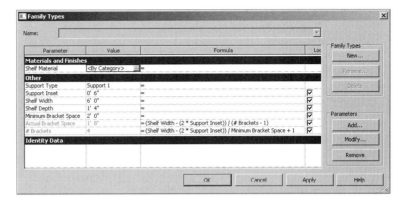

Creating and Editing Type Catalogs

Now let's consider all the possible permutations of this shelf. Imagine the following:

◆ 2 Materials (Wood and Glass)

◆ 2 Support Types (Support 1 and Support 2)

◆ 2 Support Inset Lengths (3″ and 6″)

◆ 3 Shelf Widths (2′, 4′, 6′)

◆ 3 Shelf Depths (8″, 12″, 16″)

How many Type permutations might exist?

Easy! $2 \times 2 \times 2 \times 3 \times 3 = 72$ Types

That's a lot of types to build and load into a project, especially if you really only want to use just a few of the types in your project. You have a couple of options:

◆ Some of the type parameters may work as instance parameters. That can reduce the number of types significantly. For example, if the material parameters became instance parameters, you could reduce the number of types by half. But still, that's far too many types.

◆ You can create a type catalog. This lets you to store all the types in a text file that allows you to be selective about which iterations are loaded into the project. So instead of dozens and dozens of different types, you can just load the ones that you want. This will keep your file much lighter. Also, if you need to create additional types, it's a simple matter of adding the values to the type catalog.

Type catalogs can be intimidating at first because small errors will cause either the type catalog or the corresponding family to fail, so just go slow and test frequently. You don't want to test the catalog at the end of your process and be faced with untangling spaghetti.

We'll start simple. First, keep in mind that the type catalog needs to be in the same location as the family that it references, and it should have the same name. So in this case the family is called `Parametric Shelf.rfa`, so the type catalog will be called `Parametric Shelf.txt`. In addition, spelling counts, and parameter names are case sensitive as well, just like when you're working in the Family Editor.

Parameter values can be expressed as length, area, volume, angle, force, linear force, and "other." For this example, we'll be using length (for lengths) and other (for Family Types). We'll use decimals when appropriate. While we could create this in Excel and export as a comma-delimited text file, we'll walk you through creating the type catalog as a text file (which is a little bit harder, but we will explain a lot in the process).

1. Create a text document in the same location as your Parametric Shelf family. This can be done by right-clicking the desktop of your computer and selecting New ➤ Text Document from the context menu (Figure 15.73).

FIGURE 15.73
Creating a text document

2. Rename the file to match your shelf family, and open it (Figure 15.74).

FIGURE 15.74
Opening the type catalog

3. Begin by adding the Type Names that match the Family Types. We've already created one type as well (Figure 15.75). Don't worry about matching all the values—we can change them in the type catalog. Just get the names correct for now.

This is the header text that we'll need in our type catalog. Note the comma at the beginning of the header line (by default this is the Type Name). Also note that there is no comma at the end.

FIGURE 15.75
Family Types to
be matched

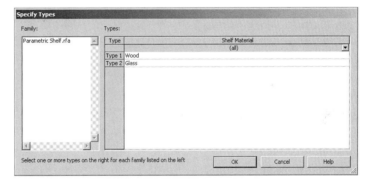

4. Let's start simple and test by specifying only the shelf material in the type catalog:

,Shelf Material##other##

Type 1,Wood

Type 2,Glass

5. After you save the text file and family, you should test the type catalog. Open a new project, and start to load in the project (see Figure 15.76).

FIGURE 15.76
Resulting type
catalog

6. Now let's start to add the other header values and types in the type catalog. Be sure to save and test frequently:

```
,Shelf Material##other##,Shelf Width##length##feet,Shelf
Depth##length##feet,Support Inset##length##feet,Minimum Bracket
Space##length##feet,Support Type##other##
Type 1,Wood,4,1,0.5,2,Support 1
Type 2,Glass,6,1,0.5,2,Support 1
```

Figure 15.77 shows the result when you attempt to load the family into the project.

FIGURE 15.77
Completed type
catalog

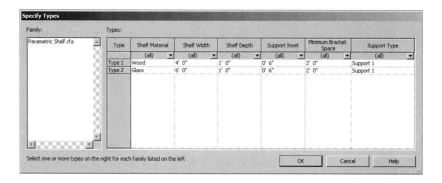

Now that you've created the type catalog in a text editor, you'll want to consider editing (or even creating) it in Excel. The important thing is that you'll need to import and export the catalog in a specific way.

1. For importing the type catalog, be sure you import the file as comma delimited. Open Excel and then select File ➤ Open. Browse to your text file and open it. Be sure to select Delimited in the first dialog box and you'll see your type catalog as shown below (Figure 15.78).

FIGURE 15.78
Type catalog
opened in Excel

2. Select Comma as the delimiter in the second dialog box (Figure 15.79).

FIGURE 15.79
Select Comma as
the delimiter.

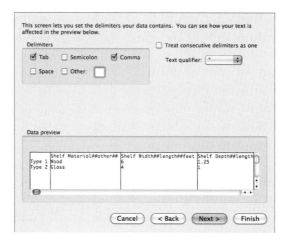

3. Now that you have your open catalog, you can fit the columns to the proper width and begin to add additional types. We've also added two additional types in this example (Figure 15.80).

FIGURE 15.80

Adding new types

4. It's important to save the file with the appropriate settings. Select File ➤ Save As and select Comma Separated Values (.csv), but go ahead and save yourself an extra step by changing the file suffix to `.txt`. And you may want to save as a different filename so as not to overwrite your original file until you've tested it (Figure 15.81).

FIGURE 15.81

Saving the type catalog from Excel

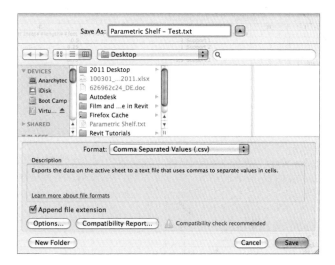

5. Finally, be sure to test all the types in your type catalog in an empty project. You can do this by attempting to load all the types. You'll be given a warning if one of the types cannot be loaded (Figure 15.82).

FIGURE 15.82

Type catalog warning

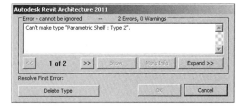

From left to right, Figure 15.83 shows Type 1 through Type 4, respectively. If you want to download the Shelf family and type catalog, look in the Chapter 15 folder on the book's web page for the files `Parametric Shelf.rfa` and `Parametric Shelf.txt`.

FIGURE 15.83
Completed family
types

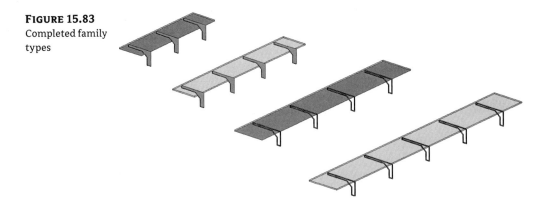

The Bottom Line

Understand the Family Editor.   Before you start modeling a piece of content in the Family Editor, take a moment and think about how you expect that piece of content to "behave" in your project. Don't be afraid to model a first pass quickly. But also be thinking ahead with regard to how it might change. The role of the Family Editor isn't just an environment to model geometry; it also determines how the content that you create will behave in the project environment.

Master It   Choosing the right template is critical. Some flexibility is allowed by allowing you to convert from one family template to another. But this is not always the case. Why would you want to choose a door template rather than a generic model template?

Choose the right family template.   Some categories and parameters are more important than others. If you choose poorly, there's no backing up. You may simply have to start over and create the family correctly.

Master It   Why are you concerned whether a family component should be hosted or not? What would happen if you select a hosted template and then decide it should be nonhosted (or vice versa)?

Use testing parameters.   Reference planes, points, and lines are the "bones" of your component. Parameterize the bones, and the geometry will follow along. Be sure to test the parameter and reference relationships before you start assigning geometry.

Master It   Why build, parameterize, and test the references first? Why not just model the geometry?

Know why formulas are important.   Sometimes parametric behavior will depend on the parameters that directly control it, but often these parameters will be expressed as a relationship to something else.

Master It   Why are formulas so important? Why not just create the parameters you need and then modify them as needed in the project environment?

Chapter 16

Stairs and Railings

Creating extraordinary stairs and railings in Revit can be fairly challenging at times. Iterating and resolving your design idea is a lot like working in a spreadsheet, and designing in a spreadsheet without some graphical feedback can be fairly frustrating. On top of this, stairs and railings are often quite sculptural in addition to being functional, and there's just so much sculpture you can get to with the in-the-box functionality.

There's a lot that the Stair and Railing tools in Revit can accomplish that even advanced users don't always realize, but often it's the exceptions that trip people up. In this chapter, we'll cover some common scenarios of stairs and railings by using the tools in the usual ways and then also using them a bit creatively.

In this chapter, you'll learn to:

- ◆ Understand the key components of stairs and railings

- ◆ Design beautiful custom stairs with default toolset

- ◆ Create elegant exceptions to the out of the box stairs and railings tool

- ◆ Implement best practices

How to Approach Stairs and Railings

Designing and reiterating complex stairs and railings in just about any software application can be difficult. It's likely that you'll need to deeply understand the rules and constraints of the application; in effect, you're learning the *language* of the application. And in order to be able to communicate fluently in that language, you need to be able to think fluently. You almost have to be able to think beyond the individual words and begin to arrange whole ideas.

Regardless of how well you know how to use a particular application, you have to contend with imagination and creation of elegant and sometimes complex design issues. Sometimes stairs and railings may be quite straightforward and functional (think of a steel or concrete egress stair) where there's not a lot of room for thinking outside the box. But in many cases, stairs and railings are conceived as feature elements within a space. They'll be touched and experienced up close. They may be extraordinarily complex and sculptural—an almost "inhabited" sculpture (Figure 16.1).

Image courtesy of Dougal McKinley

FIGURE 16.1
Detail of the feature stair in Apple's 5th Avenue retail store

When these two worlds collide—"amazing design idea" meets "perceived software functional limitation"—the result is understandably a lot of frustration for an entire design team, especially when you look back at the kinds of designs that were imagined and realized with simple paper and pencil. Computers were supposed to make this easier, right? Fortunately, you have a few options. Figure 16.2 illustrates the kind of stair that would challenge almost any 3D modeling program.

FIGURE 16.2
Complex feature stairs

For example, you can use a generic modeling application such as SketchUp, Bonzai, 3ds Max, Maya, Rhino, and so on to model your stair and railing designs. Of course, stair and railing creation will require greater "fluency" compared with modeling other, more rectilinear objects. But there's a drawback. Even though you'll eventually come to understand the rules for creating and manipulating geometry in a generic modeling application, what still remains difficult is the design idea and managing design iteration. And although many of the generic applications on the market give you the "tools" to design complex form, they seldom give you the "rules" to manage the iteration of your design.

In Revit, the situation is often reversed: you'll frequently have the "rules" to iterate and manage your design. But the tools of geometry creation can be limiting at times. In other words, Revit is purpose-built for designing building elements and relating them to the rules of likely constructed relationships (doors associate with walls, furniture associates with floors, and so on). Revit isn't simply another "generic" modeler. The application is biased toward relationships specific to designing a building and maintaining those relationships as the design changes. But to make things a bit more complicated, there's another layer. Within the general language of Revit, there's a specific language to creating stairs and railings (Figure 16.3). The image below illustrates the baluster placement dialog for a very complex baluster condition.

FIGURE 16.3
Edit Baluster
Placement
dialog box for
complex railings
configuration

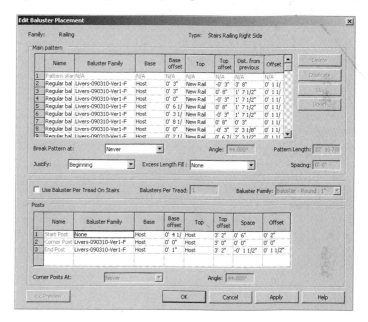

From a design iteration standpoint, it's important that your building elements understand their relationships to other elements. They will also need to view, schedule, and maintain change appropriately. To accomplish this, you can use the inside-of-the-box stair and railing functionality in some interesting, innovative ways. But in many cases, the inside-of-the-box functionality will simply not suffice:

◆ The functionality you require may not yet even exist. If this is the case, your options are pretty straightforward: you'll use other out-of-the-box functionality to create a reasonable, geometrically accurate representation of what you need. It won't be an "official" stair or railing. The upside is there may be some other desirable by-products when using non–stair and railing functionality. But the downside is that you'll have to be careful where the meta-data ends up, particularly with regard to scheduling. We can almost guarantee that you'll have to use some filtering in your schedules.

◆ The functionality that you require may be so indefinable that you might as well stop wait-ing for an out-of-the-box solution and start looking for elegant hacks. In other words, when the system of rules you're trying to create can't be defined by a system of rules, look else-where. When you expect the exceptions will occur more frequently than the rules, you're looking at quickly approaching diminished returns. The unpredictability of attempting to define the overall system isn't worth the effort.

Our approach has always been to try to find the solution that is both technically correct and aligned with the best intentions of the use of BIM (the life cycle of "cradle to cradle"). But at the same time, we believe that you should strive to take *implementability* into account. We have two simple approaches to determining when to use an in-the-box solution and when to think out of the box:

◆ Is what you're trying to design best defined as spreadsheet or sculpture? If what you're designing can be described within a spreadsheet, then it's likely that you'll be able to use the Stair tool out of the box (like an egress stair). But if what you're trying to design cannot easily be defined within the confines of a spreadsheet (i.e., Stair Tool dialog box), it's likely you'll be working outside the box of the default Stair tool. This is because there are just too many exceptions and peculiarities to make using the default Stair tool worthwhile.

◆ Just because your design might not fit within the confines of the Stair tool, it doesn't mean that you can't maintain a proper balance of project part/whole relationships when using other tools like the Family Editor. Remember that the Family Editor will allow you to maintain many relationships in a project by editing single elements and then reloading to maintain design iteration.

So in conclusion, it's important that whatever your approach, inside or outside of the stair and railing toolbox, your solution should maintain a balance of "efficient predictability." Design efforts are distributed across people and teams, and it's important that your approach is not so unique that anyone else would not be able to understand how to modify your design when it changes (and it will). And with that, let's move on to describing some essential parts of stairs and railings.

Key Components of Stairs and Railings

Details of what each of the instance and type parameters do and how they affect your railing and stair design have been covered in other books and the Revit user forums. This section is about the parts of the functionality that are important to being able to create interesting stairs and railings.

Components of Railings

The critical parts of a railing are the profiles, different kinds of balusters, and how they are placed within the definition of a railing.

Profiles   You can have as many profiles per railing as you like (Figure 16.4), but you can't have more than one profile per family (RFA) file. And all the profile families need to be a closed loop—no gaps or overlapping lines allowed. Furthermore, all the profiles will be swept parallel to their host.

FIGURE 16.4
Multiple profiles
per railing

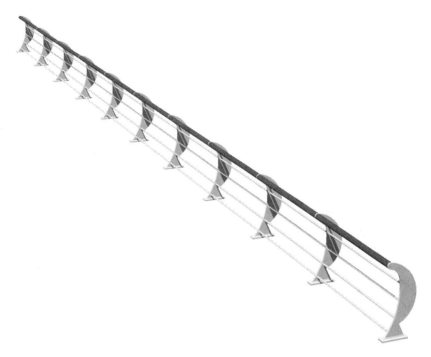

FIGURE 16.4
Multiple profiles
per railing

Balusters   There are three kinds of balusters:

◆ *Baluster posts* have built-in parameters to control the height of the baluster so that it can grow vertically (Figure 16.5).

FIGURE 16.5
Baluster post
template

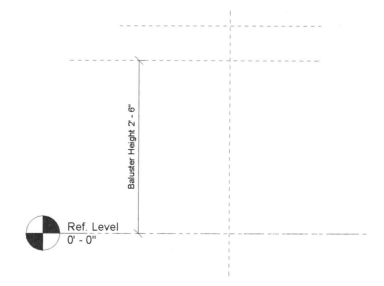

◆ *Balusters* have parameters that control the vertical length of both the top and bottom of the baluster. But there are also reference planes that will control the angle of the top and bottom of the baluster. This is helpful for maintaining angular relationships to a stringer or handrail (Figure 16.6).

FIGURE 16.6
Baluster template

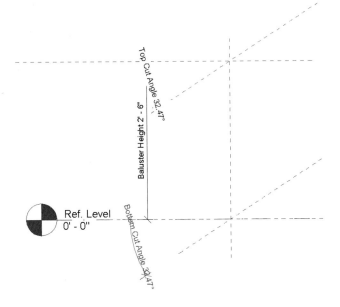

◆ *Baluster panels* have controls much like the baluster. But there are additional reference planes to control the overall width of a desired panel (Figure 16.7).

FIGURE 16.7
Baluster panel
template

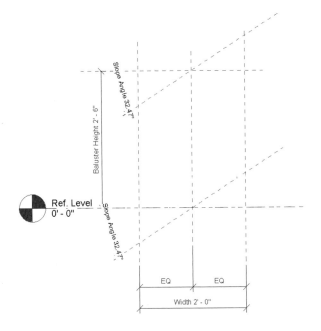

The railing profiles and all the different balusters come together to be controlled from a railing's Type Properties (Figure 16.8). Within this dialog box there are separate dialog boxes for the railing. For this particular example, we'll use the in-the-box Guardrail – Pipe family that's part of your standard Revit template.

FIGURE 16.8

Type Properties of a railing

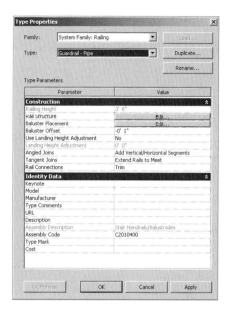

Selecting the Rail Structure option will show you all the profiles that are associated with this railing type (Figure 16.9). As mentioned earlier, you can have multiple profiles associated with a railing, but each profile needs to be a separate family file.

FIGURE 16.9

Edit Rails dialog box

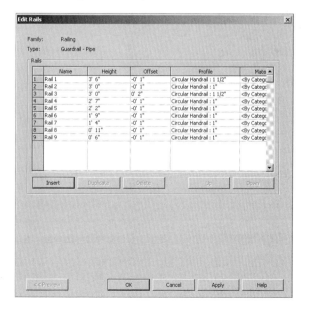

Selecting the Baluster Placement option will show you all the balusters that are associated with this tailing type (Figure 16.10). As you can see, there are options for the main pattern, the posts, and an option for how the balusters will be used on stairs (Figure 16.10).

FIGURE 16.10

Baluster Placement dialog box for Guardail – Pipe family

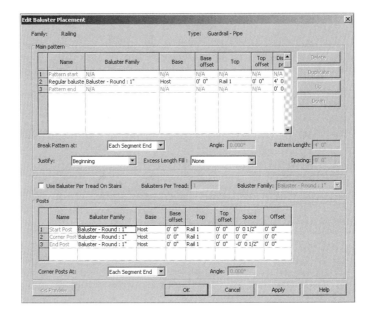

The Main Pattern section of the dialog box is where you would assemble all your baluster types and then space and host them accordingly. You can also decide how you want the pattern to repeat (or not repeat) itself at ends of sketched line segments.

The Posts section is used to specify which baluster is used at start, corner, and end conditions (and the frequency of corner posts).

That's about it with regard to the properties of railings; we've just covered the most important features necessary to create great railings using both in- and out-of-the-box techniques. Now let's discuss the important and fundamental parts of stairs.

Components of Stairs

The critical parts of stairs are the nosing profile, stringer, tread, and railing. Railings are allowed unique conditions when used with stairs.

Nosing Structure   This is one closed loop that can be associated with the front and both sides of the tread.

Stringers   The default stringers can only be rectilinear in form and may only be placed on the left, right, and middle of the stair. There may be multiple middle stringers.

Treads   Basically you can control the depth and the thickness. The actual shape of the tread in plan is controlled in Sketch mode. Keep in mind that when changing the thickness of the tread, the top of the tread is maintained.

Balusters/Railings   There is an important override option that allows you to specify the number of balusters per tread when the railing is used with stairs (as well as specify the baluster).

Now that we've covered the key components of stairs, let's start to investigate railings using techniques that are more common to Revit. Once you understand these rules, you'll better understand how and why to "stretch" them to create more complex configurations.

Railings In and Out of the Box

We consider in-the-box techniques to mean using the functionality in interesting and useful ways and leveraging intended functionality. But keep in mind that the metadata may or may not remain associated with the category of element that you're creating. For example, you can use the Railing tool to create railings, but you can also use it to distribute repetitive elements along a path that may not be railings at all. As a result, your schedules will need to be watched carefully so that certain elements are properly counted and undesirable data will be ignored.

Railings Inside the Box

Using a 3D pattern to represent geometry is not a new idea in Revit. We use pattern files to represent ceiling tiles, masonry patterns in walls, and other host elements. Using 3D patterns is a great way to go easy on your computer as well. And there are a couple of places where using model patterns is useful for creating specific types of railings.

First, indicating wire mesh panels for railings is not that hard, and it'll keep you from dealing with unnecessarily high levels of detail. The technique is also great when the wire mesh panels are curved (Figure 16.11).

FIGURE 16.11
Patterns
representing
wire mesh

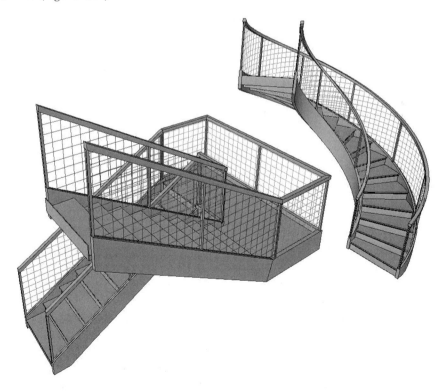

The technique is simple and can be accomplished in just a few steps:

1. You'll need a piece of geometry to represent the "zone" of the mesh. This can be easily created in the Family Editor as a profile family. In this case, the profile is ½" × 2'-6". Take care of the insertion point (Figure 16.12). This is important to keep the top of the profile properly associated with the top handrail when used with stairs.

FIGURE 16.12
Wire mesh profile

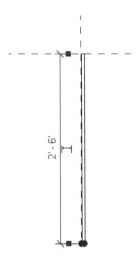

2. Save the family and load into a default project. For this exercise, let's start with a simple railing of Railing – Handrail Rectangular. Duplicate and rename it to **Railing – Wire Mesh**, and then we'll modify it.

3. Change the baluster placement from 0'-4" to 4'-0". This will give you plenty of space between the balusters and make room for the wire mesh (Figure 16.13).

FIGURE 16.13
Making room for
the wire mesh

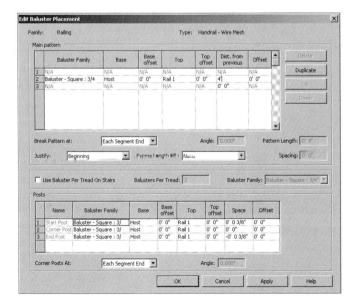

4. Now let's edit the rail structure. Duplicate the existing handrail and change the elevation. Then add another region and associate it with the wire mesh profile that you previously created (Figure 16.14).

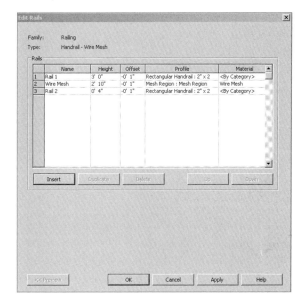

5. Finally, you'll need to create a new model pattern (Figure 16.15) and associate this pattern with the profile of the wire mesh. For this example, use a 2″ × 2″ crosshatch pattern at 45 degrees. And don't forget to set the Transparency value for shading to 100%.

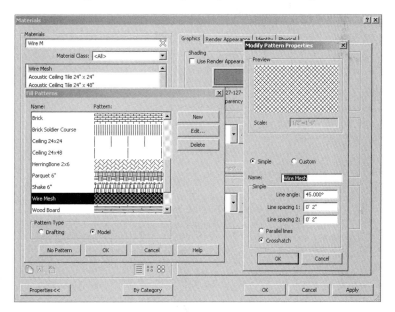

When you finish, a portion of your railing should look like Figure 16.16.

FIGURE 16.16
Finished wire
mesh railing

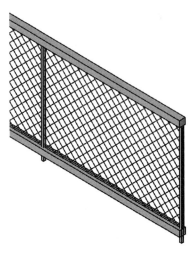

Now go ahead and create some stairs. When you're finished, swap out the default railing for your newly created wire mesh railing (Figure 16.17).

FIGURE 16.17
Mesh railing
for stairs

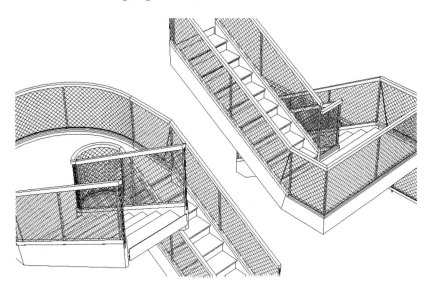

Keep in mind that this technique is great for indicating fences with vertical or horizontal battens (rather than building them out of actual geometry). This file is also available for download from the book's web page (www.sybex.com/go/masteringrevit2011) in the Chapter 16 folder; look for the Wire Mesh Railing and Stair.rvt file.

RAILINGS AS REPETITIVE SYSTEM

Unfortunately, Revit doesn't yet allow components to be quickly and easily distributed along a user-defined path. In some cases you could use "line"-based families, but these don't work in curved conditions. Having a technique that works in both straight and curved conditions is probably the best option. So in the meantime, we think you should consider using the Railing tool to distribute elements along paths.

When using railing functionality to distribute elements along paths, keep in mind these three rules:

◆ You'll likely want to nest your family into a baluster family template (rather than creating it directly as a baluster). This is because the existing parameters in the baluster family will often cause your geometry to fly apart if it needs to move up and down as a single element.

◆ Don't expect your nested element to schedule or tag. If you need the elements to schedule or tag individually, you probably want to place them individually (or use another technique like a line-based family).

◆ Don't share parameters of nested families in an attempt to schedule. It won't schedule—it'll break.

In some cases, you'll want the railing family to have associated profiles, like the shading device in Figure 16.18. The railing profiles are used to create the shading fins, and the balusters are the support elements.

FIGURE 16.18
Railing as shading device

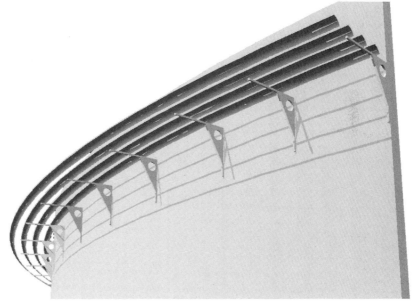

But railings don't have to contain handrail profiles. Follow these steps to delete a railing profile:

1. Set the Top value of the railing to **Host.**

2. Give the baluster a positive Top Offset value.

3. Delete the railing profile. This hosts the baluster by the host rather than the railing profile. Picking any of the balusters will allow you to edit the sketch. But the profile of the railing won't be seen until you select any one of the elements and edit their associated sketch.

Using railings to quickly and evenly distribute components along a path is great during design and allows for quick iteration. Outdoor elements are particularly appropriate for distributed placement, like a lampposts (Figure 16.19). In this example, a lamppost has been nested into a baluster family.

FIGURE 16.19
Lamppost nested into a baluster family

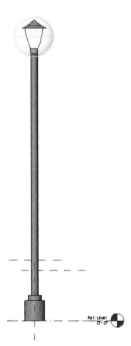

Once this lamppost has been nested, you'll be able to create a custom "railing" with the lamp designated as the "baluster." This will allow you to quickly and easily distribute lampposts along a sketch at very specific intervals that can be modified as a parameter. So for example, if the lamppost was originally distributed on 60′ centers, you could very quickly redefine it to occur on 40′ intervals (Figure 16.20).

You can use this for any repetitive elements that must be placed on center and evenly distributed along a path. Other uses might include pipe bollards and outdoor planting.

FIGURE 16.20
Lampposts distrib-
uted along a path
as a baluster family

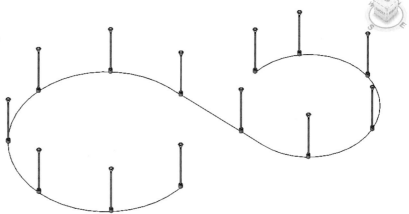

FIGURE 16.20
Lampposts distrib-
uted along a path
as a baluster family

Even a design pass at light rail tracks (including railcars) can be distributed along paths (Figure 16.21). In this case, the rail sleepers are balusters and profiles are used to create the rails and the rail bed. The monorails are easy too. The vertical supports and railcars are balusters, and the suspended track is the rail profile. This file can be downloaded from the Chapter 16 folder; look for the `Monorail and Railway Railing.rvt` file.

FIGURE 16.21
Transportation
components as
railings

Railings Outside the Box

Railings outside of the box are meant to be railing-like, geometrically speaking, but they're not created with the Railing tool. Usually this occurs when the railing is a small, unique, or highly repetitive element.

Generally speaking, maintaining order in Revit projects is often about managing repetitive relationships. These repetitive elements may be managed by creating family components, groups, and even separate Revit files. For railings, there is an obvious choice: create the railing, then create a group of the finished railing and then copy that group throughout your finished project.

Unfortunately, it's often faster to manage and update hundreds of components than it is to update hundreds of groups. The railing may also be prefabricated and installed onsite as a single component, perhaps filed under the Revit category of Specialty Equipment. If you decide to use the category of Specialty Equipment, keep in mind that the category won't cut; you'll always see a projected elevation. So, choose a category (like Generic Model) if you need to see the family cut in section.

What kind of highly repetitive railing conditions are we referring to? Sport stadiums, theaters, hotel balconies, apartment buildings, and so on all have railing conditions that are highly repetitive. Railings modeled as a singular component in the Family Editor are perfect for these kinds of situations where only a few family components can cover hundreds of conditions (Figure 16.22).

FIGURE 16.22
Example of repetitive railing condition

Custom handrail joins are known to frustrate Revit users. But again, if modeled in the Family Editor and associated with the railing, it's a challenge that can often be easily overcome. What's important is that you'll need some context to model your custom condition. So go ahead and model the context of what you need as a starting point:

1. Open a default template and sketch a stair with dimensions shown so that there's really no reason to have a railing between the two runs, but the railing should still be continuous (Figure 16.23). Note that there is only 6" separating each run.

2. Associate the Handrail – Pipe railing with the stairs and the problem is obvious: how to properly model the join between the railings (Figure 16.24)?

3. In order to model the join between handrails, it'll be helpful to have some context. Activate a section box around the desired portion of the handrail. Then export this 3D section (Figure 16.25).

FIGURE 16.23
Stair sketch in plan

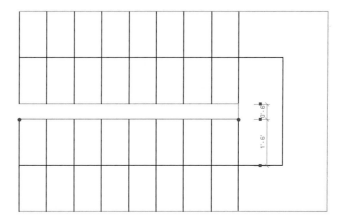

FIGURE 16.24
Example of
unjoined handrails

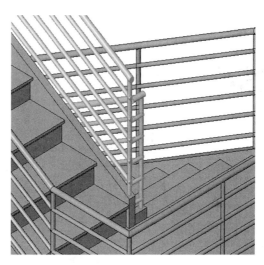

FIGURE 16.25
Exporting the rail-
ing context

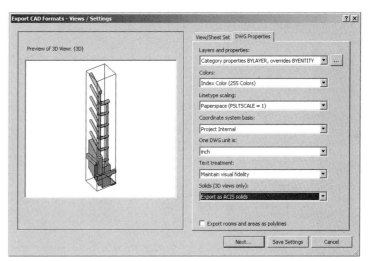

4. Since the handrail join will be part of your baluster, go ahead and duplicate the default round baluster family and name it `Baluster - Round with Join.rfa`. Now import this 3D context into your duplicate baluster family. Also, before you start to model the connections it may helpful to create some reference planes (Figure 16.26).

FIGURE 16.26
Use reference planes in context with the imported railing geometry.

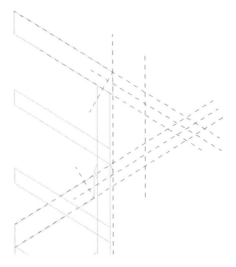

If modeling in a nonstandard 3D view is a challenge, try to model what you're creating in a standard 3D view and then rotate your component into place. You'll still be able to edit it afterward. In this case we've modeled half the join and then mirrored the other half (Figure 16.27) in context with the portion of the exported handrail.

5. Once you're done modeling the connection, you may either delete the exported context or deselect its visibility settings in the Instance Properties of the imported file.

FIGURE 16.27
Modeled handrail join in context with railing export

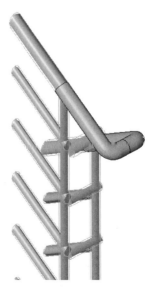

6. Back in the project environment, you'll want to delete the portions of the handrail sketch that are shown in Figure 16.28 as highlighted in blue. Keep in mind that the lower portion of the railing will be completed as a separate, hosted sketch. You won't need to model the railing connecting the upper and lower runs. Finally, the lower, hosted railing run will be the default Type Baluster – Round, not the custom baluster that we are making.

7. Duplicate the remaining portion of the inner handrail and rename to **Handrail – Pipe – Inner Section**. This will differentiate it from the default Handrail – Pipe. Now you can edit the value of the end post to the baluster family that we've just created (Figure 16.29).

8. Through a system of careful measurements (as well as a bit of trial and error), you'll want to elevate, rotate, and finally nudge the handrail join portion of the baluster family until it's in the correct position with regard to the upper and lower handrail runs (keeping in mind that the lower run is a separate sketch). Just remember to reload the baluster family into the stair project to make sure that your adjustments are correct.

FIGURE 16.28
Deleting the blue portions of the inner handrail sketch

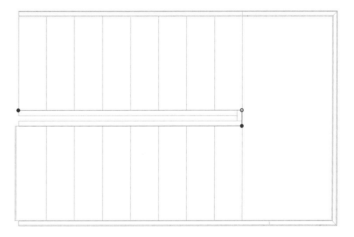

FIGURE 16.29
Edit the end post to associate with the handrail join.

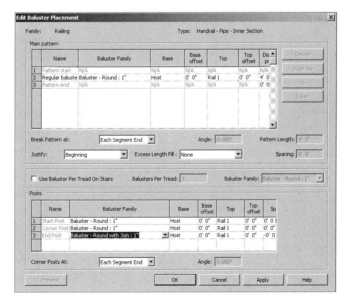

After a few moments, you'll end up with a custom connection, as shown in Figure 16.30. The great thing about this technique is that it works with multistory stair conditions. You can download the completed project in the Chapter 16 folder at the book's web page; the file is named c16 Custom Handrail Join Project.rvt.

FIGURE 16.30
Completed handrail join

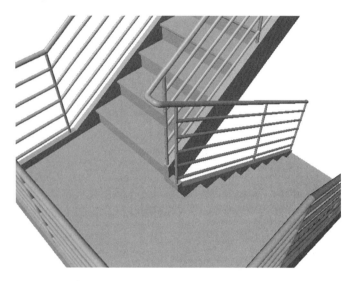

Although the three-run stair has to do with stairs as well as railings, we'll go ahead and cover it here. You can't have overlapping sketches when using the Railing or Stair tool, so you're obviously going to have to create two separate sketches. This is where most people run into problems: they divide the sketch at one of the landings.

We've found that a better technique involves breaking the stair and railing in the middle of the second run, not at the landing. Here's how:

1. Open a new project using the default template. Then open your South Elevation and create a new Level 3, as shown in Figure 16.31.

2. Return to Level 1 to start your stair sketch. You'll notice that the moment the sketch starts, you're expected to create 18 risers to complete half of the three-run stair—which means that each run will be 12 risers (36 total risers divided by three runs). So sketch your first stair with 12 risers, then a landing and another 6 risers (Figure 16.32).

FIGURE 16.31
Creating Level 3

FIGURE 16.32
Half of the
three-run stair

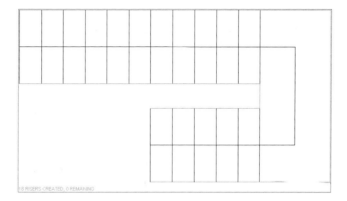

3. Now mirror the stair at the end of the second run. Change the direction of the second run so that the landings meet correctly.

4. Modify the Instance Properties of the stair to start at Level 2 and finish at Level 3, as shown in Figure 16.33. You'll also notice that there's an "extra" tread overlapping the landing. Not to worry—we'll fix that in a moment.

FIGURE 16.33
Changing the
properties of the
mirrored stair

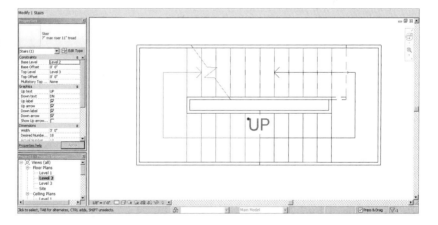

Go to the default 3D view and you'll notice that the second run doesn't meet the first run properly (Figure 16.34). That's because the stair you just mirrored starts with a riser (which you don't need).

5. Go to the stair properties of the mirrored stair, and duplicate the stair type. We're going to change the Type Properties of the second run.

6. Change the Extend Below Base value to –1'-6" and deselect the Begin With Riser option (since we already have a riser, from the end of the first run of stairs).

7. Click OK. You'll be given a warning that the actual and desired number of risers are different. Ignore the warning. Now return to Level 2 and edit the sketch of the second stair. You'll notice that you need another tread to complete the stair.

FIGURE 16.34
Initially the stairs don't meet properly.

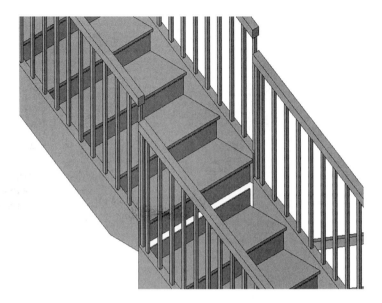

8. While in Sketch mode, simply press and drag the run line of the lower run to add an additional tread. Then move the entire sketch over 11″ so that the treads between the end of the first stair and the beginning of the second stair don't overlap. Finish the sketch. This will complete the connection between the first and second stair (Figure 16.35).

FIGURE 16.35
Completed stair connection

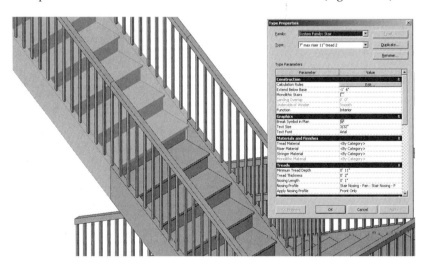

9. Duplicate the Type Properties of the upper railings. Then edit the Type Properties of the lower railings so that the Space value of End Post is 0. Set the Start Post value of the upper railing to None. Set the Justify value for the Baluster Placement of the lower railing to End and the same value for the upper railing to Beginning. You'll get the result shown in Figure 16.36.

FIGURE 16.36
Adjusting the Type
Properties of the
upper and lower
railings

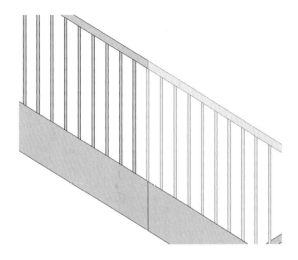

You can use this same process to create a spiral stair that is continuous and would otherwise overlap in Sketch mode (Figure 16.37). You can download the stairs in this example in the Chapter 16 folder on the book's web page; it's named `Three Run Stair.rvt`.

FIGURE 16.37
Continuous three-
run straight and
spiral stairs with
railings

The most challenging of railings often require exceptions and the ability to manually locate balusters or panels that are not part of the overall railing definition. If you were to try to define each of these exceptions as a different railing type, your project would have an overflow of railing types. This can be pretty easily accomplished, but not with the Railing tool.

By using the Curtain Wall tool, you'll be able to create railings by modeling the balusters and panels inside the Curtain Panel family template (Figure 16.38). The other nice thing about this technique is that this "railing" will contain space since it's really a wall. That makes this perfect for mezzanine conditions that require room or space calculations—certainly more efficient than creating redundant room separation lines!

FIGURE 16.38
Curtain panel as a railing

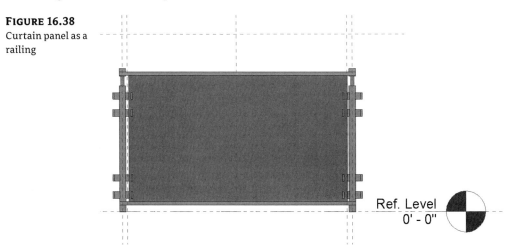

Start by creating a single panel in the Curtain Panel template. The family may contain not only the panel for the railing, but also the balusters. Once you load this panel into your project, you can create Curtain Walls with predefined panel widths (Figure 16.39).

But since curtain panels allow you to unpin predefined grids (as well as create other grid locations) you'll be able to quickly and easily make exceptions to the rules that you previously defined (Figure 16.40).

FIGURE 16.39
Curtain panel railing with custom baluster locations

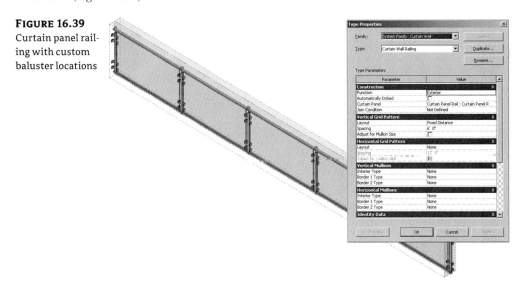

FIGURE 16.40
Adjusted baluster locations

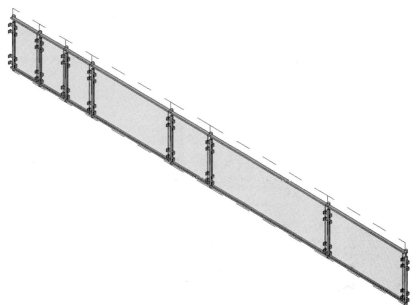

When you're creating railings as curtain walls, be sure to filter your schedules accordingly. If you want to download this example project, it's in the Chapter 16 folder and is named `Curtain Wall Railing.rvt`.

These in- and out-of-the-box techniques should give you some great ideas for making custom railings faster and more interesting than you could ever have imagined.

Stairs In and Out of the Box

Using in-the-box techniques means you're using the built-in functionality of the Stair tool to create conditions that may not have been originally intended by the factory. Sometimes this is done to overcome a limitation in functionality. But it most cases you'll be using the functionality to create conditions that are common in complex stair conditions.

As for the out-of-the-box techniques, sometimes there's just no way to anticipate every unique and sculptural design condition. In these cases, we'll show you techniques that aren't exactly using the Stair tool as designed. But the results will geometrically resemble stairs (and their railings).

Stairs Inside the Box

CERT
OBJECTIVE

You shouldn't overlook the nosing profile as a device for creating interesting shapes that complete the tread, because the shape of the nosing is not limited to traditional nosing profiles. Any shape that needs to extend beyond the face of the tread is OK. Just remember that you're limited to a single profile per tread and stair run (Figure 16.41). You'll also want to pay particular attention to the insertion point of the nosing profile because the intersection of the reference planes coincides with the top of the tread and the face of the riser.

FIGURE 16.41
Custom nosing
profile

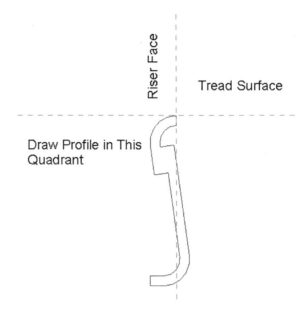

FIGURE 16.42
Continuous tread
and nosing profile

Figure 16.42 shows an example from a real stair that was designed to have each tread fabricated from a single plate and then rolled to form the face of the riser above it. Then each of these treads can be welded behind the lip of the tread above it. It's a fairly elegant idea that can be accomplished by using a custom nosing profile to create the appearance of a continuous tread (Figure 16.42). Look closely and you can see where the actual tread ends and where the nosing profile begins. But don't be distracted by the lines since they can be hidden (if necessary) when you're creating the final details.

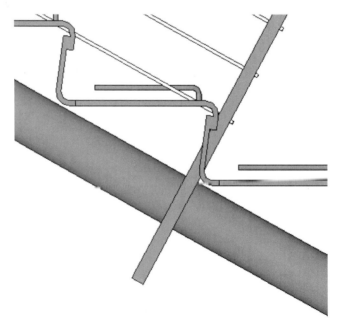

Make sure that if you're using a custom profile to represent both the nosing and the riser that you set Riser Type to None. If you don't, the profile won't be assigned correctly; it will overlap the default riser. Figure 16.43 shows the final stairs using the custom profile. As for the custom railing conditions, we'll get to that later in this chapter. If you want to investigate this stair further, it's in the Chapter 16 folder and is called `Henrys Stepp.rvt`.

FIGURE 16.43
Resulting stair

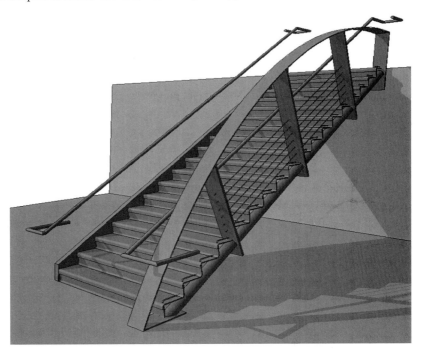

Next, let's move on to default stringers in Revit. These are good for creating a number of standard residential (wooden) or steel (commercial) conditions. What's important is that the default stringers in Revit can only be rectilinear and may be positioned to either side of the stair (left and right) and the middle. If you want a custom shape, you're out of luck if you're using default stringer. So don't! When you want to create a custom stringer profile (left, right, middle, or otherwise), simply use the Railing tool (Figure 16.44). The stair will host this railing containing the custom stringer profile (or just the custom profile, with no handrail).

FIGURE 16.44
Use the Railing tool
to create a custom
stringer profile.

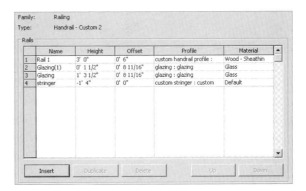

Notice in Figure 16.44 that the last profile is not really part of the traditional portion of the railing. Instead, this profile is used to indicate a custom stringer profile (Figure 16.45). But it's been assigned to the railing in order to maintain a particular relationship to their stairs.

FIGURE 16.45
Railing profile

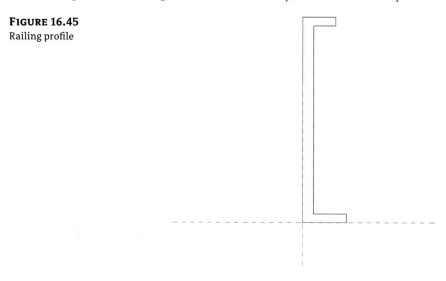

In Figure 16.46, we've isolated the railing from its stairs in order to illustrate the finished railing: the handrail, two glazed and continuous panels, and the custom stringers.

FIGURE 16.46
Completed railing profile

This railing with a custom stringer profile is perfect for a multitude of stair conditions, straight or curved or even a combination (Figure 16.47). This technique finishes off the stair nicely and exposes the structure in interesting ways.

FIGURE 16.47
Finished stairs

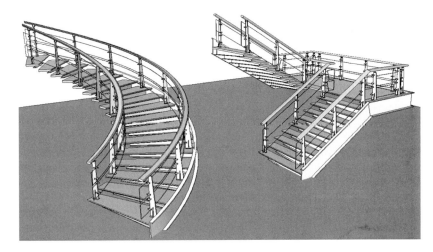

Although the stringer usually occurs to the left or right of the treads, this is certainly not always the case. In some situations you'll want to create a middle stringer using a custom profile. Just remember that this will be a railing that will be hosted by the stair and may not even contain a handrail, just the profile for the stringer (Figure 16.48). In this case, the railing is still being hosted by the stairs—it's just that there's just not any railing geometry above the tread.

FIGURE 16.48
Custom middle
stringer profile

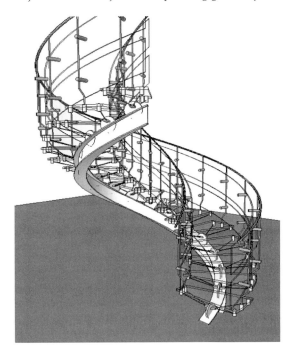

Straightforward tread shapes can be pretty boring at times, so let's move on to custom tread conditions. In situations where you need to be a bit more inventive, you're going to create a custom baluster. This technique can either create a custom support element for the default treads or it can indicate the actual tread.

But instead of the baluster being vertical, it's going to be horizontal. This horizontal baluster will be used in conjunction with the default tread. This baluster may even completely envelop the tread.

FIGURE 16.49
Baluster as tread support

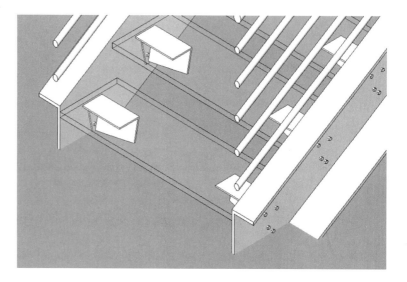

First, we need to discuss a few rules for creating an interesting tread support for the default tread (Figure 16.49):

♦ Not every baluster needs a railing. If your baluster support isn't going to be a part of the "real" railing, just create another "railing" that is hosted by the stairs. Sketching another path for your custom railing that only contains the tread support baluster can accomplish this in a few steps. Another technique is to copy an existing railing, then paste it to the exact same location and change the type to your custom supporting baluster.

♦ The Baluster Family category needs to be used for the component that will act as the tread support. Otherwise, it can't be associated to the railing.

♦ If you have a complex support element, it may be helpful to model the desired support element as a generic family. When you're finished, nest this generic element into the baluster family. You may want to do this because the baluster templates have hard-wired reference planes and parameters (which is fine if you're making a baluster that needs to geometrically flex). But in this case, we've found that these reference planes and parameters may cause your baluster to fail when you load it in the project as a result of these parameters flexing. By modeling the geometry elsewhere and nesting it, you avoid this hassle since it moves as a single component.

♦ Designating the level of detail is crucial. Assigning Coarse, Medium, or Fine as well as Orientation leads to much faster graphics regeneration, view panning, and model rotation. So if you're nesting one component into another family, the detail that you're assigning at the deepest level will be respected through nesting (Figure 16.50).

FIGURE 16.50
Single component
that will be used as
a tread support

FIGURE 16.50
Single component
that will be used as
a tread support

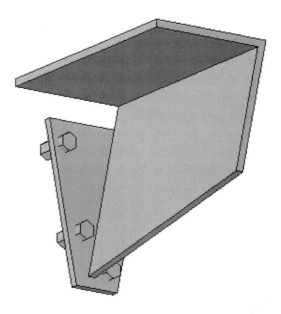

Once the component is complete, you can nest it into a baluster template, as shown in Figure 16.51. If necessary, it's also possible to parameterize the dimensions in the nested configuration.

FIGURE 16.51
The generic model
nested into a bal-
uster family

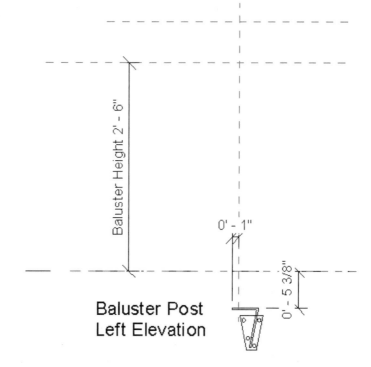

Baluster Height 2' - 6"

0' - 1"

0' - 5 3/8"

Baluster Post
Left Elevation

The completed stairs are shown in two different configurations in Figure 16.52. Many configurations are possible once you correctly define a single stair type. If you'd like to investigate this stair more closely, go the Chapter 16 folder at the book's web age and download c16_Angled_Support_Stair.rvt.

FIGURE 16.52
Completed stairs

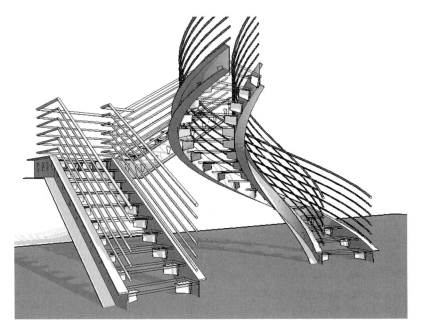

Note that a custom baluster support might be modeled to contain the real balusters that are intended to support railings. This can simplify and shorten modeling time. In the example shown in Figure 16.53, the baluster support geometry also contains the railing elements on both the right and left side. If you want to examine this stair more closely, it's in the Chapter 16 folder and is called Support Tread.rvt.

The previous support baluster can be brought together with a custom profile for the center stringer, handrails, and glazed panels (Figure 16.54). You can download this example from the Chapter 16 folder; it's called Center Baluster Support.rvt.

CONTROLLING THE BALUSTER SUPPORTS

Don't forget to control the number of baluster supports per tread. Revit has an easy way to accomplish this through the railing option Use Baluster Per Tread On Stairs.

Once you've begun to experiment with creating balusters as tread supports for stairs, you'll notice you have options for making more complete and finished conditions.

FIGURE 16.53
Complex baluster
support with
balusters

FIGURE 16.54
Complex support
with balusters

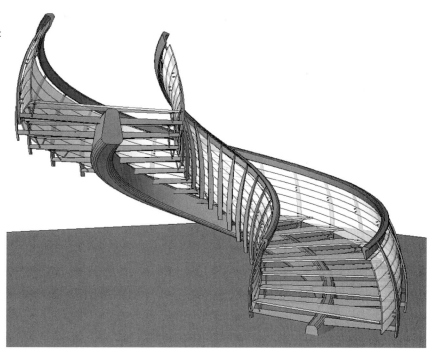

Start and end posts are useful and can help complete the structure of your custom railing and baluster system, particularly if you want to properly anchor and connect your custom stair and railing. The example in Figure 16.55 uses only start and end posts to anchor the custom railings and stair structure. It builds on the previous example of using a baluster as a support element for a tread.

FIGURE 16.55
Baluster as a support element

To finish this stair, we need to create start and end posts that anchor the stair. As with the previous handrail join exercise, you'll want to model the bulk of the custom stair with the custom railing. Then you'll export the stair parts for importing into the baluster template (or generic model template that will be nested into the baluster template).

Figure 16.56 shows the results after the start and end posts are modeled.

When it all comes together, the results can be elegant and interesting (Figure 16.57). All of this is available through the default Stair tool. You can download this stair from the Chapter 16 folder; it's called Tube Stair.rvt.

FIGURE 16.56
Finished start and end posts with a connection

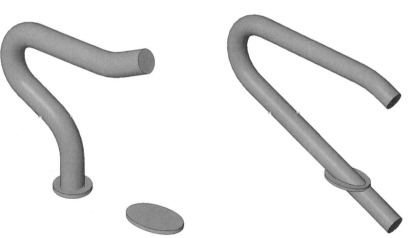

FIGURE 16.57
Finished stair with
baluster supports,
as well as start and
end posts

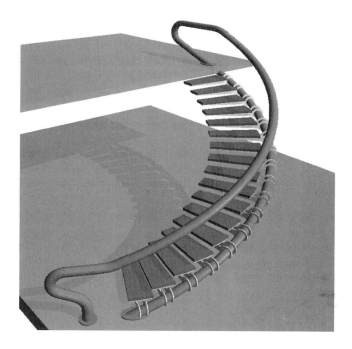

Now let's go one step further. There's no reason that the baluster support element needs to exactly conform to the shape of the tread. And there's no reason that the support element can't contain the actual baluster that is intended to support the handrail.

Take a look at the support element in Figure 16.58. Not only does it contain the support element, but the support element has been modeled to exceed the shape of the tread that will be modeled by the Stair tool.

Keep in mind that we've modeled the support element as a generic model and then nested it into a baluster post template (Figure 16.59). Again, this keeps the baluster together so it's not affected by the built-in reference planes and parameters.

FIGURE 16.58
Support and bal-
uster as a generic
model

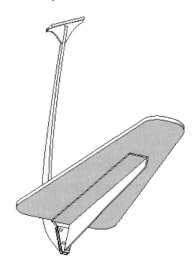

FIGURE 16.59
Baluster and support nested into a baluster post template

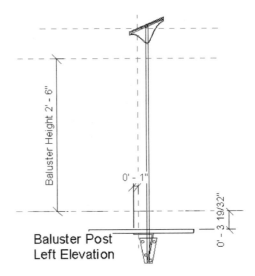

Once this custom baluster post is loaded into the project, simply associate it with the stair and its railings. Remember to select the One Baluster Per Tread option. When finished, the default tread is simply an inlay to the more complete tread support (Figure 16.60). In more complex conditions, it may be desirable to envelop the entire tread with the support geometry. This will allow you to create complex tread shapes that are not dependent on the default tread and use the functionality of the stair and Railing tools to properly locate, rotate, and elevate each of your custom treads. If you want to examine this stair further, check out the file Curved Tread Support.rvt in the Chapter 16 folder.

FIGURE 16.60
Finished stair with integrated baluster and support

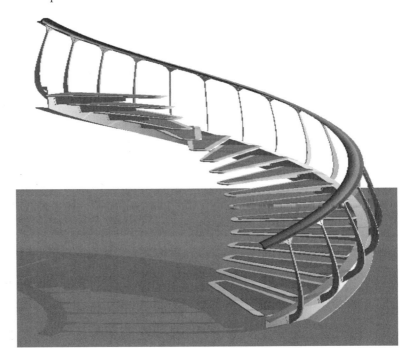

Figure 16.61 shows an example using this technique. The tread support elements have been modeled using blends in order to sweep under the metal plate while changing direction from vertical to angle. This will accommodate the angled pipe rail that will support the stair.

FIGURE 16.61
The top and underside of tread support

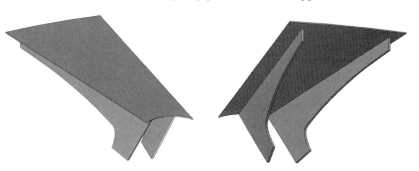

Treads come together in a particularly interesting stair and railing configuration. There is obviously a more conventional outer railing for this stair. But the inner railing doesn't have any elements that occur at hand height. The entire inner railing exists to support the baluster supports (that in turn support the default treads). The end post is being used to anchor the entire structure through the second level. You can find this example, Highlights.rvt, in the Chapter 16 folder. Figure 16.62 shows the finished stair. Note that the large structural element is actually a baluster that's been designated as the end post.

FIGURE 16.62
Completed stair with large end post

Stairs Outside the Box

As we approach out-of-the-box techniques, the goal is to create stairs that may not fully adhere to strict interpretation of BIM in that the metadata may not correspond to the geometry. But this is usually the only option to complete a design where there's no in-the-box technique. At least you'll be confident that your project will be properly coordinated from a geometric and documentation point of view.

Just be a bit more careful when you use these techniques. The metadata—the information part of BIM—isn't being coordinated properly. So you'll want to take particular care with regard to tagging and scheduling.

Let's start with the stair from the previous section (Figure 16.63).

FIGURE 16.63
Finished stair with integrated baluster and support

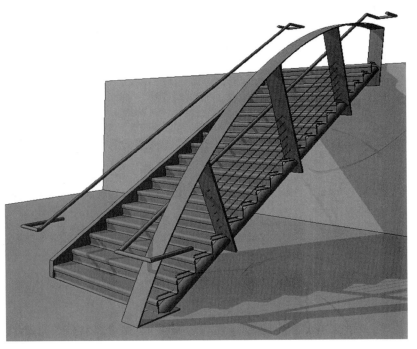

While the railings on the left side of the image seems pretty straightforward, the curved railing on the left may seem a bit challenging, the three balusters inside the curved element are perpendicular to the run of the stair, and the cable starts and stops before completing the run (which is the default condition). However, this is actually accomplished in a few easy steps.

This example nests geometry modeled in the generic family template and then nests that geometry into a baluster post template. The baluster is then assigned as the start post to create the entire railing. The nice thing about using the start post is that whenever you create the stair, the "railings" are automatically added, even if you create a multistory stair condition.

Once again, there are a few steps to follow, which by now should be rather familiar.

First, model what you can with the out-of-the-box tools. Even if you can only model the treads, this will help give you context to the rest of the system; then export the treads from a 3D view and import it into a generic model family. In this case, everything that can be modeled as the stair is shown in Figure 16.64.

FIGURE 16.64
Completed stair
before exporting

FIGURE 16.64
Completed stair
before exporting

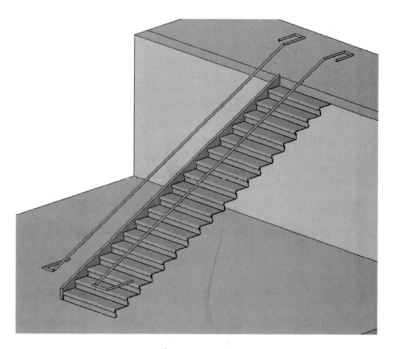

After exporting this stair in 3D and importing it into the Family Editor, you can model your design in context with exactly how it will be used. Figure 16.65 is the resulting form that will be used assigned to the stair's railing as a start post.

FIGURE 16.65
Baluster post as a
complex railing

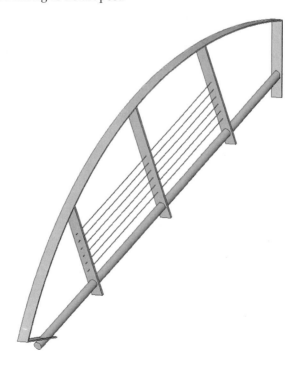

This is a valuable technique for creating complex and difficult-to-predict railings for stairs. The important part of this technique is to use the out-of-the-box Stair tool to model whatever is easily possible for context. Once again, here are the steps:

1. Export the stair in 3D.

2. Import the exported file into a generic model family.

3. Model your complex railing design in context with the imported 3D (keeping in mind that reference planes are helpful).

4. Nest the finished family into a baluster post family.

5. Associate this baluster family as the start post for the railing.

Here's another example of using this technique to overcome and otherwise complex condition that simply could not be created using the default Stair and Railing tools. The stair in Figure 16.66 is modeled with the default tools: Stair, Baluster, and Railing. This creates all that is necessary for modeling the wire cable net that will be used to complete the stair.

FIGURE 16.66
Parts of default stairs

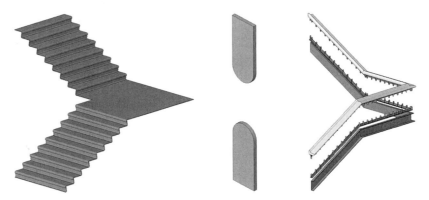

Once this geometry is exported, it's ready to be used as context for modeling the cable net that will be assigned as the start post for the stair (Figure 16.67). If you want to study this stair and railing further, check out the file Cable Stair.rvt in the Chapter 16 folder.

Now we'll talk about other challenging configurations. In many cases, it's not the parts that make up the entire stair that is the challenge. Often it is the overall configuration that vexes people (like creating the three-run stair we previously discussed).

A solid spiral wall to be used as a railing or a support element can easily be created in the Family Editor and then associated with the stair as a start post. Of course, this geometry could also be created as an in-place element. But then you'd lose the advantage of being able to quickly and easily relocate the stair in your project (or create a multistory condition).

In Figure 16.68 you can see the default tread with a baluster being used as a support element. What's interesting about this configuration is that rather than being configured as a circular stair, the path is made of two concentric arcs.

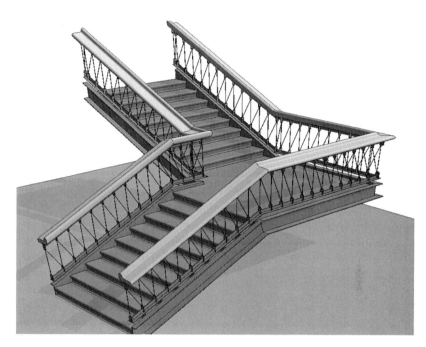

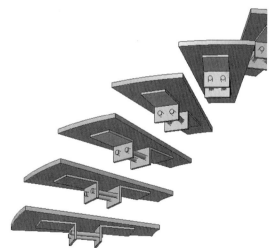

Rather than create this as an in-place family under the stair, we'll model the swept blend as a baluster post in order to associate it with the beginning of the custom baluster. In order to make sure that we have the path exactly right, we'll copy the path of the custom railing that's associated to the support baluster (Figure 16.69).

FIGURE 16.69
Copied path of the
custom railing

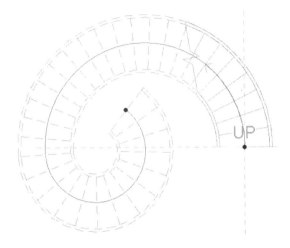

Now you can use this path as you create each of the blended sweeps (creating only one swept blend per path). In this case the blends are being modeled so that there's a 3″ gap between the undersides of the default treads. The final swept blend in shown in Figure 16.70.

FIGURE 16.70
Finished swept
blend

Figure 16.71 shows what you get when it all comes together. The swept blend has been created in a baluster template. This baluster is then loaded into the project environment and associated with the railing that contains the overall support baluster (Figure 16.71). This is also useful if you have to create walls that need to follow either side of a stair. If the condition exists only once, you may opt to create this in-place.

But if it occurs more than once or might be rotated and relocated (as well as occur on many levels), we recommend that you create this as part of the stair and railing definition. Then it'll be easier to maintain relationships throughout the project. To investigate this stair, download the Concentric Stair.rvt file from the Chapter 16 folder.

FIGURE 16.71
Finished stair
condition

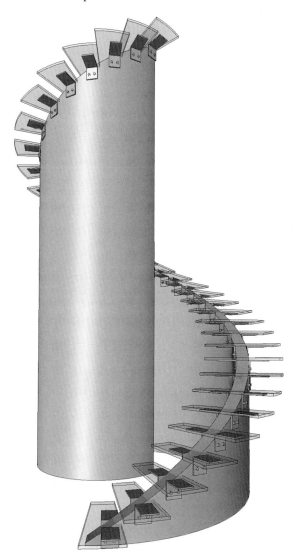

Another condition that results in a lot of confusion is creating a circular run that ends aligned from where it begins. This is also quite easy to accomplish once you understand the proper steps.

First, as you start to create the circular run, you'll notice the number of required treads. In the case of the default stairs and default template, 18 risers are required. Start by creating half that number, or 9 (Figure 16.72).

FIGURE 16.72
Sketching half the
required risers

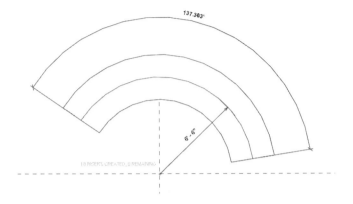

Once you've created the first half of the stairs, rotate and mirror the nine risers (Figure 16.73).

FIGURE 16.73
Align and mirror
half the risers.

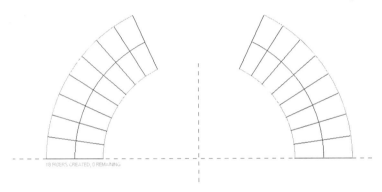

Now here's the tricky part: sketch the remaining boundaries manually. In other words, don't elect to finish the run and think that Revit will automatically complete the boundary for you (which works with more conventional configurations; see Figure 16.74).

FIGURE 16.74
Finished stair
boundary

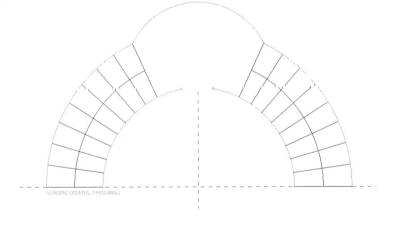

Now you're ready to finish the stair sketch with the confidence that the end of your stair is aligned with where it begins (Figure 16.75). To study this stair, download the `Curved and Aligned Stair.rvt` file from the Chapter 16 folder.

Another type of stair that creates a lot of confusion is a stair with split runs. In other words, it may start as one run but then it splits (typically at the landing) and becomes two separate runs. The challenge is that many users will create the first stair as a complete run. Then they will create a shorter run from the landing to the second level. If only it were easier… Well, it is!

Simply create half the stair and then mirror the results. Although this might create a line along your first run, the line can be hidden, and in the long run, the stair will be easier to modify and update. So let's get started:

1. The entire stair is going to be 3'-0" wide, but the first run is going to be 6'-0" wide. The shape of the sketch is shown in Figure 16.76.

FIGURE 16.76
Half the split stair

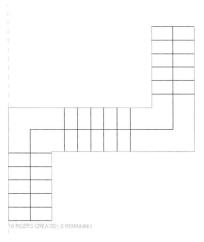

2. Once you finish the stair, edit the railing as shown in Figure 16.77. This will get rid of the railing through the middle of the landing and between the first run.

FIGURE 16.77
Editing the sketch
of the railing

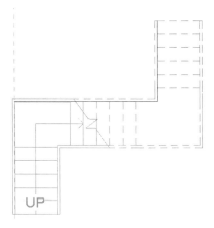

3. Now finish the stair and mirror the results. That was easy enough! But now you have to get rid of the default stringer that associated with the stairs (Figure 16.78).

FIGURE 16.78
Remove the default
stringer.

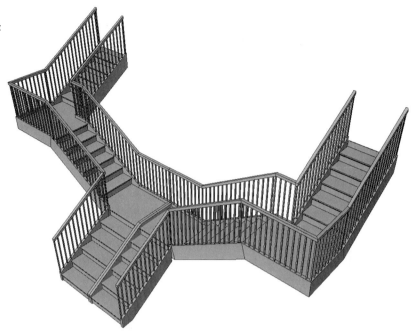

4. Edit the properties of the stairs and remove both the left and right stringers. Then create a profile of the same dimensions and associate it with the railing. But rather than create a new profile, make things easy on yourself by duplicating the Rectangular Handrail profile that you already have in your project. Be sure to also modify the Type Properties of the handrail profile (Figure 16.79).

FIGURE 16.79
Modified
handrail type

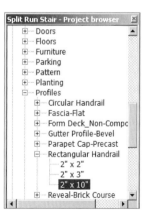

5. Now associate this profile with the handrail that is associated with the stairs, as shown in Figure 16.80.

FIGURE 16.80
Adding the hand-
rail profile

The custom stringer profile now exists as part of the railing definition. Now you have a split run stair that can be easily modified if the design changes (Figure 16.81). This stair can be downloaded from the Chapter 16 folder; look for Split Run Stair.rvt.

FIGURE 16.81
Finished split
run stairs

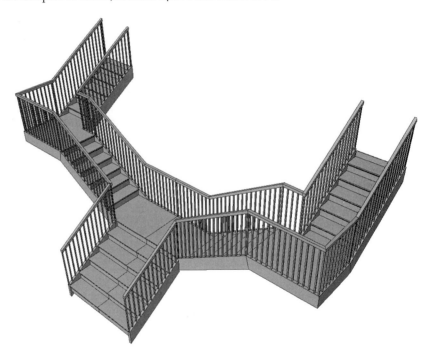

Now let's put it all together. When it comes to feature stairs, few stairs are as immediately recognizable as the glass stairs and walkways that have been designed for Apple by Bohlin Cywinski Jackson (Figure 16.82). Although these stairs seem incredibly challenging, there's very little about the Apple stairs that *can't* be modeled out of the box!

Even though the stairs are very sculptural, there are quite a few repetitive relationships that are easily identified and defined. Of course, what doesn't strictly conform to the rules of the Stair tool will have to be modeled elsewhere. First, let's model the treads and landing. We're assuming some dimensions since we don't have the actual drawings or measurements to work from: 2" thick, 6'-0" wide, and a 4'-0" interior radius (Figure 16.83).

FIGURE 16.82
5th Avenue Apple
stair in New York

FIGURE 16.83
Finished tread
configuration

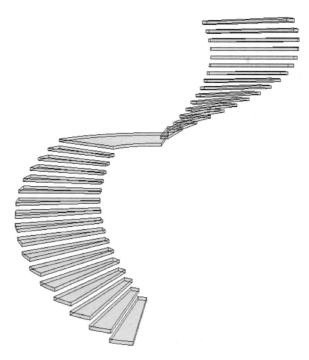

A small support "pin" is used to support the treads. One pin per tread supports the inner portion of the tread, but two pins per tread support the outer portion (so right away we'll have to create two separate handrail types for the stair). Figure 16.84 shows the pin family.

FIGURE 16.84
Support pin as a baluster

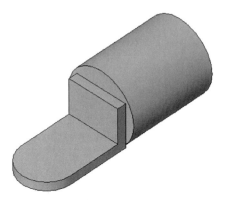

With this in mind, we're able to place the pin as a baluster after modeling it as a generic model and then nesting it into a baluster family template (not a baluster post), which will allow it to conform to the elevation of the landing. Since the pin is so small, it is also given a "fine" level of detail assignment so it doesn't show up unless the view is set to Fine.

As just mentioned, two handrail types are needed, since they will host different baluster definitions. The inner handrail has one pin support per tread, whereas the outer handrail has two pin supports per tread (Figure 16.85).

FIGURE 16.85
One and two pins per tread with handrails

As for the start and end posts, two families are needed: one for the start configuration and another for the end. They include the horizontal extension beyond the end of the railing sketch. Once you've added these posts, the stair really starts to come together (Figure 16.86).

FIGURE 16.86
Treads, support balusters, and railings

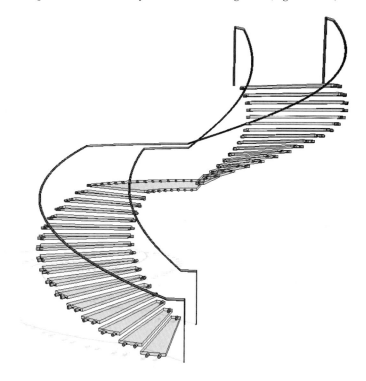

This concludes the portion of the stair that can be modeled out of the box. Export this 3D context for the remainder of the stair, which will be modeled as a generic family and then nested into a baluster post and assigned as a start post. There's a third railing in this stair (which contains no railing profile). This "invisible" railing is hosted by the stair and creates the remaining elements, as shown in Figure 16.87.

Two swept blends form the upper and lower glazed and curved panels, and a regular sweep forms the panels at the landing. At the same time, a single extrusion forms the center, glazed cylinder. When all this geometry is modeled, a single void (in plan) is extruded vertically and creates all the discrete panel separations at one time.

The panel supports and the actual balusters that will support the railing are modeled elsewhere and then nested into this family. This approach will allow the object to be quickly updated from a single location. Keep in mind that the handrails in the project will be used to host the baluster "pins" (one or two per tread); the actual handrail supports will be nested into this family. Each panel has a single baluster element (Figure 16.88).

FIGURE 16.87
Glazed panels with connections

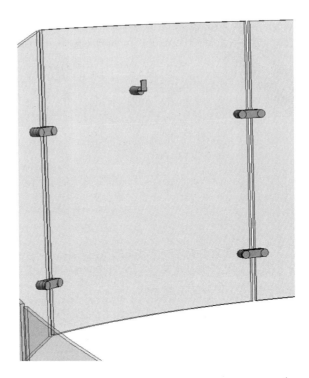

FIGURE 16.88
Final geometry before nesting into baluster family

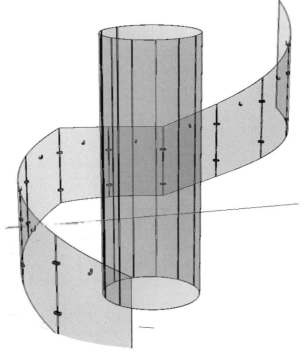

Now you're ready to associate this baluster post with a center railing (which contains no handrail). A couple of details are shown in Figure 16.89.

FIGURE 16.89
Completed stair
and details

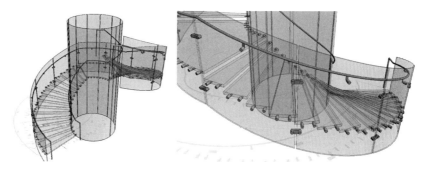

Figure 16.90 shows the finished stair. Yes, there's a lot more to the stair than this: the platform, elevator, landing, and so on. At the end of the day, there's nothing to keep you from modeling the entire stair in the Family Editor and then placing it in the project as a generic model. In some cases, this is exactly the kind of modeling control that complex and sculptural stairs need. Are they stairs? No, they're probably more like inhabitable sculpture. And trying to design sculpture in a spreadsheet is harder than just modeling what you want in the Family Editor. But what about "parameters," you ask? Well, sometimes defining the parameters takes more time than making the change manually in one place and then reloading the results into your project. If you're interested in downloading this stair, it's in the Chapter 16 folder; look for `Apple Stair.rvt`.

FIGURE 16.90
Completed stair,
panels, and core

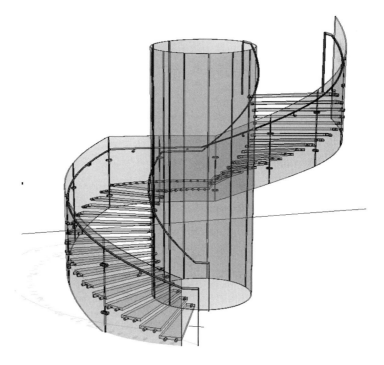

 **Real World Scenario**

IMPORTANT BEST PRACTICES, AND DON'T FORGET THE BEER!

Here are some best practices to consider with regard to creating complex stairs and railings:

◆ Don't forget to nest your family components whenever possible and appropriate. This will keep the component together when associated with some other template that contains hardwired parameters and reference planes. It'll also save you and your team a lot of time during design changes and iteration.

◆ Don't struggle with creating the stairs in this chapter. If you get stuck, you can download the sample stairs from this chapter and use them for a starting point when creating your custom stair. Just remember it's usually easier to build and test a custom stair or railing in a sample project first. Then copy and paste or use Transfer Project Standards to get the custom stair or railing from the test project to your actual project. Download sample files for this document at the book's web page. You'll probably want to copy your custom stairs and railings in an easy-to-access project that contains row upon row of finished and polished examples (since they can't be kept as family components).

◆ The level of detail and visibility is crucial if you care about graphic refresh times and printing. As you model the components of your custom stairs and railings, assign appropriate orientation and level of detail (Coarse, Medium, or Fine). You'll notice a difference when you pan and rotate your model.

◆ Take care to filter schedules. Using a curtain wall as a railing may have certain advantages, but you also want to make sure that your schedules are accurate.

Overall, be careful when reaching into your bag of tips and tricks! You need to weigh the cost of implementing a new process against the cost of doing what's familiar. Make sure that you're maintaining a balance between *predictability* and *efficiency*. There are frequently two extremes that you need to avoid:

◆ The first error involves doing what is highly predictable but not very efficient. In other words, most people will grasp the solution that you intend to implement; they'll fully understand the technology and technique. But they'll also quickly realize that managing design changes and iteration will be highly manual and time-consuming. And the rest of the team will doubt your leadership and understanding of the technology and processes.

◆ The second extreme is that you'll manage to create a highly efficient uber-solution, but one that is not very predictable to the project team (much less a recently introduced outsider). In other words, it'll almost be *too* efficient. Only you or perhaps a few team members will understand what you've created. Everyone else on the team will resist making any changes to your creation out of fear that they'll break it.

So, what's important with creating interesting and innovative stairs and railings is that you manage to strike a balance between these two extremes. Just remember these four simple characteristics:

Beneficial   Not just to you, but to the project team

Efficient   Implementation and changes that are fast and predictable

Elegant   Understood by the team and by any last-minute new members

Repetitive   Can be used on many projects

If you can't remember these guidelines, the handy acronym of BEER should help. When you are not sure which solution is the best one to follow, your team will tend to gravitate to whatever allows them to have a beer at the end of the day.

In other words, whatever allows them to decompress, reenergize, and come back to work the next day refreshed, focused, and enthusiastic will ultimately win out. And keep in mind that this principle isn't just important to stairs and railings or Revit or BIM; it's important to having an interesting life.

The Bottom Line

Understand the key components of stairs.   Having a complete understanding of the components of stairs is important. You don't want to set about breaking the rules until you understand how best (and when) those rules can be broken.

> **Master It**   What are the essential parts of stairs?

Know when not to use railings.   From model patterns to geometric intricacy, there's a lot that can be created with the Railing tool. When this doesn't work, look to the Curtain Wall tool for "railings" that can contain space and allow "balusters" to be conveniently unlocked.

> **Master It**   Why would you not use a railing to manage repetitive relationships? What if you need to accurately distribute geometry along a path?

Know when to use stairs.   Designing in a spreadsheet is hard. Step back and consider what you're trying to accomplish. If you'll look at the components that make up stairs, you'll see some interesting opportunities.

> **Master It**   How would you create a continuous tread that wasn't monolithic? What would you do if you wanted to create a custom stringer? Are balusters always vertical and used to support handrails? What if your particular stair just can't be modeled in the Stair tool?

Implement best practices.   There are specific best practices when creating custom stairs and railings. Pay attention to nesting geometry, maintaining the right level of detail, and filtering schedules so the metadata ends up in the right place.

> **Master It**   Is it possible to create solutions that are too efficient? What's the big deal with detail levels? And finally, what's the most important thing to remember before creating an elegant workaround?

Part 5

Documentation

Up to now, we've discussed how to take create a Revit model and use BIM to derive interesting forms, create parametric content, and perform analysis on your design. Part 5 will focus on how to document those designs both in the construction document phase (CDs) and ultimately present those drawings to project stakeholders.

Chapter 17

Detailing Your Design

As you've seen so far, you can show information in Revit in a variety of ways, from 3D perspectives to axons to perpendicular views, be they plans or sections. In each of these cases, the geometry is typically modeled based on a design intent, meaning that your goal isn't to model everything but enough to demonstrate what the building is going to look like. To this end, it becomes necessary to embellish parts of the model or specific views with detailed information to help clarify what you've drawn. These take the shape of 2D detail elements in Revit that you will use to augment views and add extra information.

In this chapter, you'll learn to:

◆ Create details

◆ Add detail components to families

◆ Learn efficient detailing

Creating Details

Even when creating details, Revit has a variety of parametric tools to allow you to leverage working in a BIM model. You can use these tools to create strictly 2D geometry or to augment details you are trying to create from 3D plans, sections, or callouts. To become truly efficient at using Revit to create the drawings necessary to both design and document your project, it's important to become acquainted with these tools—you will find yourself using them over and over again throughout your process.

All of these view-based tools are located on the Detail panel of the Annotate tab (Figure 17.1). This small but very potent toolbox is what you will need to familiarize yourself with in order to create a majority of the 2D linework and components that will become the details in your project. To better understand how these tools are used, let's step through each of them.

FIGURE 17.1
The Detail panel of the Annotate tab

Detail Line

The Detail Line tool (Figure 17.2) is the first tool located on the Detail panel of the Annotate tab. This tool is the closest thing you'll find to CAD drafting. It allows you to create view-specific linework using different line weights, tools for drawing different line shapes, and many of the same manipulation commands you would find in a CAD program.

FIGURE 17.2
The Detail
Line tool

Detail lines are view specific—they will only ever appear in the view in which they're drawn. They also have an arrangement to their placement, meaning that you can layer them underneath or on top of other objects. This is especially important when you begin using regions, detail lines, and model content to create your details.

Using the Detail Line tool is fairly easy. Selecting the tool will change your ribbon tab to look like Figure 17.3. This new tab will have several panels that allow you to add and manipulate linework.

FIGURE 17.3
The Detail Line
toolset

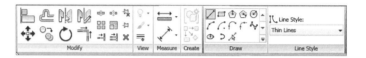

There are three major panels on this new tab: Modify, Draw, and Line Style. Because of their use sequence (selecting the line type, creating the shape, and modifying the line), we'll talk about them in order from right to left.

Line Style This panel is a drop-down menu that allows you to choose a line style and line weight in which to produce the linework in this view. This drop-down (Figure 17.4) has all the default Revit line styles as well as any custom ones you might have made for your project or to accommodate office standards. The active line will be the one displayed in the drop-down window before it's expanded.

FIGURE 17.4
The Line Style
drop-down menu

New line styles can be added at any time in the project, and many offices find it necessary to add custom line styles beyond the Thin, Medium, and Wide ones available in Revit out of the box. To add more styles or to just see the complete list, choose Additional Settings from the Manage tab and select Line Styles (Figure 17.5).

FIGURE 17.5
Modifying the line
styles

This will open the Line Styles dialog box. By expanding the Lines node at the top, Revit
will report a full list of the line styles available in the model (Figure 17.6).

FIGURE 17.6
The Line Styles
dialog box

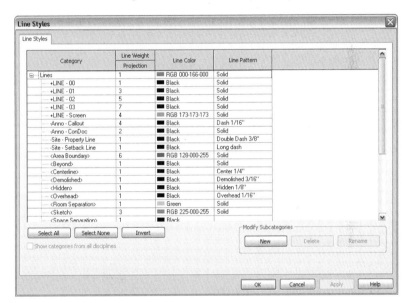

Draw   The Draw panel (Figure 17.7) contains a number of shapes that are quickly available to draw within your view. The tools allow you to create lines, boxes, circles, splines,
ellipses, and arcs. The last tool in the bottom row is the pick tool. This tool allows you to
select a line or portion of a model element (say an edge) and add a line over the top of it.

FIGURE 17.7
The Draw panel

Modify   The Modify panel (Figure 17.8) allows you to modify any of the linework already placed within the view. This panel contains several tools you can use to modify lines. Tool icon size is based on frequency of use; the larger icons are the tools you will tend to use most. The larger tools, from left to right, are Align, Offset, Mirror (axis), Mirror (line), Move, Copy, Rotate, and Trim.

FIGURE 17.8
The Modify panel

Regions

CERT
OBJECTIVE

The next tool on the Detail panel of the Annotate tab is the Region tool (Figure 17.9). *Regions* are areas of any shape or size that you can fill with a pattern. This pattern (much like a hatch in AutoCAD) will dynamically resize with the region boundary. Regions layer just like detail lines do and can be placed on top of, or behind, linework and model objects. Regions also have an opacity and can be completely opaque (covering what they are placed on) or transparent (letting the elements show through).

FIGURE 17.9
The Region tool

There are two types or regions: filled regions and masking regions. *Filled regions* allow you to choose from a variety of hatch patterns to fill the region. These are commonly used in details to show things like rigid insulation, concrete, plywood, and other material types. *Masking regions*, on the other hand, come in only one flavor. They are white boxes that can have (or not have) discernable borders to them. Masking regions are typically used to "hide" or *mask* certain content from a view that you don't want shown or printed.

When selecting the Region tool, you will be taken directly into Sketch mode, and you'll have a series of tools very similar to those for drawing detail lines. The Draw panel allows you to create any number of shapes with all the associated tools to move, copy, or offset the linework.

When creating either kind of region, it's important to note that you cannot complete Sketch mode unless the region is a closed loop. This means that there needs to be a continuous, closed line that creates one single shape. Multiple shapes are not supported when making regions. If you need more than one shape, you'll have to create more than one region.

Another aspect of regions is the linework that borders the region. When beginning the Region tool, you'll be able to choose the line style from the Line Style drop-down (similar to creating detail lines) that you want to use for the border of the region. You can change line styles for any of the segments of the region and even make them all different if needed.

One especially useful segment line style is the <Invisible> line. When drawn in Sketch mode, this will appear as a gray line, but once the sketch is completed, it will become an invisible line, allowing you to create boxes or other region shapes without discernable borders. When used with a masking region, it can create a completely invisible box that will allow you to hide elements that are unwanted in a particular view. Figure 17.10 shows the same masking region in two instances, one selected and the other not selected. You can see how the masking region visually disappears, covering the filled region.

FIGURE 17.10
A masking region selected and not selected

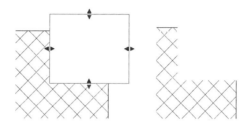

Filled regions have slightly more options since, unlike with a masking region, you can control the region's pattern. When selecting the Filled Region tool, you'll still need to create a boundary for the region to fill. Now, however, you can also select a region type from the Properties Palette (Figure 17.11). Region types are another type of Revit family. Creating a region type in one view allows the same region to be used in any other view, and modifying the properties of a region in one view changes it in all the other views.

FIGURE 17.11
Selecting a filled region type from the Type Selector

You'll notice that many of your region names in Figure 17.11 show material types. You'll typically end up using several common material types, so it's a good idea to get these regions into your office template.

STANDARDIZING REGION NAMES

Having some sort of standard applied to your region names can help you organize the Filled Region drop-down in a logical way that is easy to understand by the project team. You'll notice in Figure 17.11 that we've organized the region names around a two-number MasterSpec division prefix. Since MasterSpec is tied to the keynoting system as well, project teams tend to be familiar with the naming convention. This also keeps similar material types sorted together rather than sorted alphabetically. Take Concrete and Precast Concrete as an example. You can see in Figure 17.11 that those material types are very close together in the drop-down list based on their prefix.

The filled regions also have additional properties. By highlighting any placed region, you can go to its Type Properties (Figure 17.12). These properties allow you to control the fill type, opacity, line weight, and color of the region.

FIGURE 17.12
Type Properties for
a filled region

FILLED REGION TYPES

Beyond the ability to control opacity (transparent or opaque), two other filled region types are available. These types, Model and Drafting, create region patterns with different properties and will scale in different ways. Both of these regions can be created by going to the Filled Region properties and selecting Duplicate.

Drafting Regions

Drafting regions (Figure 17.13) are a region type typically used for patterns. Some examples of a drafting region hatch might be diagonal lines in an area plan, or crosshatched lines to show the difference between two departments.

FIGURE 17.13
Filled Region
drafting patterns

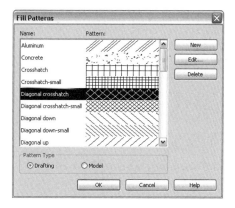

Drafting regions are created by specifying a distance between two or more lines relative to the printed sheet. In the example of diagonal lines, you might adjust the properties so the lines are ¼″ apart. This means that regardless of the view scale, the diagonal lines will always be ¼″ apart on the printed sheet. As you scale the view up or down, the lines will appear closer or farther apart, with the sheet view always remaining consistent.

Model Regions

Model regions (Figure 17.14) are the other type of filled region you can create. Model regions keep a consistent spacing relative to the model, not the view. You might use a model region to show ceiling tiles or brick courses, or to show a 4″ grid in a bathroom tile pattern. Model regions will keep their scale relative to the model. So, in the example of a 4″ bathroom tile, you would create a 4″ perpendicular crosshatch model pattern. As you change the scale of the view this region is inserted into, the lines within the region will always be 4″ apart while they will appear closer together or farther apart on the printed sheet.

FIGURE 17.14
Filled Region
model patterns

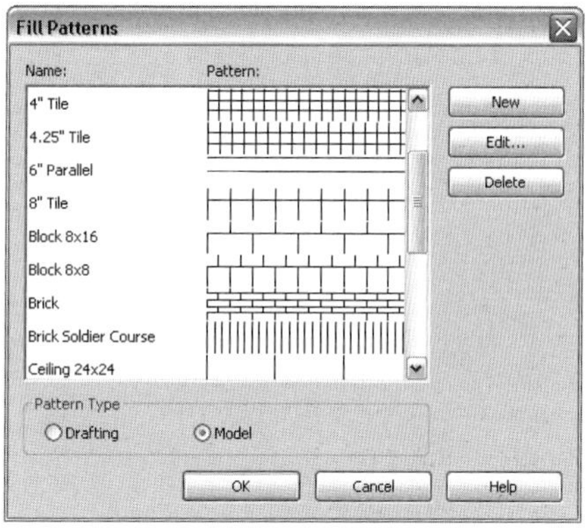

CREATING A NEW FILLED REGION TYPE

To create a new filled region type, you need to begin by duplicating an existing region and modifying its properties. To create a new type, follow these steps:

1. Select the Filled Region tool and click the Edit Type button in the Properties Palette.

2. Click Duplicate in the Type Properties dialog box.

3. Name your new region type and click the button in the Fill Pattern field.

4. Make sure you have the proper type of filled region (Model or Drafting) selected at the bottom of the Fill Patterns dialog box; then click the New button.

5. In the New Pattern dialog box (Figure 17.15) you'll have two additional options for creating a pattern. To create a simple pattern, choose the Simple radio button. This will allow you to create a pattern based on a regular line spacing that is parallel or perpendicular to the other lines in the pattern. Selecting Drafting or Model orientates the spacing to the sheet view or the model accordingly.

FIGURE 17.15
New Pattern
dialog box

For more complex pattern types, you can choose the Custom radio button (Figure 17.16). Here, you can name the pattern and import one from an external PAT file such as an ACAD pattern file. Make sure that when you import the pattern, you scale it exactly how you'd like it to appear. Once it is imported, you cannot rescale the pattern and you will be forced to recreate it.

6. With the pattern type imported or set, click OK. The last variable to set for a pattern type is Orientation In Host Layers (Figure 17.17). This drop-down menu allows you to select from three options for the orientation of the pattern within the region:

FIGURE 17.16
Importing custom
patterns

FIGURE 17.17
Orientation In Host
Layers options

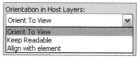

Orient To View   This option will keep any directionality associated with the pattern relative to the view. If the view is rotated, the pattern will be rotated as well. This is also the default selection.

Keep Readable   This option will rotate the directionality of the pattern relative to the bottom or right side of the sheet the view is placed on. It will act much like annotation text does and automatically align itself to the nearest readable side.

Align With Element   This option is specifically useful if you want the orientation of the pattern aligned with the region boundaries. A classic example of this is in rigid insulation. Rigid insulation is typically shown as a perpendicular crosshatched pattern oriented to the slope of the roof. By defining this pattern within the material type for Rigid Insulation, we're able to have the slope of the insulation pattern follow the slope of the roof (Figure 17.18).

FIGURE 17.18
Aligning the
pattern with the
element

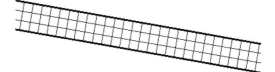

Note that this orientation type doesn't allow you to rotate a filled region—it only associates directionality with model elements.

7. When you're finished, click OK enough to exit all the dialog boxes. These same region patterns that you've created for a filled region can also be associated with material surfaces or cuts using the Settings ➤ Materials dialog box.

Components

The Component drop-down menu allows you to insert a wide array of component types into your model. These are 2D detail components, or collections of detail components in the case of a repeating detail. Detail components are schedulable, taggable, keynotable 2D families that allow an additional level of standardization within your model. Some examples for things you'd use detail components are blocking in section, steel shapes, metal studs in plan or section—just about any replicated 2D element that comes in a standardized shape.

DETAIL COMPONENTS

Detail components (Figure 17.19) are 2D families that can be made into parametric content. In other words, a full range of shapes can be available in a single detail component. Because they are families, they can also be stored in your office library and shared easily across projects.

FIGURE 17.19
Detail components

To add a detail component to your drawing, select Detail Component from the Component drop-down list located on the Annotate tab and use the Type Selector to choose from ones that are already inserted into the model. If you don't see a detail component you want to insert in the Type Selector, click the Load Families button on the Modify | Place Detail Component tab and insert one from the default library or your office library.

Adding Detail Components and Embellishing the View

Making a detail component is much like creating a 2D family. Let's step through making a simple 2D Detail component.

From the book's companion website (www.sybex.com/go/masteringrevit2011), download the Jenkins.rvt file and open the view, Exterior Detl, Typ. You'll create some detail components and regions to get started with a typical window detail. The first thing you'll want to do is use the Callout tool to create a new detail of the window sill. Create a new callout and name it **Exterior Window Sill, Typ**. The starting view will look like Figure 17.20.

FIGURE 17.20
The window sill
detail before
embellishment

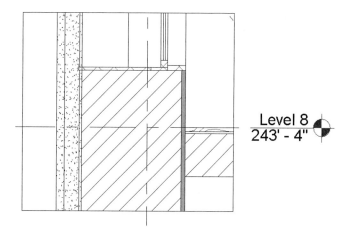

Then follow these steps:

1. You'll notice that you have some detail elements that can't exist in real-life construction. For example, you'd never run the sheetrock back behind the floor slab, and there's no room for flashing or blocking below the window. You'll need to modify this view to rectify these conditions. Let's start with the floor slab and fix the sheetrock. To do this, we'll cover a portion of this area with a filled region. Select the Filled Region button from the Annotate tab.

2. Set the line style to invisible and create a box bounding the floor slab (Figure 17.21). You'll notice three of the boundary lines are on cut planes: the top and bottom edges of the box. Select these edges and use the Line Style drop-down to change the line weight to Medium.

FIGURE 17.21
Modifying the
boundary of the
filled region

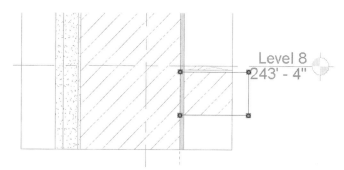

3. Click the Edit Type button in the Properties Palette to open the Type Properties dialog box. Since there is no defined region type that is identical to existing materials, we'll need to make one. Click Duplicate, name the new region type **00 Existing**, and click OK.

4. Now you need to modify the settings:

   Fill Pattern: Set this field to Drafting and choose ANSI31.

   Background: Opaque

Line Weight: 1

Color: Black

Click OK when you're done.

5. Now that the region is defined, click the green check mark to complete the sketch. Your finished filled region will look like Figure 17.22.

FIGURE 17.22
Modifying the boundary of the filled region

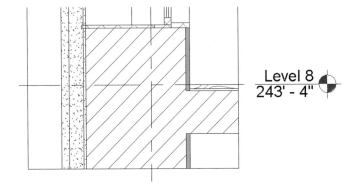

6. As part of the window sill condition, say you know you have a 1″ gap between the bottom of the window sill and the existing masonry opening. This isn't reflected in the window detail currently because the window family was created to cut a square opening just big enough for the window. For this detail, you need to create a masking region under the window sill so you can add some other components like blocking. Choose the Masking Region tool from the Region fly-out on the Annotate tab.

7. With Line Style set to Thin Lines, create a box 1″ deep under the window sill (Figure 17.23).

FIGURE 17.23
Adding a masking region

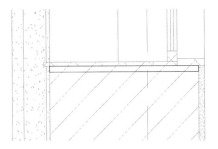

8. With the box created, click the green check to complete the sketch. The finished sill will look like Figure 17.24.

FIGURE 17.24
The completed
sketch

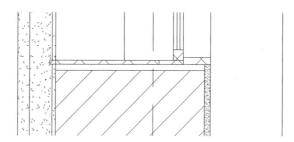

The next step is to add some detail components for blocking and trim. Click the Application button, choose File ➤ New ➤ Family, and choose `Detail Component.rft`. When creating detail components, like any other family, you'll start with two reference planes crossing in the center of the family. This crossing point is the default insertion point of the family. The first family, blocking, is straightforward:

1. Start by selecting the Masking Region tool on the Home tab and drawing a box with the lower-left corner at the origin. The box should be 1″ high and 3½″ wide. You're using the Masking Region instead of the Lines tool so you can have a clean, white box that you will be able to use to layer over other elements you might not want to see.

2. On the Home tab, click the Lines tool and draw a line across the box denoting blocking. The family should look like Figure 17.25.

FIGURE 17.25
Creating a blocking
detail component

3. With the drawing finished, click the Application button, select Save As ➤ Family, and name the family **06 Blocking**. Place it in a folder with the Jenkins model.

4. With the family named, click the Load Into Project button to add the family to the Jenkins model.

5. On the Annotate tab, click the Detail Component button. The component you inserted will be the one that will become the default component, and you will be able to see the name 06 Blocking in the Type Selector. Insert a piece of blocking at the left, right, and center of the sill (Figure 17.26).

FIGURE 17.26
Inserting and plac-
ing the blocking

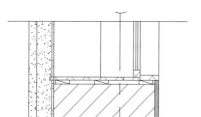

6. With the blocking inserted, you want to make one more detail component for the baseboard. Create a detail component using the same steps as earlier measuring ½" wide by 6" high and called **06 Baseboard**. The reason you want to create these elements as families and not just as filled regions is so that later in the detailing process you can annotate them using the Revit keynote tool (explained in Chapter 19, "Annotating Your Design"). Families will have a lot more functionality and versatility later down the line for faster documentation. With the baseboard added, the detail looks like Figure 17.27.

FIGURE 17.27
The sill detail
with base

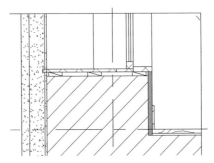

7. Not all of the detailing will be able to be completed using components. Sometimes, it is easier and more effective to simply use linework to create the necessary features in a detail. For these purposes, you want to create some flashing at the window sill. To do this, we're going to use the Detail Line tool. Choose the tool and choose Medium Lines from the Line Style drop-down menu.

8. Using the Detail Line tool, draw in some flashing for the window sill (Figure 17.28).

FIGURE 17.28
Adding flashing
using detail lines

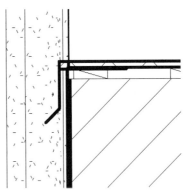

Arranging Elements in the View

So far you have created all of the content in order and have not had to change the arrangement of any of the elements. However, knowing how to change arrangement is an important part of detailing so you don't have to draw it all in exact sequence. Arrangement allows you to change the position of an element, such as a line or a detail component relative to another element. Much like layers in Photoshop or arrangement in PowerPoint, Revit allows you to place some elements visually in front or behind others. Once an element or group of elements is selected and the Modify menu appears, on the far right you'll see the Arrange panel (Figure 17.29).

FIGURE 17.29
The Arrange panel

From here, you can choose among four options of arrangement:

Bring To Front This brings the selected objects all the way to the front of the stack. In Figure 17.30, you have two detail lines on top of a masking region, which is also on top of a filled region. Select the detail lines and choose Bring To Front, and the lines are now on top of all the other elements.

FIGURE 17.30
Bring To Front

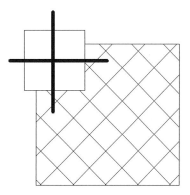

Bring Forward This option brings the selected elements one step closer to the front in a given sequence. In Figure 17.31, we've selected the masking region and chose Bring Forward, and now it appears on top of one of the detail lines. Note that each of the detail lines is its own layer within this stack.

FIGURE 17.31
Bring Forward

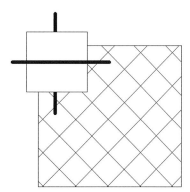

Send To Back   This option does the exact opposite of the Bring To Front tool and will send an object all the way to the back of the stack. In Figure 17.32, we've chosen the masking region again and sent it to the back.

FIGURE 17.32
Send To Back

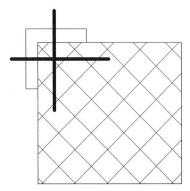

Send Backwards   The fourth option, Send Backwards, will step the selected elements one step backward in the stack. In Figure 17.33, we've chosen the horizontal detail line and sent it backward; it now appears behind the filled region.

FIGURE 17.33
Send Backwards

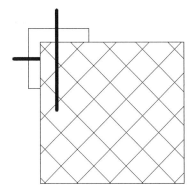

REPEATING DETAIL COMPONENT

**CERT
OBJECTIVE**

Repeating elements are common in architectural projects. Masonry, metal decking, and wall studs are some common elements that repeat on a regular interval in architectural projects. Revit's tool to help create and manage these types of elements is called the repeating detail component and is located in the Component fly-out on the Annotate tab (Figure 17.34).

FIGURE 17.34
Choosing
Repeating Detail
Component

This tool allows you to place a detail component in a linear configuration where the detail component repeats on a set interval. This allows you to draw a "line" that then becomes your repeating component. The default Revit repeating detail is common brick repeating in section (Figure 17.35). Creating elements like this not only lets you later tag and keynote the materials, but allows you some easy flexibility over arraying these elements manually.

FIGURE 17.35
A brick
repeating detail

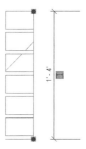

Before you create a repeating detail component, we'll cover the properties behind one so you can get a better idea of how they work. Selecting the Brick component and choosing its Properties gives you the Type Properties dialog box shown in Figure 17.36.

FIGURE 17.36
Type Properties
dialog box for a
repeating detail

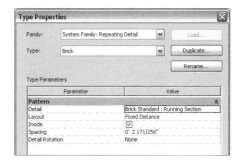

Here's a brief description of what each of these settings does:

Detail   This setting allows you to select the detail component to be repeated.

Layout   This option offers four different modes:

> **Fixed Distance**   This represents the path drawn between the start and end point when the repeating detail is the length at which your component repeats at a distance of the value set for spacing.

> **Fixed Number**   This mode sets the number of times a component repeats itself in the space between the start and end point (the length of the path).

> **Fill Available Space**   Regardless of the value you choose for Spacing, the detail component is repeated on the path using its actual width as the Spacing value.

> **Maximum Spacing**   The detail component is repeated using the set spacing, and the number of repeated components is set so that only complete components are drawn. Revit creates as many copies of the component as will fit on the path.

Inside   This option adjusts the start point and end point of the detail components that make up the repeating detail.

Spacing   This option is active only when Fixed Distance or Maximum Spacing is selected as the method of repetition. It represents the distance at which you want the repeating detail component to repeat. It doesn't have to be the actual width of the detail component.

USING REVIT TO PERFORM MATH

In the example of the brick, you have a distance of $2^{171}/_{256}''$. Since brick repeats every three bricks in 8", you don't have to know the exact distance between each brick. Revit is formula driven, so you can enter **=8"÷3** into this field, and it will calculate the distance for you.

Detail Rotation   This option allows you to rotate the detail component in the repeating detail.

With these settings in mind, you need to create a custom repeating detail for the sill detail you've been working on. The exterior of the building is terracotta brick and will have visible joint work every 8".

1. Begin by selecting a new Detail Component family. Click the Application button, select New ➢ Family, and choose `Detail Component.rft` from the list.

2. Create a masonry joint 6" long and ⅜" high with a strike on one of the short ends (Figure 17.37) using a filled region. Save the family as **04 Grout** and load it into the project.

FIGURE 17.37
The grout detail component

3. Now, back in the project, choose the Repeating Detail Component tool. Choose Edit Type from the Properties Palette and Duplicate from the Type Properties menu. Name the new type **04 Terracotta Grout** and click OK.

4. You need to change the properties of this new type to reflect the detail component you just created and its spacing. Change the following fields:

   Detail: Set this to **04 Grout**, the family you just created.

   Spacing: Set this value to **8"**.

   You can leave the rest of the fields alone. Click OK when you're finished. The Type Properties will look like Figure 17.38.

FIGURE 17.38
The repeating
detail's Type
Properties

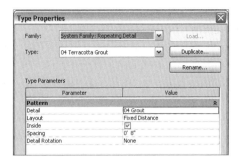

5. Since you're still in the Repeating Detail command, you can simply begin drawing a "line" with the repeating detail. Starting at the base of the view, draw a line all the way up the left edge, placing the new joint over the terracotta exterior.

6. You can further finesse the appearance by placing one of the joints directly below the window sill. This will appear placed on top of the flashing you drew earlier, so select the flashing detail line and choose Bring To Front. The completed detail will look like Figure 17.39.

FIGURE 17.39
The finished
window sill detail

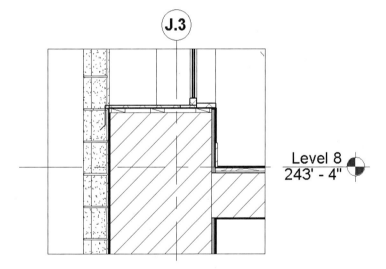

Although this detail still needs annotations before you could think about placing it onto a sheet, you can begin to see how you have used the 3D geometry of the model and were able to quickly add some embellishment to it in order to create a working project detail. For now, save this detail. You'll return to it later in the chapter.

Insulation

The best way to think of the Insulation tool is like a premade repeating detail. You'll find this tool on the Detail panel of the Annotate tab (Figure 17.40).

FIGURE 17.40
The Insulation tool

Selecting this tool allows you to draw a line of batt insulation, much like a repeating detail. Figure 17.41 shows a typical line of insulation.

FIGURE 17.41
The insulation in the model

When selecting the insulation tool, you can modify the width of the inserted insulation from the Options Bar (Figure 17.42). The insulation is inserted using the centerline of the line of batt, and you can shorten, lengthen, or modify the width either before or after inserting it into your view.

FIGURE 17.42
Modifying the Insulation width in the Options bar

Detail Groups

Detail groups are similar to blocks in AutoCAD and are a quick alternative to creating detail component families. These are collections of 2D graphics and can contain detail lines, detail components, or any collection of 2D elements. While you will probably want to use a detail component to create something like blocking, if you plan to have the same blocking and flashing conditions in multiple locations, you can then group those conditions and be able to quickly replicate them in other details. Like blocks in AutoCAD, manipulating one of the detail groups will change all of them consistently.

There are two ways to make a detail group. Probably the most common is to create the detail elements you'd like to group and then select all of them. In the contextual Modify tab that shows up, click the Create Group button (Figure 17.43). When you're prompted for a group name, name the group something clear rather than accepting the default name Revit wants to give it (Group 1, Group 2, and so on).

FIGURE 17.43
Selecting elements
and then creating
a group using the
Modify menu

The other way to create a detail group is by clicking the Create Group button in the Detail Group fly-out on the Annotate tab (Figure 17.44). You will then be prompted for the type of group (Model or Detail) and a group name before you can select any elements for the group.

FIGURE 17.44
Click the Create
Group button on
the Annotate tab,
then select the ele-
ments.

When selecting the elements, you'll be taken into Edit Group mode. Your view will have a yellow transparency overlaid on top of it, and elements within the view will appear gray. To add elements to the group, click Edit Group ➢ Add button (Figure 17.45). Here you can also remove unwanted elements from your group. When you're finished, simply click the Finish check.

FIGURE 17.45
The Edit Group
panel

You can place any group you've already made using the Place Detail Group button from the Detail panel of the Annotate tab (Figure 17.46). Groups insert like families, and you can choose the group you'd like to insert from the Type Selector on the Properties Palette.

FIGURE 17.46
Inserting a detail
group

Linework

Although not part of the Annotate tab, the Linework tool is an important feature in creating good line weights for your details. Revit does a lot to help manage your views and line weights automatically, but it doesn't cover all the requirements all the time. Sometimes the default Revit lines are heavier or thinner than you'd desire for your details. This is where the Linework tool comes in handy; it allows you to modify existing lines in a view-specific context.

To use the Linework tool, choose the Linework button from the View panel on the Modify tab. This will add the familiar Line Styles Type Selector panel on the right of the tab and allow you to select a line style from the list. Simply choose the style you want a particular line to look like and select that line in the view. The lines you pick can be almost anything; cut lines of model elements, families, components, whatever. Selecting the line or boundary of an element will change the line style from whatever it was to whatever you have chosen from the Type Selector. Figure 17.47 shows a before and after of your sill detail with the linework touched up.

FIGURE 17.47
Before and after
the linework tool

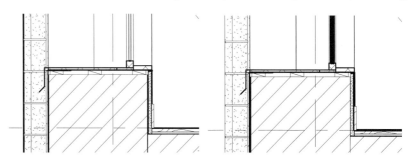

You can also choose to remove lines using this tool. By selecting the <Invisible> line type, you can make some linework disappear. This is a good alternative to having to cover unwanted linework with a masking region.

DETAIL COMPONENTS AND PROJECT TEMPLATES

If you find you are inserting the same detail components over and over again, load them into your project templates and make them readily available when you begin any new project.

Adding Detail Components to Families

Earlier in this chapter, you investigated how to embellish a view by adding detail components, detail lines, and other elements. By doing so, you not only made the detail you were working with more complete, but you also added content to the model that could be reused in other details. Combining these principles, you can extend this theory to family creation where you can modify 3D families to include elements from 2D details.

Since you have the ability to change the level of view detail from Coarse to Medium to Fine within your project, you can use these settings in connection with detail components to modify families and add even more versatility to them. You can begin embedding detail components into the families for typical conditions and eliminate even more repetition when adding components to typical conditions.

Building these types of families is not complicated, but it does require a bit of knowledge about how a family is created and assembled and a bit of planning around the building design and detailing. In the chapter's example, you have found that the window you detailed earlier in this chapter is a typical window and a typical condition in many other parts of the building. Since this window type will show up in all the sections throughout the project, you'll now add some of the common features from the detail components directly to the family so you don't have to draw and redraw them every time this window appears.

Adding Details to a Window Family

Since you already created the sill condition in the window detail, it will be an easy reference when working on the family. Start by opening the Jenkins model you downloaded earlier in this chapter and locating the Callout Of Exterior Detl, Typ view you have been working on. This view (Figure 17.48) shows a window sill condition with some flashing and blocking.

FIGURE 17.48
The window sill detail

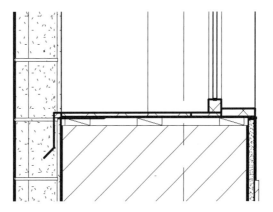

1. Begin by selecting a window and choosing Edit Family from the context menu. The detail you are working from is a section condition and there's no section described in this family. To add one, from the View tab choose the Section tool and cut a section through the plan of the window looking the same direction as your project detail.

2. Since you are adding elements to this section, assume you've decided to add some additional information about the window itself. During the course of the design, you've chosen a window manufacturer and gone to their website to download sill, head, and jamb conditions, and you want to create another detail component from this file. Click the Application button and select New ➤ Family ➤ Detail Component.rft.

3. From the Insert tab, choose Import CAD and navigate to the ASCMDDH3a.dwg file you downloaded from the manufacturer's website (or in this case, from the book's companion website). Before you import the file, you need to make some adjustments to this dialog box. Change the following fields:

    Colors: Black and White

    Layers: Specify

    Import Units: Inches

This will import the CAD file at the right scale and allow you to choose the layers you want to import. When your dialog box matches Figure 17.49, click Open.

FIGURE 17.49
Importing a
CAD detail

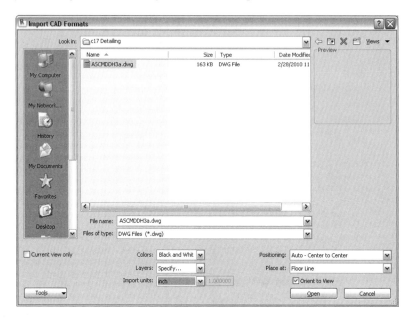

4. Before the CAD detail completes its import, you get to choose which layers you'd like to import. When the Select Layers/Levels To Import/Link dialog box appears, uncheck the following layers (Figure 17.50):

Pel_Defpoints

Pel_Hatch

Pel_TXT

Then click OK.

FIGURE 17.50
Selecting layers
to import

The imported CAD file will look like Figure 17.51. You'll need to perform a bit of cleanup before you can make this into a usable detail component.

FIGURE 17.51
The Imported
CAD file

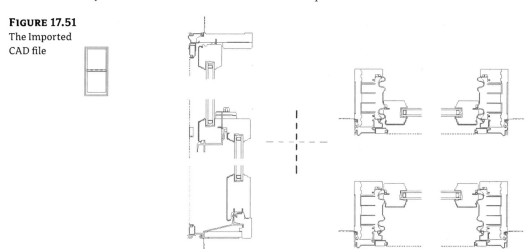

5. Highlight the imported CAD file and from the Modify tab choose Full Explode (Figure 17.52). This will break the CAD file down into individual components and allow you to not only edit some of the level of detail but also remove elements you don't need.

FIGURE 17.52
Exploding the
CAD file

6. From this point, you can delete all of the other CAD information except for the sill condition. That bit can also be cleaned up and much of the detail removed. Many times downloaded CAD files have more detail in them than will show well graphically in detail drawings, so cleaning out some of the extra linework will benefit visibility later when you print. The cleaned detail should look like Figure 17.53.

FIGURE 17.53
The final sill detail

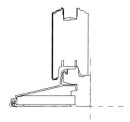

7. While the remaining linework is what you want to use in your detail component, you don't want to use the CAD lines that we've imported. You need to convert those line styles to Revit line styles so you don't clutter the project file with extraneous line types. In your window sill detail, select all the linework. Once the lines are selected, choose the Line Styles drop-down menu from the Modify tab. For this detail, you want to change all the line styles to Detail Items, so select that from the drop-down list (Figure 17.54).

FIGURE 17.54
Changing the
line styles

8. Before you can finish this detail, there is one more element that needs to be added. If the detail was inserted as it is right now, any model elements would appear through the line-work, and you want this detail to layer over the top of any other information. To do this, you need to add a masking region around the detail. Choose the Masking Region tool from the Annotate tab and, using the Pick tool, pick the border of the sill detail to form a closed loop and create the masking region shown in Figure 17.55.

FIGURE 17.55
Making the
masking region

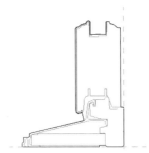

9. With the addition of the masking region, you're ready to save the detail and load it into the project. Save the detail to the project's family location and name it **08 Window Sill**. When this is done, click the Load Into Project button and load the detail into the Double Hung window family (Figure 17.56).

With the final missing detail component created, you can begin adding the other elements
to this detail. You want to create some of the common conditions that appeared in the earlier
detail: the blocking, flashing, and masking region.

1. In the Section 1 view of the window detail, click the Component button. Start by placing
   the window sill you just created. Place it over the modeled window so it creates an extension of the existing condition (Figure 17.57).

FIGURE 17.57
Adding the win-
dow sill detail to
the window family

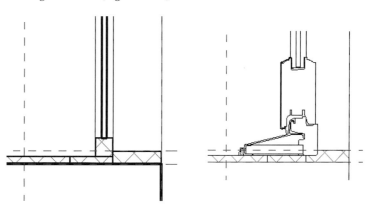

2. Next, similar to how we added additional detail earlier in the project, you will want
   to embellish this new addition to the detail. Start with the masking region. Select the
   Masking Region tool from the Annotate tab. Revit will ask you to select a work plane on
   which to draw your masking region. From the Name list, choose Center, which is the reference plane that cuts the window in half in plan (Figure 17.58).

FIGURE 17.58
Select a reference
plane for the mask-
ing region.

3. Create the masking region the same as before: 1″ tall and the width of the wall (Figure 17.59). Be sure to constrain the vertical dimension to 1″ and lock the other edges to the reference plane (top) and wall edges (left and right). This will allow the masking region to resize with the wall should they be different sizes when the window family is imported into the model.

FIGURE 17.59
Drawing the masking region

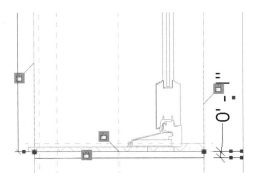

4. On top of the masking region, you will want to add the blocking. Choose the Detail Component button from the Annotate tab and then choose Load Family from the Modify context menu. Browse to the 06 Blocking family you created earlier and load it into the project. Place the blocking in the same locations you placed it earlier. It should look like Figure 17.60 when finished.

FIGURE 17.60
Placing the 06 Blocking detail component

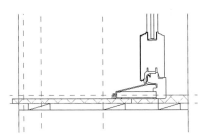

5. As a last item to create, you will need to add the flashing to the detail. In a family, there are no detail lines but instead symbolic lines.

6. Symbolic lines are used to show 2D projections or cuts for 3D families. They are commonly used to create any of the 2D linework in a family you will need since not everything in the families are modeled. One of the most familiar uses of symbolic lines is the plan project of the door swing. In this detail, use the symbolic line Frame/Mullion [Cut] (Figure 17.61) to create the necessary flashing.

7. The finished flashing will look like Figure 17.62. At this point, we're done adding information to the detail and you can move on to modifying some of the elements we've inserted to add some additional flexibility to the family.

FIGURE 17.61
Adding symbolic
lines

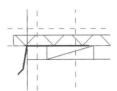

FIGURE 17.62
Finishing the
flashing

🌐 Real World Scenario

DOORS AND SYMBOLIC LINES

In the architecture industry, doors are typically modeled in a closed position but shown as open and with a door swing direction in plan view. To get this dual representation, in the Family Editor turn off the visibility of the door panel (extruded solid form) in the plan view and draw the 90-degree open door panel and its swing using symbolic lines.

Symbolic lines can be controlled using the same visibility settings available for detail components and the solid model elements in the family. You can use the same logic and draw the dashed lines that represent the door opening direction in elevations.

At this point, you could insert the window family back into the project and have it look identical to the detail you created earlier. While it will have the desired look you want, when the detail is drawn at ½″ = 1′-0″ scale (as it is in the project) these additional elements will make the detail look muddled when you show this window at larger scales. So that you can use this same family regardless of scale, you want to modify the Visibility settings.

Visibility Settings

The Visibility Settings tool, found on the Modify tab, allows you to control when elements appear in families based on several variables. Visibility settings are controlled by the Coarse, Medium, and Fine settings for the detail level within a view. These settings are completely independent of any of the family type parameters.

Depending on whether the element you want to control the Visibility settings for is a drafting or model element, you'll have different options to control the visibility. For a model element, you can see from the Family Element Visibility Settings dialog box (Figure 17.63) that you can set if the element is visible in:

Plan/RCP

Front/Back

Left/Right

When cut in section

All of the detail levels (Coarse, Medium, Fine)

FIGURE 17.63
The Family Element Visibility Settings dialog box for model elements

For drafting elements, the number of options is more limited. Since these elements only appear in one view, you have the choice to control the detail level and whether the elements selected are visible when the family is cut in section (Figure 17.64).

FIGURE 17.64
The Family Element Visibility Settings dialog box for drafting elements

For the detail you have been working on, all of the elements you will want to manipulate are 2D. Select the inserted blocking, sill detail, and masking region and click the Visibility Settings button. Uncheck the boxes for Coarse and Medium detail level. You also want to select Show Only If Instance Is Cut. The Family Element Visibility Settings dialog box should look like Figure 17.65.

With this complete, click OK. The modifications to this family are now finished, and you can load it back into the model and test the changes we've made. Click the Load Into Project button.

FIGURE 17.65
The Family Element Visibility Settings

First, delete the blocking, masking region, and flashing you added earlier in the chapter. Now, you can quickly cycle through the levels of detail to see how the new family's visibility changes with the detail level. Figure 17.66 shows the window sill in Coarse detail. Note that part of your existing conditions for the building show the existing walls in a gray fill. Figure 17.67 shows the wall condition in a Medium detail level. Here you do not yet see the details we've added, but the gray fill is replaced by the masonry hatch. Finally, in Figure 17.68, at a Fine level of detail, you can see the elements you added to the family appear in the view. Since you have this window installed in multiple locations within the model, the same views will be present any time you cut the model in section.

FIGURE 17.66
The Window detail
at Coarse

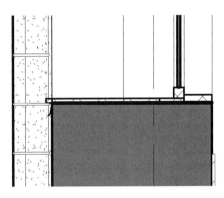

FIGURE 17.67
The Window detail
at Medium

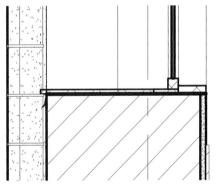

FIGURE 17.68
The Window detail
at Fine

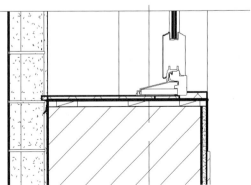

Learning Efficient Detailing

As you get more practice creating details in Revit, you'll find certain workflows support more flexibility and speed. Here are some tips to keep in mind when creating your details:

◆ If your modeling is reasonably detailed to begin with, the detailing will go much faster because you will need to add fewer components. However, you must strike a balance and not make an overly detailed model, because that would negatively impact performance. When wondering what to model or what to make into a detail component, ask yourself the following questions:

   ◆ Will I see or use this in other views in the project?

   ◆ Will it affect other aspects of the project (like material takeoffs)?

   ◆ How large is it? (Our office tends to use 2D detailing for details 1½″ and smaller.)

◆ Remember to import only CAD files that you have already cleaned up. Only bring in what you need to reduce your overhead and keep file performance optimal.

◆ There is no limit to how much information you can place in a detail component. If you will be seeing similar conditions throughout the model, put in as much as you can.

◆ You can use detail components at every scale within the model, so it is a great way to draw the information only once.

◆ If the lines describing geometry merge when printed into a single graphic element, there's little point in showing that geometry at that scale. You might consider making the model simpler.

Real World Scenario

FIXING AN OOPS

The first time this detail was loaded into the model, it didn't create Figure 17.65 quite like it is shown. Part of creating families is knowing how to fix them when they don't quite turn out the way you expect. In the case of this window family, the first time it was loaded into the project, it looked like this:

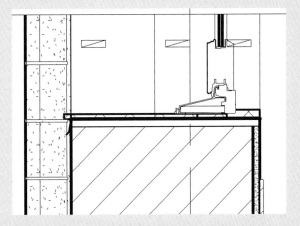

Clearly, it is not possible or desirable to install blocking at the location this blocking is shown at. In this case, the problem occurred because the blocking family wasn't locked to a reference plane and when the window changed heights to accommodate all the family types, it left the blocking floating in space.

The fix for this condition is to open the window family again and use the Align tool to lock the top of each piece of blocking to the reference plane (shown here). When the family is reinserted into the model, it appears correctly.

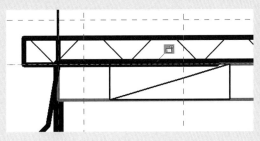

The Bottom Line

Create details.   Details in Revit are a combination of 2D elements layered on top of 3D model elements or sometimes just stacked on top of each other. Creating good, easy-to-read details typically requires some embellishment of the 3D model.

Master It   What are the three primary categories of detail elements and how are they used?

Add detail components to families.   You can make creating details in Revit easier by adding some of the detail elements directly to the family. In this way, when you cut sections, make callouts, or enlarge plan conditions, your "smart" details can begin to construct themselves.

Master It   Since you don't always want elements to appear in every scale of view, how can you both add detail elements to your families while still limiting the amount of information that is shown in any given view?

Learn efficient detailing.   As you master detailing in Revit, you'll begin to learn tips and tricks to make your process of creating details more efficient.

Master It   To help you assess how much effort you should be putting into your details, what are three questions you should be asking yourself before starting any detail?

Chapter 18

Documenting Your Design

While the industry continues to move toward a 3D BIM model as a construction deliverable, today we still need to produce 2D documents for a construction set. Fortunately because of Revit, you can create these sets with more accuracy and dependability than in the past. In this chapter, you will work on taking the elements you have modeled and detailed and creating documentation.

In this chapter, you'll learn to:

- ◆ Document plans
- ◆ Create schedules and legends
- ◆ Use details from other files
- ◆ Lay out sheets

Documenting Plans

In this chapter, we'll introduce a scenario that will mimic what might happen on a real project in preliminary design. We are going to assume that you'll be using the Jenkins.rvt model from the book's companion web page: www.sybex.com/go/masteringrevit2011.

Here's the story: you have recently completed some preliminary design work in advance of your upcoming client meeting. You will need to lay the plans, elevations, and perspectives out on some presentation sheets for the meeting, but you will also need to include some building metrics such as area plans and schedules of overall spaces. You have also been thinking through some of the details and would like to show a few of those as well. Secretly, you had some detail work on a similar project that never made it off the ground, so you plan to borrow some of those details you were interested in using on that other project and bring them into this one. With this scenario in mind, you need to create some area plans, schedules, and legends. You need to import your design ideas, some of which some were done in another Revit project and some of which were done in CAD. Finally, you must create a presentation sheet and lay out all of these views so you can print them prior to your meeting.

In the following sections, you'll start with the area plans. For the purposes of program verification, you have decided you need to establish the building areas for the existing building so the client can get some preliminary pricing back from the contractor. Before you create your area plans, we'll discuss some of the various ways Revit can calculate areas.

Room Areas

The simplest way to calculate areas in Revit is to use the room objects. Room tags can report room name, department, area, and any of the other properties of a room. These properties can also be scheduled and tabulated to report the total area. With rooms, however, the areas that they report are limited to how those spaces are defined. With the Jenkins model open, choose the Home tab, then the fly-out menu on the Room & Area panel. Click Area And Volume Computations, which opens the Area And Volume Computations dialog box (Figure 18.1). You can see here what the options are for calculating areas in Revit. The choices are as follows:

◆ At Wall Finish

◆ At Wall Center

◆ At Wall Core Layer

◆ At Wall Core Center

FIGURE 18.1
The Area And Volume Calculations dialog box

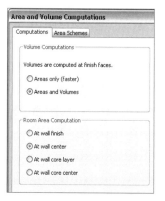

Each setting is global for the project. Although this ensures a level of consistency for room calculations, it makes it difficult to use the room objects to calculate areas. Room calculations, however, can give you an accurate net area or "carpet area." This value refers to the area between the finished wall surfaces that would be occupied space. This value can also be reported in the room tag or schedule by selecting the first choice, At Wall Finish, from the Area And Volume Calculations dialog box. Select this option and click OK.

Let's see how this is reflected on the floor plans. Open the Level 3 floor plan. In this plan, we have already established the rooms and added tags. The tags, however, do not reflect the room areas. To modify this setting, follow these steps:

1. Select any of the room tags and from the Properties Palette, choose Edit Type.

2. In the Type Properties dialog box, choose the Show Area check box. Click OK to exit the dialog box.

Now you should see the areas reflected in the room tags, shown in Figure 18.2.

FIGURE 18.2
Room area
reflected in the
room tag

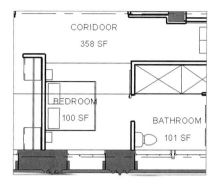

If you select any one of these room tags, you can also see the area that it is calculating (Figure 18.3). When adding rooms, you are not limited to only rooms that are bound on all sides with walls. If you note the bedroom in Figure 18.3, there isn't a wall on the top of the room. Using Room Separation Lines, which can be found under the Room flyout on the Room & Area panel of the Home tab, you can create room boundaries without being limited to adding walls.

FIGURE 18.3
The room object
shows what area is
being calculated.

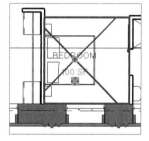

Since this area calculation type doesn't take wall thickness or glazing into account, let's look at some other ways to calculate areas using area plans. Although this is certainly useful, it does not accommodate calculation of the precise areas you will need to verify your program or perform cost takeoffs.

Area Plans

Area plans are views of the model used to calculate defined two-dimensional spaces within the model according to prescribed calculation standards. Some of the types of standards used to calculate areas are as follows:

Gross Area   Gross area is the overall area of a floor or footprint of the building extending to the outside face of the exterior walls.

Rentable Area   Rentable area typically refers to all the spaces within the interior surface of the exterior walls and the interior surface of exterior glazing and doesn't count areas such as mechanical rooms, elevator cores, stairwells, and some restrooms. Rentable space can also be defined as usable area or BOMA area.

Usable Area   This area refers to the space in a floor plate that is usable to a tenant. It doesn't typically count the floor areas taken up by columns, walls, shafts, or mechanical rooms, but would count restrooms, janitorial closets, and storage as usable areas.

BOMA Area   BOMA stands for the Building Owners and Managers Association. Widely used in the United States by architects, developers, and facilities managers alike, it was created to help standardize office building development and spatial needs. BOMA uses its own set of standards for calculating areas; these standards are similar in some ways to those for rentable area but have some nuances relating to exactly where the area boundaries between spaces falls. More information on BOMA standards can be found at www.boma.org.

Revit allows you to choose from two predefined area schemes, Gross and Rentable, or it gives you the option to create your own scheme based on standard area calculation variables. To add to the list of available area types, choose the Area And Volume Computations button located on the Home tab and under the Room & Area fly-out (Figure 18.4).

FIGURE 18.4
The Room &
Area fly-out

When the Area And Volume Computations dialog box (Figure 18.5) opens, choose the Area Schemes tab. Here you can add new areas by clicking the New button. Since we want to calculate Rentable area and already have a definition of that, click OK.

FIGURE 18.5
The Area Schemes
tab in the Area and
Volume Computa-
tions dialog box

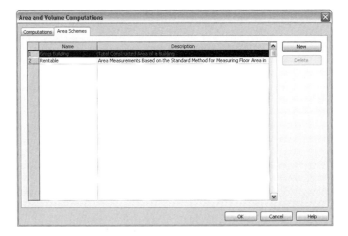

CREATING AN AREA PLAN

For our example, you need to create an area plan for your presentation. You can create an area plan from two locations in Revit: one is located on Room & Area panel of the Home tab (Figure 18.6).

FIGURE 18.6
The Area Plan tool
on the Home tab

The other is located on the Create panel of the View tab (Figure 18.7). Both locations will produce the same result. Choose one of those Area Plan buttons. The result will be a dialog box asking you to choose a level from which to make a new area plan.

FIGURE 18.7
The Area Plan button on the View tab

The New Area Plan dialog box (Figure 18.8) allows you to create a new area plan. The drop-down menu will give you the choice to select an area plan type from the list available in the Area And Volume Computations dialog box. You can select a level (or multiple levels by holding down the Ctrl key) to create an area from and set the scale of the area plan.

FIGURE 18.8
Creating a new area plan

For our purposes, choose Level 3, leave the scale at 1/8″ = 1′-0″, and click OK.

This will create a new area plan for you under a new node in the Project Browser: Area Plans (Rentable). Expanding that, you'll see Level 3. You'll also notice the plan took a vertical orientation. This is because when the building was modeled, it was modeled with Project North being up (up being north in Revit). We've modified the view creating a True North so the view sits horizontal on the sheet, allowing us to capitalize on more sheet real estate. Creating the drawing using North as "up" in Revit allows the sun shading to be accurate.

Let's rotate the view back to True North by choosing True North from the Orientation menu in the Properties Palette (Figure 18.9). This will only rotate the building within the view—so feel secure that you haven't manipulated any building geometry.

FIGURE 18.9
Rotating the
building using the
Properties Palette

Now you'll be able to see our initial area plan. We have to point out a few things about the area plan. When looking at the area plan on your screen, you'll notice a purple line running around the inside face of the exterior wall. This is the area boundary line in Revit. Revit has attempted to calculate your plan area based on some predefined rules. For the most part, Revit does a fairly good job of figuring out what the boundaries are, but from time to time those lines need some adjusting.

In this example, Revit missed three areas: the closet by the leftmost bedroom, the closet just off the living room, and what will eventually become the fire exit on the rightmost side of the building. To create an accurate area plan, you must make adjustments to these areas. Follow these steps:

1. Let's start with the closet across from the bedroom. You need to extend the purple area plan lines back into the closet and trim the line running across the face of the closet area. To do this, choose the Home tab. On the Room & Area panel, select the Area fly-out and choose the Area Boundary Line tool (Figure 18.10).

FIGURE 18.10
The Area Boundary
Line tool

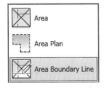

Once the tool is selected, you'll see the ribbon change to the familiar Modify context menu. The tool by default will be in a pick mode, meaning it will allow you to simply pick the walls you want bound by the area plan and it will place the area line for you based on the embedded rule system for calculating areas. In our example, you want to draw the lines yourself, so choose the Line tool and draw a line inside the closet and trim the line crossing the closet. The sketch should look like Figure 18.11.

FIGURE 18.11
Trimming out the
closet area lines

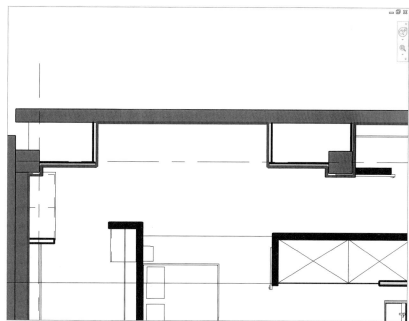

FIGURE 18.11
Trimming out the
closet area lines

2. Now pan to the right side of the floor plan. Do the same thing to the closet off the living area and close the opening on the right wall. The finished sketch will look like Figure 18.12.

FIGURE 18.12
Modifying the area
lines on the right
side of the plan

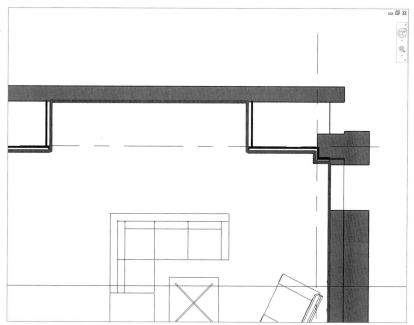

ADDING AN AREA

Like room elements, area plans need a closed boundary in order to place an area element. They have properties to which you can add attributes and that are "taggable." You can have any number of areas visible in an area plan. Unlike rooms, however, areas are view specific, and the areas will only appear in the view they are added to.

Back in the Area fly-out on the Home tab, choose the Area tool (Figure 18.13).

FIGURE 18.13
Adding an area

The Area tool will place an area similar to placing a room, and it will give you a bound area with a large X in it (Figure 18.14). Placing the area will also report to you the area of the space bound by the purple area lines. In Figure 18.13, the area is reported as part of the tag.

FIGURE 18.14
The placed area
element

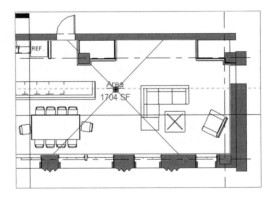

Unbound areas will have a slightly different display (Figure 18.15), letting you know that somewhere there is a gap in the purple linework that will need to be closed in order to properly report the area.

FIGURE 18.15
An unbound area

AUTOMATIC AREA CALCULATIONS

When first creating an area plan, Revit automatically creates area boundary lines. Those lines are locked by default to the walls on which they are created. This can be a helpful feature during the design process. When your design changes and walls are relocated, the area boundaries move with them, keeping your area plans always up-to-date.

MODIFYING AREA PLANS

Areas, like rooms, can be modified at any time during the design process. They can be modified dynamically if the area lines are locked to a wall or other element that has been moved as part of the design, or they can also be modified manually.

If you delete an area line, you'll get the warning message shown in Figure 18.16. This message tells you that you have removed one or more of the boundary lines for an area and Revit is alerting you to the fact that it can no longer calculate the area as closed.

FIGURE 18.16

Modifying an area boundary

This warning will also be present in the Warnings dialog box. If you are in the midst of modifying a space, finish your modifications and replace any area lines that you've deleted or removed as part of the design change. Once the area is whole, it will recalculate the space.

CREATING COMPLEX AREA PLANS

In some cases, as when designing for specific clients like the General Services Administration (GSA), you might have to create and maintain a series of numerous area plans for each floor. At times, larger clients have the need for more robust area plans detailing spaces for gross area, rentable, and individual department areas. All these additional calculations can slow file performance, depending on the complexity of the building. One way around this is to make a separate project file for the area plans and then link the building project to this secondary file. By linking the building model to a file with area plans, you can improve model performance by not adding that overhead to your project file. You can also quickly create or print area or department plans without interfering with the workflow of the rest of the team.

In this section, you've created an area plan that will give you a graphic representation of the space you've defined with area lines. But what if you want to show this same information in a spreadsheet format? All you need to do is set up a view type in the model that allows you to look at this same information in a different format. For this, you can use a schedule.

CERT
OBJECTIVE

Creating Schedules and Legends

Schedules are lists and quantities of elements and element properties within the model. They itemize items, including building objects such as walls, doors, and windows; calculate quantities, areas, and volumes. They also list elements such as the number of sheets, keynotes, and so on. Schedules are another way to view a Revit model. Once created, they are constantly kept up-to-date with any changes that occur to the model itself.

Legends are a way to graphically display building components, elements, or annotations. Legends can be created for displaying information such as door types, wall types, key plans, or general notes. Legends are unique in their behavior as a view because they are the one view in Revit that can be placed on multiple sheets.

Schedules

In a project workflow, creating schedules of objects, areas, or quantities is usually one of the most laborious tasks for architects. When this process is performed manually, it can take a very long time and typically results in errors, requiring much checking and rechecking of the information. In Revit, all the elements have information about their properties defined within the model. You also have the option to add additional information or categories to any existing element. For example in Revit, doors have properties such as size, material, fire rating, cost, and so on. All of this information can be scheduled and quantified.

Revit lets you schedule elements based on their properties. This means that almost anything placed in a Revit model can be scheduled and quantified. Because the schedule is linked to the element within the model, making changes to the schedule itself makes changes to the element in the model, and vice versa.

Revit has several types of schedules. They can all be accessed from the Create panel of the View tab. The Schedule fly-out is shown in Figure 18.17. There are five primary types of schedules you can create using Revit:

FIGURE 18.17
Schedules in Revit

Schedule/Quantities This is the most commonly used schedule type in Revit. This schedule allows you to list and quantify all the element category types in Revit. You would use this type to make door schedules, wall schedules, window schedules, and so on.

Material Takeoff This type of schedule can list all the materials and subcomponents of any Revit family category. You can use a material takeoff to schedule any material that is placed in a component or assembly. For example, you might want to know the cubic yardage of concrete within the model. Regardless of whether the concrete is in a wall or floor or column, you can tell the schedule to report the total amount of that material in the project.

Sheet List This schedule allows you to create a list of all the sheets in the project.

Note Block   This schedule lists the notes that are applied to elements and assemblies in your project. You can also use a note block to list the annotation symbols (centerlines, north arrows) used in a project.

View List   This schedule shows a list of all the views in the Project Browser and their properties.

Each of these schedule types has a host of categories that you can mix and match to make schedules and track elements within the model. All of these schedules are broken down into some common elements that allow you to build and customize your schedules. Let's step through what these are and how they can be used.

To begin a schedule, select one of the choices we've listed from the View tab. In our example, we're going to select Schedule/Quantities since it is the most widely used of schedule types. Selecting any of these schedule types will give you the New Schedule dialog box (Figure 18.18).

FIGURE 18.18
Creating a new schedule

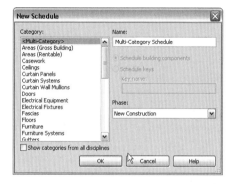

This dialog box will allow you to choose the category you would like to schedule. As you pan through the list on the left, you can see a host of different schedule categories:

Areas (Gross and Rentable)	Gutters	Rooms
Casework	Lighting fixtures	Site
Ceilings	Mass	Slab edges
Curtain panels	Mass floors	Specialty equipment
Curtain systems	Mechanical Equip.	Stairs
Curtain wall mullions	Parking	Structural columns
Doors	Planting	Structural foundations
Electrical equipment	Plumbing fixtures	Structural framing
Electrical fixtures	Property line seg.	Topography
Fascias	Property lines	Wall sweeps
Floors	Railings	Walls
Furniture	Ramps	Windows
Furniture systems	Roofs	

If there aren't enough categories for you to choose from to create customized schedules, Revit provides a venue to add additional options. At the bottom-left corner of the New Schedule dialog box is the Show Categories From All Disciplines check box. Selecting this check box gives you the ability to schedule elements from MEP and Structural categories. This can be useful when you have those disciplines supplying Revit files to you and you are linking them to your architectural model.

Revit also allows you the opportunity to create some schedules that span categories. The first option in the dialog box in Figure 18.18 is the <Multi-Category> schedule. You might want to schedule all the casework and furnishings in a project simultaneously, or all the windows and doors if they are being ordered from the same manufacturer. A Multi-Category schedule allows you to combine a number of different categories into one schedule. One of the limits of this schedule type is that you cannot schedule host elements (walls, floors, ceilings, and so on) but only their materials and family components.

With this description in mind, let's look at the other options when creating a schedule. Choose Walls and click OK. This will give you a new dialog box called Schedule Properties. Here, you can set the various properties of a schedule that define not only how it looks but what information it reports. There are five tabs across the top: Fields, Filter, Sorting/Grouping, Formatting, and Appearance. Each of these controls different aspects of the schedule. Let's step through each of them and look at how they affect the look and reporting of the schedule:

Fields The Fields tab (Figure 18.19) lets you select the data that will appear in your schedule. For the wall schedule, it shows all the properties available in the wall family (we chose Family And Type, Type Mark, and Volume). The list of available fields on the left will vary based on the family you chose to schedule. If you've added any project-based parameters to those family categories, they will be available here as well. Also notice the option Include Elements In Linked Files at the lower-left corner. Enabling this option will allow you to schedule across multiple files and can be a great tool for larger projects.

FIGURE 18.19
The Fields tab

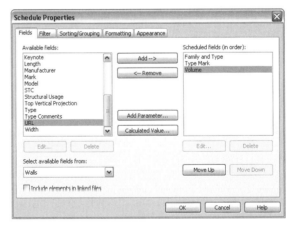

Filter On the Filter tab (Figure 18.20), you can filter out the data you don't want to show in your schedule. Filters work like common database functions. As an example, you can filter out all the sheets in a set that don't begin with the letter A. Or you can filter a material list so that it only shows items containing Concrete.

FIGURE 18.20
The Filter tab

FIGURE 18.20
The Filter tab

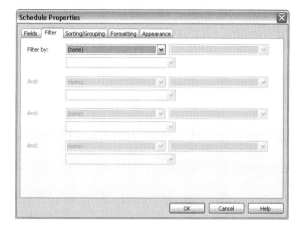

Sorting/Grouping   The Sorting/Grouping tab (Figure 18.21) lets you control the order in which information is displayed and which elements control that order. For instance, if you are creating a sheet index, you can choose to sort by Sheet Number or Sheet Name, depending on how you'd like the information displayed. You can also decide whether you want to show every instance of an item or only the categories for a family by using the Itemize Every Instance check box at the bottom.

FIGURE 18.21
The Sorting and
Grouping tab

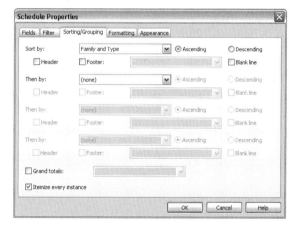

Formatting   The Formatting tab (Figure 18.22) controls the display heading for each field and whether the field is visible on the schedule. It also controls other elements of the field such as justification, display name, and orientation of the header. This tab also allows you to use the Calculate Totals check box. Not all Revit fields will calculate their total values at the bottom of the schedule. By highlighting the field on the left, you can check the Calculate Totals box and show a sum at the bottom for any numerical column.

FIGURE 18.22
The Formatting tab

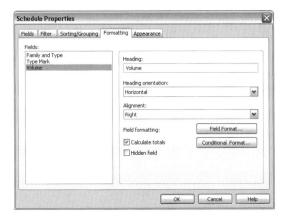

Appearance   The Appearance tab (Figure 18.23) controls the graphical aspects of the schedule, such as font size and style of text for each of the columns and headers in the schedule. It also allows you to turn the schedule grid lines on and off, and modify the line thickness for the grid and boundary lines.

FIGURE 18.23
The Appearance tab

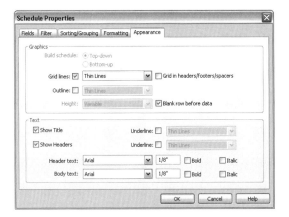

Once you've established the fields and look of your schedule, clicking OK gives you a preliminary layout. The schedule's layout can be modified at any time during the project but gives you a basis from which to begin. To modify the schedule at any time, simply click the Element Properties button or right-click and choose Element Properties from the context menu.

Schedules have their own special tab on the ribbon that is active when you are viewing the schedule outside of a sheet. The tab (Figure 18.24) allows you to select the properties, add and delete rows, and show or hide columns within the schedule.

FIGURE 18.24
The Schedule tab

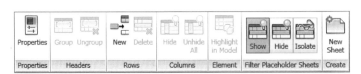

Another key feature of this menu bar is the Highlight In Model button (grayed out in Figure 18.24). This button allows you to select any element within the schedule and locate that element within the model. Let's say you want to locate a particular door from your door schedule. Highlight the door and click the Highlight In Model button, and Revit will take you to a different view with that door highlighted. This can be a useful way to locate elements in the model especially for larger models.

Now that you have an idea of the elements that compose a schedule, let's return to the demonstration workflow and create a Rentable Area schedule based on the areas we've defined earlier in this chapter.

MAKING A RENTABLE AREA SCHEDULE

To make a Rentable Area schedule, start by selecting the Schedule/Quantities button from the Schedule fly-out on the View tab. You will get a dialog box similar to Figure 18.25.

FIGURE 18.25
Creating a
Rentable Area
schedule

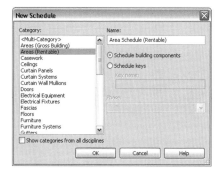

To create the schedule, follow these steps:

1. From the Categories list, select the Area (Rentable) schedule type and click OK.

2. On the Fields tab, notice that the available fields in an area table are much more limited than they were in the Walls table in the previous example images. For this schedule, you need only three fields: Level, Name, and Area. Choose those from the Fields list on the left and, using the Add button, push them to the right (Figure 18.26).

FIGURE 18.26
Adding fields to the
area schedule

3. Next, choose the Sorting/Grouping tab. From the first pull-down, choose to sort by Level and check the Itemize Every Instance box at the bottom (Figure 18.27).

FIGURE 18.27
Sorting the
schedule by level

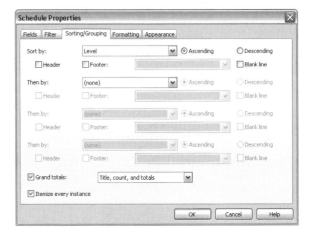

4. In this schedule, you want to make the areas read as they would in a spreadsheet—right-justified and totaled. Choose the Formatting tab and select Area from the list on the left. Change the justification to Right and check the Calculate Totals box (Figure 18.28)

FIGURE 18.28
Formatting the
schedule

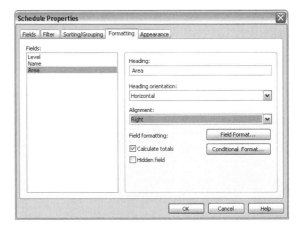

5. Leave the rest of the schedule as the defaults, and click OK. Since you have defined only one floor with an area plan, you will see only one floor in the schedule (Figure 18.29). However, you'll notice that this reported the same area as you had shown in the earlier area plan, and once the schedule is formatted, it will dynamically fill itself in as you add additional Rentable floor plans.

FIGURE 18.29
The Schedule tab

ADDING SCHEDULES TO YOUR TEMPLATES

On a typical project, you will find that you will use the same schedules time and time again. Spend the time to make them consistent with your office's graphic standards, and add them to your office template. That way, you won't have to make them over and over again. As you add content to your model, the schedules will automatically populate, in effect, filling themselves out.

You will find yourself making the same schedules for each and every project. Take the ones you find the most universal and make them a part of your default template. As you add content to the model, these will start to auto-populate.

If you have a schedule in another project and you want to add it to your project, there's no need to re-create it. Open both projects in the same instance of Revit. Go to the sheet that the schedule you want to copy is on. If it's not on a sheet, you'll need to place it on one. Then simply highlight it and copy it (press Crtl+C) to the clipboard. In your destination project, go to any sheet and press Crtl+V to paste it. Once the paste is finished, the schedule should be there with all the formatting from the previous project but with all the information from your current model.

CREATING A SHEET LIST

The Sheet List schedule allows you to create a list of sheets in your project. You'll find it on the View tab under the Schedules fly-out (Figure 18.30).

FIGURE 18.30
The Sheet List schedule

In Revit 2011, this schedule has a new feature that allows you to create placeholders for sheets that are not yet created or will not be a part of your discipline's drawings. This can be used to create full sheet schedules, including all consultant drawings. It also allows you to create place-holder entries in the sheet schedule before you've created the sheets.

In the sample workflow, you have created an area plan for Level 3. Eventually, you want to create an area plan for each of the floors of the building. You haven't created them yet, but you want to create our sheet list, including the area plans that you will create later. To do this, begin by selecting the Sheet List tool from the Schedules fly-out.

1. You'll see the now familiar Revit schedule dialog box open to the Fields tab. On this tab, you need to select two fields from the categories on the left and move them to the column on the right. Select the Sheet Number and Sheet Name categories (Figure 18.31).

FIGURE 18.31
Creating the
sheet list

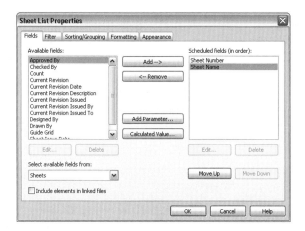

2. On the Sorting/Grouping tab, choose to sort by Sheet Number and make sure the Itemize Every Instance check box is checked (Figure 18.32).

FIGURE 18.32
Sorting by Sheet
Number

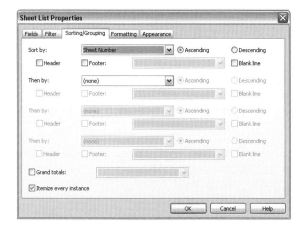

3. Choose the Filter tab. You'll be creating a sheet index for your presentation sheets, so you don't want to include all the sheets in the set. You already have some of the construction documentation sheets in the file (the A series sheets) and you don't want those reported in our schedule. To do this, you want to filter out all the sheets that don't begin with the letter P (for Presentation).

A. On the Filter tab, choose to filter by Sheet Number.

B. From the next pull-down, choose Begins With.

C. And in the third field, enter the letter **P**. The filter should look like Figure 18.33. Be sure to use a capital P, as the Boolean queries in Revit are case sensitive.

D. Click OK.

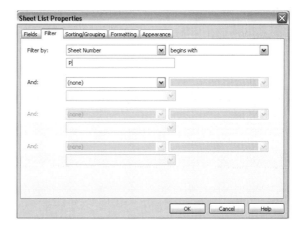

FIGURE 18.33
Filtering out sheets

What you should have is a schedule with nothing in it. This is because at this point, you haven't created any sheets beginning with a P to use in your presentations. Now you need to populate the sheet list.

1. To begin adding sheets to the sheet list, click the New button in the Rows panel (Figure 18.34). This will give you a row with a blank for both of our headings, Sheet Number and Sheet Name.

FIGURE 18.34
Adding rows to
the schedule

2. To get your sheet list populated, add three lines for the third, fourth, and fifth floors, creating sheet numbers P103, P104, and P105, similar to Figure 18.35.

FIGURE 18.35
Adding sheets
to the list

3. You can continue populating the schedule in this way, adding any sheet names you need or plan to have in the presentation package. However, since you have a Level 3 Area Plan already established, you need to now create a sheet out of it. To do this, you will reuse the line you already created for sheet P103 and simply link a sheet to it.

  A. Start by highlighting the row P103 from the schedule and selecting the New Sheet button from the ribbon. This will give you a dialog box similar to Figure 18.36.

  B. Here, you have a couple of choices to make. You will want to select the type of sheet you'd like use from the selection list at the top. For these sheets, Choose the Sheets – Presentation 11x17 from the list at the top.

      c. You also need select the sheet number and name you'd like to tie this new sheet to from our schedule. Choose P103 – Third Floor from the list at the bottom (Figure 18.36) and click OK.

FIGURE 18.36
Converting
the schedule into
a sheet

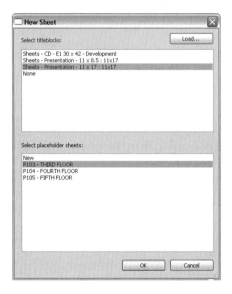

This will create a sheet from the line item in the schedule using the same name and sheet number. The new sheet will appear under the Sheet node in the Project Browser.

Legends

CERT
OBJECTIVE

Legends are unique views in Revit as they are the only view type you can place on more than one sheet. These can become great tools for things like general notes, key plans, or any other view type that you will want to have consistent across several sheets. It's also important to note that anything you place inside a legend view—doors, walls, windows, and so on—will not appear or be counted in any schedules. Legend elements live outside of any quantities present in the model.

    The Legend tool is located on the View tab. There are two types of legends (Figure 18.37) you can create from this menu: a legend, which is a graphic display, or a keynote legend, which is a text-based schedule. Both legend types can be placed on multiple sheets, but for this exercise, you'll focus on the legend. The keynote legend will be handled in more detail in Chapter 19.

FIGURE 18.37
The Legend tool

As part of the sample workflow, say you want to present some of the wall types as part of your presentation package to demonstrate the Sound Transmission Class (STC) of the walls and the overall wall assembly. Since these wall types will be appearing on all the sheets where we are using them in plan, you'll make them using a legend.

To make a legend, choose the Legend button from the View tab under the Legends fly-out. Creating a new legend is much like creating a new drafting view. You'll be presented with a New Legend View dialog box (Figure 18.38) where you can name the legend and set the scale. For this legend, name it a Wall Legend and choose 3/8″ = 1′-0″ for a scale.

FIGURE 18.38

Creating a legend

The legend you've created will look like a blank view. At this point, it's up to you to add content. The simplest type of legend would be adding notes such as plan or demolition notes that would appear in each of your floor plans. You could do this simply by using the Text tool and adding text within this schedule view.

You want to add more than just text to the legend, however. To add wall types (or any family for that matter), expand the family tree in the Project Browser and navigate to the Wall family. Expand this node and then expand the Basic Wall Node. Select the Interior – Gyp 4⅞″ wall type and drag and drop it into the view (Figure 18.39).

FIGURE 18.39

Drag and drop the wall type from the Project Browser.

With the family inserted into the view, it will appear as a 3′ long plan wall. Change your view type from Coarse to Medium or Fine so you can see the detail within the wall. With that done, highlight the inserted wall and let's look at the new Modify | Legend Components menu in the Options Bar (Figure 18.40).

FIGURE 18.40

The Legend Options Bar

| Modify | Legend Components | Family: | Walls : Basic Wall : Interior - Gyp 4 7/8″ | ▼ | View: | Section | ▼ | Host Length: | 1′ 6″ |

This menu will be consistent for any of the family types you insert. The menu consists of three sections:

Family This drop-down menu allows you to select different family types and operates just like the Type Selector does for other elements within the model.

View The View option lets you change the type of view from Plan to Section.

Host Length This option changes the overall length (or in the case of sections, height) of the element selected.

Let's make some minor adjustments to the wall. Let's change View to Section and change Host Length from a foot to 18″.

The wall now looks like a sectional element. By adding some simple text we can embellish the wall type to better explain the elements you're viewing (Figure 18.41).

FIGURE 18.41
Creating the Wall
type section

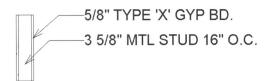

Using Details from Other Files

It is not uncommon to have details in your Revit model that came from CAD. Sometimes these are details taken from a manufacturer's website, and sometimes they can be details drawn in other projects or from an office library and you simply want to reuse them in your project rather than having to re-create them. Regardless of where they have originated, Revit has the ability to work with 2D detail elements and import or link them into the model for use in your project.

Revit allows you to both link and insert CAD files into your model to be used in your documentation. You can find both of these functions on the Insert tab. There are several file types you can both insert and link into Revit: `.dwg`, `.dfx`, `.dgn`, `.sat`, and `.skp`. There are benefits and drawbacks to using either a linking workflow or an importing one. In the following sections, we'll step through the differences between the two and discuss when and why you'd like to use either one of those methods.

Linking vs. Importing

You will find that you will want to get CAD data into your Revit model at a variety of stages in the project process. Sometimes it could be the building site you've received from your civil consultant; sometimes it's manufacturer details you need for documentation. In each case, the CAD files can be temporarily imported or linked, or permanently become part of the documentation. In addition, the size of these CAD files can vary greatly. Knowing when to import and when to link can help save a lot of frustration later on in your project by helping to keep the file sizes low and the model easy to manage.

LINKING

The Link CAD tool (Figure 18.42) is on the Insert tab on the Link panel. This panel also controls all the other types of linking you might want to do for external files such as DWF markups or decals (images).

FIGURE 18.42

The Link CAD tool

We recommend you use linking when you have files that will update through the design process. This can be a 3D site drawing that you'll be receiving regularly from your civil engineer or 2D CAD details you'll receive from another drafter on your project who isn't familiar with a Revit workflow. By linking the files, you'll ensure that as those external files get updated and that the information in Revit will reflect those changes. Linking creates a live connection between the model and the external files—much like an Xref in AutoCAD.

Linking files also works best when you are working on a smaller team or smaller project and are not sharing your Revit files with others in the same discipline. As an example, if you are working on a large project and teamed with another architectural firm and you are both sharing files and details, linking might not be the best workflow for you. When transferring Revit files between team members, you'll need to make sure to include all the linked files and make sure they are located in a similar directory path. If not, you'll receive an error message like Figure 18.43, and those files won't appear within the model.

FIGURE 18.43

Unresolved References dialog box

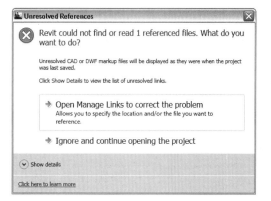

IMPORTING

The Import CAD tool is on the Import panel of the Annotate tab (Figure 18.44). The Import panel contains additional tools to import files from other sources. From here, you can import views from other Revit files as well as images and manage those imports through another dialog box.

FIGURE 18.44
The Import
CAD tool

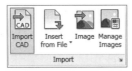

Use the Import CAD function when you want to embed files within your model. This might be valuable when you want to insert 2D or 3D geometry to trace over and you don't want to link the file. Or, if you have completed details done in CAD and you want to make them a permanent part of your model, you can do that through an import.

When importing CAD data, it will insert itself as a single object—like a family—in the model. You can manage layers by turning them on and off in the Visibility/Graphic Overrides dialog box, but you'll be unable to edit any of the geometry without exploding the CAD file. If you want to explode the file, simply highlight it and choose Full Explode or Partial Explode from the menu; however, we don't recommend this. Think of Revit like a database full of objects. An inserted CAD file is a single object in the database. An exploded CAD file can be thousands. Each time you explode a CAD file, you're adding overhead to your model that you might not be able to remove later. Good file management will help you keep your files small and able to react quickly.

 Real World Scenario

TIPS ON IMPORTING CAD DETAILS

At times in the project, your workflow will necessitate using 2D information from a past project, manufacturer's library, or other resource in your current Revit project. To optimize the performance of your imported CAD files within your model, we recommend you take some steps to prepare the CAD file before import. Here are some general tips to help your import process:

◆ If the file you'd like to import contains hatches or annotations, delete them before importing and use filled regions and the Revit Text or Keynote tool for annotations. This will help keep your graphics consistent (in the case of hatch) and allow you to edit the verbiage and location of any notes.

◆ Import only one detail at a time so you can take better advantage of Revit's ability to manage sheet referencing. If you have a series of details organized in a single CAD file that you want to use in documenting your project, isolate each detail, save it as a separate file, and then import.

◆ Make sure you import the CAD details using the proper line weights, colors, and styles. Check your CAD file before importing into Revit to make sure it is consistent with your office's standards.

◆ If the imported geometry is something you really want or need to edit, it's better for your model and overall file size to import the CAD file into a detail component (if it's 2D) and explode it and edit it in the family editor. This way, when you import it into your project file, it is still a single object rather than thousands.

◆ Revit doesn't allow line segments shorter than ¹⁄₃₂″. Although this is seemingly a very small line, many manufacturer details have small segment lines in them. When CAD details are exploded in Revit, those short lines will be deleted and can leave your linework looking incomplete.

Options During Import/Link

The Import CAD Formats and Link CAD Formats dialog boxes are nearly identical in functionality and look (Figure 18.45). There are, however, a series of options you'll want to understand in order to get the results you want from linking or importing files.

FIGURE 18.45

The Import CAD Formats and Link CAD Formats dialog boxes

Current View Only   Selecting the Current View Only check box (located at the left of the dialog boxes) brings the linked or imported file into *only* the view that is currently active. Typically, when importing or linking in CAD details, you don't want the detail to show up in every view. More often than not, you'll want to make sure this check box is selected as it will limit the number of views in which your linked file will appear. If you import with this option unchecked, the linked file will be visible in every model view (not drafting views) in the project and any new views you will create. You can control the visibility of CAD information through the Visibility/Graphic Overrides dialog box. If you import your CAD file into one view and would like to have it in others, you can easily copy and paste it from one view to the next.

Colors   The default view background in CAD is black, so the colors used in are easily visible on a black background. When you import a CAD file into Revit (which has a white background), many of the colors usually used in CAD such as yellow, light green, magenta, or cyan are often difficult to read. Revit recognizes this issue, and in the Colors section of the Import/Link dialog box you have the option to invert these colors or change them to straight black linework.

Layers   The Layers drop-down menu gives you the option to import or link in all the layers, only the layers that were visible at the time the CAD file was last saved, or a selected group of layers from a secondary dialog box. (Layers are a DWG-based naming convention. Revit allows the same functionality with levels from DGN drawings.)

Import Units   The Import Units section of the Import/Link CAD Formats dialog box allows you to let Revit autodetect the scale at which the imported or linked drawing was created and convert accordingly. You also have the option to manually scale the imported geometry if you want to change scale factors upon import.

Positioning   The Positioning option allows you to align the inserted file with your current model geometry. By default, CAD files insert at their origin (0,0,0) and will insert that at the origin of the Revit file. This location juxtaposition is not always ideal as sometimes it means the CAD file is inserted several miles away. By modifying the Positioning value, you can choose to locate inserted CAD files by Center To Center (the default) or Manual, or by using shared parameters.

Place At This option allows you to choose the level in which you are inserting the CAD file in the case of a multilevel view, such as an axon. In our case, since you have chosen to insert the CAD file while Level 3 was our active view, the option is grayed out.

Reusing Details from Other Revit Projects

We've discussed that you sometimes want to reuse details or geometry from other projects done in CAD. But what happens when you want to reuse details from projects completed in Revit? Thankfully, there are a couple of simple ways to take your Revit details and drawings with you from one project to the next.

SAVING A SINGLE DETAIL

Everyone is familiar with the problem that you have a detail very similar to the one you need to create in a previous Revit project. Now the question is, how do you get it into your project? In the case of a single, 2D detail, it can be quick work to get the file from one project to the next.

1. The first thing to do is open the file with the detail you'd like to collect and open the view this detail is in. Once it is open, select all the geometry within the view (Figure 18.46) and create a group using the Group button on the Home tab.

FIGURE 18.46
Find the detail and select the geometry.

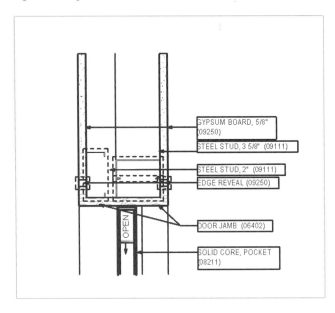

2. The group will by default be created as a detail group (since all your geometry is only 2D). Give the group a unique name, making sure the name is unique enough not to overlap with any view names in your current project or the project you're going to import into (Figure 18.47).

FIGURE 18.47
Creating a detail
group

3. With the detail grouped and named, in the Project Browser expand the Groups node. Now, expand the Detail Group node and find the detail you just created. Right-click the detail and choose Save Group from the context menu (Figure 18.48).

FIGURE 18.48
Saving the detail
group

4. As part of the Save As process, you'll get the Save Group dialog box (Figure 18.49). This will allow you to create a separate RVT file for your group—basically a stand-alone project file. Save the group in a location where you'll be able to find it again and close your project file. There's no need to name the group as the new file will name itself the same as the group name.

FIGURE 18.49
The Save Group
dialog box

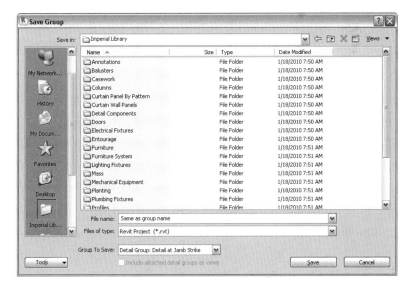

5. Open the destination project file. On the Insert tab, choose Insert 2D Elements From File (Figure 18.50).

FIGURE 18.50
Inserting the group

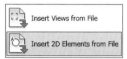

6. This will give you the Open dialog box. Simply navigate to the group you just made and select it. It will give you a preview in the upper-right corner so you can verify that the geometry was exported properly. Highlight the group name and choose Open (Figure 18.51).

FIGURE 18.51
Saving the detail
group

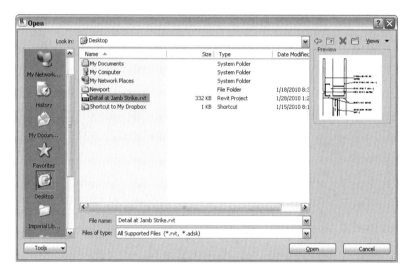

7. Once the file is inserted into the project, all you need to do is drop it into a view. Because this will probably be a stand-alone detail in its own view, create a new drafting view at a scale matching the view you just exported. In the Project Browser, expand the Group node and then the Detail Group node. You'll see the group listed there that you just imported. Select the group name from the list and drag and drop it into the new view (Figure 18.52). It will insert as a group, which you can then ungroup if you would like to make further edits.

FIGURE 18.52
Inserting the group
into a new view

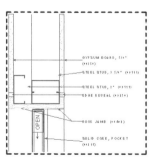

SAVING MULTIPLE DETAILS

As you create more and more details in Revit, you will inevitably want to save some of them to an office library or some sort of localized resource so you can quickly locate the good ones again. Revit allows you to selectively save multiple views from a single project into a separate, stand-alone file. This workflow will work for both 2D and 3D content.

A quick way to get any view isolated to an external file is to simply right-click the view in the Project Browser and choose Save To New File from the context menu. It might take Revit a few moments to compile the view content, but you will be presented with a dialog box asking you to locate the new file. Once the view is exported, it functions like any other RVT files. You can open these new views directly and edit or manipulate any of the content or elements within the file. You'll also see a streamlined version of the Project Browser having only the nodes that relate to the content you've exported.

A secondary way to export multiple views is to click the Application button and choose Save As ➤ Library. This command allows you to save multiple views into a single RVT file that acts as a library for those views.

1. Start by opening the file with the views you want to save. Click the Application button and select Save As ➤ Library ➤ View (Figure 18.53).

FIGURE 18.53
Saving multiple views into a library

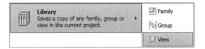

2. This will give you the Save Views dialog box (Figure 18.54). It will show a list of view names on the left and a preview window on the right side. Simply click the check box for each of the views you want to save out into a separate file. Once you have all your view names established, click OK.

FIGURE 18.54
Exporting multiple views to a separate file

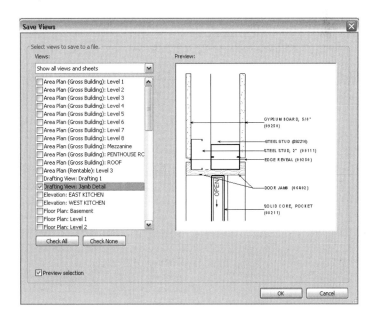

Revit might take a few moments to export the views depending on how many you've chosen and how large the overall file size is. Once the process is completed, you'll have a separate file to import those views back into Revit. This import process is just as simple as exporting. To import the views:

1. Open the project you'd like to import the views into and choose Insert From File from the Insert tab (Figure 18.55). Choose Insert Views From File.

FIGURE 18.55
Inserting views
from a separate file

2. The new dialog box will look very similar to the Save Views dialog box. You will have a list of the views you can import from the column on the left and a preview of those views on the right. Check the box for the views you want to import and click OK (Figure 18.56).

FIGURE 18.56
Importing
multiple views
into a project

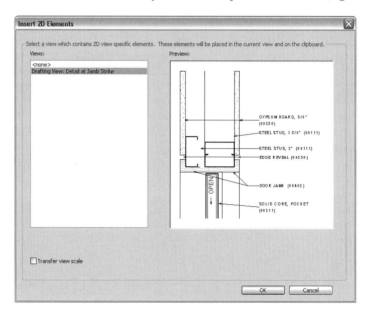

Laying Out Sheets

Throughout this chapter, you have created and imported several different kinds of views from area plans to schedules to legends to details. Eventually, you will need to lay those out onto sheets so they can be printed or exported as PDF and sent to clients or team members for review.

Creating sheets in Revit is very easy. As you've already seen, you can create sheets through a Sheet List schedule. You can also create sheets by right-clicking the Sheet node in the Project Browser and selecting New Sheet from the context menu. Regardless of which method you use to create them, in the following sections we'll walk through laying these views out on sheets and show you how to manipulate each view further once it's placed on a sheet.

Adding the Area Plan

Since you have already created a series of views for Level 3, let's use the sheet you've already made for this purpose. Open the P103 – Level 3 sheet in the view window by double-clicking it in the Project Browser. Now, let's add your first view—the area plan. To do this, simply drag and drop it from the Project Browser and onto the sheet. The view will show at the proper scale and with a View Title already established. You can then drag the view across the sheet to place it where you'd like to have it, which in this case is centered at the top of the sheet.

After placing the view, however, you'll notice that the purple area lines are still visible. If you print the sheet at this point, Revit will print those lines as thick, black lines that border your floorplate. This would be highly undesirable, so you need to do some view management to turn those lines off. One way you can do this is by double-clicking the view from the Project Browser and working within the view itself. Since you have the view already established on a sheet, there's no reason to go back to the original view when you can work on it directly through the sheet.

Right-click the view on the sheet and choose Activate View from the context menu (Figure 18.57).

FIGURE 18.57

Activating a view to make modifications

Activating a view is like working in model space through paperspace in CAD. You're working on the actual view but you're doing so while it is placed on the sheet. This gives you the benefit of seeing how changes to the view will affect the layout of the view on the sheet. At times, it could be undesirable to enlarge the crop window for the view to show more information on the sheet. Doing so will take up valuable sheet real estate and will need to be balanced by the amount of space the other views on this sheet need as well. Working through the sheet allows you to see how this all works live on the sheet so you can make any adjustments on the fly. You'll also notice that once the view is activated, all the surrounding materials (the sheet and any other views) turns gray (Figure 18.58). This is to help alert you to the fact that you're working in the view and are not active on the sheet.

FIGURE 18.58
When the view is activated, surrounding information is grayed out.

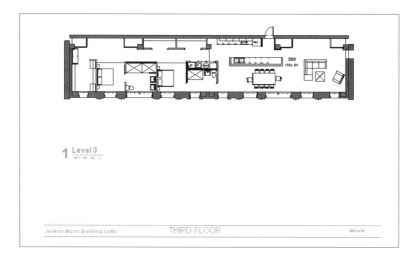

In this view, however, you want to make some modifications to the visibility and turn off the area boundaries so they are not visible when you print. To do this, open the Visibility/Graphic Overrides dialog box by pressing **VG** on your keyboard or navigating to the command via the context menu.

In the Visibility/Graphic Overrides dialog box, pan down in the Model tab (activated by default), and choose the Lines node. Uncheck the box for <Area Boundaries>, and click OK. The boundary lines should disappear from the view.

Now, you're ready to get out of the activation mode and add some additional views to the sheet. To do this, right-click anywhere within the view and choose Deactivate View from the context menu (Figure 18.59).

FIGURE 18.59
Find the detail and select the geometry.

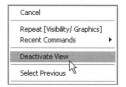

DEACTIVATE ACTIVATED VIEWS

Keep the following in mind: once you activate a view and complete your edits, you must also deactivate it. As you can see on the sheet, activated views gray out the surrounding sheet context. If you were to print at this point, the sheet would print as gray with only the activated view showing in black.

With the view on the sheet, you will want to make some other adjustments to help clean the sheet layout up a bit. One thing you will want to do is modify the View Title's location and length. To do this, click the view itself and the View Title will activate, showing in purple. This might sound a bit counterintuitive, but selecting the View Title itself will allow you to relocate the view and title around on the sheet.

With the View Title active, you'll notice the blue grip at the end of the title line. By grabbing this grip, you can shorten it to a length more appropriate to the length of the text. You can now also grab the View Title itself by clicking and holding the left mouse button down and drag the title closer to the view itself (Figure 18.60).

FIGURE 18.60
Move the view title by selecting it, not the view.

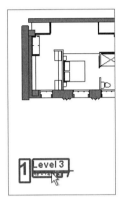

Adding the Schedule

With the largest view, the area plan, on the sheet, you can use the bottom portion of the sheet to lay out your other views. For the second view, let's add the area schedule you created. To do this, simply drag and drop it from the Project Browser in much the same way you added the area plan. The inserted view will look like Figure 18.61. You'll notice some differences in how this view looks from the way a schedule looks when it's not on a sheet. Specifically, you can now see the header text and the fonts you chose back in the schedule properties. You'll also be able to see the grid lines and their associated line weights from the Appearance tab of the schedule properties.

FIGURE 18.61
Adding a schedule to a sheet

With the schedule on the sheet, it looks a bit tight. Once located, you have the ability to redefine the column spacing so you can make any visual adjustments to the schedule while it is on the sheet to help it read better. These adjustments do not change the actual schedule—just its appearance on the sheet itself.

To do this, simply highlight the schedule by selecting it. The schedule will turn blue, and you'll have a few new grips to help you make adjustments (Figure 18.62). The blue inverted triangles will allow you to modify the column widths. Simply grab them and drag them left or right to change the column sizing.

FIGURE 18.62
Modifying the schedule on the sheet

You'll also notice a blue cut symbol . This cut symbol lets you break the schedule into parts while on the same sheet. This can be especially handy if you have a long schedule like a room schedule or door schedule and it has too many rows to fit on your sheet vertically. Selecting this tool will break the schedule in half (and you can break it into half again and again) so that you can take advantage of the horizontal real estate. If you choose to separate your schedule in this fashion, it will still retain all the necessary information and all the portions will continue to automatically fill themselves out dynamically as a single schedule would. You also have the opportunity to change the overall height of the schedule once it is broken up by grabbing the grips at the bottom of the schedule and dragging up and down (Figure 18.63). Doing this will draw or push rows from the adjacent schedule portion so all of your information is continuous.

FIGURE 18.63
Changing the schedule height

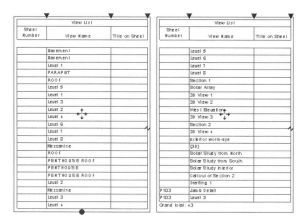

Real World Scenario

GETTING THE VIEWS TO LOOK THE WAY YOU WANT

On a typical project, there will be multiple views shown in the same way. These can be plans, elevations, or sections, but you will find yourself laying out crop boundaries, scale, visibility graphics, and many other settings for each of these views. Rather than creating them all manually, use view templates, which are a great way to apply settings to a view or to transfer settings between views.

The simplest way to do this is to get one of your views (say a plan) set up visually just the way you want it. Once that is done, right-click the view in the Project Browser, and choose Save As View Template. Then, you can right-click all your remaining plans in the Project Browser and choose Apply View Template from the context menu, and they will all take on the settings of your previous view.

In addition, you can go back and change these settings manually at any time by selecting the Manage tab and then View Templates from the Settings fly-out menu.

FINISHING THE SHEET

Now that you have those two views on the sheet, it is a simple matter to add the remaining views. To add the wall legend you created, you will drag and drop it from the Project Browser in much the same way you did with the other two views (Figure 18.64).

FIGURE 18.64
The wall legend
placed on the sheet

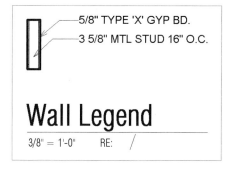

In this case, the wall legend came onto the sheet needing very little modification. Following this same workflow, you can also add a detail from one of our imported details to the sheet completing P103 (Figure 18.65).

FIGURE 18.65
The finished sheet

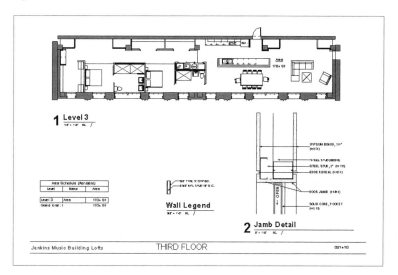

The Bottom Line

Document plans.   Floor plans can create visual graphics that help to define how a space is laid out. However, Revit provides other tools such as area plans to help you describe space.

Master It   List the four types of area plans that you can create and note the two that Revit creates automatically.

Create schedules and legends.   Schedules are another view type in Revit; they allow you to show information about the model in a nongraphic format. Schedules can also be used to dynamically report quantities of elements inside the model.

> **Master It**   Understand how to create schedules in Revit and report additional information about the elements in the model. How would you create a simple casework schedule showing quantities of types?

Use details from other files.   In many project workflows, you will need to incorporate details from other projects. Reusing these details can aid in the speed and efficiency of project documentation.

> **Master It**   There are several ways to reuse details from other projects. Name one and list the steps to perform the tasks necessary to quickly move a detail from one project to another.

Lay out sheets.   Eventually in a project process it will become necessary to create sheets that will become the documentation set. Knowing how to create a good sheet set provides you with another venue to communicate with contractors, clients, and other team members.

> **Master It**   To properly create a sheet set, you need to understand the dynamic of adding views to a sheet. In Revit there is only one way to add views to a sheet. What is it?

Chapter 19

Annotating Your Design

No set of documents is complete without the annotations to describe the drawings. Even when working in Revit and using a digital, parametric model, you will still need to provide annotated documents. It is necessary to add dimensions, tags, text, and notes to the drawings to properly communicate with owners, contractors, and the rest of the design team.

In this chapter, you'll learn to:

◆ Annotate with text and keynotes

◆ Use tags

◆ Adding Dimensions

◆ Set project and shared parameters

Annotating with Text and Keynotes

Notes are a critical part of communicating design and construction intent to owners and builders. No drawing set is complete without descriptions of materials and the work (Figure 19.1).

FIGURE 19.1
An annotated detail

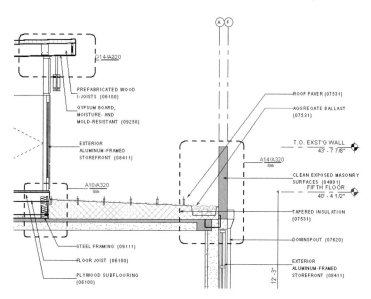

Revit has two ways for you to note your drawings. Both are located on the Annotate tab and highlighted in Figure 19.2. One of these methods is the Text command (shown on the left), and the other is the Keynote command (shown on the right).

FIGURE 19.2

Text and keynotes

The Text command in Revit consists of a field you can enter type into with or without a leader, bullets, or numbers. Text can be used for annotations, sheet notes (such as General Notes), legends, or generally anywhere you need to add a description or a note. Keynotes are predescribed text fields that are linked to elements and materials through a data file. Keynotes can be scheduled and standardized across the project but can't be directly edited within Revit. Both keynotes and text have specific uses across the project. Let's look at both.

Using Text

Text is quick and easy to add to any view (including 3D views) and, like other drafting elements, is view specific. Text added to one view will not appear in any other location within the model, nor will the actual type that you insert into the text box hold any sort of parametric values.

You can access the Text tool from the Text panel on the Annotate tab (shown earlier in Figure 19.2).

To begin adding text, simply select the Text tool, choose a location to insert the text, and start typing. You'll be presented with the standard Revit crosshair, but it will have a small A in the lower corner to let you know you are adding text and not other elements. The Text tool will allow you to write much as you do in applications like Microsoft Word. Once you are done typing, simply click outside the text box.

Your finished text box will look like Figure 19.3. You'll also notice that once you're finished with your initial text, you have a few tools available:

Grips The round grips on either side of the text box allow you to resize the box.

Move There is a move icon that appears in the upper-left corner of the text box. In addition, hovering your mouse anywhere within the highlighted text will also display a move cursor. You can click and drag from within the box or click the move icon on the upper-left corner to relocate it. When you're moving text with the move icon (or the Move command), the text *and* leader will relocate together. When moving text by dragging, the leader end will remain pinned while you relocate the text box. These methods allow you to move either the text or the text and the leader, depending on your need.

Rotate The upper-right corner will show a rotate icon. Clicking this icon will allow you to rotate the text box as you would any object within Revit. Remember that text within Revit will always position itself to be read from the bottom or right side of the screen, drawing, or view.

The Text family behaves like other Revit families, and text families maintain a parametric relationship throughout the project. Making changes to a text family in one location (changing font, font size, color, and so on) changes all the instances of that family throughout the model. To modify a text family, simply select a block of text or choose the Text tool. This will open the Type Selector, shown in Figure 19.4.

FIGURE 19.3
A highlighted
text box

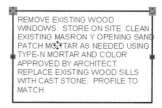

FIGURE 19.4
Type Selector
for text

Here, the controls are rather limited and deal primarily with Instance parameters for an individual instance of text (alignment, location, and so on), which you can also set on the Ribbon. The Type Selector also allows you to change type or edit the text family. Click the Edit Type button, and it will open the text family's properties. Figure 19.5 shows the properties for Text 3/32″ (75 mm) Arial.

FIGURE 19.5
Type Properties
dialog box

In this dialog box, you have more control over the style of the text. Here you can modify typical text properties, such as font style and size and width factor, and you can add formatting to the font, such as bold, italic, and underline.

At any time within the Text command or when the text box is selected, there are additional tools available on the Ribbon. The Format panel is divided into four sections that allow you to modify the instance of the text you've placed. Figure 19.6 shows the Format panel. Let's look at this panel in some more detail to better understand the toolset:

FIGURE 19.6
The Format panel

Leaders   The leftmost section of this panel allows you to designate the type and style of leader you want to add to your text box. By default, the upper-left A is selected (as in Figure 19.6), which designates that no leader is currently added. The other choices all will add a leader to the text. Reading from left to right, the options are no leader, a single segment leader, a double segment leader, and an arced leader. Leaders can be added at any time when you're placing or editing text and can also be removed at any time. Remember that when you're removing leaders, they will disappear in the order they were added.

Leader Location   The second portion of this panel dictates leader location. Leaders can be added to the left or to the right and at the top, center, or bottom of the text box. Figure 19.6 shows the default with a left leader springing from the upper left of the text; leaders that spring from the right side typically come from the end of the text box (at the bottom). A double-segmented leader springing from the left and right will look like Figure 19.7.

FIGURE 19.7
Text with a leader

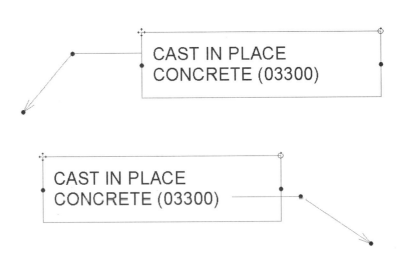

Format   The third portion of the text box controls the format of the text. These features—justification, bold, italicized, and underline—can also be modified using the Properties dialog box shown previously in Figure 19.4.

Bullets   The rightmost portion of the Format panel allows you to add a bulleted or numbered list to the text box. By default, this style of formatting is not added, but by selecting the text box or the text within the box, you can add bullets, number, or letters to the text. Figure 19.8 shows the bulleting and numbering options.

FIGURE 19.8
Textnotes with bullets

Using Keynotes and Textnotes

Keynotes are written annotations that relate text to specific elements or materials in the model using an external file. You can control the formatting of the font style, size, and justification in the same manner you can format standard text, but keynotes and textnotes behave more like a typical Revit family. Using keynotes, you can insert different family types of text into the model, just as you would door or window families. These inserted families contain text that is not directly editable but instead is tied to an external TXT file. Inserting a keynote allows you to choose a value from the file and apply it to a material or element. Because keynotes and textnotes act as families in Revit, they can also be scheduled where standard text cannot. Although the Revit command is called Keynote, Revit can produce keynotes, textnotes, or a combination of both. Before we discuss how to add those note types, we'll cover the differences between a keynote and a textnote.

A keynote is a short numeric reference followed by a two-letter suffix. The keynote references a list or schedule located on the same sheet the note is placed that has a longer definition of the note. As an example, a keynote on a detail might read "033000.AA" with a leader pointing to an element in the drawing. The associated list on the side of the sheet would read "CAST IN PLACE CONCRETE." Figure 19.9 shows an example of a keynote legend.

FIGURE 19.9
A keynote legend

KEYNOTE LEGEND	
03300.AO	CIP CONC FLOOR SLAB (03300)
04810.BF	STONE CLADDING (04810)
05120.AC	STEEL BEAM (05120)
05310.AH	COMPOSITE FLOOR DECK (05310)
05500.BB	STEEL COLUMN (05500)
05500.BU	STEEL ANGLE (05500)
06105.AB	WOOD FURRING (06105)
06105.AC	PLYWOOD (06105)
06105.AD	1X IPE WOOD SUNSCREEN (06105)
07210.AB	RIGID INSULATION (07210)

In contrast to keynotes, textnotes are the full, written description directly within the detail or view without the numeric reference key. Figure 19.10 shows an example of a textnote.

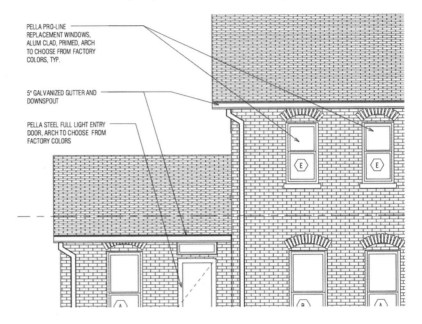

There is no wrong system to use, and Revit supports both ways of annotating sheets. Regardless of the method you use, the keynotes will adhere to the same process for use. Once an element is tagged with a keynote, it will retain that keynote in all other views in the model. If an element that has been tagged with a keynote in one view is then annotated in another view, it will automatically pull up the same keynote value. This can become a very powerful tool you can use to add consistency throughout the model for annotated elements.

The Keynote command is located on the Annotate tab. When you select the Keynote tool, you have three note type options:

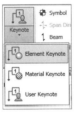

Element Use Element notes to keynote elements and assemblies within the model such as walls, doors, floors, or other family instances. This type of note is typically used if you want to annotate an entire assembly (such as a wall). Moving the Element keynote leader arrow off the wall will dynamically change the value of the note based on the element it points to. The keynote value can be preset for different family types within a template in the element's properties. We'll go into how to do that later in this chapter.

Material   Using the Material note type will allow you to annotate specific materials within any elements. You can add notes for materials like concrete, gypsum board, rigid insulation, metal studs, and the like. Moving the Material keynote leader arrow off the wall will dynamically change the value of the note based on the material it points to. Material notes can also be predefined as part of your template. Material notes can be used in conjunction with Element notes.

User   This option allows you to select any model-based component in Revit and define a custom keynote for it. Notes defined this way differ from those defined as Element or Material because they're not unique to the particular object selected. Once you move the keynote leader arrowhead, the note will not dynamically change. User-defined notes are static in that sense. They can be used in conjunction with Element and Material notes on any object but cannot be predefined.

You can use all of these note types in conjunction with one another. Using an Element note to add a keynote to a wall doesn't mean you cannot also use a Material note to call out the individual materials in the wall assembly.

Keynote Behavior and Editing

A core concept of the Keynote tool is how the notes react with in the model. Keynoting an object in Revit lets you associate a text or numeric value with a family's keynote parameter. This value is consistent for every instance of that element within the model or project. For example, all walls have a type parameter called Keynote that lets you set the keynote value. If you keynote a wall, anywhere within the model, the keynote value in the type parameter will reflect that note. Consequently, any other wall of that type will be prepopulated with that keynote value. Changes to this keynote value will dynamically update the type parameter value and update any keynotes placed within the model tagged to this wall.

It's important to think of a keynote as a family type because keynotes will act more like a Revit family than they will like text. Keynotes behave similar to other Revit families in that you cannot edit the keynote directly within the model. All keynotes within the model are tied to an external TXT file. This TXT file is the only location where the value of the keynotes can be edited. This file can be modified at any point to add or remove notes and the edits can happen while the project is actively open. Figure 19.11 shows a sample portion of the file.

FIGURE 19.11
The Keynote TXT file

```
Division 03        Concrete
030000    Concrete Division 03
033000.AA          C.I.P. CONCRETE (033000) 030000
033000.AG          LIGHTWEIGHT CONCERETE FILL (033000)     030000
034100.AA          PRECAST STRUCTURAL CONCRETE (034100) 030000
034500.AB          PRECAST ARCHITECTURAL CONCRETE (034500)     030000
034900.AA          GLASS-FIBER-REINFORCED CONCRETE (034900)     030000
Division 04        Masonry
040000    Masonry  Division 04
042000.AM          CMU (042000)      040000
042000.BE          FACE BRICK (042000)      040000
042300.AB          HOLLOW GLASS BLOCK (042300)     040000
044300.AB          STONE MASONRY (044300)      040000
Division 07        Insulation
070000    Insulation and Sealants      Division 07
071326.AQ          BOARD INSULATION (071326)      070000
071800.AF          SHEET FLASHING (071820) 070000
072100.AD          CONCEALED BUILDING INSULATION (072100) 070000
074213.AA          METAL WALL PANEL ASSEMBLY (074213)      070000
076100.AA          SHEET METAL ROOFING (076100)     070000
Division 08        Doors and Windows
080000    Doors and Windows        Division 08
084413.AV          INSULATED SPANDREL PANEL (084413)      080000
085200.BG          MULLION (085200) 080000
```

This external file is designed to keep the annotations consistent by storing them in one repository. Every time you add or change a note value and reload the TXT file back into the Revit model, all of the notes of that type dynamically update.

You can edit this TXT file or add one to the project at any time. You can have multiple keynote files for various projects, but you can have only one TXT file per project at a time. Revit does not allow for multiple keynote files to be linked to the model simultaneously.

MANAGING KEYNOTES

A great way to ensure consistent use of notes throughout multiple projects is to create a master keynote file for your various project types. This master note list can be linked to elements and materials with your project template so that you can immediately begin inserting common notes into any project. Since this file will commonly be long as a master list, project teams can make a copy of the list and place it in their project directories. They can then safely delete the notes they won't be using over the course of the project, giving them fewer options to hunt through when they need to add a keynote.

Having a centrally controlled keynote file also allows project management a level of control over the consistency of the notes that you won't be able to get if you use regular text. Spelling accidents or mislabeling can happen in a project. Using regular text, it's easy to overlook a note that reads "CIP CONCRETE" on one detail and "CAST-IN-PLACE CONCRETE" in another. By placing all the notes into one centralized file, the project manager or project architect has better control over how the note reads and ensures consistency throughout all the sheets and details.

Because the keynote file is a separate TXT file, remember that when transferring files to other offices or clients you'll need to include the TXT file as well as the RVT file if you are going to share information. If you don't send the TXT file, others will be able to see all of your notes but won't be able to change or edit any of them.

THE KEYNOTE FILE

There are three Keynote text files in Revit that come with Revit by default. You can find all of them in `C:\Documents and Settings\All Users\Application Data\Autodesk\RAC 2011\Imperial Library`; they are called `RevitKeynotesImperial.txt`, `RevitKeynotesImperial_2004.txt`, and `RevitKeynotesMetric.txt`.

Edit any of these files in Notepad or Excel, and follow the format already established within the file. Let's look at this format of this file so you can understand how to customize the keynotes.

The first few rows of the file (Figure 19.12) designate the grouping of the notes. In this example, they consist of a label (Division 03) followed by a tab and then a description (Concrete).

FIGURE 19.12

The Keynote TXT file header

```
Division 03  Concrete
030000 Concrete    Division 03
033000.AA  C.I.P. CONCRETE (033000) 030000
```

Directly below this header is a secondary, or minor, grouping. This secondary grouping follows the same format as the primary group and provides better control over how the keynotes are displayed within Revit. This line follows the same format as the first: Label (033000), then a tab, then a description (Concrete), then another tab, then another description (Division 03). In this line, the description needs to match, identically, the label in the line above. This designates the second line as a subset to the first line. You can add as many or as few subgroups as you'd like. In our case, we have subcategories for each division, but that's not necessary.

Below the grouping are the contents of that group. These lines are articulated in the following format:

Label, Tab, Description (note body), Tab, Grouping

In the previous example in Figure 19.12, this reads as follows:

033000.AA [tab] C.I.P. CONCRETE (033000) [tab] 033000

where the [tab] is an actual tab, not the text.

To get an idea of how this will all look once loaded into Revit, Figure 19.13 shows you the Keynote dialog box with Division 7 expanded.

FIGURE 19.13
The Keynote file loaded into Revit

Using the keynote file approach lets you add, remove, or edit notes and groups of notes. This might seem frustrating to have to open and load a separate TXT file every time you want to add or remove notes from the keynote list. However, remember that this also maintains consistency and a level of control over the master list that isn't available with simple text. Although it might be slow at stages to get all the project notes into the TXT file, it also means that your time to check and verify the notes is dramatically reduced.

Should managing keynotes directly in a TXT file not be a workflow you would like to maintain, there are some tools available online to help you accomplish this using a better graphic interface. Emc2 has a great tool (www.emc2architects.com/revit_tools.html) that will manage your keynote list, create headings and subheadings, and format the TXT file in a way that Revit can read. Tools like this are great for speeding up the editing process for keynotes and maintaining proper formatting of the TXT file.

KEYNOTE SETTINGS

Now that the Keynote TXT file is established and you've begun populating it with annotations, you need to link it to the Revit model. Loading this file into the Revit project is simple and needs to happen only once during the project. Additionally, loading this keynote file is a project setting, not a user one, so once the file is linked, all the users will have access to the keynotes.

To access the keynote settings and load the keynote text file, choose the Tag fly-out from the Text panel on the Annotate tab (Figure 19.14) and choose Keynoting Settings.

FIGURE 19.14
Choosing Keynoting Settings

This command will open the Keynoting Settings dialog box (Figure 19.15). Here, you can define the project's keynote file as well as adjust some other settings. To load the keynote file, click the Browse button and navigate to the TXT file you've created.

FIGURE 19.15
Keynoting Settings dialog box

The following are some of the other variables you can set in the Keynoting Settings dialog box:

Path Type Path Type defines how Revit looks for your text file using one of three methods:

Absolute The Absolute option follows the UNC naming conventions and navigates across your network or workstation for a specified location.

Relative This option locates the text file relative to the Revit project file. If you move the Revit file and the text file and maintain the same folder structure, Revit knows where to look for the keynote file.

At Library Locations This option lets you put the text file in the default library location defined in the File Locations tab of the Options dialog box (Application button ➤ Options).

Numbering Method   Numbering Method defines how the keynotes are numbered:

By Keynote   This option allows you to number keynotes as they come from the associated text file.

By Sheet   With this option enabled, Revit numbers the keynotes sequentially on a per-sheet basis.

LOADING KEYNOTES

Once the keynote TXT file is loaded into Revit, it is available for the team to use. As we've mentioned, changes can be made to this file on the fly while the project is open and active. Although this is true, when changes are made to the keynote file and the project is opened, the keynote file will need to be reloaded into the project for the changes to be visible to other team members. There are two ways to do this:

◆   Open the Keynoting Settings dialog box and browse back out to the TXT file and reload it. Once this is done, you'll need to Synchronize With Central (if the project is workshared) and your team members will also need to SWC to gain access to the changes.

◆   Close and reopen your Revit project file.

KEYNOTE TYPES

To add keynotes to a Revit model, choose one of the three keynote types from the Annotate tab; then in your view, select the object you want to annotate and insert a keynote. Keynotes insert in an arrowhead, segment, note sequence. The arrowhead location will also define the element or material if you are using one of those note types. If the object doesn't have a note already defined, you'll be prompted to pick a note from the keynote list. Figure 19.16 shows a sample of this list.

FIGURE 19.16
Choosing a keynote to insert

Before inserting a keynote, we'll cover the three types of notes and explain how each might be used.

Element

Element notes will annotate an assembly (walls, floors, roofs, and so on) or a component or family (doors, windows, furniture, and so on) within the model. Once keynoted, the assembly or component will capture the keynote value within the object's Type properties. In Figure 19.17 you can see the Keynote value is filled in for the Roof type, Basic Roof.

FIGURE 19.17
Keynote value
in the object
properties

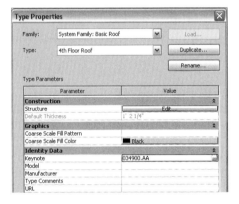

Alternatively, you can set this value through the object properties. By clicking the button next to the keynote value 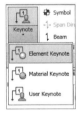, you will open the Keynote list, which allows you to preselect a keynote for the element. For elements that are more universally used from project to project (such as cast-in-place concrete walls), you can preset values within your project template. The Element keynote is the first option you can select from the Keynote fly-out (Figure 19.18).

FIGURE 19.18
Keynoting
elements

When using an Element note to tag an assembly within Revit, simply click anywhere on the assembly. A tagged roof condition looks like Figure 19.19.

FIGURE 19.19
Using the Element
keynote on a roof
assembly

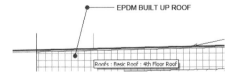

Material

Material notes define the materials within a model. Whereas the Element notes can be used to define an assembly, Material notes can be used to define the materials within that assembly. For example, you can use an Element note to annotate a gypsum board wall assembly and a Material note to designate the layers of gypsum board and the metal stud in between.

To tag materials using the Material Keynote, select the Material Keynote button and hover your mouse over the materials comprising an assembly. As you hover over the various materials, you'll notice that predefined materials will show the note value and undefined materials will give you a question mark. Tagging the same roof assembly, you can specify all the materials that make up the roof element (Figure 19.20).

FIGURE 19.20
Keynoting
materials

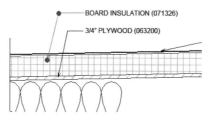

The Material Keynote tool is the second tool located on the Keynote fly-out on the Annotate tab (Figure 19.21). You'll notice that once you begin using any of the keynote tools, the last tool used will take the default icon location in the Text panel. In Figure 19.21, you'll see that this is currently set to the User keynote.

FIGURE 19.21
Material keynote

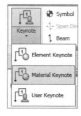

Like Element notes, Material notes can also be predefined. To predefine these note types, choose the Material button from the Manage tab (Figure 19.22).

FIGURE 19.22
Predefining the
Material keynotes

Selecting the Materials button opens the Materials dialog box. To predefine a material's keynote, select it from the list on the left and choose the Identity tab (Figure 19.23).

FIGURE 19.23
The Identity tab of
a material

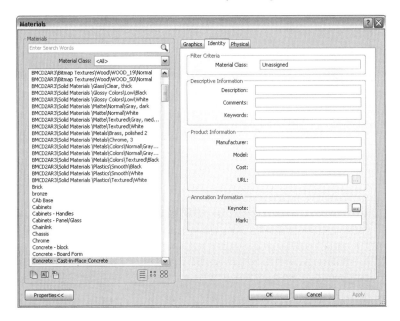

At the bottom of this tab is the Keynote field. Selecting in this field will allow you to click the same ⬚ button you selected when predefining an Element keynote. You'll be presented with the Keynotes dialog box and can select a note to apply to your material (Figure 19.24).

FIGURE 19.24
Adding a keynote
to a material

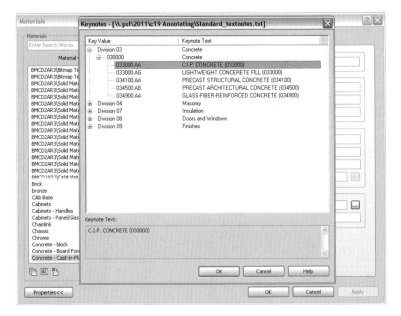

Defining the note will enter a value into the Keynote field, as shown in Figure 19.25. As with Element notes, you can predefine a number of keynote values as part of your project template.

FIGURE 19.25
A material with a
defined keynote

User

User Keynote is the third tool on the Keynote fly-out (Figure 19.26). User notes are different from Element and Material notes because they are view specific and cannot be predefined. Although they are still tied to the same TXT file and will update in the same manner as other notes, they are not tied to any geometry in Revit. User notes are meant to be used for all the instances when you don't have a modeled element or material but you still need to define a note. Some examples of things you wouldn't necessarily model would be sealant, backer rod, or flashing.

FIGURE 19.26
The User keynote

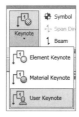

User keynotes are used primarily in drafting views. To use any keynote, a given view must have at least one model element or component visible within it. In the case of a drafting view, you will need to insert a 2D component (such as wood blocking or a steel stud) because keynotes cannot be used to note linework. Because User notes are not locked to specific model geometry, once they are inserted they can easily be copied or moved around within the view and pointed to any element. In this way, if you have sealant or flashing shown as linework, you can add a User note to the view, and then adjust the note leader and the note value to call out the sealant properly. You can change the value of a user keynote at any time simply by double-clicking the note value; this modification will not affect any other notes within the project.

KEYNOTE LEGENDS

Depending on your choice of keynote and your workflow, you might want to create a legend on each sheet for your notes. You might want only the keynotes that are on a given sheet to appear in the legend. Or you might want to have one legend for the entire project that will show all keynotes used in the project.

These lists usually reside on the side of the drawing near the title block information and can take one of two forms. The first type is all-inclusive and shows every note within the project. This style has the benefit of consistency between sheets in the set. The same note will always be in the same location in the list. The other type of keynote list includes only the notes that show up on a particular sheet. This has the advantage of supplying a list of notes customized for each sheet without extraneous information. Creating either list manually has traditionally been challenging. One of the benefits of Revit is the ability to automate either list, thus removing much of the chance for error in the process. Let's review how to create both types of lists.

Creating a keynote legend in Revit is simple: choose the Legend button on the View tab and select Keynote Legend from the drop-down list (Figure 19.27). Once you click the Legend button, go ahead and name the keynote legend, and then click OK.

FIGURE 19.27
The Keynote
Legend button

You'll be presented with what looks like a typical schedule dialog box called Keynote Legend Properties. There are only two fields available in a keynote legend, and by default, they are both loaded into the Scheduled Fields side of the Fields tab (Figure 19.28). Those fields are as follows:

Key Value   This field contains the numeric value of the keynote.

Keynote Text   This field contains the text value for the keynote.

FIGURE 19.28
The Fields tab of
the keynote legend

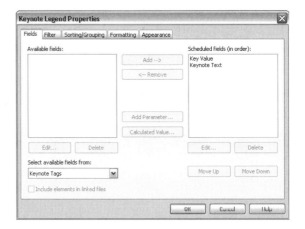

A keynote legend works like any other schedule as far as formatting and appearance goes. By default, the sorting and grouping are already established because the key value is used to sort. The one special item of note is located on the Filter tab. At the bottom of this tab is a feature unique to this type of schedule: a Filter By Sheet checkbox (Figure 19.29). Selecting this box gives you the ability to filter the list specifically for each sheet set; leaving the box deselected will supply a full list of the keynotes over the entire project.

FIGURE 19.29

The Filter By
Sheet checkbox is
located at the bottom
of the Filter
tab in the Keynote
Legend Properties
dialog box.

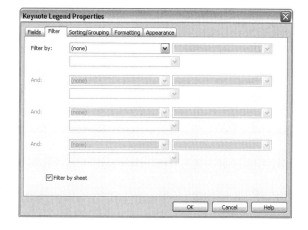

As with any legend, these can be placed on sheets again and again within the project. You're not limited to only one instance of the legend on a sheet as you are with other view types. Additionally, if you choose the Keynote legend that filters by sheet, it will dynamically modify the note list based on individual sheet contents. As views are added or removed from a sheet or notes are added to the project, the keynote legends updates accordingly.

Keynote legends are considered to be another type of legend view and will appear under the Legends node of the Project Browser.

A SCHEDULE FOR KEYNOTES

Creating a schedule for keynotes is a great way to find single-use notes and typos in a project. If you are working on a project team, there's always a chance that someone could be inserting an incorrect keynote into the project. Scheduling the notes is an efficient approach to managing this process and gives you the tools to verify consistency. Scheduling keynotes allows you to do three things:

◆ List all the notes within a project and verify their spelling and accuracy.

◆ Find odd or one-off instances. Sometimes this can mean the note was accidentally placed in lieu of another note.

◆ Make sure all the keynotes in the project are represented in the specifications.

THE KEYNOTE FAMILY

Revit comes with a default Keynote family that allows you to produce both keynotes and text-notes using the default keynote TXT file. The family name is `Keynote Tag.rfa`. This family has four family types that let you change note styles within the project. You can see the four note styles in Figure 19.30.

FIGURE 19.30
Keynote styles
available in the
default tag

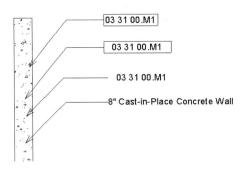

The four default styles are

◆ Keynote Number

◆ Keynote Number – Boxed – Large

◆ Keynote Number – Boxed – Small

◆ Keynote Text

Each of these notes pulls information from the text file we discussed earlier in this chapter and reports it at the end of the leader.

Annotating with Tags

Tags are text labels for elements such as doors, walls, windows, rooms, and several other objects that architects typically need to reference in a set of drawings. These tags typically refer to other schedules or information in other portions of the drawing set and are unique to the view they are inserted within. In Revit, tags are intelligent, bidirectional symbols that report information stored in an object's properties. You can enter a value directly into the family properties or right into the tag itself.

Once you've tagged an element and given the tag a value, the element will retain that value until you remove it. The value lives with the elements within Revit; it is not a property of the tag. This allows you to delete or remove tags without any fear of losing the data entered into the tag. It also means that once an element is tagged with information in one view, that same element will report that same information in any other view that it is tagged in without you having to have the information entered twice. To explain this a bit better, take the example of a door tag.

You've placed a door tag in a view. The tag initially had a "?" as a value, meaning that the door number was blank. You've entered a door number of **3-1**. In another view, you can now tag the same door and have it automatically display a value of 3-1. You can also delete any, or even all, of the door tags for that door and have new tags you place also report the door number of 3-1.

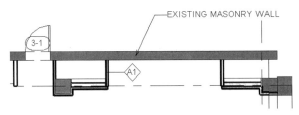

In Revit 2011, you can also tag elements which are in linked models. While you cannot edit the properties of these elements (e.g. you cannot change the wall type or door number) you can add tags to any of the linked elements as you can if the same elements were part of your project file.

Tags are versatile elements in Revit. A tag can display a door number, but it can just as easily display any other properties of the door, such as fire rating, cost, or material type.

Inserting Tags

Tags can be automatically inserted when another element, such as a door or room, is placed within the model (by checking the Tag On Placement option in the Options Bar), or they can be inserted later in the project. The options to place a tag are all located on the Tag panel of the Annotate tab (Figure 19.31).

FIGURE 19.31
Revit tags

When you're adding tags, it's not necessary to find or choose the right tag—Revit will do that for you. Tag types are specific to the elements to which they are being tagged. For example, you can use a door tag to tag a door, but you can't use a door tag to tag a wall or other element within Revit. Figure 19.32 shows you some of the tags that are available; there is a tag for each type of object within Revit. You can customize each of the tag family types so you can graphically differentiate your door tags from wall tags, room tags, area tags, and so on.

FIGURE 19.32
Revit tag types

When inserting the tag, you'll have several options regarding tag placement available in the Options Bar (Figure 19.33).

FIGURE 19.33
The Options Bar
when placing a tag

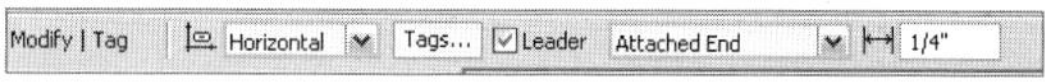

Modify | Tag   Horizontal   Tags...   ☑ Leader   Attached End   1/4"

Orientation   This first option allows you to orientate the tag horizontally or vertically. Tags, like text, will always read from either the bottom or right side of the sheet or view.

The Tags Button   Clicking this button opens the Tags dialog box, where you can load various tags.

Leader   The final three options deal with the tag leader. You can check the Leader check box on (or off) to have a leader show (or not show). While attached leaders are the default for Revit tags, the Attach End drop-down can be changed to not associate the end of the leader with the element you've selected. Using the Unattached End option allows the leader to float free of the object. The final option of this set for leaders is the default leader length. By default, the value is set to ½″. When you're placing tags like wall tags that have leaders perpendicular to the wall they are tagging, it is a good idea to set a default length you are comfortable with. You can adjust the tag location after inserting them, but sometimes it's easier to set a good default value in leader length.

Using the Tag Toolbox

CERT
OBJECTIVE

On the Annotate tab, you'll find there are several methods you can use to insert tags into Revit. Each of these tools allows you to tag elements within a view in different ways. Each has different uses and can be used in conjunction or separately to help document your project.

Tag By Category   The Tag By Category button is possibly one of the most frequently used Tag commands. As we mentioned before, several tags are available in Revit, allowing you to tag a host of elements in the model. Click the Tag By Category button (shown in Figure 19.34) when you want to tag one element at a time, regardless of its category.

FIGURE 19.34
Tag By Category
button

Using this tag command will allow you to select a door, a window, a wall—whatever single element you want to apply a tag to in the model. As you hover over elements, Revit will show the tag that corresponds to that element, allowing you to place it. Should the element you are trying to tag not have the associated tag loaded in the Revit file, Revit will prompt you to load it (Figure 19.35). You'll be presented with a dialog box asking you to load a tag, which you can do either from Revit's default stock or your own office library.

FIGURE 19.35
Loading a tag

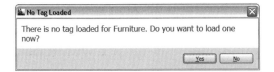

Tag All   The Tag All command (Figure 19.36) will do exactly that—tag all the elements within a given view.

FIGURE 19.36
Tag All

Tagging all the elements, however, doesn't mean that you have to tag everything within a view. That would be messy since everything within your view gets a tag. Revit will tag elements by the groups that you select. So, for example, you can tag all the doors. Or you can tag all doors, walls, and rooms—or any combination of any list of elements. When you select the Tag All command, Revit will present you with the Tag All Not Tagged dialog box (Figure 19.37). This dialog box displays a list of the elements in the view for which you have already loaded tags. Here, you can specify which elements can get tagged, what tag will be used, and if that tag will have a leader assigned to it. Use the Control key on the keyboard to select more than one element from the list. When you've selected the categories you would like tagged, click OK.

FIGURE 19.37

Tag All Not Tagged dialog box

Tagging all the elements within a view can be a wondrous time saver—but only if you're OK with Revit choosing the location for each of the tags. In some cases, like rooms, Revit will place the tags in the middle of the rooms. For most spaces, that will work just fine. For other tag types, such as walls or doors, you might have to adjust tag locations to make sure everything reads properly.

Room Tag and Area Tag   These two tag types work in much the same way. They will tag the room elements or area elements, depending on the type of view you happen to be in. In the case of Figure 19.38, we are in a plan view that has no areas, so only the Room tag is active. To tag rooms or areas, simply select the tag type you want and select the room or area object. By default, when you place rooms or areas initially, Revit will automatically tag them for you.

FIGURE 19.38

Room and Area tags

Material Tag   The Material Tag (Figure 19.39) is an interesting tag type that can best be described as a hybrid between text and a keynote.

FIGURE 19.39
The Material
Tag tool

This tag is actually a text box and leader, much like the Text command, and like Text, it will allow you to type a value into the text box. Like a keynote, the material that you tag will remember its note and the next time you tag an element, it will produce that same text. Change the text in one location and it will change it everywhere. To make this a bit clearer, let's use an example. From the book's companion website (www.sybex.com/go/masteringrevit2011) download the Jenkins.rvt file for Chapter 19.

1. Open one of the floor plans. In our example, we've chosen Level 3.

2. Choose the Material tag from the Annotate tab. Hovering over one of the existing, exterior walls, you'll see a question mark, as shown in Figure 19.40.

FIGURE 19.40
Tagging the exterior wall material

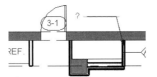

3. Place the tag and type **EXISTING MASONRY WALL** in the text box. Then click to insert a new tag.

4. As you hover over some of the interior walls, you'll notice that Revit will present you with the question mark, indicating materials that are not yet defined. Hover over the exterior wall, however, and you'll notice that the tag value automatically fills itself in (Figure 19.41).

FIGURE 19.41
Material tags keep their value.

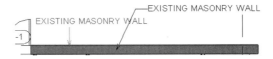

Using these tag types can be a good alternative to using the Revit keynote system. This allows you some versatility over the note—you can type the text when adding the note—while also ensuring consistency across the project. This tag type only works with materials and can't be used on detail components or any linework.

Multi-Category Tag The Multi-Category tag is a new tag type in Revit. This tag allows you to use the same tag style in a project to tag elements of different categories (Figure 19.42).

FIGURE 19.42
The Multi-Category tag

This tag type can be useful in a number of ways. Let's say you want to tag several elements in a floor plan and call out their manufacturer and unit cost. Historically, you would have to create a few different tags to tag Furniture, Systems Furniture, Casework, and any other category you had wanted to tag. Now, a single tag type can do this for you. Let's step through making a Multi-Category tag.

From the book's companion website (www.sybex.com/go/masteringrevit2011**), download the** Jenkins.rvt **file for Chapter 19.**

1. Open one of the floor plans. In our example, we've chosen Level 3.

2. Click the Application button and choose New ➤ Family. This will take you to the default Revit family templates. Open the Annotation folder and choose Multi-Category Tag.rft.

3. In the Family Editor, place a label. Once the label is located on the screen, the Edit Label dialog box opens. Here you'll see a long list of the family categories that are common across multiple family types—Assembly Code, Cost, Family Name, and Model, among others. The full list is shown in the Edit Label dialog box in Figure 19.43. To make our simple tag, select Manufacturer and Cost.

FIGURE 19.43
Adding labels

4. Finish the family and load it into the project.

5. Now, select an element in the floor plan. In our example, we've chosen the dining room table. When the tag is placed, you will see the familiar question mark, indicating this element has no predefined value for either Manufacturer or Cost. Place the tag and double-click the question mark.

6. The Change Parameter Value dialog box (Figure 19.44) opens. Enter a value for both Manufacturer and Cost, and then click OK.

FIGURE 19.44
Changing the
parameter value

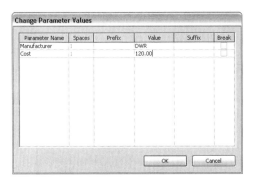

7. As you hover your mouse over other elements in this view, you'll notice the same behavior as with other tags. Elements that have predefined values will show the tag filled in while other elements without values will have question marks. Add a few more tags and you can begin to see some of the versatility of the Multi-Category tag.

Adding Dimensions

Dimensions are used to convey the distance or angle between elements or parts of elements. In Revit, a dimension is a bidirectional annotation that essentially tags distance or size. This means that you can edit the distance directly within the dimension string to move elements to a specific distance apart; likewise, the dimension updates automatically as the distance between elements changes. Dimensions are annotations, making them view-specific elements that appear only in the view where they're drawn. The Dimes ion tools are located on the Annotate tab.

Like all annotations in Revit, dimensions adjust to the scale of the drawing. They will always appear at the proper scale in the view. If you change the view scale, the dimensions automatically resize.

By default, a linear string of dimensions only dimensions parallel entities. Nonparallel elements by their very nature have a dynamic dimensional relationship. Dimensions in Revit always read from the bottom or from the right following the standard architectural sheet layout conventions. To place a dimension, choose any dimension tool and begin selecting entities in a sequence. You can keep selecting multiple entities in a given direction creating a dimension string across your drawing.

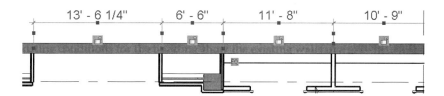

  Once the dimensions are placed, you can relocate them at any point either an individual dimension or for an entire string. Select the dimension and grab the blue square grip. By selecting and holding on this element you can move the witness line to a new host element without having to recreate the entire dimension string.

Annotating with Project and Shared Parameters

Every element in Revit has a list of parameters that has been assigned to it by default. Some of these parameters, such as Assembly Code and Mark, can be consistent throughout all the elements in Revit. Others, such as Length, Height, or Volume, are specific to element groups that could contain those kinds of parameters. The list of default parameters is available to describe most of what you need, but periodically you will want to add parameters to elements. These new elements, like the default ones, can be tagged and scheduled.

Depending on how you'd like to use a custom parameter, you can add them to your elements in Revit in a few ways:

◆ If all you want to do is schedule the new parameter, you have a couple of options:

   ◆ Add the parameter directly within the schedule itself. This will add a new parameter to your element family. Adding your parameter using this method adds it only to the element family in the schedule. For example, say you want to schedule the STC (Sound Transmission Class) of a wall. You could add this property directly within the wall schedule and the new parameter would only be available to objects in the Wall category.

   ◆ Your second option if you only want to schedule parameters is to add the parameter directly into the project itself. Using this method, you can still schedule the new parameter, but you will have the option to add it to multiple categories. So, if you want to add a parameter for Unit Cost, you can add that to both your door and window categories at the same time.

◆ If you want to be able to both schedule *and* tag your parameter, you will need to create what is called a *shared parameter*. This parameter is created as part of a separate file that is shared between the tag family and the element family you've created. An example use of this kind of tag might be for door hardware security. You can create a tag that will allow you to designate whether or not a door has a card reader to gain entrance to a room.

In the following sections, we will discuss how to create both of these parameter types as well as the pros and cons of each.

Creating Custom Project Parameters

You can create custom project parameters at any time in the project cycle. Depending on how you create the parameters, you can assign them to one or more element categories within the model. You can also assign them to elements that have already been created or to element categories for elements that you have yet to create.

We'll step you through how to make a custom parameter that will be schedulable but not tag-gable. For this example, pretend you are working on an existing building and reworking a space. Much of what is on-site will need to be demolished, but you would like to reuse all the elements that are salvageable. As you are documenting the existing conditions, you will want to schedule the elements you'd like to keep. To do this, you'll make a parameter called *Reuse*.

1. To add a new project parameter, click the Project Parameters button on the Manage tab. This will display the Project Parameters dialog box (Figure 19.45). Click the Add button.

FIGURE 19.45
Adding labels

2. In the next dialog box, Parameter Properties, you will be asked to define a list of proper-ties for the new parameter. Let's step through what these selections will be. Figure 19.46 shows a view of the completed dialog box.

FIGURE 19.46
Setting the param-eter properties

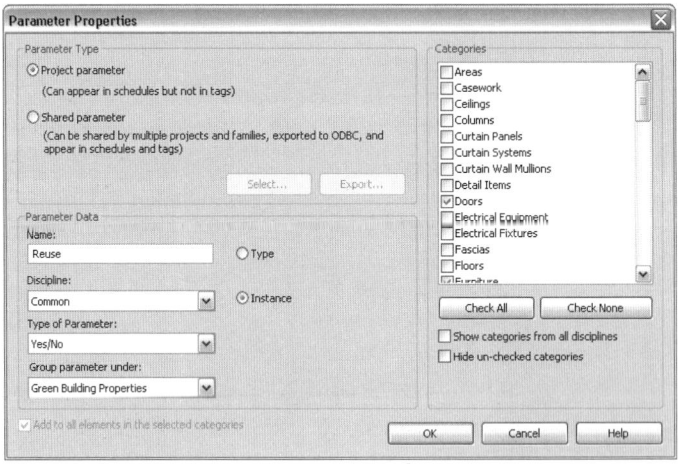

◆ Project Parameter or Shared Parameter is the first choice you'll need to make. We'll get to shared parameters later, so for now, leave it at the default of Project Parameter.

◆ Name is used for describing the parameter. For this example, name the parameter **Reuse**.

◆ The Discipline drop-down menu will give you three choices: Common, Structural, and Electrical. Leave the default selection, Common, for your parameter.

◆ Type Of Parameter dictates what kind of parameter you have. As you can see from Figure 19.47, there are a variety of parameter types. It's important to understand some of these options and, more specifically, their differences. If you start creating formulas with your parameters, you'll quickly understand how imperative it is to use the proper type. For instance, you cannot multiply Angle × Volume. Text cannot be added to a formula. Integers do not have decimal values. Many of these values are easy to understand if you apply a bit of logic. For our example, use the Yes/No type.

FIGURE 19.47
Parameter types

◆ Type Or Instance Parameter controls the uniqueness of the parameter itself. Probably the best way to explain the difference between these two options is to describe a couple of use cases:

  ◆ Type parameters are used for parameters that will be consistent across a type. This type is defined as a subset of a family. Let's take a door family, for instance. In the door family, you will want to define types that are 36″ (926 mm), 34″ (876 mm), 32″ (826 mm), and 30″ (726 mm) doors. To do so, you'd use a type parameter. When you insert the door, you can choose between these predefined types in the Type Selector drop-down.

  ◆ Instance parameters are used in cases where you might have too much variety or uniqueness of an element property to want to define a series of types. A good use for an instance parameter is to specify the length of a countertop. When you insert the countertop into your model, you'll be able to drag the length of the counter to fit your needs rather than have to choose a predefined length from the Type Selector.

Both parameter types can be mixed within a given family. In this example, use an instance parameter because you want to designate on an element-by-element basis whether something is reusable.

◆ Group Parameter Under is an organization tool. When you open your Element Properties, depending on how many parameters you add, you can acquire a long list. This tool allows you to group new parameters into any given category.

◆ Category is where you define all the category types that our Reuse parameter will be associated with. There are 58 categories in Revit to which you can assign this parameter. For our example, choose Doors, Windows, and Furniture. Categories are flexible. If you decide you need to change categories after you create your parameter, you can easily come back and modify your selection.

3. Once you're finished, click OK. This will take you back to the original dialog box where you can choose to add another parameter or, in our case, just click OK to exit the Parameter Properties dialog box completely.

Back in the model, you can now select a door (because it is one of the categories you chose) and see that you have added a Reuse parameter to it in the form of a checkbox (Figure 19.48).

FIGURE 19.48
The Reuse parameter in the family

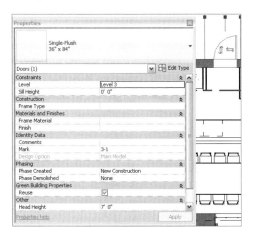

Now that you've created a custom parameter in the project, it's even easier to create one while in a schedule. You can create a custom parameter while creating a schedule or after the fact by simply modifying one. To create a parameter, simply click the Add Parameter button in the Schedule Properties dialog box (Figure 19.49). This will open the same dialog box as clicking the Project Parameter button, with the exception that the Categories selections will be grayed out because you can only create parameters in schedules for the element being scheduled.

FIGURE 19.49
Adding a parameter while in a schedule

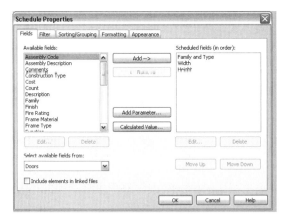

Creating Custom Shared Parameters

When you want to schedule *and* tag a custom parameter, you will need to use shared parameters. In the earlier example, you learned that shared parameters are useful for creating a tag for the STC rating on a wall, scheduling which doors have security systems as part of the door hardware set, or specifying which equipment in a lab will require special gases (oxygen, argon, others). None of these parameters exist by default in any of the Revit families, but they are all values that you might want to tag or schedule, depending on the type of project you are working on.

These same parameters do not exist in any of the tags as well, so in order to tag these parameters, you need to create the parameter type in both the tag and in the element family.

Don't worry—it's not as complicated as it all sounds, but you will need to follow some steps fairly closely. Once you have added a shared parameter to your project, you cannot modify it. If you want to change it, you'll need to delete it and re-add the parameter. So, it behooves you to make your choices thoughtfully.

Let's look at the workflow behind creating a shared parameter. You'll do this with an example of creating a custom wall parameter called STC so you can tag the sound transmission class of the wall types. To get started, navigate to the book's companion website (www.sybex.com/go/ masteringrevit2011) and download the Jenkins.rvt file in the Chapter 19 folder.

CREATING THE SHARED PARAMETER

The first thing we need to do is create a new, shared parameter file. This file will be what talks and translates the values of the shared parameter between the tag, family, and project.

1. To create a shared parameter, click the Shared Parameter button on the Manage tab. This will open the Edit Shared Parameters dialog box (Figure 19.50).

FIGURE 19.50
Creating the shared parameter

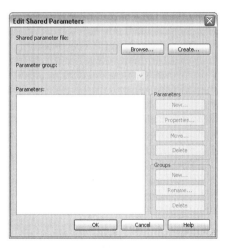

2. Now, click the Create button to open the Save As dialog box. Name your shared parameter file. For our example, we've named it **STC**; however, if you plan to make more than one shared parameter, you might want to name it something more universal. All of the shared parameters for a given project will ultimately live in the same file. Choose File ➢ Save As and give the file a name and location that will make sense to the project team. Then click OK.

3. Now you need to give the shared parameter a group. This group is a hierarchical collection. So, for the wall's STC, you will want to create a group called **Wall Properties** (Figure 19.51). This grouping allows you to easily sort different parameters within project categories. Name the group, and click OK.

FIGURE 19.51
Naming a group

4. Once you have a group, you'll see the Parameter buttons are now active. Click the New button, and let's create a shared parameter. Name the parameter **STC**. Leave the Discipline setting at Common. For Type Of Parameter, choose Integer. Since STC ratings are whole numbers, you can use the Integer type and eliminate any decimal places you'd have if you used Number as the type (Figure 19.52). Once you've entered the settings, click OK.

FIGURE 19.52
Naming the parameter and setting the type

5. You should see the new STC parameter in the Edit Shared Parameters dialog box. Click OK to exit this dialog box.

You've now created a shared parameter. The next step is to assign it to a category.

ASSIGNING THE SHARED PARAMETER TO A CATEGORY

The shared parameter is now defined, but we don't have it associated with any categories yet.

1. Click the Project Parameters button on the Manage tab to open the Project Parameters dialog box. You'll see the Reuse parameter you created earlier (Figure 19.53). You want to add a new parameter, so click Add.

FIGURE 19.53
Putting the shared parameter into the project

2. The Project Parameters dialog box opens. This time, select the Shared Parameter radio button, and then click Select. In the resulting dialog box, browse to the STC file you just created. Select the file and click OK. You'll see that many of the fields are now grayed out. This is because you have already preselected this information. For a category type, select Walls (Figure 19.54).

FIGURE 19.54
Assigning the shared parameter to a category

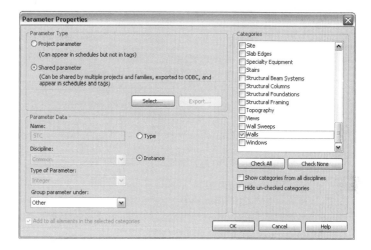

3. Click OK to exit the dialog box. You'll see the new shared parameter (STC) next to your previous project parameter (Reuse) in the Project Parameters dialog box (Figure 19.55).

FIGURE 19.55
The shared parameter is now part of the project.

4. Now that the STC parameter is part of the project, you can begin assigning values to it. Open Level 3 and select one of the walls. By scrolling down in the Properties Palette, you'll notice that the STC parameter is now at the bottom (Figure 19.56). Enter a value of **45** and click Apply or mouse out of the pallet.

FIGURE 19.56
Giving the new
parameter a value
in the project

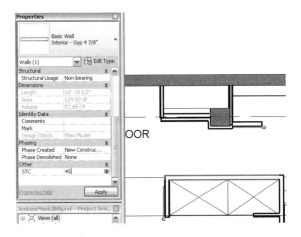

TAGGING THE SHARED PARAMETER

So far, you've created a shared parameter and added it to the Walls category, and you're able to add values to it. These are all features you could have leveraged with a project parameter. The benefit of using a shared parameter is being able to tag it. The final step in this process is creating a tag and tagging the STC parameter in the wall.

1. The first thing you'll need is a new tag. Since you're tagging a wall, there isn't a default wall tag type, so you'll need to make a generic tag and apply it to a wall condition. Click the Application button and select New ➤ Family. In the New Family – Select Template File dialog box, open the Annotations folder, select `Generic Tag.rfa`, and click OK (Figure 19.57).

FIGURE 19.57
Selecting the
Generic Tag file

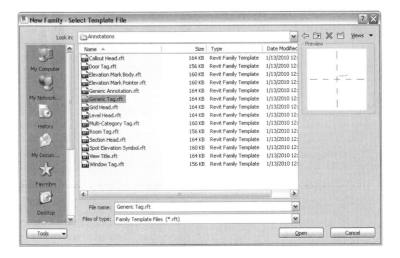

2. Next, you'll assign the correct category to the tag. By default, a generic tag is just that: generic. You want it to report information from the Doors category, so at the top of the Home tab, click the Family Category And Parameters button (it has a small file folder in the lower-right corner), shown in Figure 19.58.

FIGURE 19.58
Opening the
Family Category
And Parameters
dialog box

3. With the Family Category And Parameters dialog box open, choose Wall Tags from the bottom of the list (Figure 19.59), and click OK.

FIGURE 19.59
Selecting the Wall
Tags category

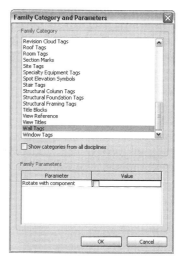

4. With the proper category selected, you need to add a label for your tag. Click the Label button on the Text panel of the Home tab (Figure 19.60).

FIGURE 19.60
Adding a label

5. For our first label, you want to add a mark (Figure 19.61). This will call out the wall type from the Wall schedule in your documents and help you associate the proper wall with the STC rating. Select the Mark parameter and place it above the green grid in the family.

FIGURE 19.61
Adding the Mark
parameter

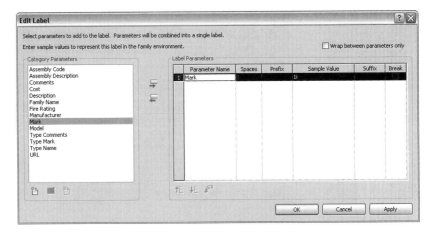

6. With the Mark parameter placed, let's add the STC parameter. Choose the Label tool again, and this time, click the Add Parameter button at the bottom of the Category Parameter column 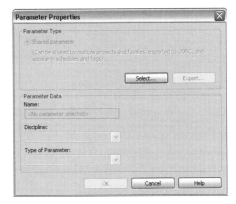. This opens the Parameter Properties dialog box (Figure 19.62). Click Select to open the Edit Shared Parameters dialog box. Select STC and click OK, and then click OK again.

FIGURE 19.62
Choosing the
shared parameter

7. You'll now see the STC parameter in the list. Select it and drag it to the right side of the dialog box (Figure 19.63). Click OK to close the dialog box and place this label under the green dashed line and under the mark.

8. With all the labels added, you can brush up the tag with a bit of linework to help differentiate the tag from the rest of the drawing. For our example, we've created a simple, divided box, shown in Figure 19.64. Once this is done, you're ready to load it into the project by clicking the Load Into Project button.

FIGURE 19.63
Adding the STC parameter to the tag

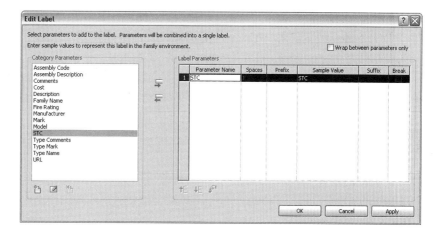

FIGURE 19.64
The sample door tag

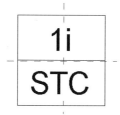

9. Back in the project, you're ready to tag the wall. Choose Tag By Category from the Annotate tab, and select the wall you have already given a value of 45 to for the STC. You'll see the wall type and STC rating populate within the tag (Figure 19.65).

FIGURE 19.65
The shared parameter now shows up in the tag within the project.

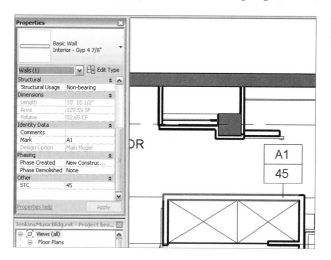

And that's it. Once you've stepped through this workflow a few times, it will quickly become old hat, and you'll be able to add custom parameters to projects and tag them without a second thought. One thing to keep in mind, however, while you're doing all of this is that once you have added a shared parameter to your project, you will not be able to change any of the properties of the parameter itself. If you set the parameter to Integer and really wanted Number, you'll need to go back, delete the parameter, and start over. Also remember when working with a team, shared parameters work much like keynotes with their external TXT files. If you are sharing the project file with the idea that it will be edited by another team, be sure to include the shared parameter file.

The Bottom Line

Annotate with text and keynotes.   Although a picture is worth a thousand words, you will still need notes in order to make drawings understandable and be able to call out key elements in each view. Understand how to create and modify text and keynotes for a complete set of documents.

> **Master It**   To properly utilize the keynoting feature, you'll need to understand what each of the three keynote types do and how they're used. List each and explain how they can be used in a project.

Use tags.   Tags are text labels for elements such as doors, walls, windows, rooms, and several other objects that architects typically need to reference in a set of drawings. These tags typically refer back to other schedules or information in other portions of the drawing set and are unique to the view in which they are inserted .

> **Master It**   Inserting tags quickly can be a good way to make documentation time more efficient. How can you quickly tag a number of elements in the model at the same time?

Adding Dimensions   Dimensioning is a critical part of the project documentation allowing you to communicate the distance elements are from one another.

> **Master It**   Adding dimensions is a necessary part in any project. However, in a project workflow, you will typically want to change the location of a dimension's witness line without having to recreate the entire dimension. How do you move a witness line without remaking the entire dimension?

Set project and shared parameters.   Revit lets users add as many custom parameters to an element as are needed to document the project. These parameters can be both tagged and scheduled, depending on how they are made.

> **Master It**   You need to add a custom parameter for your project to track the percentage of recycled content in materials. What's the best way to go about doing this?

Chapter 20

Presenting Your Design

Although Revit is most often used to create parametric content for documentation, it is often necessary to show designs to clients and other project stakeholders to get buy-in. Revit has tools that can be used to embellish views or create new graphics to help present the design.

In this chapter, you'll learn to:

◆ Add color fill legends

◆ Use visualization techniques in your design

Adding Color Fill Legends

There are many times in the project process where you will need to go beyond simple documentation and portray the spaces in the building in a different way. For example, you may need to communicate design intent, spatial adjacencies and allocations, or materiality. Since Revit knows what these things are in your model (as long as you've labeled them), you can use Revit's parametric capabilities to do more than just documentation and show these other types of spatial parameters.

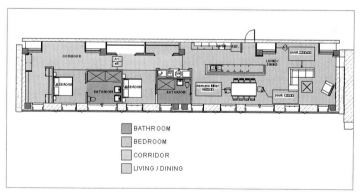

Revit's tool for creating these types of views is called the color fill legend. You can use this tool in nearly any view—plans, sections, elevations, and so on. It allows you to assign different colors to just about any of the field properties within the view. Here are some quick examples of the types of views you can create:

- Floor plans showing departments.

- Floor plans showing areas based on square footage. An example might be rooms smaller than 500 square feet as one color, rooms that are between 500 and 1,000 square feet as another color, and rooms bigger than 1,000 square feet as a third color.

- Building sections showing different departments in different colors.

- Plans, sections, or elevations portraying room finish types.

There is an almost endless list of the types of color fills you can create using Revit to help communicate a wide variety of project-specific details. The Color Fill Legend tool is located on the Room & Area panel of the Home tab (Figure 20.1).

FIGURE 20.1
The Legend tool

To better demonstrate some of the uses of color fills, let's step through making a simple color fill plan showing room types.

Making a Color Fill Legend for Rooms

In many projects, it becomes necessary to display plans with some additional information about the spaces. Typically during the design phases, clients need to see how different departments are located adjacent to one another. Even in a simple residential design, it can be helpful to see how public spaces such as kitchens and living areas are located relative to the more private spaces of bedrooms and bathrooms.

In the sample project, the Jenkins building, say you want to visually show the various space types in the floor plans. You want to graphically demonstrate where living areas, bathrooms, bedrooms, and circulation spaces are in the design. To get started, open the `Jenkins.rvt` model that's on the book's companion web page: `www.sybex.com/go/masteringrevit2011`.

Open Level 3, the same level you've been working on for other aspects of this project. You need to create a color fill legend that will represent the spaces discussed earlier. To do this, follow these steps:

1. Open Level 3 in the `Jenkins.rvt` file and click the Legend button in the Room & Area panel of the Home tab. This will activate the color fill legend and ask you to place a legend somewhere in the active view. This placeable legend will look like Figure 20.2, which is not terribly descriptive. That's OK. Once the legend is placed, you can then define its characteristics. Place the legend below the plan.

FIGURE 20.2
Placing a color fill legend

2. Once the legend is placed, you'll be presented with a dialog box similar to Figure 20.3. This will prompt you to choose from a list of space types and color schemes that have already been established within the model. If you have already created a color scheme that you want to use in this view, it would be a simple matter of selecting both from this list and clicking OK, and the legend and view would be complete. Since this is your first color scheme for the floor plans, you still need to define what schemes and colors you will want to use. Accept the defaults and click OK.

FIGURE 20.3

Choose Space Type
And Color Scheme
dialog box

3. Once the legend is place, you can then define the type of legend you want to use for the floor plans. Select the legend and in the Modify | Color Fill Legends context menu, click the Edit Scheme button (Figure 20.4).

FIGURE 20.4

Editing the color
scheme

4. When editing the color scheme, it will open the aptly named Edit Color Scheme dialog box (Figure 20.5). This dialog box allows you to define a series of color schemes on the left side and give these schemes colors and attributes on the right. For this project, you want to define a scheme type that will allow us to color the rooms based on room name.

FIGURE 20.5

The Edit Color
Scheme dialog box

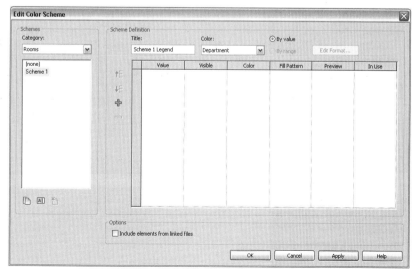

5. To begin defining this scheme type, select Scheme 1 in the field on the left, and then click the Rename button (the center icon) below that field. This will allow you to rename the default scheme to something more practical (Figure 20.6). Rename the scheme to **Rooms** and click OK.

FIGURE 20.6
Renaming the default scheme

6. Now, in the right panel, you need to name the legend and choose the legend type. In the Title field, rename the default value to **Room Legend**. Figure 20.7 shows the Color drop-down list options associated with room information. All these types can be used to generate various room-based color fill fields and used in different plan types. For this example, select Name from the list.

FIGURE 20.7
Color fill legend options for rooms

7. Once the Scheme definition of Color is chosen, you will see the field on the right (the Scheme Definition) populate with all the room names currently in the model. By default, Revit will assign color values to each of these rooms (Figure 20.8). Before you move forward with the color fill legend, let's stop for a minute to look at the options in this portion of the dialog box. Here, you have the ability to change a number of variables that will help you define the look and feel of the legend.

FIGURE 20.8
Making changes in the Scheme Definition dialog box

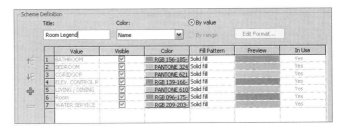

CERT OBJECTIVE

A. One of the first things you'll likely want to change is the colors. Revit's default selections for color schemes might or might not be what you will ultimately want to use in your legend. As many firms typically have standards for color types for different plan areas, once you've defined these elements, it's a good idea to add them to your office template. That way, you'll be ensured of a consistent look and feel across multiple projects.

For the legend here, you can change any of the colors by selecting any of the buttons in the Color column. This opens a dialog box like the one in Figure 20.9 and allows you to select color types based on RGB values or Pantone colors. Once you have the proper color selected, click OK.

FIGURE 20.9
Renaming the default scheme

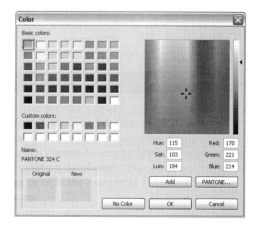

B. Once you have defined the colors, take note of a couple of other features. The first is the Options area under the Scheme Definition field. There is a single check box that allows you to pull values from linked projects. If you are working on a large building that is split into multiple files, this is a good way to tie all that information together into a single graphic.

C. The other option you have is the ability to include various room names (in this example) on any given legend. Remember, views in Revit are specific to each view, and while you might drop the same legend on multiple views, each view will have the option to make minor edits to the legend. In this case, the element you can edit is which room names appear on the legend. As you can see in Figure 20.10, there are several room names that won't appear in the view. Rooms such as the Water Service room and the Elev. Control Room are functionally necessary for the building, but probably not necessary to show when you are defining living spaces on Level 3. Uncheck those rooms in the list and click OK.

FIGURE 20.10
Defining which rooms will appear in the legend

8. After clicking OK, you'll notice that all the spaces will dynamically change to reflect the modifications you made in your legend properties. The rooms will change color and fill based on room name (just like you asked Revit to do). Although the colors are great and they have predefined the spaces for you (Figure 20.11), you still need to do a bit of cleanup to make this view presentable as a presentation view.

FIGURE 20.11
The floor plan after legend colors are defined

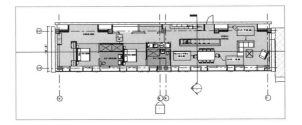

9. With the color fill legend defined, let's finish up the plan so it's more of a presentation-based plan and less for documentation. Open the Visibility/Graphic Overrides dialog box by pressing **VG** on the keyboard or by choosing it from the right-click context menu. In the dialog box, choose the Annotation Categories tab and deselect Sections, Grids, Elevations, and Dimensions; then click OK. The final plan will look like Figure 20.12.

FIGURE 20.12
The final color fill plan

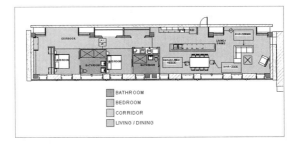

You have created a color fill legend and placed it within a view, and you've seen a number of the settings and properties of the legend. Those settings reflect how the color fill legend will look and react to the plan or view it's placed in, but there are other settings you can modify as well. The legend key itself has several property types that control fonts and sizes. Select the legend and let's look at the Properties dialog box to explore some of these other properties you can modify.

Figure 20.13 shows the properties for color fill legend. Notice that in this dialog box, you can change the font size and type as well as the size of the color swatches that appear in the legend.

FIGURE 20.13
Color fill legend's
Type Properties
dialog box

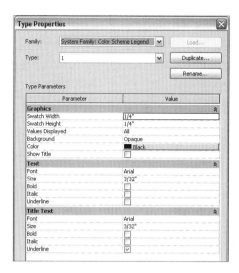

Other Types of Color Fill Legends

With the Room color fill legend defined, you have seen an example of how to create color fill legends. A variety of other legend types are available, and some of these types allow you to define your own parameters when creating the legend itself. Let's step through this process again using a different legend type so you can see how you define your own parameters in a color fill legend.

The next legend type you will create is based on areas. Whereas the Room legend was defined by rooms that were already placed on plans, the Area legend is defined by area types you will need to define within the legend properties.

1. Working with the same Level 3, select the Color Fill Legend and click the Edit Scheme button again. In the dialog box that opens, click the Duplicate button and name the new scheme **Areas** (Figure 20.14).

FIGURE 20.14
Creating the new
Area legend

2. From the Color drop-down list, choose Area (Figure 20.15). You'll notice that all the room names and colors will disappear; they are replaced with an empty Scheme Definition field.

FIGURE 20.15
Choosing the Area
scheme

3. Since none of the area types are defined for you in order to establish colors and types, you'll need to define your own. There are two buttons to the left of the Scheme Definition field that look like a green plus and red minus sign (Figure 20.16). These buttons will allow you to add and remove field choices from the list. Select the green plus button and add four values to the table.

FIGURE 20.16
Adding values to
the color fill legend
table

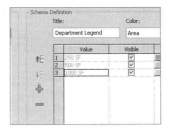

4. With these values added to the table, you have some new options in the Scheme Definition field that you can modify to best suit your desired display type. Figure 20.17 shows the new Scheme Definition field. Here you can add areas to the leftmost column that will define spaces and colors with the model. By changing the minimum area size under the At Least column, you can define the colors and spaces. In this column, add the following values: **200**, **350**, and **500**.

FIGURE 20.17
Modifying the values in the Scheme Definition field

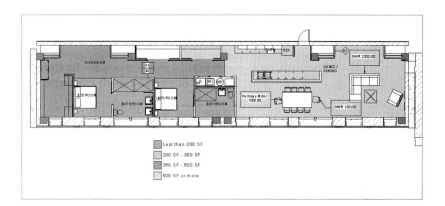

5. Click OK to update the color fill scheme from room names to room areas. Figure 20.18 shows the updated plan view. You'll notice that the rooms have colors defined based on their size rather than their name.

FIGURE 20.18
The finished floor plan

In both of these schemes, you have created family types for the legends. If you want to create another plan view based on the room name scheme, it's a simple matter of placing the legend in a view and selecting the desired type in the Color Filled Legends dialog box.

Understanding Other Visualization Techniques

Beyond the color fill legends, Revit has other ways to help you visualize your design. These tools can aid in visualizing your designs not only in 2D views like plans and sections, but also in 3D axonometric and perspectives. Using a combination of the Visual Style tool located in the View Control bar and some other new features in the 2011 release, there are a variety of new ways to view your model information.

Visual Style

The Visual Style tool is located in the View Control bar at the bottom of the drawing area in Revit. Selecting this tool opens the list shown in Figure 20.19. You are given the option to change how your view is represented depending on the style of view you want to create.

FIGURE 20.19
Visual style
options

By choosing different visual styles, you can represent the view in different ways, depending on the effect and presentation style you want to use. You can pair these styles with various shade and shadow options to create several effects for graphic displays. Figures 20.20 through 20.24 demonstrate each of the separate visual styles available with and without the shadows turned on.

FIGURE 20.20
Hidden Line style

FIGURE 20.21
Shaded With
Edges style

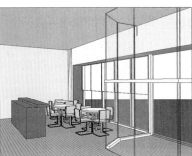

The Consistent Colors setting automatically activates the Sun and Shadow settings. You'll notice when choosing this selection in the View Control bar that the Sun and Shadow settings have been disabled (Figure 20.23) not allowing you to turn them off.

FIGURE 20.22
Consistent Colors style

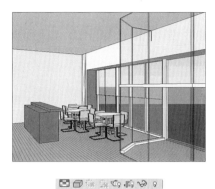

FIGURE 20.23
The Consistent Colors setting is active; the Sun and Shadow settings in the View Control bar are disabled.

FIGURE 20.24
Realistic style

Depending on which of these features you use, it can quickly diminish your computer's performance. The more visually accurate the image displayed, the more resources it tends to take for your specific workstation. For these instances, it's usually best to set up the view and not use it to manipulate model elements or content, or create the view settings and only apply them to the view when you're ready to create a visualization and not use them during production.

These same view types can be reflected outside the building as well. The exterior view is shown in Figures 20.25 through 20.28.

FIGURE 20.25
Hidden Line style

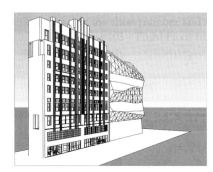 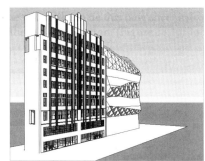

FIGURE 20.26
Shaded With Edges
style

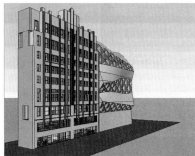 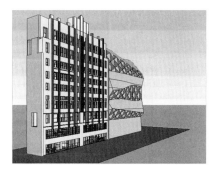

FIGURE 20.27
Consistent Colors
style

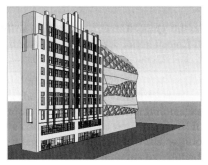

FIGURE 20.28
Realistic style

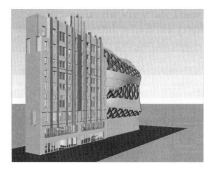 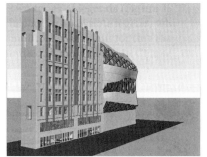

You'll notice that in these exterior views, we've added a gradient sky to the model. This visualization feature can be added to any exterior view and is controlled through the Graphic Display Options dialog box (Figure 20.29). You can select the Gradient Background check box and then control the gradient colors through the Sky, Horizon, and Ground colors listed. Color selection is very similar to the selection process for choosing color fill regions, as discussed earlier in this chapter in the Adding Color Fill Legends section.

FIGURE 20.29
Enabling Gradient
Background in the
Graphic Display
Options dialog box

Another feature of this dialog box is the Ambient Lighting check box. Checking this box will require a lot of your system resources—both in RAM and in processor—so choose this only for visualization reasons and don't try to use it to perform geometric manipulations. This feature will allow you an even more realistic view of the model. To enable this check box, however, you will need to have Hardware Acceleration enabled first. You can find this feature by clicking the Application button and selecting the Options tab. Then choose the Graphics tab (Figure 20.30), where you'll see the Use Hardware Acceleration option under Graphics Mode.

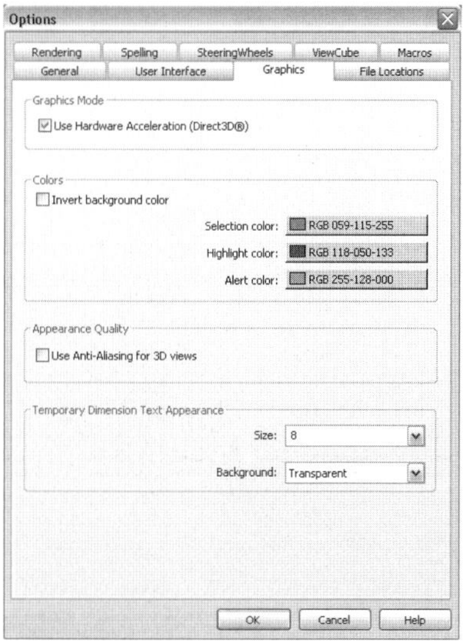

FIGURE 20.30
Use Hardware
Acceleration

Select the Use Hardware Acceleration check box; then click OK. You can now enable the Ambient Lighting setting. You can see the results both inside and outside the building in Figure 20.31.

FIGURE 20.31
Ambient lighting applied to the interior and exterior views

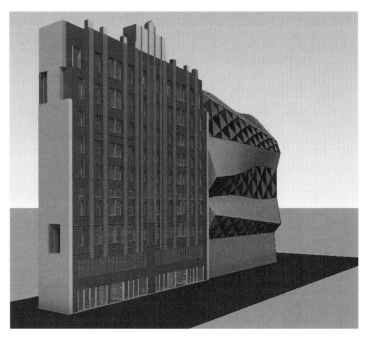

This feature combines a representation of the ProMaterial applied to the element (set under the Materials dialog box) and the current lighting scheme. To look at this feature in another way, the two chairs shown in Figure 20.32 are the same chair. One is shown using a Shaded With Edges style and the other is Shaded With Edges but with the Ambient Lighting feature activated. You can see the vast difference in display style.

FIGURE 20.32
The same chair shown using Shaded With Edges without and with Ambient Lighting activated

Analysis Display

A final element that can be used in presentation materials is Analysis Display. This feature can be found in the View Properties of any view in Revit (Figure 20.33) right below the Color Scheme button.

FIGURE 20.33
Analysis Display

When you select the Analysis Display field in View Properties, it will open a New Analysis Display Style dialog box. Here you can choose from two preset analysis display styles (Figure 20.34). Give the display type a name and click OK.

FIGURE 20.34
Creating a new analysis display style

Click OK to open the Analysis Display Styles dialog box, which contains controls similar to the ones available with color fill legends. Here you can create new styles for display and set the variables and color gradients using the Settings, Color, and Legend tabs (Figure 20.35).

FIGURE 20.35
The Analysis Display Styles dialog box and the Settings, Color, and Legend tabs

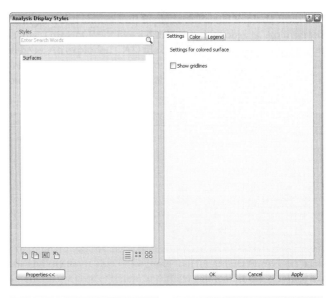

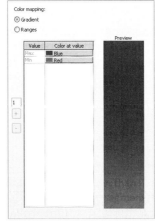

Although this feature doesn't have much use graphically beyond what we described, it can be tapped by third-party APIs for use with other analysis packages.

The Bottom Line

Add color fill legends.   Color fills are a great way to color views in Revit for use in various presentation displays and graphics.

Master It   There are a variety of ways to graphically display information in Revit using color fills. Setup can initially take a bit of time to get things organized, but once you create them, the legends can easily be transferred between views and projects. Describe how to add a color fill legend, once created, to your project template.

Use visualization techniques in your design.   Revit has a variety of ways to help you visualize your designs—both while designing and during presentation. Understanding where these features are located and how and when to use them can help expedite the presentation process, depending on the look and feel you want to create with your images.

Master It   List several ways using the View Control bar that you can modify the graphic settings of a view.

Part 6

Construction and Beyond

In the previous chapters, we focused on the architect's role in design and construction using Revit. As the uses of Revit continue to expand beyond documentation, we want to touch on several other uses of the tool beyond the traditional scope of the designer. In the following chapters, we are going to discuss several uses of Revit and how it can be used to augment design and documentation after construction documents are complete.

For this section, we worked with leading industry experts in these individual fields. More information about each of the contributors can be found in their respective chapters.

Chapter 21

Revit in Construction

In this chapter, we will explore the use of Revit in the construction phase by design teams and builders. For design teams, the use of Revit usually entails markups, sketches, and revision management; however, a builder may approach BIM tools in unique ways. As of 2010, there are many different BIM programs available for builders to use in preconstruction and construction phase tasks, so we will not pretend that Revit is used by the majority of construction organizations. Instead, we will offer two case studies of companies currently using Revit for these tasks and show you some of the benefits they realize.

In this chapter, you'll learn to:

◆ Add revisions to your project

◆ Use digital markups

◆ Understand how a builder uses Revit

Adding Revisions to Your Project

ABOUT THE CONTRIBUTING AUTHORS: LAURA HANDLER, JOSH LOWE, AND MIKE WHALEY

Laura Handler oversees Tocci's Virtual Design and Construction (VDC) process utilizing Building Information Models (BIM). In this key position, Handler manages the VDC team, including modeling, coordination and optimization for all of Tocci's projects. She advances Tocci's use of VDC, through research & development efforts. Apart from her duties at Tocci, Handler is very active in the industry. She serves on the leadership committee of the BIMForum as a Leader at Large and participates actively in local organizations, including the Boston Revit Users Group, Boston Society of Architects BIM and IPD Committees and the Associated General Contractors of Massachusetts. Handler presents frequently, locally and nationally, on VDC, IPD and Tocci's use of this groundbreaking process. Her blog, bimx.blogspot.com, is widely regarded as one of the best sources of information regarding VDC and BIM. She was recently selected as one of Building Design+Construction's 40 Under 40 in 2009.

Mike Whaley is a graduate of the University of Wisconsin-Milwaukee. During the first 26 years of his career he worked as an Architect, his professional focus was on project management of corporate, healthcare and municipal facilities. In 2005, Mike joined the J. H. Findorff & Son team, where he serves as Director of the Preconstruction services. His role is to lead the early collaboration and integration between owner, designer and contractor. Mike's technology initiatives have spearheaded Findorff to be an industry leader in the use of Building Information Modeling and Construction Visualization software. This advancement in preconstruction has improved collaboration, project understanding while demonstrating increased efficiency in the field, and project savings. In addition to his BIM initiative Mike has been instrumental in the implementation of the first full three part IPD project for Findorff.

Josh Lowe is a graduate of the University of Wisconsin-Milwaukee where he received a Bachelor of Science, Architectural Studies and a Certificate in Urban Planning. In 2004, Josh joined the J.H. Findorff & Son team, where he is currently a Construction Visualization and Integration Specialist. He is responsible for integrating trades during construction as well as promoting lean construction by leveraging the power of Building Information Models in the field to increase productivity. In addition to the utilization of BIM models for projects, Josh also is involved in the research and development of new BIM applications.

Revisions allow designers and builders to track changes made to a set of construction documents during the construction phase of a project. Since the construction documents usually consist of numerous sheets, this methodology allows everyone on the team to track and identify which changes were made and when they were made during construction. The purpose is not only to ensure correct construction but also to create *as-built* documentation recording how the building was actually created to be delivered to building owners upon occupancy.

In a typical drawing set, revisions will look like Figure 21.1 when they are created in Revit and issued as part of the drawing set. Revision clouds themselves are created within views that are placed on the sheets. The Revision tag is also placed within the view, but once the view is then placed on a sheet, the revision will appear in the sheet properties and on any Revision schedule on the sheet itself.

FIGURE 21.1
A typical revision

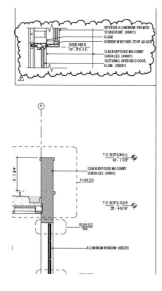
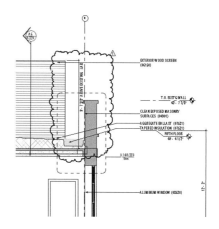

To create a revision cloud in your project, select the Annotate tab, and choose Revision Cloud from the Detail panel (Figure 21.2). This will place you in a revisions cloud drawing mode, similar to a Sketch mode, and will allow you to bubble the revised detail or drawing. When you're finished, click the green check to complete the sketch and your annotation is done.

FIGURE 21.2
The Revision tool

Typically in a project process, you won't have only one round of revisions to a document set. Revit provides controls for this and gives you the ability to name and date the various revisions in your project to better track them. The Sheet Issues/Revisions tool is located in two places in Revit. You can find it either on the View tab as the Revisions button or on the Manage tab under Additional Settings (Figure 21.3).

FIGURE 21.3
Opening the Sheet Issues/Revisions dialog box

Either of these tools will open the Sheet Issues/Revisions dialog box (Figure 21.4). Here you can add, merge, issue, and define the behavior of revisions. Let's review the major components of this dialog box.

FIGURE 21.4
The Sheet Issues/ Revisions dialog box

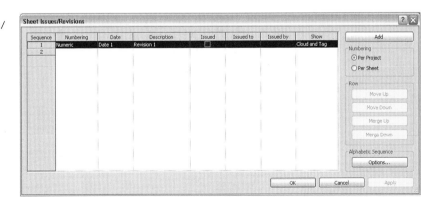

Numbering   You can choose to number revisions By Sheet or By Project in Revit. This is a global setting for the whole project but can be swapped one for the other at any point. Which method you choose mainly depends on how your firm chooses to track revisions. By Sheet allows you to have as many revisions as you want within the drawing set, but on each sheet, the revision numbers always start with 1. In the example shown in Figure 21.4, the tags and revision schedule are unique for each sheet, depending on how many revisions are on each sheet with each revision on each sheet presented sequentially. This means you are chrono-logically numbering/tracking the changes that happened on one particular sheet, not all the changes that happened in the entire project.

Using By Project will tag your revision clouds based on the global sequence established in the project. In this example, all revisions with the same issue date would have the same revi-sion number. So you can potentially skip a revision number on any given sheet. Either num-bering method can be set in advance and added to your project template.

Revision Table   The Sheet Issues/Revisions dialog box starts with one default revision already in place, even though you may have not made a revision yourself. This is only to give you a place to start—no revision will appear in your title blocks until you add revision clouds to your views. Each revision has a fixed number of parameters that you can enter. As you can see in Figure 21.4, the parameters include Numbering, Date, Description, and an Issued check box, in addition to Issued To and Issued By columns and options for showing clouds and tags.

The Add Button   This function is used to create a new revision. The new revision will auto-matically be placed in sequential order and only the sequence number will be automatically updated. You'll need to add your own description and date.

Revision Numbering   The Numbering option allows you to number each revision numeri-cally, alphabetically, or not at all. If you choose alphabetic sequence, the sequence is defined in the Alphabetic Sequence options. Click the Options button in the lower right of the dialog box to set your sequence and remove letters you don't want to use. For instance, some firms don't use the letters *I* or *O*. Figure 21.5 shows a sample of the dialog box. By default, an entire alphabet will appear here. The None option will allow you to add project milestones—non-numbered entries that appear in revision tables—to sheets without having to add revision clouds.

FIGURE 21.5
Sequence options allow you to use any order of letters or numbers.

Revisions   To issue a revision, click the check box in the Issued column. This will lock the revision clouds placed on sheets or in views associated with that revision, preventing them from being moved, deleted, or otherwise edited. The parameter values in the dialog box will gray out and become noneditable. This is to guarantee that the clouds and data do not change downstream once you issue a set of drawings.

REVISIONS IN A LIVE MODEL

During the construction process, the Revit model is still always changing. When you issue a revision, keep this in mind: while the clouds can become fixed in the project, the model will not be. As you continue to make revisions to the model it will always be up-to-date. So, if you need to maintain an archive of all project phases or each revision, be sure to export the sheets either as DWF or PDF files as a snapshot of the sheets at time of issuance.

Revision Clouds and Tags This controls the visibility of revision clouds and revision tags that have been issued. As issues occur, you may want to hide just the clouds or just the tags from previous revisions. This portion of the dialog box allows you to control individual visibility of those individual elements. For example, if you've issued a revision and then add revisions later and want to clean up your drawing, you can choose to show the issued revision *as the tag only*—typically a small triangle with the revision number inside it (Figure 21.6) or not show anything at all by using the None option.

FIGURE 21.6
A typical
revision tag

Figure 21.7 shows the options available in the Show drop-down list.

FIGURE 21.7
Use the Show drop-down list to hide clouds or tags of issued revisions.

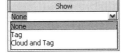

Placing Revision Clouds

To place a revision, open a view in which changes to the model have occurred and use the Revision Cloud tool found in the Detail panel on the Annotate tab. Start drawing bubbles around the area you are calling out as a revision in a clockwise direction. Revit automatically creates a line that makes a *cloud* (or series of arcs), as shown in Figure 21.8. When you're finished creating the cloud, click the Finish Sketch button at the top-right side of the Ribbon.

FIGURE 21.8
Adding a revision
cloud to a view

FIGURE 21.8
Adding a revision
cloud to a view

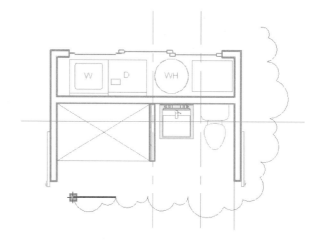

Like other objects in Revit, the graphics for revision clouds are controlled from the Object Styles dialog box (shown in Figure 21.9), accessed on the Annotation Objects tab. The default Revit setting for the line thickness is 1. We recommend that you change this to something like 7 in your project template to give it the pop you will typically see in revisions.

FIGURE 21.9
Changing the line
weight and style of
the revision cloud

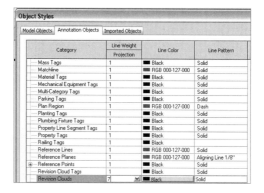

By default, each new revision cloud will be assigned to the last revision in the Sheet Issues/Revisions dialog box. If you need to change the revision that a cloud belongs to, select the cloud and use the Properties Palette to change it (Figure 21.10).

FIGURE 21.10
The revision
cloud's Properties
dialog box

As soon as you have placed a revision cloud on a sheet, any revision schedules placed in your title block will update to include the revision number, description, and the date you assigned in the Sheet Issues/Revisions dialog box earlier (Figure 21.11).

FIGURE 21.11
The updated title block with the revision information

Enter address here   Project No.   05129

Schematic Design

G Date **07/20/05**

Revision	Description	Date Issued
1	Revision 1	5.01.2010

F

Tagging a Revision Cloud

Revision clouds can be tagged like many other elements in Revit. Like other tags, these are intelligent and designed to report the revision number or letter that has been assigned to the revision cloud. To place a revision tag, use the Tag By Category tool in the Tag panel on the Annotate tab.

If a tag for revisions is not in your template, you will be warned that no such tag exists in your project. To continue, simply load a revision tag. The default Revit tag loaded by default in Revit is named `Revision Tag.rfa` and is located in the default Annotations folder created with a standard installation.

Once you have a tag loaded, you are ready to tag revision clouds. Hover the cursor over a revision cloud and click to place the tag. You will see a preview of the tag prior to placing it (Figure 21.12). Once the tag is placed, you can drag it around the cloud to reposition it, and turn on and off the leader, and it will stay associated with the cloud.

FIGURE 21.12
Tagging a revision cloud

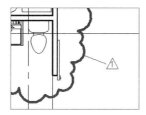

DISABLING THE LEADER

You can choose to use a leader line between the tag and the cloud depending on your preference or your office standards. In many cases, the tag just needs to be near the cloud and a leader is not necessary. Disable the leader by selecting the tag and clearing the Leader option in the Options Bar.

BIM and Supplemental Drawings

The process of making supplemental drawings (SDs) entails making a change to an existing drawing and then issuing that change as a separate package during the construction process. Sometimes this can be a single 8½″ × 11″ or 11″ × 17″ sheet where the new detail is then pasted over the old one in the document set. From a workflow perspective, this can be a little disruptive in Revit for a couple of reasons:

◆ When in Revit, placing the new detail into a smaller sheet to issue the individual drawing can lead to other problems. Since there is only one instance of the view, it requires you to take views off your Construction Document sheet and place the detail in a new sheet. The problem is the new sheet/detail is meant to replace a portion of your original document set, so your set is now out of sequence. You will need to either remove the view from the sheet it was issued on temporarily (and remember to put it back) or duplicate the view and hope that you do not need to make last-minute additional changes.

◆ A Supplemental Drawing, once issued, is like a snapshot in time. It becomes a numbered change made to the drawing set at a given date. Because the model and all the views in the model always reflect the most current state of the project, making separate SD sheets and views within Revit will show any additional changes made to that view.

As a best practice, some architects leave all the revisions directly on the sheets where they were originally issued. The sheets can be printed to PDFs, and the PDFs (with the revision clouds) are imported into Adobe Illustrator or a similar application (where they can be properly scaled and cropped to the view or detail being revised and then placed on a template to be issued for the revision). This process not only creates a historic record of the revision, but also allows you to avoid issuing the full sheet while keeping your model up-to-date.

Using Digital Markups

Autodesk Design Review offers a digital and efficient way to view and mark up 2D and 3D documents for review. This workflow is different from revisions and is geared more toward informal design review rather than the management of sheet issues. For example, if your drawings must be reviewed for quality control and overall design comments by a senior designer who might not be Revit savvy, this tool can streamline the process. The senior designer, consultant, or any other third party can make comments and review changes directly in the digital file and return them to the Revit user who needs to follow up on those reviews.

Design Review publishes files in a DWFx format. If you export the drawing sheets from Revit to DWFx, when the DWFx is linked back into Revit, Revit will automatically place the DWFx under the corresponding sheet. So there is no need on your part for any sort of alignment or placement of the revisions.

Design Review is a free tool that you can download from the Autodesk website: `www.autodesk.com/designreview`.

Once it's installed, you can open any DWFx or DWF file produced by any Autodesk or non-Autodesk software packages.

Publishing to Design Review

The DWFx format allows others to examine your design without needing to own or know how to use Revit. The files are also small, which makes them easy to email, something you cannot do with a large Revit file. There are two ways to share your model using Design Review: as 2D information or as 3D information. If you publish to 3D, you create a single 3D representation of your model. Publishing to 2D can create either a view or a whole collection of interconnected views and sheets all packaged as one file.

DWF Exports

You can export to DWF from any view in Revit. To export your views or sheets, select the Application menu and choose Export ➤ DWF (Figure 21.13).

Figure 21.13
Exporting to DWF

The DWF Export Settings dialog box (Figure 21.14) will open. You can choose which views/sheets to export; the default is your current view. You can choose to include or exclude any sheets or views using the Include column. When you've made your selection, click Next. By default, all your views and sheets will be combined into a single DWF file. If you want a separate file for each view and sheet, clear the option Combine Selected Views And Sheets Into Single DWF File. Let's walk through this:

1. Open the Jenkins.rvt model on the companion web page, www.sybex.com/go/masteringrevit2011.

2. Click the Application button, and select Export ➤ DWF to open the dialog box shown in Figure 21.14.

3. Select ALL SHEETS from the Export drop-down list.

FIGURE 21.14
The DWF Export
Settings dialog box

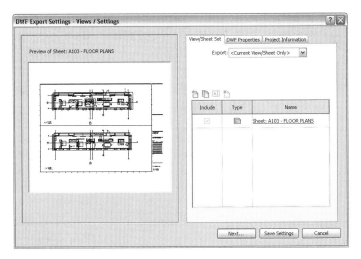

4. To check the export size, open the DWF Properties tab and click the Print Setup button. In the resulting dialog box, you can set explicit sizes for your export. Click the option <Use Sheet Size> to let Revit autodetect sheet sizes based on the title blocks you are using in the project.

5. Click Next and specify the name of the file and a location in which to save it. Make sure you are combining all sheets into a single DWF file.

Marking Up the Model Using Design Review

Once you have exported a DWF, you can open it in Design Review and add textual markups that can then be shared with your team and linked back into Revit. Figure 21.15 shows the exported DWF opened in Design Review.

FIGURE 21.15
Opening the DWF
in Design Review

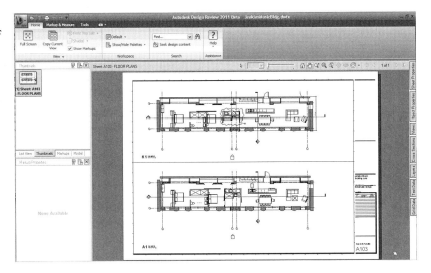

Choose the Markup & Measure tab to begin adding comments or markups to the DWF (Figure 21.16).

FIGURE 21.16

Using the DWF markup tools

Using the shapes and draw tools on this tab, you can add clouds, arrows, and text to insert your comments or changes into the drawings. Once all your changes are created, save the file and it will retain all your changes. Figure 21.17 shows an example of a markup. While this is shown in black and white, markups can be done in a variety of colors and line weights to give them extra visibility on the page.

FIGURE 21.17

A marked-up DWF

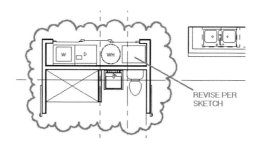

Importing a Design Review Markup

Once you've added markups in Design Review, save the file. You can then link the marked up DWF file back into the Revit project. On the Insert tab, choose DWF Markup (Figure 21.18).

FIGURE 21.18

Linking in a marked-up DWF

When a DWF file is selected, Revit will link and show only the markups, not the entire DWF file. If there are no markups in the DWF file, nothing will be visible in Revit. If your file does contain markups, Revit will alert you to which sheets in the set will have comments that need to be addressed. Figure 21.19 shows a sample of the dialog box that Revit presents when inserting a marked-up DWF. In this example, there is one sheet with markups.

FIGURE 21.19
Revit shows which
sheets have associ-
ated markups.

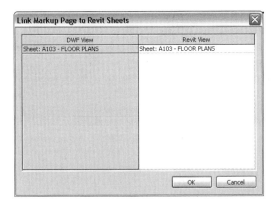

Note that markups can only be linked to sheets. If you export a view and mark it up, it will not show up in Revit. Always work from sheets when using Design Review for markup transfer.

You cannot move or delete linked DWF markups—they appear with a pin if selected. You can do a number of things to graphically indicate that you've dealt with a markup:

Change its graphic appearance. Let's say you have 20 redline markups on your sheet. You need to keep track of which ones you've picked up. One way to do this is to graphically override each markup as you make the requested modifications. Select the markup, right-click, choose View ➤ By Element, and click Override Graphics. Choose a color to indicate "done." Yellow works well because it suggests a highlight marker.

Hide it. This approach is similar to the graphic override, but you hide the markup altogether. Select the markup, right-click, and choose Hide In View ➤ Element.

Remove it. You can remove markups by choosing Manage Links from the Manage tab. In the Manage Links dialog box, select the DWF Markups tab, select the markup, and click the Remove button. This removes all markups associated with the link.

Revit for the Contractor

Now that we have reviewed some basic functionality a design team might use in the construction phase, let's take a look at how a builder (contractor, subcontractor, or construction manager) uses Revit in the industry today.

Revit is often referred to as a design application; however, contractors are using Revit more frequently as both a model authoring and project analysis tool. The increase in contractors' use of Revit parallels the increased trend of contractors adopting BIM. According to the 2009 McGraw Hill Construction SmartMarket Report *The Business Value of BIM*, "contractors are gaining ground faster than any other group," with 50 percent of contractors interviewed for the report using BIM in 2009, compared to 13 percent of contractors interviewed in 2007. Although contractors use Revit to obtain different results than design professionals, many of the processes and functions are the same; they are merely applied in unique ways.

A contractor might use Revit in one of several scenarios. Likely to be the most popular situation is the case in which builders will utilize Revit to construct their own virtual model of a project based on 2D drawings they receive from design teams. While this book encourages open sharing of 3D intelligent design data, the fact remains that many projects still share *flattened* plans, sections, and elevations for the construction phase.

Another interesting use case is that of a contractor using Revit in conjunction with architects and engineers in an integrated project delivery (IPD) environment. In this case, the perceived risks of sharing complete model data are mitigated by the IPD contractual requirements. Design, engineering, and construction teams work together to ensure the ultimate success of the project. This process requires adequate planning and development of a robust BIM execution plan.

It is important to note that construction managers may only need to support the coordination of data by other builders or provide guidance in construction phasing, staging, or cost control. Although Revit can provide much of this functionality, many other powerful tools are available in the marketplace today. Programs from Autodesk such as Navisworks Manage and others such as Vico Office Suite, Synchro Professional, Solibri Model Checker, and Beck DProfiler are developing increased interoperability with Revit. For a more complete overview on the use of these tools, please read Brad Hardin's *BIM and Construction Management* (Wiley Publishing, 2009).

In the following case study, contributed by Josh Lowe and Mike Whaley of J. H. Findorff & Son, Inc., you will see that Findorff finds ways to use Revit to convert 2D design data and to generate working documents for their self-performed construction tasks. It covers BIM uses in preconstruction planning and in the construction phase by a contractor implementing Revit for the sake of their own productivity. Whether you are an architect, engineer, or builder, we hope you will find this case study informative and inspirational.

 Real World Scenario

CASE STUDY: J. H. FINDORFF AND SON, INC.

Established in 1890, J. H. Findorff and Son, Inc., is a southern Wisconsin general contractor and construction management company with offices in Madison and Milwaukee. While employing an average of 600 construction professionals, they complete more than $300 million in construction annually. Findorff self-performs concrete, masonry, carpentry, steel erection, and drywall with their own teams. Their primary markets include healthcare, education (K–12), higher education (two-year and four-year), and a mixture of other commercial projects.

USING REVIT FOR PRECONSTRUCTION PLANNING

Using an intelligent 3D model to plan construction phase activities has several advantages over traditional approaches. Plans and uninformed spreadsheets not only take longer to produce but expose the opportunity for errors and misinterpretation. A model-based approach can support such activities as creating virtual mockups, planning for site safety, and work staging. Contractors can also use Revit in ways similar to that of an architect, as demonstrated in other chapters of this book.

One of the very first applications of Revit for Findorff was realizing the visualization capabilities of 3D images. On a major hospital project that involved multiple tower cranes, an early Revit model was used to demonstrate to the Med-Flight helicopter team how the tower cranes would look as the helicopters approached the hospital during construction. This involved modeling the existing hospital and site as simple massing elements in one overall model with the helicopter landing pads. Combined with models of the tower cranes (including their swing zones as shown here), this model allowed multiple flight path approaches to the hospital to be simulated.

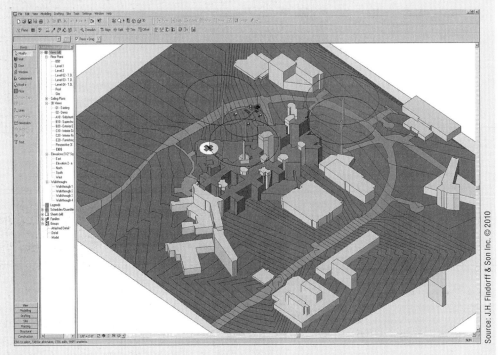

The model was then used to produce a series of animations that were presented to the hospital staff and flight crews. This mockup allowed construction to proceed with the confidence of the hospital administration, staff, Med-Flight pilots, and even field staff that the cranes and the helicopter approach would ensure the appropriate level of safety.

In another example, a Revit model of a project's major building components was linked to the project schedule in Navisworks, creating an animation, as shown here.

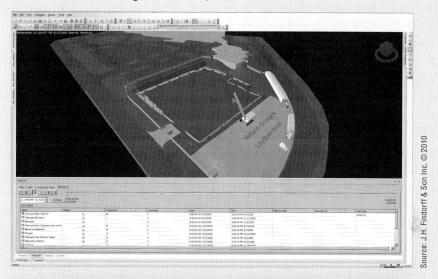

Upon review of the 4D simulation, construction team leaders realized the sequence of the construction would require that structural steel framing from the staging area be hoisted over part of the building that would was occupied. As this was an unacceptable safety condition, the construction sequence was modified, thus avoiding potential delays and unsafe conditions during actual construction.

From the very beginning, the Findorff project management staff realized the power of Revit as a site planning and utilization tool. A site utilization plan can include the basic elements of construction to determine where to place a job trailer or store materials. Families have been developed to represent typical job site elements to expedite modeling of sites, as shown here.

Source: J.H. Findorff & Son Inc. © 2010

Beyond the placing of basic elements on the site plan, Revit is being utilized to create site models to analyze traffic and circulation patterns and sequencing for delivery of materials. In addition to site utilization, Findorff also uses Revit for schedule coordination, phasing and sequencing studies, detailed staging plans for specific field applications, and clash detection for our MEP trade partners.

An interesting example of site phasing was a project that required a continuous concrete pour of more than 3,000 cubic yards. To further complicate this process, access to the formwork was more than 30 feet (10 m) below grade between and behind four existing buildings. To develop a productive solution to these issues, models of the concrete pump trucks with all of their characteristics for reach, swing, and setup requirements were developed. Then, using the site model and the models of the concrete pump truck, the project managers and site superintendants conducted multiple test layouts in the model, as shown here:

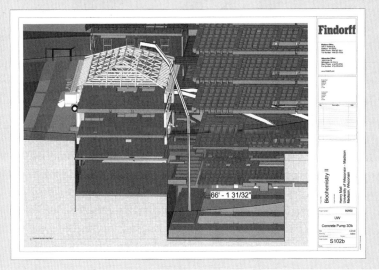

The model was also used to map the site access for all of the concrete trucks, including staging. The pour was completed overnight without moving the concrete pumps or adjusting any of the staging, as shown here. The Revit model is shown on the left. The right image is a photograph from the night of the pour.

USING REVIT DURING CONSTRUCTION

Contractors such as Findorff are finding an increased return on their investment in training and development of BIM resources. During the construction phase, Revit can be one of many valuable tools in a builder's virtual toolbox. An example of this is using Revit models aggregated in Navisworks to allow all MEP trades to merge into the structural and architectural models for spatial coordination (shown here).

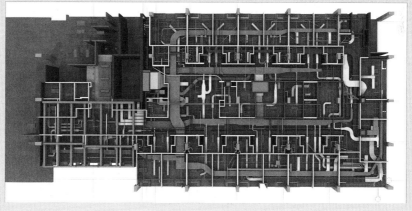

Source: J.H. Findorff & Son Inc. © 2010

In this project, the team faced a start delay of six weeks due to a delay in getting an agency's approval. Working with all of the subcontractors, the team modeled every component above the ceilings and then agreed to a detailed sequence of installation. Many of the trades also used this as an opportunity to prefabricate many of their system components. Not only did the project recover the time lost in the agency review delay, it was completed two months ahead of schedule.

CONSTRUCTION SET-OUT DRAWINGS

Concrete and masonry lift drawings are not new to the construction industry. Concrete superintendants and foremen have been doing lift drawings on grid paper by hand for years. Revit simply takes this process to a new level with increased efficiency and information. Findorff creates concrete lift drawings by building their own models of foundations using the architect's and engineer's drawings for reference. This allowed them to create a series of lift drawings based specifically on the exact methods of construction rather than solely on the design intent. One example of such a drawing is shown here:

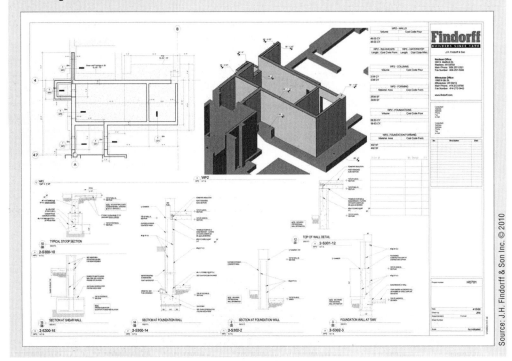

Such drawings aid in the construction process by clearly identifying the work to be completed. They can contain a variety of intelligent information, including the following:

◆ Steel embeds

◆ Concrete openings

◆ Architectural elements

◆ Details

◆ Quantities

◆ Cost codes

◆ Labor requirements

Advanced visualization based on accurate modeling techniques can detect potential design conflicts before they can adversely affect the on-site team. Such discrepancies are usually remedied by the modeler and reflected in the lift drawings for little or no cost. If such questions occur in the field during the installation of formwork or during a concrete pour, the cost in lost time would be substantial and probably require expensive change orders.

In addition to detecting and resolving potential conflicts in the execution of the design intent, the construction modeler will engage the project manager and superintendant to determine the optimal sequencing for each concrete pour. All major details associated with each pour are linked to the lift drawings as well as critical information, including volume of concrete, required labor, and productivity measures. These items are all generated from intelligent families of concrete objects that were created within Revit.

The use of modeling for foundations has progressed from simple foundation lift drawings to very sophisticated slab lift drawings, and the level of information and content in the lift drawings has expanded exponentially. Now lift drawings contain openings, sleeve locations, and embed information. In effect, contractors are now producing concrete field shop drawings, even modeling critical rebar areas if a conflict between rebar and formwork is anticipated. Detailed phasing models are also created using view filters to color specific parts of a model based on their construction order, as shown here:

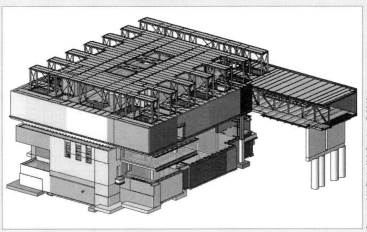

Source: J.H. Findorff & Son Inc. © 2010

Masonry lift drawings are a natural next step after the development of concrete lift drawings. The productivity savings from completing concrete lift drawings can be equally applied to the development of similar masonry documents. Masonry lift drawings coordinate information relating to masonry work, including but not limited to, openings, elevations, area of insulation, lintels, stone banding, sills, flashing, winter protection, block/brick counts, and manhours, as shown here.

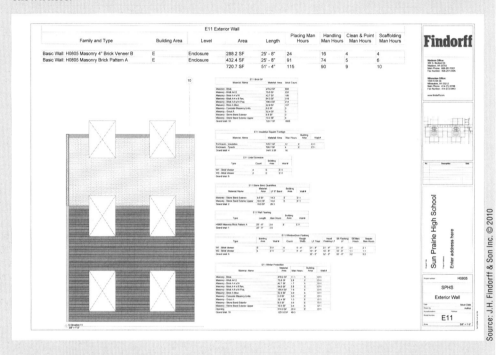

Unlike concrete lift drawings, the breakdown on the pieces became less important and information was given based on individual elevations. The drawings then became planning tools for the field that allowed for more efficient and accurate brick ordering, crew planning, site utilization, staging/delivery management, and constant updated quantity checks throughout construction. This approach resulted in only a 1 percent variation from what was ordered to what was used.

In the following case study, contributed by Laura Handler of Tocci Building Corporation, you'll find that Tocci uses Revit in a different way from Findorff. While the previous case study focused on an implementation of what you might call *lonely BIM*, the following illustrates a company dedicated to the notion of *social BIM*. This case study examines how Tocci applies the principles of integrated design and project delivery in a collaborative environment with a project's design team.

Real World Scenario

CASE STUDY: TOCCI BUILDING CORPORATION

Tocci Building Corporation (www.tocci.com) provides building and construction services throughout the Northeast and Mid-Atlantic, as well as program management and team integration throughout the United States. Through its affiliate company, Q5 LLC (www.q5thecompany.com), Tocci provides virtual design and construction (VDC) and integrated project delivery (IPD) facilitation to projects around the world. Managed by third-generation CEO (Chief Enabling Officer) John Tocci, the company began investigating and testing BIM software tools as early as 1999. By 2006, Tocci had selected the Revit suite of products for model authoring and mandated full use of VDC on all projects. Since then, Tocci has built a robust VDC team and trained all employees to utilize models on a day-to-day basis on projects.

Tocci performs work in the institutional, hospitality, and commercial markets and is nationally known as a leader in VDC and IPD. In 2009, Tocci completed the first pure IPD project on the East Coast, the Autodesk AEC Headquarters, with KlingStubbins and Autodesk, Inc.

CONSTRUCTION VISUALIZATION

Tocci is nationally known as a leader in virtual design and construction and has been implementing Revit for many years. They have used it in ways similar to those described in the previous case study on Findorff. Simple massing models are used to visualize major project phasing milestones, schedules and color filters facilitate preconstruction planning, and material quantities are extracted from the model to generate accurate bills of materials. One simple and innovative way Tocci utilizes the visualizations of a data-rich building information model is by placing high-resolution renderings throughout the jobsite. These images are extracted directly from the Revit project using camera views situated according to key work areas requiring clarification as shown in the following graphic. This enables subcontractors to better understand the overall design intent of a space while they execute their part of the work.

Another specific example of construction visualization is Tocci's use of phasing in Revit and some manual organization of geometry to generate visual construction phase projections—also known as a *look-ahead*. You can split objects such as walls and floors and then place them in specific phases, one for each week of a construction phase projection. Phase placement will drive both the data in your Revit views as well as quantity information in schedules, so it is critical that it is done carefully.

Using phase filters applied to 3D views shows where the project should be at the end of the week. The phase-filtered schedules communicate the picks of steel and volume of concrete to be poured that week (as shown here). For this project, the three-week projections were used to order materials and to communicate to subcontractors. This process helped keep the project on schedule and reduced material waste.

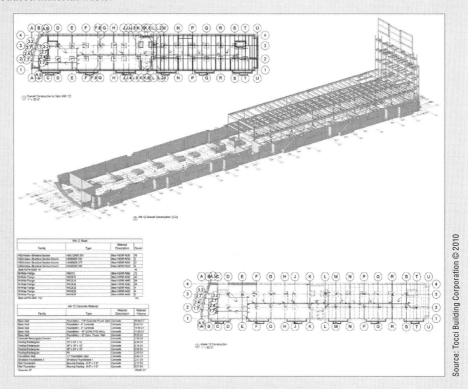

Planning for Integrated Project Delivery Using BIM

As described in Chapter 7, "Working with Consultants," collaboratively working in Revit requires advanced planning, often taking shape in the BIM execution plan (BEP). Although the BEP covers all BIM use on a project, Revit standards and protocols will be a large part of the BEP if a team elects to use Revit for model authoring or other BIM uses.

Although there are many BEP templates out there, including the buildingSMART Alliance's BIM Project Execution Planning Guide, Tocci Building Corporation uses an internal template that was originally developed in 2006 and has been continually refined since then. The concept of a BIM execution plan was developed in a digital charrette between Johnson & Johnson, KlingStubbins, Tocci Building Corporation, and EMCOR through the BIMForum (www.bimforum.org) to jointly streamline the BIM-enabled process. The concept was incorporated into ConsensusDOCS 301, BIM Addendum as the documentation that defines the level for which a building information model or models may be legally relied on. It has been incorporated into many other documents since then.

The BEP template and planning process described here was used by Tocci Building Corporation and KlingStubbins on the Autodesk AEC Headquarters, in Waltham, MA, the first pure IPD project on the east coast of the United States. On this project a single building information model, made up of several linked Revit files, was used during design and construction.

Step 1: Picking the People   Before any BIM planning can be done, the BIM leads on the project must be determined. A BIM lead represents one of the BIM-enabled major project participants on the project. Start by selecting a BIM lead to represent architecture, construction, and the owner, if each party is BIM-enabled. Select BIM leads to represent other design disciplines or subcontractors as needed. BIM leads should be actual project participants, and possess technical BIM experience and a disposition toward collaboration.

Step 2: Reviewing the Project Phases   The project phases and schedule should be reviewed, so the BIM leads can plan BIM use and standards over the course of the project. Include these in the BEP for reference.

Step 3: Determining BIM Uses   Although a BIM can be used in a multitude of ways, each project will use a model in different ways due to the constraints of the project (schedule, complexity, needs, or team members). Determining BIM uses in the planning process will help your team focus on the most appropriate level of detail and model collaboration protocols. A list of potential BIM uses can be found on the Penn State website for BIM Project Execution Planning at www.engr.psu.edu/ae/cic/BIMEx. This list includes information specific to each use, including potential value, resources required, and team competencies required.

Step 4: Selecting Software   Given the large number of software programs available, it is often difficult to figure out which ones are necessary. However, once you determine your BIM uses, project software selection will become clearer. The BIM leads may need to engage design consultants or subcontractors to make the final selection.

Step 5: Establishing Standards   For each discipline, standards must be set forth for model authoring. Additionally, software-specific standards should be set for each software program needed. Because many participants will already have company-wide standards set up, compromise will be required during this step. Some of the shared standards to consider for Revit include the following:

◆ Filenaming conventions

◆ Component naming conventions

◆ Material naming conventions

◆ Workset organization

◆ Phasing standards

◆ Shared parameters

◆ Units and tolerance requirements

Step 6: Determining Model Access   With so many entities involved in Revit with an IPD project, access rights will need to be determined. For each model and person, think about the following questions:

◆ Is live access needed or would a regular update suffice?

◆ Does the person need to make edits to or extract information from the model?

◆ Do they require model geometry or just parameters?

◆ Does the participant just need to view the model?

Answering these questions helps determine if the participant should access the model live via VPN or by co-locating, versus downloading the model regularly via tools such as FTP. It will also help determine what software each person needs and if certain parts of the model should be restricted (if that is technically possible).

Step 7: Defining the Level of Detail   One of most time-consuming parts of BIM execution planning is determining the level of detail required at each stage for each component type. This is casually referred to as "who models what, when, and how." For each object type, detail geometry definitions and parametric information required at each project stage is documented based on the project BIM uses. With walls, for example, this includes making decisions on the following:

◆   When walls need to change from nominal to actual dimensions

◆   When layers need to be defined

◆   When layers need to be broken

◆   When and how fire-rating data is input

◆   What parameters wall tags will display

Step 8: Mapping Workflows for Model Uses   A workflow needs to be defined and documented for each BIM use, so all parties understand the details of the use and how it fits into the overall project. Workflow is often discussed with level of detail (LOD), but it needs to be focused on and finalized. A simplified example is shown here.

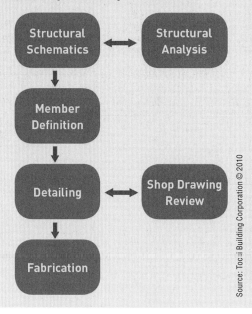

Source: Tocci Building Corporation © 2010

DESIGN TO FABRICATION

In the IPD project for Autodesk's AEC Headquarters, KlingStubbins and Tocci had utilized, to the greatest extent possible, a process that supported the stewardship of data from the earliest design concepts through fabrication and installation. This process is perhaps best illustrated in the development of custom wood ceiling panels for a special customer area of the project. After a concept was conceived by the architect with input from the builder and fabricator, custom families in Revit were created to optimize the layout of the panels.

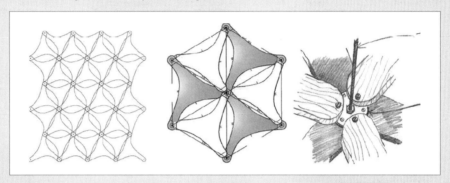

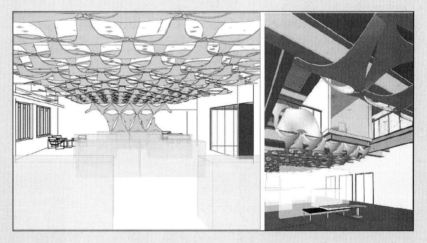

Once the panels were arranged throughout the space in the desired configuration, modelers from KlingStubbins and Tocci were able to collaborate with fabrication modelers at RB Woodcraft in Syracuse, NY, to further refine the design based on optimal constructability. Autodesk Inventor was then used to assimilate the form and generate 2D shop drawings.

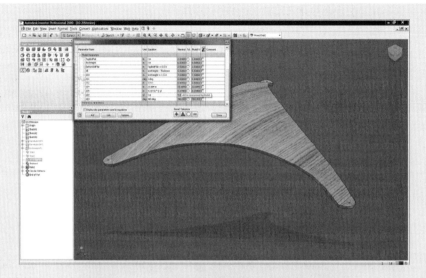

When the custom panels were installed, it completed the vision of both the design and construction team while controlling cost, reducing waste, and keeping the project on schedule.

Modeling for Construction

The process of using Revit for design is different than using it for conversion of 2D drawings into a construction phase model. As we have demonstrated in previous chapters of this book, generic element types and component placeholders support rapid iteration of design concepts. In contrast, a builder will likely be dealing with a design that will not change drastically throughout the construction phase. As such the builder can generate models with a higher level of detail and precision. As you will see, this approach is necessary for a builder to ensure their models are accurate and constructible. In this section we will discuss the concepts of modeling for construction and how this process may be different when working with a design team in an integrated project delivery method.

The simplest way to explain how to model like a builder is this: *model it how it's going to be built*. This guiding principle must be applied to accuracy, level of detail, tolerances, and technique. Here are a few examples to illustrate each of these concepts:

Accuracy   Objects need to be modeled so that they are accurate in 3D instead of merely *appearing* accurate in 2D plans. As shown in Figure 21.20, the foundation modeled on the left would appear correct in plan; however, the 3D geometry doesn't correctly represent the design intent. The foundation model on the right is the same condition modeled accurately. An accurate 3D model supports quantity extraction, coordination efforts, and direct-from-model total station layout.

FIGURE 21.20
The foundation modeled on the left would appear correct in plan but is incorrectly modeled. The model on the right is the accurately modeled condition supporting other BIM uses.

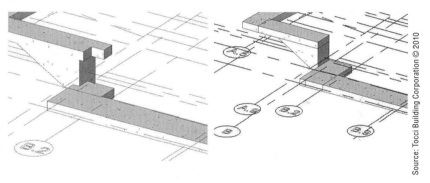

Source: Tocci Building Corporation © 2010

Level of Detail   Although the performance issues in Revit limit the level of detail that can be modeled across an entire project, it is helpful to model extreme levels of detail in specific areas—to ensure that the detail is fully coordinated in 3D, meets the design intent, and is understood by all stakeholders, enabling seamless execution of the design intent. In some cases, this means modeling blocking or pre-rock; in others it means modeling every detail of a specific assembly.

As shown in Figure 21.21, the exterior wall detail depicts flashing, backer rod, caulking, trim and finishes—among other elements created using In-Place Families. This detail was created in the architectural file for the project and placed on a specific workset named Exterior Wall

Detail (its global visibility was set to not be visible in all views). The detail could also be segregated from the overall model by using a linked file or design options.

Source: Tocci Building Corporation © 2010

FIGURE 21.21

A highly detailed exterior wall model depicts flashing, backer rod, caulking, trim, and finishes, among other things, using In-Place Families.

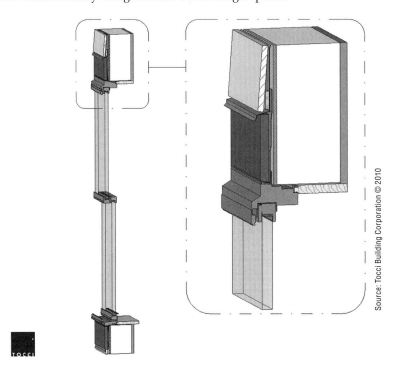

Tolerances Although modeling in Revit is considered accurate, the tolerance of the modeling can be adjusted. If tolerances aren't set tight enough, issues can arise when using a model for construction. Different construction uses require different tolerances, so it is important to select the tolerances for the entire project based on the most demanding use. Revit allows for a project-wide unit tolerance as small as $\frac{1}{256}''$ or 0.001 mm, but also allows tolerances to be overridden for specific dimension styles. Rather than using dimension styles to round dimensions to appear correctly, builders require the objects to be modeled accurately. In the example shown in Figure 21.22, the impact of tolerance on modeling is demonstrated. The intended dimension between the two walls shown was $2'-\frac{1}{2}''$, but when placed, it was modeled at $2'-\frac{105}{256}''$. To make the dimension appear correctly in plan, a rounded dimension style can be used (in this case $\frac{1}{4}''$ rounding would work), but if the geometry was extracted for execution (i.e., fabrication or total station layout) the as-built dimension would be closer to $2'-\frac{7}{16}''$. Although $\frac{1}{16}''$ may seem like a negligible distance, on a large project such discrepancies can accumulate to a significant length.

Source: KlingStubbins and Tocci Building Corporation © 2010

FIGURE 21.22

The impact of unit tolerance on modeling

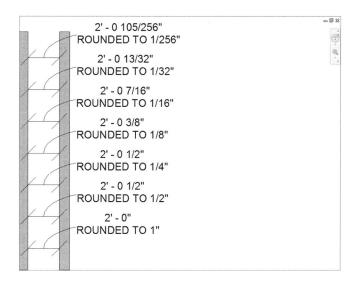

FIGURE 21.23

Modeling workflow used by KlingStubbins and Tocci Building Corporation on the Autodesk AEC Headquarters

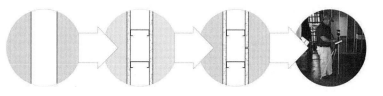

Technique   It is in modeling technique that "model it how it's going to be built" takes on additional meaning. It isn't enough that the geometry is being modeled accurately; it needs to be organized based on construction methods. For instance, foundation walls and slabs are split to reflect pour sequence or the layers of walls are modeled separately to reflect construction sequence. Figure 21.23 depicts the wall-modeling workflow used by KlingStubbins and Tocci Building Corporation on the Autodesk AEC Headquarters in Waltham, MA. During concept design, walls were modeled generically. Once the floor plan was approved, KlingStubbins established wall types and Tocci Building Corporation created construction-ready walls where each layer of material was modeled as a separate wall. KlingStubbins further detailed the walls, breaking the finish to reflect reveals. Finally the geometry was used to execute the work with total station layout.

Modeling Walls for Construction

To help illustrate this method of modeling specifically for construction, this section will walk you through the process of modeling a single 10′ × 10′ room, including a soffit from scratch. The following process was developed to support more accurate phasing simulation and automated on-site layout by splitting the overall assembly of wall components into separate wall types. You should approach each project with careful consideration of the common goals set forth in a BIM execution plan. This level of detail may not be required in all cases.

1. Open the file c21-Walls.rvt from this book's companion web page at www.sybex.com/go/masteringrevit2011. Look at the basic wall types that have been created for use in the file: Core 1, Drywall PT 1, and Drywall PT 2, as shown in Figure 21.4. This assumes that the design team only defined one partition type with two different paint finishes. For an actual project, start by creating the wall types that are defined by the partition schedule and the exterior details.

2. Select the Home tab in the ribbon and choose the Wall tool. From the Properties Palette, select the "Core 1" wall type. In the Options Bar, set Height to Unconnected: 10'-0" and Location Line to Wall Centerline.

3. Model the room as shown in Figure 21.24. Since the interior of the room is to be 10' × 10', model the walls 10' to 1¼" away from each other, to allow for both a layer of 5/8" drywall to be added on each side in the next step.

FIGURE 21.24
Wall cores
modeled

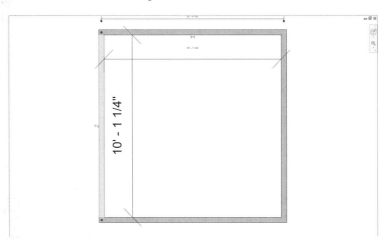

4. Activate the Wall tool again if necessary and select the wall type Drywall PT 1 from the Properties Palette. In the Options Bar, set Height to 10'–0" and the Location Line to Finish Face-Interior. Model the interior drywall layer snapping to the inside face of the Core 1 wall type you modeled in step 3. Create these segments in a counterclockwise direction; otherwise, you may need to flip the orientation of the walls using the spacebar on your keyboard.

   You might find it easier to use the Pick Lines geometry method to place these wall component segments rather than drawing them from point to point. Also make sure that the Detail Level of the current view is set to Medium or Fine.

5. Once the drywall layer is modeled, use the Align tool to align it to the core wall and lock the constraint. Make sure that the drywall layer is locked to the core wall and not vice versa. This is accomplished with the Align tool by picking the core wall first, then the drywall layer. You may need to use the Tab key to cycle through the common faces to select the correct layers in the correct order. Be sure to watch the status bar to verify the references of the elements you are aligning.

The purpose of aligning and locking walls is so that the finish moves with the core. Try moving a core wall and notice how the finish wall moves with it. Move the wall back to its original location.

6. After the wall components are aligned and locked, go to the Modify tab in the ribbon and select Join from the Geometry panel. Join each finish layer to its core layer.

The purpose of joining the walls is so that doors and windows cut through all wall layers. Place a door in one of the completed walls and notice how the object cuts all the wall layers. Delete the door.

7. To add the drywall layers to the outside of the core layers, repeat steps 4–6 except use the wall type Drywall PT 2, set Location Line to Finish Face-Interior, and model the walls in a clockwise direction. Repeat the process of aligning, locking, and joining the finishes to the core walls.

8. Now, let's consider how to use this technique in a slightly more complicated situation. Select all three layers of the wall on the left side of the room and on the Properties Palette change the Base Offset to 7′-0″ and the Unconnected Height to 3′-0″ to create an opening as shown in Figure 21.25.

FIGURE 21.25
The wall base offset and unconnected height is modified to create an opening.

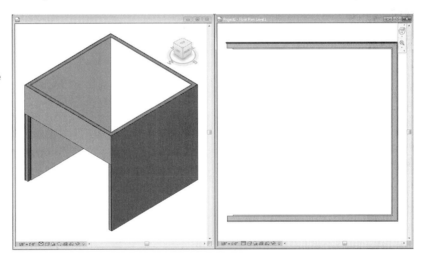

9. There are several methods that can be used to wrap the drywall finish around the exposed ends of the stud walls: (1) modify the profile of the finish walls or (2) model new walls. To use the latter method, create a finish wall using the same methods in steps 4–6, only changing the unconnected height to 7′-0″. When joining the finish wall to the core, make sure to also join the finish wall to adjacent finish walls, as shown in Figure 21.26.

FIGURE 21.26
Finish layers are
added to the ends
of the walls.

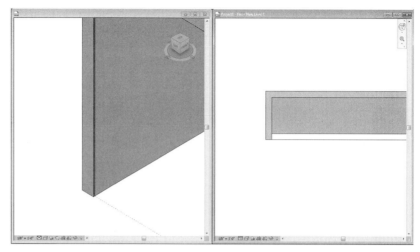

FIGURE 21.26
Finish layers are
added to the ends
of the walls.

10. To finish the soffit assembly as shown in Figure 21.27, create a ceiling at the soffit, using ceiling type Drywall PT 2 to "cover" the exposed core wall.

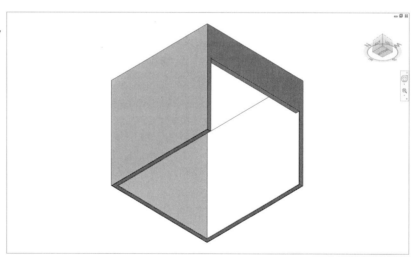

FIGURE 21.27
The soffit assembly
is complete.

Once walls are modeled with this level of accuracy, it becomes easier to extract quantities, link the model to a phasing simulation, and export geometry to a total station for layout in the field. It also enables accurate representation of real-world construction conditions. Figure 21.28

illustrates a condition where the drywall layers are modeled only a short distance above the ceiling assembly, which is a common construction method for interior partitions.

FIGURE 21.28
The unconnected height of the drywall is easily modified to reflect the actual design intent of the detail.

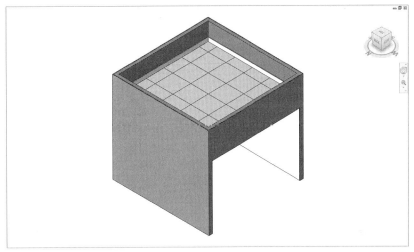

The Bottom Line

Add revisions to your project.   You need the ability to track changes in your design after sheets have been issued. Adding revisions to a drawing is an inevitable part of your workflow.

   Master It   Add revisions to your project that automatically get tracked on your sheet.

Use digital markups.   DWFs provide a lightweight means to digitally transfer and mark up multiple sheets in a document set.

   Master It   Explain the workflow using DWF markups.

Understand how a builder uses Revit.   We talked about several scenarios where builders might use Revit models during construction.

   Master It   List two ways builders use BIM and the immediate benefits of each method.

Chapter 22

Revit in the Classroom

Using Revit in the classroom has particular and unique challenges that differ from using Revit in an architectural design and production environment. First, the design exercises are often deliberately more contrived than they would be in the business environment. It's important that students face the kinds of complex design issues that in the "real" world would often be given to an entire team of people.

Second, the design process needs to be more gestural and discovery based. It needs to be paced and show process in order to give the jury points of discussion and response. Students should get to a point of design and then stop and build consensus rather than go beyond the intention of a particular exercise. Although at first this can be frustrating, in time students learn there's little value in racing to do something twice.

Third, it's often difficult for students to look to outside influences for both technical inspiration and techniques. They feel that if the idea didn't "originate" with them that it can't be valid or as valuable as an idea that was without external influences. This can't be further from the truth, and it's important for students to realize that architecture is often an expression of aggregate ideas. They should learn that you can often excel by rigorous observation to get at the important principle at the core of a particular design expression.

Fourth, a studio is a hectic place, and professors often view technology as a shortcut to lazy thinking. So, students should be careful not to use Revit in a way that expresses they were not engaged with the design idea. Just because a particular technology allows them to do something faster doesn't mean that it allows them to do something better. Students need to be aware that it's important to be rigorous with their design tools instead of a pencil or a computer.

And finally, a studio is a highly competitive environment. Seeing the work of others can be both inspiring and threatening. The important thing is that this culture forces students to try harder, to work smarter, and to be prepared to do more than they thought possible at the beginning of another semester in studio.

That's what this chapter is all about. If you're a student learning to use Revit for the first time or looking for ideas and inspiration to help you push your Revit skill beyond where you thought possible, this chapter is just what you need.

In this chapter, you'll learn to:

- ◆ Develop a workflow for Revit
- ◆ Overcome common objectives
- ◆ Challenge yourself as a student

Revit in the Studio Environment

ABOUT THE CONTRIBUTING AUTHORS: ADAM THOMAS AND JEREME SMITH

Adam Thomas and Jereme Smith currently study architecture and business administration at Southern Polytechnic State University in Atlanta, Georgia. Together, they operate the BIM and design-focused website www.archdesignlabs.com. Additionally, they create video tutorials that are hosted as podcasts on iTunes, and they're both working part-time in design practices—all this while being full-time students!

They believe that being architecture students who live and breathe BIM gives them a particularly unique and valuable insight. Not everyone can be as dedicated to teaching students about programs such as Revit for use in design applications. It takes a lot of time, effort, and patience, but they find the results rewarding.

Both Thomas and Smith heard about Revit a few years before either had even finished high school. But it wasn't until their second year studying architecture that their interest in BIM started to increase. After a few brainstorming sessions, they decided to push to use Revit for all their studio projects.

They were enthusiastic—but also in for a shock. By their third year, they decided that Revit wasn't being used to think about design in an integrated, holistic manner. Initially, they were discouraged but found the challenge interesting. As a result, they successfully developed a unique process and approach for using Revit in architecture school. They call their approach the "Three Ds of Revit."

In addition to Revit, they integrate and teach other design programs, including Photoshop, Illustrator, Bentley MicroStation, form*Z, SketchUp, 3ds Max, and Autodesk Impression. Although this is a broad list of applications to be responsible for from an implementation standpoint, they strongly believe there are far more advantages than disadvantages.

The advantages are numerous. First, student-to-student relationships are more personal and allow for more intense discussion. Next, since they're working with fellow students, everyone is more comfortable and finds it easier to relate to the design challenges and rigors of architecture school because they've recently been in the same situation.

But there are a few disadvantages. Since everyone is a student, the lack of hierarchy is particularly challenging. And, of course, architecture students have no short supply of opinions! Finally, students usually lack real-world experience—just because you can model it in the computer and the results look really sexy doesn't mean it will work in the real world!

The following sections describe Thomas and Smith's "Three Ds of Revit" approach. Ultimately, it's important to note that you don't consider the following sections to be an overly prescriptive step-by-step process with no alternatives. Rather, consider this a guide—a "template for modification and manipulation that welcomes the idea of abstraction and degeneration."

The Three Ds of Revit

While contemplating how to incorporate Revit in an architectural studio environment, Thomas and Smith soon found themselves running into many problems with Revit when used "out of the box." For whatever reason, there was a tendency for design students using Revit for the first time to begin using it in an almost counterproductive way. Essentially, these students were allowing Revit to do the designing for them.

For example, Revit has a stair template. But this shouldn't mean that each project should use that same standard stair. Or just because the default height of walls is 10′ tall does not mean every space in your project should have a 10′ ceiling height. Observing these tendencies for design students to use Revit without understanding its full potential initially created a lot of frustration.

This is because students who don't approach Revit with an appreciation for its real potential often misrepresent to other students as well (not to mention professors) the potential advantages of using BIM. So, with this in mind Thomas and Smith set out to correct the way Revit is utilized and taught and implemented in the classroom. After a lot of patience and effort, Thomas and Smith arrived at what they call the "Three Ds of Revit": design, develop, and demonstrate. Overall, it's a straightforward and ultimately successful approach to teaching Revit integrated design. It may seem strange to narrow Revit (which is such a dynamic program) down to just three simple concepts. But in architecture, according to Thomas and Smith, even the most complex ideas can be reduced to simple principles, concepts, and illustrations.

Once you start to follow these concepts closely, you begin to understand the underlying logic of using Revit Architecture in an educational design environment. Not only will this aid your design process and efforts, ultimately you'll become more productive. Yet your designs will be more complex, resolved, and satisfying.

So, what is Thomas and Smith's "Three Ds of Revit" all about? What about all the other books that teach Revit for use in the classroom? They teach something like Figure 22.1.

FIGURE 22.1
Teaching Revit for design production

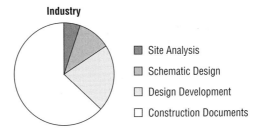

What Thomas and Smith are proposing with the "Three Ds of Revit" approach is a little different. They are suggesting that although using production drawings is important, this isn't taking advantage of BIM. Thomas and Smith believe that a more appropriate BIM approach is to focus on the design and communication process. Overall, it might take the same amount of time, but the value is shifting from production to more design analysis and communication (Figure 22.2).

FIGURE 22.2
Teaching Revit for design communication

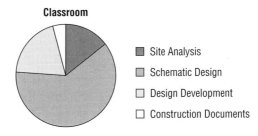

Overall, it's critically important that you learn how to use Revit to work expressively and artistically. You can't allow the technology to think for you but to communicate what you're thinking. Technology should express *that* you create, not necessarily *how* you create. Otherwise, we'll all use the tools to become lazy designers—and our responsibility as architects will inevitably suffer.

The following sections highlight Thomas and Smith's approach to the three Ds.

Design

A question that Thomas and Smith often hear from both new students to architecture school and students who are new to Revit is, "How do you design in Revit?" The answer is simple: massing. But actually, Thomas and Smith believe that a better question would be, "How could I use Revit to enhance communication about my design?"

This is because design is the something that simply cannot be rigidly conformed to a train of thought or even a single application. In their process, Revit should be seen as a tool that is aiding an initial design process. But Revit should never delegate. Never.

Knowing when to navigate to Revit, what to utilize in Revit, and how to express your design concepts externally becomes imperative to a productive ongoing design and iteration processes. Through much discussion and practice, Thomas and Smith have determined areas where Revit can help during your design process.

Believe it or not, as much as Thomas and Smith love computers—they stress to classmates over and over that Revit cannot replace what raw hand sketching and physical modeling can do—there's just no one "right" answer. All of these tools are an important part of the design discovery process. So what Thomas and Smith stress is that in the right hands, Revit can help to show both qualitative and quantitative experiences. Communicating these principles in either hand sketching or physical model massing is difficult. But this step is often necessary before you use Revit to finalize both at the same time.

MASSING

The Massing tool is single-handedly one of the most powerful yet often underutilized tools in Revit. For whatever reason, students are often compelled to start creating the building out of walls, floors, furniture, entourage, and so on. But it's important that they concentrate on making the "design" first. The walls, floors, and so on, will come later (Figure 22.3).

FIGURE 22.3
Even simple massing communicates design intent.

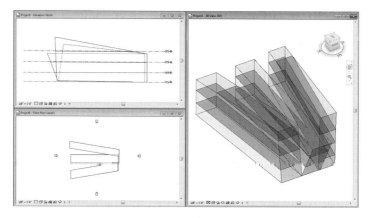

The reason massing works so well during this early design process is because it allows the users to quickly show the quality of the space and form they are trying to envision. It allows them to create a believable metaphor without becoming too literal too soon. The Massing tool allows you to utilize solids and voids to create a volumetric space, from which views and plans can be extruded to produce schematic plans, sections, perspectives, and so forth. Those drawings can then be printed and used as trace overlays for further exploration with digital and analog tools. This is covered in more detail in the advanced modeling and massing tutorials of Chapter 9, "Advanced Modeling and Massing."

The advantages of using these reference drawings in the design phase create an enhanced understanding of the initial concept. The design is more refined as the accuracy of scale and proportion are increased. Ultimately, those highly resolved masses should be used in the development phase for both applied context as well as detail.

This overall massing process eliminates a lot of the wasted time students usually spend on dozens of models unable to be leveraged into anything substantial.

 Real World Scenario

EXAMPLE WORKFLOW

The following is a typical example of how Thomas and Smith approach a design massing workflow that is both analog and digital—in their own words.

We want design to be an open-ended process. Keep in mind that any of the examples may be taken out of sequence or even repeated in a different order based on your own design approach.

PROGRAM ANALYSIS/SPATIAL RELATIONS

When you are first given a project, the first thing you should do as a student is familiarize yourself with the program. We encourage our students to not "jump in" too soon. Consider spatial percentages and color-coding systems, and slowly begin a bubble diagram that also takes into account the requirements and steps needed to complete the project. Remember that even at this early stage this is an iterative process.

HAND SKETCHING

Throughout the process you should continuously sketch gestural ideas that communicate the development of your thinking. And keep in mind that those same sketches will be used for inspiration or referencing when translating to Revit for use as underlays as you move between analog and digital tools (as shown here):

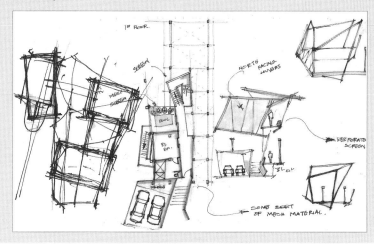

SITE STUDIES

Important relationships (and even restrictions) such as setbacks and major circulation routes around the site should be assessed at this stage. It's important that you start to relay sight lines and building datum. Panoramas and other visual studies of the actual site should be sketched and calculated intuitively before creating representation in the computer. This will help you carefully consider site proportions and context before turning to the computer for a digital representation.

ROUGH MASSING MODELS: ANALOG

Since the level of scale and detail will still be quite broad, you should also experiment with conceptual studies of your models and in context with the spatial relationships of the site. Consider manually creating rough sectional models made of cardboard, wood, chip board, or any other number of materials.

The great thing about not going to the computer too soon is that your analog methods force you to work slower. Now to some of you, the word *slower* may hold a negative connotation. But what we mean to convey is that working with "inefficient" tools also allows you to be more contemplative. You don't want to rush an idea of what you are trying to mold and shape in Revit (as shown here):

ROUGH MASSING MODELS: DIGITAL

Now you have the opportunity to translate those massing studies and sketches into 3D space and form using Revit's massing tools. Even with early massing you can begin preliminary analysis of spaces, surfaces, views, composition, areas, and so on.

These digital masses also lend themselves to being placed in context on a Revit site by linking each of your different iterations of your RVT projects. Once you set up your camera and views with various lighting settings, you can use the same values with each of your various massing studies to render your views (as shown here):

PRELIMINARY ENVIRONMENTAL STUDIES

Since you want to think of your design in a holistic manner, you should begin to look at the sun and orientation of your contextual studies at the exact location of the site in order to reveal site dynamics of sun and shadow direction and angle. Animated lighting studies and solar radiation studies can yield important results.

Of course, rendering has its advantages. But keep in mind that Revit allows real-time shadow studies. Key dates and times can be placed on views and studied side by side to see the effects a new conceptual high-rise's shadow will have on surrounding buildings (as shown here):

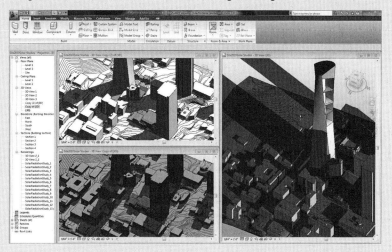

Of course, solar radiation is an important consideration. These studies can be accomplished quickly and easily by using a free plug-in provided by Autodesk Labs at http://labs.autodesk.com/ (as shown here):

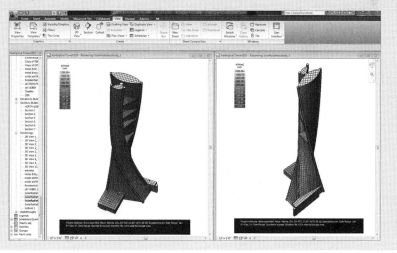

Depending on the complexity of your digital mass, you will probably want to start referencing floor level heights as they relate to the overall building form. Start by creating floor area faces in your massing study and then add your floors by face later. This functionality is particularly useful in large, geometrically complex designs, as the edge of the slab is not something easily coordinated. Fortunately, Revit is able to maintain these relationships for you and your design team.

Once you've created your floor area faces, it's often a good idea to create schedules of floor areas and compare them to the surface and volume areas of your masses. Not only does this ensure that you are within the required square footage but it also can be used to determine ratios of efficiency (how much surface area is being used to contain a given volume). You don't want to go through the effort of creating rooms and tagging them to find out your program isn't going to work at a micro level before you've checked it at a macro level first. However, if your project is particularly small, floor area faces may not be necessary as room schedules are more useful in smaller projects. The individual spaces can simply be compared to whole floor plates.

DIGITAL AND ANALOG

In our experience we want to make it clear that it's not about "digital versus analog." It's more about finding elegant ways of allowing both to coexist and complement the other. So after multiple iterations and studies, it's usually a great idea to print out scaled plans as underlays for further plan- and section-specific iterations and investigation with the freedom provided by hand drawing and trace overlays.

Staring at a blank screen to create a "hard" or "finished"-looking iteration can be unrewarding. We've found that after numerous rough ideas are worked on by hand, all of those same drawings can be scanned and imported into Revit. Using the Scale command, you can ensure an accurate scale. Simply create multiple views of your floor plan for each of your scanned iterations (as shown here):

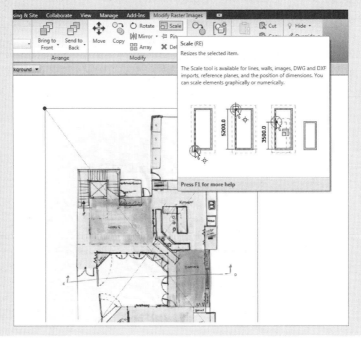

Once they are imported and scaled, don't think that you have to start using specific wall types to define your spaces. Although this may seem counterintuitive at first (because you might have to change them later), you'll find that it's quite freeing. It allows you to think more about the nature of the space and less about the walls. We recommend using generic wall types to dAaefine both walls and curtain walls (a 1″ thick wall with a transparent material) and openings without frames or panels to define doors and windows.

This defines your space and the intent of your design without being too literal. When you decide to be more specific, you know what needs to be resolved to a higher level of detail. The results can be quite satisfying and you can keep the analog version within Revit so you can compare it with your digital iteration, since we've found that changes are likely to occur moving from one to the other. It's not likely that your digital reiteration of your analog sketch is going to be a highly literal reinterpretation (as shown here):

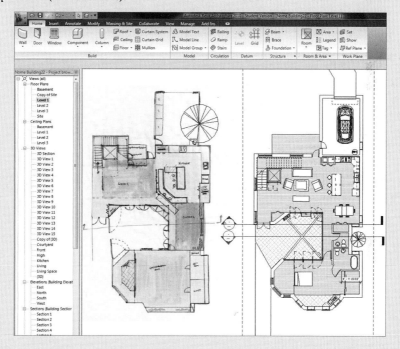

PERSPECTIVE VIEWS

Now that you've worked hard to establish formal and spatial relationships, you'll want to envision that space through perspective cameras or even animated walkthroughs. This will allow you to experience how a sequence of spaces unfolds in an early presentation.

After you've tweaked your design based on the perspective and walkthrough views, you'll be prepared to take your work to a third-party application for laying out boards. Get as much done as you can in Revit—this will save a lot of time later (rather than having to edit your project in a photo-editing tool). But don't think that you'll be able to use Revit alone for creating emotive and elegant layout boards.

First, export or print your generic massing perspectives and interior/exterior views. Some will be rendered, but many will be real-time shaded views (with and without shadows). And even though the initial design phase is complete in the computer, it is important to filter that product back through the hand. You'll often find there are still missing parts of your project that you need to view and embellish that you forgot or were simply not be able to model.

It's our experience that this back and forth between Revit and hand modeling and sketching is nearly always 50/50. One tool or technique tends to balance and complement the other. Besides, if you are not comfortable modeling complex masses in Revit (or in any computer application), you should use your hand skills and then interpret it into Revit once you have a better understanding of its components.

On the other hand, if you have taken the time to better understand the modeling tools in Revit, you can become fairly capable of designing and manipulating more in the computer itself. Another benefit is that working in the computer can often give you the freedom to increase the complexity of the design.

It depends on how comfortable and advanced you are with Revit; it is better to iron out some of those details in drawing and making forms before inputting into Revit. Many times how you model something in Revit is related to how it will be assembled in construction. Utilizing those rough-drawn details often helps you detail in Revit much more easily.

The design process is not straightforward. There will be instances where you have to go back and completely rethink your process after seeing the final product. Or you may have to keep going from hand to computer to hand back again to computer. This can easily be accomplished in Revit without losing much time. You may even have to return to the design phase after completing items in the develop phase. Design essentially never ends and should always be fresh in your mind.

Develop

As you move from early design and begin to develop your ideas, you'll find that you will begin to provide more subjective context. You'll add features and details that others can use to connect with your design on a personal level. But be careful, because you only need to model what is important. You can carry this step too far too soon.

For example, let's say you've designed a residential project that is solely created from recycled materials. Is it more important to show the exterior context of the recycled materials or the bathrooms inside the home? This is a difficult question to answer – even though it seems like such a straightforward question. The reason is that this level of detail is often too much information and too soon in your design process. Thomas and Smith say they've seen many students get so caught up in making things look "nice" that they forget or lose sight of their design intention.

Now expand this principle on a large, complex, and highly technical exercise, and you'll see how getting immersed in the details too soon can slow you down. This is particularly true when you consider the computing resources of a typical architectural student. Your laptop can't handle dozens of carefully laid-out and geometrically detailed 3D restrooms, especially when your design only needs to indicate them in a few plans.

So, you don't want to overly detail your project because it's likely just going to slow your computer down. But more importantly, it's going to slow your process down. You'll have created far too much "clutter" in your presentations. Finally, adding all this detailing takes valuable time that you simply can't waste in order to finish your project.

CREATING CUSTOM CONTENT

Once you have finished your schematic design, you are going to want to start developing, but not overdeveloping, the most important parts of your model. Unfortunately, this is the stage that most people start to let the computer just *tell* them what to do. The result will leave jurors simply scratching their heads and wondering why you are saying one thing but showing something completely different. Many times Thomas and Smith say they've seen people tell their teachers that the computer simply will not let them create the shape they are thinking about. But in almost every instance, this certainly wasn't the case.

Usually this comes down to being able to create custom shapes, forms, and content that are critical to rigorous design. Revit is never going to be able to create all these unique design elements for you. So, you'd better get started understanding how to create them yourself. The following are just a few of the important areas where creating custom content can turn a mediocre design into something special:

Curtain Panels   A common misconception with new Revit users, according to Thomas and Smith, is that you can only create walls in Revit that are preloaded into the program. That means you can only create normal-looking exterior and interior finishes, and that is simply not the case. Another thing Thomas and Smith hear all the time is that you can't create slanted, angled, or curved walls when using Revit. Another commonly heard objection is "I can't create my own custom mullion or glass system."

However, it is quite simple to create different wall configurations and forms. The most straightforward method is to start with a mass. Thomas and Smith believe that for any shape you can mass, you can create basic, complex, or curtain walls to conform to that mass. Figure 22.4 is just one of the examples of how Thomas and Smith make Revit work for them.

FIGURE 22.4
Custom curtain panels

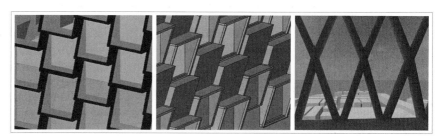

Structures   One of the strangest statements Thomas and Smith say they've heard is that Revit is only a parametric building modeler. The key word is *building*, but Revit can be used to create so much more than just buildings. They tell people all the time that if you can dream it, you can use Revit to create it. Figure 22.5 shows a bridge completed only in Revit; this was simple to take from the schematic phase all the way through final rendering. The possibilities are endless—just let your mind take control and allow yourself to make Revit work for you (Figure 22.6).

FIGURE 22.5
Bridge structural and material iterations

FIGURE 22.6
Completed
rendering

Furniture and Details   Just remember that designing the building isn't going to be enough. The detail that goes into the building and the detail of the components that you place within the building are meant to demonstrate your ability create a well-resolved solution.

This means that you'll have to become familiar with the Family Editor. You'll be able to take your projects to new levels of uniqueness and understanding by creating your own furniture, railings, columns, mullions, and many other objects (Figure 22.7). You simply can't use the out-of-the-box content by the time you are into the develop phase.

By adding custom families, you prove that you understood your project and cared about your project so much that you created every detail (Figure 22.8).

FIGURE 22.7
Creating custom
furniture

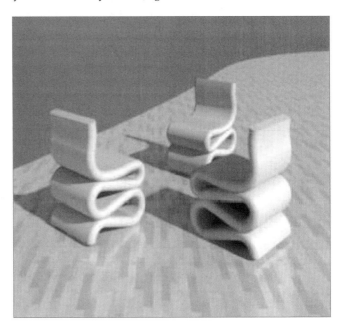

It seems that no matter how little Thomas and Smith sleep and how long they work, there's never enough time to finish a design idea. But as time is running out and your projects are still looking for a little extra, Thomas and Smith have found that taking an out-of-the-box family and editing it to resemble what you are thinking about is an easy way to add more clarity to your design and allow jurors to look at your project rather than being distracted by your use of fully out-of-the-box doors and windows.

FIGURE 22.8
Custom shelving and casework for a library project

Materials and Patterns   According to Thomas and Smith, the easiest way to make a project uniquely yours is to edit the materials and render appearances of everything you use. There is no excuse for using stock colors and render patterns from preset walls and families when Revit contains hundreds of other rendering patterns that come with the program.

If you want your walls to be aluminum instead of brick, make them aluminum and pick the actual color and pattern you want the aluminum to be. When you're finished with your project, you should be able to go back and know that you made a conscientious decision to include every pattern and color you see and stand by those decisions proudly (Figure 22.9).

FIGURE 22.9
Mobile medical
lab project

Demonstrate

According to Thomas and Smith, there comes a point in every design process that you must take what you have designed and present it in a deep, meaningful, yet easy-to-understand way. This is the point that you need to start refining and pulling your drawings out of Revit for integration into other programs like 3ds Max, Photoshop, Illustrator, and Impression. As great as Revit is for design and production, architecture is often about communicating the emotive, intangible impressions of your design. Before you export your views and renderings, there are a few things that you want to do.

EDITING LINE WEIGHTS

Creating and editing your own line weight gives more depth to your drawings and provides a clearer level of understanding to your project. Sometimes these settings can be captured in a template and applied to a view or project. But even then, you'll likely want to make exceptions within a single view in order to accentuate a particularly important part of your design (Figure 22.10).

You'll also want to add a sense of scale and proportion. And while Revit has 3D Entourage like people, trees, and cars, these will show up throughout your project, which is not always desirable. We've found that a better process is to embellish your views with 2D detail content that is already oriented to your views and won't clutter up other views of your project. Two-dimensional content can come from your Revit library, but it can also come from a screen capture of your favorite "sketchy" 3D program or even a scan of a hand sketch that you created. Remember to save these images as PNG files to give them transparent backgrounds.

EXPLODED AND DIAGRAMMATIC VIEWS

Don't forget to create a variety of views of the drawings you need, like exploded axons, and 3D sections, section perspectives, plans, callouts, and renderings. Keep in mind that copying the view and manipulating visibility and material settings will allow you to sequence the design and discovery process that you need to communicate to the jurors.

FIGURE 22.10
Adding scale to
2D views

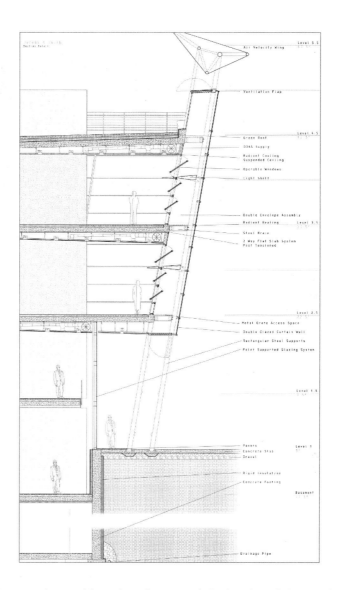

Diagramming in Revit can be quickly and easily accomplished with visibility graphics. The simple shortcut VG gives you the ability to filter, prioritize, and distill important information in your project. One example is a series of exploded axons showing all the components of a pre-fabricated home created by simply manipulating the visibility graphics; Figure 22.11 shows an example by student Brenton Klopp.

Colors, material, and transparency can also be manipulated using either the automated grouping of similar elements by category or by selecting individual components you want to express (Figure 22.12). After adjusting in Revit, the images can be exported to Photoshop for composition or even kept in Revit and composed on a sheet.

FIGURE 22.11
Prefab design
project by
Brenton Klopp

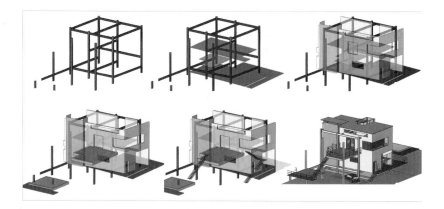

FIGURE 22.12
Stacked and
exploded views

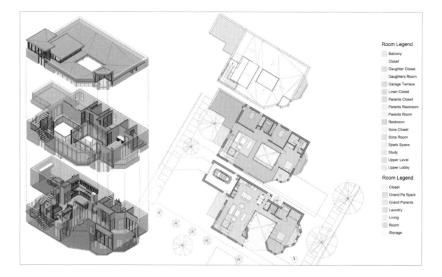

Studio Tips and Tricks

A very wise New Zealander once said:

> *Even fools can learn from their own stupid mistakes. The real trick is to learn from the
> mistakes of some other poor bastard.*

R. G. McKinley

Isn't that the truth? An architectural studio can be a wonderful, rewarding, and yet incredibly stressful place. This advice will carry you far in architectural school and probably your career in architectural practice.

The students with the best design ideas are easily overwhelmed with having to hone presentation and communication techniques. Many times the best design suffers from poor presentation.

What students fail to realize is that their design doesn't stop with the design of their project. They also must take into account the design of the communication of their design. Both should be well planned ahead of time—because at the end of the day, there's simply no faster way to design than in Revit. But if you don't plan ahead and incorporate time-saving techniques, your overall experience will suffer. Therefore, it's important to share some critical but often overlooked tips and tricks that work well in the architectural studio environment. The following sections highlight Thomas and Smith's tips for students.

Multiwindowing

With the advent of cheaper computer hardware, students have the ability to purchase larger, more complex computer systems. Some of these systems include multiple monitors. A useful, often overlooked tool in Revit is the Tile Windows command. To tile multiple views of the model or other projects side by side, select the View tab and select Tile (Figure 22.13). This functionality is covered in more detail in Chapter 2, which discusses the principles and UI of Revit.

Keep in mind that these views are active, allowing you to see changes made in plan, section, and vice versa in real time. This is important because in design you should always be thinking about the implications of your design in multiple dimensions.

This approach works with any number or type of views because of the parametric relationships between all views, sheets, and schedules. Although Revit does not have a multimonitor setting, a great fix is to simply take the program out of full screen mode and then stretch the single window across all your monitors. You can then place and resize multiple project views across all your monitors (Figure 22.14).

FIGURE 22.13
Tile Window function

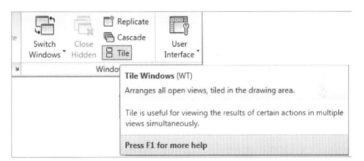

FIGURE 22.14
Tile Window across multiple monitors

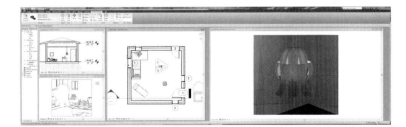

Duplicate, Duplicate, Duplicate

It's important to duplicate all your settings and views before proceeding to a new idea. The reason is that after putting in hours of work and finally coming to the end of your project, you will need to start producing your boards for design review. And if you have not duplicated your important ideas before moving on, you will have lost all the example iterations that got you to where you are before review. You don't just want to communicate your *destination*. You need to communication the *trip* as well.

In addition to duplicating settings and views, you'll want to duplicate geometry as well. These duplicates can live as separate families (Component or In-Place), in linked projects, or within different design options. A common mistake when using Revit's massing environment is to simply manipulate one mass or idea without duplicating the results. You must remember to duplicate finished ideas before further manipulating your last mass into another significantly different idea. Duplicating content, whether masses, host families, or system families, is covered in much more detail in Chapter 15, which discusses the Family Editor.

At this stage it's not going to stress your computer to copy your masses over and over again. If you don't duplicate your ideas, it will prevent you from returning to previous concepts and developing them if you decide to take an important change in direction. The massing studies shown in Figure 22.15 were duplicated before any major changes to form and parameters to ensure the ability to return to previous ideas.

FIGURE 22.15
Duplicating multiple massing options

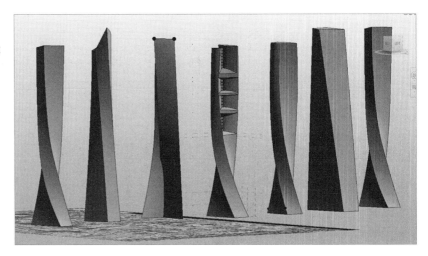

Level of Detail

As you finish your project, it is increasingly important to know when and how to detail your project. The most important thing to remember is not to detail everything in your model, because it is not necessary for rendering purposes and it takes time to detail your project. To learn more how the level of detail is determined and managed, refer to Chapter 15, which discusses the Family Editor.

When you start to detail your project, think of the areas that are most important and set up all the views you want to be displayed during your final presentation. Then only increase the level of detail in the areas that you have noted to be important features in your design. If you're particularly pressed for time, only increase the detail in parts of the model that you can see once rendered. Otherwise, you're spending time adding detail that won't even be clear to the jurors.

When creating content that will significantly increase the level of detail in a single model, always test the content in another empty test file first. View it in plan, elevation, section, and 3D views and render it as well. This will indicate whether the level of detail you're creating is worth the effort to duplicate when you transfer the family into the actual project.

Multiple Models

On particularly large projects, it may be helpful to separate repetitive portions of your design as distinct projects and then link them together in Revit. This will allow you to quickly and easily control the visibility of large portions of your projects. Linking large projects is covered in Chapter 15.

Revit is unique in that it's really the only "Whole Building BIM" application that can integrate the architecture, structure, mechanical, site, and documentation design elements into a single file. But given our computers as students, it's sometimes a lot of information to put into a single file and keep it all manageable. So don't feel embarrassed if you put each of these elements in separate files and then link them together.

Visualization Options

Rendering is much more than making a photorealistic image. What you're attempting to do is create an impression by communicating more than the sum of all the parts. Students forget this, and Thomas and Smith believe this is where a lot of students struggle.

Rendering should be considered as much as an art as a science. The challenge is that students are comfortable (at first) with letting the computer figure out the realistic quality of the rendering and then thinking that they're done. This isn't enough.

Sometimes you may want a photorealistic rendering. But in many other cases (especially early in design), this can be distracting. Don't be afraid to experiment with Revit's built-in rendering. But don't be afraid to try other rendering and visualization tools that exist as other applications.

EXPORTING

Yes, Revit is an amazing design tool. But you need to remember that Revit also gives you the option to easily export to a number of different 2D and 3D programs. For example, if you feel more comfortable detailing in 2D in AutoCAD, Thomas and Smith encourage you to export your Revit file to DXF or DWG. If you are more familiar with embellishing, detailing, and rendering in 3ds Max, then you should use that tool. The point is not to feel as though you cannot use any program except Revit. Stay smart and use Revit to your strengths and use other programs when necessary.

Once you have created all the drawings you need, export the absolute best drawings you can to help you once you get into third-party programs. According to Thomas and Smith, you can use a number of programs in order to do postproduction work on your project images and drawings. Each application has its advantages and disadvantages:

Autodesk Impression   The first program is Autodesk Impression, which allows you to quickly create stylized images. Once finished with Impression, it is often best to save the images out and compose and edit them in either Photoshop or Illustrator. Both programs are great for final composition, but students think that these two applications are really the same thing. They are fundamentally different. Photoshop has a lot more control in some areas than Illustrator, but operates in DPI while Illustrator operates in vectors (Figure 22.16).

FIGURE 22.16
Autodesk
Impression

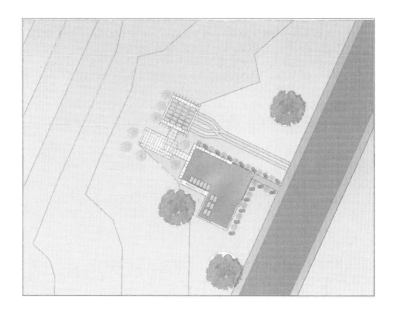

Adobe Photoshop   Adobe Photoshop is a pixel-based software developed primarily to edit photos and images. Photoshop is a useful program for postproduction in many respects. Colors as well as filters can be edited and applied in Photoshop to produce abstract representations of designs. Entourage can also easily be included, though scaling appropriately may be difficult.

Another thing to keep in mind when exporting to Photoshop is using the TIF format for images. Revit allows you to export renderings in the TIF format, which in turn allows you to quickly and professionally remove the background of your exported render. Then when you're using Photoshop, you can easily control and merge a new background for better impact. Rendering the same view multiple times just to get just the "right" sky is incredibly tedious. But selecting an image to underlay in your rendering is very fast and can be easily controlled and manipulated.

This technique is often really useful for "stacking" images that need to show both rendered and documented information like text, sections, and callouts. Once the rendering of a plan, section, or elevation is complete, a great technique is to combine the rendering with an export of your documentation (Figure 22.17).

The images and drawings exported from Revit to Adobe Illustrator are great. But unfortunately, Illustrator lacks a lot of the image-editing features of Photoshop. In terms of complete control over linework, line quality, and line weights, Illustrator is number one. On the other hand, when it comes to renders and pixel-based images, Photoshop is the best program to use.

3ds Max   For advanced users, it can be beneficial to export Revit models to 3D Studio Max. This will give you the most control when it comes to render settings. Also, creating complex animations that are detailed (even allowing animations of objects and other effects) is far more impressive than the simple walkthroughs that are possible in Revit. So if you are willing to learn another application at a level at least as deep as you'll need to know Revit for design, we recommend learning 3D Studio Max for visualization. Fortunately, Revit templates are available in standard 3D Studio Max and 3D Studio Max design for easy transfer of your project (Figure 22.18).

FIGURE 22.17
Combining rendering and documentation, courtesy of Jonathan Pharis

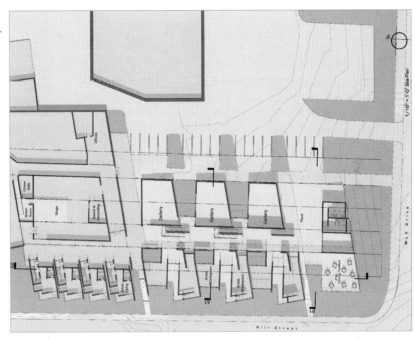

FIGURE 22.18
Hotel project modeled in Revit and rendered in 3D Max

Rendering

When it comes to rendering, there are a few essentials any student should keep in mind. First, you need to realize that time and quality are inversely proportional. Your life as an architecture student has enough compromises with regard to time. Plan to plan. Thomas and Smith say they're often asked which tool is best for this. Their suggestion? Excel. You need to get used to listing what you're going to do and assign reasonable amounts of time to each task. Back this out of the deadline and now you know when to start. If you tend to need more time, take the results and multiply by some number larger than one.

In the studio environment, everything you do is likely dependent on something else. Such dependencies are crucial when it is close to deadline. Here are a few things to keep in mind in regard to time and quality.

No matter what you are rendering, Thomas and Smith have found that the setting Exterior: Sun Only is going to be your fastest render in terms of lighting schemes. Interior: Artificial Plus Natural is going to take considerably longer due to the number of lights and their complexity (Figure 22.19).

FIGURE 22.19
Fast lighting settings

Pay particular attention to your clip plane as well as your section box. Many times Revit will render everything in the scene when all you need is a certain room. This becomes especially important when rendering large design projects.

The type of materials, their size, and number of cutouts can affect the render time. For instance, a 10′ wall covered in an aluminum screen will take a lot longer to render than the same wall covered in simple matte paint of any color. This is due to Revit having to calculate light passing through all the holes of the screen versus a simple flat surface (Figure 22.20).

A good rule of thumb when it comes to rendering quality versus time is to keep the uncompressed image size around a 10MB file size. The number will change depending on camera view size and the printer quality. But this is important for those of you working on laptops.

FIGURE 22.20
Some materials will render faster than others.

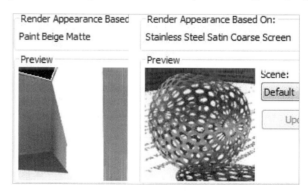

When it comes to powerful desktops, you may be able to select a larger image when necessary. We recommend that in most cases keep it under 10MB for a manageable render time (Figure 22.21).

Thomas and Smith say they've found that the render setting High is your best all-around setting. In their experience, the amount of improvement given with a Best render is minuscule compared to the added time necessary to accomplish it, considering that it can often be two or three times as long as the High quality render setting. And always wait to do high renderings for final presentations. They typically use Draft and Low to test lighting and placement before rendering at the High setting (Figure 22.22).

FIGURE 22.21
Keep images under 10MB.

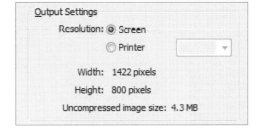

FIGURE 22.22
Set your render quality to High for finished renderings in Revit.

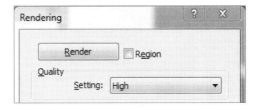

Another frequently overlooked setting is the Adjust Exposure option. This is a helpful feature, especially for a rendering at night and with artificial lighting. In many cases, an image might come out black in a Nighttime or Artificial Only setting. Don't delete the resulting image as faulty until after you've tried adjusting the exposure values (Figure 22.23). Rendering and visualization are covered in more detail in Chapter 12.

FIGURE 22.23
The exposure settings shouldn't be overlooked.

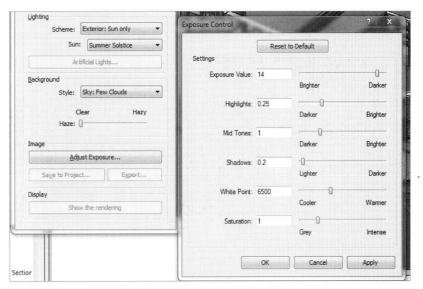

Student Projects

This section showcases projects that several students have completed in order to show just how much can be done with Revit if you put your mind to it.

Jereme Smith

This project is a third-year assignment and was essentially a nature center focused on the juxtaposition between man and nature (Figure 22.24). Smith says, "In my design I saw this juxtaposition not as a man versus nature scenario, but a dialogue between the two. Literally speaking, man is nature, and thus anything made by man is theoretically speaking nature. Therefore, the difference between the two becomes the process of manipulation of natural elements to create something that may appear less natural, or altered."

FIGURE 22.24
Nature center

He continues, "In my design I sought to create a space that would act as a buffer or transitional space between the manipulated and the nonmanipulated, the disturbed and the undisturbed; a space foreshadowing that of the natural environment it is set in. The building becomes a rite of passage between the man-made and the non-man-made" (Figure 22.25).

Adam Thomas

This project was a recycled home completed in Third Year Studio, where students were to reenvision the modern home to incorporate many "green" technologies (Figure 22.26). Thomas says, "Revit was used to create the entire building inside and out, and complex families were used to create the recycled blocked skin that served as a thermal mass for the home" (Figure 22.27).

FIGURE 22.25
Axonometric
parts

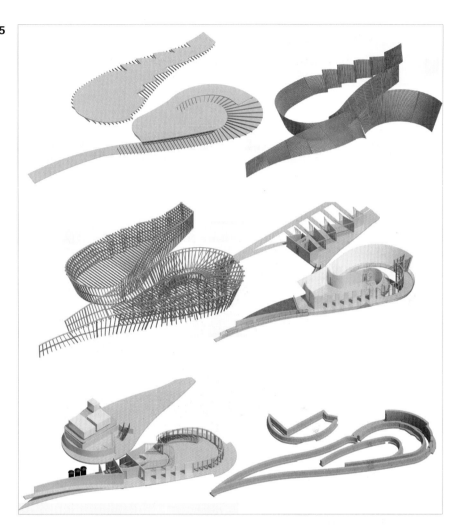

FIGURE 22.26
Recycled house

FIGURE 22.27
Interior
rendering

 Real World Scenario

OVERCOMING COMMON OBJECTIONS

Thomas and Smith explain, in their own words, what to do if you meet objections from professors.

Not every professor embraces technology as fast as students do. And although some professors see technology as a positive and contributing tool to the design process, we've seen many professors biased, if not openly hostile, to using computers in their classrooms.

To those students who are currently in situations where using the computer is frowned on, here's what we tell many of our students and classmates: don't shy away from important and valuable knowledge that can have such a positive impact on your life as a student and your career in architecture.

Always continue to learn and expand your knowledge of the computer, embrace its advantages, and understand its disadvantages. Do not let the professor dictate your own method of design. The field of architecture is one that is very subjective. What one professor sees as a horrible idea, another sees as intriguing. This does not suggest that any project is a great one in the right eyes, but what it does suggest is that if the process and fundamental elements are in place, it has the potential to become a successful design, regardless of what someone else thinks of the technology using to express it behind it. What's important is that you embrace design as a rigorous process. Don't use the computer to be less rigorous and thoughtful. Use the computer to be far more rigorous and interested than otherwise.

The same goes for Revit and its implementation. If used properly in the correct situations, it will be beneficial. Learning when those instances occur is part of your own personal discovery. What we have done in the past when restricted is use Revit for our own exploration and analysis in *addition* to the requirements. It is simply easier to understand things in a 3D environment.

For final presentation boards, we reference plans and sections as well as perspectives done in Revit to ensure accuracy. This is not cheating—it's our design, after all. These drawings are detailed—we use only massing and light studies to help with proportion, depth, and scale. All of the final boards are redone by hand by using underlying Revit drawings as references. Then we add details where needed.

Do not get this process confused with simply tracing. Tracing is a passive act that does not require a critical eye. Referencing is an active process that requires you to continually reflect on and refresh your procedure.

The computer is not going to go away—it's just going to evolve. In fact, we believe the use of the computer and its integration into the fields of architecture, engineering, and so on is going to increase exponentially. We as students should embrace this. It is now the task of the student, the architect, and the professor to collaborate, teach, learn, and discuss. We should embrace the overall technology of the design process. Otherwise, we should give up our position as architects to those who *are* willing to work with the computer to create wonderful, amazing projects.

Omar Foster

The program for this design called for a dwelling that would accommodate a couple and was to be integrated within the structure of an existing bridge. Foster's intent was to invert the seeming stable and logical structural appearance of a dwelling place and a bridge. He conceptualized the design by flipping a structural model upside down and warping the structural elements (Figure 22.28).

Revit was instrumental in bringing the design to fruition on three fronts. First, Revit helped create numerous digital studies models, communicating the integration of structural expression and interior space. Second, it created a 3D base master file; the designer was able to go through many more iterations than possible if he'd had to create physical models of every iteration. Third, Revit allowed the designer to create a far more comprehensive finished product. Revit allowed Foster to work in a holistic, iterative manner, rather than working in a linear method of physical studies, refining physical studies, producing floor plans, sections, elevations, renderings/perspectives, and so on (Figure 22.29).

FIGURE 22.28
Bridge house detail

FIGURE 22.29
Overall elevation

FIGURE 22.29
Overall elevation

Jonathan Pharis

This project featured the adaptive reuse of an existing structure. An art gallery sought to expand their present offices into a complex that catered to a group of artists' creative needs and interests. The existing building was modified and expanded, using the same structural grid and similar materials (Figure 22.30). Ultimately, the redistribution of materials about the extended structure became a pivotal feature of the design and sequencing of the spaces (Figure 22.31).

FIGURE 22.30
Overall site and
exterior views

FIGURE 22.31
Interior light
and detail

Brenton Klopp

The intent of Klopp's building design is to be a fashion museum in Tokyo, Japan. The idea behind the design was to create a rigid geometric underlay with a seemingly free-form and free-flowing shape. The building itself was created in Revit, and the façade and skin were created in Rhino. Because both programs are completely compatible with each other, the skin was able to go through many iterations while the base model stayed the same. Having a program that can accept many other file formats and have them successfully incorporated into designs is crucial for both computer-generated modeling as well as for school (Figure 22.32).

FIGURE 22.32
Design studies and exterior views

The Bottom Line

Develop a workflow for Revit.   For those interested in getting started with Revit, it's important to establish a workflow in Revit that seamlessly connects you with your design. Don't be afraid to be more deliberate in your approach to technology. Don't just race to finish, or you may find yourself racing to do something twice.

Master It   What kind of workflow can you use to get started in Revit? How can you be sure to pace yourself in the rigor of a studio?

Overcome common objections.   If you're a high school student headed for your first studio environment, you will be faced with those who may oppose you and your ideas. Instead of reacting, you'll want to focus on the principle that your professor is trying to communicate. At the same time, you don't want to give up on what is most beneficial to you, your values, and your career.

Master It   When the professor refuses to allow students to use computers and Revit in your studio, what can you do?

Challenge yourself as a student.   The examples shown in this chapter were a good representation of individuals currently in the studio environment producing thoughtful, well-researched, context-sensitive projects utilizing Revit. Fourth-year or even third-year students did many of the projects shown. Many of these students have the potential to redefine the way we use and see Revit and the design process.

Master It   The design process can become introspective, singular, and artificial when so much design actually produces little more than paper. What can you do to challenge yourself as a student? What can you do to push yourself?

Chapter 23

Revit and Virtualization

Virtualization isn't just about running Windows applications on Mac hardware. It's about maximizing your computing investment by running multiple operating systems and applications simultaneously. Running virtualized operating systems also helps protect your host computing environment by isolating the virtual machines from the host machine and each other, which is great for testing new versions of software and isolating programming efforts (rather than risk testing on the host machine). In addition, virtualization takes full advantage of multicore environments.

A multicore processor is like having multiple computers in one PC. Running Revit on VMS means that when one computer-intensive task starts, you'll still be able to manage other tasks. For example, while rendering your project in one VM, you can create a family component in another, while saving your project to the central file on another VM—all at the same time.

Until recently, Autodesk didn't officially support running its applications in virtualization. But this changed in the fall of 2009 when official support was announced. Although most components of virtualization run at nearly full speed, emulated graphics for 3D-intensive applications are certainly a challenge for virtual environments. However, there have been some recent and exciting developments in this area that are removing even the most stringent barriers to adoption. In this chapter, you'll learn to:

◆   Understand the benefits of virtualization

◆   Take advantage of virtualization

What Is Virtualization?

ABOUT THE CONTRIBUTING AUTHOR: PETER STREIBIG

Peter Streibig holds a bachelor of science degree in architecture from the University of Virginia and has over 10 years' experience in architecture. He manages and coordinates information and communication technology. His role is particularly challenging: incorporating emerging technologies in a high-profile and high-design firm. He also understands the importance of keeping the emphasis on architecture while maintaining a stable, approachable, and sophisticated (mixed-platform) computing environment.

Virtualization was originally pioneered more than 40 years ago by IBM in order to distribute costly mainframe resources and run multiple applications. At the time, computers were far too expensive to be tied up computing single tasks. Virtualization allowed the host computer to run many more "virtual" computers at the same time—duplicates of the host computer. Pretty cool!

Eventually the necessity and cost of maintaining expensive, distributed computing decreased, so eventually virtualization was no longer necessary. The decrease in mainframe computing coincided with advances in personal computers (PCs). And personal computing meant that end users finally had the ability to run both their operating system and their applications locally, right at their desk—on their personal computer. So, in some aspects, computing was becoming more and more "decentralized." Another viewpoint is that they've actually become "hyper-centralized," because nearly everyone has a computer right at their desk!

By today's standards, early PCs were quite primitive. "Top-of-the-line" personal computers came with a 60MHz processor and a 250MB hard drive. Only 15 years later, the phone in your pocket probably has a 400MHz processor (a more than 6 increase) and an 8GB hard drive (a more than 30 increase in capacity).

As for today's personal computing, processor speeds once measured in megahertz (MHz) are now measured in gigahertz (GHz), and single processing systems have given way to processors that may in turn contain multiple "cores." This means that a single processor system may be composed of two or more independent cores. And it's not uncommon to have computers with multiple processors. That's a lot of computing power. And in many cases, it's a lot of underused computing power.

Did you know that you might actually have a computer with multiple processors, each of which contains multiple cores? That means you effectively have many potential computing environments. For example, if your computer contains two quad-core processors, you potentially have eight simultaneous computing environments!

You're probably beginning to understand why virtualization is making a comeback. Those 40-year-old computing principles are being applied to personal computing. A multicore CPU will allow applications to run simultaneously and faster (within a single operating system). Virtualization allows multiple operating systems to run concurrently on the same computer.

This is because each VM is allocating the physical resources of the multiprocessor/core computer while "virtualizing" other physical hardware resources required by an operating system. So each virtualized session contains its very own operating system—Windows, Linux, and so on. And within those virtualized operating systems, multiple applications are able to operate.

A lot of great applications run in Windows, but some very industry-specific applications run in Linux. Others may only run in Mac OS X (which is Unix based). Virtualization allows you to create a fantastic best-of-breed solution, where you get to choose not only the application but also the operating system for that application.

WHAT ABOUT MAC OS X?

In September 2009, Autodesk began officially supporting virtualization (including Mac OS X hardware) for a number of Autodesk products: AutoCAD, AutoCAD LT, Autodesk Inventor Professional, 3ds Max, and the Revit platform.

Although both VMware and Parallels can run Autodesk's Windows-based applications, Autodesk and Parallels signed agreements signifying that Parallels would be Autodesk's preferred virtual solution. It should also be noted that Autodesk extended official support to Boot Camp earlier in 2009.

Autodesk already supports five native OS X applications. So, who knows what's in store for Mac users. Maybe even native support for Revit!

Just imagine that not too long ago, radios were AM only, and then later FM, and eventually both AM and FM. Even the first TVs were VHF (channels 2–13) and then later UHF (channels 14–83) was added. But if you wanted AM and FM, or VHF and UHF, you had to buy two radios and two televisions! Well, that certainly seems unimaginable now. Yet now the same goes for personal computing. You no longer have to buy multiple computers to run multiple operating systems because you effectively already have multiple computers in your "one" computer. You're just not taking advantage of them!

Figure 23.1 illustrates this with four concurrent "spaces" in Mac OS X (which is being used as the host computer). In turn, this host computer is running two virtual machines. One of the VMs is of Windows XP, which is running Revit 2010 (upper right). The other VM is running Vista 64, which is running a beta of Revit 2011 (lower right). And at the same time, the upper and lower spaces on the left contain instant messaging sessions, email, web browser, and word processing applications (running on the host computer).

FIGURE 23.1
Multiple virtual machines running on a single host computer

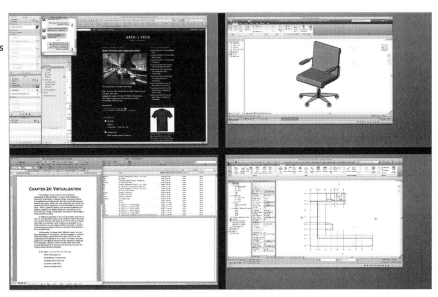

To get started with virtualization, you'll need a computer with multiprocessors (or a single processor with multiple cores). You'll also need to have enough memory to allocate to your host and your guest (or virtual) computers: 4GB of RAM will do nicely. How many real and virtual processors you have will help you determine how many computing environments can run simultaneously. For example, if you have four processing cores and 8GB of RAM (and you want to allocate each computer (real or virtual) at least 2GB of RAM, then you'll be able to run up to four computers at the same time (one host computer and three guest computers).

The Host Computer

The *host* computer is the actual physical machine along with its operating system (OS). Windows, Linux, and Mac OS X may all operate as the host computer and operating system. In turn, the host computer will simply host the virtual OSs. And in turn those virtual operating systems will run their virtualized applications (this is the guest computer). Standard x86 hardware and Intel or AMD architecture may host virtual machines.

The Guest Computer

The *guest* computer is simply a virtual machine. The VM contains the virtual OS, applications, and even user files (like a document, spreadsheet, and so on) all contained in a single file.

The guest may reside on the same hard drive as the host machine. But the guest machine may also be stored (as well as backed up) on another hard drive or even external hard drive or other portable media.

Essentially, each VM exists as a separate, virtual disk image. And yet files on the host machine may be accessed by either the host or guest machine, or vice versa. For example, a Microsoft Word document residing on a host machine (running OS X) may be accessed, opened, and saved by a guest VM running Microsoft XP and Microsoft Office. And the guest VM may contain files accessed by the host machine. It's really quite flexible.

As a result, it's important to keep in mind that the files that you need to access within a VM (or guest machine) need not reside "inside" the VM. Your files may reside on the host machine or even at a location that can be accessed by either the host or the guest, such as a LAN or WAN network drive or even an external hard drive.

Advantages of Virtualization

Basically, it's all about flexibility and being able to select a best-of-breed solution that suits your business and working style. Having to choose one "right" personal computer for work (or your family, for that matter) is a thing of the past. Instead, you can choose one right host—likely the one that suits a majority of your needs. Then you're free to virtualize the other operating systems and applications that you'll run from your host of choice.

IT/Support Advantages

From the standpoint of IT and end-user support issues, there are numerous advantages when allowing end users to utilize virtual environments. First, the rollout of approved disk images is greatly simplified (containing both OS and applications—and even user files and templates if necessary). Everything is self-contained in a single file. Rolling out prebuilt images of VMs can make new installations and upgrades easier, predictable, and far less time-consuming. Even installing operating systems in VMs takes far less time because you're writing the data to RAM.

Another advantage is that the entire OS and all required applications may be quickly restored. In the event of a corrupted hard drive (where the VM resides), a duplicate VM can be replaced in a matter of minutes rather than hours or days. Just copy the at-risk VM to a new hard drive as you would any other file. No reinstalling the OS, applications, user settings, and preferences, and so on—it's all already there in the VM.

If you are in the position of having to support legacy operating systems and applications, then virtualization is a no-brainer. Rather than having to maintain aging hardware, out-of-date operating systems, and legacy applications, you can simply emulate everything in a single file.

This keeps your teams and project managers happy while you don't having to worry about maintaining or replacing aging equipment.

And if you've been in IT for only a short time, it doesn't take long to experience a first-person account of the unintended consequence of a rogue OS or software update or patch that completely ruined an otherwise useful computer! In these cases, two people (at least) are stuck: the person who was until a few moments ago being quite productive and the person who will have to trouble-shoot the computer back into usefulness—in other words, you. Well, virtualized computer software and operating systems can be tested first in virtualization without the risk of impacting the host system.

Finally, networking and hardware connectivity and emulation may be completely isolated from the host machine. This allows for virus containment of the VM without risking the host machine or other virtual machines on the host. Just delete the suspect VM and restore from a backup (or roll the VM back to a previous state).

End-User Advantages

There are also numerous, compelling advantages for the end users running virtual machines. First, computing resources may be easily allocated to the guest OS and applications depending on specific requirements. Of course, 3D-centric applications will need more resources. But word processing and spreadsheets will require far less. Less hardware-demanding applications won't compete with operating systems and applications, which require more resources, and all of this can be defined within the settings of each VM.

Second, customized VMs and applications can be created for individual users quickly and easily. Of course, economies of scale often prevail in large organizations, where choosing the "right" hardware, OS, and applications is paramount. But with virtualization, you can define best-of-breed solutions for your associates and deploy them quickly and easily. This "mass customization" can go a long way toward employee satisfaction. And not only this, but in many cases, portability is also a key concern. So, it's important to keep in mind that a modest external hard drive can contain dozens of virtual machines. Let the end user choose the "computer" that's right for them. And if that computer fails, simply take the portable hard drive to another computer for minimal downtime.

End users may operate multiple VM simultaneously, which takes full advantage of multicore computing resources. Of course, the licensing of operating systems and applications is an important business concern. Yet, network licensing of operating systems and applications allows users to run multiple operating systems and applications at the same time while being fully compliant from a licensing standpoint. The virtual machines simply need to be able to access licenses from the network, which is not much different from how the host computer already operates.

Of course, every computer crashes, even virtual ones! But if an application or OS within a VM crashes, the host OS and remaining VMs are isolated. As a result, your host computer is typically not affected by a crash of the guest computer. The end user simply restarts the virtual machine and its applications.

But even when computers don't crash, it's still pretty easy to tell when they're "struggling" to complete one task before they allow you to start another. This is referred to the "white screen of death"—since your computer simply hangs with a white screen until it's done with whatever it was working on and ready to let you do something else.

When running processor- and memory-intensive applications and processes in virtualization, end users can quickly select another VM and continue working in another application and process, avoiding the dreaded "white screen of death." In other words, although Revit is saving to Central, or completing a rendering in a virtual machine, you're free to work in another virtual machine or the host computer while the task in the VM completes. Multitasking indeed!

And finally, not only will the end users be able to choose the best-of-breed operating system and applications, but as we've illustrated earlier, they'll also be able to run them concurrently! There's no rebooting between operating systems or other sessions. Nor will your end users need to keep multiple computers within arm's reach to multitask. It's all there in one single computer!

Practical Limitations

Just like any computer, there are practical limitations to running virtual computers. Depending on the application that you're running in virtualization, response times are going to be nearly as fast as running it natively—or significantly slower. Real-world experience indicates that bottlenecks in speed tend to occur in applications that are graphically intensive: video, video games, and 3D graphics.

From the standpoint of your host computer, it's important that each of your virtual machines have one (or more) processors preallocated to the virtual machine. This means that every time you start your VM, the host computer will dedicate a processor of your host computer to the VM.

Keep in mind that when your VM is opened, the entire computer—operating system, applications, files—will try to operate in RAM, rather than writing back and forth to your hard drive. So, how much memory you allocate to a VM is really important. But there is a point of "diminished returns" because the more memory that you allocate to the guest machine, the less will be available to the host machine. But since the host machine is responsible for running your virtualization software, the less memory available to your host machine will impact how efficiently your guest machine will run.

The file size being opened by your virtualized application (on your virtual machine) will also impact how efficiently your guest machine runs. Keep an eye on your virtualized task manager. As a rule of thumb, we suggest that you allocate at least 20× in memory of your opened Revit file. So if you have a file that is 100MB in size, you'll want to allocate at least 2GB in memory to that Revit file alone. But keep in mind that you also have the operating system and the application to consider.

Interestingly enough, virtual machines will run nearly as fast as if they were running natively as the host operating system. In some cases that require intensive reading and writing to the physical hard drive, your virtual machine may actually perform better than running on a host machine because in many cases it is faster to write data to RAM. So, where is the bottleneck we all keep reading about? Graphics.

Virtual machines do their best to emulate graphics cards, but just as the VM preallocates dedicated processing, there's no substitute for the "real" thing. Graphics emulation will get you close when it comes to most business applications (word processing, spreadsheets, and so on). But graphics-intensive applications will stress your virtual machine.

What is needed is dedicated graphics. In other words, just like the VM relies on a dedicated, physical processor, a virtual machine that is tasked with running graphically intensive applications could take advantage of dedicated graphics hardware. We'll talk about this later in the chapter when we discuss some exciting recent developments in virtualization.

DEDICATED GRAPHICS THROUGHPUT

In the second half of 2009, Parallels introduced Parallels Workstation Extreme. This software was developed to take particular advantage of HP workstations with multiple, specifically designed graphics cards. Each of these graphics cards is meant to be dedicated to a virtual environment. The result is near-native speeds in a virtualized environment. For many, this will remove the final objection to running graphics-intensive applications (like Revit) in virtualization.

For the time being, this specific hardware solution by Intel and NVIDIA is only available on HP Workstations. But of course this will evolve over time. Many Apple users are hoping this technology will be certified on their hardware. Overall, the ability to design in one environment, while being able to test and analyze in another, will be an exciting culmination with regard to the promise of BIM. Virtualization will allow a best-of-breed solution to flourish, where the best design software may run on Windows and the best analysis software may run in Linux—all managed from a single workstation.

For more information, visit www.parallels.com/products/extreme/.

Creating Virtual Machines

There are two primary methods of creating a virtual machine. You can start from scratch and create a clean installation of your desired operating system (Figure 23.2), or if you already have a computer that you know you want to use, you can convert your physical computer to a virtual one.

FIGURE 23.2
Creating a new virtual machine in Parallels

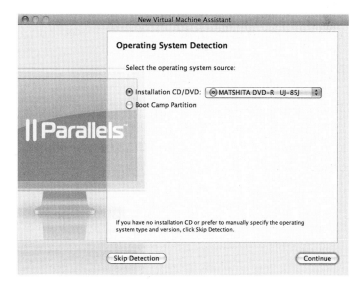

Starting from Scratch

If you want to start from scratch and create a clean installation of an operating system and applications, simply start your VM software and select File ➢ New. This will allow you to begin the process of installing the desired operating system. The process of creating a VM happens much faster than installing an OS on regular computer hardware because you're able to input most of your user settings upfront (such as licensing information) even before your start to create your virtual machine.

Depending on the operating system, expect the VM to restart a few times during the process. But overall it should take significantly less time to create a VM than to install an operating system on a host computer. When the installation is complete, remember to check for recent updates to the operating system. We've found that downloading and installing these updates (which usually require the guest computer to reboot after install) can take as long to complete as the installation of the whole operating system.

What about network and Internet access on the VM? Unless you intend to completely isolate your guest computer from the network and Internet, it's a good idea to install virus protection software just as you would on any host computer. Fortunately, both VMware and Parallels offer subscriptions to virus protection software as part of the purchase of either virtual solution.

Keep in mind that after you've created your clean install (and installed any suggested critical updates), you may not want to start installing any applications right away. Why? Because you've just spent a fair amount of time creating a brand-new virtual computer! So, before you start spending a lot of time installing applications and moving files to your guest computer, why not create a copy for safekeeping? The original clean install will be updated from time to time through system updates. But the copy will be a starting point for installing your applications.

By creating a copy of your new guest computer, you'll have a great starting point for testing out new applications without risking the rest of your virtual environments. And when you're done testing a new application, simply delete the VM and copy a new one. In some cases, installing an application on a clean, duplicate guest computer is faster than going through the process of uninstalling an application and reinstalling it in the same VM.

Physical to Virtual

In some cases, you don't want to spend the time to create a VM that is a duplicate of a physical machine, particularly if it means trying to re-create a physical machine that contains an operating system, numerous applications, and dozens of user-created files that has grown and evolved over time. Trying to exactly re-create such a physical computer would be nearly impossible, especially if the physical computer you're trying to duplicate is a work-issued desktop or laptop that contains applications and settings that you can't install or duplicate.

Fortunately, both Parallels and VMware have applications that allow you to turn your physical computer into a virtual computer, in effect migrating the entire computer into a VM. This is commonly referred to as physical-to-virtual (P2V) technology. The applications to complete the P2V migration are provided on a complimentary basis by the software vendors. Obviously it's in their interest to get you to give virtualization a try! Not only that, but both Parallels and

VMware offer 30-day trials of their virtual solutions so you can create or convert a trial virtual computer.

To download Parallels Transporter, go here:

`www.parallels.com/products/pvc45/technology/transporter/`

To download VMware Converter, go here:

`www.vmware.com/products/converter/`

Once you've downloaded either (or both) P2V conversion solution, simply install the application, start it, and follow the on-screen directions. It's pretty straightforward, but it may take some time (up to a few hours), and while the conversion is taking place, it's best to not attempt to work on the host computer.

When the conversion is complete, you'll have a single file that is very close to the size of the used capacity of your physical computer. For example, if your physical computer's operating system, applications, files, settings, and so on take up 60GB of space on your hard drive, you'll have a 60GB file when the P2V conversion is complete. Therefore, it's important to have more free space on your hard drive than you're presently using before you start the conversion process. Or better yet, you can write the conversion (the creation of the virtual computer) to another hard drive, even an external hard drive.

Prepare yourself when you open this VM for the first time. Expect everything to look and feel the same as your physical computer. But the first time you launch your virtual machine, expect to be at least a little "giddy" when everything is just there and looks the same. All the settings, software, files—even the desktop—will look just like your physical computer, except now your physical computer may reside on an external hard drive that is no longer dependent on a specific location. Any computer that contains the virtual software is capable of running your virtual computer. So if your workstation or laptop is unavailable or in need of repair, you can still be up and running!

 Real World Scenario

RUNNING REVIT IN VIRTUALIZATION

It's always interesting to us the reaction that virtualization gets from many suspecting individuals. If it's really that good, why haven't you heard about it before, right? Well, it's likely that your company is already using virtualization on the server side of your IT department. There are some advantages to running mission-critical applications on virtual machines (like your email server) so if one application fails, the rest of the server is not affected.

But virtualization is somewhat new on the end-user side. And although you might feel comfortable testing virtualization yourself or on a case-by-case basis, what about end-user virtualization in an enterprise environment?

At Autodesk University 2007, Peter Streibig and Phil Read presented "Running Revit in Virtualization." As you can imagine, a lot has changed since then. Both hardware and software have evolved—more memory allocation, multiple processors, and so on. So we've asked Peter to contribute to this book and update us on what's been going on in virtualization over the past two years. But first, some background information on the amazing design firm where Peter works.

BOHLIN CYWINSKI JACKSON

Bohlin Cywinski Jackson (BCJ) is the design firm behind such notable projects as the Pacific Rim Estate near Seattle; the Pixar Animation Studios in Emeryville, California; and a series of high-profile stores for Apple Inc. that are located around the world. New York City's Fifth Avenue store is shown here.

The firm has received more than 350 regional, national, and international awards for design, including the Architecture Firm Award of the American Institute of Architects—the highest honor bestowed on an architectural practice by the institute.

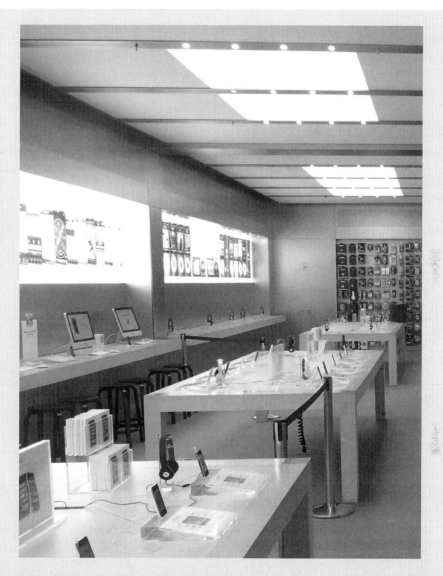

BCJ was founded in 1965 and has offices in Wilkes-Barre, Pittsburgh, Philadelphia, Seattle, and San Francisco. The firm is known for exceptional design rigor as well as their commitment to the particularity of place and user. This extraordinary aesthetic is based on a quiet rigor that is both intellectual and intuitive.

The firm's principals and nearly 200 staff practice architecture and offer a broad range of related services. Their breadth and depth of skills and experience enable the practice to address a wide range of challenges—difficult sites, demanding budgets and time constraints, unusual technological requirements, and the integration of new construction with existing buildings and contexts. The firm responds to the particular circumstances of each situation, alive to the subtleties of place—man-made or natural, to the varied natures of client and user, to the character of institutions, and to the means of construction.

BCJ is also noted for exceptional and humane design, ranging from modest houses and recreational facilities to larger academic, research, civic, and corporate buildings. Their problem-solving approach emphasizes thorough research and analysis of each project's unique human, technical, and economic circumstances. They believe the best design comes from an alert and balanced response to the particular circumstances inherent in each situation.

In an essay about their firm's work, Gold Medal–winning architect Joseph Esherick comments, "What is remarkable is the degree to which BCJ achieve the highest possible technical standards of construction, of energy management, of sophisticated program requirements, and still preserve such freshness and openness."

TECHNOLOGY HISTORY

It's particularly interesting to note that BCJ has always been a Macintosh shop (a noted irony considering its design history). They consisted of longtime MicroStation users, first on the Macintosh, but they later transitioned their workstations to the Windows platform for CAD starting with version 7 of MicroStation.

Apple's switch to the Intel platform provided the opportunity to return to the Macintosh, with options of running Windows virtualized (with Parallels or VMware) or by booting directly into Windows via Apple's Boot Camp technology. For low-end consumer computers, Apple can cost a premium. But for high-end workstations and laptops BCJ believes the current advantage of overall price, flexibility, build quality, and subsequent ease of maintenance make Apple products an easy choice.

When looking to make the move from CAD to BIM, Bohlin Cywinski Jackson investigated many of the BIM products available. Revit simply proved the most developed and complete solution available. The depth of resources available in the Revit community, and the number of colleagues, consultants, and collaborators using Revit made the decision to move to Revit even easier.

Initially, BCJ used both Parallels and VMware for their virtual computing environments. Both VMWare and Parallels provide simple, easy-to-maintain virtual solutions. But since that time they've begun to transition solely to Parallles.

For workstations, BCJ uses Mac Pro towers running at 2.6GHz and 2xQuad Core Xeons with10GB of RAM and VMware for virtualization. But for laptops, they selected the MacBook Pro running at 2.5GHz and containing Core Two Duo processors with 8GB RAM and Parallels for virtualization.

BEST PRACTICES

Overall, the employees have a brief accommodation period while learning how the two systems (host and guest computers) interact and how to best use the systems together. The company will periodically host an employee seminars and refresher sessions on getting the most from virtual machines.

In their experience, the isolation of running Windows and Revit from other primary tasks on the host computer running the Mac OS X environment has proven its worth when Windows crashes or has problems booting. They keep exact copies of VMs on hand for just such a case. If a virtual machine becomes suspect or corrupted, the end users simply shut down their VM and rename both images (the original for the backup, and vice versa), thereby swapping the backup for the original. Then they restart the VM and are up and running.

This flexibility has proved invaluable during tight deadlines, especially when someone is working late or on weekends when support from other associates or IT staff might be limited.

Another protective layer that BCJ utilized is adding a secondary hard drive to users' machines for hosting their virtual images. The additional backup copies are kept on the system drive in anticipation of hard drive failure. If the system drive fails, the user can simply shut down, take their virtual images on the second Apple drive sled, and move it to another Mac Pro and slide it in place. Then they can open their image by double-clicking on it or choosing it through Parallels or VMware. In such cases, the total downtime is about 15 minutes.

As for best practices, Peter highly recommends regularly discussing and sharing user experiences with other user users. It's important to gain as much as possible from their perspective. User experience often suggests potential tweaks to configuration, workflows, and preferences. Overall, sharing this knowledge is the best way to get a smooth, consistent environment for everyone involved.

Obviously there are a number of options an administrator can set right at the start. Creating a master image to roll out for the users significantly reduces setup time. It also provides a great platform for testing updates, upgraded or new software, and settings before impacting everyone's work.

Some particularly important issues from an administrative standpoint are that both Parallels and VMware Tools need to be reinstalled on all updates and occasionally at random maintenance intervals (possibly due to Windows updates). Additionally, Parallels and VMware Tools (like many other Windows-based applications) require Windows administrator-level permissions to install properly. Usually this can be accomplished by a "first-run" setup logged in as administrator, and then switching to the user's account.

It's important to note that Parallels and VMware updates require an administrative password on the Macintosh side of things. The process that Peter typically uses is the following:

1. Schedule an hour with the user to shut down Parallels or VMware.

2. Make a backup copy and then install the new version and upgrade the image.

3. Reinstall Parallels Tools. It's a good idea to test the VM for a bit, changing and tweaking any new settings as necessary.

4. Shut down and make another (new) backup copy. Then restart and get back to work (don't forget to delete the old VM).

Keep in mind that updating takes a significant amount of work. There are updates for two operating systems involved (OS X and Windows), not to mention all the related applications on both the host and guest computers. Peter manages this by testing all the updates himself and then after a couple of weeks (and a fair number of waiting upgrades have amassed), he schedules time with users to upgrade and update. And it's best to do the updates early in the morning or late in the evening.

Using Apple Remote Desktop, Peter can "push" new images to clients even while they continue to work, reducing transition time later, when the 40GB OS images are ready on the local machine for his administrative access. Mac OS system upgrades are sped up with the use of an in-house Apple Software Update Server that downloads the updates once and then distributes the updates to the client machines over the local network. This provides much faster installs for the workstations, while reducing overall Internet bandwidth impact.

HARDWARE SETTINGS

BCJ began using investigating virtualization back in 2007. At that time they began implementing both VM Ware and Parallels. VMware was found more suitable for workstations and Parallels was better for laptops.

But over the past three years, Parallels has won out over VMware for a couple of reasons. Overall, they've been more pleased with the performance from Parallels (verified by higher Windows Experience Scores), including higher video RAM throughput and more core support in multicore machines. The following graphics show the specific settings in Parallels for both laptops and workstations. Keep in mind that current Apple laptops are limited to two cores, whereas BCJ uses workstations with four cores (a few of them have eight).

The hardware settings in Parallels reside on three tabs in the configuration panel. These settings control the general options, the options for applications, and the options for hardware. The General options are shown here. The important thing about this setting is that out of 8GB of RAM, the user is allocating 4GB of RAM to the virtual machine.

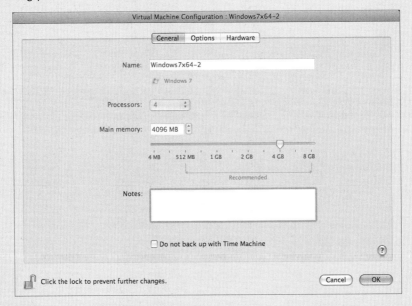

The Options tab contains a setting that allows you to control the startup and shutdown of the virtual machine. They have opted not to automatically start up the VM when the user logs into the host computer.

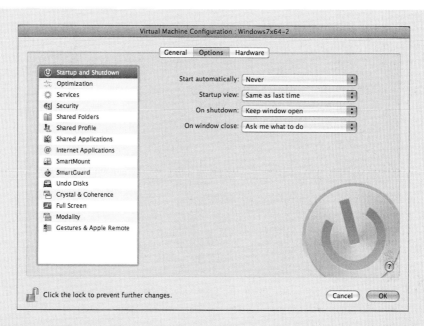

Optimization is important when using virtualization for 3D-intensive applications like Revit. Notice that BCJ is optimizing performance toward the virtual machine (rather than the host machine), as shown here, and they're leaning toward better performance (rather than extending battery life). Note that auto-compression has been disabled.

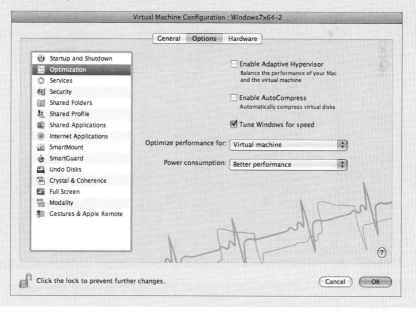

Services allow you to share the time and date settings of the host computer. This option has been selected, as shown here.

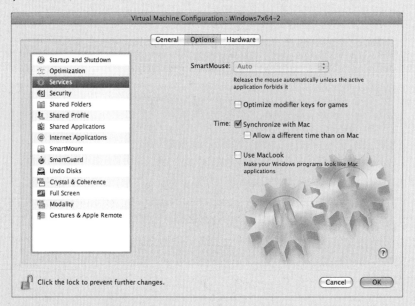

If you want to isolate your virtual environment from your host computer, this can be done through the Security settings. But by doing so, you won't be able to launch project files from the host machine. This option has not been selected, as shown here.

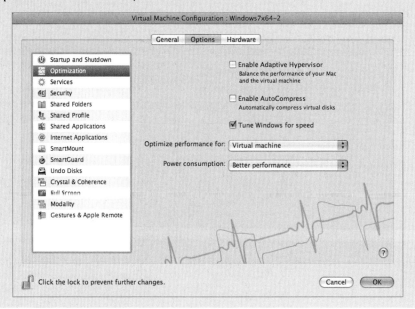

Creating a shared folder allows you to designate a specific location to share files between the host and virtual computers. But this option is not needed in an already networked environment.

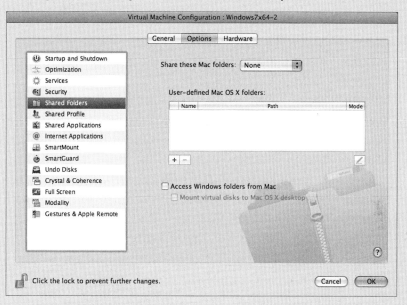

Shared Profiles has not been selected either, as shown here. This is more useful if you're working the majority of time from the guest OS rather than the host OS. This is not typically the case, because most users of virtualization utilize the guest OS for access to a few, very important applications.

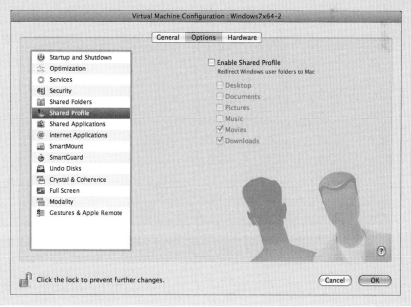

By sharing applications, you're able to launch files that reside on the host OS by the guest OS, as shown here. This is not being utilized.

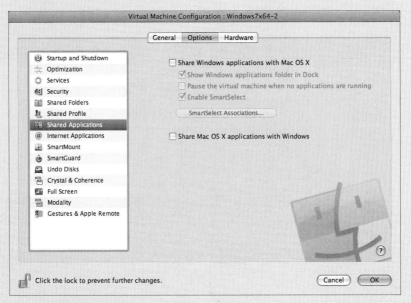

Internet applications create consistent experiences between the guest and host OS. The default settings are being used, as shown here.

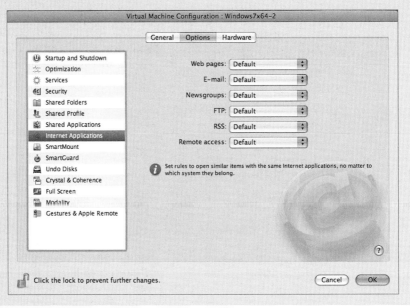

SmartMount allows other hardware, drives, and folders to map to the guest OS from the host OS. These options are not selected, as shown here.

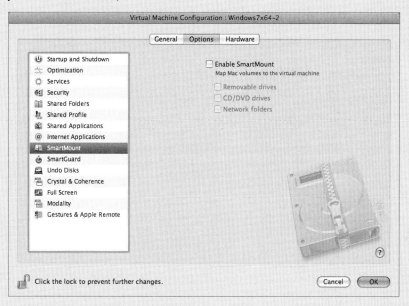

SmartGuard allows you to automatically create snapshots of your entire virtual machine, so in the event of corruption you can in effect roll back your VM to a previous state. BCJ did not enable SmartGuard, as shown here, because they have other backup methods.

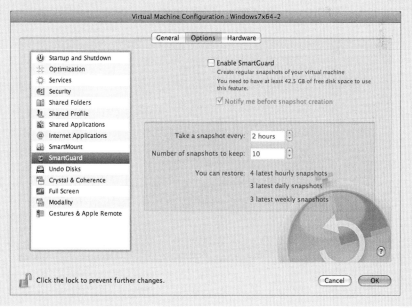

The ability to create an undo disk means that all the operations from the moment of starting the virtual session are not permanently stored. This is great for testing purposes but not needed in this case, as shown here.

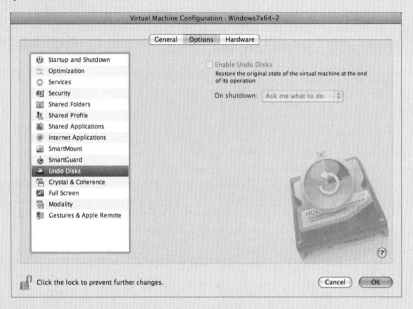

BCJ has opted to show the Windows system tray in the Mac menu bar rather than show applications in the Dock, as shown here.

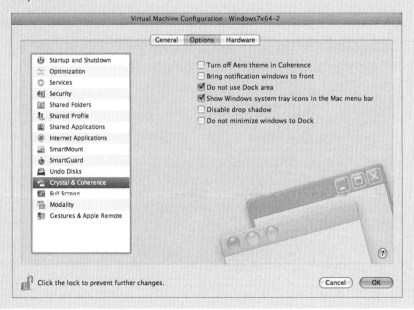

Full-screen mode is entered by moving your cursor to a predefined screen corner. This is a convenient way to share the same window. But keep in mind that users have another option in Mac spaces that allow you to create panels out of your desktop.

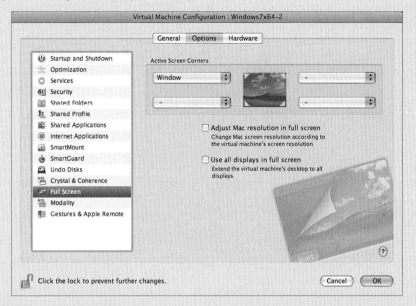

Note that BCJ has deselected the option that forces one window to stay on top of another window, as shown here. This allows you to see through the guest machine to the host machine.

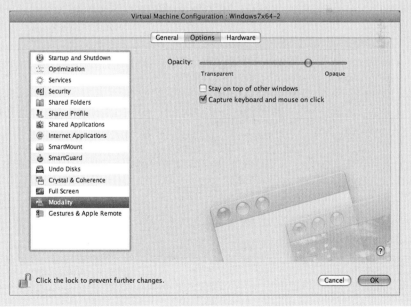

Neither gestures nor remotes have been selected, as shown here. This means that the track pad will respond more conventionally in the guest OS.

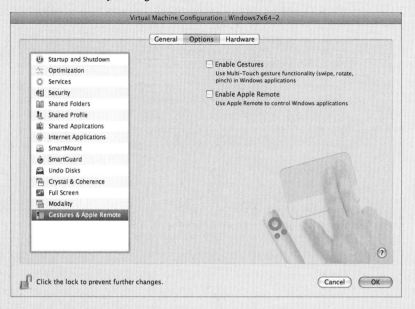

Now we can begin to discuss some of the important hardware virtualization settings. The default boot order is shown here.

Using Revit in virtualization will require as many video resources as you can manage. In fact, most operations in virtualization are nearly concurrent in speed, as if running on a host OS. But there is a bottleneck with regard to video card simulation. As mentioned earlier, HP has created some interesting alternatives by dedicating video hardware to virtual machines. But these alternatives are not available in laptops or with Apple hardware.

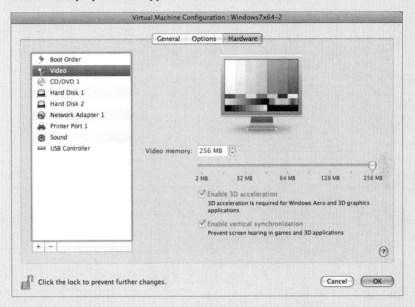

BCJ has deselected the default option to share the CD/DVD player with the guest OS, as shown here. Again, these virtual machines are just for running Revit and little else. So, they're very lean from a resource and hardware standpoint.

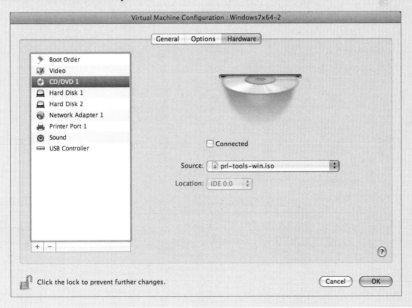

Two hard disks are shown. You may only have one on your system. BCJ recommends having a separate drive that is used only for storing the virtual machine. Hard Disk 1, as shown here, is used for the host OS applications and files.

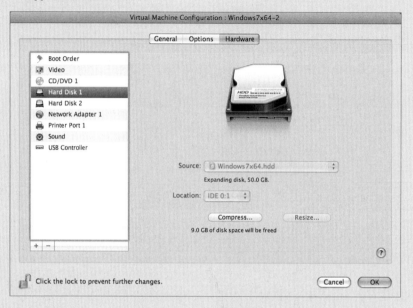

Hard Disk 2 is used to store the virtual machine image and nothing else, as shown here. According to Peter, performance increases when the host and guest OS don't need to share the same disk drive.

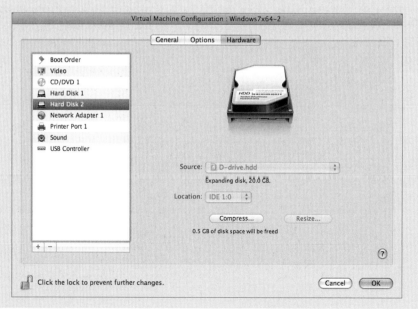

Selecting Connected, as shown here, allows the host machine to share the Internet connection of the host machine. If your intention is to keep the guest VM from accessing the Internet, then you'd want to deselect this option.

The hardware printer port is being shared, as shown here.

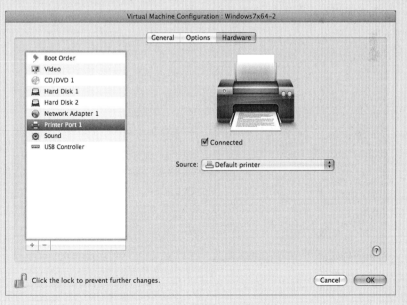

Again, the virtual machine is meant to be as light as possible from a resources standpoint. Not even sound is being shared between the host and guest, as shown here.

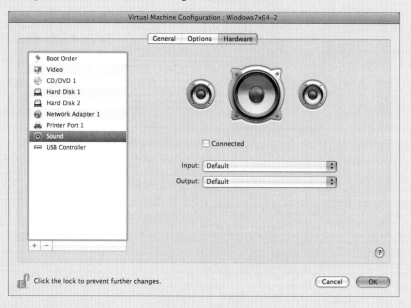

No USB devices are being shared, as shown here. When a USB device is plugged into the host computer, it will only show up on the desktop of the host machine.

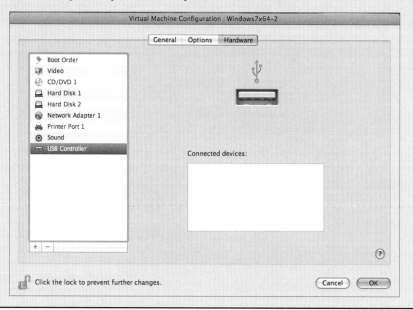

The Bottom Line

Understand the benefits of virtualization. There are advantages of virtualization for both IT support as well as end users.

Master It What are the advantages of virtualization?

Take advantage of virtualization. Having to maintain multiple operating systems is hardly uncommon. But rather than maintain obsolete hardware and applications, why not utilize virtualization and maintain best-of-breed solutions?

Master It What's the easiest way to try out virtualization?

Chapter 24

Under the Hood of Revit

If you are an experienced AutoCAD user, it is likely you have had some experience with creating or using customized scripts or routines to increase your productivity based on unique needs. You may have also seen such add-on programs attempt to offer similar object-like behavior as seen in Revit today (remember Auto-Architect by Softdesk?). Unlike the more generic platform of AutoCAD, Revit is a specific application designed for architecture and engineering. As such, Autodesk has slowly and deliberately opened up the application programming interface for customization by others. This chapter will help you understand how to create your own commands and applications to extend the power of Revit to meet your needs.

In this chapter, you'll learn to:

◆ Understand the basics of the Revit API

◆ Understand the new `.addin` manifest file method used to load custom command and applications into Revit

◆ Set up and build your own custom external applications and commands

Introducing the Revit API

ABOUT THE CONTRIBUTING AUTHOR: DON RUDDER

Don Rudder is currently working as a BIM manager for HOK San Francisco, providing Revit customization development and support. Don has an extensive background in .NET, AEC, and Web development. His background is primarily in the MEP disciplines where he has served as designer, CAD Manager, and customization consultant.

All great applications provide a means to extend their functionality through some sort of API, and Autodesk Revit is no different. The software community's desire to customize and extend software applications to suit their specific needs has been around as long as software itself. The integration of an efficient means to accomplish application customization will usually have some effect on an application's popularity in the marketplace.

One of the most important reasons that a software company would provide a powerful application programming interface (API) in their product is to allow customers to purchase their product in a state that may not be exactly what is needed but is easily molded to suit their needs, resulting in a larger market share than if a useful API was not provided. The Revit API supports in-process dynamic link libraries (DLLs) only and runs on Microsoft's .NET Framework (www .microsoft.com/net). Only single-threaded access is supported, but future releases of the API will likely support multithreading. Since the API runs on the .NET Framework, it supports all native .NET programming languages. Although most of the examples found online and in the Revit 2011 SDK are written in the C# language, Visual Basic .NET (VB.NET) is equally capable of providing the same functionality. The choice between .NET programming languages is purely up to the programmer.

There are two types of DLLs you can develop with the Revit API: external commands and external applications. The differences between the two types are distinct in both lifetime as well as scope.

External Commands

External commands are accessible from the Add-ins tab under the External Tools drop-down button. External commands have access to the current document as well as any elements selected when the command is executed. Commands can be registered into Revit through the `Revit.ini` file or by using an `.addin` manifest file new to the Revit 2011 API. This new feature will be explained in greater detail later in this chapter in the section "External Utility Registration Options."

The memory lifetime for external commands lasts only from the time the command is clicked, to when the command returns success or failure. Any objects created or held in memory by the command are destroyed when the command is completed. Data will not persist in memory alone from one external command to another. If data persistence is needed from one external command to another, you will need to employ a means to store this data either by parameters or by an external database.

THE *IEXTERNALCOMMAND* INTERFACE

The `IExternalCommand` interface is a required implementation for all Revit API commands and must accompany a public function named `Execute` to access it at runtime. Empty boilerplate samples of this interface are shown here in both VB.NET (Listing 24.1) and C# (Listing 24.2).

LISTING 24.1   VB.NET IExternalCommand Example

```
Imports Autodesk.Revit
Imports Autodesk.Revit.Attributes
Imports Autodesk.Revit.DB
Imports Autodesk.Revit.UI

<Regeneration(RegenerationOption.Manual)> _
<Transaction(TransactionMode.Automatic)> _
Public Class Command
    Implements IExternalCommand
    Public Function Execute(ByVal commandData As UI.ExternalCommandData, _
            ByRef message As String, _
            ByVal elements As DB.ElementSet) _
            As UI.Result Implements IExternalCommand.Execute
        Try
            ' Command implementation
            Return Autodesk.Revit.UI.Result.Succeeded
```

```
        Catch ex As Exception
            Return Autodesk.Revit.UI.Result.Failed
        End Try
    End Function
End Class
```

LISTING 24.2   C# IExternalCommand Example

```
using  Autodesk.Revit;
using  Autodesk.Revit.Attributes;
using  Autodesk.Revit.DB;
using  Autodesk.Revit.UI;

[Regeneration(RegenerationOption.Manual)]
[Transaction(TransactionMode.Automatic)]
public class Command : IExternalCommand
{    public Autodesk.Revit.IExternalCommand.Result
Execute(Autodesk.Revit.ExternalCommandData commandData,
        ref string message, Autodesk.Revit.ElementSet elements)
    {
        // Command implementation
    }
}
```

Required Execute Function Parameters

It is good practice to always trap the main functionality attempt within a `try` statement. This provides a stable means of trapping any complications that may arise during the command startup:

```
Public Function Execute(ByVal commandData As ExternalCommandData, _
                        ByRef message As String, _
                        ByVal elements As DB.ElementSet) _
                        As Result Implements IExternalCommand.Execute
    Try
        ' Functionality extends from here
        Return Result.Succeeded
    Catch ex As Exception
        ' If something goes wrong, exit and return failed
        Return Result.Failed
    End Try
End Function
```

Three return states exist for the IExternalCommand interface. The only result that will allow changes to be committed to the model is IExternalCommand.Result.Succeeded. All others will roll back any changes made by the command. The three return states are shown here:

```
Return IExternalCommand.Result.Succeeded
Return IExternalCommand.Result.Failed
Return IExternalCommand.Result.Canceled
```

COMMANDDATA

The CommandData parameter provides access to both the application information and the model database information. Information for the current view is also accessible through this parameter.

MESSAGE

The Message parameter serves as a means of reporting error information to the user upon returning a result of Failed. The Message parameter will only be displayed if the command status returns Failed. There is a limit of 1,023 characters for this message; longer strings will be truncated.

ELEMENTS

The Elements parameter provides access to objects currently selected while the command is executed.

External Applications

External applications are loaded when Revit starts and remain loaded until Revit shuts down. One of the biggest advantages that applications have over commands is that applications provide access to Revit document events. Applications are typically accessible from the Add-Ins tab of the ribbon, but the 2011 API now also provides a means to add application ribbon items to the Analyze tab in Revit MEP 2011.

THE *IEXTERNALAPPLICATION* INTERFACE

The IExternalApplication interface is a required implementation for all Revit API external applications. External applications must accompany OnStartup and OnShutdown functions that fire off when Revit launches (OnStartup) and when it closes (OnShutdown). Empty boilerplate samples of this interface are shown here in both VB.NET (Listing 24.3) and C# (Listing 24.4).

LISTING 24.3   VB.NET IExternalApplication Example

```
Imports Autodesk.Revit.UI
Imports Autodesk.Revit.UI.Events
Imports Autodesk.Revit.Attributes

<Transaction(TransactionMode.Automatic)> _
<Regeneration(RegenerationOption.Manual)> _
Public Class App
    ' Required Interface...
```

```
    Implements IExternalApplication

    Public Function OnStartup(ByVal a As UIControlledApplication) _
    As Result Implements IExternalApplication.OnStartup
            ' OnStartup implementation
    End Function

    Public Function OnShutdown(ByVal a As UIControlledApplication) _
        As Result Implements IExternalApplication.OnShutdown
            ' OnShutdown implementation
    End Function

End Class
```

LISTING 24.4   C# IExternalApplication Example

```csharp
using Autodesk.Revit.UI;
using Autodesk.Revit.UI.Events;
using Autodesk.Revit.Attributes;

namespace ClassLibrary1
{
    [Regeneration(RegenerationOption.Automatic)]
    public class Application : IExternalApplication
    {
        Public Result OnStartup(ControlledApplication application)
        {
            // OnStartup implementation
        }

        Public Result OnShutdown(ControlledApplication application)
        {
            // OnShutdown implementation
        }
    }
}
```

External Utility Registration Options

There are now two options for registering external commands and applications into the Autodesk Revit user interface.

.ADDIN MANIFEST FILE METHOD (PREFERRED)

The Revit API now offers the ability to register API applications into Revit using an `.addin` manifest file. Manifest files will be read automatically by Revit when they are placed in one of two locations on a user's system:

Windows XP

◆ `C:\Documents and Settings\All Users\Application Data\Autodesk\Revit\Addins\2011\`

◆ `C:\Documents and Settings\<user>\Application Data\Autodesk\Revit\Addins\2011\`

Windows 7

◆ `C:\ProgramData\Autodesk\Revit\Addins\2011\`

◆ `C:\Users\<user>\AppData\Roaming\Autodesk\Revit\Addins\2011\`

All files named `.addin` in these locations will be read and processed by Revit during startup. It is possible to load multiple elements within a single manifest by nesting multiple `AddIn` elements into one `.addin` file. An example `.addin` file adding our example `ExternalCommand` looks like this:

```xml
<?xml version="1.0" encoding="utf-8" standalone="no" ?>
<RevitAddIns>
 <AddIn Type="Command">
  <Assembly>C:\Revit Projects\ExampleCommand.dll</Assembly>
  <AddInId>72d6cd76-5462-4c97-b56c-5468b08ba742</AddInId>
  <FullClassName>ExampleCommand.Command</FullClassName>
  <Text>Batch Family Export Utility</Text>
  <VisibilityMode>NotVisibleInFamily</VisibilityMode>
  <LongDescription>Batch export all family files as external RFA files. ↵
Each file will be saved into a subdirectory named by its category ↵
beneath the parent directory selected by the user.</LongDescription>
  <TooltipImage> C:\Revit Projects\Preview_BatchFamilyExport.PNG</TooltipImage>
 </AddIn>
</RevitAddIns>
```

The example `ExternalApplication.addin` file would look like this:

```xml
<?xml version="1.0" encoding="utf-8" standalone="no" ?>
<RevitAddIns>
 <AddIn Type="Application">
  <Name>ExampleApplication</Name>
  <Assembly>c:\Revit Projects\ ExampleApplication.dll</Assembly>
  <AddInId>fb36c4b0-d4c2-4ead-96db-81f48407e57a</AddInId>
  <FullClassName>ExampleApplication.Application</FullClassName>
 </AddIn>
</RevitAddIns>
```

The `.addin` XML schema utilizes the XML tags described in Table 24.1.

TABLE 24.1:   `.addin` XML Schema

TAG	DESCRIPTION
Assembly	The full path to the add-in assembly file. Required for all ExternalCommand and ExternalApplication objects.
FullClassName	The full name of the class that implements IExternalCommand or IExternalApplication. Required for all ExternalCommand and ExternalApplication objects.
AddInId	A GUID that represents the ID of this particular application. AddInId must be unique for a given session of Revit. Autodesk recommends you generate a unique GUID for each registered application or command. Required for all ExternalCommand and ExternalApplication objects. The property UIApplication.ActiveAddInId provides programmatic access to this value, if required.
Name	The name of application. Required; for ExternalApplications only.
Text	The name of the button. Optional; use this tag for ExternalCommand objects only. The default is External Tool.
Description	Short description of the command, will be used as the button tooltip. Optional; use this tag for ExternalCommand objects only. The default is a tooltip with just the command text.
VisibilityMode	Provides the ability to specify if the command is visible in project documents, family documents, or no document at all. Also provides the ability to specify the discipline(s) where the command should be visible. Multiple values may be set for this option. Optional; use this tag for ExternalCommand objects only. The default is to display the command in all modes and disciplines, including when there is no active document. Previously written external commands that need to run against the active document should either be modified to ensure that the code deals with invocation of the command when there is no active document, or apply the NotVisibleWhenNoActiveDocument mode.
AvailabilityClassName	The full name of the class in the assembly file that implemented IExternalCommandAvailability. This class allows the command button to be selectively grayed out depending on context. Optional; use this tag for ExternalCommand objects only. The default is a command that is available whenever it is visible.
LargeImage	The path to the icon to use for the button in the External Tools drop-down menu. The icon should be 32 × 32 pixels for best results. Optional; use this tag for ExternalCommand objects only. The default is to show a button without an icon.

TABLE 24.1: .addin XML Schema *(CONTINUED)*

TAG	DESCRIPTION
LongDescription	Long description of the command; will be used as part of the button's extended tooltip. This tooltip is shown when the mouse hovers over the command for a long amount of time. You can split the text of this option into multiple paragraphs by placing <p> tags around each paragraph. Optional; use this tag for ExternalCommand objects only. If neither this property nor TooltipImage is supplied, the button will not have an extended tooltip.
TooltipImage	The path to an image file to show as a part of the button extended tooltip, shown when the mouse hovers over the command for a longer amount of time. Optional; use this tag for ExternalCommand objects only. If neither this property nor TooltipImage is supplied, the button will not have an extended tooltip.
LanguageType	Localization setting for Text, Description, LargeImage, LongDescription, and TooltipImage of external tools buttons. Revit will load the resource values from the specified language resource DLL. The value can be one of the 11 languages supported by Revit. If no LanguageType is specified, the language resource that the current session of Revit is using will be automatically loaded.

REVIT.INI METHOD

In Revit 2011, the registration method utilizing the Revit.ini file is still supported; however, it will not be supported in future releases of the API. This is because it does not offer any of the new capabilities of the .addin manifest method. Be aware that updaters may not be registered from external applications registered using the Revit.ini method because Dynamic Model Update registration requires a valid AddInId.

Create a backup copy of your Revit.ini found in the C:\Program Files\Autodesk\Revit Architecture 2011\Program\ directory. Only after you have backed up your Revit.ini file, launch Notepad and open Revit.ini for editing. Press Ctrl+F, and search within Notepad for the text string [ExternalCommands]. If your Revit.ini does not contain this entry, we will need to add it to the end of the file.

The [ExternalCommands] portion of the Revit.ini requires a line directly beneath it entered as ECCount=#, where # would be replaced by the total number of external commands being loaded into the Revit.ini file. If you have two external commands, the entry would read ECCount=2.

```
[ExternalCommands]
ECCount=1
```

Each externally defined command requires four lines to describe the name, the class, the assembly filename, and a description. Only the description line is optional.

In the following example external command entry, the number preceding the = represents the command's loading order into Revit. Commands must be numbered in sequence without any skipped numbers:

```
ECName1=Batch Family Export
ECClassName1=BatchFamilyExporter.Command
ECAssembly1=C:\BatchFamilyExtractor\bin\Debug\BatchFamilyExporter.dll
ECDescription1=Batch Family Export Utility...
```

In the previous code, the entry for ECName will display in the Add-Ins tab of the ribbon beneath External Commands for your command.

ECClassName requires the namespace of the project to be loaded followed by the class name containing the IExternalCommand reference. The required format is NameSpace.Classname. In this example, our namespace is BatchFamilyExporter, and our class containing the IExternalCommand reference is Command.

ECAssembly requires the full path and filename of the DLL file to be loaded containing the external command.

ECDescription is optional and will display in the status bar of Revit.

Selecting a Development Environment

Several development environment options are available for building and debugging .NET Revit API utilities. Although Visual Studio 2008 Professional is preferred, it is not free. Microsoft provides free express versions of Visual Studio 2008 in both VB.NET and C# on its website at www.microsoft.com/express. These express versions provide more than enough functionality to generate a fully featured .NET Revit API utility.

A new .NET programming language known as F# is quickly emerging as the next generation of .NET technology. F# has been so successful that Microsoft has promoted it to a "first-class" language in Visual Studio 2010. See www.fsharp.net for more information.

VISUAL STUDIO DEBUG SETTINGS

Debugging a Revit command or application in Visual Studio 2008 requires that you first enter the full path and filename to your Revit.exe in the Start External Program field in the Debug tab of the Project Properties dialog box, as shown in Figure 24.1. The Revit API does not yet provide a means to interact with the Revit application in an externally defined stand-alone executable file. Entering the full path and filename to a Revit file in the Command Line Arguments field will launch that file when the project enters debug mode.

DEBUGGING ON A 64-BIT OPERATING SYSTEM

You will not be able to edit your code in break mode on a 64-bit operating system in Visual Studio 2008. Use a 32-bit operating system as your development station as a workaround.

FIGURE 24.1
Setting debug
options in Visual
Studio

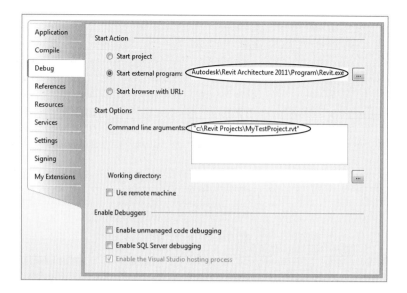

Revit 2011 Software Development Kit (SDK)

The Revit 2011 SDK is available on the Revit 2011 installation disk and in the downloadable installation package; however, you can download the latest version of the SDK from Autodesk's website at www.autodesk.com/revit. The SDK contains several working samples of code written in both the C# language as well as VB.NET. Examples range from simple element modifications to family creation. The "Getting Started with the Revit API" document included with the SDK will help you with the examples provided.

The Revit 2011 API requires the .NET Framework Version 3.5 as a prerequisite, but since this same framework version is required to install and run Revit in general, it is not necessary to build your applications with this as a runtime prerequisite. If you choose to build your application using a .NET Framework version newer than 3.5, you should build your application to verify the installation of your required framework version at runtime.

What's New in the Revit 2011 API

If you are planning on updating any existing Revit API utilities to run in Autodesk Revit 2011, be prepared to make some rather major changes to your code. If you have any familiarity with previous versions of the Revit API, you will immediately notice some differences as you explore the new version.

The changes introduced in this version are going to make Autodesk Revit much more powerful in the long run because it will become possible to accomplish things that you just couldn't do in previous versions of the API. Not only are there new features, but other features have been redesigned to improve performance, such as the way elements are accessed and iterated within loops.

DLL Split

There was just one lonely DLL in previous releases of the API representing the entire thing. There are now two DLLs, each with its own scope, in the Autodesk Revit API:

`RevitAPI.dll`   This DLL now contains only methods used to access the Autodesk Revit application, documents, elements, and parameters at the database level.

`RevitAPIUI.dll`   This is a new DLL and contains all API interfaces related to manipulation and customization of the Revit user interface. This DLL provides access to the Revit command and application interfaces required by all external command and applications to run inside Revit.

- ◆ `IExternalCommand` and `External Command`–related interfaces
- ◆ `IExternalApplication` and related interfaces
- ◆ Selection
- ◆ `RibbonPanel`, `RibbonItem`, and all `Ribbon` subclasses
- ◆ `TaskDialogs` (new)

Access to the document- and application-level interfaces through both the `RevitAPIUI.dll` and the `RevitAPI.dll` is now provided through a split of the `Document` and `Application` classes.

`Autodesk.Revit.UI.UIApplication`   This class provides access to the UI-level interfaces for the Revit application, including the ability to add `RibbonPanels` and the ability to obtain the active document in the Revit user interface.

`Autodesk.Revit.UI.UIDocument`   This provides access to UI-level interfaces for the document, such as the contents of the selection and the ability to prompt the user to make selections and pick points.

`Autodesk.Revit.ApplicationServices.Application`   This provides access to all other application-level properties.

`Autodesk.Revit.DB.Document`   This new `DB.Document` class provides access to the document-level properties. The `ExternalCommandData` interface provides access to the `UIApplication` object as well as the active document view. From the active `UIApplication` object, you can obtain the active UI document as either a family or a project model. You can also construct the `UIApplication` from the `Application` object, and the `UIDocument` from the database-level document at any time.

New Transaction Interfaces

Transactions are a means to prevent corruption by only allowing changes to be made when all required methods and conditions succeed. "All or nothing" is a good way to describe a transaction. Transactions roll back any changes contained within the transaction when a requirement or method does not return successfully. Transactions are common in complex database programs and are critical for ensuring that a complex operation succeeds as intended.

The 2011 API now provides a much more comprehensive system for handling transactions for changes being made to the model. There are three main transaction classes included in the

Revit 2011 API. The most notable is the ability to manage subtransactions. Each of the three transaction types listed here share these four common methods:

Start   Starts the context

Commit   Commits all changes to the document

RollBack   Discards all changes to the document

GetStatus   Returns the current status of a transaction object

The Commit and RollBack methods also return a status indicating whether or not the method was successful. Available status values for Commit and RollBack include the following:

◆ Uninitialized

◆ Started

◆ Committed

◆ RolledBack

◆ Pending

In the methods mentioned here for Commit and RollBack, the Pending method is set after an attempt to either submit or roll back a transaction object but because of failures, that process could not be completed yet and is waiting for the end user's response (in a modeless dialog). Once the failure processing is finished, the status will be automatically updated (to either Committed or RolledBack status).

In the Revit 2011 API, events no longer automatically open transactions. Because of this change, the document won't be modified during an event unless one of the event's handlers modifies it by making changes within a transaction. If your application requires changes to anything in the document, these transactions are no longer optional.

Transaction

All transactions must be named, and only one can be active at any given time. Transactions cannot be nested within other transactions. Each transaction will be represented as one "undo" in Revit upon successful completion. A series of three successful transactions would be represented as three individual undos in Revit, and so on.

Subtransaction

Subtransactions are optional and can be used to enclose a set of Revit model modification commands. Subtransactions are a convenience feature that allows a developer to break up more complex tasks into logical, smaller, and more manageable tasks.

Subtransactions can only be created within an already opened transaction and must be closed (either committed or rolled back) before the transaction is closed (committed or rolled back).

Unlike transactions, a subtransaction may be nested, but any nested subtransaction must be closed before the enclosing subtransaction is closed. Subtransactions do not have names, nor do they appear as actions in the Undo command in Revit.

TRANSACTION GROUP

Transaction groups are optional and allow several independent transactions to be treated as a single transaction all at once. A transaction group can only be started when no transactions have been opened yet, and can be closed only after all enclosed transactions are closed (rolled back or committed). Transaction groups can be nested, but any nested group must be closed before the enclosing group is closed.

When a transaction group is to be closed, it can be rolled back, which means that all already submitted transactions will be rolled back at once. If not rolled back, a group can be either submitted or assimilated. In the former case, all submitted transactions (within the group) will be left as they were. In the later case, transactions within the group will be merged together into one single transaction that will bear the group's name.

Regeneration Options

To help improve the speed of a custom application or command as it interacts with the elements in a project, new regeneration options are available within the Revit API. In previous versions, all actions on model elements would force the model to update or regenerate automatically. Within the 2011 API, you can now specify automatic or manual regeneration. There is no default for this option and you *must* apply it to legacy application classes to allow your application to function in Revit 2011.

The new `Autodesk.Revit.Attributes.RegenerationAttribute` custom attribute should be applied to your implementation class of the `IExternalCommand` interface and `IExternalApplication` interface to control the regeneration behavior for the external command and external application. There are two supported values:

`RegenerationOption.Automatic`   This option is the equivalent behavior with Revit 2010 and earlier versions of the Revit API. This option will regenerate after every model-level change. The performance of multiple modifications within the same file will be slower than `RegenerationOption.Manual`. This mode is provided for behavioral equivalence with Revit 2010 and earlier; it is obsolete and will be removed in a future release.

`RegenerationOption.Manual`   This is the preferred option and will not regenerate after every model-level change. Instead, you may use the regeneration APIs to force an update of the document after a group of changes. Because this mode suspends all updates to the document, your application should not read data from the document after it has been modified until the document has been regenerated, or it runs the risk of accessing outdated information. This will eventually be the only regeneration option mode in future releases of the Revit API.

In the empty boilerplate samples shown here, you will see the definition of the manual option in VB.NET (Listing 24.5) and the automatic option in C# (Listing 24.6).

LISTING 24.5   VB.NET External Application Example

```
Imports Autodesk.Revit
Imports Autodesk.Revit.UI
Imports Autodesk.Revit.ApplicationServices


<Regeneration(RegenerationOption.Manual)> _
Public Class Application
    Implements IExternalApplication
```

```
Public Function OnStartup(ByVal a As UIControlledApplication) _
        As Result Implements IExternalApplication.OnStartup
    Try
        ' Application starts here
        Return Result.Succeeded
    Catch ex As Exception
        Return Result.Failed
    End Try
End Function

Public Function OnShutdown(ByVal a As UIControlledApplication) _
    As Result Implements IExternalApplication.OnShutdown
    Return Result.Succeeded
End Function

End Class
```

LISTING 24.6   C# External Application Example

```
using Autodesk.Revit;
using Autodesk.Revit.UI;
using Autodesk.Revit.ApplicationServices;

[Regeneration(RegenerationOption.Automatic)]
public class Application : IExternalApplication
{
    public Autodesk.Revit.UI.Result OnStartup(ControlledApplication application)
    {
      // OnStartup implementation
    }
    public Autodesk.Revit.UI.Result OnShutdown(ControlledApplication  application)
    {
      // OnShutdown implementation
    }
}
```

Namespace Changes

One of the more obvious changes made to the API in this release is the renaming of namespaces. These new names help improve consistency and make the API more suitable for future expansion. Most notable are the changes to the MEP namespaces to Mechanical, Electrical, and Plumbing.

Figure 24.2 shows a small excerpt from the `Revit 2011 API Namespace Remapping.xlsx` file included with the Revit 2011 SDK available for download from the Autodesk website.

This figure shows from left to right the class name, the previous 2010 namespace, the new 2011 namespace, and finally any notes explaining the change in the last column of the document. This spreadsheet will help get you on your way to understanding the namespace changes made to the Revit 2011 API.

FIGURE 24.2

Namespace remapping spreadsheet available with the Revit SDK

	A	B	D
1	2010 class	2010 namespace	2011 namespace
2	Autodesk.Revit.ACADExportOptions	Autodesk.Revit	Autodesk.Revit.DB
3	Autodesk.Revit.ACADImportOptions	Autodesk.Revit	Autodesk.Revit.DB
4	Autodesk.Revit.APIObject	Autodesk.Revit	Autodesk.Revit.DB
5	Autodesk.Revit.Application	Autodesk.Revit	Autodesk.Revit.ApplicationServices
6	Autodesk.Revit.Areas.AreaScheme	Autodesk.Revit.Areas	Autodesk.Revit.DB
7	Autodesk.Revit.Areas.BoundarySegment	Autodesk.Revit.Areas	Autodesk.Revit.DB
8	Autodesk.Revit.Areas.BoundarySegmentArray	Autodesk.Revit.Areas	Autodesk.Revit.DB
9	Autodesk.Revit.Areas.BoundarySegmentArrayArray	Autodesk.Revit.Areas	Autodesk.Revit.DB
10	Autodesk.Revit.Areas.BoundarySegmentArrayArrayIterator	Autodesk.Revit.Areas	Autodesk.Revit.DB
11	Autodesk.Revit.Areas.BoundarySegmentArrayIterator	Autodesk.Revit.Areas	Autodesk.Revit.DB
12	Autodesk.Revit.BuildingSiteExportOptions	Autodesk.Revit	Autodesk.Revit.DB
13	Autodesk.Revit.BuiltInCategory	Autodesk.Revit	Autodesk.Revit.DB
14	Autodesk.Revit.ButtonData	Autodesk.Revit	Autodesk.Revit.UI
15	Autodesk.Revit.CADExportOptions	Autodesk.Revit	Autodesk.Revit.DB
16	Autodesk.Revit.CADImportOptions	Autodesk.Revit	Autodesk.Revit.DB
17	Autodesk.Revit.Categories	Autodesk.Revit	Autodesk.Revit.DB
18	Autodesk.Revit.Category	Autodesk.Revit	Autodesk.Revit.DB
19	Autodesk.Revit.CategoryFilter	Autodesk.Revit	Autodesk.Revit.DB
20	Autodesk.Revit.CategoryNameMap	Autodesk.Revit	Autodesk.Revit.DB
21	Autodesk.Revit.CategoryNameMapIterator	Autodesk.Revit	Autodesk.Revit.DB
22	Autodesk.Revit.CategorySet	Autodesk.Revit	Autodesk.Revit.DB
23	Autodesk.Revit.CategorySetIterator	Autodesk.Revit	Autodesk.Revit.DB
24	Autodesk.Revit.Collections.Array	Autodesk.Revit.Collections	Autodesk.Revit.Collections

Additional Ribbon Customization Options

Perhaps one of the most powerful improvements made in the Revit 2011 API has to do with the ribbon control additions. The ability to dock a custom text box into the Quick Access toolbar (QAT) for uses ranging from command entry with full argument syntax support to family search is now right at your fingertips. This opens doors for generating simpler customizations without having to create a clunky dialog interface.

New Ribbon Controls

The ability to create ribbon items with all the same features as the default ribbon items is a major improvement in this version of the API. You can now add long descriptions that display when you hover over a custom ribbon control as well as tooltip images. The list of ribbon improvements is quite extensive. For example, new controls that can be added to the ribbon in Revit 2011 include the following:

SplitButton   Creates a pull-down button with a default push button attached.

RadioGroup   Creates a set of ToggleButtons, where only one of the set can be active at a time.

ComboBox   Creates a pull-down containing a set of selectable items, which can be optionally grouped.

TextBox   Creates an input field for users to enter text; an event has also been added to pass the contents when Enter is pressed.

SlideOut Panel Similar to a flyout panel that slides down from a ribbon panel when clicked. These panels can contain any of the standard ribbon components.

Custom Panels to the Analyze Tab Custom panels can also be added to the Analyze tab in Revit MEP 2011 as well as the Add-Ins tab via a new overload of `Application .CreateRibbonPanel()`.

New Ribbon Control Methods

As a result of the ribbon control enhancements, some preexisting ribbon methods have been modified, as shown in Table 24.2.

TABLE 24.2: Changes in Ribbon Control Methods

METHOD/PROPERTY	DESCRIPTION
`RibbonPanel.AddButton()`	Replaced with `RibbonPanel.AddItem()`
`RibbonPanel.AddStackedButtons()`	Replaced with `RibbonPanel.AddStackedItems()` overloads
Property `RibbonPanel.Items`	Replaced with method `RibbbonPanel.GetItems()`
Property `PulldownButton.Items`	Replaced with method `PulldownButton.GetItems()`
Method `RibbonPanel.AddPushButton()`	Removed; use `RibbonPanel.AddItem()`
Method `RibbonPanel.AddPulldownButton()`	Removed; use `RibbonPanel.AddItem()`
Method `RibbonPanel.AddToPulldown()`	Removed; use `PulldownButton.AddItem()`
Method `PulldownButton.AddPushButton()`	Removed; use `PulldownButton.AddItem()`

Building a Batch Family Extractor

Now that you have a basic understanding of the Revit API, let's build a custom command and a custom application to call it. The code samples for the external command and external application are written in VB.NET using Visual Studio 2008.

The sample command will iterate through all family symbols in the model and export them to individual RFA files to a user-selected directory location. Each family file will be saved into a subdirectory named by its Revit family category name. The sample application will generate a custom ribbon button you will use to launch the custom external command. Harvesting content from existing projects will never be easier.

Creating the Visual Studio Projects

All external commands and applications are now required to have unique globally unique identifiers (GUIDs) in order to load into the Revit user interface. This means that each command and application is better managed as individual Visual Studio projects.

Visual Studio allows multiple stand-alone projects to be loaded into a *master* project, allowing you to easily manage multiple projects written in any supported .NET language in one convenient master environment.

This example demonstrates how to configure the `ExternalCommand` as one Visual Studio project and the `ExternalApplication` as another. You will then create a third *master* project into which you will load the two subprojects.

1. Create a new Visual Basic Class Library project in Visual Studio 2008. Make sure that the .NET Framework is set to 3.5. Name it **ExampleCommand** (Figure 24.3) and click OK.

2. Save the ExampleCommand project to disk and create another project using the same settings, but this time name it **ExampleApplication** and save it alongside the ExampleCommand project.

3. Close both of the command and application projects and create a third project. This time select the Empty Project template and name the solution **ExampleProject**, as shown in Figure 24.4.

FIGURE 24.3
Create a new class library in Visual Studio.

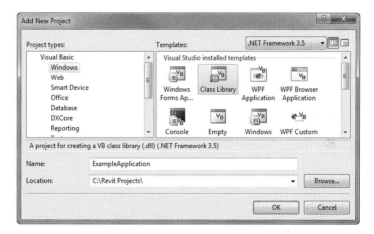

FIGURE 24.4
Create a new example project in Visual Studio.

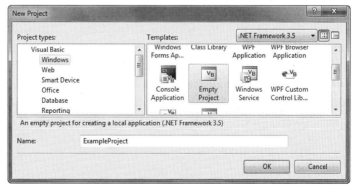

4. Add the ExampleCommand and ExampleApplication projects to this new ExampleProject project by selecting File ➤ Add ➤ Existing Project. The sample command and application projects can be debugged and managed through this master project.

Adding Namespace References

All Autodesk Revit 2011 IExternalCommands and IExternalApplications now require two namespace references: RevitAPI.dll and RevitAPIUI.dll.

Right-click the title of the Visual Studio 2008 project name in the Solution Explorer and select Add ➤ Reference. Alternately, you can select Project ➤ Add Reference from the main menu. Navigate to the Program folder of your Revit installation (usually in C:\Program Files\ Autodesk\Revit Architecture 2011), and add these two references to your project, as shown in Figure 24.5.

FIGURE 24.5
Adding API references to your Visual Studio project

The ExternalApplication project requires two additional references to Presentation Core and Windows Base for the ribbon image functionality. Both of these references are available from the .NET tab of the Add References dialog box.

Class and Form Configurations

With the namespace references out of the way, the next step in our project configuration is to name the default IExternalApplication and IExternalCommand interface classes to something logical. The names of these classes can be anything you want but we recommend that a consistent naming strategy be used to make it easier to manage. We typically use the name of Command for commands and App for applications.

COMMAND CLASS

Select Class1.vb in the ExternalCommand project, and change its name to Command.vb in the Visual Studio properties window. This class will serve as the main external command class containing the IExternalCommand interface necessary to gain access to the Revit user interface.

SETTING *COPYLOCAL* TO FALSE

The CopyLocal property for references added to a project using the Browse method will typically default to True. This property should always be set to False for the Revit API DLLs.

Select the RevitAPI.dll and RevitAPIUI.dll references and set their CopyLocal property to False in the Properties Palette, as shown here:

Import Namespaces

The command class requires three namespace imports. The Revit and Revit.UI namespaces are used to get at the main program and user interface functionalities. The Revit.Attributes namespace is used to access the regeneration and transaction features that are now required by the Revit 2011 API.

```
Imports Autodesk.Revit
Imports Autodesk.Revit.UI
Imports Autodesk.Revit.Attributes
```

Transaction and Regeneration Mode Attributes

The Transaction and Regeneration attributes are now required for all Revit 2011 API commands and applications. These two attributes must be called immediately before the class declaration and after any namespace imports.

The transaction serves as a container of changes that can be rolled back if a failure occurs. The regeneration options can now be set to manual, preventing Revit from regenerating on each and every modification made by your utility. This basically opens the door for speed and efficiency in your functions.

```
<Transaction(TransactionMode.Automatic)> _
```

```
<Regeneration(RegenerationOption.Manual)> _
Public Class Command .......
```

Listing 24.7 shows the completed Command class code.

LISTING 24.7   The Completed Command Class

```
Imports Autodesk.Revit
Imports Autodesk.Revit.UI
Imports Autodesk.Revit.Attributes

''' <summary>
''' Demonstrates how an ExternalCommand is added to the Revit user interface.
''' </summary>
<Transaction(TransactionMode.Automatic)> _
<Regeneration(RegenerationOption.Manual)> _
Public Class Command
    Implements IExternalCommand ' All ExternalCommands ↵
    must implement IExternalCommand
    ' Handy way to post build version info to a form
    Public Const appDate As String = "(YYYY-MM-DD) - "
    Public Const appVer As String = "V#.#"

    Public Function Execute(ByVal commandData As ExternalCommandData, _
                      ByRef message As String, _
                      ByVal elements As DB.ElementSet) _
                      As Result Implements IExternalCommand.Execute
        Try
            Dim rvtApp As UI.UIApplication = commandData.Application
            Dim rvtDoc As DB.Document = rvtApp.ActiveUIDocument.Document
            Dim oForm As New formMain
            Dim sAppVersion As String = rvtDoc.Application.VersionNumber
            ' Pass the Revit document along with any other variables to the form
            oForm.Initialise(rvtApp, rvtDoc, appDate, appVer & ↵
            " for RAC" & sAppVersion)
            oForm.ShowDialog()
            ' ExecuteCommands must return either Succeeded, Failed, or Cancelled
            Return Result.Succeeded
        Catch ex As Exception
            ' If something goes wrong, exit and return failed
            message = "Command load failed"
            Return Result.Failed
        End Try
    End Function
End Class
```

APPLICATION (APP) CLASS

Select `Class1.vb` in the ExternalApplication project and change its name to **App.vb** in the Visual Studio properties window. This class will serve as the main external application class containing the `IExternalApplication` interface for adding our ribbon panel to the Revit user interface.

The sample application class will add a pushbutton to the Add-Ins ribbon as well as a sample text box demonstrating how to capture the `EnterPressed` event for this control. The text box control introduction to the Revit 2011 API is in our opinion the most useful addition to the UI namespace of the Revit 2011 API.

Import Namespaces

The sample external application needs six namespace imports to achieve the functionality needed as shown here. `Revit.UI.Events` is required for the textbox `EnterPressed` event example. Each of the System imports are required to add images to our ribbon controls.

```
Imports Autodesk.Revit.UI
Imports Autodesk.Revit.UI.Events
Imports Autodesk.Revit.Attributes

Imports System.Windows.Forms
Imports System.Windows.Media.Imaging
Imports System.Reflection
```

Immediately following the namespace imports, we set the transaction mode to automatic. In an effort to make the program run faster, we then set the regeneration option to manual, as shown here, in an effort to make the program run faster.

```
<Transaction(TransactionMode.Automatic)> _
<Regeneration(RegenerationOption.Manual)> _
Public Class App ......
```

Listing 24.8 shows the completed App class code.

LISTING 24.8   The Completed App Class

```
Imports Autodesk.Revit.UI
Imports Autodesk.Revit.UI.Events
Imports Autodesk.Revit.Attributes

Imports System.Windows.Forms
Imports System.Windows.Media.Imaging
Imports System.Reflection

''' <summary>
''' Demonstrates how an ExternalApplication is added to the Revit user interface.
''' </summary>
<Transaction(TransactionMode.Automatic)> _
<Regeneration(RegenerationOption.Manual)> _
```

```vb
Public Class App
    ' Required Interface...
    Implements IExternalApplication
    ' Fired off by OnStartup
    Public Sub AddRibbonPanel(ByVal a As UIControlledApplication)
        ' Share the execution path with supplemental command paths
        Dim myPath As String = Assembly.GetExecutingAssembly.Location.Substring( _
            0, (Assembly.GetExecutingAssembly.Location.LastIndexOf("\") + 1))
        Dim rvtPanel As RibbonPanel = a.CreateRibbonPanel("Samples")
        ' Use the 'New' method to create pushbuttons
        Dim rvtData As New PushButtonData("ExampleCommand", _
            "Batch Family Export Utility", _
            myPath & "ExampleCommand.dll", _
            "ExampleCommand.Command")
        rvtData.ToolTip = "Example Batch Family Export Command"
        ' Add the pushbutton to the ribbon panel
        Dim myButton As PushButton = rvtPanel.AddItem(rvtData)
        ' Add a textbox that will return its entered value when enter is pressed
        Dim txtData As New TextBoxData("MyTextBox")
        ' Add the textbox to the ribbon panel
        Dim txtBox As Autodesk.Revit.UI.TextBox = rvtPanel.AddItem(txtData)
        txtBox.Value = "Textbox Event Example"
        txtBox.Image = New BitmapImage(New Uri(myPath & "enter.png"))
        txtBox.ToolTip = "A sample message dialog displaying the entered data..."
        txtBox.ShowImageAsButton = True
        txtBox.PromptText = "Enter Text and Press Enter"
        ' This passes the event data to our event handler function
        AddHandler txtBox.EnterPressed, _
            New EventHandler(Of TextBoxEnterPressedEventArgs)↵
            (AddressOf Me.TextBoxPopup)
    End Sub

    Public Sub TextBoxPopup(ByVal sender As Object, _
                            ByVal args As TextBoxEnterPressedEventArgs)
        ' This reacts with the string entered into the textbox...
        MessageBox.Show(sender.value, _
                    "Textbox Value!", _
                    MessageBoxButtons.OK, _
                    MessageBoxIcon.Exclamation)
    End Sub

    Public Function OnStartup(ByVal a As UIControlledApplication) _
    As Result Implements IExternalApplication.OnStartup
        Try
            ' Add the ribbon part to the Add-Ins tab
            AddRibbonPanel(a)
```

```
            Return Result.Succeeded
        Catch ex As Exception
            Return Result.Failed
        End Try
    End Function

    Public Function OnShutdown(ByVal a As UIControlledApplication) _
        As Result Implements IExternalApplication.OnShutdown
        Return Result.Succeeded
    End Function

End Class
```

The User Form

The sample command will need a user form as a means to interact with the user. Right-click ExternalCommand in the Solution Explorer and select Add ➤ Windows Form to add a user form to the project. Name this form **formMain** and click OK.

Adding the Controls

The next step is the design of the user form along with all required controls necessary to provide the functionality we need. Save the project and open the design view of the formMain class. Figure 24.6 illustrates what the completed form design should look like.

FIGURE 24.6
Example of a completed form in Visual Studio

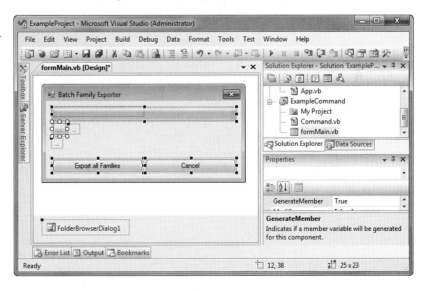

You can be creative as to your placement of these controls so long as they are of the correct control types and match the names listed here. The controls are listed in order from top to bottom, going left to right, as illustrated in the previous example.

FolderBrowserDialog Control: FolderBrowserDialog1   Add a FolderBrowserDialog from the toolbox to the form named **FolderBrowserDialog1**. This will serve as a helper dialog box to navigate and select an alternate directory for the RFA file family exports. This control only displays in the form design tray and will not necessarily display on the form itself.

Progressbar Control: ProgressBar1   Provides progress information to user. Place this control along the top of the form as illustrated earlier.

Label Control: LabelExport   The example form design shows the LabelExport control placed underneath the left corner of the progress bar along the top of the form. This label displays as the main prompt to the user on load.

Button Control: ButtonBrowse   Place this control beneath the progress bar and set its text to **....** This button will be used to launch the folder browse dialog box. Double-click the ButtonBrowse control and enter the following code:

```
Private Sub ButtonBrowse_Click(ByVal sender As System.Object, _
                            ByVal e As System.EventArgs) _
                            Handles ButtonBrowse.Click
    ' Browse to select the parent export path
    Me.FolderBrowserDialog1.ShowDialog()
    If Me.FolderBrowserDialog1.SelectedPath.ToString() <> "" Then
        Me.LabelExportPath.Text = ↵
        Me.FolderBrowserDialog1.SelectedPath.ToString()
    End If
End Sub
```

Label Control: LabelExportPath   Place a label control named **LabelExportPath** to the right of the ButtonBrowse control. This label will display the path to the selected export directory.

Label Control: LabelFileName   Place a label control beneath the ButtonBrowse button named **LabelExport**. This label will display the current family file as it is being processed by the main export functions.

Button Control: ButtonExport   The bottom-left button, named ButtonExport, is used to launch the export command and commit the start of the export process. Set the text for this button to **Export all Families**. Double-click this button control to create the basic code structure for the click event. The code behind this button is shown in "The Main Export Function" section later in this chapter.

Button Control: ButtonCancel   The bottom-right button, named ButtonCancel, is used to close the command without performing any actions at all. Set the text for this control to **Cancel**. Double-click the Cancel button and enter the following code:

```
Private Sub ButtonCancel_Click(ByVal sender As System.Object, _
                            ByVal e As System.EventArgs) _
                            Handles ButtonCancel.Click
    Me.Close()
End Sub
```

Adding the Private Form Class Variables

The following lines are used to make the Revit application, current Revit project model, and default export path available to all functions within the form class. These declarations will go just beneath the form class declaration:

```
Private rvtDir As String = ""
Private rvtApp As UI.UIApplication = Nothing
Private rvtDoc As DB.Document
```

Adding the Supplemental Form Functions

The command example is quite simple in function but still requires a few supplemental helper functions:

Initialization It is common to utilize an initialization subroutine within a form as a means of introducing any required parameters to the form as it is being launched. This provides an easy way to pass object variables to the form that can then be used within the form class.

Among the objects that we are interested in passing over to the user form are the Revit application object, current Revit project model, a string representing the build date, and another string representing an arbitrary build version, such as V1.0.

This function will also set our default export path to the directory of our model using the central model file path if the project is workshared.

```
Public Sub Initialise(ByVal app As UI.UIApplication, _
                      ByVal document As DB.Document, _
                      ByVal myAppDate As String, _
                      ByVal strAppVer As String)
    ' Hide the progressbar until we need it
    Me.ProgressBar1.Visible = False
    ' Form title with version
    Me.Text = "Batch Family Exporter - " & myAppDate & strAppVer
    ' Expose Revit doc and app
    rvtDoc = document
    rvtApp = app
    ' Set default export path adjacent to model location
    ' If workshared, use the central model path
    If rvtDoc.IsWorkshared = True Then
        Try
            rvtDir = Path.GetDirectoryName ↵
            (rvtDoc.WorksharingCentralFilename) _
            & "/Exported Families/"
        Catch ex As Exception
            ' Detached model will not have a file path
        End Try
    Else
        rvtDir = Path.GetDirectoryName(rvtDoc.PathName) & _
        "/Exported Families/"
```

```
            End If
            ' The proper formatted file path...
            Me.LabelExportPath.Text = Replace(rvtDir, "/", "\")
        End Sub
```

CheckValidFileName   While Revit provides its own means of preventing invalid file-naming characters from making their way into family names, you can use this function as a precautionary means. This filename validity snippet is useful anytime you are exporting files and need to verify that the characters used in the filename are valid.

```
    Public Shared Function CheckValidFileName↵
       (ByVal fileName As String) As String
        CheckValidFileName = fileName
        For Each c In Path.GetInvalidFileNameChars()
            If fileName.Contains(c) Then
                ' Invalid filename characters detected...
                ' Could either replace characters or return empty
                CheckValidFileName = ""
            End If
        Next
        Return CheckValidFileName
    End Function
```

The Main Export Function

The main export function in the sample project is all nested inside the `ButtonExport_Click` subroutine. There will be a lot going on inside this routine. The meat of the function is where the family symbols are filtered out of the Revit document and then iterated one by one and exported out as external RFA family files into a subdirectory named using the family's Revit category name.

The Element Collection Filter   The Revit 2011 API provides a much more efficient and robust means of filtering elements for selection as well as iterating elements within these collections.

```
    ' Filter to get a set of elements that are elementType
    Dim filter As New DB.ElementIsElementTypeFilter
    Dim collector As New DB.FilteredElementCollector(rvtDoc)
    collector.WherePasses(filter)
```

Element Iteration   Once the elements have been gathered from the model using an element filter, we can iterate through them quite easily. This snippet illustrates the element iteration code:

```
    Dim iter As IEnumerator = collector.GetElementIterator
    Dim element As DB.Element
    Dim FamInst As DB.Family = Nothing
    Dim famSymb As DB.FamilySymbol = Nothing
    Dim category As DB.Category
    Do While (iter.MoveNext())
        element = iter.Current
```

```
        If (TypeOf element Is DB.FamilySymbol) Then
            category = element.Category
            If Not (category Is Nothing) Then
                Try ' Create the category subdirectory
                    exportPath = rvtDir & category.Name & "/"
                    Directory.CreateDirectory(Replace _
                    (exportPath, "/", "\", , , CompareMethod.Text))
                Catch ex As Exception
                    ' Category subdirectory exists
                End Try
                Try ' family variable to Element
                    famSymb = element
                    FamInst = famSymb.Family
                    sFamName = FamInst.Name
                    ' Verify famname is valid filename and exists
                    If Dir$(exportPath + sFamName & ".rfa") = "" And _
                            CheckValidFileName(sFamName) <> "" Then
                        Me.LabelFileName.Text = "...\" & _
                            category.Name & "\" & _
                            FamInst.Name
                        Dim famDoc As DB.Document = rvtDoc.EditFamily(FamInst)
                        famDoc.SaveAs(exportPath + sFamName & ".rfa")
                        famDoc.Close(False)
                    End If
                Catch ex As Exception
                    ' Prevent hault on system families
                End Try
            End If
        End If
    Loop
```

Listing 24.9 shows the completed formMain code.

LISTING 24.9   The Completed formMain Code

```
Imports Autodesk.Revit
Imports System.IO

Public Class formMain

    Private rvtDir As String = ""
    Private rvtApp As UI.UIApplication = Nothing
    Private rvtDoc As DB.Document

    Public Sub Initialise(ByVal app As UI.UIApplication, _
                          ByVal document As DB.Document, _
                          ByVal myAppDate As String, _
                          ByVal strAppVer As String)
```

```vb
        ' Hide the progressbar until we need it
        Me.ProgressBar1.Visible = False
        ' Form title with version
        Me.Text = "Batch Family Exporter - " & myAppDate & strAppVer
        ' Expose Revit doc and app
        rvtDoc = document
        rvtApp = app
        ' Set default export path adjacent to model location
        ' If workshared, use the central model path
        If rvtDoc.IsWorkshared = True Then
            Try
                rvtDir = Path.GetDirectoryName↵
                (rvtDoc.WorksharingCentralFilename) _
                & "/Exported Families/"
            Catch ex As Exception
                ' Detached model will not have a file path
            End Try
        Else
            rvtDir = Path.GetDirectoryName(rvtDoc.PathName) & _
            "/Exported Families/"
        End If
        ' The proper formatted file path...
        Me.LabelExportPath.Text = Replace(rvtDir, "/", "\")
    End Sub

    Public Shared Function CheckValidFileName(ByVal fileName As String) As String
        CheckValidFileName = fileName
        For Each c In Path.GetInvalidFileNameChars()
            If fileName.Contains(c) Then
                ' Invalid filename characters detected...
                ' Could either replace characters or return empty
                CheckValidFileName = ""
            End If
        Next
        Return CheckValidFileName
    End Function

    Private Sub ButtonExport_Click(ByVal sender As System.Object, _
                            ByVal e As System.EventArgs) _
                            Handles ButtonExport.Click
        ' Return a qualified export path
        rvtDir = Replace(rvtDir, "\", "/", , , CompareMethod.Text)
        Dim sFamName As String = ""
        Dim exportPath As String = ""
        Try ' If the parent export directory is missing, create it
            Directory.CreateDirectory _
            (Replace(rvtDir, "/", "\", , , CompareMethod.Text))
        Catch ex As Exception
```

```vb
    ' Message to show any errors
    MsgBox(Err.Description, MsgBoxStyle.Information, Err.Source)
End Try
' Filter to get a set of elements that are elementType
Dim filter As New DB.ElementIsElementTypeFilter
Dim collector As New DB.FilteredElementCollector(rvtDoc)
collector.WherePasses(filter)
' Iterate the elements
Dim iter As IEnumerator = collector.GetElementIterator
' Variables for element handling
Dim element As DB.Element
Dim FamInst As DB.Family = Nothing
Dim famSymb As DB.FamilySymbol = Nothing
Dim category As DB.Category
' Quickly count for progress bar
Dim iCntFam As Integer = 0
Dim iCnt As Integer = 0
Do While (iter.MoveNext())
    element = iter.Current
    If (TypeOf element Is DB.FamilySymbol) Then
        iCntFam += 1
    End If
Loop
' Reset for export process
iter.Reset()
' Start the progressbar
Me.ProgressBar1.Visible = True
Me.ProgressBar1.Minimum = 0
Me.ProgressBar1.Maximum = iCntFam
Me.ProgressBar1.Value = iCnt
' The export process
Do While (iter.MoveNext())
    element = iter.Current
    If (TypeOf element Is DB.FamilySymbol) Then
        Me.ProgressBar1.Value = Me.ProgressBar1.Value + 1
        category = element.Category
        If Not (category Is Nothing) Then
            Try ' Create the category subdirectory
                exportPath = rvtDir & category.Name & "/"
                Directory.CreateDirectory(Replace _
                (exportPath, "/", "\", , , CompareMethod.Text))
            Catch ex As Exception
                ' Category subdirectory exists
            End Try
            Try ' family variable to Element
                famSymb = element
                FamInst = famSymb.Family
                sFamName = FamInst.Name
```

```
                              ' Verify famname is valid filename and exists
                              If Dir$(exportPath + sFamName & ".rfa") = "" And _
                                    CheckValidFileName(sFamName) <> "" Then
                                  Me.LabelFileName.Text = "...\" & _
                                    category.Name & "\" & _
                                    FamInst.Name
                                  Dim famDoc As DB.Document = ↵
                                   rvtDoc.EditFamily(FamInst)
                                  famDoc.SaveAs(exportPath + sFamName & ".rfa")
                                  famDoc.Close(False)
                              End If
                          Catch ex As Exception
                              ' Prevent hault on system families
                          End Try
                  End If
              End If
          Loop
          Me.Close()
      End Sub

      Private Sub ButtonCancel_Click(ByVal sender As System.Object, _
                                 ByVal e As System.EventArgs) _
                                 Handles ButtonCancel.Click
          Me.Close()
      End Sub

      Private Sub ButtonBrowse_Click(ByVal sender As System.Object, _
                                 ByVal e As System.EventArgs) _
                                 Handles ButtonBrowse.Click
          ' Browse to select the parent export path
          Me.FolderBrowserDialog1.ShowDialog()
          If Me.FolderBrowserDialog1.SelectedPath.ToString() <> "" Then
              Me.LabelExportPath.Text = ↵
               Me.FolderBrowserDialog1.SelectedPath.ToString()
          End If
      End Sub
  End Class
```

Additional API Resources

If you are interested in learning more about the Revit API, here are some online resources for your reference:

◆ Autodesk Developer Center and Developer Network (ADN): www.autodesk.com/adn

◆ The Building Coder (a blog by Jeremy Tammik): thebuildingcoder.typepad.com

♦ Autodesk Revit API Discussion Group: `discussion.autodesk.com/forum`
`.jspa?forumID=160`

♦ DevTV: Introduction to Revit API Programming: `download.autodesk.com/media/adn/`
`DevTV_Introduction_to_Revit_Programming_new`

Using Revit Journals

As you work in Revit, all of your actions are recorded in journal files. These files, which can be found in `C:\Program Files\Autodesk\Revit Architecture 2011\Journals`, are basic text files that can be opened and reviewed in any text editor such as Notepad or Notepad ++ (`notepad-plus.sourceforge.net`). If you have ever had any kind of complicated support issue, you may have been asked to send your journal files to Autodesk for review. With the journal files, the Autodesk support team can replay the actions captured in an active Revit session. Journal files can also be used to perform some simple automated tasks.

WARNING ABOUT USING REVIT JOURNALS

You should be aware that Autodesk does not support any kind of scripting via use of the journal files. Use these suggestions at your own risk and do not test them on active project data.

Family Upgrade Method

One simple example of a journal script is the family upgrade utility, which is a simple journal-based script that will launch Revit and open a series of families you specify, thus upgrading them to the latest version. This utility is included with your Revit installation package and can be found after you extract the installation package in the subfolder: `Utilities\Common\ ContentBatchUtility`.

Before running the script, you must first copy the `Upgrade_RFA.txt` and `Upgrade_RFA.bat` files into the root directory of the library you want to upgrade and then run the `Upgrade_RFA` `.bat` file to generate a list of files to upgrade. This BAT routine will create another text file named `famlist_rfa.txt`; don't change the name of this file or move it. The `Upgrade_RFA.txt` file is a Revit journal file. If you open the journal file, you will find the main function listed as a subroutine between the code `Sub` and `End Sub`, as shown in Listing 24.10.

LISTING 24.10   The Main Function in the Family Upgrade Journal Script

```
Sub upgrade(namepath, file)

Jrn.Command "Menu", "Open an existing project , 57601 , ID_FILE_OPEN"
  Jrn.Data "File Name" _
         , "IDOK", namepath

 Jrn.Command "Internal" , " , ID_REVIT_SAVE_AS_FAMILY"
```

```
Jrn.Data "File Name"  , "IDOK", namepath

Jrn.Command "Menu" , "Close the active project , ID_REVIT_FILE_CLOSE"

End Sub
```

To execute the journal script, simply drag the Upgrade_RFA.txt file onto the Revit desktop icon. Revit will launch and open each RFA file in the list. As you can see in Listing 24.10, the actual journal commands being passed to Revit are quite simple. ID FILE OPEN opens the project, whereas ID REVIT SAVE AS FAMILY saves it in the new version.

Local File Script and AutoHotkey

You can find another example of journal scripting in a local file utility developed in collaboration between David Baldacchino, David Kingham, and James Vandezande. This utility was created in an open source scripting language called AutoHotkey (www.autohotkey.com). This language is easy to learn and can be an excellent learning platform for aspiring programmers. You can download the local file utility from the AUGI Forums at forums.augi.com/showthread.php?t=65897.

The local file utility has several iterations for each of the developer's respective companies, but at its core, it performs basic file functions to create local copies of Revit central files and then automatically opens them with journal-based scripts. Let's take a look at that portion of the utility.

Other parts of the script will identify the central file and locations for a user's local copies. Once a local copy of the central file has been created, journal commands are generated and written to an actual journal file:

```
Set Jrn = CrsJournalScript
Jrn.Command "Menu" , "Open an existing project , 57601 , ID_REVIT_FILE_OPEN"
Jrn.Data "File Name"  _
, "IDOK", "%DESTINATION%\%LOCALFILE%.rvt"
Jrn.Data "WorksetConfig"  _
, "Editable", 0
  Jrn.Data "MessageBox"  _
        , "IDOK", "This Central File has been copied or moved from↵
  ""%DRV%\%DSCPLN%\%Folder%\%C1%"" to ""%DESTINATION%\%LOCALFILE%.rvt"".".↵
  & vbCrLf & "" & vbCrLf & "If you wish this file to remain a Central File ↵
  then you must re-save the file as a Central File. To do this select ↵
  ""Save As"" from the ""File"" menu and check the ""Make this a Central ↵
  File after save"" check box (under the options button) before you save."↵
  & vbCrLf & "" & vbCrLf & "If you do not save the file as a Central File↵
  then it will be considered a local user copy of the file belonging to↵
  user ""%USERNAME%""."
Jrn.Command "Menu" , "Workset control , 33460 , ID_SETTINGS_PARTITIONS"
```

The journal file is then executed by passing it to the Revit program executable, which is similar to actually dropping a journal file on the Revit desktop icon in the family upgrade method.

Notice the syntax of the journal launching code is quite similar to running an application with optional parameters at the Windows command prompt. The following line runs `Revit.exe` with the journal file (%JournalFile%) in a maximized application window:

```
Run %AppPath%\Program\Revit.exe "%JournalFile%", Max
```

The Bottom Line

Understand the basics of the Revit API.   The need for some users and developers to extend the functionality of Revit is supported by the Revit application programming interface (API). Revit's software development kit (SDK) provides sample code and instructions for building add-ons to the application.

Master It   What are the two types of dynamic link libraries you can develop for Revit?

Understand the new `.addin` **manifest file method used to load custom command and applications into Revit.**   The Revit API for 2011 now offers the ability to register API applications into Revit using an `.addin` manifest file.

Master It   How is the `.addin` manifest method different from previous versions?

Set up and build your own custom external applications and commands.   You can start to create your own custom applications and commands for Revit using either Microsoft Visual Studio or a free tool such as Visual Studio Express or SharpDevelop.

Master It   How do you make the Revit API functions available in your developing environment?

Chapter 25

Direct to Fabrication

The use of BIM in the industry has exploded over the past decade to include a variety of uses both before documentation commences and after construction begins. So far, we have covered many of the ways you can use Revit to augment this design through the construction process. With the "direct to fabrication" process, you are taking that entire cycle of concept to realization and compacting it into a single, fluid process.

In this chapter, you'll learn to:

- ◆ Understand the concepts of digital fabrication
- ◆ Use digital fabrication on a project
- ◆ Model cleanly and accurately

Understanding the Concepts of Digital Fabrication

ABOUT THE CONTRIBUTING AUTHOR: JEFFREY MCGREW

Jeffrey McGrew comes from a deep background of professional design, Architecture, and the industry of construction. For the last three years he has been the co-owner of the Design Build company, Because We Can, which has immersed him in product and furniture design from small decorative pieces to complete interior spaces, all with a heavy focus on leveraging CNC-driven tools and Building Information Modeling. He is finishing his Architectural Licensing exams, and plans to have them completed this year. In his non-existent moments of spare time he likes to draw, read, and learn more about tools and programming. Occasionally he gives presentations on BIM at local and national conferences, though wishes he spent more time making bad rock songs in Garageband, going to Tiki Bars, and keeping the Because We Can '67 Dodge van running.

Jeffrey McGrew, Founder, Because We Can, LLC
www.becausewecan.org

Much of this book so far has been about the *I* of BIM. This *I* represents all the rich *information* that you can put into your Revit projects and how to make best use of it. We have also discussed a lot about the *M* of BIM, *modeling*. We've explored how to make buildings and families and how to use models for documentation, clash detection, and rendering. Although both of these elements are wonderful advantages of BIM, this chapter will begin to consider the *B*, or *building*. When talking about digital fabrication, regard this building not as a noun but as a verb.

Digital fabrication is the process where you take data-rich models from your BIM model and feed them directly to automated, computer-driven tools to make physical models or parts of your project. It is *building* directly from the BIM—no drawings needed! It's not a flying car, but it sure is the future, and it's a lot more accessible than you might think. By the end of this chapter, you should be ready and inspired to begin making things directly from your BIM projects!

Types of Fabrication

Automated tools or computer numeric control (CNC) tools tend to fall into two main categories: additive fabrication and subtractive fabrication.

ADDITIVE FABRICATION

Additive fabrication is where a computer-controlled tool deposits, adds, or stacks material a layer at a time to "print" your 3D models. Some of the types of additive fabricators are 3D printers, "fabbers," and robotic placement arms. We'll discuss each of these in a bit more detail and talk about how they might be used:

3D Printers These machines glue together thin layers of powder or plastic to build up your part a layer at a time. They are good for quickly making models and small, durable plastic parts; however, only the higher-end devices have the ability to make things from more durable materials (like metals) or create models in multiple colors.

"Fabbers" This is a subset of 3D printers that extrude plastic, resin, wax, frosting (really!), or even concrete. Imagine a robotic hot glue gun that can build up models a thin layer at a time. They have an advantage over traditional 3D printers in that they can make "real" items, because the media they use tends to be a lot more durable. In the case of printing to wax, the models can be used in lost wax casting to make molds.

Robotic Placement Arms Ever see those huge robot arms that weld cars together? Think of these as their smarter little brothers. These can be used to stack bricks, blocks, or other elements with perfect precision to literally build walls and forms.

SUBTRACTIVE FABRICATION

Subtractive fabrication is the process where a computer-controlled tool removes, cuts, or otherwise carves away material to produce 3D models. Some of the machine types that fall into this category are CNC mills, CNC lathes, CNC routers, CNC punch mills, CNC wire benders, and laser and water-jet cutters. Each has a unique use and cost associated with this type of fabrication.

CNC Mills These are traditional metalworking mills made robotic. They are great for cutting almost any type of material accurately, but these machines tend to be limited in the size of parts they can produce and are somewhat slow. With CNC mills, the cutting head typically stays stationary, and the material is moved or tilted around it.

CNC Lathes These are traditional metalworking lathes made robotic. They are also a powerful tool for accurately cutting most materials but can be slow and limited in part size. With these machines, the cutting head moves while the material is spun along its long axis, allowing it to cut out different forms than other CNC machines.

CNC Routers   A router is a rotary cutter mounted to a robot arm or gantry-style system that moves over the top and around the material being cut, which is stationary. This workflow is great for making big things quickly, and most of these machines can cut full sheets of plywood or larger stock. However, CNC routers are not as accurate as the mills and lathes, and can have a difficult time cutting harder materials like steel.

CNC Punch Mills   A CNC punch mill is a traditional metalworking punch or press made robotic. They are able to punch out and fold sheet metal and are commonly used for automated production of HVAC ducting, metal siding panels, and curtain wall elements.

CNC Wire Benders   In a CNC wire bender, steel wire or rebar is fed while a special robot hand bends it or cuts it to length perfectly. CNC wire benders are ideal for mass production of custom-bent rebar or metal chair legs.

Laser and Water-Jet Cutters   These machines are similar to CNC routers, except that rather than a rotary cutting tool, they use a high-power laser or hyper-concentrated stream of water to cut the materials. They are great for producing parts with very tight tolerances and perfect corners, or when used to cut from thin materials. However, they tend to be able to cut clear only through materials (making fully 3D parts more difficult). Also, although the water-jet is amazing in that it can be used to cut pretty much anything imaginable, laser cutters can run into problems with certain materials and can cause burning, slagging, or even exploding!

Cutting by Axis

Another factor that is common with these machine types is the concept behind numbers of axes any of the machines might have. Commonly, machines are referred to as a *three-axis*, or a *five-axis*. What this means is how many directions the machine's blade can move in. Figure 25.1 demonstrates some of the differences between axis types.

FIGURE 25.1
Types of CNC axes

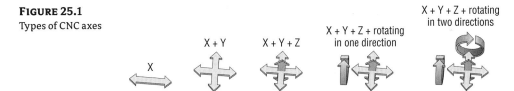

One Axis   Two Axis   Three Axis   Four Axis   Five Axis

Most CNC machines are three-axis; they can move back and forth (x- and y-axes) and up and down (z-axis), but can't tilt or turn the cutter or material to cut at angles. They are confined to cutting in only one plane or on one side of a piece of material. Typically, this is not a limiting factor in design as this allows you to make fully three-dimensional parts with complex surfaces, sculptural profiles, and so on.

A five-axis machine can move in the x-, y-, and z-axes, and it can also rotate or tilt the cutter or material. This means that a five-axis machine has the ability to produce more complex shapes automatically or without someone moving or changing the material. There are even six-axis and seven-axis machines, where not only can the cutter move and tilt, but the material being cut can move and rotate and tilt as well.

In all of these types, one thing to keep in mind is that higher-axis machines tend to be a lot more expensive to purchase or hire, and most of what you want to do can probably be done with a lower-axis machine—it's just going to take longer or require a little more creativity.

You shouldn't feel like a lower number of axes is limiting to your design. A two-axis machine, such as a water-jet or laser cutter, can cut through materials or be used to etch or engrave a surface by lessening the power of the device. However, once cut, these flat parts can be assembled together to create virtually any type of form. The cut material can also be folded or bent after cutting to create even more complex shapes. The only real limit is the designer's ability to create an element and then think through the process of disassembly, fabrication, and reassembly.

BIM to Digital Fabrication: The Process

Now that you have an understanding of the parts and machine types involved in digital fabrication, let's talk about process. In any digital fabrication workflow, there are five important steps you need to consider in order to work with Revit and CNC machines:

Inspiration   You have an incredible idea for something, or selected a part of our project to produce via CNC tools. Now what? At this early stage, you design like you always do, but with a couple of new ideas in mind and a few things to watch out for:

Mass Customization   Because the robots don't care if every part is unique or exactly the same, you can take advantage of this simple fact to produce totally custom elements without an increase in price. For example, each panel within a facade, screen, or other design element can be completely unique, no two alike, so that when the overall element is assembled it forms a larger picture or shape. Or, as another example, you can simply have every door in your project have a different hewn pattern carved into it. The only limit here is your time to model each element (or your ability to write scripts that automatically generate the models for you!).

Mass Production   Taking advantage of the same robots and their disinterest in unique or repetitive work, you can mass-produce elements that want to be built. Parts can be designed for easy assembly, like Scandinavian furniture, so that they only go together one way, auto-align to their joints, and snap together like a big puzzle. Additionally, making custom assembly or layout jigs is trivial. This in turn makes it so some building processes can be greatly optimized, even though what you're making is completely custom.

Configuration   So, you've established your big idea. Now you have to capture the design intent in your model with CNC production in mind. You need to take your inspiration, and envision it well enough to have a plan of how to make it, what it's going to be made from, and the other details of production.

Rationalization   As your third step, you have to turn those design models into fabrication models by adding in all the joints, parts, and pieces. This is where the rubber meets the road in terms of our Revit modeling—now it has to be 100 percent real. This step is about moving from conceptualization to a virtual version of your final product.

Isolation   Before you can produce your parts, you'll need to isolate them within your model. Sections, custom 3D views, and proper modeling go a long way to making this an easy process. You'll also need to be able to export the Revit models to the various formats that will work with our CNC machines. Each machine type and manufacturer will accept (or not accept) different model formats. Some common ones are STL, SAT, and IGES. Do some text runs for exporting and importing from Revit to CNC to detect subtle problems in workflow that can impact the final product of your design.

Fabrication Finally, the fun step: exported models are turned into jobs for the robots, and they are set in motion to make your project!

Now let's see how that process works in a real-world example.

 **Real World Scenario**

TIPS TO PLANNING YOUR FABRICATION

CNC machines are no more a magic bullet for your building than BIM is for your drawings. So, here are some tips you'll need to keep in mind:

Understand the limits of your materials. Certain materials, like plywood, can vary in thickness from sheet to sheet. Some plywoods can't be laser-cut effectively. If you design with these factors in mind and specify the materials with some forethought and knowledge, you can avoid expensive mistakes. Plan ahead for what materials you want to use, and research and test them prior to production.

Understand the limits of your machines. Certain tools are better suited to certain tasks. While you could make a presentation model using a CNC router, it might be a lot faster to use a 3D printer. And while you could use a CNC router to cut metal curtain wall parts, a water-jet might be the better solution. Additionally, certain machines have limits on the material size or thickness you can use with them. Plan ahead, talk to your fabricator, and do your research.

Understand the limits of your modeling. Sadly, while Revit is an amazing tool, there are simply things it's not so great at modeling. When it comes to more sculptural pieces, you may need to use some other modeling tool along with Revit.

Using Digital Fabrication on a Project

Now that you have an understanding of the concepts and tools involved, let's take a look at a real-world example. Say you have a pretty typical interiors project: an office remodel. You used Revit to produce space plans (Figure 25.2), complete with multiple options as well as some interior renderings of the proposed space (Figure 25.3).

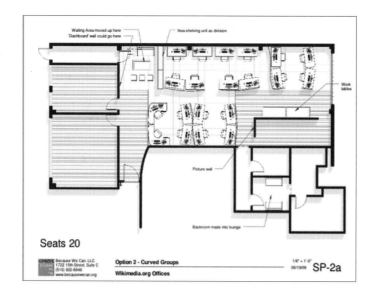

As part of the design process, you need to create furniture purchase lists and quick cost estimates. However, you're also slated to produce a custom reception desk. After several version and meetings with the client, they decided on a nice, clean, gentle curving desk (Figure 25.4).

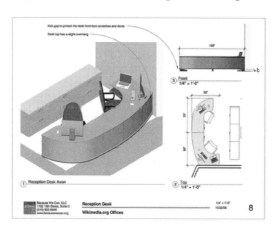

Now that you've completed the first step (the inspiration), next you have to take the idea and turn it into a reasonably constructible model. In this phase, you don't need to model every detail yet—just enough to capture your design intent and to get pricing for client review. So now you need to go from the simple form you've created during design and begin adding more detail, configuring what the final product will eventually become. Figure 25.5 shows the same model with an embellished level of detail. This phase would be similar to design drawings in a typical architectural set.

In this example, you'll be making this from plywood, and you are limited to the common size of a sheet: 4′ × 8′ (2440 × 1220mm). To best economize the stock, the longer form needs to be broken down into two parts. You'll also be bending a thin piece of face plywood to make that curve, so we'll need a lip to capture this piece and a frame behind it.

FIGURE 25.5
Working drawings for the reception desk

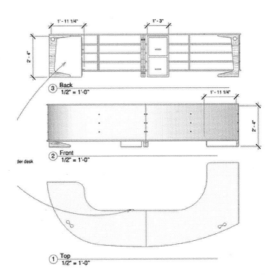

At this stage you could also do more BIM-enabled calculations on the desk if needed. Material takeoffs are easy—you have a rough area of plywood now. If this was a structural element, you could import the model into Revit Structure and then use the analysis package to properly test material strength. If this was a daylighting element, you could perform renderings in Revit, or export to 3ds Max Design or even Ecotect, to see how well the design performs in shading, bouncing light, or glare conditions within our project.

Although you could simply model elements for CNC fabrication in a non-BIM program, such as AutoCAD, SketchUp, or Rhino, you would then lose out on all that BIM "goodness" of analysis, collision detection, and more. Finally, you can now use this reception desk family within your project, right alongside all the rest of the work, instead of having models living in other, separate platforms.

Back in the example project, the client signs off on the design and costs. Configuration is done, so it's time to move on to rationalization. Now, you'll need to take the Design Model family in Revit, which initially captured the design intent of your reception desk in a reasonable, buildable way (and looked really good in the renderings) and begin creating a fabrication model. The Fabrication Model family in Revit is fully detailed to be ready for fabrication. Every joint and bit now need to be modeled so that all the elements fit together properly. Figure 25.6 shows an example of this type of condition.

FIGURE 25.6
An example of a joint created in a Revit family

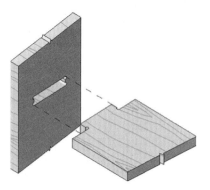

 Real World Scenario

MAKING FABRICATION EASIER

An essential part of fabrication from a Revit model is keeping your base planes of your solid objects in the proper place. It's always a challenge in Revit editing a sketch like the one shown here. In this image, you are in Sketch mode showing a table surface. While the surface of the table will be built at 30″ (762 mm) high, the sketch here is at the ground level. Working in this way makes it difficult to visually align adjacent surfaces.

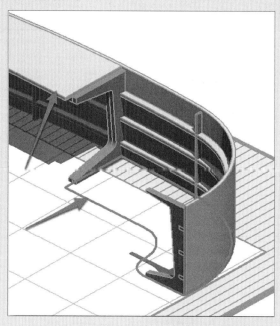

A better way to edit this element is to redefine the work plane of the solid. By setting the plane to be the actual desk surface, you can see that our sketch now lives in the same spot as the element, as shown here. It's now easier to use the pick line tools and to snap to other elements in the family, thus facilitating joint modeling.

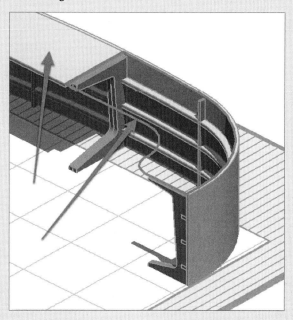

Remember that although normally in Revit design intent is good enough, when working with a fabrication model, the CNC machine will cut to the same tolerance that you design to. A more accurate model will mean a better final product.

Breaking the Model into Parts

Now that the design has been settled and it's fully detailed as a fabrication model with joints and assembly in mind, you now have to break down your model into its various parts. These parts will then be exported in a file format our robot or CNC machine will understand. In this example, because our desk is pretty simple, you can use section views to cut up the model into its various views, isolating the individual parts you need the machine to create (Figure 25.7).

These sections or isolated elements can be exported to various file types such as DXF, DWG, or SAT files, which will in turn be imported into our CAM software.

FIGURE 25.7
Using sections to break the model into individual components

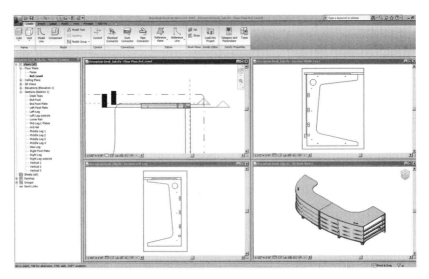

Fabricating from Revit

Now you're ready to start fabrication. Computer-aided manufacturing (CAM) software is the "setup" software used to send a job to the robot or machine you're working with to create the design. This CAM software can be anything from something as simple as a printer driver (in the case of a laser cutter), to a plug-in, to a complete stand-alone application solution.

If you're not doing this entirely in-house but working instead with a fabricator, they will likely have a favorite CAM software they will want to use. Meeting with your fabricator early on and testing some sample exports is vital to success. File exports such as DWG, DXF, or SAT files can vary in compatibility between applications.

In this example, we'll show a CAM tool called Aspire from Vectric. Vectric will easily take DXF files, so when you import them from Revit, they look like Figure 25.8.

One benefit about using quality CAM software is the features it has that are domain specific. Aspire is focused at CNC routers, and it has tools like an automated nesting feature that lays out parts on sheets for us automatically (Figure 25.9).

FIGURE 25.8
Importing the BIM model into a CAM package

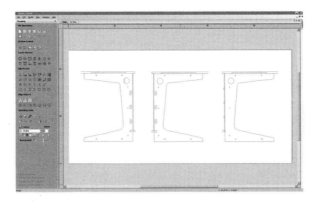

FIGURE 25.9
Elements auto-
matically nested in
Aspire

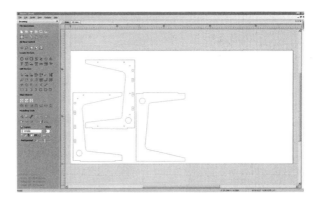

This is why it's best to collaborate early on with your fabricator; otherwise, you might waste time doing something their systems do automatically and quickly (such as part nesting) or working to export to a file type that their machines cannot accept.

Once the job is imported and nested, you or your fabricator can define how each piece should be cut. Figure 25.10 shows some element editing in the native fabrication software.

FIGURE 25.10
Modifying the
elements before
cutting begins

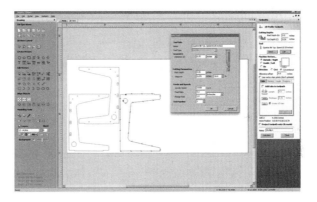

In this example, the cut jobs are then run on the CNC router to fabricate the parts (Figure 25.11).

FIGURE 25.11
Cutting the parts
on a CNC router

When cutting is complete, the BIM model is used as a reference for assembly. In Figure 25.12, you can see the skeletal frame of the reception desk assembled on the workroom floor.

FIGURE 25.12
Assembling
the fabricated
elements

And voilà! A custom reception desk quickly and affordably fabricated, directly from the BIM model, with no shop drawings needed (Figure 25.13).

FIGURE 25.13
The final
reception desk

Tips and Tricks for Better Fabrication

Although the workflow we have described in this chapter is a thorough, high-level overview of fabrication, many nuances to the process might require special attention depending on the desired end result. Here are some tips and tricks gleaned from the field to help you finesse the process and achieve the results you're looking for:

◆ One huge asset to a digital fabrication workflow is the ability to make quick prototypes during the configuration and rationalization steps discussed earlier in this chapter. Nothing makes you certain your design works than making a prototype and jumping up and down on it. Half-size or scaled prototypes are also easy to make, and clients love models to help them visualize the final design.

♦ Sometimes the fabrication model will have to be done with another software tool during the rationalization step. For example, Figure 25.14 shows another reception desk, this time with fancy CNC-carved wings on the front.

FIGURE 25.14
A reception desk
with a more
detailed design

This desk was entirely modeled in Revit as well and produced via the same CNC process used in the previous example. However, Revit wasn't very good at modeling the small, complex shapes of the wings with the typical Family Editor (Figure 25.15). To generate the form, the wing element was exported from Revit and imported into Blender, a 3D modeling software like Autodesk 3Ds Max.

FIGURE 25.15
The sketched
Wing Design

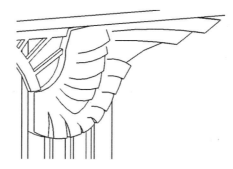

In Blender, the wings were edited into a much more complex form (Figure 25.16). Placeholders were left in Revit, and as long as the joint where the placeholder met the rest of the Revit model didn't change, you could trust that the final parts would all fit together, even though the wings were being done in a different modeling package.

FIGURE 25.16
The complex wing
form modeled in
Blender

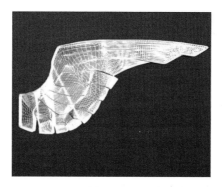

◆ Another thing to watch out for is in the isolation step. Much can go wrong here! Problems can arise from issues during file conversions. For example, when exporting solids that used splines in their sketches from Revit to DXF, it can tend to sometimes "wander" when imported into the CAM software. Figure 25.17 shows two images, one exported from Revit and the other imported into the CAM software. Notice the differences in the final form.

FIGURE 25.17
Watch file exports to make sure the model imported into the CAM software is what you exported from Revit.

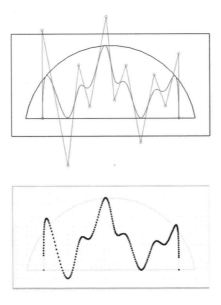

Differences from export to import will make the final model not fit together.

◆ Sometimes manufacturing details can come into play with certain approaches. For example, when making things from folded sheet metal, you need to take into account things like the K-factor, where metal will thicken and shorten when bent depending on the material type and the tooling. If you model something in Revit, and export it to Rhino or 3ds Max, and simply "unfold" it, it might not work once laser cut from steel. However, if you exported that same element to Inventor, and unfolded it there using their sheet metal toolset, it would work. Picking the proper tool to assist based on material type can be critical depending on the design.

If you remember nothing else to aid your workflow when designing for direct to fabrication, remember these two things:

Test assumptions. Talk with your fabricators, your service bureau, or research your in-house machine with several tests. Don't assume too much. CNC machines can make a lot of parts very quickly, which means that they can also make a lot of problems very quickly.

Model clean. By creating families in Revit, setting categories, and making the model 100 percent accurate, you'll find it a lot easier to isolate the parts later on and be certain they work prior to fabrication.

The Bottom Line

Understand the concepts of digital fabrication.   Before you can create furniture and other elements using digital fabrication, it's important to understand both the tools involved and the principles used in the process.

Master It   Understanding the process involved in fabrication will help you master the steps. List the five steps outlined in this chapter that are necessary for digital fabrication.

Use digital fabrication on a project.   In the example of creating a reception desk in Revit, you went through a real example of direct to fabrication from a BIM model. Understanding the steps in this process can help you replicate these same steps on other projects and designs.

Master It   In this chapter, we discussed the need to think about the end of the process before starting the beginning. Consider the outcome and what that might be to help inform the best equipment and methods to derive that outcome. Describe two important points in this process and how they help create a better final product.

Model cleanly and accurately.   Once you go through the process of fabrication, you can refine your process and make it more efficient for future production, developing your own tips and tricks along the way.

Master It   Modeling cleanly and accurately is one of the primary ways to build skill in digital fabrication. Describe some of the ways to model in this fashion.

Chapter 26

Revit for Film and Stage

Buildings may last for a long time, but "film is forever"! Revit provides extraordinary advantages for film and stage design professionals, from concept design to construction management. If you're in the film and stage industries (or interested in learning more about an incredibly creative and rewarding design environment), this chapter will give you some insight.

What's really important is learning how to quickly and easily communicate ideas much faster than using traditional 2D tools (which don't lend themselves to 3D) and far more efficiently than 3D tools (which don't lend themselves to construction documentation). Revit has the best of both worlds, and it provides an intuitive, integrated solution that helps everyone involved in the process of making the imagined real.

We'll profile how one set designer in the film industry, Bryan Sutton, has used Revit in his projects. In this chapter, you'll learn to:

◆ Design "scenically"

◆ Use Revit in the design to production process

◆ Use Revit for previsualization

Revit in the Film Industry

ABOUT THE CONTRIBUTING AUTHOR: BRYAN SUTTON

Bryan Sutton is an incredibly talented set designer in Vancouver, British Columbia, Canada, who has been using Revit to design sets for major motion pictures since 2001. Vancouver is a center of commercial television, and film production in North America.

Right up front, you should know that Revit has not widely established a technical presence in the set design industry. Instead, this space is dominated by 3D and SketchUp, Rhino, 3ds Max, and Maya. But Revit has begun making inroads in recent years.

One reason for the recent interest in using Revit in the film industry is Bryan Sutton and his initial posts in the Autodesk User Group International (AUGI) forums in fall 2004. When he posted a few renderings of the airlock door from the first *Fantastic Four* movie, he immediately grabbed the attention of the growing Revit community.

From that time, there has been a growing interest in using Revit in film and stage production. But of all the designers in that industry, Sutton is considered one of the most talented Revit users not only in his industry but in the world. He has developed a style and approach to Revit that has moved beyond technical proficiency to a masterful art form. That's why we'll share his experiences using Revit with you in this chapter.

Sutton first began toying with computers primarily as a production tool but then quickly began to focus on parametric design technologies. All this was happening while he was working as a carpenter building sets for commercial productions. Some of the first tools he used were AutoCAD, 3ds Max, and Strata. Very soon he started doing production drawings and found he had an advantage in understanding both the set design and the accompanying construction processes.

In Sutton's industry, it's not enough to be technically or architecturally trained. What's important is that you understand how to design "scenically." The design and documentation needs to be suggestive—and what lies beyond the façade should be taken into account.

Sutton's understanding of the importance of designing "scenically" quickly led him to look beyond the traditional 2D CAD tools. So, after starting with AutoCAD, Sutton began to experiment with other 3D tools such as Rhino and IronCAD. It was IronCAD that opened his eyes to the realm of *parametrics*—the ability to build relationships and affect many changes at once. But the workflow was still lacking an integrated process: what was being designed in 3D was being exported for documentation. And design changes discovered during documentation required editing elsewhere: back to the 3D file, export, and so on.

Fortunately, Sutton discovered Revit from the same friend who had introduced him to IronCAD. He immediately realized that here was an integrated environment for doing architectural work that didn't care where you made the change: 3D, 2D, documents, and even schedules. Sutton was hooked. And he began using Revit 1.0 (just before version 2.0) on set designs for commercials.

In spite of his extraordinary and exceptionally aesthetic approach to using Revit, Sutton is the first to admit that unfortunately he can't "draw himself out of a paper bag." His advice? Hand-sketching is critical for the early design process. You need to be able to draw quickly and elegantly—and according to Sutton, sketching is the language of communicating design ideas.

You can find more information on Sutton at www.imdb.com/name/nm1340613/.

Using Revit in the Design to Production Process

Using Revit in the architectural profession has unique processes and characteristics. The same is true in the production process of film and stage set design. Of course, there's going to be some overlap considering that both spaces need to be occupied by people. But you'd be surprised how little "real" architecture is in the set design industry.

In this section, we'll walk you through the process of using Revit in the film and stage industries. And since you're familiar with the industry, only Revit might be unfamiliar. But if you're an architect already familiar with Revit, the quality and craft of the film and stage industries is going to both impress and challenge you.

Understanding the role of a set designer is easier if you understand some adjacent roles in the production process. Roles that used to be distinct are now overlapping and merging throughout the production process. For example, the director of photography and the director of visual effects used to have distinct roles. The director of photography was traditionally in charge of the production filming, while the production designer was traditionally in charge of the overall "look and feel" of the production. But these two roles are meshing together because of computer-generated imagery (CGI) and visual effects. Both roles should understand the real and virtual sets so that the digital environments have the same look and feel of the physical sets.

Digital tools have reinforced the need to have the entire production team work together in constant communication. Working in 2D can quickly lead to confusion. Even creative people struggle with reading 2D plans, sections, and elevations. Just like in traditional architecture, any miscommunication is expensive in both time and money. And just like with architecture, the production has a deadline—*the release date*. This deadline cannot move.

Revit offers the ability to provide so much communication in one elegant tool—you get 3D, 2D, visualization, and scheduling in a single environment. But what's compelling with Revit is its bidirectional nature. You can work directly from the production drawings to change the model; you can model in context with a production sketch as an underlay. Being able to quickly and easily create parametric content is key to a successful process.

At the end of the day, Revit is just better organized for creating buildings than using a generic 3D modeling tool like SketchUp, Rhino, or 3DMax. According to Sutton, as a set designer he uses Revit for more than 95 percent of his job, with the occasional modeling in Rhino.

In the following sections, we'll walk you through the process of the overall workflow that takes a project from the earliest production sketches through fabrication and construction.

Design Interaction

As soon as the earliest sketches arrive from the art director, it becomes incredibly important to stay away from the "coldness" of computer renderings. They tend to be too hard and lack important emotive qualities—or may even look too finished. You need to focus on techniques to keep the design "loose" early on. This keeps the design open and tends to invite input from the director and others. In Figure 26.1, note how the materials are muted rather than literal representations. Although the glass is transparent, if you look carefully you'll notice there are hash marks on the glass. This is an important graphic gesture. It also communicates materialness in elevation.

FIGURE 26.1
Muted materials and hash marks on glazing

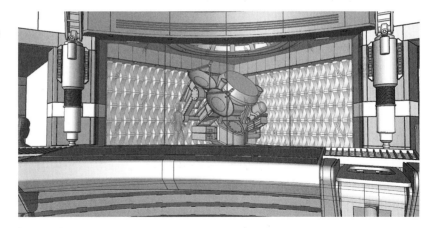

This same hand "sketchiness" doesn't just apply to 2D plans, elevations, and sections. Even when rendering, you'll want to overdramatize lighting effects by placing geometry-less studio lights. The gaffer (who is in charge of lighting) and director of photography are keenly interested in lighting effects. So in many cases, you (or more likely, someone else) will need to take a rendering you've created in Revit or Maya and then work on it in Photoshop in order to exaggerate lighting or to soften it. The idea is that you're trying to bring more emotive qualities to the rendering than may be present (Figure 26.2).

FIGURE 26.2
Softened, emotive
lighting effects

Lead Time and Production

Although design teams tend to work on in their own silos (that are focused on different parts of the movie), expect to work in a collaborative environment. Everyone needs to understand how the vision of the art director will allow the movie to flow from one scene to the next.

Illustrators may or may not start with a 3D model. But if they do start with a 3D model, it'll likely be just enough to have provided context for their early design concepts and sketches. Lots of hand drawing will go on top of these images. If you're provided with digital copies of the model and sketches, expect to remodel the geometry because it won't be useful in Revit for more than context. The same goes for the digital sketches. But at least it's a start!

Deadlines are likely going to be very, very tight. Where standard architecture practice allows for months, in the film industry you'll have weeks. And where standard practice allows for weeks, you'll have days. Expect to work 12-hour days, 5 days a week and anywhere from 4 to 8 months for a major motion picture (with a break of a few months between productions). That's *not* 4 to 8 months for resolving design to documentation—it's for resolving *concept to construction*. And the detail to be resolved is going to have to be extraordinary, as shown in Figure 26.3.

FIGURE 26.3
Gritty realism
in *X-Men: The
Last Stand*

Construction can start from a napkin sketch in cases when the design is not *too* complicated. On more complicated projects, it's likely that you'll be working on site and very near to the construction and other production teams—as in the same building, down the hall, or possibly in the same "war room." Some pieces of your design may be repetitive and contain parts that have to fit together with a high degree of precision. When this is the case, it's likely these pieces will be prefabricated via CNC and then assembled on site. Fortunately, you can export other formats from Revit that quickly lend themselves to fabrication (such as `*.sat` or ACIS).

Sutton has worked on a number of "third-act" sets. Third-act sets are known for being large, complex, and/or highly themed because they'll be seen near the end of the movie and must leave a lasting impression. In the case of *Watchmen*, the Karnak set took months to create, and the Revit model was used to resolve issues ranging from design to camera angles to rigging for stunt work (Figure 26.4). Overall, remember that it's critical to stay a week or two ahead of the construction team because of the amount of lead time required by the set decorators after construction concludes.

FIGURE 26.4
Detail of glazing in Karnak

Even with all the early attention to detail during the design process, occasionally parts of sets will need to be pulled apart and rebuilt. But keep in mind this is extremely disruptive to the entire production process. The deadline has been set years in advance, and the budget is inflexible. The tolerance for rebuilds is becoming more unlikely now that 3D is becoming so common in the design process.

Scheduling

While quantities are important, in the middle of all this design iteration and visualization production, some standard architectural techniques may not translate into designing for film and stage. For example, it's unlikely that you'll be creating discrete schedules as you normally would. So rather than noting quantities on schedules, you'll tend to note them on sheets. This makes it simple and keeps as much information in one place as possible. You'll also indicate spacing—but again not the hard numbers.

Details

In the same way that traditional architectural schedules aren't used (but rather, quantities are noted in context with documentation), details are shown in the context of the elements being detailed. So, rather than "segment" your work into different groups (plans, elevations, sections, and so on), it's more likely that you'll be assembling your work in context, which is more like traditional architectural hand-drawn techniques. For example, being able to see both design intent and resolution at the same time is important. Plans, elevations, sections, and 3D views will likely be assembled together (not apart). This is particularly true as set builders can be given a lot of creative leeway, and you're often giving them enough information to get started. Prop builders, fabricators, and sculptors—they all love to have 3D representations! Taking an artist's sketch and putting it in context of the construction documents communicates the spirit of design intent (Figure 26.5).

FIGURE 26.5
Design intent and resolution on the same sheet

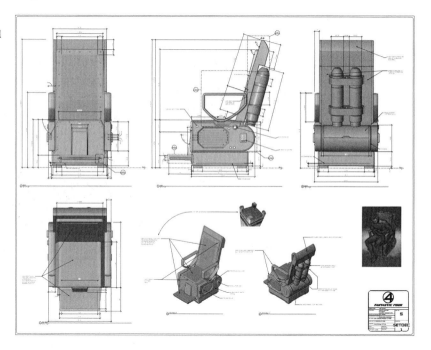

Dimensions

While we're discussing documentation, remember that dimensions in context with shaded views are better suited for resolving depth than mere hidden line views. Much of what you'll be designing in film and stage production are curved, imaginative kinds of forms. These shapes aren't visualized well in black and white, 2D kinds of views. But if you change the views to shaded, curved elements are far more expressive. If you need to embellish 3D and perspective views, simply add the text and other notes outside the view once the views have been placed on the sheet.

Be sure to demonstrate finesse with regard to visualization that is suitable for communication as well as presentation—and sometimes these are different things. In other words, how you illustrate design intent comes in many styles and influences. But what's important is to be able to make deliberate design decisions while illustrating a certain aesthetic *lack* of resolution. Because so many people are going to influence the final product, you must visualize your work in a way that doesn't raise unnecessary objections while building consensus as quickly as possible.

Level of Detail

Level of detail is critical in the film and stage industries. Don't expect to model to the level of detail standard in architectural practice. In other words, you're *not* going to be able to model in 3D at a low level of detail and then document in 2D a greater level of detail. If the component calls for hardware, you'll probably model it. In this industry, geometric detail is vitally important. It'll be leveraged for documentation through visualization. What you model is what gets built—you're not going to be allowed to leave much if any to guesswork or imagination (Figure 26.6).

FIGURE 26.6
Expect to model
to a high level
of detail.

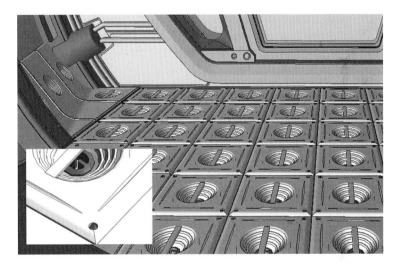

Fabrication

Fabrication is essential. Computer numerical control (CNC) plays a large part in the set design industry and utilizes five-axis machining, laser cutting, and water cutting (which was used to create the lattice work in Figure 26.7 and the door panels in Figure 26.8). Speed and accuracy are huge benefits and provide unmatched precision for preassemblage.

FIGURE 26.7
CNC lattice work
for pagoda from
*Fantastic Four: Rise
of the Silver Surfer*

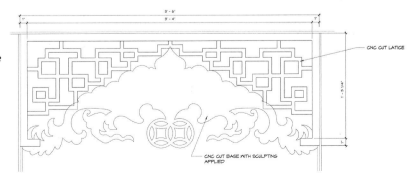

FIGURE 26.8
CNC door panel detail for pagoda from *Fantastic Four: Rise of the Silver Surfer*

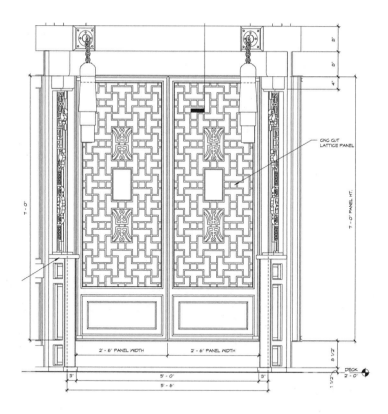

Five-axis tools usually mill high-density foam "sign board" if a more finished surface is required. If the surface needs to be less finished and a bit more porous, less dense Styrofoam is used (typically used for simulating concrete).

But for *very* tight, automotive-quality finishes, CNC machines are used to make the molds, which are then treaded and used as negatives for fiberglass casting, a process that was used to manufacture the "Fantasticar," as shown in Figure 26.9. And although Revit *wasn't* used to model the Fantasticar, it was used to model the dashboard elements that were used in the car—and its garage.

FIGURE 26.9
"Fantasticar" garage and support elements from *Fantastic Four: Rise of the Silver Surfer*

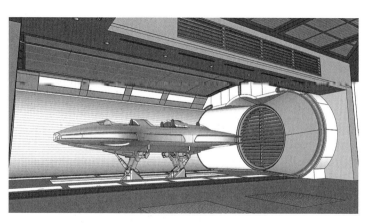

Geometry modeled in Revit will usually be taken to Rhino for *unfolding* a developable surface—like the airplane fuselage for *Snakes on a Plane*. But the structural ribs that were modeled in Revit were resolved by water cutting (Figure 26.10).

FIGURE 26.10
Cockpit interior of airplane fuselage from *Snakes on a Plane*

Construction

Some of the differences that you'll encounter in the film and stage industries compared to architecture will resonate when you get to construction. This is not to say that architectural projects aren't highly detailed—just that they're detailed differently. In film and stage production, you'll model not only what will be seen but in some cases what will *not* be seen. For example, when modeling, take into account the green screens beyond the actual sets as in Figure 26.11. Being able to accurately previsualize their size and locations during the design standpoint is important.

FIGURE 26.11
Green screens surround the Karnak set from *Watchmen*

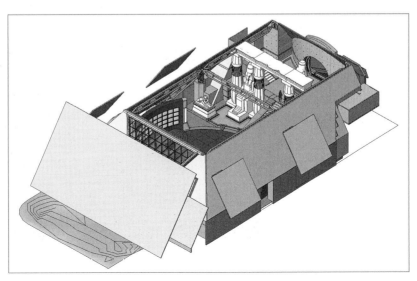

Previsualization in Revit

Remember that when you're designing "scenically," you're going to be focusing on maintaining the emotive quality of the design without getting into too much detail. As the design progresses, geometric "intent" will give way to specific content. But even then, someone will take over what you've started and give the final look and feel to your work. You're not just trying to show the literal "geometry" of what needs to be constructed—you're also trying to maintain the emotive quality and connection to the earliest production sketches.

Form/Transparency

Concentrate on illustrating differences between what is solid and what isn't. The context of what is *beyond* the immediate space is important. Note the equipment in the room beyond the center space. For example, in Figure 26.12 the materials in Reed's science lab are muted and suggestive—but not too literal. Color is used to distinguish between different materials rather than to express specific materiality.

Real World Scenario

TEMPLATE OR NO TEMPLATE?

Surprisingly, Bryan Sutton doesn't keep a project template. He says not starting from a template "keeps it simple." However, details are often reused, and Sutton has created a set of custom line styles to indicate "wild walls" (where the walls have deliberately designed breaks so they can be opened for camera access).

Components and system families are *not* typically reused from project to project in the film industry—everything is highly customized from project to project (unless a sequel is being considered). Rather, Sutton uses a more elegant process of employing generic elements as placeholders during the early design stages. These component and system families are sufficient to indicate the design intent of placement, spacing, and locations—the "big ideas" of the design. As the design is refined, he'll swap out the placeholders with more specific elements that share the same category and insertion point. Being able to swap out one "idea" for another quickly and easily is something that Sutton remarks "is what's really nice about Revit."

FIGURE 26.12
View through
Reed's lab
from *Fantastic
Four: Rise of the
Silver Surfer*

Lighting/Shadows

Even before materials are assigned, lighting plays an important role in adding emotive, dramatic context to the design. You have a couple of options since Revit allows shadows in real time but only a single light source, as illustrated in Figure 26.13. Beyond this you're going to need to render.

While the objects in Revit can contain the actual "lights" that can be controlled at time of rendering, this may not be enough. So keep in mind that studio lights (lights without lighting fixtures—just the light source) can be added to the project as well, a technique that was used to visualize Figure 26.14. These kinds of lights are useful for overdramatizing lighting effects and overcoming otherwise hard edges of shadows at the time of rendering.

FIGURE 26.13
Real-time shaded view

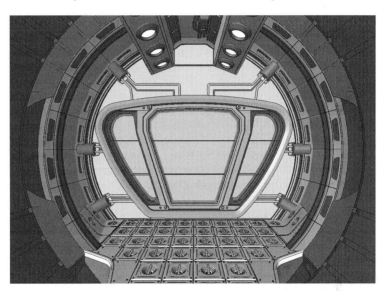

FIGURE 26.14
Rendered view through the airlock, *Fantastic Four*

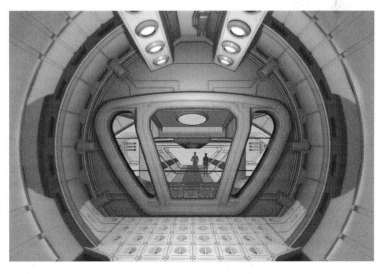

Materials

When materials are added, they're probably going to be understated during the design process. More detailed and specific materials assignments will be assigned by CGI artists (who will probably benefit from using your files as a starting point). In Figure 26.15, the horizon is being subtly suggested—but not as a hard, horizontal line in the distance that separates earth from sky. Any more detail would be a distraction!

FIGURE 26.15
Rendering of walkway structure, *I, Robot*

Rendering and Visualization

Renderings are critically important to the design process in the film industry, and you'll have to communicate simultaneously with regard to form, space, lighting, material, opacity, transparency, and so on, as shown in Figure 26.16. But in some cases, you'll want to be able to render one theme at the exclusion of others.

FIGURE 26.16
Creating a matter-rendering filter

Rendering conceptually as any solid color is a quick way to rationalize and objectify the design. This can be quickly and easily done in Revit using phasing. All you need to do is create a new phase filter called Matte Rendering. Be sure all the phase filter assignments are set to Overridden. (To learn more about phasing, see Chapter 11, "Phasing, Groups, and Design Options.") This is shown in Figure 26.17, as phase filters are being overridden; Figure 26.18 illustrates material assignments associated with a particular phase.

FIGURE 26.17
Overriding
phase filters

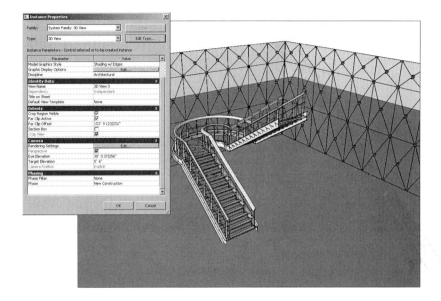

FIGURE 26.18
Applying material
assignments via
phasing

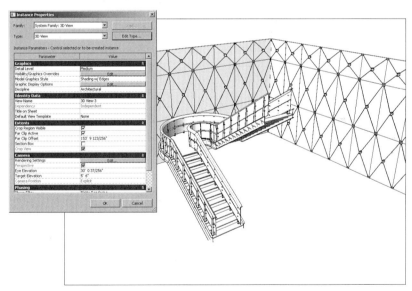

Using the Phasing dialog box, set the Graphic Overrides values of both shaded and rendered material assignments of the Complete phase to a solid, white (or off-white) matte material, as shown in Figure 26.19.

FIGURE 26.19
Overriding the sur-
face and materials

FIGURE 26.19
Overriding the sur-
face and materials

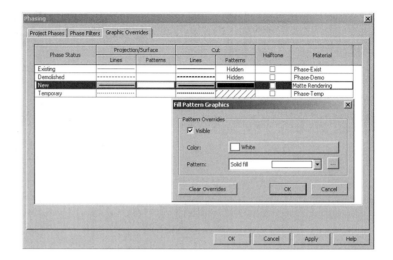

Create a 3D View, then open View Properties and set Phase Filter to Matte Rendering. Figures 26.20 and 26.21 show the results (before and after).

When you render with these settings, the result will be a monolithic scene that doesn't require you to manually manipulate the materials one by one for shaded views or renderings.

Keep in mind when using this technique that glass will render as opaque. If you want to render with glass as translucent, you'll want to render twice and create a composite view. First, turn off any glass via Visibility Graphics (Categories or Subcategories), and then render the view. Now create a composite view with the glass turned both on and off, and then set the transparency of the view with the glass turned on to around 20 percent. Figure 26.22 shows the final result.

FIGURE 26.20
Rendering without
glass

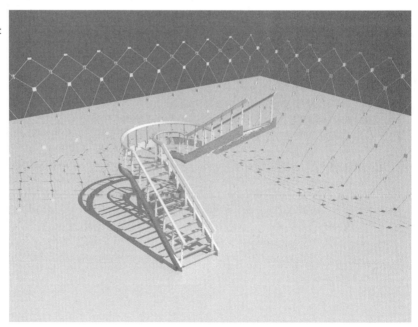

FIGURE 26.21
Rendered
with glass

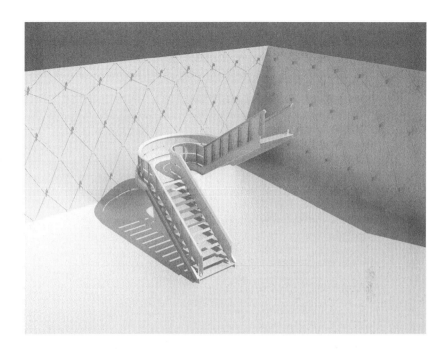

FIGURE 26.22
Final
composite view

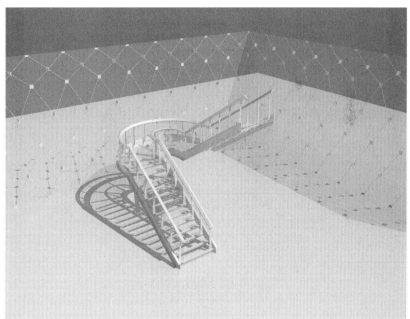

Creating a hidden line composite view is just one more step beyond creating a composite rendered view (Figure 26.23). Hidden lines are helpful for distinguishing objects that are small, translucent/transparent, or at some distance from the viewer because they accentuate the edges of objects. In these cases you can export a hidden line view and then overlay with a rendered view in order to accentuate edges (Figure 26.24).

With this kind of composite view, it's easy to see why they're so effective and desirable. In Figure 26.25, it's apparent that important details are missing! But in the next image, the details are clearly visible through highlighting the edges of those objects from an exported hidden line view (Figure 26.26).

FIGURE 26.23
Hidden line export

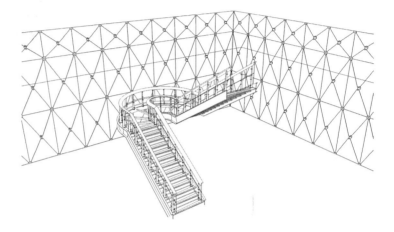

FIGURE 26.24
New
composite view

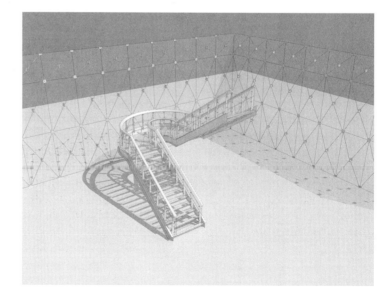

FIGURE 26.25
Detail before hidden line composite

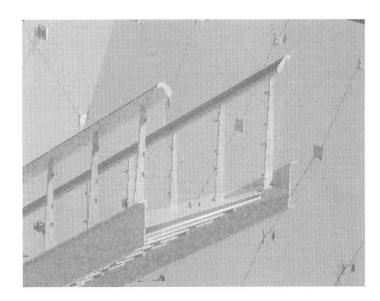

FIGURE 26.26
Detail after hidden line composite

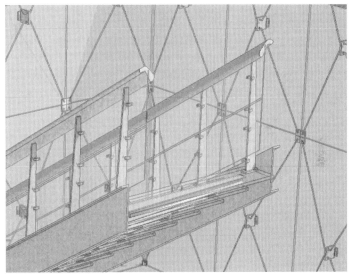

Photorealistic Renderings

Photorealistic renderings are certainly important to the design process as a set designer, but if your work is meant to resolve constructability, it may turn out that you're not responsible for creating highly emotive, finished views. Be aware that from within Revit, you are limited to the geometry that is in the Revit file.

But even if Revit were capable of creating any form imaginable, keep in mind that another person needs to render in their language of choice. And after years of fluency in one language, it's not likely that they're going to change languages to render in Revit. Additionally, they'll subject their renderings to significant postproduction in an image editor. So, be prepared to work with the visualization specialist by exporting Revit to another format (DWG, 3DS, FBX, and so on).

Exploded Views

Live exploded 3D views can be quickly and easily assembled in a couple of ways. The first technique involves creating a section box around part of your project and then selecting and copying this section box (Figure 26.27). Copying a section box automatically creates another section box with the same view.

FIGURE 26.27
Real-time section views through airlock, *Fantastic Four*

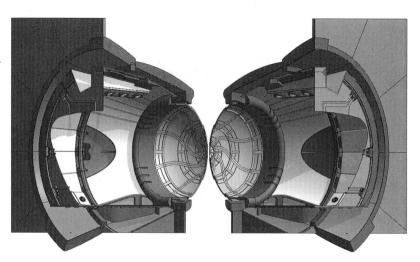

Another option is to isolate elements in duplicated views (with or without a section box). When you assemble the views together (on a sheet) you'll be able to pull them apart, creating the effect that the object is being pulled apart. This will help illustrate individual elements that will be prefabricated for assemblage.

Revit to CGI Workflow

According to Sutton, the film and stage industries in Vancouver overwhelmingly use Maya. And before FBX exporting, getting your file to a usable format wasn't always too successful. Fortunately, FBX has really helped. But in some cases you'll export to 3DDWG (and usually as ACIS solids). Autodesk Mudbox is frequently used for high-resolution close-ups (ZBrush).

Your Revit file is often a useful starting point for the CGI work that complements the physical sets, which can be exquisitely detailed, as in the Karnak main hall in *Watchmen* (Figure 26.28).

What's nice is that everything should line up between the physical and digital designs. But don't be alarmed if much of your work needs to be "rebuilt" in Maya.

FIGURE 26.28
Karnak main hall,
Watchmen

STACKING VIEWS

You should anticipate how the views should stack. It's not yet possible to reorder the front/back relationships of views *after* the views have been placed on sheets. So the views in the "background" need to be placed on the sheet *first* and the views that need to be in the "foreground" should be placed *last*. The image shown here displays the real-time exploded views through the airlock on *Fantastic Four*.

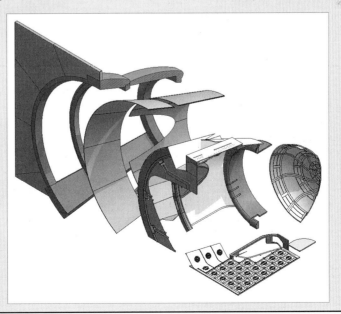

First, people like to have full control in a familiar "language" (application) that they have used for years. The deadlines are demanding and there's no room for unpredictable outcomes. Since Maya is being used extensively in the industry, it's likely that Revit files will get leveraged in Maya.

Second, the level of detail that you've produced in your Revit file (you know—the level of detail that is way beyond standard architectural practice) will likely be unnecessarily high for the CGI artist, as illustrated in Figure 26.29. Rendering is still incredibly expensive and time consuming. So any shortcuts to shorten rendering times (without sacrificing quality) are welcome. As a result, the CGI artists often use materials to represent granular geometric details—the kind of details that you've just modeled with geometry in Revit to resolve construction (Figure 26.30)!

FIGURE 26.29
Karnak glazing detail

FIGURE 26.30
Karnak detail; note the chamfering of bolts.

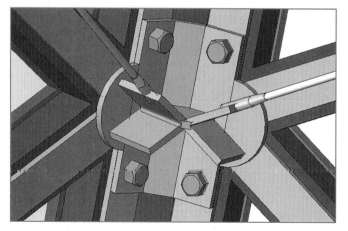

Best Practices for Film and Stage

Best practices for using Revit in the film and stage industries may have a lot in common with standard architectural practices, but sometimes they'll be significantly different. We'll cover both the similarities and the differences in the following sections.

Level of Detail

As mentioned earlier, the *level of detail* that you will model in these types of projects will greatly exceed what is customary in a standard architectural project, where a high resolution of detail is either not necessary for construction or is resolved in 2D with detail components during documentation. In this industry, modeling generically in 3D and then attempting to show more detail in 2D can be a distraction to an exacting art director. So don't be surprised if you're expected to model to less than an inch in detail—and expect what you model to be a fairly literal representation of what will be built.

Geometric Flexibility

Maintaining flexibility during design is critical to a successful project because once production starts, everything starts moving quickly. Use generic representations of an approximate size and category. As the design progresses, you can easily swap these "design placeholders" out for more specific elements.

Design Alternatives

In the film and stage industries, phasing and design options will also be used in 3D and documentation views to illustrate alternatives where pieces of the set need to convey some sort of movement—for example, if an object needs to be opened and closed or extended and retracted. In this case, simply assigning a unique phasing or design option to those elements will allow you to filter the views to only show one condition or another at a time.

In the case of the Comedian's (Eddie Blake's) apartment in *Watchmen*, phasing was used to illustrate the shattered curtain panel. The existing panel was unbroken, while the proposed panel was shown in the broken state (Figure 26.31).

FIGURE 26.31
Use phasing or design options to show alternatives

Nesting Geometry

Nesting is extremely useful for creating a component once and then using it in many different components (Figure 26.32). The advantage is that it's significantly faster (sometimes more than 95 percent faster in some cases) to update family components rather than groups. Keep in mind that a lot of the elements that you'll model will themselves contain nested components. This allows you to manage and update repetitive relationships quickly (Figure 26.33).

FIGURE 26.32
Nesting showing the door open in VIKI brain, *I, Robot*

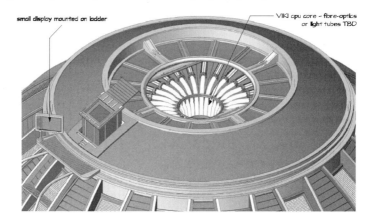

FIGURE 26.33
Nested components in VIKI brain, *I, Robot*

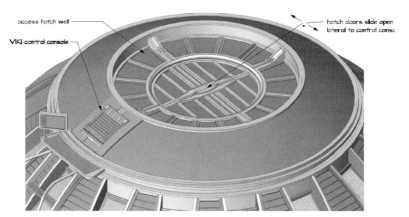

Family Category

Choosing the right family category is also important, but not in a way that often comes up in standard architecture practice ("Hmm…furniture or furniture system?"). Most of the time, the Generic Model category will suffice. But there remain a couple of subcategories that are really important.

First, you will have to select a Lighting category if you anticipate using the component to render lighting effects. Second, use face based rather than hosted.

Either face-based or hosted components can "cut" their host. With a face-based family, you need to model a void to cut the face, whereas with a hosted family, you must add an opening or a void. That's not so much of a difference, right?

Wrong. If you select hosted, you need to also know what kind of host is going to be cut (Wall, Floor, Roof, or Ceiling). But in this industry, what is a floor one moment might be a ceiling the next. And what is a wall today may turn out to be a roof later! So, specifically selecting a hosted category (which requires you to know what sort of host is going to be cut) can lead to disastrous results when the design changes (and it will…a lot)! Using a face-based family avoids this nasty consequence.

Another reason is that face-based families will easily orient themselves to the face of either component or system families, whether in the project or a nested family environment.

Finally, a face-based family can cut the face of both system families (in a project environment) as well as when nested into another component family. Overall, face-based families offer a lot of flexibility during the design process.

Keep in mind that in many cases nested components are likely to end up in multiple families as well as the project environment. This adds another layer of complexity when you find yourself in the awkward situation of having to open and edit multiple families in order to make whole project changes to a nested component. This is where "sharing" the parameters of the nested components will save you a lot of time and trouble.

Here's how: if you expect that the nested family is going to be nested into other families—or used directly in the project—you'll want to consider setting the Family parameter of the nested family to Shared (Figure 26.34).

FIGURE 26.34
Select Shared
in the Family
Parameters.

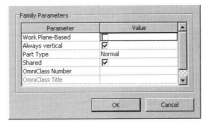

Simply select the originally nested component and edit its Category And Parameters setting. Select the Shared option and then reload this nested component in your family. The next time this family (containing the nested and shared component) is loaded into your project, both the component and the nested/shared component are loaded into the project. Whenever you edit this special shared/nested family (from either the project or one of the many families it's nested into), it will update everywhere in the project.

BE CAREFUL WITH SHARING

Remember, once an element is "shared" and loaded into the project, you cannot "unshare" that family!

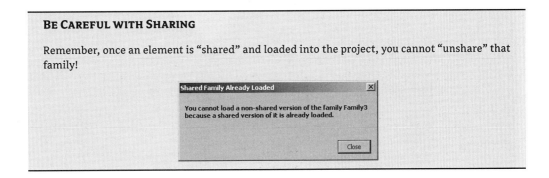

Advanced Geometry Creation

Modeling complex forms in Revit often differs from modeling in other 3D applications. Think of sculpture. First you can create something by building a formwork and then casting what you want within that form. This is an additive approach.

In Revit, the process, sculpturally speaking, is more subtractive. In other words, the complex form that you're trying to create is going to be accomplished by creating more geometry than necessary and then "carving" away the results with a void. This can be accomplished by building up "layers" of geometry (and perhaps joining them). But when you add voids, selectively cut only certain layers of the geometry.

See Figure 26.35 for a simple example. Although the family looks complicated, it is composed of only *five* elements: two solids and three voids. This file is also available for download from the Chapter 26 folder as the Complex Cube.rfa file.

FIGURE 26.35
Creating complex forms through layering geometry and voids

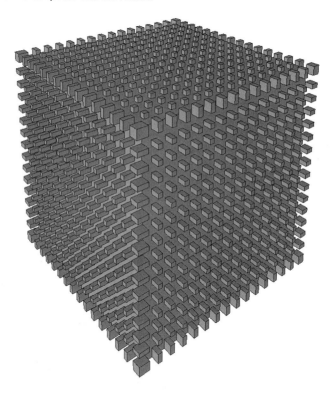

Carving geometry to resolve a desired shape is a simple technique but absolutely essential for being able to quickly create and (more importantly) iterate complex forms in Revit, such as the airlock door in Figure 26.36. According to Sutton, nonlinear solid/void relationships give Revit the edge over other more generic modeling tools (Figure 26.37).

FIGURE 26.36
Single section of
the airlock door

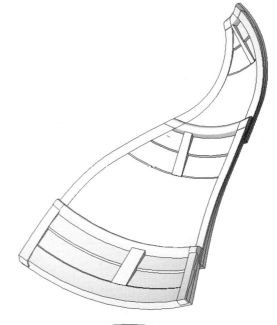

FIGURE 26.37
Completed airlock
door, *Fantastic Four*

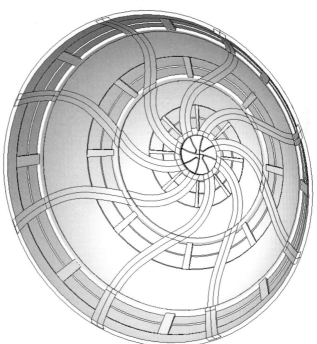

The file of the airlock door (`Airlock Door.rvt`) is also available for download from the Chapter 26 folder. It's a great example of using overlapping solids and selectively placed voids to cut away portions of geometry while leaving adjacent solid geometry intact. This technique was skillfully used to cut away the reveals that surround the airlock door (Figure 26.38).

FIGURE 26.38
Final rendering of the airlock door assembly, *Fantastic Four*

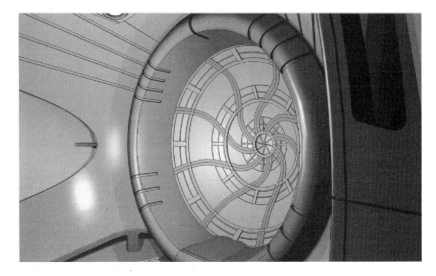

Worksharing

Worksets are typically not needed in the film and stage industries unless the project is large or contains a campus-like collection of other Revit projects. Although this atmosphere is highly collaborative, it's also task-centric—one person dedicated to working on one part of the project or file is not uncommon. So, using worksharing to distribute Revit files across multiple team members is not common.

Industry Examples

Having worked in the film and stage industries using Revit since 2003, Sutton has successfully managed a number of design challenges. The following are just a few production-related stories.

I, Robot

I, Robot was Sutton's first feature film and really quite special. After working for a number of years in set design at the scale of commercial production, it was "trial by fire." The sets were much larger, as well as multistory, as shown in Figure 26.39.

Sutton had to take over from an architect, and in some cases, the drawings were hard to read. In other cases, one design view would not align with another view, and in this industry coordination is extremely important because of the short deadlines.

In Sutton's words, "Revit really saved the day." Views were always consistent and always agreed with each other. The precision was always there, even considering the detail in the access walkway and platform surrounding the computer core (Figure 26.40). Revit was used to count the number of spider brackets used for the railings and other hardware.

FIGURE 26.39
Atrium walkway
rendered in Revit:
I, Robot

FIGURE 26.40
Platform and VIKI
brain core, *I, Robot*

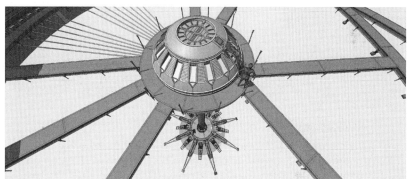

Ultimately, the VIKI brain that had been modeled in Revit for constructing the physical sets was leveraged for CGI work. This gave the CGI artists some great starting points (Figure 26.41). Again, precision was key.

FIGURE 26.41
Shaded detail per-
spective of VIKI
brain, *I, Robot*

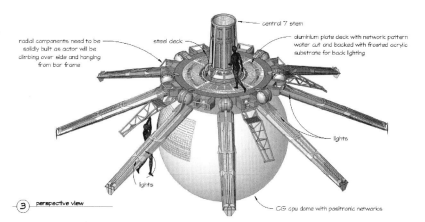

Fantastic Four

Fantastic Four was the next feature film that Sutton helped design in Revit. In this project, the level of detail increased because so many renderings were being done directly in Revit for this movie, starting with the interior of the space station (Figure 26.42).

FIGURE 26.42
Space station interior, *Fantastic Four*

Of course, these were the days of AccuRender—and many extra studio lights were placed in order to avoid the hard shadows that were common at the time. The shadows in AccuRender had hard edges and required a lot of artificial lights placed around the space, especially considering the detail and lighting of the ceiling (Figure 26.43). Fortunately, the implementation of Autodesk mental ray has improved the process.

The ceiling was challenging to model, according to Sutton, because there were so few straight lines. But he was able to do it with Revit using a lot of built-up solid and void relationships. The sweeps going along the edges of the ceiling and down to the floor was particularly challenging, as shown in Figure 26.44.

When you can't get the model "just right," you have the geometry as context for documentation. This saves a lot of time over the back and forth compared to modeling in 3D, exporting, and then documenting in 2D.

FIGURE 26.43
Space station ceiling, *Fantastic Four*

FIGURE 26.44
Space station interior, *Fantastic Four*

X-Men: The Last Stand

This project built on the challenges of the previous projects. Sutton soon found himself being selected to design the third-act set (see the section "Lead Time and Production" earlier in this chapter). The island of Alcatraz was going to be third-act set and would be used for the big fight scene at the end of the *X-Men* film. It turned out to be an interesting challenge, because it involved a lot of both indoor and outdoor sets, such as the exterior Alcatraz set (Figure 26.45).

Fortunately for the third-act set, you're likely to be given a bit more lead time. It's got to be detailed—and it's going to be used for a lot of the "money shots" at the end of the movie. For *X-Men*, it also had to include a debris field that was supposed to suggest the ripped apart end of the Golden Gate Bridge (Figure 26.46).

FIGURE 26.45
Alcatraz set,
*X-Men: The
Last Stand*,
looking toward
prison complex

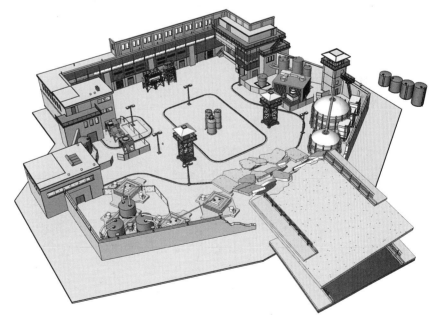

FIGURE 26.46
Alcatraz set,
*X-Men: The
Last Stand*,
looking toward
collapsed bridge
structure

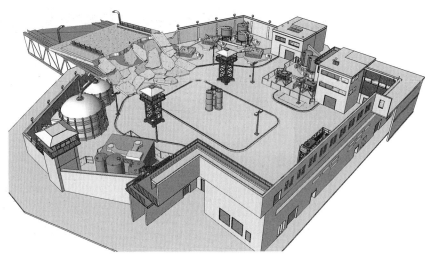

Snakes on a Plane

Originally, for *Snakes on a Plane*, actual pieces of aircraft fuselage were going to be used in context of the set pieces that remained to be built. So, the new challenge was integrating pieces of actual planes into Revit for context. But in the end, they rebuilt the plane and gutted the existing plane for parts and set dressing (Figure 26.47).

FIGURE 26.47
Airplane section,
Snakes on a Plane

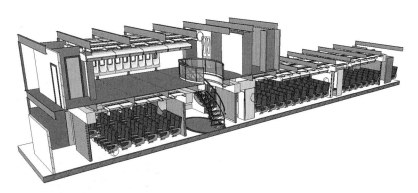

Some of the 3D shapes were a challenge. For instance, the fuselage consisted of complex shapes. But in the end, nearly the whole plane was designed in Revit, even the cockpit area (Figure 26.48). Overall, it was a "smaller" production.

FIGURE 26.48
Cockpit rendering,
Snakes on a Plane

FIGURE 26.48
Cockpit rendering,
Snakes on a Plane

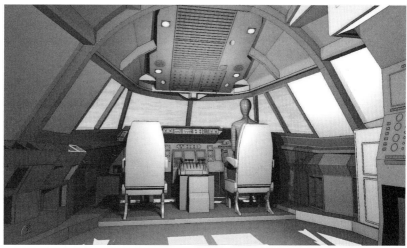

Fantastic Four: Rise of the Silver Surfer

This project was rewarding—the people working on the project were great. According to the production designer, Revit helped "save the movie." The set pieces, like the highly complex and detailed pagoda shown in Figure 26.49, required intricate structural elements and carefully cut screened panels.

FIGURE 26.49
Exterior of the
pagoda, *Fantastic
Four: Rise of the
Silver Surfer*

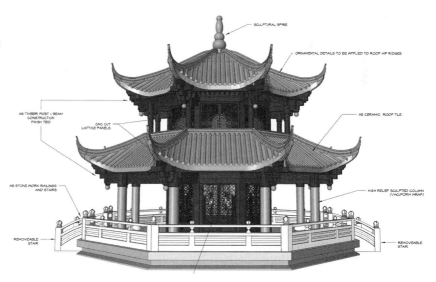

In the case of the pagoda, full-sized sheets were printed and used as stencils for cutting the lofted, structural ribs. In other cases, CNC machines were used to cut out the door and panel pieces designed in Revit (Figure 26.50).

FIGURE 26.50
Pagoda upper screen detail, *Fantastic Four: Rise of the Silver Surfer*

Night at the Museum: Battle of the Smithsonian

For this movie, numerous set pieces were designed in Revit. But there was one particularly interesting challenge: a replica of the Wright Flyer, as shown in Figure 26.51, the world's first powered aircraft to achieve controlled, sustained flight. Apparently a company exists that makes replicas for museums and other displays. In this case, though, the replica needed to be 85 percent smaller than the original. Oh, and the wings had to have proxy elements built of fiberglass so that the actor could walk on them during production.

FIGURE 26.51
Wright Flyer, *Night at the Museum: Battle of the Smithsonian*

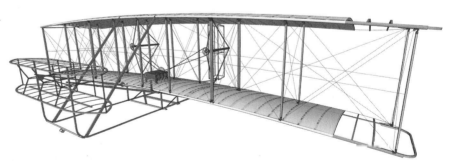

While reviewing copies of drawings originally from the Smithsonian, Sutton wasn't sure that it could be done in Revit. The detail in the drawings was extraordinary. But once he began to visualize and understand the parts that made up the whole—the ribs, the frame, and the engine—it all became quite clear. And in the end, according to Sutton, it was great fun modeling the Wright Flyer in Revit.

In fact, in addition to the air and space set, even smaller details like the afterburner for the F104 was modeled in Revit (Figure 26.52).

FIGURE 26.52

F104 Afterburner, *Night at the Museum: Battle of the Smithsonian*

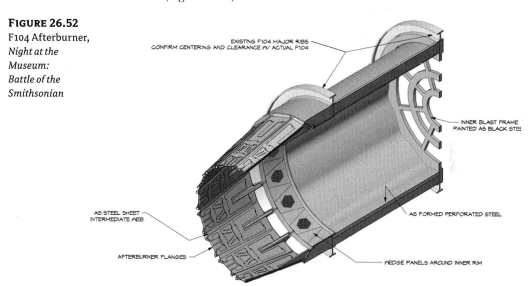

EXISTING F104 MAJOR RIBS
CONFIRM CENTERING AND CLEARANCE W/ ACTUAL F104

INNER BLAST FRAME
PAINTED AS BLACK STEEL

AS STEEL SHEET
INTERMEDIATE WEB

AS FORMED PERFORATED STEEL

AFTERBURNER FLANGES

WEDGE PANELS AROUND INNER RIM

Watchmen

Watchmen is a graphic novel (originally released as a limited 12-comic book series). It was created by writer Alan Moore, artist Dave Gibbons, and colorist John Higgins and published during 1986 and 1987. Although attempts to create a live action film began shortly after the graphic novel's success, some deemed the complex narrative "unfilmable."

Numerous production starts and stops continued until Warner Brothers brought in Zack Snyder (the director of *300*) and principal photography began in 2007. Snyder even created his own storyboard sketches to fill in the action between the key frames of the novel. According to Sutton, "It was fantastic working for the director who creates his own version of storyboards. He has a very visual approach. I actually used the sketches for reference within the context of the design and construction documentation."

Another detail that Sutton looked forward to during the *Watchmen* film and production was the opportunity to work with Alex McDowell, the production designer (McDowell's previous efforts include *Fight Club* and *Charlie and the Chocolate Factory*). Sutton had long admired McDowell's work.

The Karnak set was the third-act set and would be extremely detailed. At the direction of McDowell, the bolt heads were modeled in Revit with chamfers (Figure 26.53).

Once again, phasing was used extensively to turn off and on large portions of the model to visualize the various stages of construction and production. The glazing system was also extensive.

FIGURE 26.53
Interior of Karnak,
Watchmen

Ultimately, the model was so complex that major portions of the model were done as large collections of nested families, as shown in Figure 26.54. This was done to manage the amount of highly detailed repetition.

FIGURE 26.54
Complex structure
family Karnak set,
Watchmen

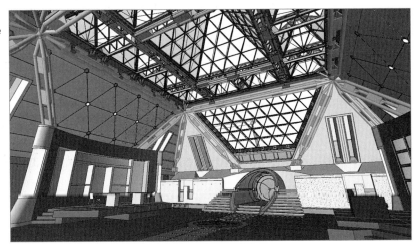

Creating individual families and then nesting them into a single, large family maintained design iteration. This large family assemblage was then loaded and placed into the project (Figure 26.55). Admittedly, families of this scale might not be a standard architecture best practice, as it would obviously affect scheduling. But the advantage to the exception in this case is pretty obvious. Rather than creating separate projects and linking them together, you're creating really large families and loading them into the project. (Figure 26.56).

FIGURE 26.55
Support elements for Dr. Manhattan's lab, *Watchmen*

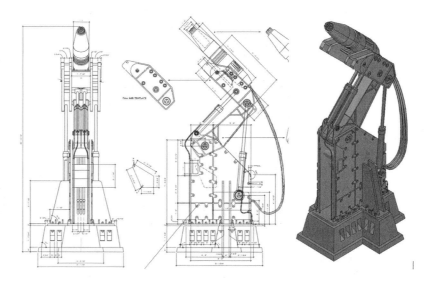

FIGURE 26.56
Tachyon corridor in Karnak, *Watchmen*

Design iteration could then be managed by opening the "master" family and then drilling down to get to the single nested family, as in Figure 26.57. Then the nested families would be reloaded into the master family. Then this master family would be reloaded into the project file, illustrated by the single cell in Figure 26.58.

FIGURE 26.57
Portion of
Tachyon panel

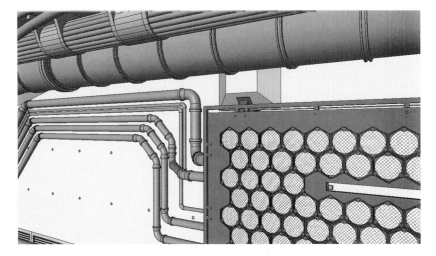

FIGURE 26.58
Detail of nested
Tachyon cell

The Bottom Line

Design "scenically."   According to Sutton, profiled in this chapter, designing "scenically" takes precedence over designing too literally. This might be different from standard architectural practice, but it's critical in the film and stage industries.

> **Master It**   How would you design "scenically," and how does this differ from standard architectural practice? What can you learn from the film and stage industries to keep the emotive quality high?

Use Revit in the design to production process.   While standard architectural practice entails design to documentation, the film and stage focus is from concept through construction.

> **Master It**   With an emphasis on level of detail and tight, repetitive elements and finishes, what would you do to help maintain time and budget? How might you suggest creating intricate repetitive design elements in your next project?

Use Revit for previsualization.   When using Revit in the film industry, you need to keep the design "loose" during the early concept stages. You'll have to match the look and feel of the art director's vision. Keeping the materials muted will be far less distracting than being too specific. One of the great things about Revit is that you'll be able to emotively visualize in the same environment as you analytically rationalize. This will come in handy when the director, director of photography, and then art director all want a different question answered at the same time!

> **Master It**   How can you express constructability to a high level of detail, particularly when the object is going to be assembled from many individual parts? Why rely on standard architectural practice of documenting in plan, section, and elevation views?

Chapter 27

Revit in the Cloud

You have probably heard a lot about cloud computing and software as a service (SaaS), but what about moving your high-performance graphics workstations to the cloud so that you can run Revit and other BIM analysis tools? This chapter describes the strategies for building a *private cloud* that includes high-performance graphics workstations.

A private cloud differs from the public cloud (such as Amazon Web Services or Google) in that the cloud-computing infrastructure is controlled and owned by the private business that deploys it. Although a business may consume various computing resources from a public cloud at times, it's our opinion that every corporation will have their own private cloud in which they can utilize public cloud offerings if they so choose. CIOs who always have a "plan B" want their firm to be able to keep working in the event that the entire Internet is down. And you cannot do that if all your computing is done in a public cloud.

In general, most of the current discussion on cloud computing has been dealing with the servers (or back-end systems). Only recently have businesses begun to put their desktops into the cloud. Little, the company we'll profile in this chapter, has a cloud that is the first AEC *workstation cloud* in production and on track to reduce Little's laptop hardware expense by 67 percent ($2 million) over the next 10 years. The benefits realized by virtualizing the servers can now be realized by virtualizing the desktops.

Why is this solution viable now? What has changed? There are several reasons. First, the cost of network bandwidth and latency has decreased. You can now get 10MB of metro Ethernet for the same price a T1 (1.5MB) used to cost (at least in the United States). Also, Windows 7 and Remote Desktop Protocol (RDP) have gotten much better at moving screen images of media-rich applications. Finally, hardware costs are coming down and rack-mounted server-class workstations are within the reach of many firms.

In this chapter, you'll learn to:

◆ Understand the business benefit of a high-performance workstation cloud

◆ Implement a high-performance workstation cloud

◆ Know which future desktop cloud computing technologies to watch

Business Benefits of a High-Performance Workstation Cloud

ABOUT THE CONTRIBUTING AUTHOR: CHRIS FRANCE

Chris France, CIO at Little Diversified Architectural Consulting (Little), has specialized in Information Technology & Communications for over two decades. He started his career at IBM Federal Systems in New York as a software/systems engineer, and progressed to leadership roles for major DOD systems. From IBM, he traveled to Charlotte, North Carolina, to work for Bank of America where he led efforts to re-engineer, merge, and consolidate the information technology of major bank acquisitions. Prior to becoming the CIO of Little, he consulted in the technology-intense Wachovia Capital Markets.

Chris not only leads Little's Information Technology Strategy, Planning and Operations, but he also consults with clients to ensure that their diverse technology needs are addressed and incorporated during the design process. He is constantly changing the technology "rules" to give businesses competitive advantage. BIM Clouds are just the beginning.

In this chapter, we'll walk you through the process that led Little, the company of one of this book's authors, to maximize the business benefits from a high-performance graphics workstation (HPGW) cloud. For a number of years, Little did what many firms today are doing: putting high-end workstations under the desk of users who required the horsepower. BIM, visualization, and other business dynamics of decreasing time-to-market demand that we utilize hardware as best as possible. Over time, Little found a better way.

Since 2009, the economy has been challenging for all organizations, and companies have had to rethink everything. One of the driving forces behind cloud innovation is BIM. With BIM, designers are now able to construct a fully documented, 3D building on a computer before they build it on-site. This requires a lot of computer power as well as a few obstacles to overcome. Little's cloud strategy "kills 11 birds with one stone" and has many applications outside of the architecture, engineering, and construction (AEC) industry as well.

Growing Desktop Computing Needs

As an architectural and engineering firm, Little has heavy desktop computing needs, similar to the gaming industry. The company's industry applications require a lot of simulation, analysis, rendering, and 3D modeling in order to design buildings, and it had been on a two-year refresh cycle for the laptops. Each year, Little spent between $250,000 and $300,000, and the laptops were getting more expensive as the company added more software capability. In 2009, the company could not afford to refresh the laptops as usual, but the company still had increasing desktop needs. Switching to a workstation cloud strategy allowed the company to shift to a four-to five-year refresh cycle by providing access to high-performance workstations. The laptops could easily operate as "cloud access devices," and new laptops could be purchased for less than $1,000 when needed. Now the laptops are kept until the wheels fall off.

Collaborating Over Wide Area Geography

As a multioffice firm, Little's designers would be assigned to a project based on their expertise and the needs of the client project. It was very common to have people in Orlando; Washington, DC; and Charlotte, NC working on the same building model. While the software vendors are working on solutions to make their products operate over a WAN and infrastructure companies can provide WAN accelerators, this still was not good enough. Was it too much to ask to have the distributed project teams working just as if they were sitting in the same office? The company didn't think so. By shifting everyone to the cloud, Little was able to give that "same office" experience to a distributed project team.

Collaborating with Outside Firms on the Same Model

The next logical step in BIM model development was to accommodate the standard industry practice of hiring consultants to help design the building. Many firms do not have all the design resources within their company. They regularly work with outside engineering, fire protection, or acoustical consultants, but everyone is working on the same building (and the same model). Now that many of these consultants are using BIM tools, it would be ideal if they could all work on the same model just like employees of the same firm can do. But without the cloud technology, project teams are forced to trade models via an FTP or project websites on set schedules. Real-time collaboration is difficult between external entities. Although Little has not yet had a project that required real-time collaboration with outside consultants, it has the technology in place to allow it to happen when the need arises.

IT Infrastructure Cost Consolidation

Although the genesis of Little's cloud was to solve the BIM computing problem, it has yielded other benefits. Virtualization is another IT industry strategy that is central to building high-performance clouds. Increases in hardware and network performance, coupled by a corresponding reduction in price, have made virtualization very attractive to IT leaders. Virtualization was initially justified based on hardware cost reduction. In Little's case, it had 57 physical servers now running on two physical servers ($170,000 vs. $35,000). Storage is virtualized as well; it manages approximately 50TB of data. Had Little not virtualized its storage when it did, it would have had to add a large number of IT staffers to manage various physical data volumes. Virtualization enabled Little to avoid an annual expense of $700,000. By using a combination of this sophisticated virtualization software, Little wanted to see the same reductions in the laptop/desktop infrastructure.

Regional Office IT Infrastructure Cost Consolidation

Little recently consolidated two of its Los Angeles offices into one for better efficiency. Faced with a decision to buy a large, 2TB+ storage area network (SAN) or network attached storage (NAS), the company opted instead to move the LA office "to the cloud." With the cloud infrastructure that was in Charlotte, the company had on-demand resources to accommodate this expansion of disk and consolidation of office space. This strategy has allowed the regional office to operate exclusively in the cloud with no local storage; Little plans to move its other three offices to the cloud by the end of the year. Again, it is just like being in the same office; the physical location of the office does not matter.

General-Purpose Business Applications

Sure, designers love the raw power an $8,000 workstation can bring to them, but what about the rest of us? With Little's virtualized high-performance graphics workstation, this technology is affordable to all firms, in all industries, and for all applications. Can you imagine the productivity enhancements of running Outlook, Microsoft Office 2007, Financial, HR, or other business applications on an HPGW? Seven to ten BIM designers can work on one of these workstations. Depending on the business applications, a firm may be able to run 20 to 30 users on such a box. An $8,000 HPGW running 30 business users costs $267 per user. Isn't that worth the productivity gained?

Of course, you will have to test your applications to see whether they are "RDP friendly," but many of the modern applications work fine in RDP. The accountants love tearing through their crystal reports on this cloud workstation.

Full Mobility

How many employees work exclusively in their physical office all the time? With the consolidation of real estate leased space, more workers telecommuting from home, and more freelancers and consultants competing for jobs all over the place, people need to be able to run all their office applications anytime, anyplace, just as if they were in their office. This has been difficult up to now because people had applications on their laptops and their data scattered between local and remote sources. There have been improvements from the WAN accelerator companies that allow individual users access to accelerate their laptop traffic, but again, this is still not good enough. With a secure remote cloud gateway, you will be able to access your HPGW, which is sitting right next to your data on a gigabit LAN. Their laptop is nothing more than a cloud access device for most of their computing.

Home workers now have more options. They still need a broadband Internet connection, but instead of working on their laptop connected to their home Internet connection, they can use Remote Desktop Protocol (RDP) from their laptop to access the remote high-performance workstation and use its computing resources, as shown in Figure 27.1. This workstation, coupled with the 20MB corporate Internet connection, provides a much better and faster computing experience. This is because the HPGW is better than their laptop and the corporate Internet connection is way better than their residential broadband.

FIGURE 27.1
Using Remote Desktop Connection to work with a Revit model via the cloud computer

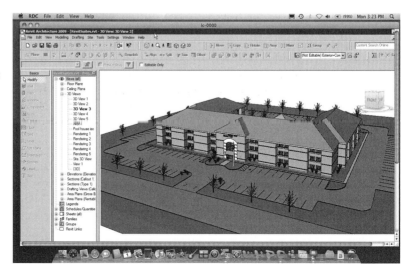

As shown in Figure 27.2, a Mac can be used just as easily as a Windows computer to work with the cloud. In fact, you could even use a smartphone such as the iPhone as the "cloud access device." All it needs is an RDP client, as shown in Figure 27.3. Although you may not want to work with Revit on an iPhone, you can at least access and view a model if required.

FIGURE 27.2

Using a Mac to work with Revit on the cloud

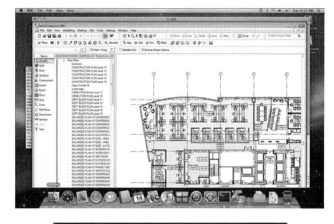

FIGURE 27.3

Accessing Revit on the cloud with an iPhone

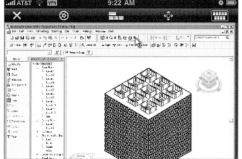

IT Automation and Support Reduction

Although a cloud strategy does not change your software licensing agreements with your software vendors or the related costs, it is much easier for your IT staff to deploy and manage new applications. Many software applications have a network or concurrent licensing model. This means that anyone can work on any workstation as long as there is an available license in the pool. If everyone in the company needs access to a particular application, the traditional approach was to use sophisticated scripting or software automation to push an application to 200+ laptops. This is time-consuming and problematic because it is hard to update a laptop that rarely connects to the corporate network.

Little can run the entire company on 20 HPGW (aka cloud computers). These 20 HPGW are stationary, located in a datacenter, and available 24/7. It is much easier for IT to update these 20 stationary computers than 200 mobile computers. Depending on the application and number of users, you can put it on one cloud computer, and people just log in to it when they need to run it. Problem solved.

Business Continuity, Disaster Recovery, and Security

How many firms back up their user desktops and laptops? Not many do this, because of the time and disk requirements. But IT knows that many people have all kinds of corporate and client information on their laptops. With the cloud strategy, you can keep corporate and client information "in the cloud" where it is backed up and replicated. Without the cloud, if your laptop is stolen or the hard drive crashes, you are out of commission until your IT department can get you a new laptop or rebuild it after it is repaired. With an HPGW cloud, if there is a failure, there is no data lost since it is on the SAN. And there is no downtime.

Little has spare capacity on the cloud just for disaster recovery purposes. For example, if cloud box LC-0000 goes down (LC stands for Little's Cloud), IT tells the people assigned to that box to log into LC-5000 and keep on working. Their profiles and user data migrate over with them. If their cloud access device (such as their laptop) fails, IT can hand them a spare laptop and they can keep working. If they are on the road, they can walk into any electronics store and buy a $400 laptop to access the cloud. And finally, security is greatly enhanced, particularly for the client data. People can leave their data in the cloud and not have to bring it to the local laptop. If there is a situation where people need to present and thus need data locally, it will just be a copy and not the source.

Locked Down Corporate Desktops, Unlocked Personal Laptops

How long has IT tried to lock down corporate desktops so that they will be consistently available for business? Now try to balance that requirement with people's need for autonomy, local software innovation, and the ability to respond to clients' needs without having to check in with IT every time.

Little's cloud offers the best of both worlds. The company locks down its cloud computers and does not allow any personal applications or data. The local laptop, in effect, becomes the place for personal data, pictures, and applications (such as iTunes). If people want to back up their laptop, the company recommends that employees purchase their own USB hard drive or buy a subscription to an online backup service. If people blow away their local settings and data or their laptop becomes infected with spyware, IT can quickly replace their laptop. Their business applications and data remain unaffected.

Rendering an Animation Farm

Most large design firms have a 3D animation studio where they create photorealistic renderings of their buildings. Many take it to the next level of making short movies, fly-throughs, or full cinematic storytelling to give clients a better sense of what their new facility will look like. These rendering programs have to crunch frame by frame of a video and could take several days to complete. By having an HPGW cloud, these studios can use the cloud at the same time people are using it, just at a lower processor priority (see Figure 27.4). When people go home, these programs crank up and fully utilize the CPU all night long. On some jobs, we have seen rendering times drop from 53 mins/frame to 7.3 secs/frame. With all this additional number-crunching ability, regular renderings get done quicker. It is also encouraging Little's designers to move into high-definition (HD) rendering to achieve a higher level of quality, client "wow" factor, and enhanced competitive capability.

FIGURE 27.4
The cloud HPGW also does double duty as a rendering farm in addition to running BIM applications.

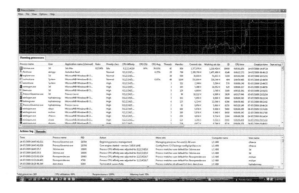

Implementing a High-Performance Workstation Cloud

This section provides an overview of the two main steps Little took to create their virtualized high-performance graphical workstations. The virtualization of other IT assets such as servers and storage are also crucial to the full workstation cloud strategy. Figure 27.5 shows a schematic diagram.

FIGURE 27.5
HPGW cloud

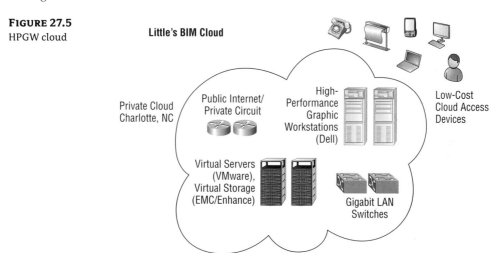

Virtualizing Your Servers and Storage

As a method to save money in buying new server hardware, Little began testing VMware's ESX software. After an initial pilot on low-risk servers, the company worked out tools and techniques, and now all servers are placed into a virtual infrastructure. This led to significant reductions in Little's hardware expense, and the company has seen greatly increased operational capabilities such as "instant" provisioning, disaster recovery, and business continuity. It has enabled the IT department to be able to deliver on the corporate challenge to "do more with less."

Next, Little chose to virtualize its storage to save money and to be able to manage a mountain of data with existing IT staff. The company standardized on the EMC CX500 and has a big pot of disks that are carved as needed for applications and servers. That "pot-o-disk" is approaching 50TB on two redundant EMCs.

Virtualizing Your High-Performance Graphics Workstations

Virtualized workstations are workstations that are not virtualized in the way most IT people think of virtualization. Little does not use VMware's ESX server or any other virtual desktop infrastructure (VDI) like Citrix XenDesktop or VMware View. The company uses a utility that allows it to share the Windows 7 64-bit operating system with many users at the same time. So from an IT perspective, this is a shared piece of hardware. From an end user's perspective, it looks and feels like a virtual desktop.

To derive the same virtualization benefits for the desktops that the company had realized with its servers and storage, it tested various desktop virtualization products. However, the company did not virtualize the Graphics Processing Unit (GPU), which led to poor performance—a cloud that would be slower than users' laptops. The key to getting the users to move to a workstation cloud was to provide not just the same experience as their laptop, but an experience that was *way* better than their laptop. Little wanted a workstation cloud that people couldn't touch with their laptop computers.

What if you took a baby-step toward desktop virtualization and used a hybrid approach? Little had a vision where it could have a smoking-fast workstation sitting in a datacenter that the company could get to via various remote desktop protocols. But this wasn't good enough. That approach still needed a one-to-one mapping of people to workstations. This didn't save Little any money. But what if you could turn a single-user workstation into a multiuser workstation— call it a workstation server? To end users, it would look virtualized and be in the "cloud." To the IT staff, it would be a piece of shared hardware. Little challenged its IT staff to come up with a concept to build this—and they did. Based on its benchmark testing, Little was able to put 10 people on these shared workstations.

Here is the "the secret sauce" of Little's strategy:

Hardware

◆ Rack-mounted workstation

◆ Two 3.0GHz Xeon quad-core processors (8 cores total)

◆ 32GB of RAM

◆ 1.5GB of Video RAM

◆ Fast local hard drive

◆ User/design data mapped to virtualized storage on the company's SAN

◆ Client access device: Their primary Windows laptop

Software

◆ Microsoft Windows 7, 64-bit desktop operating system

◆ Utility software for multiuser access, load balancing of CPU, network, and memory resources.

◆ Remote Desktop Protocol (RDP) used for client remote access

Software Licensing

You might wonder if this strategy violates any end-user licensing agreements (EULAs) for Autodesk or Microsoft. The short answer is no. All users consuming software resources are fully licensed.

Autodesk's EULA does not allow virtualization, hosting, or service bureau–type provisioning of their software, and a BIM cloud is neither. This approach is a private cloud owned by the customer, who has purchased all required licenses either in a networked or stand-alone version. Autodesk also states they will not support ICA or RDP connections even though these work for most functions. If you do need to place a support call, simply do it from the console of the cloud box and not on an RDP connection. It is this author's opinion that Autodesk does eventually need to support RDP/ICA and virtualization for their products and update their EULA. This will actually generate more Revit revenue as it will make the hardware more affordable for smaller firms.

Microsoft's EULA allows you to connect to a remote workstation via RDP as long as you have a licensed Windows device (such as a laptop). For the non-Microsoft devices such as Macs or IPhones, you must purchase a Windows OS license for that device to access a remote workstation.

Based on the size of Little (225 people), it can provide design services on 20 HPGW cloud computers. These workstations will *not* need to be refreshed every two years like users' individual laptops. Little estimates that they will upgrade their cloud computers every four to five years, with maybe a component upgrade in the interim. The primary laptops will need to be replaced only when they die—and the company is hoping to get four years out of them. With most of the computing load moved off the laptops, when the company does need to replace laptops they will cost $800 to $1,000 rather than $2,200 to $2,500. Little figured it was better to spend $1 million over 10 years than $3 million to buy desktop computing hardware.

Does this solution work internationally? Technically it does, but we would say practically it does not. The network latency across oceans is too great to get a smooth desktop experience. Little has logged into the cloud from an AirCard, and it was OK. Typing was slow, but you can do basic things. The latency on the AirCard was 180ms, and that is similar to what you would experience over the oceans. So, depending on how globally you are working now, it may be better. But it is not the "same as being there" performance. In the United States, however, the performance is rock-solid, with coast-to-coast latencies of 50 to 55ms. It works so well that Little is able to run its Los Angeles office entirely in the cloud with no local storage, as mentioned earlier. If a company has an international footprint, you could set up clouds on each continent so you would not have to cross the ocean to work.

Implementing a Dual-Purpose BIM Cloud and Render Farm

Once your Revit people are working on their new BIM cloud, you'll realize just how little your desktops and laptops are utilized. Our *people* are utilized—just not always on their computer. They have to attend client meetings, develop business, go to the job site, red-line printed documents, or do some hand-sketching. This utilization solution is similar to concurrent licensing to maximize the utilization of your Revit software. For large firms, you can buy fewer seats of Revit because not everyone is designing at the same time.

The same concept applies to your desktop. If users aren't consuming a Revit license, they are probably not consuming other computing resources (like CPU and memory). Wouldn't it be nice if those rendering groups could use the excess computer resources? Well, they can, but you have to be smart about it. It will not go over too well if the rendering studios are pegging the CPU so that the human designers can't work. That is why you need to manage the CPU, memory, and disk resources of your cloud boxes. Now when all this is truly virtualized it will all be done automatically, but in the meantime you have to get creative with your manual procedures.

CPU-Constrained Rendering

Many utilities allow you to manage running processes on a computer. Find one you like, and then figure out which processes are pegging the CPU. Then bind them to half of your available CPUs.

Little is running two quad-core Xeon CPUs, which give the company eight cores. They assign four or five cores to their rendering processes so that the other cores are available to humans. They also set the priority of these processes below the human processes. That way, if the humans need more cores, they will get them by taking CPU resources from the rendering jobs. By having CPU resources available to humans all the time, you are always able to take back CPU from rendering. Then when the humans log off and go home, the rendering jobs kick back up. Little has tried many combinations of assigning CPUs to the rendering jobs, and the 50-50 split seems to yield the optimal performance.

Memory-Constrained Rendering

Some animations programs won't use much CPU, but they will take all the available memory. You can say they don't play nicely with others. To solve this problem, Little found a free virtual product that runs on Windows 7 64-bit and could see all eight cores. They installed a Windows desktop OS inside this virtual machine and then gave it only 4GB of RAM. Now that animation program can render all day long and only consume 4GB of RAM. This restriction gives the VM a lower priority so it doesn't take resources from humans when they need it.

Disk-Constrained Rendering

Disk-constrained rendering is a little trickier and harder to monitor. First, hard disk resources are another computer resource that can become constrained, thus reducing your performance. Next, some applications are particularly disk I/O intensive, which is variable and hard to measure with pinpoint accuracy. Finally, application types (Revit vs. 3ds Max), the size of files, and the methods the designer uses all create different disk I/O scenarios.

All of this together means that if you have multiple people on the same computer making similar demands on the hard drive, the computer will slow down. You can minimize this constraint by adding multiple hard drives into the computer. One common solution is to put the operating system on the C: drive but locate the user Revit models on the D: drive, which is a separate disk.

In Little's case, the company is opting to put user and Revit models on a SAN that is separate from the cloud box. Not only will this improve disk performance, but it also makes users' data available in the event their cloud computer is down.

In the pilot version of Little's BIM cloud, the company allowed the users to work in the C:\ My Documents folder, which will be slower (but not really noticeable) if there are many people working at the same time. The way around this is to move their user profiles to the SAN. Users can log into any cloud box and see their profile. It works very much like the Windows roaming profile, but it's easier to manage and works more consistently.

Little has decided to blast this out to all their users once it has the Windows 2008 Active Directory online. The Group Policy management for Windows 7 is much better, so they plan to wait.

Lessons Learned

Here are some of the lessons Little has learned so far from production users on the cloud:

◆ With multiple users using the same workstation, you can see how underutilized your laptops really are. Most of the time, they are sitting idle when people are in meetings or out in the field. This makes laptops ripe for consolidation.

◆ Not all users' computing needs are the same—some consume much more memory and CPU than others. Your IT staff can work with them to see whether the need is legitimate or whether there was a training issue.

◆ Memory can be the biggest constraint. Early on at Little, they had a "cloud burst" by having too many people consuming memory on one box. They locked up the box. By reducing the number of designers per box from 8 to 7 and adding more memory, the cloud bursts were eliminated.

◆ Some applications do not lend themselves well to a remote desktop strategy. Little had to tweak its AutoCAD program because the mouse pointer "crosshair" caused too much data to be sent—and this is tiresome if a user is working in AutoCAD all day long. They have found a solution to this problem using an accelerated RDP client that works better for AutoCAD-based products. Real-time video compositing also works better with local hardware. And if you use Revit workshare *monitoring* (not worksharing), you'll be disappointed in the cloud. Worksharing is fine, but you can have only one instance of the monitoring going at the same time on the same box. Because Little's STCs are so fast, they don't use monitoring. Be sure to test your mission-critical applications first on a small pilot with hardware you already own. The cloud approach is better, but not perfect.

◆ You can drive utilization of these boxes to nearly 100 percent. When people aren't using them, you can turn these into a "rendering farm" that generates computer animations. Since these processes run at a lower priority than user applications, they can be running at the same time as people are designing. Any additional capacity is used for new users and disaster recovery purposes.

◆ Running on the cloud is faster from home than a laptop hooked into a broadband cable service.

◆ People forget where they leave their stuff. IT people take remote desktops for granted since they use them every day. It takes a little coaching and practice on the users' part to realize what's going on. But once they catch on, they are all over this new computing method.

Desktop Cloud Computing Technologies to Watch

There are three main strategies for desktop cloud computing:

◆ Remote connection to physical desktop OS (the strategy that Little chose)

◆ Remote connection to a physical server OS

◆ Remote connection to a virtual desktop OS running on a physical server OS

Each strategy has its advantages, and its viability will change over time.

Remote Connection to a Physical Desktop OS

This strategy is a twist on an age-old strategy. Using RDP to access a remote desktop has been around forever, it seems. As desktop RDP matures, more and more applications work in this scenario. So it is not a far leap to take RDP from a one-to-one desktop mapping to a many-to-one desktop mapping. For most firms (fewer than 700 people), this is the most effective and afford-able strategy.

Little will stick with this infrastructure until the performance, cost, and manageability of the other solutions exceed this one. The company will keep its current cloud hardware for five years and then decide whether there is a compelling business reason to change. And if that compelling reason comes before the company is ready to decommission this hardware, Little will just reimage the cloud machines with the new solution. Because the company has 20 cloud computers, it will be easy to migrate in a controlled fashion.

Remote Connection to a Physical Server OS

Another remote desktop, multiuser strategy is a Terminal Server option. There are different vendors in this space, but the concept is the same. You take a server, with server-class hardware, and a server operating system, and you create a window (or terminal) for each user who wants to access the resources on that server. The "terminal" name comes from the old mainframe days when you had a mainframe computer that supported as many as 3,270 terminals via a hardware connection.

Eventually, this same concept was brought to the Windows/software world. A user would have a desktop computer (or laptop) running some type of remote client software (like RDP or ICA). They would then launch this remote client software, and it would "point" to a terminal session on the server. Once the connection is made, a complete Windows desktop shows up as a window on the user's local desktop. This can be kind of confusing at first because most people are used to working on the console (or main screen) of a computer. So, rather than having your Windows desktop fill your entire screen, you have a smaller window that contains a Windows desktop. To confuse people even more, you can maximize your subwindow to make it look like your console. Yes, it is easy to forget where you are computing! So, now that you have opened a desktop on a remote computer, you can start using the applications on that desktop just like you were sitting in front of it.

Technically this approach works, but it does not have the robust graphics support that a workstation has, plus the hardware and software costs more to implement this solution.

However, just to be on the safe side, this was Little's plan "B" strategy if the company couldn't get the desktop terminal services solution to work with all their applications. But to use a Terminal Server product, you would have to then stick a high-end desktop graphics card into a server. Windows 2008 Server would pick it up, but Little was not confident how well the terminal server products would use it in all situations.

In the end, Little did a limited test with Windows 2008 Server, Terminal Server, and Revit, and it seemed to work fine. This is a proven solution that will certainly allow you to share a sin-gle piece of hardware with multiple users. You will, however, pay more for the server features even if you do not need them. In any event, the company couldn't justify why it would want to run Revit on a server OS when it runs better on a desktop OS. On the flip side, it would be easier to scale and manage this solution. You might want to consider this option if your firm employs more than 700 people. The following are major vendors in this space:

◆ Citrix XenServer

◆ Microsoft Windows 2008 R2 Remote Desktop Services

Remote Connection to a Virtual Desktop OS via a Physical Server OS

As of this writing, this strategy is the newest technology and is not quite ready for prime time for high-performance workstations because the horsepower just isn't there for graphic and 3D-intensive applications. However, we think this is the Promised Land. Perhaps in three to five years the technology will be baked and affordable. This strategy will scale to large design firms, IT support will be automated, and computing resources (CPU, memory, disk, NIC) will be automatically optimized and load-balanced. The industry term for this strategy is *virtual desktop infrastructure* (VDI), and there are many players in this space, such as the following:

◆ VMware View

◆ Citrix XenDesktop

◆ Calista Technologies (acquired by Microsoft)

◆ Oracle's Sun VDI

These vendors offer similar solutions, but the real test in the AEC space is to find the one that does the best job at accelerating the graphics. Most seem to be focused on the corporate desktop rather than the designer workstation.

The Bottom Line

Understand the business benefit of a high-performance workstation cloud.   Cloud computing benefits not only Revit but all your corporate applications. Mobile laptops have just as much horsepower available as the highest-end workstations. And rather than having that expensive hardware available only to a few users, you can make it available to anyone who needs it—at any time.

> **Master It**   Consider the up-front cost of a high-performance workstation cloud over three years as compared to your previous and anticipated expenditures. How can you take advantage of the business benefits of putting your design tools in the cloud?

Implement a high-performance workstation cloud.   Once you feel comfortable with your Revit cloud computing infrastructure performing better than your current desktop computing infrastructure, don't be surprised if there is resistance by some diehard desktop users who refuse to let go of their workstations.

> **Master It**   Since price isn't the issue, where do you think you still might encounter cultural barriers to implementing cloud-based solutions?

Know which future cloud computing strategies to watch.　　Technology is going to keep evolving. The VDI industry is moving quickly and rapidly evolving. You want to be well positioned to take advantage of the best technology for your firm at the best price point possible.

Master It　　Most firms in the AEC space have well under a few dozen employees. If smaller firms have the advantage of being nimble when it comes to adopting and implementing new technology quickly, why is cloud computing such a great fit?

Appendices

In this section you will find:

Appendix A

The Bottom Line

Each of The Bottom Line sections in the chapters suggests exercises to deepen skills and understanding. Sometimes there is only one possible solution, but often you are encouraged to use your skills and creativity to create something that builds on what you know and lets you explore one of many possible solutions.

Chapter 1: Beyond Basic Documentation

Leverage the BIM model.   Understanding the level of risk your firm is willing to take in new technologies will help you establish goals for your future use of BIM.

Master It   Using the three areas of firm integration (visualization, analysis, and strategy), define how those areas overlap for your firm or project.

Solution   Remember, there is no wrong answer in mapping a path forward for your firm or project. The important thing is to identify which areas are critical to the workflow of your firm to help you focus your future efforts.

Know how BIM affects firm culture.   Not only is the transition to BIM from 2D CAD a change in applications, but it's also a shift in workflow and firm culture. Understanding some of the key differences helps to ensure project and team success during the transition.

Master It   What are some of the ways that BIM differs from CAD, and how does this change the culture of an office or project team?

Solution   BIM shifts the level of effort in different phases of the project. This creates new responsibilities and workflows that the team needs to become aware of in order to maintain a level of predictability within the project workflow. Since BIM is also hosted out of a single file instead of several, isolated files, BIM changes the level of interteam communication on a project.

Focus your investment in BIM.   One of the key elements to understanding BIM beyond documentation is simply to have an awareness of the possibilities. This allows you to make an educated decision as to what direction your firm or project would like to go.

Master It   List some of the potential uses of a BIM model beyond documentation.

Solution   Spatial validation, visualization, facility management, construction visualization, blast analysis, and whole building analysis are all potential uses of a BIM model.

Chapter 2: Principles of Revit

Understand Revit project organization.   Revit has been available for about 10 years, and yet, after a decade, it remains unique in its approach to "whole-building BIM." The compelling advantage of being able to design, document, and manage your project across multiple disciplines—the architect, structural, and mechanical disciplines—is something that you can only do in Revit, and understanding project workflow in Revit is key to getting off on the right foot.

Master It   Thinking back to the Revit organization chart shown in Figure 2.1, what are the main components of a Revit project, and how can you use them apply to your design process? How do these categories directly affect your design workflow?

Solution   The top-level categories of a Revit project are Datum, Content, Views, and Management. They correspond to the design process of maintaining relationships, repetition, representations, and restrictions. Keep these corollaries in mind as you move sequentially from schematic design, design development, construction documentation, and construction management.

Understand Revit interface organization.   In addition to understanding how your project is organized, to use Revit well you must understand how the user interface is organized. Once you grasp both these concepts, you'll be ready to move ahead.

Master It   The "big" areas of the Revit UI are the Ribbon, properties, the Project Browser, and the drawing area. How do these areas work together, and what tabs correspond to an iterative design process?

Solution   The Home tab is where you'll turn in your early design process since it contains datum, system families, component families, and spaces. As the design develops, you'll establish your views from the View tab. When you start to get into documentation, you'll work from the Annotate tab. And having panels from the Modify tab pulled off and close at hand will keep you from having to go between one contextual tab and another.

Chapter 3: The Basics of the Revit Toolbox

Select, modify, and replace elements.   There are many fundamental interactions supported by Revit to select just what you need and to modify elements efficiently.

Master It   How can you quickly select only the door tags in a plan view and switch them to another type?

Solution   First, window-select around the entire plan. Then, on the Filter tool in the Modify ribbon, select only the Door Tags category, close the Filter dialog box, and change the type in the Properties Palette.

Edit elements interactively.   The editing tools in Revit are similar to those found in other CAD and BIM software programs. Tools such as Move, Copy, and Trim are available on the Modify tab of the ribbon.

Master It   How do you create a parametric repetition of an element?

Solution   Select an element and activate the Array tool from the Modify tab of the ribbon. Specify a linear array with the Group And Associate option and choose either Move To 2nd for a specific element spacing or Move To Last for a consistent overall length with varied element spacing.

Use other editing tools.   Beyond the basic editing tools are more advanced commands to help you consistently and intelligently populate a building model with content.

Master It   How do you copy model elements in the same location for a multistory building?

Solution   Select the required elements and copy them to the clipboard (Ctrl+C). From the Clipboard panel in the Modify tab, select Paste ➢ Aligned To Selected Levels and then choose the levels to which you'd like to paste the copied content.

Creating site context for your Revit project.   The site tools in Revit allow you to create context for your building models including topographic surfaces, graded regions and property lines.

Master It   Describe the different methods used to create a topographic surface.

Solution   A topographic surface can be created by placing points at specific elevations relative to Revit's internal project coordinates, by using an imported 3D CAD file from a civil engineering software program, or by using a text file that contains the XYZ coordinates of a field of points.

Chapter 4: Configuring Templates and Standards

Define settings for graphic quality and consistency.   The fundamental building blocks for any template are the customized settings to object styles, line styles, fill patterns, materials, and more.

Master It   How can a complex custom fill pattern be imported into Revit?

Solution   Using Notepad and an existing hatch pattern definition from AutoCAD, add the text `;%UNITS=INCH` or `;%UNITS=MM` and `;%TYPE=DRAFTING` or `;%TYPE=MODEL`. Save the result as a PAT file and import it into Revit via a new fill pattern.

Organize views for maximum efficiency.   The project template can be used to capture a framework supporting your visual and organizational standards.

Master It   How can you customize the Project Browser to support your business needs?

Solution   On the Manage tab, create custom project parameters assigned to views. These parameters can then be included in customized browser organizations, which you can access on the View tab in User Interface ➢ Browser Organization.

Create custom annotation families.   Developing a graphic style to match your standards will usually require some annotation families to be edited or created from scratch.

Master It   Can a single label display more than one parameter? How are custom view tags loaded into a project?

Solution   When editing a label in the Family Editor, add as many parameters into a single label as necessary. You can even use live, custom formatted measurement parameters of the model element being tagged. Custom view tags must be loaded into a project or project template, assigned to a system family tag type, and then assigned to a view type.

Start a project with a custom template.   Making your custom template available for new projects ensures all future projects will maintain the same level of graphic quality and efficiency you expect.

> **Master It**   How do you set your own custom project template to be the default for new projects?

> **Solution**   Click the Application button, select the Options button, and navigate to the File Locations tab. Click the Browse button for the Default Template File field and navigate to the location of your custom project template. From now on, click the Application button, select New ➤ Project, and select New in the Recent Files window—or click Ctrl+N—to use your new template as the basis for the new project.

Develop a template management strategy.   Organizing your standards, content, and settings while using Revit's tools to transfer content will make your effort more efficient.

> **Master It**   How do you insert your standard details from one Revit project to another? How do you transfer settings such as materials?

> **Solution**   2D content such as standard details can be stored in a separate Revit project files and loaded when needed. One way to do this is with the Insert Views from File tool in the Insert tab. Select an RVT project file, and then choose eligible views such as drafting views, sheets, or schedules. They are transferred into your active project with all associated parameters. To transfer settings and styles such as materials, select the Manage tab and click Transfer Project Standards. Remember to open another project from which you'd like to transfer settings before running this tool.

Chapter 5: Managing a Revit Project

Understand a BIM workflow.   Understand how projects are completed in BIM and how the use of Revit on a project can change how information within a project is created.

> **Master It**   Explain one of the primary differences between a more traditional 2D CAD-based workflow and producing documents using Revit.

> **Solution**   In a 2D CAD-based workflow, documents are created by team members creating plans, sections, elevations, and details all as separate drawings and then manually coordinating that content to for the project set. In a BIM or Revit workflow, the plans, sections, elevations, and perspectives are a byproduct of creating the virtual building model and are coordinated through updates made to the model itself.

Start a BIM project.   Since Revit is a change in workflow, it is also important to understand the change in staffing and who is needed to perform what roles on a project.

> **Master It**   What are the three primary roles in a Revit project and what are the responsibilities of those roles?

> **Solution**   Every successful Revit project will need three roles accounted for. These roles do not need to be individual people; one person can assume all three roles at any point in

the project. The roles are Architect, Modeler, and Drafter. These roles are responsible for understanding and articulating the design, creating model content, and laying out and annotating the documentation respectively.

Work in a large team.   Many projects require multiple team members. Some require having a very large team assembled on a project. Working with a large team in Revit is a matter of collectively managing a series of smaller models. Know how to manage these smaller models.

Master It   How many people is too many to have working in a single Revit file? What do you do when you reach that limit?

Solution   Typically, six to eight people is about the realistic working limit for the number of separate users within a Revit file. When this number is hit, the team needs to decide a good way to split the model up into smaller models that can then be linked back together.

Create details in Revit.   Revit is a combination of model content in 3D and annotations and embellishment in 2D to create any document set. It is important to understand when to use 3D within a model environment and what elements are best done in 2D to maintain model integrity and keep the model responsive.

Master It   What are the three questions you should ask yourself before modeling or drafting any views in Revit?

Solution   Asking yourself these three questions will help you form a good understanding of whether your detail needs to be modeled or drafted in Revit. You should ask yourself the following:

- How often will the detail be seen (in how many views)?

- What scale will the detail be shown in?

- How good am I at using Revit?

Perform quality control on your Revit model.   Since you have several people using one file to create possibly hundreds of drawing sheets, it's important to keep a model clean of errors and functioning well. Performing regular maintenance on your model is essential to maintaining a file stability and functionality. Should a file happen to become corrupted, you stand to lose the work of the entire team. Understand how to maintain a model and how to regularly check under the hood.

Master It   There are several ways to keep an eye on the model so it stays responsive and free of corruption. List some of these ways.

Solution   Here are some of the ways to maintain oversight of the model:

- Watch the file size. Jumps in file size or an excessively large file will point to possible problems or poor model performance.

- Schedules are a good way to track content within a model.

- Regularly check the Errors And Warnings dialog box and be sure to keep the overall error count low.

Chapter 6: Understanding Worksharing

Understand key worksharing concepts. Once the team has created local files, it is necessary to understand how to keep both the local file and central file up-to-date as changes occur on the project. This ensures that everyone is working from an updated and recent copy of the model at all times.

Master It Once you've begun working out of your local file, how do you publish your changes to the central file? How do you download changes from the central file to your local file?

Solution The easiest way to do this is by using the Synchronize With Central command, which is accessible from the Collaborate tab and is also accessible from the Quick Access toolbar.

Use worksharing in your project. Knowing how to activate and utilize worksharing is indispensible to working in a team environment using Revit.

Master It How do you transition a single-user Revit file to a multiuser environment using worksharing?

Solution To activate worksharing, click the Workset button on the Collaborate tab. This will initiate the worksharing feature and divide your model up into the two default worksets. To allow others to access the model, you will need to perform a File ➢ Save As and save the file to a network location. After this, close the file. Each team member then makes a local copy of this network file and then works exclusively within their local copy.

Manage workflow with worksets. Once the central file has been created, you'll need to organize and structure the model into logical worksets to maintain workflow with Revit.

Master It How do worksets differ from layers in 2D CAD? What are some logical ways to create worksets within a model?

Solution 2D CAD layers were logically divided around individual elements in isolated files. In Revit, since everything is in one file and we are working with 3D objects, not just model lines, we need to use worksets to divide the building in different ways. Some logical workset divisions would be Shell and Core, Interiors, FF&E, and Site.

Understand element ownership in worksets. Editing elements in a central file means you have sole ownership over further changes to those elements. Understanding the permissions will be critical to working in a team.

Master It How do you edit an element in the model if someone has already taken permission of it in a worksharing environment?

Solution Trying to edit the element will initiate a request for permissions within Revit. By alerting the other team member of your desire to have ownership of this element, they can grant your permission request using the Editing Requests button from the Collaborate tab.

Chapter 7: Working with Consultants

Prepare for interdisciplinary collaboration. Proper planning and communication are the foundation of effective collaboration. Although only some client organizations may require a BIM planning document, it is a recommended strategy for all design teams.

Master It What are the key elements of a BIM execution plan?

Solution An effective BIM execution plan will first list the goals and uses of building information modeling as well as the scope of the data to be developed. It will also list the software platforms to be utilized, information exchange process, delivery strategy, and technology infrastructure.

Collaborate using linked Revit models. The most basic tool for collaboration is the ability to view consultants' data directly within the context of your own model. Project files from other disciplines can be linked and displayed with predictable visual fidelity without complex conversion processes.

Master It How can worksharing complement the use of linked Revit models?

Solution Placing each linked model on a unique workset allows team members to choose when to load or unload the linked models without affecting their teammates. Worksets within linked models can also help manage graphic quality using the ability to load or unload worksets globally.

Use Copy/Monitor between linked models. The Coordination Monitor tools establish intelligent bonds between elements in a host file and correlating elements in a linked model. They also support a workflow that respects the needs of discrete teams developing their own data, perhaps on a different schedule than that of other team members.

Master It How can grids in two different Revit projects be related?

Solution The Copy/Monitor tool allows you to copy an element from a linked file into a host file and monitor the linked element for changes.

Run interference checks. Interference checking—also known as *clash detection*—is one of the most important uses of building information modeling. It is the essence of virtual construction and has the greatest potential for cost savings during the physical construction process.

Master It How do you find interfering objects between two linked Revit models?

Solution On the Collaborate tab, find the Coordinate panel and choose Interference Check ➤ Run Interference Check. If you are using linked models, select the desired linked project in the Categories From drop-down list while keeping the other column set to Current Project. Select the desired object categories in the left and right columns (for example, choose Structural Framing from a structural model and Ducts from an MEP model). Click OK to run the check. The results can be exported to a report for coordination with others.

Chapter 8: Interoperability: Working Multiplatform

Use imported 2D CAD data. CAD data can be integrated into your Revit project in a number of ways: as plans of existing conditions, as fixture layouts from consultants, or as standard details from your company's library.

Master It How can CAD details be used within Revit?

Solution Create a new drafting view for a single detail. From the Insert tab, choose Link CAD and select a DWG detail file. During linking, set the colors to Black and White. Make sure the scale of the drafting view matches the notation scale of the CAD detail. Use the Query tool to turn off unwanted layers within the linked file.

Export 2D CAD data. The ability to deliver quality 2D information to other constituents involved in your project is as important as importing it into Revit. Appropriately formatted views, standardized layer templates, and proper coordinate settings will result in happy team members and a smooth coordination process.

Master It Does Revit comply with the National CAD Standard?

Solution You have the ability to map Revit model categories to standardized layers in the Export Layers dialog box. Access this tool by clicking Application button and selecting Export ➤ Options ➤ Export Layers DWG/DXF. Load industry standard layer conventions using the Standard button.

Use imported 3D model data. Model data generated outside of Revit can be integrated into your projects as whole building systems, massing studies, or unique components.

Master It How can a building's structural model created with Bentley Structure be integrated into Revit?

Solution Create a structural framing family into which the DGN model will be inserted. When the family is finished, the DGN geometry will be displayed as any other Revit structural framing component.

Export 3D model data. Your modeled elements don't have to remain in the Revit environment forever. Data can be exported to 3ds Max, Google SketchUp, AutoCAD MEP, and more.

Master It How can I coordinate my architectural Revit model with an engineer using AutoCAD MEP?

Solution The engineer will likely require one DWG model per level for efficient coordination. Create duplicate floor plans for exporting and adjust the View Range settings for Top to Level Above, Offset: 0 and Bottom to Associated Level, Offset: 0. Create duplicate 3D views for each level, right-click the ViewCube, and choose Orient To View ➤ Floor Plans and find the corresponding floor plans. These 3D views can be batch-exported to DWG format and referenced by the MEP engineer in her designs.

Work with IFC imports and exports. Industry Foundation Classes is a vendor-neutral model format designed to support interoperability in the AEC industry. It is widely used by some major BIM platforms available around the world.

Master It How is an IFC model integrated into Revit for coordination?

Solution You can open an IFC file by clicking the Application button and selecting Open ➢ IFC. Once open, the data can be saved as an RVT Revit project file and linked into another Revit file for continued coordination.

Chapter 9: Advanced Modeling and Massing

Create and schedule massing studies. Starting the design process with actual building elements can lead to a lot of unexpected frustration. Walls lead to rooms, which get room tags and eventually scheduled. But if you've failed to fulfill the program, you'll wonder where to start over!

Master It You're faced with creating some design studies of a large hospital complex. How would you go about creating a Revit project that would allow you to create a massing study and schedule it against the design program?

Solution Massing studies allow you to create schedules of the surface, floor areas, and volumes of a mass. This is incredibly helpful for resolving design ideas before committing to walls, floors, and other building geometry.

Know when to use solid and surface masses. While solid masses and surface masses can both be used to maintain relationships to host geometry like walls and roofs, surface masses can't be volumetrically scheduled or contain floor area faces.

Master It You've been asked to create a complex canopy system for the entry to a hotel project. The system will consist of a complex wave of triangular panels. What kind of mass would you create?

Solution You're probably going to be better off not creating a solid mass since you don't need a solid—you only need a surface. It's best to use solids when you have to calculate the overall design program; floor areas, surface, and volume. For limited, surface-based relationships, just use surface massing. They'll help you resolve the overall design idea first. Then you can move on to patterns and eventually component-level geometry.

Use mathematical formulas for massing. Not all massing is going to be intuitive, in-the-moment decision making. By discovering the underlying rules that express a form, it is possible to create the formulas that can iterate and manipulate your massing study. So rather than manually manipulate the mass, you simply manipulate the formulas related to your mass.

Master It What's the best way to discover and create these formulas?

Solution Never stop sketching! Staring at a blank spreadsheet is a one-way road to frustration. Sketch the idea and try to discern the rules that make the form change and morph into your design idea. Once you think you've discovered the rules that contain the idea, go ahead and start testing the rules in Revit. Once you find that the idea or principle is valid, it's simply a matter of scale.

Chapter 10: Conceptual Design and Sustainability

Embrace sustainable design concepts.   Understanding the concepts behind sustainable design is an important part of being able to perform analysis within the Revit model and a critical factor in today's design environment.

Master It   What are four key methods for a holistic sustainable design?

Solution   Four key methods for a sustainable solution are (1) understanding a building's climate, (2) reducing building loads, (3) using free energy when possible to power those loads, and (4) using efficient systems.

Leverage schedules.   Using schedules in Revit helps you track many of your design elements throughout the whole design process. These schedules can also be used to validate programmatic information during conceptual design.

Master It   Explain how to create a schedule from a conceptual mass that will show the programmatic areas for each floor level.

Solution   After the mass is created, insert it into the project. Select the mass and from the Modify | Mass tab, click the Mass Floor button and apply floors to the mass. Finally, create a schedule of mass floors showing Level and Area.

Use sun shading and solar paths.   Understanding the effects of the sun on a building design is a critical way to create and form space. Revit has tools to help you identify how the sun will affect the design and where shade and shadow will fall inside and outside the building over the course of the year.

Master It   How can you use the tools in Revit to produce still and animated solar studies from interior and exterior views in order to understand shading and the sun's effect on the building and space?

Solution   Use the Graphic Display Options dialog box to set the global location of the project. Next, establish a time of day to view the effects of the sun. Create key interior and exterior views of the project and apply these sun settings to the new views. To see the effects of the sun at that time throughout the year, animate the solar study for each week throughout the year.

Prepare and export your model for energy analysis.   Being able to predict a building's energy performance is a necessary part of designing sustainably. Although Revit doesn't have an energy modeling application built into it, it does have interoperability with many applications that have that functionality.

Master It   Explain the steps you need to take to get a Revit model ready for energy analysis.

Solution

1. The building has to have walls, floors, and roofs. Those all need to meet and join so there are no unrealistic gaps in the model.

2. Make sure each of the regions in the model has a room element inserted into it and the room element's height is set to the bottom of the floor above.

3. Under Area And Volume Calculations, turn on Room Volumes.

4. You're now ready to export the model to gbXML and import that into an energy analysis application.

Analyze your project for daylighting.   Not only can proper daylighting in a building save energy, but it can make the inhabitants happier and healthier. Through analysis, you can now quantify the amount of light you're getting in any space and measure the footcandle readings before you begin building. This allows you to iterate the design-making modifications to maximize your daylight while balancing the amount of glazing against solar heat gain and mechanical needs.

Master It   Understand how much daylight you need to perform certain tasks. How much daylighting is needed for the following:

- ◆ Working in an office
- ◆ Reading a book
- ◆ Working on or reading something small for an extended period of time

Solution

- ◆ 25 footcandles is the average needed as defined by the USGBC.
- ◆ 15–40 footcandles depending on the print size.
- ◆ 200–2000 footcandles depending on the size and task.

Chapter 11: Phasing, Groups, and Design Options

Use phasing.   Time is such an important element to the design process and nearly impossible to capture with traditional CAD tools. Don't use phasing for construction sequencing (there's a better way). Embrace phasing for *communication*, not just *illustration*.

Master It   How can you use phasing to communicate your design across a series of key stages? What kind of project is best suited to phasing?

Solution   Phasing works great in the presence of existing conditions, some of which need to be retained, and others that need to be demolished before proposed design can proceed. Actively search for a tenant fit-out to start using Revit.

Know why you shouldn't mirror groups.   Groups are great for creating collections of both host and family component geometry. Just remember to use best practices and you'll avoid a lot of common roadblocks. Everything still schedules, as you'd expect. And creating exceptions in groups allows you to make subtle changes without creating a new group.

Master It   Why shouldn't you mirror groups?

Solution   Although mirroring works conceptually, it breaks in implementation. Just because you can mirror something in Revit doesn't mean that it can actually be manufactured that way. And even more confusion can result if the mirrored object has to be powered, accessed, maintained, etc. in an impossible condition.

Mirroring groups has been known to create so much hassle that you are better to avoid it. And we'll keep pushing the factory to restrict mirroring of family components as a parameter, as well as groups.

Make design options for design iteration.   Like groups, design options work great when you work within the rules. Design options are intended for design iteration that is bounded and well defined—not for putting multiple buildings in one project file. Remember that links, groups, and phasing can exist within design options. Always keep hosted elements with their host when using design options.

Master It   Suppose you have a multistory tower. How could you show repetitive curtain wall options?

Solution   Put the different curtain wall options in different files. You can link these files within one Revit file. Then associate each of the different lines with a different design option. Eventually you set and accept the primary option. Then bind the link. They'll all become groups within your project.

Chapter 12: Visualization

Create real-time and rendered analytic visualizations.   Analytic visualization is about communicating information about your project in a nonliteral way, and it's very important! It's not about showing real materials in the project but using filters to visualize important metadata.

Master It   During the renovation of a space, you want to reuse the doors rather than throw them away. How would you illustrate this?

Solution   Assign an instance parameter to the doors called Recycled. Then apply this value to all the doors fulfilling these criteria in your project. Now you can use this parameter to create a view filter to illustrate where these reused doors are being used.

Render emotive photorealistic visualizations.   Photorealistic visualization is also about communicating design ideas but in emotive ways that are much closer to how the space will be experienced, including real lighting, materials, and entourage. Just remember that the time it takes to calculate and render your views will change dramatically based on the quality and resolution of your views.

Master It   Would the rendering for a PowerPoint presentation differ from a rendering being printed for a marketing brochure?

Solution   The rendering for the PowerPoint presentation needs only to be about 150dpi while the rendering for the printing needs to be 300dpi. A 300dpi image will take much longer to render than a 150dpi image, even though they'll look the same on the screen.

Understand the importance of sequencing your visualization workflow.   The sequence of design—building, content, materials, and cameras—is not the same as the sequence for visualization (geometry/cameras, lighting, materials). Lighting is far more important than materials of actual objects. Get the lighting right, and the materials will look great, but not the other way around.

Master It How do you create a rendering environment that replaces the actual materials with matte materials in order to study the effects of lighting on your design?

Solution Until View Filters allow elements actual rendered materials to be overwritten in a view, use phasing. Create a filter that overrides the materials and assign this analytic filter to the view that you're rendering with lights. After you achieve the desired lighting effects, go ahead and start re-rendering the view showing the actual materials.

Chapter 13: Walls and Curtain Walls

Use extended modeling techniques for basic walls. Walls in Revit are made from layers of materials that can represent generic placeholders for design layouts to complete assemblies representative of actual construction.

Master It How can you customize the profile of a wall?

Solution A wall can be attached to another object such as a roof, floor, or reference plane. Select a wall, activate the Attach Top/Base tool, and pick the object to which the wall should be attached. You can also edit the profile of a wall in elevation by selecting a wall, activating the Edit Elevation Profile tool, and modifying the sketch of the wall.

Create stacked walls. Exterior walls are usually composed of several combinations of materials with varying thicknesses. These various wall types can be combined into a single entity called a stacked wall.

Master It How do you create a stacked wall?

Solution You must duplicate an existing stacked wall type within a project. In the Type Properties, open the Edit Assembly dialog box and add any combination of basic walls into the stacked wall structure.

Create simple curtain walls. A curtain wall is an assembly of parts including curtain grids, panels, and mullions. They can be created in predefined types with regular horizontal and vertical spacing along with specific panel and mullion types.

Master It How do you add a door to a curtain wall?

Solution Use the Tab key to select a single panel in a curtain wall segment. If the panel is part of a predefined system, you must unpin the panel first. From the Type Selector, choose a curtain panel door family.

Create complex curtain walls. Revit's conceptual massing environment can be used to create complex curtain wall configurations. Pattern-based panel families can be loaded into the massing environment and populated on a divided surface. These populated surfaces can then be loaded and placed in a project model for documentation and scheduling.

Master It How do you create a complex divided surface?

Solution From Revit's Recent Files window, select New Conceptual Mass. Add a second level to the family and draw a curved line on each level. Select the two lines and click Create Form; choose the Planar Surface option. Select the new form and click the Divide Surface button on the ribbon.

Chapter 14: Floors, Ceilings, and Roofs

Understand floor modeling methods.   Floors are one of the most fundamental, sketch-based system families used in a Revit model. You can customize them to accommodate a variety of assumptions at various stages of design.

Master It   How can you create a structural floor with integrated metal decking?

Solution   You can create a structural floor by going to the Home tab of the ribbon and clicking Floor ➤ Structural Floor. This tool activates the Structural parameter in a floor's instance properties. Once this is activated, edit the floor's type properties to add a Structural Deck layer and assign a deck profile.

Model various floor finishes.   Thick and thin floor finishes can be created in Revit to support tagging, scheduling, and quantity takeoffs.

Master It   How would you represent a thin finish material in your project such as carpet?

Solution   Activate the Split Face tool from the Modify tab of the ribbon, select a floor, and define the boundaries of the area to be assigned as the thin material. Then activate the Paint tool, select the appropriate material, and click the split face you created within the floor.

Create ceilings.   Ceilings are sketch-based system families that can host objects such as light fixtures and HVAC diffusers.

Master It   What's the best way to model a ceiling within a space?

Solution   Ceilings are best created in a ceiling plan. Activate the Ceiling tool from the Build panel in the Home tab of the ribbon. Specify a value for the Height Offset From Level setting of the ceiling in the Properties dialog box, and use Automatic Ceiling to fill a bounded space with a ceiling object.

Understand roof modeling methods.   Roofs can be modeled as simple single-pitch shed roofs or complex extrusions of sinuous curves.

Master It   What is the best way to create a single vault roof?

Solution   That roof is best created with the roof by extrusion method. Go to the Home tab of the ribbon and click Roof ➤ Roof By Extrusion. Specify a wall or reference plane as the work plane and switch to an elevation, section, or 3D view. Draw the profile of a vaulted roof and click Finish Edit Mode. Adjust the extents of the extrusion as desired.

Work with advanced shape editing for floors and roofs.   A small but powerful toolset is available for extended editing of floor and roof objects. These tools allow you to create warped floor slabs and tapered layers of roof assemblies.

Master It   How do you create a drainage point in a flat roof slab?

Solution   Select a roof object and activate the Add Split Line tool from the Shape Editing panel in the ribbon. Draw two crossing lines from the four corners of the roof boundaries. Activate the Modify Sub Elements tool and select the point where the Split Lines cross. Change the value that appears to create a low drainage depression in the slab.

Chapter 15: Family Editor

Understand the Family Editor.   Before you start modeling a piece of content in the Family Editor, take a moment and think about how you expect that piece of content to "behave" in your project. Don't be afraid to model a first pass quickly. But also be thinking ahead with regard to how it might change. The role of the Family Editor isn't just an environment to model geometry; it also determines how the content that you create will behave in the project environment.

Master It   Choosing the right template is critical. Some flexibility is allowed by allowing you to convert from one family template to another. But this is not always the case. Why would you want to choose a door template rather than a generic model template?

Solution   Balusters, Curtain Panels, Detail Components, and Hosted elements all have specific, predefined behavior. Plan ahead when you're creating these categories. Objects that need to "cut" their host—like doors and windows—must be created in templates that are hard-wired to contain a portion of the host that will be cut. This allows you to create the door and also cut the host in the way that it needs to cut in the project.

Choose the right family template.   Some categories and parameters are more important than others. If you choose poorly, there's no backing up. You may simply have to start over and create the family correctly.

Master It   Why are you concerned whether a family component should be hosted or not? What would happen if you select a hosted template and then decide it should be nonhosted (or vice versa)?

Solution   Hosted objects typically need to create an opening in their host and then maintain a particular relationship to that host. For example, if the host is deleted, the hosted family is deleted as well. If you choose a hosted template and need to convert the family to a nonhosted component, you'll essentially have to start over.

Use testing parameters.   Reference planes, points, and lines are the "bones" of your component. Parameterize the bones, and the geometry will follow along. Be sure to test the parameter and reference relationships before you start assigning geometry.

Master It   Why build, parameterize, and test the references first? Why not just model the geometry?

Solution   Testing the references and parameters before you add geometry keeps things simple and helps you troubleshoot parametric behavior before building the geometry. Remember to keep parameterized dimensions outside of Sketch mode so you and others can easily find them later. After you've tested the parameters and references successfully, you can be confident that your geometry will behave predictably.

Know why formulas are important.   Sometimes parametric behavior will depend on the parameters that directly control it, but often these parameters will be expressed as a relationship to something else.

Master It   Why are formulas so important? Why not just create the parameters you need and then modify them as needed in the project environment?

Solution   Formulaic relationships help maintain rules within a family so that changing one rule can have an effect on many others. Using formulas therefore allows you to drive one parameter based on the value of another, and the result can drive a length, material, or other rules-based value. When you have many, many parametric type permutations, it's better to not weigh your project down with a lot of options that you'll probably never use. Whenever this happens, don't load all the possible types in your project—just turn to a type catalog in order to select only the family types that you need. Since you don't want to have to remember all of these relationships manually, allow Revit to maintain them for you.

Chapter 16: Stairs and Railings

Understand the key components of stairs.   Having a complete understanding of the components of stairs is important. You don't want to set about breaking the rules until you understand how best (and when) those rules can be broken.

Master It   What are the essential parts of stairs?

Solution   Baluster posts, balusters, and baluster panels along with handrail profiles are the essential parts of any railing. Nosings, stringers, and treads are the essential parts of stairs. Having a firm understanding of how these components react to their respective dialog boxes is critical.

Know when not to use railings.   From model patterns to geometric intricacy, there's a lot that can be created with the Railing tool. When this doesn't work, look to the Curtain Wall tool for "railings" that can contain space and allow "balusters" to be conveniently unlocked.

Master It   Why would you not use a railing to manage repetitive relationships? What if you need to accurately distribute geometry along a path?

Solution   Modeling these railings as components in the Family Editor is often faster than creating groups and then copying them throughout the project. Railings are also helpful for creating geometry that needs to be distributed along paths, even if the results aren't actually railings. Finally, don't use geometry when a model pattern will do. This will keep your project light.

Know when to use stairs.   Designing in a spreadsheet is hard. Step back and consider what you're trying to accomplish. If you'll look at the components that make up stairs, you'll see some interesting opportunities.

Master It   How would you create a continuous tread that wasn't monolithic? What would you do if you wanted to create a custom stringer? Are balusters always vertical and used to support handrails? What if your particular stair just can't be modeled in the Stair tool?

Solution   Try using the nosing profile to complement the shape of your tread. And don't forget that a handrail profile can be used to create a custom stringer profile with little trouble. Although balusters often support handrails, this is not always the case. Balusters may also consist of the support element that will support the tread. A complex baluster family associated with the railing as the start post can create the most complex railing conditions quickly and easily. But if all else fails, remember there's still the Family Editor.

Just model it just the way you want it and then put it in the project. It's probably more sculpture than stair at this point. Modeling it in the Family Editor means that you'll be able to move, elevate, rotate, and copy the results throughout the project. If you have to make changes (and you will), you'll simply open the component in the Family Editor.

Implement best practices.   There are specific best practices when creating custom stairs and railings. Pay attention to nesting geometry, maintaining the right level of detail, and filtering schedules so the metadata ends up in the right place.

Master It   Is it possible to create solutions that are too efficient? What's the big deal with detail levels? And finally, what's the most important thing to remember before creating an elegant workaround?

Solution   You're not the only person working on the project! Design is a team sport, and any out-of-the-box exceptions to the rules need to be understood by the entire team. "Overmodeling" is often misunderstood to mean "too much geometry," but geometry is critically important to understanding how your design is going to be assembled. So if you'll take the time to assign levels of detail to components, it'll help refresh views and printing. Finally, remember that the best solution is the one that is implementable. If your team doesn't understand your "custom hack," then you're not playing a team sport, and the project will ultimately suffer.

Chapter 17: Detailing Your Design

Create details.   Details in Revit are a combination of 2D elements layered on top of 3D model elements or sometimes just stacked on top of each other. Creating good, easy-to-read details typically requires some embellishment of the 3D model.

Master It   What are the three primary categories of detail elements and how are they used?

Solution   Detail lines are used to create two-dimensional linework of various weights and styles. They are used for drafting, much like you would draft in a CAD application. Filled regions and masking regions are the two region types that are used to apply patterns (even if that pattern is a solid-white field) against your details. These can help to show context such as materiality. Components like detail components and detail groups are used to create 2D families that can be used and reused in a variety of details within the model. They are historically used to create elements like blocking, metal studs, metal deck, and so on.

Add detail components to families.   You can make creating details in Revit easier by adding some of the detail elements directly to the family. In this way, when you cut sections, make callouts, or enlarge plan conditions, your "smart" details can begin to construct themselves.

Master It   Since you don't always want elements to appear in every scale of view, how can you both add detail elements to your families while still limiting the amount of information that is shown in any given view?

Solution   Using the detail levels (Coarse, Medium, and Fine), you can control the visibility of any element within a family to show, or not show, at those settings. By controlling the detail level, you can keep the family simple in a Coarse view and add more detail as the drawing gets increasingly complex.

Learn efficient detailing.   As you master detailing in Revit, you'll begin to learn tips and tricks to make your process of creating details more efficient.

Master It   To help you assess how much effort you should be putting into your details, what are three questions you should be asking yourself before starting any detail?

Solution   Will I see or use this in other views in the project?

Will it affect other aspects of the project (like material takeoffs)?

How large is it?

Chapter 18: Documenting Your Design

Document plans.   Floor plans can create visual graphics that help to define how a space is laid out. However, Revit provides other tools such as area plans to help you describe space.

Master It   List the four types of area plans that you can create and note the two that Revit creates automatically.

Solution   The four types of area plans are: rentable area, gross area, usable area, and BOMA area. Revit provides automatic calculations to show rentable and gross areas.

Create schedules and legends.   Schedules are another view type in Revit; they allow you to show information about the model in a nongraphic format. Schedules can also be used to dynamically report quantities of elements inside the model.

Master It   Understand how to create schedules in Revit and report additional information about the elements in the model. How would you create a simple casework schedule showing quantities of types?

Solution

1. On the View tab, choose Schedule/Quantities from the Schedule button.

2. Choose Casework as a schedule category.

3. On the Fields tab, choose Family And Type followed by Quantity.

4. On the Sorting tab, choose to sort by Family And Type; make sure Itemize Every Instance is checked. When that's done, click OK.

Use details from other files.   In many project workflows, you will need to incorporate details from other projects. Reusing these details can aid in the speed and efficiency of project documentation.

Master It   There are several ways to reuse details from other projects. Name one and list the steps to perform the tasks necessary to quickly move a detail from one project to another.

Solution

1. Start by opening the file with the views you want to save. Click the Application button, and select Save As ➤ Library ➤ Views.

2. This will give you the Save Views dialog box. It will show a list of view names on the left and a preview window on the right side. Simply click the check box for each of the views you want to save into a separate file. Once you have all your view names established, click OK.

3. To import the views, open the project you'd like to import the views into and choose Insert From File from the Insert tab. Choose Insert Views from File.

4. The new dialog box will look very similar to the Save Views dialog box. You will have a list of the views you can import from the column on the left and a preview of those views on the right. Check the box for the views you want to import and click OK.

Lay out sheets. Eventually in a project process it will become necessary to create sheets that will become the documentation set. Knowing how to create a good sheet set provides you with another venue to communicate with contractors, clients, and other team members.

Master It To properly create a sheet set, you need to understand the dynamic of adding views to a sheet. In Revit there is only one way to add views to a sheet. What is it?

Solution Views can be added to a sheet by dragging them from the Project Browser and dropping them onto the sheet. From that point, they can be edited or manipulated to properly place them relative to other views that might appear on that sheet.

Chapter 19: Annotating Your Design

Annotate with text and keynotes. Although a picture is worth a thousand words, you will still need notes in order to make drawings understandable and be able to call out key elements in each view. Understand how to create and modify text and keynotes for a complete set of documents.

Master It To properly utilize the keynoting feature, you'll need to understand what each of the three keynote types do and how they're used. List each and explain how they can be used in a project.

Solution Element keynotes annotate assemblies such as walls, floors, and roofs. Material keynotes designate materials within Revit, such as concrete, gypsum board, or rigid insulation. User keynotes are not tied to an element or a material and can be used to note other aspects of the view or detail.

Use tags. Tags are text labels for elements such as doors, walls, windows, rooms, and several other objects that architects typically need to reference in a set of drawings. These tags typically refer back to other schedules or information in other portions of the drawing set and are unique to the view in which they are inserted .

Master It   Inserting tags quickly can be a good way to make documentation time more efficient. How can you quickly tag a number of elements in the model at the same time?

Solution   Use the Tag All tool. This tool allows you to load several tags for different elements at the same time and populate a view with all those tag types at once. You will probably need to manipulate the location of some of the tags, but most should be placed cleanly and accurately, saving you time for other portions of the project.

Adding Dimensions.   Dimensioning is a critical part of the project documentation allowing you to communicate the distance elements are from one another.

Master It   Adding dimensions is a necessary part in any project. However, in a project workflow, you will typically want to change the location of a dimension's witness line without having to recreate the entire dimension. How do you move a witness line without remaking the entire dimension?

Solution   Highlight the dimension string and grab the blue grip that is below the text string. By clicking and holding on this element, you can now select a new host for the witness line.

Set project and shared parameters.   Revit lets users add as many custom parameters to an element as are needed to document the project. These parameters can be both tagged and scheduled, depending on how they are made.

Master It   You need to add a custom parameter for your project to track the percentage of recycled content in materials. What's the best way to go about doing this?

Solution   Since the items you want to track need to be scheduled but not tagged, it's easiest do to this with a project parameter. Add one to the project for a percentage of recycled content, and then track that in a Multi-Category schedule showing all the material types you want to track.

Chapter 20: Presenting Your Design

Add color fill legends.   Color fills are a great way to color views in Revit for use in various presentation displays and graphics.

Master It   There are a variety of ways to graphically display information in Revit using color fills. Setup can initially take a bit of time to get things organized, but once you create them, the legends can easily be transferred between views and projects. Describe how to add a color fill legend, once created, to your project template.

Solution   To add a color fill legend from a project to your project template, add it to a view and add the view to a sheet. Legends can be transferred like schedules: once they are added to a sheet, they can be copied to the clipboard and then pasted to the sheet in the project template. This will transfer all the colors, fonts, and other settings from the project to the template.

Use visualization techniques in your design.   Revit has a variety of ways to help you visualize your designs—both while designing and during presentation. Understanding where these features are located and how and when to use them can help expedite the presentation process, depending on the look and feel you want to create with your images.

Master It   List several ways using the View Control bar that you can modify the graphic settings of a view.

Solution   The View Control bar has several ways you can modify a view visually. The Visual Style tool allows you to flip through several display options, including Wireframe, Hidden Line, Shaded With Edges, and Realistic. The View Control bar also allows you to turn shadows on and off as well as manipulate the solar settings to create a variety of graphics to help visualize and communicate the overall design.

Chapter 21: Revit in Construction

Add revisions to your project.   You need the ability to track changes in your design after sheets have been issued. Adding revisions to a drawing is an inevitable part of your workflow.

Master It   Add revisions to your project that automatically get tracked on your sheet.

Solution   Use the Revision Cloud tool and the Revit Revision cloud tag family. Using those tools to create revision clouds ensures that they will automatically be tracked on the sheets they appear on.

Use digital markups.   DWFs provide a lightweight means to digitally transfer and mark up multiple sheets in a document set.

Master It   Explain the workflow using DWF markups.

Solution   Once your views are drawn and placed on sheets, export the sheets to a DWFx format. They can be shared with the Quality Assurance team for markup. QA will open the DWFx in Design Review and create the comments, and then send the marked-up set back to the design team. This set is then linked back into the drawing set and the markups will be visible on the drawing sheets.

Understand how a builder uses Revit.   We talked about several scenarios where builders might use Revit models during construction.

Master It   List two ways builders use BIM and the immediate benefits of each method.

Solution   Revit can be used by a builder in preconstruction planning to determine potential safety conflicts or manage complex phasing. Builders can also use Revit in the construction phase to document and plan ongoing trade work or support design to fabrication efforts in an IPD project.

Chapter 22: Revit in the Classroom

Develop a workflow for Revit.   For those interested in getting started with Revit, it's important to establish a workflow in Revit that seamlessly connects you with your design. Don't be afraid to be more deliberate in your approach to technology. Don't just race to finish, or you may find yourself racing to do something twice.

Master It   What kind of workflow can you use to get started in Revit? How can you be sure to pace yourself in the rigor of a studio?

Solution Use Thomas and Smith's "Three Ds of Revit," which are *design*, *develop*, and *demonstrate*. These three simple words that can lead to an elegant and streamlined workflow for students interested in getting started in Revit. Start by first learning the project's program and translating that to initial sketches and idea models. Start your *design* with those thought in mind. Begin to Mass the model using the massing tools to get a better understanding of the idealized form, space, light, and shadow. Then improve on the massing model through multiple duplicated iterations.

Once satisfied, you can further *develop* that model using details such as sophisticated curtain systems and refining all the details through annotations in Revit.

With the detailing complete, it is time to demonstrate what you have done through diagramming, multiple 3D views, and sections as well as finalized renderings.

Overcome common objections. If you're a high school student headed for your first studio environment, you will be faced with those who may oppose you and your ideas. Instead of reacting, you'll want to focus on the principle that your professor is trying to communicate. At the same time, you don't want to give up on what is most beneficial to you, your values, and your career.

Master It When the professor refuses to allow students to use computers and Revit in your studio, what can you do?

Solution Even when the answer will become clear, do not allow a professor a friend or anyone for that matter to impose ideas on you. Set yourself up immediate-, middle-, and long-term goals. Determine the steps needed to achieve them and live your dream.

Use Revit (and other design programs) to investigate, iterate, and implement your design. When you arrive at a satisfying solution, print out your Revit files and use them as underlay references for your hand-drawn work.

Challenge yourself as a student. The examples shown in this chapter were a good representation of individuals currently in the studio environment producing thoughtful, well-researched, context-sensitive projects utilizing Revit. Fourth-year or even third-year students did many of the projects shown. Many of these students have the potential to redefine the way we use and see Revit and the design process.

Master It The design process can become introspective, singular, and artificial when so much design actually produces little more than paper. What can you do to challenge yourself as a student? What can you do to push yourself?

Solution Enter design competitions that utilize team efforts. Architectural practice is built around teams of people with different interests, abilities, and specialties. Start working in teams now. Take the lead in some teams on one project. Defer leadership on other projects. This will give you far more insight into the real practice of architecture than working along on projects where you are responsible for everything that must be done.

Chapter 23: Revit and Virtualization

Understand the benefits of virtualization.   There are advantages of virtualization for both IT support as well as end users.

Master It   What are the advantages of virtualization?

Solution   Virtualization allows your end users to run their specific suite of applications without an overreliance on their host computer. People can test existing and developing technologies without risking damaging hardware and other network connections. Computer upgrades are a snap. Rollouts of new images can be easily controlled from a central location.

Take advantage of virtualization.   Having to maintain multiple operating systems is hardly uncommon. But rather than maintain obsolete hardware and applications, why not utilize virtualization and maintain best-of-breed solutions?

Master It   What's the easiest way to try out virtualization?

Solution   The first step is converting a physical machine to a virtual one. Virtual machines can either be created from scratch or migrated from existing physical machines. Either solution is fine. It depends on what you're trying to accomplish. Migrating an existing machine is a great way to get started, especially if you don't want to have to spend a lot of time installing applications and files and replicating a lot of hard-to-remember user settings. Parallels and VMware office 30-day trials along with free physical-to-virtual migration tools. You may be surprised at the ease of use and performance.

Chapter 24: Under the Hood of Revit

Understand the basics of the Revit API.   The need for some users and developers to extend the functionality of Revit is supported by the Revit application programming interface (API). Revit's software development kit (SDK) provides sample code and instructions for building add-ons to the application.

Master It   What are the two types of dynamic link libraries you can develop for Revit?

Solution   External commands are limited lifetime routines that have access to the current project as well as any elements selected. External applications are loaded when Revit starts and remain active until Revit is closed.

Understand the new `.addin` manifest file method used to load custom command and applications into Revit.   The Revit API for 2011 now offers the ability to register API applications into Revit using an `.addin` manifest file.

Master It   How is the `.addin` manifest method different from previous versions?

Solution   In previous versions of Revit, custom applications had to be registered in the `Revit.ini` file with a limited number of options. The `.addin` manifest file is based on a robust XML schema allowing additional customization of the application.

Set up and build your own custom external applications and commands.   You can start to create your own custom applications and commands for Revit using either Microsoft Visual Studio or a free tool such as Visual Studio Express or SharpDevelop.

Master It   How do you make the Revit API functions available in your developing environment?

Solution   The Revit API namespace references must be added to every .NET project. In Visual Studio, right-click the title of the project name in the Solution Explorer and select Add ➢ Reference. Navigate to the Program folder where Revit is installed and select the files `RevitAPI.dll` and `RevitAPIUI.dll`.

Chapter 25: Direct to Fabrication

Understand the concepts of digital fabrication.   Before you can create furniture and other elements using digital fabrication, it's important to understand both the tools involved and the principles used in the process.

Master It   Understanding the process involved in fabrication will help you master the steps. List the five steps outlined in this chapter that are necessary for digital fabrication.

Solution   The five steps to digital fabrication are the following: inspiration, configuration, rationalization, isolation, and fabrication.

Use digital fabrication on a project.   In the example of creating a reception desk in Revit, you went through a real example of direct to fabrication from a BIM model. Understanding the steps in this process can help you replicate these same steps on other projects and designs.

Master It   In this chapter, we discussed the need to think about the end of the process before starting the beginning. Consider the outcome to help inform the best equipment and methods to derive that outcome. Describe two important points in this process and how they help create a better final product.

Solution   Two of the steps listed in the project example were talking directly with your fabricator early on in the project process and understanding how CAM software would accept different model exports. Understanding these processes helps reduce data loss and maximize intent between design and eventual product.

Model cleanly and accurately.   Once you go through the process of fabrication, you can refine your process and make it more efficient for future production, developing your own tips and tricks along the way.

Master It   Modeling cleanly and accurately is one of the primary ways to build skill in digital fabrication. Describe some of the ways to model in this fashion.

Solution   Some of the methods for modeling a fabrication element cleanly are using the proper families in Revit for materials; avoid taking shortcuts in modeling; be geometrically accurate and show detail in the model; show joint work; and align congruent faces of elements.

Chapter 26: Revit for Film and Stage

Design "scenically."   According to Sutton, profiled in this chapter, designing "scenically" takes precedence over designing too literally. This might be different from standard architectural practice, but it's critical in the film and stage industries.

> **Master It**   How would you design "scenically," and how does this differ from standard architectural practice? What can you learn from the film and stage industries to keep the emotive quality high?
>
> **Solution**   Keep the materials suggestive. Concentrate on expressing transparency and opacity. Adding additional lights (that aren't part of any real light fixture) can soften shadows and sharp edges.

Use Revit in the design to production process.   While standard architectural practice entails design to documentation, the film and stage focus is from concept through construction.

> **Master It**   With an emphasis on level of detail and tight, repetitive elements and finishes, what would you do to help maintain time and budget? How might you suggest creating intricate repetitive design elements in your next project?
>
> **Solution**   CNC is being used more and more in the film and stage industries when repetitive elements need to be created quickly. CNC machines are essential to creating components that need to fit together with a high degree of quality and fit.

Use Revit for previsualization.   When using Revit in the film industry, you need to keep the design "loose" during the early concept stages. You'll have to match the look and feel of the art director's vision. Keeping the materials muted will be far less distracting than being too specific. One of the great things about Revit is that you'll be able to emotively visualize in the same environment as you analytically rationalize. This will come in handy when the director, director of photography, and then art director all want a different question answered at the same time!

> **Master It**   How can you express constructability to a high level of detail, particularly when the object is going to be assembled from many individual parts? Why rely on standard architectural practice of documenting in plan, section, and elevation views?
>
> **Solution**   Live exploded views allow you to visualize the component parts and sequence of assemblage without exporting to another tool. Just create a 3D view and duplicate in order to isolate different parts of the assembly. All the duplicated views can be assembled together on a single sheet.

Chapter 27: Revit in the Cloud

Understand the business benefit of a high-performance workstation cloud.   Cloud computing benefits not only Revit but all your corporate applications. Mobile laptops have just as much horsepower available as the highest-end workstations. And rather than having that expensive hardware available only to a few users, you can make it available to anyone who needs it—at any time.

Master It Consider the up-front cost of a high-performance workstation cloud over three years as compared to your previous and anticipated expenditures. How can you take advantage of the business benefits of putting your design tools in the cloud?

Solution One size doesn't fit all. Start with putting your commodity applications in the cloud, such as word processing, email, and spreadsheets. As you get comfortable, start putting more hardware-intensive design tools in the cloud.

Implement a high-performance workstation cloud. Once you feel comfortable with your Revit cloud computing infrastructure performing better than your current desktop computing infrastructure, don't be surprised if there is resistance by some diehard desktop users who refuse to let go of their workstations.

Master It Since price isn't the issue, where do you think you still might encounter cultural barriers to implementing cloud-based solutions?

Solution The cultural barrier of people thinking of a computer as "theirs" can be a significant barrier to success. But once people realize that "their" computer in the cloud has greater advantages, flexibility, and reliability than "their" computer under their desk, this is an easy cultural hurdle to overcome. Get people to trust the cloud in stages—with non-design applications (such as email and word processing) as a great place to start.

Know which future cloud computing strategies to watch. Technology is going to keep evolving. The VDI industry is moving quickly and rapidly evolving. You want to be well positioned to take advantage of the best technology for your firm at the best price point possible.

Master It Most firms in the AEC space have well under a few dozen employees. If smaller firms have the advantage of being nimble when it comes to adopting and implementing new technology quickly, why is cloud computing such a great fit?

Solution Small businesses can't afford big outlays to hardware that is nearly obsolete the moment it's installed anyway. And besides, desktop virtualization and cloud computing isn't going away. Use this opportunity to create a strategic business differentiator in the minds of your design partners, contractors, and owner.

Tips, Tricks, and Troubleshooting

This appendix provides some tips, tricks, and troubleshooting to help keep your project files running smoothly. Listed here are some pointers to keep you from getting into trouble, as well as a peppering of time savers and other great ideas.

In this appendix, you'll learn how to:

◆ Optimize performance

◆ Use best practices

◆ Learn tips and shortcuts

Optimizing Performance

It should make sense that a smaller file on a good network will run the fastest. There is no "typical" Revit file size, and they can range anywhere from 10MB to over 300MB. Much of that variation depends on the level of detail in the model itself, the presence of imported geometry (2D CAD files, SketchUp, and so on), the number of views you have, and the overall complexity. Obviously, your hardware configuration will also be a factor in determining the speed and operation of your models.

You can optimize your hardware in a number of ways to get the most out of the configuration you have. You should first look at the install specifications and recommended hardware specs for a computer running Revit. Autodesk has published those requirements on its website, and they are updated with each new version of Revit. You can find the current specs at www.autodesk .com/Revit; choose System Requirements under the Product Information heading.

Beyond the default specifications, you can do a number of things to help keep your files nimble. Here are some other recommendations:

Use a 64-bit OS.   Revit likes RAM, and the more physical RAM it can use, the more model you can cache into active memory. Windows now offers several versions of a 64-bit OS. Windows XP, Windows Vista, and Windows 7 all have 64-bit capability. This allows you to bridge the 32-bit limit of Windows XP and earlier. The older operating systems were limited to only 2GB of RAM per application. A 64-bit OS allows you to use as much as you can pack into your machine.

If you have a 32-bit OS, use the 3GB switch.   If you have a 32-bit OS such as Windows XP, need to get your project done, and don't want to deal with the upgrade, use the 3GB switch.

This setting allows you to grab an extra gigabyte of RAM from your computer for a maximum of 3GB. To take advantage of this switch, you'll need to load Windows XP Service Pack 2 and follow the instructions found on the Autodesk support site at www.autodesk.com/support; choose Revit Building from the menu, and read the support article on enabling the 3GB switch. Of course, you need more than 2GB of RAM in your workstation.

Figure out how much RAM your project will need.   Before you email your IT department requesting 12GB of RAM, figure out how much you're actually going to use on your project. Your OS and other applications like Outlook will use some of your RAM, but you can calculate how much RAM Revit will need to work effectively. The formula is as follows:

Model size in Explorer × 20 + Linked File Size(s) × 20 = Active RAM needed

Let's look at a couple examples of this to demonstrate how it works. You have a Revit file with no linked files and your file size on your server is 150MB. So 150 × 20 = 3,000 or 3GB of RAM to operate effectively. In another example, you have a 120MB file, a 50MB structural model linked in, and four CAD files at 1MB each:

(120 × 20) + (50 × 20) + (4 × 20) = 3480MB or 3.5GB of RAM

Once you've put as much RAM into your workstation as is practical, your next recourse for improving model performance is to reduce your file size so you're not using as much RAM. Here are some tips to do that and thereby improve your file speed.

Manage your views.   There are two things you can do using views to help improve performance. First of all, the more views you open, the more information you will load into active RAM. Close windows you're not using to help minimize the drain on your resources. You can always close all the windows but your active one using the Close Hidden Windows tool. Choose the View tab and click the Close Hidden button (Figure B.1). It's easy to have many views open at once, even if you're concentrating on only a few views.

FIGURE B.1
Closing hidden
windows

The other way to manage your views is to get rid of the ones you don't need. Revit allows you to make different views within your model quickly and easily. This can sometimes lead to having a lot of views (sometimes hundreds) that you aren't using in your document set and don't plan to use. Adding too many views can raise your overall file size even if you haven't added any geometry. Get rid of those unused views—typically views that are not on sheets—to help keep your file running smooth. We discuss how to create a schedule to help identify the unused views in Chapter 5, "Managing a Revit Project."

Delete or unload unused CAD files.   There are many times in a project process when you'll want to load content from another source as a background. This could be a client's CAD as-built drawings or a consultant's MEP design. You might link or import these files into your drawing and, during the busy course of the project, forget about them. As you've seen from the earlier tips on RAM use, all these small files add up. Getting rid of them can speed your file up and is simply just good housekeeping. If the file is linked, you can unlink it using the

Link CAD button on the Insert tab. If they are inserted, right-click an instance of the file and choose Select All Instances from the context menu. Clicking Delete now will delete all the instances in the entire model as opposed to only the active view.

Don't explode imported CAD files.   A CAD file, when imported into Revit, is a collection of objects that is managed as single entity. If you explode a CAD file, the single object immediately becomes many objects—and these all take up space in the file requiring more resources from Revit to track and coordinate.

If you're importing DWG files, leave them unexploded as much as possible. If you need to hide lines, use the Visibility/Graphic Overrides dialog box to turn layers on and off. Explode *only* when you need to change the imported geometry, and start with a partial explode to minimize the number of new entities. Figure B.2 shows the tools available in the Options Bar when you select an imported or linked DWG file. Also note that lines smaller than ⅟₃₂″ are not retained with CAD files are exploded. This can result in unusable imports.

FIGURE B.2
Explode options

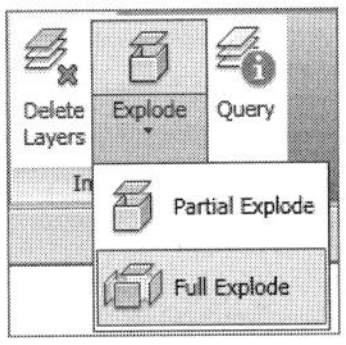

A better workflow than importing your CAD files directly into the project is to import them into a Revit family and then load that family into the project. This will also aid in keeping accidents from happening, like a novice user exploding Qathe files. This workflow is covered in more detail in Chapter 5.

Turn on volume computation only as needed.   Calculating the volumes on a large file can slow your model speed down immensely. These are typically turned on when exporting to gbXML, but sometimes teams forget to turn them back off again. Volumes will recalculate each time you edit a room, move a wall, or change any of the building geometry. Turn these off using the Area & Volume Computations dialog box found on the Room & Area panel on the Home tab (Figure B.3).

FIGURE B.3
Choose the
area calculations
to minimize
unneeded
computations.

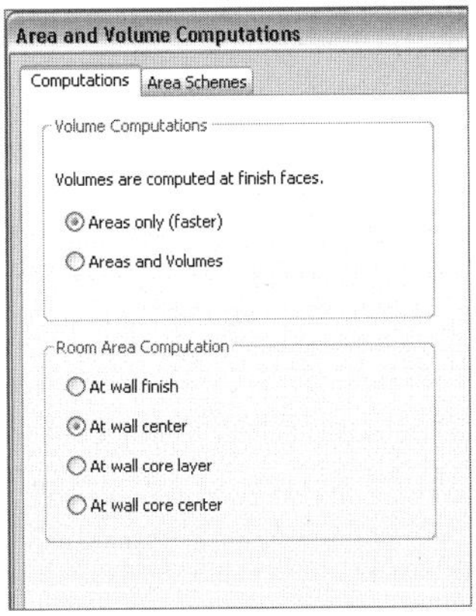

Using Best Practices

Good file maintenance is critical to keeping your files running smoothly and your file sizes low. Here are some best practices and workflows identified in other areas of the book but consolidated here as a quick reference. For more information on managing a Revit workflow, please refer to Chapter 5.

Manage the amount of information shown in views.   Learn to manage the amount of information needed in a given view. Don't show more than you need to show in a view by working to minimize your view depth and level of detail. Here are some simple tips to keep your individual views working smoothly:

Minimize the level of detail.   Set your detail level, found in the View Control bar, relative to your drawing scale. For example, if you're working on a ⅟₃₂″ (1:50) plan, you probably don't need Detail Level set to Fine. This will cause the view to have a higher level of detail than the printed sheet can show, and you'll end up with not only black blobs on your sheets but views that are slow to open and print.

Minimize view detail.   Along with the amount of detail you turn on in the view using the Detail Level tool, make sure you're not showing more than you need to. For instance, if you have wall studs shown in a ⅟₁₆″ scale plan or the extruded aluminum window section shown in a building section, chances are it will not represent right when printed. Turning off those elements in your view will keep things moving smoother as well as printing cleaner.

Minimize view depth.   View depth and crop regions are great tools to enhance performance. As an example, a typical building section is shown in Figure B.4. The default behavior causes Revit to regenerate all of the model geometry the full depth of that view every time you open the view. To reduce the amount of geometry that needs to be redrawn, drag the section's far clip plane (the green dashed line when you highlight the section) in close to the cutting plane.

FIGURE B.4
Minimizing the view depth

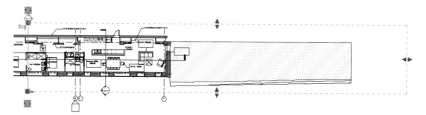

Model only what you need.   While it is possible to model to a very small level of detail, don't fall into the trap of overmodeling. Be smart about what you choose to model and how much detail you plan to show. If it's not conveying information about the project, maybe it's not really needed. The amount of information you do or do not model should be based on your project size and complexity, your timeframe, and your comfort level with the software.

How much to model: use these three rules of thumb.   When trying to decide how much detail to put into a model or even a family, there are three very good rules of thumb to help you make the right decision for the particular element you're looking to create.

Scale   What scale will this detail be seen in? If it's a very small-scale detail, it might be simpler to just draw it in 2D in a drafting view.

Repetition   How many times will this detail appear in the drawing set? If it will appear only in one location or only one time, it might be easier to just draft it in 2D rather than try to model the element. If it will appear in several locations, modeling is probably the better solution. The more exposure an element has in the model (the more views it shows in) the more reason you have to model it. As an example, doors are good to model. They show in elevations and plans all over the sheet set.

Quality   How good at modeling families in Revit are you? Honestly? Don't bite off more than you can chew. If you're new to Revit, keep it simple and use 2D components. The more projects you complete in Revit, the better you'll understand the change to a BIM workflow.

Don't overconstrain.   Embedding user-defined constraints into families and the model help keep important information constant. However, if you don't need to lock a relationship, don't do it. Overconstraining the model can cause problems later in the project process when you want to move or modify locked elements. Constrain only when necessary. Otherwise, let the model be free.

Watch out for imported geometry.   While Revit has the ability to use geometry from several other file sources, use caution when doing so. Remember that everything you link into Revit takes up around 20 times the file size in your system's RAM. So, linking a 60MB NURBS-based ceiling design will equal 2GB of RAM and more than likely slow down your model. Deleting unused CAD files, using linking rather than importing, and cleaning up the CAD geometry before insertion will help keep the problems to a minimum.

Purge unused files.   You will find that you won't use every family or every group you create in your model. Revit has a tool that will allow you to get rid of those unused elements to help keep your file sizes down to a reasonable level. This tool, Purge Unused, can be found on the Manage tab on the Setting panel. If your file is very large, it can take several minutes to run, but eventually you'll be presented with a list (Figure B.5) of all the unused elements within your file.

FIGURE B.5
Use the Purge
Unused dialog box
to reduce file size.

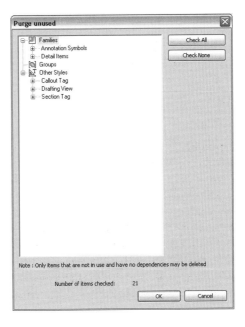

Using this tool is typically not recommended at the beginning of a project while you are still trying many design solutions and file sizes tend to be fairly small.

Model correctly from the beginning.   As you refine your design, it's critical to model correctly right from the beginning, not taking shortcuts, so you don't have to fix things later. If you can begin by thinking about how your project will be assembled, it will save you a lot of time later in the process. It's good practice to plan ahead, but remember that Revit will allow you to make major changes at any stage in the process and still maintain coordination. If you are still in early phase of design and do not know the exact wall type, use generic walls to capture your design intent; changing them later will be simple.

Managing Workshared files   When employing worksharing on a project, there are additional tools and tips you'll want to follow. Check out Chapter 6 for more details.

Make a new local copy once a week.   In a workshared environment, your local copy can begin to perform poorly or grow in file size while the central file remains small and nimble. If this is the case, it might be time to throw out the old local copy for a new one. As a general practice, if you're accessing a project on a daily basis, it's a good idea to make a new local copy once a week.

Divide your model.   For larger projects or campus-style projects, you can break up your model into smaller submodels that are linked together. You can also do this on a single, large building. Dividing a model up helps to limit the amount of information you are loading into a project at one time.

If you decide to divide your project, make your cuts along lines that make sense from a holistic-building standpoint. Don't think of the cuts as you would in CAD, but think about how the actual assemblies will interact in the building. As an example, don't cut between floors 2 and 3 on a multistory building unless you have a significant change in building form or program. Here's a list of some good places to split a model:

- At a significant change in building form or massing

- At a significant change in building program

- Between separate buildings on the site

- At the building site

Fixing File Corruption

From time to time your project files will begin to experience duress and possible corruption. This can happen for any number of reasons; network problems, file size, too many errors, gremlins. If your file begins crashing, don't panic. There are a few things you can do before calling Revit Support. Here are some suggestions to help get you back on track:

Review warnings.   Each time you create something that Revit considers a problem, a warning is issued. Warnings will accumulate if left unresolved. Think of all these errors as unresolved math calculations. The more there are, the more your computer will have to struggle to resolve them, and eventually you will have performance issues or file instability. To review the warnings, click the Warning button on the Manage tab. You'll get a dialog box like Figure B.6, which will allow you to search for and resolve the problem objects.

FIGURE B.6
Resolving errors

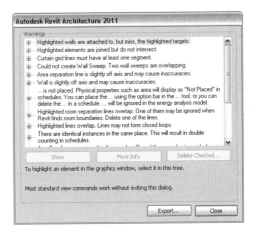

Reduce your file size. Sometimes when file corruption occurs it's due to a file that has grown beyond capacity of the machines using it. Reduce your file size using the tips above to make the model more manageable and resolve some of the errors.

Audit the file. Another way to deal with file corruption is to perform an audit on your file. You can find this tool in the lower-left corner of the File Open dialog box (Figure B.7). Auditing a file will review the data structures and try to correct any problems that have occurred. When it is completed, it will ideally be a fully functioning file again.

You can audit either a local file or the central file itself. Whenever you audit a file, you'll want to make a new central copy and have all of your project team create new local copies. The last thing you'll want to do is have someone with file corruption in a local copy synchronize those problems back to your newly fixed central file.

FIGURE B.7
Auditing a file

Learning Tips and Shortcuts

Beyond all the things you can do to hone your Revit skills, you will begin to learn a number of tips and shortcuts as your experience grows using Revit. Here is a compilation of some of those tips and tricks:

Let Revit do the math. Revit is like a big calculator and it's very good at doing math correctly. Don't want to spend the time trying to figure out what your room size is after you subtract a 3⅝″ and ⅝″ piece of gypsum board from an 11″–2″ room? Don't. If you need to modify a dimension, simply add an equal sign and a formula (Figure B.8) and Revit will calculate the value for you.

FIGURE B.8
Performing calculations in Revit

Add a sloped ceiling. You want to add a gypsum soffit to the bottom of a stair or you want a sloped ceiling? Well, you can't do that with the ceiling tool. But you can with a ramp. Make a gypsum board ramp and align it to the bottom of your stair or angle it to create your sloped ceiling plane.

Make elevators visible in your plans. You want to create a shaft that will penetrate all the floors of your building and put an elevator in it that will show in all your plans. You could do this with an elevator family and cut a series of holes in the floors by editing floor profiles, but sometimes those holes stop aligning on their own recognizance. Fortunately, you can do both things at once using the Shaft tool found on the Opening panel of the Home tab. Here, you can not only cut a vertical hole through multiple floors as a single object, but you can also insert 2D linework to represent your elevator in plan (Figure B.9). Every time the shaft is cut, you're certain to see the elevator linework.

FIGURE B.9
Adding elevators to a shaft

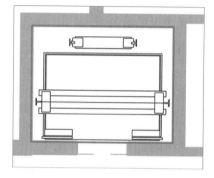

Orient to view. Creating perspective views of isolated design elements can be quick and easy in plan or section, but let's say you want to see that same element in 3D to be able to work out the details.

1. Create a plan region or section cut isolating the area in question. If you're using a section, make sure to set your view depth to something practical.

2. Open the default 3D view or any axon of the project.

3. Right-click the ViewCube, select Orient To View, and select your view from the context menu.

4. Now, your 3D view will look identical to your section or plan region, but by rotating the view, you'll be able to see that portion in 3D.

—Submitted by Mark

Tune your shortcuts. Revit now allows you to edit your keyboard shortcuts without the hassle of rooting through your hard drive looking for a TXT file. To edit your shortcuts, click the Application button and select Options. Choose the User Interface tab and then the Customize button. The Keyboard Shortcuts dialog box (Figure B.10) will allow you to edit those shortcuts. Consider making common shortcuts the same letter. So, instead of pressing VG to get to your Visibility/Graphic Overrides dialog box, make the shortcut VV for quicker access.

FIGURE B.10

Editing your keyboard shortcuts

—Submitted by John S. from St. Paul, Minnesota

Drag and drop families.   You need to load a family into Revit, you have the Explorer window open, and you know where the family is, but you don't want to go through the laborious effort of navigating across your office's server environment to get there. No problem. You can drag and drop Revit families from Explorer directly into the project file.

—Submitted by Tony D. from Kansas City, Missouri

Copy a 3D view.   You made the perfect 3D view in your last project, and you can't figure out how to get it into your current project. Fortunately, there's a way to copy views from one project to another. Open both files in the same instance of Revit.

1. In your perfect view, right-click the 3D view in the Project Browser and choose Show Camera from the context menu.

2. Press Ctrl+C to copy the selected camera.

3. In your new model, use Ctrl+V to paste the camera and your view and all its settings are now there.

Use a quick cut poche.   Want to change everything that's cut in a view without having to select every family and change its properties? A quick cut poche is, well, quick:

1. Open the view you want to modify.

2. Using a crossing window, select all the elements within the view.

3. Right-click and choose Override Graphics ➢ By View from the context menu. As shown in Figure B.11, you can choose any filled region in the project and assign it to anything that is cut within your model.

FIGURE B.11
Using Override
Graphics for a
quick poche

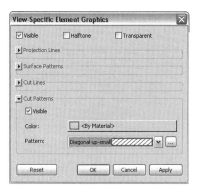

—Submitted by Tobias H. from Boston, Massachusetts

Move your ribbon. Did you know that you can reorganize the tabs on the ribbon and place them in any order you'd like? Hold down the Ctrl key and select a tab (like Home). You can drag it left or right to change the order they appear in.

—Submitted by Tobias H. from Boston, Massachusetts

Additional Resources

A number of resources are available to help you along the way and improve your Revit use, help you solve problems, or create new content. In our digital age, there is a wealth of information online to help you learn or communicate with users far and wide. So, before you spend hours trying to solve a particularly challenging problem on your own, you might check some of these tools:

Revit Help Menu Open the Revit Help menu by clicking the question mark icon in the upper-right corner of the application. This tool will give you a basic synopsis of all the tools, buttons, and commands available in the application.

Subscription Support If you have purchased Revit on subscription, Revit Subscription Support offers web-based support. Their responses are speedy, their advice top-notch, and chances are they've seen your problem before. Subscription Support can be accessed online at `subscription.autodesk.com`.

AUGI Autodesk User Group International (AUGI) is a source for tips and tricks as well as excellent user forums. The forums are free to participate in, and it's a great place where you can ask questions, find answers, or discuss project workflows. AUGI is located online at `www.augi.com`. Once you're there, look for Revit Architecture.

Revit City Looking for content or families? Revit City offers another free online resource and has a growing database of families posted by users. See `www.revitcity.com`.

YouTube Here's a great reason to tell your IT department you need access to YouTube. Autodesk has its own channel that has some great content, it's free, and it has hundreds of short videos showing you how to perform specific tasks in Revit. See `www.youtube.com/user/autodesk`.

AECbytes   AECbytes is a website dedicated to following the trends in the AEC industry, with a strong focus on BIM, technology, and the direction of the industry, put together by Lachmi Khemlani. See www.aecbytes.com.

What Revit Wants   Revit Professionals is an online resource put together by Luke Johnson that is peppered with great tips and workflows with everything from tips on creating graphics to dealing with crashes. See www.whatrevitwants.blogspot.com.

The Autodesk Certification Exams

Autodesk has selected *Mastering Autodesk Revit Architecture 2011* to be an official training guide for its Revit Architecture 2011 certification exams. There are two levels of certification: the Certified Associate level and the Certified Professional level. The exam for the Certified Associate level consists of 30 computer-administered questions that include multiple choice, matching, and point and click. The exam for the Certified Professional level is a performance-based test that requires you to perform tasks in Revit Architecture in addition to answering questions.

To help you focus your studies on the skills you'll need for these exams, we've included three tables in this appendix. Table C.1 lists the Assessment Test Objectives, Table C.2 lists the Certified Associate Exam Sections and Objectives, and Table C.3 lists the Certified Professional Exam Sections and Objectives. These tables also direct you to the chapters in this book that will help you master the objectives for each exam.

If you would like more information about Autodesk's certification program, please visit the website www.autodesk.com/certification.

Revit Architecture 2011 Exam Preparation Roadmap

Autodesk certifications are industry-recognized credentials that can help you succeed in your design career – providing benefits to both you and your employer. Autodesk certifications are a reliable validation of skills and knowledge, and can lead to accelerated professional development, improved productivity, and enhanced credibility.

Autodesk highly recommends that you structure your examination preparation for success. This means scheduling regular time to prepare, reviewing this exam preparation roadmap, using Autodesk Official Training Guides, taking an Assessment test, and using a variety of resources to prepare for your certification. Equally as important, actual hands-on experience is recommended.

The Revit Architecture 2011 Certified Associate exam consists of 30 questions that assess your knowledge of the tools, features, and common tasks of Autodesk Revit Architecture. Question types include multiple choice, matching, and point and click (hot spot). The exam has a one-hour time limit (in some countries the time limit may be extended).

The Autodesk Revit Architecture 2011 Certified Professional exam is a performance-based test. The exam is comprised of 20 questions. Each question requires you to use Revit Architecture 2011 to create or modify a data file, and then type your answer into an input box. The answer you enter will either be a text entry or a numeric value. The exam has a 90-minute time limit (in some countries the time limit may be extended).

To earn the credential of Revit Architecture 2011 Certified Professional, you must also pass the Revit Architecture 2011 Certified Associate exam. You can pass the exams in any order.

To recertify from Revit Architecture 2011 Professional to Revit Architecture 2011 Professional, you need only pass the Revit Architecture 2011 Certified Associate exam.

Assessment Tests

Autodesk assessment tests will help identify areas of knowledge that you should develop in order to prepare for the certification exam. At the completion you will be able to review the items you missed and their correct answers. Contact an Autodesk Certification Center for more information at http://autodesk.starttest.com.

ATC® Instructor-Led Courses

The Autodesk Authorized Training Center (ATC®) program is a global network of professional training providers offering a broad range of learning resources. Visit the online ATC locator at www.autodesk.com/atc.

Recommended Experience Levels for Revit Architecture 2011 Certification Exams

Actual hands-on experience is a critical component in preparing for the exam. You must spend time using the product and applying the skills you have learned.

2011 CERTIFIED ASSOCIATE EXAM

Mastering Revit Architecture 2011 course (or equivalent) plus 100 hours of hands-on application.

2011 CERTIFIED PROFESSIONAL EXAM

Mastering Revit Architecture 2011 course (or equivalent) plus 400 hours of hands-on application.

TABLE C.1:   Assessment Test Objectives

TOPIC	OBJECTIVE	CHAPTER
1. Revit Terminology	Describe Revit Architecture and the Revit environment	Chapter 2
	Define parameters and parametric relationships	Chapter 1
	Describe bidirectional associativity	Chapter 1
2. User Interface	Explain the function of the Project Browser	Chapter 2
	Describe the Options Bar	Chapter 2
3. Modeling	Identify and describe processes for accessing the materials library, creating new materials, and adding material information	Chapter 4

TABLE C.1:   Assessment Test Objectives   *(CONTINUED)*

TOPIC	OBJECTIVE	CHAPTER
	Identify and describe processes for loading a component into a building project (furniture, door, window, etc.)	Chapter 3
	Apply knowledge about how to create elements such as floors, ceilings, or roofs	Chapters 13, 14
	Use appropriate tools to place a door, window, or other hosted element	Chapter 3
	Change the boundaries of a room using separation lines	Chapter 18
	Describe properties of a room	Chapter 18
4. Views	Describe how to define global visibility settings in a project	Chapter 2
	Explain how to generate a view from its referring symbol	Chapter 2
	Demonstrate how to create a duplicate view for a plan, section, elevation, drafting view, etc.	Chapter 2
	Describe ways to alter element visibility in a view. Explain ways to modify a view's extents	Chapter 2
	Describe ways to alter element graphic representation in a view	Chapter 11
	Differentiate how to place a view (plan, section, elevation, schedule, etc.) on a sheet	Chapter 11
	Discuss the relationship between the view on the sheet and its referring symbol	Chapter 2
5. Elements	Differentiate between different wall types	Chapter 13
	Demonstrate knowledge about how to associate a model element with a datum element	Chapter 15
	Discuss the importance of coordinating datum elements with model elements	Chapter 15
	Apply knowledge about how to add and modify a new level	Chapter 2
	Apply knowledge about how to use align, trim, extend, offset, etc.	Chapter 3
	Apply knowledge about how to use move, copy, mirror, rotate, etc.	Chapter 3
	Explain how to modify an element's instance parameters	Chapter 3
	Define instance and type parameters	Chapter 3

TABLE C.1:   Assessment Test Objectives   *(CONTINUED)*

TOPIC	OBJECTIVE	CHAPTER
	Identify key features of each family category	Chapter 2
6. Documentation	Apply knowledge about how to place a string of dimensions	Chapter 19
	Apply knowledge about how to add/remove a witness line in a dimension string	Chapter 19
	Explain how a tag functions	Chapter 19
	Demonstrate how to tag elements (doors, windows, etc.) by category	Chapter 19
	Explain how to add an additional leader to text	Chapter 19
7. Collaboration	Explain linking Revit files	Chapter 7
	Explain how to modify the visibility of elements in a linked file	Chapter 7

TABLE C.2:   Certified Associate Exam Sections and Objectives

TOPIC	OBJECTIVE	CHAPTER
Modeling	Create an in-place mass	Chapter 9
	Apply an element by face	Chapter 9
	Define floors for a mass	Chapter 9
	Demonstrate how to generate a toposurface	Chapter 9
	Create a building pad	Chapter 16
	Demonstrate how to model railings	Chapter 11
	Demonstrate how to use design options	Chapter 11
	Demonstrate how to work with phases	Chapter 15
	Edit a model element's material (door, window, furniture)	Chapters 10, 12
	Demonstrate how to create a stair with a landing	Chapter 16

TABLE C.2:   Certified Associate Exam Sections and Objectives   *(CONTINUED)*

TOPIC	OBJECTIVE	CHAPTER
	Explain how to change a generic floor/ceiling/roof to a specific type	Chapters 13, 14
	Use appropriate tools to attach the top or base of a wall to a roof or ceiling	Chapter 13
Views	Define element properties to be included in a schedule	Chapter 18
	Organize and sort items in a schedule	Chapter 18
	Demonstrate how to create and manage legends	Chapter 18
	Demonstrate how to control visual styles	Chapter 18
	Explain how to move the view title independently of the view	Chapter 20
	Demonstrate how to manage view position on sheets	Chapter 20
Elements	Demonstrate how to create a stacked wall	Chapter 13
	Use Revit family templates	Chapter 15
	Explain how to make a new family type of a given model element (door, window, column)	Chapter 15
	Explain how to modify an element's type parameters	Chapter 15
	Describe the difference between a hosted family from a component family (wall vs. door)	Chapter 15
	Explain how to create and/or modify each family category	Chapter 15
Documentation	Discuss the benefits of a dimension string vs. a series of individual dimensions	Chapter 19
	Set the colors used in a color-scheme legend	Chapter 20
	Identify rendering settings in Revit	Chapters 10, 12
	Demonstrate how to place and modify detail components and repeating details	Chapter 17
	Demonstrate how to create and modify filled regions	Chapter 17
Collaboration	Demonstrate knowledge about worksharing	Chapter 6

TABLE C.3: Certified Professional Exam Sections and Objectives

TOPIC	OBJECTIVE	CHAPTER
Modeling	Apply knowledge about Review Warnings in Revit	Chapter 5, Appendix B
	Identify and describe processes for accessing the materials library, creating new materials, and adding material information	Chapters 10, 12
	Create an in-place mass	Chapter 9
	Apply an element by face	Chapter 9
	Define floors for a mass	Chapter 9
	Demonstrate how to generate a toposurface	Chapter 3
	Demonstrate how to model railings	Chapter 16
	Demonstrate how to use design options	Chapter 11
	Demonstrate how to create elements such as a floors, ceilings, or roofs	Chapters 13, 14
	Demonstrate how to create a stair with a landing	Chapter 16
Views	Demonstrate how to create a duplicate view for either a plan, section, elevation, drafting view, etc.	Chapter 2
Elements	Create a vertically compound wall from a basic wall	Chapter 13
	Demonstrate how to create a stacked wall	Chapter 13
	Change elements within a curtain wall (grids, panels, mullions)	Chapter 13
Documentation	Demonstrate how to tag elements (doors, windows, etc.) by category	Chapter 19
	Identify rendering settings in Revit	Chapter 12
	Explain how to control which lights render	Chapter 12
Collaboration	Demonstrate how to copy and monitor elements in a linked file	Chapter 7
	Apply interference checking in Revit	Chapter 7
	Use project base points and survey points	Chapter 7

Index

Note to the Reader: Throughout this index **boldfaced** page numbers indicate primary discussions of a topic. *Italicized* page numbers indicate illustrations.